MASS SOCIETY IN CRISIS

SOCIAL PROBLEMS AND SOCIAL PATHOLOGY

Bernard Rosenberg THE CITY COLLEGE, NEW YORK

Israel Gerver U.S. DEPT. OF HEALTH, EDUCATION, AND WELFARE

F. William Howton THE CITY COLLEGE, NEW YORK

THE MACMILLAN COMPANY, NEW YORK

COLLIER-MACMILLAN LIMITED, LONDON

FIRST PRINTING

MR. GERVER'S CONTRIBUTION TO THIS WORK WAS
MADE IN HIS PRIVATE CAPACITY. NO OFFICIAL
SUPPORT OR ENDORSEMENT BY THE U.S.
DEPARTMENT OF HEALTH, EDUCATION, AND
WELFARE IS INTENDED OR SHOULD BE INFERRED.

LIBRARY OF CONGRESS CATALOG CARD NUMBER: 64-12212

THE MACMILLAN COMPANY, NEW YORK
COLLIER-MACMILLAN CANADA, LTD., TORONTO, ONTARIO

PRINTED IN THE UNITED STATES OF AMERICA

*The second quarter of the twentieth century saw
more than five million people killed by the Germans
because of their "race," uncounted millions
killed by the Russians and Chinese because of
their politics, and well over one hundred thousand
killed by the Americans through atomic bombing
of Japanese cities. This book is dedicated to the memory
of these and other victims of the total politics
and total weapons of our time.*

Preface

NO ONE taking a cool view of our time can find much comfort in it. And our view is far from cool. We do not claim to be disinterested observers of the tragicomic scene before us, Olympian scientists above the melée, removed, disengaged, value-free. The present state of affairs troubles us greatly—else we would not have bothered to put this book together.

Civilization may be *in extremis*; human sensibility is under fire; we are threatened on every side. At such a time he who remains in his accustomed groove could indeed find that it will be his grave.

What follows was selected, arranged, commissioned, and written with much soul searching over a period of years. The reader should not expect to find in these pages a comprehensive reflection of social science literature bearing on all our pathology; we have tried to incorporate the fundamentals, however, and to emphasize critical evaluation. Our basic intent has been to redirect the student of society from paying exclusive attention to a range of social problems limited by the perspective of an earlier generation of sociologists who set and defined it. In the light of present concerns what was of indisputably central importance thirty years ago includes much that can only be called trivial today and leaves out matters that are at the very heart of our vital interests in the '60's.

Another bone we have to pick with colleagues who represent the conventional approach to the study of social problems is that they sometimes foster in the mind of the public an overconfidence in the efficacy of social science. Deflating this illusion is part of our task. When given the chance they clamor, for economists seldom perform wonders in helping us grapple with our ailing economy—or psychologists with mental disorder or sociologists and criminologists with juvenile delinquency. Investing quite limited means with magico-religious power does service neither to science nor society. If in seeking his lost faith secular man succeeds in deifying science he will destroy it, especially a science still in swaddling clothes. There are stirrings in sociology, unmistakable signs of growth; but making a god-hero out of the infant is more likely to produce a monster than to speed its moral and intellectual development.

We gratefully acknowledge the help of our wives in producing this book: Sarah Rosenberg, Joan Gerver, and Louise Howton. Their advice and criticism did much to sustain the whole enterprise, as did our shared hopes of a better world for our children: Deena, Daniel, Jane, Michael, Erica, and two Josephs. We would like also to express our sense of solidarity with members of the Humanistic Underground, as one of them has dubbed that segment of our profession. Thanks, then, for inspiration and friendship, to: Joseph Bensman,

v

Judith Kramer, Dennis Wrong, Arthur Vidich, Lewis Coser, Albert Salomon, Reinhard Bendix, and Hans Gerth. Donna Whiteman ably assisted with typing and other essential tasks. Finally, we thank our Macmillan editor, John Dennis Moore, for his help and forebearance.

BERNARD ROSENBERG
ISRAEL GERVER
F. WILLIAM HOWTON

Contents

The Morning After

November 23, 1963

As though a diamond were to split apart and show
Its central core was soft with pus that all the glitter
Could not at last contain, could not at last disguise
Or keep from stinking, is that how it is with us?
The mighty civilization, racing to the moon,
Pressing the money from the chambers of its heart?

Now, citizen, consider. It will do no good
To say the man who pulled the trigger was insane
Or Communist-inspired. That excuse may serve by day,
But what of the night, the evil hatred born of fear
That eats the heart? Did that man, by his distant kill,
Reflect the people of our country to themselves?

Another man, having as yet much life to live,
Rich yet ambitious, honorable even in
The ways of power, one elected by the people
To express the intricacies of their will through tangled paths
In the mechanical jungle of this world, has died
Of his election. Does that death express our will?

Our will to hatred and the arrogance of wealth,
To smugness and expediency and want of charm,
To politics as foolish as intemperate,
And, product of these, our will to be indifferent
To sufferings that enduring wrong permissively
Sustains among our own, excluded and kept poor,

Despised and beaten for the color of their skins,
And savagely deprived of even the little learning
Our universities afford—all this because
Their ancestors were haled to us in prison-holds,
In chains, in filth; thus we rewrite the Word of Christ:
"If once you smite a man, give him the other fist."

Our will, I mean, to money and armor more than all,
Our stingy computation of the overcost
Of charity, or kindness, or common honesty,
Our deathy phantasies about "Defense" and that
"Security" that could not, when the moment came,
Secure the life of the one man who stood for us.

The people elevated him; it is fair to say
He died because of all the people, of his party
And of the party opposed. As though the nation's will,
So evenly divided and balanced as to be

source: Reprinted from the *New Leader,* December 9, 1963.
Used by permission.

Near paralyzed, as in a catatonic state,
Had suddenly expressed itself as trigger-happy.

Sorrow, America, sorrow has always been
Easy for us because we love ourselves so well,
And it may be we love ourselves so well because
We're always able to dredge up the extra tear
In favor of survival, after we have made
The great refusals that leave survivors blind with grief.

Sorrow is easy, America, we are a people
Quick to the handkerchief. Maybe our tears can be
Impounded behind a dam and used to turn the wheels
Of some concern whose wastes will more pollute the waters.
Maybe our tears will poison all the Russians. Maybe.
Sorrow, America, and while you sorrow, think.

—HOWARD NEMEROV

*First Hiroshima, then Nagasaki: this is
the Nagasaki A-bomb (1945).*

*"A tree grows in Nagasaki"—a view
from the ground.*

*"The Hiroshima maidens"—pictured is one of several groups of
young Japanese women disfigured in the Hiroshima bombing who
were subsequently brought to the United States to undergo a series
of plastic surgical operations (1956).*

(Top) A transport arrives at Auschwitz. (Crematoria chimneys can be seen in the background.) Photo taken by an SS guard in 1944. (Bottom) Transport cars for the bodies inside the Auschwitz crematory. Fresh flowers are kept in memory of the victims.

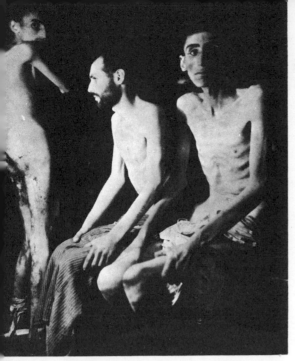

With the collapse of Nazi Germany the existence of hundreds of concentration and extermination camps became incontrovertibly evident. The frightful misery pictured here was not untypical of what the Allied forces found generally. The original caption, dated April 16, 1945, reads as follows: "These Russian, and Polish slave laborers interned at Buchenwald Concentration Camp averaged 160 pounds each prior to entering 11 months ago. Their average weight is now 70 pounds. Many had died of starvation when U.S. troops of the 80th Division took over the camp."

Wide World Photos

This captured German photograph shows a camp band playing "the death tango" (a tune ordered especially composed by the commandant) during SS shootings of Soviet and Polish civilian prisoners in the Lvov region.

(Right) "Birmingham, Ala., May 4, 1963. 'We Don't Want a Riot'—Rev. James Bevels, Negro integration leader, uses a bull horn in an attempt to disperse large crowd of racial demonstrators. Bevels told the crowd that a disturbance 'like this could easily cause a riot.'"

(Top Left) "Jackson, Miss., May 31, 1963. 'Demonstrators on the Run'— Faced with a human barricade of Jackson police, Negro demonstrators run from scene in Jackson this afternoon. Negro girl to left of center dropped contents of purse and was undecided about leaving them. She did. Police arrested several hundred and charged them with parading without a permit, in the latest racial crisis."

(Bottom Left) "Jackson, Miss., June 3, 1963. 'Repeat Performance'—Six Negroes were arrested this afternoon in Jackson for 'parading without a permit' as they picketed a downtown store in another demonstration against the city's racial policy. Trusties carry demonstrator to paddy wagon as portion of group waits on curb. Policeman at right holds American flags and signs they carried."

Wide World Photos

Negroes seek their rights in the North as well as the South. A protest parade and rally in White Plains, N.J.

Wide World Photos

A Moslem lies dead on the sidewalk of a busy street in Algiers, mostly ignored by a European passersby who became accustomed to such sights. He was shot by a European terrorist for no other reason than that he was "there," in all likelihood, and as part of a general policy of avenging similar acts of terrorism by Moslems against Europeans.

An armed French soldier stands guard at the entrance to the Casbah (Moslem Old Quarter), Algiers, during the height of the rebellion. The regular army's mission—ultimately hopeless—was to protect both Moslem and European civilians against terrorist attacks by irregulars (guerrillas) from the opposite side.

Symbolic of the nationalist hopes of Algerian Moslems, strong enough to sustain them through seven years of bitter and corrupting underground warfare, this cyclist proudly bears the flag of the new republic after independence.

The Tacuara, an Argentine neo-Nazi, anti-semitic organization, stages a demonstration in Buenos Aires (1962). The German Nazis had their origin in just such a group, in the 1920's.

Negroes seek their rights in South Africa as well as in the U.S. Police officer chases a demonstrator in Langa, near Capetown.

This mental patient performs acrobatics on a high voltage tower before being 'talked down.'

Wide World Photos

One of the problems confronting the scholar is that the exploits of totalitarianism have a certain morbid appeal to sick minds. The young man pictured here was picked up (Newark, N.J., 1959) for attempted suicide.

Wide World Photos

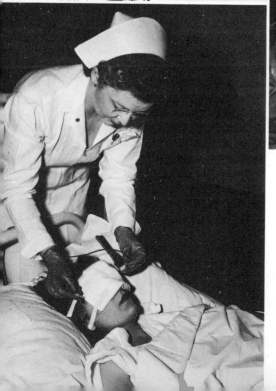

A nurse assists in administering electro-shock treatment to a patient diagnosed as suffering from manic depressive psychosis.

Wide World Photos

Unemployed auto workers tell their story to an AP correspondent in a Detroit union hall (1961). Automation's impact is evident in the loss of jobs (down 18% from 1955 to 1962) even while production is rising (up 14% in the same period).

An unemployed coal miner takes care of his children while his wife works. Coal production is up while the number of jobs is far below what it was ten years ago. In this instance the husband and father is denied his traditional role as breadwinner.

INTRODUCTION

We are living in a demented world. And we know it. It would not come as a surprise to anyone if tomorrow the madness gave way to a frenzy which would leave our poor Europe in a state of distracted stupor, with engines still turning and flags streaming in the breeze, but with the spirit gone.

Everywhere there are doubts as to the solidity of our social structure, vague fears of the imminent future, a feeling that our civilization is on the way to ruin. They are not merely the shapeless anxieties which beset us in the small hours of the night when the flame of life burns low. They are considered expectations founded on observation and judgment of an overwhelming multitude of facts. How to avoid the recognition that almost all things which once seemed sacred have now become unsettled, truth and humanity, justice and reason? We see forms of government no longer capable of functioning, production systems on the verge of collapse, social forces gone wild with power. The roaring engine of this tremendous time seems to be heading for a breakdown.

But immediately the antithesis forces itself on our minds. Never has there been a time when men were so clearly conscious of their commanding duty to cooperate in the task of preserving and improving the world's well-being and human civilization. At no time has work been so much honored as it is today. Man has never been so ready to apply all his powers to a common cause. At least hope has not yet been lost.

If, then, this civilization is to be saved, if it is not to be submerged by centuries of barbarism but to secure the treasures of its inheritance on new and more stable foundations, there is indeed need for those now living fully to realize how far the decay has already progressed. . . .

Between the extremes of despairing pessimism and the belief in imminent deliverance stand all those who see the grave evils and shortcomings of our time, who do not know how they are to be remedied and overcome, but who hope and work, who strive to understand and are ready to bear.

—J. Huizinga[1]

"Crisis" is a medical concept which originated with Hippocrates. When modern man speaks of political, economic, social, religious, or esthetic crisis, he proceeds metaphorically, and nowhere more than in sociology. Beginning more than a century ago, when Auguste Comte first baptized the discipline, sociology has been animated by a profound sense of crisis in every sphere of life. Indeed, the presence of disease and disorder, and the need to ameliorate them for man's survival, brought sociology into existence and has sustained

---

[1] J. Huizinga, *In the Shadow of Tomorrow* (New York: Norton, 1936), pp. 53–54. Reprinted by permission.

it ever since. At first, as one brilliant sociologist, Albert Salomon, has put it, there was "the nineteenth century intellectual's eschatological vision of a dying world."[2] Among those mentioned by Salomon is Jacob Burckhardt, who wrote in 1846, "I have no hope at all for the future. It is possible that a few half endurable decades may still be granted us, a sort of Roman imperial time. I am of the opinion that democrats and proletarians must submit to an increasingly harsh despotism. . . ."[3] and Proudhon, "All traditions are abused, all beliefs abolished, while the new gospel has not yet entered the mind of the masses. That is what I call the dissolution."[4]

Such are the origins of sociology as a field of study or a point of view, cradled in Europe and nurtured on crisis. That these origins have never been systematically studied (beyond the brilliant though as yet fragmentary contribution of men like Salomon) is cause for regret. They require intensive scholarly study by the historian of ideas and the sociologist of knowledge. Meanwhile, it may be said that the sociologist arose out of feverish change, revolutionary ferment, and the accompanying hope that perhaps he might equip himself to survive amidst all the wreckage.

Comte's view of the situation was relatively parochial and so was that of his great successor, Emile Durkheim. Both of these men were wracked with anxiety for their Motherland. It was the future of France, under successive republics and in her time of troubles, that passionately concerned them. They felt apprehensions of doom but did not look far beyond their own borders. It took Oswald Spengler to dramatize a greater fear that welled up in the twentieth century: *The Decline of the West*—or translated more precisely, *The Destruction of the West*—as his masterwork is entitled. Only a few decades later, Spengler strikes us as having written an optimistic book, since it only envisages *Der Untergang des Abendlandes* at a time when, not Western man alone, but mankind at large faces the possibility of universal extinction.

Is it any wonder that in a prophetic series of lectures twenty years ago Huizinga said:

In the social and cultural domain no metaphor is more apt than the pathological one. No doubt our time is full of fever. Growing pains? Possibly. There is raving; there are phantasms and senseless oppression. Or is it more than a passing overstimulation of the brain? Is there reason to speak of a derangement caused by a serious lesion of the nerve center? Every one of these metaphors has its weight of meaning when applied to the various aspects of the present state of our culture.[5]

Technically, that is, academically, social pathology is, at present, a subdivision of sociology. We treat it as such in this book. However, for long periods of time from their stormy inception, the two fields have been indis-

---

[2] Albert Salomon, *The Tyranny of Progress* (New York: Noonday, 1955), p. 84.
[3] *Ibid.*, quoted by Salomon, p. 6.
[4] *Ibid.*, quoted by Salomon, p. 75.
[5] *Loc. cit.*

tinguishable. Since Comte and St. Simon, the subject matter of one has been substantially that of the other. As the crisis deepens, notwithstanding a certain euphoria which is itself symptomatic, this virtual identity of interests becomes more apparent. To the pioneer sociologist, and he is not much more than that today, society always was the *patient*.

For some time, thoughtful Europeans have felt that their world was collapsing. But what of Americans? Optimism is deeply ingrained in our national character. We are suspicious of nay-sayers and skeptics, and the "worry-bird" is a disgraceful symbol. Yet nowhere has sociology flourished as in the United States, and nowhere has it been more clearly oriented to social problems. The pragmatic attitude created by a feeling that society was out of kilter found its ultimate expression in American sociology, which begins and ends with specific social problems. In point of fact, an excessive preoccupation with "problems" has often blinded American sociologists to the larger framework without which these problems could not be grasped. We must nevertheless face the paradox of a habitually optimistic people that produces a social science focused upon pathological behavior.

It was a contemporary *American* social philosopher, Charles Frankel, who recently observed, *a propos* the story *Frankenstein*, "In the twentieth century version Frankenstein and his monster keep house together and work out an uneasy *modus vivendi*." It is to the exorcism of this monster in his innumerable forms that the American sociologist has addressed himself from first to last, that is, from Lester Frank Ward to Robert K. Merton. The dark side of American civilization, so elusive in surface manifestations, can be seen not only in American literature, which has remained as perversely gloomy in Faulkner as it was in Melville and Hawthorne, but also in its peculiar social science. At the same time, Americans like "to do something" about their "problems," and the emphasis in sociology is fully harmonious with that trait.

To this day the sociology curriculum in American institutions of higher learning is heavily weighted with courses called Social Problems and Social Disorganization, whose unit of study may be anything from the hobo and cripple to the causes of war. We favor a different, but not altogether unpopular, name and a more coherent definition of the field. The name, if not the concept it embodies, should be given short shrift. There are persuasive reasons, based on premises already suggested, to organize relevant data under the heading Social Pathology, but it will be no more offensive to us by any other name. For we agree with Humpty Dumpty:

"There's glory for you."
"I don't know what you mean by glory," Alice said.
Humpty Dumpty smiled contemptuously. "Of course you don't—till I tell you. I meant, There's a nice knock-down argument for you!"
"But glory doesn't mean a nice knock-down argument," Alice objected.
"When *I* use a word," Humpty Dumpty said, in a rather scornful tone, "it means just what I choose to mean—neither more nor less."

By calling it Social Pathology, we choose to mean a tremendous but finite segment of the social scene. Yet our decision is a little less capricious than Humpty Dumpty's, since it rests on a solid and usable tradition.

To date, most of us have studied the darker side of social life, in one of four ways. We have subsumed the subject under these headings: pathology, problems, deviation, and disorganization. None will do; each is defective; all have been criticized. Deviation for one man is conformity for another; problems in one context are solutions in another. Our standpoint will determine whether the same activity is viewed as disorganized or highly organized.

Other equally important strictures apply to the concept of pathology. Like "crisis" it is a medical metaphor with the special discursive hazard that human society may at first be likened to, and then mistaken for, an organism. Our sociological forefathers were often subject to that illusion which has for long been dismissed as "organicism," a quaint conceit of the Social Darwinists who were swept aside along with their too literal analogy. We still have evolutionists, but none who seriously claim that culture is analogous to the human nervous system, with its own social cerebrum, cerebellum, and medulla oblongata. Since no one is now taken with that theoretical extravagance, we think it is safe and even advantageous to revive the old concept without any nineteenth-century trappings. Put to current use, the idea that there are pathological circumstances of a specially forbidding nature abroad in our world is given the centrality it deserves.

Next to "pathology," the term "dysfunction" which is so fashionable in sociology these days, takes on a pallid coloration. Habits are dysfunctional when they create upsets, cause perturbations, produce conflict, provoke strife, or foster discontent. But shall we say of mass terror, wholesale imprisonment, brainwashing, death factories like Auschwitz, the incinerators of Hiroshima and Nagasaki—mounting to global delirium in the prospect of race suicide —that they are "dysfunctional"? As well say they are signs of impropriety.

The contemporary crisis is of a different magnitude from problems like organized crime. By the same token, it has nothing to do with "the human predicament," the perennial and irremediable troubles that always beset us, our finite state, the curse of consciousness and its agonies. Men are born, they suffer, and die as "discontinuous beings," in Georges Bataille's phrase, "individuals who perish in isolation in the midst of an incomprehensible adventure . . ."[6] The possible abrupt termination of that adventure is our reality. We cannot but view it as profoundly pathological, although to do so is no more (nor less) "scientific" than to view it through other, likewise imperfect, sociological lenses.

Delimiting and defining the field is a more formidable matter, one with which we propose to deal throughout the text that follows. At this juncture, one or two guiding principles may be set forth. For example, it is not our

---

[6] Georges Bataille, *Death and Sensuality* (New York: Walker, 1962), p. 15.

intention to encompass all current problems, or even to explore any one problem exhaustively. The major weakness of existing perspectives is their omnivorousness: not only do they take in too much, but also they take it in from too many angles.

A glimpse of some fairly recent books will immediately establish that the social pathologist in this country chronically overreached himself and operated at an intolerably low level of abstraction. We should like to eschew these tendencies. About them more will be said below. On the positive side, we take one simple proposition for granted and thereby differentiate this text from much of the literature, namely, *that social problems can only be understood by the sociologist in social terms*. This is, if you like, the credo of Emile Durkheim, and with certain minor qualifications, we shall adhere to it. Before doing this we must examine the work of other schools (Part I of this book) and determine whether to reject them completely or to retain whatever is salvable.

This does not mean that we adhere to a rigid sociological determinism. Rather, we propose a certain structural and holistic emphasis in our analysis of social problems. The analysis of social problems in social terms—whether these problems appear in the domain of human extinction, mental disorder, or deviant behavior—means that we engage in certain procedures which will aid in obtaining analyzable data. Ideally, the sociological analysis of social problems requires information about (1) the distribution of the phenomenon throughout the population, (2) the differential distribution of the problem throughout subgroups of the population, (3) the institutional features of society which contribute to perpetuation of the problem, and (4) the cultural values that provide ideological support for the persistence of the problem.

Our social problems are often only incidentally conceived of as having their sources in social life. The popular preference is to ascribe their existence to external or extraneous sources, biological defects, personality disorders, or a lack of positive thinking and optimistic faith in the future of humanity. As a result of this mystical and seemingly simpler causal analysis, meliorative efforts, those aimed at some kind of solution, are rarely successful.

In casting about for a solution to a complex social problem that may have been erroneously defined in the first place, we tend to seek quick results even at the risk of acting on a misapprehension of its causes. Our American inclination is to do something in a hurry rather than to assess the sources of a problem with great care and with a view to the likeliest solution. This inclination is itself a social problem of some significance—and we treat it as such in our final section.

A Chilean politician once said, "There are two kinds of political problems: those that solve themselves and those for which there is no solution." Does the apothegm have any relevance for us? More, perhaps than we like to admit as North Americans given over to activism. To be sure, we cannot preserve our manhood and relinquish all hope for a rational solution to the problem of international tension, to the danger of thermonuclear war, of atmospheric *or* cultural fallout, the risk of being physically extinguished or spiritually anesthetized. Yet the matter of survival is so precarious that despite its urgency we are often better advised to embrace immobilism, to do nothing at all, than to act in reckless and precipitate haste.

If there is some truth to the Chilean attitude on matters of cultural life and death (the theme of Part II), then there is much more truth in it for "traditional" problems (such as those discussed in Part III). Part I of this book is a critical examination of several, mostly monocausal, approaches to social pathology in its most conventional sense. Part IV rounds out the picture foreshadowed in Part I. For every theory of the origin of social problems, with all its deficiencies, there is an accompanying panacea, whose implementation promises to generate more problems than it allays. Everyday problems are serious and vexatious, but we have not begun to understand them any better than those that threaten us with the apocalypse. Learning what we do not know and what we cannot do is the precondition for extricating ourselves from an otherwise hopeless impasse.

Part One. APPROACHES

Social scientists usually decry monistic causal theories as logically fallacious, incomplete, biased, and untestable. However, despite (or possibly because of) scientific protest, most people, in their attempts to comprehend or to solve a 'problem, favor some sort of monism. This is particularly so when the problem comes to be regarded as socially significant.

Most of us feel uncomfortable unless we can reduce complex realities to a single dimension. Thus we are tempted to seize upon categorical labels for phenomena which are not easily understood. Most teachers are familiar with resistance to careful analysis. Too many students substitute such categories as psychological, economic, sociological, and biological determinism for analysis—as if labelling explained anything.

We do not make this charge only against students. Unfortunately the prestige of scientific labels has led to general reliance on a kind of magical nominalism which is felt to explain away problematic aspects of social life, whether these be mass terror or political dishonesty. The following pages of this introductory section are devoted to a description and dissection of various mystiques, adopted by scientists and laymen alike as modes of thinking about social problems, both trivial and profound. Some of these approaches are fairly well discarded, while others are very much alive and in the vanguard of contemporary "scientific" sociological concern.

The distinguished contemporary sociologist, Robert K. Merton, once observed of his science that it was characterized by many approaches—and few arrivals. His witticism applies with special force to that part of sociology with which we are concerned in this book.

Herewith we offer a limited miscellany of those approaches to social pathology which, though they have led us nowhere, still attract a host of laymen, many scholars, and a golden flow of money. Research funds for the further exploration of sterile hypotheses seem to be inexhaustible. Apparently the resourceful man can always scare up enough backing for yet another inquiry into the alleged relationship between anatomy and criminality or between body chemistry and psychosis. Of course, we are not now, and probably never will be, able to disprove the relationship. But, as Leslie White[1] used to say, neither are we able to disprove the existence of Santa Claus. And he would add that sometimes science progresses not so much by disproving theories as by outgrowing them.

---

[1] A well-known anthropologist on the faculty of the University of Michigan.

The moon may after all be made of green cheese (science can never dismiss any unexplored possibility). Yet if an astrophysicist proposed to spend huge sums for the investigation of such lunar phenomena, he would be laughed out of court and consigned to scientific oblivion. Suppose he found support, undertook his expensive study, and failed to establish that the moon is made of green cheese. Wouldn't that be the end of it for a long time? Couldn't he or his scientific betters go on to something else? Not if our man and those who followed him down to the same dead end, generation after generation, are gripped by a will to believe.

Must we enter the twenty-first century before the *idée fixe* that first possessed Cesare Lombroso[2] is finally relinquished—the notion that criminals are biologically different from other men? In our time that idea has been cherished by the physical anthropologist Ernest Hooton (p. 13), William Sheldon, Sheldon and Eleanor Glueck, and their many admirers. Clyde Kluckhohn declares in his prize-winning *Mirror for Man* (described on its cover by Margaret Mead as "the best contemporary introduction to modern anthropology"):

One of the most famous studies in constitutional anthropology is that by Professor Hooton on the American criminal. His finding that criminals are, in general, biologically inferior has been disputed. Most reviewers have concluded that he took insufficient account of socioeconomic factors. Hooton makes it perfectly clear that criminals "do not bear the brand of Cain nor any specific physical stigmata whereby they can be identified at a glance." However, he presents a good evidence for certain associations. For example, among criminals as a group, those convicted of burglary and larceny are likely to be short and slender; those convicted of sex crimes are likely to be short and fat.

For many of Hooton's major assertions the cautious reader must probably render the Scotch verdict of "not proven." On the other hand, a demonstration that some of Hooton's methods were unsatisfactory does not mean a constitutional factor in criminality can be ruled out. . . . The hard facts . . . suggest that the biological factor deserves further study.[3]

And further (still inconclusive) study is just what it has been given, for example, by William Sheldon, a student of human body types, or "somatotypes" elaborately correlated with various forms of psychopathic and sociopathic human conduct. Of this work, Kluckhohn says, "Somatotyping must be regarded as a valuable technique still in the exploratory stage."

Sheldon, in *Varieties of Delinquent Youth* (a formidable volume that looks ominously "scientific"), purports to explain delinquent behavior not by an uncritical equation of physique and deviance, but by observing the frequency with which youngsters' so-called "D" (for Disappointingness) scores correlate with a triple rating of somatotypes. The method is impressive. Put to use for some other purpose it might even interest statisticians. Nevertheless, his analysis is on the level of magical nominalism mercilessly anato-

---

[2] A nineteenth-century Italian criminologist.
[3] Clyde Kluckhohn, *Mirror for Man* (New York: Fawcett, 1959), p. 74.

mized by Lynn Thorndyke in *The History of Magic and Experimental Science*. Thorndyke's book is replete with informative accounts of naive biological determinism, with its single-minded stress on morphological, genetic, and physiological traits, which now comes to us in the form of a refined category used as a substitute for explanation.

Sheldon finds that for his most delinquent boys, a husky "mesomorphic" type is the statistical mean. He concludes that this type is most markedly disposed to delinquency. The precise relationship is never revealed; it is only asserted. He does not tell us why ectomorphic and endomorphic children (of less athletic build) should be less inclined to break laws. Some critics have contended that mesomorphic boys may be socially induced to display greater aggression than their punier mates. Notice that neither morphological determination nor social inducement can be established (by any plausible argument) as truly or basically causal.

It should not have to be repeated—but evidently it does—that empirical data which inform us about association between two phenomena do not necessarily inform us about causation. We may be misled into confusing plausibility with necessity, and therefore into ignoring alternative hypotheses. Furthermore, continued preoccupation with biology, especially as the basis of crime and madness, may have a function transcending the goals of science —specifically, a systematic displacement of interest from potentially troublesome and controversial areas of social inquiry. This tendency also appears in other kinds of monistic nominalism.

After William Sheldon, the Drs. Sheldon and Eleanor Glueck, long famous as criminologists, drew out their calipers and applied them to the anatomy of many certified juvenile delinquents. Although their work was still in the exploratory stage, they nevertheless reported their findings in an influential book entitled *Unraveling Juvenile Delinquency*. The results, though scientifically indefensible, made a real mark—which shows no sign of being fully effaced as yet—on an assortment of social workers, field personnel, and family counselors. A syndicated column in the daily press written by Dr. Frances L. Ilg and Dr. Louise B. Ames offers a synthesis of constitutional psychology (the Hootonian or Sheldonian view) and developmental psychology (out of a Yale laboratory where every phase of growth, from birth to age fifteen, has been carefully observed and unhelpfully "averaged").

In attacking this school, one does not beat a dead horse. Yet a barnyard figure of speech may not be inappropriate, for it has been said of people pursuing this strange line of inquiry that they show less flexibility than the hen who will sit on a rock in the belief that it is an egg, but for only so long. After a while she gives up. Those bearing the banner of Lombroso cannot seem to give up. Nothing hatches, but they keep sitting on the same rock, protesting after more than a hundred years, that really, it may turn out to be an egg. Let the reader decide, once he has sampled Hooton and Hooton's critics, whether it is worthwhile to encourage more somatotyping.

In one form or another, the heredity theory, according to which criminals and other "deviants" are born, not made, is still with us. It dies hard. Next in durability, at least with laymen (and teachers, preachers, planners, reformers), if not with criminologists, is the poverty theory. Jean Valjean, as a decent but hungry man driven to steal, excites the public imagination more than a robber baron who may never have experienced anything but affluence. We now know that crime occurs at every level of society; it is as common in the upperworld as it is in the underworld. No one did as much as the sociologist Edwin Sutherland (p. 35) to destroy the idea that only poor people are habitual lawbreakers. He focused our attention on businessmen and professional men, the most respectable of them and not their disreputable confreres, who repeatedly violate the criminal code. Like racial identification, socioeconomic class turns out to explain a good deal about why some people are punished for their crimes, but very little about why they commit them. As a theory of crime causation, economic determinism is useless if only because many people in poverty are not criminals, and many of the well-to-do are. From Bonger (p. 31) to Sutherland is a major step in the direction of banishing a powerful myth.

If biologism and economism are unacceptable, so is psychologism.[4] Psychologistic explanations fashioned out of "mechanisms" said to operate only in the individual are a favorite refuge of detached scholars and active administrators interested in social problems.

The champions of psychological determinism, when they invoke it to account for any and all human phenomena, profess to have found a master key in the unique individual which will unlock all doors and thereby dispel every behavioral mystery. This is a great piece of presumption, not because psychologists are unable to throw light on the individual, but because that light might blind us to the collectivity, to society and *its* problems. The two are often incommensurable—as Herbert Blumer (p. 58) indicates in his important essay on individual and social disorganization.

It would be preposterous to deny the psychologist his province (or for him to deny sociologists theirs). Neither is this to say that disciplinary frontiers should never be crossed. We do not hesitate to shift from one type of abstraction to another, nor to appropriate useful data from any source, including that of behaviorist and depth psychology. The issue is actually that of finding limits to psychologically slanted explanations. How far can one go with them if they are not located within a broader cultural framework?

The phenomenon of personal injuries, accidents, and casualties may be used as a hypothetical case in point. When the psychologist applies himself to this problem in the spirit of magical nominalism what may emerge is a

---

[4] And all these "isms" are simply manifestations of the basic fallacy of "reductivism," a fallacy whose equally unsatisfactory antithesis is the vague and weightless concept of "multiple causation" which implies, "No, not just this, but this and that—and that and that and, well, everything."

theory of accident-proneness, or sado-masochism, or cardio-motor disability or the need to compensate for frustration. The emphasis is always individualistic and behavioristic. We, on the other hand, would feel obliged to consider the possibility that accidents are derived from a sociocultural context, that they are reflected in accident *rates*, that group and subgroup differences must be taken into account. Sex, age, ethnicity, class, and occupation are the significant variables to a sociologist examining the differential distribution of accident rates—or suicide rates, divorce rates, and crime rates. If from this perspective one can specify the location of high and low incidence, he will then perhaps be well advised to enrich his analysis by recourse to psychology for interpreting residual differences. Thus it might be that men tend to have more accidents that women, but when we correct our male and female rates for age, it becomes obvious that young men have more accidents than older men. If so, the original male-female differences becomes a function of age distribution. Then, the residual difference *may be attributable* to psychological patterns present in the younger and older male but absent in the younger and older female.

This fictitious example is meant only to suggest the possible link between psychological and sociological analysis. It is better illustrated in Durkheim's *Suicide*, a masterpiece of early empirical and theoretical sociology, still unsurpassed in its subtlety. While eager to establish the independence of sociology, Durkheim recognized and utilized social psychology as a discipline, comparable to biochemistry, combining elements from two other sciences to achieve its own point of view. That point of view is more often hopelessly confused than creatively fused with others.

The small group is a practical, self-selected unit of study for social psychologists like Charles Horton Cooley (p. 70), Kurt Lewin, and their contemporary followers. The material in this section on primary group and small group research is less a critique of these men than of a widespread propensity to generalize from their microcosmic laboratory to the macrocosm of society at large. When this is done in the area of social pathology, the consequences are particularly unfortunate. The small group is only one step removed from the individual and, its study, however, ingenious, can tell us only about the small group. The area is legitimate, its scope considerable. We can only be indebted to the social psychologist who teaches us about interaction in the family—and deceived if he claims that every social problem can be traced to the family without asking, "How did the family get that way?"—a question which is beyond his purview.

The sociologist is beset by other pitfalls, some of his own creation. More than twenty years ago, C. Wright Mills (p. 92) set forth the nature of these pitfalls and sketched their topography. He presented his findings in a classic essay called "The Professional Ideology of Social Pathologists," which we have reproduced in its entirety. Mills' findings were based upon a thorough examination of textbooks then in use; Emil Bend and Martin Vogelfanger (p. 111) have replicated Mills' study for this book, making some of the same objections, withdrawing some, and adding a few of their own; they have inspected textbooks now widely in use.

The texts of today are undoubtedly more sophisticated than those in use two decades ago. For this, their authors have many men to thank, not the least is Robert K. Merton. Merton's brilliant quasi-Durkheimian conception of social problems stemming from "Social Structure and Anomie" (the title of his famous article) (p. 122) gently helps sociology to formulate more meaningful hypotheses. We take it as a healthy sign that not even this important contribution is invulnerable to serious criticism. Joseph Bensman and Israel Gerver (p. 141) and Bernard Lander (p. 130), among others, have lately discovered that it is hard for them to conceptualize their data around Merton's schema. They offer modifications that promise to be fruitful.

To end there would be to leave the reader on a "positive" note very far from our intention in these chapters, which have actually been assembled for a "destructive" purpose, to suggest what is wrong, to raise every kind of doubt about existing approaches—the better to make way for future arrivals. Therefore, our final selection is a skillful summary of Barbara Wootton's work (p. 152). Miss Wootton has scoured the literature of criminology and observed its judicial application as a juvenile court judge. She finds that though there is a plethora of studies, none has as yet demonstrated with any rigor that the twelve commonest, or "hypothetically causative," factors of crime and delinquency have any real bearing on the question. Evidently we must start anew. Meanwhile, demolition of old and useless theories as well as the rehabilitation of those that show some promise must continue. We take it that this is an act of creative destruction.

1. BIOLOGISM

Crime and the Man

EARNEST ALBERT HOOTON

If one considers in order sane civilians, sane criminals, insane civilians, and insane criminals, he finds that each succeeding group tends to manifest greater ignorance, lowlier occupational status, and more depressing evidence of all-around worthlessness. The same hierarchy of degeneration is evidenced in physical characteristics. The lower class civilian population is anthropologically fair to middling; the sane criminals are vastly inferior, the insane civilians considerably worse than sane criminals, and the insane criminals worst of all. It would be a rash person who would venture to assert that these parallelisms of increasing inferiority in sociological and anthropological characters are fortuitous and unrelated. The specific criminal proclivities found in certain races and nationalities among the sane prisoners are carried over, to a great extent, into the offenses committed by insane criminals, of the same ethnic or religious origin. . . . (P. 382)

So I think that inherently inferior organisms are, for the most part, those which succumb to the adversities of temptations of their social environment and fall into antisocial behavior, and that it is impossible to improve and correct environment to a point at which these flawed and degenerate human beings will be able to succeed in honest social competition. The bad organism sullies a good environment and transforms it into one which is evil. Of course, I should by no means argue that man should cease to attempt to ameliorate his social environment, but, when he entirely neglects the improvement of his own organism, he condemns his environmental efforts to futility.

That racial background of inheritance which determines our skin color, our hair form, and numerous anatomical features, may also in some vague and general way influence mental and temperamental characteristics, emotional sets, and so on. But race does not make the human animal criminalistic. All existing races have survived through scores of thousands of years

SOURCE: Reprinted by permission of the publishers from Earnest Albert Hooton, *Crime and the Man*. Cambridge, Mass.: Harvard University Press, Copyright, 1939, by The President and Fellows of Harvard College.

the vicissitudes of natural and social selection and are mentally and physically sound at the core. But race undoubtedly influences choice of crime in those organic inferiors which are all too numerous within each racial group. It is the individual and familial inheritance which produce the deteriorated organism which cannot withstand environmental adversity. When a whole race is environmentally depressed, either because of coercion by other races or through inability to cope with the environment to which it has become adapted, we need not expect it to proliferate in antisocial or criminal behavior. Crime is not rampant in savage and retarded human societies. Crime flourishes rather in rich cultures where production is varied and abundant, so that constitutional inferiors are coddled and fostered, inevitably to bite the hands which have fed them. . . . (Pp. 388–89)

It may be well to state bluntly here that I have not spent the greater part of twelve years in studying criminals from any humanitarian zeal for the rehabilitation of offenders, or from any deep interest in the treatment of incarcerated felons. Such motives are laudable and the efforts of those who engage in criminological work are usually disinterested and sometimes efficacious. More power to their elbows! I wish to disabuse everyone of the idea that the function of the general human biologist is that of the family physician—to comfort or to cure individual patients. The anthropologist studies the adult male incarcerated felon as the medical research scientist would study the manifestations of cancer in its advanced stages, so that he may obtain an accurate knowledge of the most pronounced, far-reaching, and exaggerated effects of the disease. I have selected the criminal for study principally because the extreme outrageousness of criminal conduct makes the delinquent a most suitable subject for an exploration of the relation between the quality of the organism and its behavior. No scientific criminologist or penologist, however optimistic he may be of the good effects of a favorable environment and of education and moral suasion, has any particular hope of rehabilitating hardened adult criminals *en bloc*. Crime prevention is centered upon the treatment of juveniles and when it gets to be really scientific, it will have to start earlier still and concern itself with familial heredity. . . . (Pp. 390–91)

I may now, at length, confess that to the biological anthropologist the entire question of crime and the criminal bulks very small indeed in comparison with the enormous problem of checking the degenerative trends in human evolution which are producing millions of animals of our species inferior in mind and body. I deem human deterioration to be ultimately responsible not only for crime, but for the evils of war, the oppression of the populace by totalitarian states, and for all of the social cataclysms which are rocking the world and under which civilization is tottering. . . . (P. 393)

I confidently predict that it will be a comparatively easy and short matter to determine the correlations of human body types with disease. At the same time it is equally necessary, and even more necessary, to relate gross anatomical structure to physiological and mental variation in the large mass of the so-called "normal" human beings—those who are not ill, or who, in blissful ignorance of the fact that they are ill, nevertheless go on functioning and living as if they were well. Since the individual behavior of the human being is indissolubly connected with the quality of his organism and its health functioning, the study of human conduct must not be divorced from the simultaneous attack of anthropology, medicine, and psychology upon the individual. The sociologist, or if you prefer, the social anthropologist, is wholly indispensable in the cooperative effort. For our ultimate purpose is to improve human behavior through the study of the organism which produces behavior.

Intelligent and intensive work should yield in a decade a fairly detailed and accurate knowledge of the associations of manifold human types of structure with the normal variations of physiological functions, with pathological susceptibilities and immunities, with mental range and capacity, and with patterns of social behavior. We should then have learned what types of human beings are worthless and irreclamable, and what types are superior and capable of biological and educational improvement.

By the time we shall have secured exact data upon physico-psycho-sociological correlates from the study of constitution in all of its broader implications, it is possible that the human geneticists will be able to furnish us with more than an inkling of the manner whereby desirable and undesirable human combinations are produced through the mechanism of heredity. If nature can evolve better and more complicated animal organisms through the blind processes of trial and error, natural selection, and fortuitous variation, surely man with his comparatively high animal intelligence, with the transmitted cultural knowledge of thousands of years, and with a purpose hardened by the realization that the fate of his own species is at stake, can learn the mechanism of human heredity. We can direct and control the progress of human evolution by breeding better types and by the ruthless elimination of inferior types, if only we are willing to found and to practise a science of human genetics. With sound and progressively evolving human organisms in the majority of our species, problems of human behavior will be minimized, and there will be improved educability. Crime can be eradicated, war can be forgotten.

The theory of democratic government is noble and the practise of it offers the greatest opportunities for human happiness, if only the mass of the human individuals within the democracy is sound in body and in mind, and consequently social and to some extent unselfish in behavior. Progressive biological deterioration of the people leads inevitably to anarchy and dictatorships. More than ever, in the light of recent events, we have come to pin all of our faith for the future of civilization and of man on democracy. Like Noah we have builded an ark, the rains have come, and the deluge is uopn us. Do we hope to take refuge in that ark of democracy, with our sons and our sons' wives, and survive the flood? We can succeed in this hope only if we leave out some of the noxious animals who are boring from within and making that ark dangerously leaky. So it behooves us to learn our human parisitology and human entomology, to practise an artificial and scientific selection with intelligence, if we wish to save our skins. . . . (Pp. 395–98)

Crime and the Anthropologist

ROBERT K. MERTON AND M. F. ASHLEY-MONTAGU

> Of all the cants which are canted in this canting
> world, . . . the cant of criticism is the most
> tormenting.—Laurence Sterne, *Tristram Shandy*.
>
> I await these squallings with equanimity.
> —Earnest A. Hooton, *Crime and the Man*.

Professor Hooton in two works recently published in the combined fields of physical anthropology and criminology[1] has propounded some highly unorthodox theories and stated some startling conclusions. Already the popular press is heralding the more lurid of these conclusions and it may no doubt be expected that additional publicity of this sort will follow upon the appearance of the two succeeding volumes of *The American Criminal*. In this massive report, Hooton has presented the results of twelve years of research representing the most extensive investigation of the physical characters of a criminal series of populations as compared with civilian populations that has yet appeared. It may at once be stated that this work will occupy as conspicuous a place in the history of criminology as the works of his predecessors in the field, Lombroso and Goring. It is the mantle of Lombroso, patched with some pieces from that of Max Nordau, rather than that of Goring— which Hooton spurns—that has descended upon the shoulders of Hooton. He wears it most gracefully. We are convinced that this vigorously tendentious study of the American criminal will have a most stimulating effect upon that largely neglected branch of human biology which is concerned to discover the relations between body, mind, and society; or shall we say heredity, conduct, and culture? It is a work which simply bristles with controversial points.

Since Hooton's work seems destined to exert an appreciable effect upon the thought of all those who make themselves acquainted with it, as well as upon the thought of many who do not, it is desirable that the significance

SOURCE: Robert K. Merton and M. F. Ashley-Montagu, "Crime and the Anthropologist," *American Anthropologist*, 42:3 (July–September, 1940), pp. 384–408. Reprinted by permission.

[1] Earnest Albert Hooton, *Crime and the Man* (Harvard University Press, 1939). *The American Criminal: An Anthropological Study* (Harvard University Press, 1939).

of his results be critically examined from as many aspects as possible, for its implications are of the greatest importance. The study is of such magnitude that even the present forerunners of what promises to be a monumental report cannot be adequately discussed in a paper of this length. At most all that we can venture to do here is to consider some features of the framework of the research, some of its more general conclusions, and certain methodological assumptions which have been adopted. We shall hereafter refer to *The American Criminal* (the first of "three ponderous volumes, each positively bristling with statistical documentation") as *AC*, and to *Crime and the Man* (the summary volume of Lowell Institute Lectures) as *CM*.

As a consequence of his researches Hooton has been forced into the un-American position of espousing the cause of the angels. It may seem from what we say here that we have been forced into the opposite extreme of embracing the cause of the criminals. That is only apparently so. Actually, what we wish to do here is to suggest that the differences between the angels and the criminals are only skin deep; that the criminals may not have sprouted wings as the angels have done, not because it was not in them to do so, but because their wings were clipped before they were ready to try them.

Both of Hooton's works are introduced with ingenious attacks upon anticipated criticism and a series of *ad hominem* rejoinders-in-advance to any who may venture to voice their disagreement with the author's conclusions. "The categorical denials of hereditary influences in crime which are commonly emitted by sociologists" (*AC*, 4) and other "humanitarian practitioners" who "have poured out so much blood and treasure upon the investigation of the causes of crime" have not led us any nearer to a solution of the causative elements in criminal behavior. Hence, it is implied, the author's categorical affirmations that "criminals are organically inferior" and that "the primary cause of crime is biological inferiority" are more likely to do so. The statement of the case in terms of these mutually exclusive alternatives adds considerably to the dialectical flavor of the argument if not to our knowledge of the causation of crime. As we shall have occasion to see, this posing of false dilemmas is one of the more frequent polemical devices which Hooton utilizes in the analysis of his data.

Hooton defines a criminal as "a person who is under sentence in a penal institution, having been convicted for an antisocial act punishable by commitment to such an institution." (*AC*, 7.) He points out that "Crimes are obviously infractions of more or less arbitrary social rules, and whether an act is or is not accounted a crime, depends not only upon the nature of that act, but also upon the attitude of society toward it, which may differ radically from time to time and in diversely constituted political, social, and ethnic groups." (*AC*, 7.) "The criminal is a person distinguished by the commission of an overt act against society and he exemplifies for us an extreme of human conduct, thus making himself an excellent subject for the investigation of the relation of physique to behavior." (*AC*, 8.)

It is because the criminal exemplifies an "extreme" of human conduct that he was selected by Hooton for the investigation of the possible relation of physique to conduct. The object of the investigation is stated at the conclusion of the second chapter (*CM*, 33), which is significantly entitled *The Organic Basis of Crime*, as being "Specifically [the examination of] the physical characteristics of a large series of anti-social individuals in order to find out whether their varied types of delinquency are associated with their anthropological characters, and whether they are physically distinguished from those of us who are, perhaps temporarily, at large, and at least, putatively, law-abiding."

An indication of Hooton's dispassionate approach—in contrast, presumably, to Goring's "emotional preconception" which Hooton decries—is afforded by his initial comment "upon one stupid objection . . . to the effect that it is useless to study incarcerated criminals because they represent only the failures of those habitually and purposefully engaged in anti-social pursuits." (*AC*, 10.) In such an extreme form, this objection, whether "stupid" or not, would rule out most studies of criminals, since only those who are incarcerated are usually available for study. But it is still possible, and for some purposes relevant, that incarcerated criminals are not a representative sample (with respect to intelligence, economic status, race, nationality and rural-urban composition) of those who commit crimes. Selective arrests, and more importantly, selective commitments in terms of economic status and race are attested by many conversant with the facts; the differential in the case of Negroes seems to be especially marked. Hooton himself finds it convenient to adduce possible differentials in "rates of apprehension and conviction" between rural and urban criminals when he writes that "in rural life sparsity of population and restricted criminal opportunity lead . . . to easy detection and apprehension of persons responsible for crimes" in relative contrast to urban offenders. (*AC*, 288.) Criminologists have indicated additional selective elements in this connexion.) It is at least possible, then, that some of the apparent sociological and physical differentials between criminals and civilians would be eliminated, were allowances made for the selective elements in commitment. Hooton is of course at liberty to define the "criminal" as he wishes, but he is not free to assume as an unchallengeable axiom that prisoners are in all relevant respects representative of the total population of those who have committed one or more illegal acts. To insinuate an axiom is not to demonstrate a fact. This consideration is mentioned here, not so much for its intrinsic importance—the fact remains that unconfined criminals and the anthropometrist's calipers have little chance to meet—but simply to bring out the author's tendency to demolish exaggerated propositions and hence to obscure the essential issue.[2]

---

[2] It is interesting to confront Hooton's remarks with the observations of a criminologist on the question of prison samples of criminal populations. "It is probable that arrests for serious crimes are less than 10 per cent of the serious crimes actually committed in large cities. Out of 1000 consecutive burglaries and robberies of chain grocery stores

The study of the *Old American Criminal* reports on 4212 native white prisoners of native white parentage from nine states and a civilian (non-criminal) check sample of 313 (146 Nashville firemen and 167 residents of Massachusetts). Observations included at least 33 anthropometric measurements and indices, ten sociological categories and 33 morphological categories for each person. It should be noted that almost one-half of the civilian check group are firemen; in an occupation for which, Hooton observes, "the physical qualifications are rather stringent." He also notes that "the principal objection to them is that they are inclined to be fat," but feels compelled to add that they have the further liabilities of being of uniform social and economic status, in contrast to the criminal sample, and that their urban residence contrasts with the dominantly rural residence of the criminals when not incarcerated. In other words, as far as half the crucial check sample is concerned, the civilians are in many respects distinctly selected. However, it is comforting to learn that the Nashville civilians and the Tennessee villains are at least ethnically comparable.

Another part of the check group consists of Massachusetts militiamen and "in as much as enlistment in the militia is contingent upon the passing of a physical examination, it may be assumed that its members are, on the whole, of superior physique to the criminals" who, presumably, do not need to pass a formal physical examination. (*AC*, 34.) One may readily sympathize with Hooton's difficulty in obtaining a suitable check sample, but the fact still remains that a research of this magnitude proceeded with a clearly loaded check group. That the Tennessee civilian sample, with its various physical and social idiosyncrasies, proves disturbing to Hooton may be inferred from the frequency of such remarks as: "the Tennessee firemen show an unduly high mean," "the Tennessee firemen are perhaps broader in the face than an unselected (*sic*) civilian group would be," "the plump and sedentary fire-fighters," "the big-jowled firemen," "the excess weight of the Tennessee firemen," *etc.* (*AC*, 208 *ff*.) Despite all this, we are told that the Tennessee series probably "affords the more reliable results," "for the Massachusetts criminal series includes a brachycephalic French element almost absent from the civilian series." (*AC*, 216.) Another liability of the Massachusetts civilian series is the intrusion of the personal equation of "Observer C" with respect to some morphological items. Thus, the Tennessee civilian sample is the more reliable, and if this be so, then rough indeed is this

---

in Chicago in 1930–1931, only two resulted directly in arrests." "Many types of offenses are widespread but seldom result in prosecution." "The selective nature of arrest and of imprisonment make these statistics an inadequate source of information regarding the characteristics of criminals, but it is difficult to develop statistics regarding criminals who are not recorded in some manner. Apparently, therefore, the best that can be done at present is to recognize the bias in the statistics of arrests or of prisons and attempt to secure statistics in other ways regarding the classes which are not adequately represented." E. H. Sutherland, *Principles of Criminology* (Philadelphia, 1939), pp. 29, 37, 45. The various writings of Thorsten Sellin on crime indexes should further be consulted in this connexion.

roughly comparable setting of civilians." To what extent are observed "biological" differences attributable to the bias of the sample? In view of some of the inferences which Hooton later feels justified in drawing, this bias becomes a grievous inadequacy, to say the least. It should be noticed, however, that Hooton has zealously ascertained and emphasized some of these sources of bias, both slight and pronounced in his data.

An exhaustive statistical analysis of the data leads to the "important conclusion that native White criminals of native parentage are not only distinguished from each other by offense groups in sociological characteristics, but also in anthropometric and morphological features. Thus it is suggested that crime is not an exclusively sociological phenomenon, but is also biological." (*CM*, 75.) Concerning the nature of Hooton's statistical analysis we shall have something to say hereafter, but even if this were unexceptionable, we may here recall the words of Wilhelm Ostwald.

Among scientific articles there are to be found not a few wherein the logic and mathematics are faultless but which are for all that worthless, because the assumptions and hypotheses upon which the faultless logic and mathematics rest do not correspond to actuality.

But Hooton's logic, if not his mathematics, is far from faultless.

Hooton finds that "on the whole, the biological superiority of the civilian to the delinquent is quite as certain as his sociological superiority." (*CM*, 376.) "The evidence," he writes, "that the criminals are derived from the baser biological stuff of their various ethnic stocks seems to me to be conclusive, although" he adds, "it might be argued that they came from families which are the anthropological victims of environmental depression." (*CM*, 379.)

Hooton finds that the "First generation criminals seem to adhere more closely than first generation civilians to the squat, broad-faced types which are often characteristic of the foreign born emigrant from Europe," and he goes on to make the astonishing suggestion that "It seems possible that such biological inadaptability, such phylogenetic conservatism, is responsible for the association of primitive features with retarded culture in modern savages." (*CM*, 379.)

It need hardly be said that for this suggestion there exists not the slightest factual support, but unexceptionally the evidence completely and unequivocally proves the contrary; that modern "savages" are biologically at least as perfectly adapted to the environments in which they live as the white man is to his. With respect to culture, it apparently requires to be pointed out that the culture of "savages," with rare exceptions, is anything but "retarded." It is a misunderstanding of the nature of culture, and of the history of our own, to speak of the culture of simpler peoples as retarded. Primitive cultures are no less complex and developed in their own ways that our own; unless, of course, we set out with the assumption that the standards of thought and material organization which Western culture has attained, as a consequence of the countless fertilizing cross currents and eddies of other cultures to which Western man has for the past few thousand years been exposed, are the measures of all cultures. Is it necessary to point out that not more than two thousand years ago, many peoples now esteemed "retarded" by us, might have judged the ancestors of all the potential and actual readers of this article as irremediably physically and culturally retarded, with quite as much justice as is implicit in Hooton's suggestion? It would seem that Hooton might profitably include an historical dimension in his biologistic judgments.

What, furthermore, it would be interesting to know, are the "primitive features" which are thought to be associated with the "retarded culture" of "modern savages"? As far as the physical structure of "modern savages" is concerned, there is no ground whatever for the belief that it is characterized by quantitatively or qualitatively more "primitive features" than is the physical structure of Western man. It is in such pronouncements as these that Hooton reveals his strong bias in favor of the belief that certain kinds of physical characters are probably associated with certain kinds of mental and social functioning.

Two distinct interpretative tendencies run throughout the work: one, a cautious and admirably restrained effort to assay the significance of biological factors in the determination of the incidence of criminal behavior; the other, a pugnacious and flamboyant insistence on the biological determination of crime. These two views do not rest comfortably in the same book but, conveniently enough, they are usually segregated. Thus, we have such careful disclaimers of extreme biological determinism as these:

This is very far from an insistence upon the direct causal relationship between the physical minutiae of an animal and his phychological processes—much less his behavior. All of these are varied expressions of the organism bound up together in their common heredity and modified in their several directions by the common environment. (*AC*, 6.)

Similarly, it may be worth while to examine the physical characteristics of large groups of criminals to discover whether they are in any sense physically homogeneous, and if so whether they are distinguishable from non-criminals. Here again there is no necessary implication of causality—at least in the sense of a direct relationship between the physical characteristics of criminals and their anti-social conduct. (*AC*, 8.)

The lawless habits of a racial or ethnic group may be persistently linked with its hereditary physique, although in a mainly non-causal relationship. (*AC*, 296.)

These straightforward formulations of problems in criminal anthropology seem to us to be unexceptionable. But these moderate statements are soon forgotten in the fervor of formulating conclusions. In spite of all these laudable protestations that a statistical association is not to be confused with a causal relationship, Hooton insists that "the variation in physique and body build is *certainly causally* related to nature of offense." (*AC*, 296; italics inserted.) And this, despite the absence of adequate evidence to demonstrate the causal connexion which he holds to be incontestable. In an qually forthright fashion, Hooton tells his Lowell Institute audience: "You may say that this is tantamount to a declaration that the *primary cause* of crime is biological inferiority—and this is exactly what I mean." (*CM*, 130; italics inserted.) In fact, as he warms to his subject, he evidently means much more than that. Hooton believes that he now has sufficient evidence for the following dictum:

I deem human [biological] deterioration to be ultimately responsible not only for crime, but for the evils of war, the oppression of the populace by totalitarian states, and for all of the social cataclysms which are rocking the world and under which civilization is tottering. (*CM*, 393.)

He does not tell us whether the recent "bear market" on the Stock Exchange is likewise attributable to this same biological degeneration. The sibylline abandon with which one of our most eminent physical anthropologists bestows these *obiter dicta* upon a Lowell Institute audience augurs ill for the more exact correlation between fact, inference and conclusion which we have assumed to characterize the scientific method. Extrapolations such as these pique the imagination and bedevil the intellect. One of Hooton's more interesting implications is that we either accept and act upon these views or slink back into our self-constituted caverns of democratic ignorance and despair to await the impending collapse of civilization. (See his concluding remarks in *CM*.) If we are to escape the day of Biological Judgment we must act—before too long. Only the "ruthless elimination of inferior types" can save us. The concluding words of Hooton's monograph are these:

Criminals are organically inferior. Crime is the resultant of the impact of environment upon low grade human organisms. It follows that the elimination of crime can be effected only by the extirpation of the physically, mentally and morally unfit, or by their complete segregation in a socially aseptic environment. (*AC*, 309.)

In his call to arms, Hooton is especially prone to such horrendous catchwords as "biological inferiority," "organic degeneration," "biological deterioration." Thus, we are told that "criminals present a united front of biological inferiority," (*AC*, 300) and that "criminals as a group represent an aggregate of sociologically inferior and biologically inferior individuals." (*AC*, 304.) Without holding any particular brief for criminals, one may nevertheless inquire: what does Hooton concretely mean by inferiority in these connexions? As we shall see, his "answers" are either contradictory, equivocal or darkly implicit. In comparing his criminal and civilian samples—the latter, be it remembered, consist of exactly 313 persons (146 Nashville firemen and 167 Massachusetts militiamen and Boston out-patients)—he finds seven metrical and indicial items in which there are unquestionably significant *differences*[3] (which persist when civilian and criminal aggregates are com-

---

[3] Significant differences = 3 or more times the probable error (not the standard error).

pared as a whole and when intra-state comparisons of civilians and criminals are made). What are these *differences* which, we must infer, unquestionably signify *inferiority?* The first is age. The criminals are 3.80 years younger than the civilians. Youth, presumably, is to be included in this homespun category of biological inferiority. "The hoary head is a crown of glory." (*Proverbs*, xvi, 31.) It hardly comes as an unheralded discovery that the age-group of maximum criminality is in the young-adult period and that this age-group varies with the type of offense. The study of crime statistics had long ago led to this finding.

The second term involving statistically significant differences between the civilians and criminals is weight: the criminals are 11.70 pounds lighter, on the average, and this difference is 10.83 p.e. Presumably, deficiency of weight as compared with the "roly-poly" firemen, *et al.*, is a mark of biological inferiority. In view of the frequently observed associations between body weight and socio-economic status, might it not be advisable to equate the status of the criminal and check samples, before treating differences of weight as "biological" differences? Or are we to make the further assumption that socio-economic status is also biologically determined?

The five other indubitable differences involve the criminals' deficiencies in chest breadth, head circumference, upper face height, nose height and ear length. One awaits with some impatience the demonstration that these deficiencies represent biological inferiority, as one awaits the proof that these "significant differences" mean anything more than a difference between two statistics computed from separate samples of such a magnitude that the probability that the samples were drawn from the same universe is inappreciable. We already know that Hooton's samples were drawn from different universes, and what we would be interested to know is why Hooton fastened upon a difference of a biological nature, rather than upon the many other characters of difference which are socio-economically known to exist between the civilians and criminals, as the causative factor in criminality. Statistically significant differences tell us no more than that the statistics involved are of different values; they do not tell us *why* or how they came to be so. The extrapolation of the "biological" factor, to the exclusion of all others, may satisfy Hooton's critical sense, but it does not satisfy ours. Furthermore, since some of Hooton's "significant differences" between the civilians and criminals are no more than 3 or 4 times the probable error, this renders those particular differences less clearly significant. It may be mentioned here that the employment of the critical ratio, *i.e.*, difference/standard error of difference, rather than the difference/probable error of difference as used by Hooton, would have constituted a critically more exacting index of "statistical significance" of such differences as were found to exist between criminals and civilians. But in any event, the demonstration is altogether lacking that such differences as the criminals exhibit are marks of "inherited inferiority" which inevitably militates against the living of a legally acceptable life.

If one turns to the fourteen morphological items which involve unequivocal statistical differences (Table XII–12, *ff.*), these are found to include an excess proportion of criminals with small hair quantity (beard) and a deficiency of those with medium quantity; likewise, an excess proportion of criminals with straight hair-form and a deficiency of those with low waves; a deficiency of those with blue eye color, with gray and white hair color, with medium (length and breadth) necks and an excess of those with long, thin necks. These, and six other marks of biological inferiority constitute some of the major differences upon which Hooton bases his imputation of organic inferiority. To be sure, with respect to morphological, indicial and metrical items, there are other differences as well, though not as clearcut as the foregoing. It remains for Hooton to reassess the utility of his control group and to make more explicit the exact implications of the "inferiorities"— or shall we say, differences?—to which he attaches so much anthropological significance. Finally, it remains for him to demonstrate that the differences which survive a reexamination of his check sample are in no way attributable to environmental differences since he often tends to identify "the organism" and "heredity." (". . . although scientifically competent persons without exception admit the importance of the organism as a determiner of its own behavior, it is expedient for them to stress rather the contribution of environment to that behavior. This is because the heredity of an existing individual cannot be altered. . . .") (*AC,* 252.)

As we have seen, Hooton speaks much of biological inferiority. To our knowledge, in only one passage does he specifically state what he means by this term. This statement is a truly remarkable example of *petitio principii.* Hooton is quite clear as to the characters which are biological inferiorities; namely, *any of the characters which are distinctive of the criminal aggregate when compared with the civilian sample.* In effect all differential characters of the criminal population are by fiat inferiorities.[4] It is by virtue of a clearly circular definition that Hooton can arrive at the "indubitable" conclusion that "criminals are biologically inferior." The exact defining statements, placed within their original context, are deserving of repetition.

Differences between individuals or groups can be ascertained and appraised without the necessity of pronouncing judgments as to inferiority or superiority. These latter may be wholly subjective and undesirable. Certainly that is true of racial differences . . . But, when we compare convicted felons . . . with law-abiding citizens of the same race, we are contrasting the social liabilities with the social assets, and we deliberately judge criminals to be undesirable and of lesser worth than economically efficient and socially-minded men. *Thus, if we find felons to manifest physical differences* (sic) *from civilians, we are justified in adjudging as undesirable biological characters those which are associated in the organism with antisocial behavior* . . . It is the organic complex which must be estimated inferior

---

[4] In terms of such logic, the male of the species with a rate of imprisonment often tenfold that of the female is hopelessly inferior. Here indeed is a "biological" difference associated with a difference in rate of commitment. On Hooton's logic, as Sutherland has indicated, the all-too-wicked male "should be weeded out of the population."

or superior on the basis of the type of behavior emanating from such a combination of parts functioning as a unit. (*CM*, 342–343; italics inserted.)

* * *

What the significant deviation in greater nose breadth among the criminals may mean we do not know, but we should be strongly disinclined to look upon such a character as a mark of organic inferiority. With respect to the significance of this character Hooton is silent, but not so when it comes to small-headedness, for in this connexion he remarks that "Presumably or possibly, the smaller head sizes of the criminals may be associated with their indubitably inferior intelligence." (*CM*, 368.)

To leave the discussion of the anthropometric-indicial characters for a moment, what, we may well ask, does Hooton mean by the "indubitably inferior intelligence" of the criminal? It may be pointed out that 'indubitable' means "clear or certain beyond question." Hooton's statement concerning the unquestionably inferior intelligence of the criminal is explicitly based upon two sets of data: the intelligence ratings of 154 cases (inmates of the Concord Reformatory) in his crminal series and upon Sheldon and Eleanor Glueck's intelligence ratings of 466 former inmates of this Reformatory. The first series of 154 Concord matriculants is notably dull-witted, for only 19.48 per cent possess a "normal intelligence" (I.Q. 96 or above). The Gluecks found that of their 466 subjects 33 per cent had a normal I.Q. (90–110), 24.1 per cent were dull (I.Q. 80–90), 22.3 per cent borderline (I.Q. 70–80), and 20.6 feeble-minded (I.Q. 50–70). It is not our purpose to question these results. What is in question is Hooton's implied suggestion that such "intelligence tests" measure native intelligence or ability exclusively. The fact is that intelligence tests, so-called, measure innumerable factors among which native intelligence is presumably one. Whatever they may be claimed to be, intelligence tests are not a measure of that single factor alone. For children and college students it has been shown time and again that these tests do not measure native ability or intelligence apart from schooling, that the tests are largely measures of scholastic or experiential attainment. What these tests measure is an expression of the experience-capacity equation.

Altogether apart from these considerations, the Gluecks' findings are by no means invariably substantiated by other studies. In view of the widely differing techniques and "results" in this field, as recent surveys have shown, the one conclusion which seems wholly out of place is that of the 'indubitably' inferior intelligence of the criminal aggregate.[5] Murchison found, after a comparison of the Army Alpha ratings of soldiers with prisoners of the same states, that the scores of the prison population were a representative

[5] See E. H. Sutherland, *Mental Deficiency and Crime*, in Kimball Young (ed.), *Social Attitudes* (New York, 1931); L. D. Zeleny, *Feeblemindedness and Criminal Conduct* (American Journal of Sociology, 1933), pp. 38, 564–578; S. H. Tulchin, *Intelligence and Crime* (Chicago, 1939); W. C. Reckless, *Criminal Behavior* (New York, 1940).

sample of the community from which the subjects were drawn.[6] With respect to juvenile delinquents, competent observers such as Healy, Slawson, Burt and Willemse, while agreeing that some delinquents are feebleminded also agree that delinquents as a whole do not exhibit differences in intelligence which would be capable of explaining the fact of their delinquency.[7] Thus, Burt found only eight per cent of delinquents "who were backward in intelligence by at least three-tenths of their ages."[8]

Of course, authorities could be multiplied on both sides, but our purpose here has been to suggest that native intelligence is not what the intelligence tests measure, and that it is far from indubitable that criminals and delinquents are of inferior native intelligence.

As for the suggested possible or presumed relationship between head size and intelligence, it has been clearly established by the work of Pearson, Murdock and Sullivan, Reid and Mulligan, and others that there is no relation whatever between head size and intelligence or scholastic achievement.[9]

And here we may return to Hooton's characters of assumed physical inferiority. We have already seen with respect to the majority of the so-called primitive or inferior characters in the anthropometric-indicial series, that these are few in number and that they are far exceeded in number by characters of an agreed advanced and neutral or indifferent nature. When we turn to consider the 16 "primitive" characters which characterize the morphological grouping, as shown in Table III, we must frankly confess that we fail to see in any one of them any sign which may be interpreted as a mark of physical or organic inferiority, although by the arbitrary standard which we have adopted as a measure of the developmental status of such characters, these characters must remain in the "primitive" category. But there are only 32.0 per cent of these characters in this group as against 56.0 per cent of "advanced" characters. A more significant figure is obtain by taking these 16 primitive characters together with the two characters of the same class from the anthropometric-indicial series and expressing them as a percentage of the total number of combined anthropometric-indicial-morphological characters, which amount to 101. In this way we find that only 17.8 per cent of

---

[6] Carl Murchison, *Criminal Intelligence* (Boston, 1926). See also H. M. Adler and M. R. Worthington, *The Scope of the Problem of Delinquency and Crime as Related to Mental Deficiency* (Journal of Psycho-Asthenics, 1925), pp. 30, 47–56.

[7] John Slawson, *The Delinquent Boy* (Boston, 1926); Cyril Burt, *The Young Delinquent*, (London, 1925); W. A. Willemse, *Constitutional Types in Delinquency* (New York, 1932).

[8] Burt, *op. cit.*, 300.

[9] K. Pearson, *Relationship of Intelligence to Size and Shape of the Head and Other Mental and Physical Characters* (Biometrika, 1906), pp. 5, 105–146; R. Pearl, *On the Correlation between Intelligence and the Size of the Head* (Journal of Comparative Neurology and Psychology, 1906), pp. 189–199; K. Murdock and L. R. Sullivan, *A Contribution to the Study of Mental and Physical Measurements in Normal Children* (American Physical Education Review, 1923), pp. 28, 209–215; 276–280; 328; R. W. Reid and J. H. Mulligan, *Relation of Cranial Capacity to Intelligence* (Journal of the Royal Anthropological Institute, 1923), pp. 53, 322–332.

characters fall into the primitive class as compared with 49.5 per cent in the advanced class. In the light of these findings, then, is it a tenable hypothesis that the criminal is an organically inferior being? We think not. We believe it to be undemonstrated that such differences as we do find are marks of genetic or biological inferiority. We believe that Hooton's own findings, when subjected to a developmental analysis such as we have attempted, do not support his conclusion that "The evidence that the criminals are derived from the baser biological stuff of their various ethnic stocks seems . . . to be conclusive."

Hooton also imputes "sociological inferiority" to the criminal aggregate. It may be suggested, however, that his summary of significant sociological differences between the criminal and civilian samples attests above all the glaring inadequacy, in some respects, of the check sample (Table XII-126, *ff.*). This may be seen by examining the specific marks of sociological "inferiority." With respect to marital status, the excess of single men among criminals, and correlatively, the deficiency of married criminals, is acknowledged to be "partially attributable to the lower mean age of the criminals." Some differences persist, however, apart from this factor of age. The criminals' excess of divorced men is allegedly due in part "to probable suppression of divorce on the part of civilians" (for not a single divorced person appears in the civilian check sample!). *All* of the differences in occupational distribution are exaggerated, Hooton acknowledges, by the disproportionate number of public service workers (those Nashville firemen again) in the check sample. To the naive reader it would seem that the occupational distribution (and perhaps other social and physical characteristics) of the criminal sample would have appeared even more "abnormal" and "inferior" if the entire civilian sample, instead of only some 50 per cent, were constituted by the "stout" firemen.

When it comes to the third set of clearcut social differences, namely, education, the criminals are found to be, as expected, clearly deficient in duration of formal schooling. However, here again the gross results must be interpreted cautiously in view of the fact that 60 per cent of the criminal sample come from Tennessee, Kentucky and Texas. In fact, when comparison is made between the Tennessee criminal and the Tennessee firemen, some of these differences are sharply attenuated, if not reversed in direction (e.g., the criminals have a marked excess of those who have had from one to two years of high school training and a statistically insignificant excess of college men). All this is not to suggest that there are no social differences between the criminal and civilian populations—on the contrary, other exacting studies have shown many such differences—but simply to indicate the inadequacy of the particular samples utilized in this study.

Moreover, there still remains the question as to what is meant by the oft-repeated phrase, "sociological inferiority" of the criminal sample. The possibility of selective commitment on the basis of social and economic status is not explored here for the ample reason that the relevant evidence is not available. Thus, granted the reliability of the observed differences, what is concretely meant by the unqualified imputation of sociological inferiority? Fortunately, Hooton is explicit on this point. "Excess of single men and of divorced men indicate an inability or unwillingness to undertake successfully the normal family responsibilities of the adult male." (*AC*, 304.) The introduction of Hooton's personal attitude toward divorce and celibacy is illuminating, perhaps interesting, but hardly relevant. If those of us who have given hostages to Fortune are more kindly disposed toward benedicts than toward celibates, well and good; but is this a considered judgment resting in part upon twelve years of anthropological research concerning the American criminal or is its source some arcanum into which we may not be admitted? In any event, if this evaluation is to be accepted at its face value, one must also conclude that the Massachusetts civilians are in this respect "sociologically inferior" to the Tennessee civilians inasmuch as 86 percent of the latter are married whereas only 32 per cent of the Bay State representatives have attained this superior status. Moreover, on the same logic, the Massachusetts civilians are likewise inferior to the criminal aggregate since 45 per cent of the latter are confessed benedicts. The not wholly irrelevant point is that Hooton's conclusion of ingrained biological and sociological inferiority of the criminal will be and has been heralded as a finding derived by an unquestionably eminent scientist from a comprehensive analysis of objective data. In view of the painstaking and exact nature of a great part of the study, it is unfortunate that the interpretation is marred by such dicta.

Hooton continues with the proposition that "deficient education and low occupational status are bound up with mental inferiority, lack of industry and stability and general weakness of character." (*AC*, 304–305.) Within the context of Hooton's general point of view, all of these, presumably, are biologically determined. At the risk of unleashing a favorite *ad hominem* thesis of the author—critics of his extreme position are simply voicing their adherence to the "democratic doctrine of human equality" and thereby insisting that all men are created biologically equal—one might suggest that this unauthenticated statement might well await more intensive study before claiming general acceptance. The exacting researches by Gray and Moshinsky[10]—pertaining to England, to be sure, but not wholly irrelevant to Hooton's expansive assertion—find that (in a sample of 9000) 59 per cent of the children with an I.Q. of 130 and over do not enjoy the opportunity of a higher education. It must be confessed that these investigators do not examine differences in "general weakness of character," which, it must be assumed, either Hooton or others must have done.

Hooton's causal imputations and his varied attempts to attribute to the criminal "inferiorities" of one type or another can be questioned in greater detail, but the general consideration is clear. By neglecting a close, systematic examination of social, economic and cultural differences between his criminal

---

[10] J. L. Gray and P. Moshinsky, *Ability and Educational Opportunity in Relation to Parental Occupation* in L. Hogben (ed.), *Political Arithmetic* (New York, 1938), pp. 376–417. See also L. Isserlis, *On the Relation between Home Conditions and the Intelligence of School Children* (H. M. Stationery Office, London, 1923).

and civilian samples,—such differences being attributed by fiat to biological causes—by using a check sample which is highly selective in many respects and by extrapolating far beyond the data which he has so meticulously assembled, he comes to a series of conclusions which are to the largest extent questionable.

The extent to which Hooton's convictions color not only his interpretation but also his procedure may be gathered from the following statement.

A considerable part of the sociological differentiation of the body build types may be due to the inequality of their individual derivations from the nine states represented in our criminal series. Thus, short and slender men are particularly common among the Massachusetts and Wisconsin criminals, while tall-heavy men are unduly represented in the Texas sample, and tall-slender men in Tennessee and Kentucky. In Wisconsin and Massachusetts educational facilities are excellent, while the same cannot be said of Tennessee and Kentucky. Again, Massachusetts is a state with a large urban population, whereas most of the other states in our series are predominantly rural. *It is all too clear that the several state environments, physical and cultural, are quite diverse.* It may then occur to my readers that it would be possible to eliminate the complicating effects of state environment from this study of body build type by applying a correction for state sampling, such as was done in testing the physical differentiation of offense groups. *I have not applied such corrections for state sampling, because I maintain that it is the organism which creates social environment and not the reverse.* Only if each of the states possessed an exclusive physical environment and an exclusive physical type with its own particular and unvarying culture, could we conclude that environment is the common cause of body build and sociological status . . . But *if short, fat men commit rape and come from Texas, I for present purposes, am inclined to relate their criminal predilection to their bodily constitution and not to the sexuality of the Lone Star State.* (CM, 99; italics inserted.)

This interesting formulation once again presents the issue in terms of a dilemma: either "the organism creates the social environment" or the social environment creates the organism. An alternative view that homicidal patterns, for example, may be more definitely an integral part of one local culture in contrast to another and that a larger proportion of "organisms" reared in this culture may assimilate these cultural values—e.g., "the unwritten law" pattern—and act accordingly, receives no attention. On Hooton's view, to take an extreme case for illustration, head-hunting practices in New Guinea can be quite simply interpreted as manifestations of the particular bodily constitutions of the population. A critical examination of the quoted passage from Hooton's book shows most clearly the limited purview of his sociological framework of analysis.

Yet in another particular context—and it is this discriminatory inclusion of cultural considerations in one instance and not in others which appears especially indefensible—Hooton finds it advisable to distinguish between bootleggers from rural districts (largely those in the present sample) where "moonshining" is a traditional private avocation and the metropolitan bootlegger who is generally foreign-born or of foreign parentage. Likewise, when confronted with the fact that Negro and Negroid criminals are "not unequivocally inferior in physique to the humbler non-college civilians, but only to the collegians, and, in their case, the criminal inferiority is restricted to stature and some few other metric features," Hooton decides that it is the "rigid social and economic straitjacket in which the Negro is confined" which "confuses" the (imputable or expectable) anthropological differences between the Negro criminal and civilian. (*CM*, 386.) In other words, when the expected differences do not occur, socio-economic factors may be at times involved; when they do occur, socio-economic factors are on the whole irrelevant and the differences are biologically determined. *In neither case, be it noted, is there a close examination of the actual role of these non-biological factors; they are introduced or neglected in accord with the disposition of the investigator.* If socio-economic factors "obscure" (putative) biological differences between the Negro criminal and civilian, why not investigate further to see whether or not they "accentuate" apparently biological differences in other instances? Of what avail is an accurate, refined and chaste anthropometry when interpretation devolves into a "medley of *ad hoc hypotheses*"? An occasional, unpredictable nod in the direction of social and economic factors is not an adequate substitute for their systematic appraisal.

The peculiar procedure adopted by Hooton may possibly be due to the uncertain status of sociological elements in his interpretative scheme. Thus, we find him remarking that "Opportunities for theft and temptations to homicide are alike, or virtually alike, for the blond and brunet, for the Negro and the White. It is therefore remarkable that we should be able to demonstrate even a minor organic factor in the intricate web of crime causation." (*AC*, 298; in this passage the author temporarily reverts to the modest position that the organic factor is only of minor importance.) Clearly it is only in an equivocal and misleading sense that "temptations to homicide" (a formulation which largely obscures the issue) are alike for the White from a bourgeois cultural area in Massachusetts, let us say, and the lower class Negro in rural Texas or, for that matter, the White of corresponding status and origin. Or does Hooton believe himself to have demonstrated that biological differences between the two samples explain the 24:1 ratio of Kentucky to Massachusetts criminals convicted of first degree murder? And may we likewise assume biological determinants of the fact that there are proportionately five times as many Texas criminals convicted of forgery and fraud as in the Massachusetts sample? Are these discrepancies readily ascribable to biological, quite apart from the sociocultural, differences between the native white populations of the two states?[11] Is it not significant that the forgery-and-fraud group among Negro and Negroid as well as among White criminals stem largely from Texas? Possibly that "glib and oily art" of stock-swindling is less a matter of bodily type than of petroliferous regions and an established pattern of promoting chimerical "gushers."

---

[11] In this connexion it would be profitable to consult H. C. Brearley, *Homicide in the United States* (Chapel Hill, 1932).

2. ECONOMISM

Crime and Poverty

W . A . B O N G E R

What are the conclusions to be drawn from what has gone before? When we sum up the results that we have obtained it becomes plain that economic conditions occupy a much more important place in the etiology of crime than most authors have given them.

First we have seen that the present economic system and its consequences weaken the social feelings. The basis of the economic system of our day being exchange, the economic interests of men are necessarily found to be in opposition. This is a trait that capitalism has in common with other modes of production. But its principal characteristic is that the means of production are in the hands of a few, and most men are altogether deprived of them. Consequently, persons who do not possess the means of production are forced to sell their labor to those who do, and these, in consequence of their economic preponderance, force them to make the exchange for the mere necessaries of life, and to work as much as their strength permits.

This state of things especially stifles men's social instincts; it develops, on the part of those with power, the spirit of domination, and of insensibility to the ills of others, while it awakens jealousy and servility on the part of those who depend upon·them. Further the contrary interests of those who have property, and the idle and luxurious life of some of them, also contribute to the weakening of the social instincts.

The material condition, and consequently the intellectual condition, of the proletariat are also a reason why the moral plane of that class is not high. The work of children brings them into contact with persons to associate with whom is fatal to their morals. Long working hours and monotonous labor brutalize those who are forced into them; bad housing conditions contribute also to debase the moral sense, as do the uncertainty of existence, and finally absolute poverty, the frequent consequence of sickness and unemployment. Ignorance and lack of training of any kind also contribute their quota. Most demoralizing of all is the status of the lower proletariat.

SOURCE: W. A. Bonger, *Crime and Economic Conditions* (Boston: Little, 1916), pp. 667–672.

The economic position of woman contributes also to the weakening of the social instincts.

The present organization of the family has great importance as regards criminality. It charges the legitimate parents with the care of the education of the child; the community concerns itself with the matter very little. It follows that a great number of children are brought up by persons who are totally incapable of doing it properly. As regards the children of the proletariat, there can be no question of the education properly so-called, on account of the lack of means and the forced absence of one or both of the parents. The school tends to remedy this state of things, but the results do not go far enough. The harmful consequences of the present organization of the family make themselves felt especially in the case of the children of the lower proletariat, orphans, and illegitimate children. For these the community does but little, though their need of adequate help is the greatest.

Prostitution, alcoholism, and militarism, which result, in the last analysis, from the present social order, are phenomena that have demoralizing consequences.

As to the different kinds of crime, we have shown that the very important group of economic criminality finds its origin on the one side in the absolute poverty and the cupidity brought about by the present economic environment, and on the other in the moral abandonment and bad education of the children of the poorer classes. Then, professional criminals are principally recruited from the class of occasional criminals, who, finding themselves rejected everywhere after their liberation, fall lower and lower. The last group of economic crimes (fraudulent bankruptcy, etc.) is so intimately connected with our present mode of production, that it would not be possible to commit it under another.

The relation between sexual crimes and economic conditions is less direct; nevertheless these also give evidence of the decisive influence of these conditions. We have called attention to the four following points.

First, there is a direct connection between the crime of adultery and the present organization of society, which requires that the legal dissolution of a marriage should be impossible or very difficult.

Second, sexual crimes upon adults are committed especially by unmarried men; and since the number of marriages depends in its turn upon the economic situation, the connection is clear; and those who commit these crimes are further almost exclusively illiterate, coarse, raised in an environment almost without sexual morality, and regard the sexual life from the wholly animal side.

Third, the causes of sexual crime upon children are partly the same as those of which we have been speaking, with the addition of prostitution.

Fourth, alcoholism greatly encourages sexual assaults.

As to the relation between crimes of vengeance and the present constitution of society, we have noted that it produces conflicts without number; statistics have shown that those who commit them are almost without exception poor and uncivilized, and that alcoholism is among the most important causes of these crimes.

Infanticide is caused in part by poverty, and in part by the opprobrium incurred by the unmarried mother (an opprobrium resulting from the social utility of marriage).

Political criminality comes solely from the economic system and its consequences.

Finally, economic and social conditions are also important factors in the etiology of degeneracy, which is in its turn a cause of crime.

Upon the basis of what has gone before, we have a right to say that the part played by economic conditions in criminality is preponderant, even decisive.

This conclusion is of the highest importance for the prevention of crime. If it were principally the consequence of innate human qualities (atavism, for example), the pessimistic conclusion that crime is a phenomenon inseparably bound up with the social life would be well founded. But the facts show that it is rather the optimistic conclusion that we must draw, that where crime is the consequence of economic and social conditions, we can combat it by changing those conditions.

However important crime may be as a social phenomenon, however terrible may be the injuries and the evil that it brings upon humanity, the development of society will not depend upon the question as to what are the conditions which could restrain crime or make it disappear, if possible; the evolution of society will proceed independently of this question.

What is the direction that society will take under these continual modifications? This is not the place to treat fully of this subject. In my opinion the facts indicate quite clearly what the direction will be. The productivity of labor has increased to an unheard of degree, and will assuredly increase in the future. The concentration of the means of production into the hands of a few progresses continually; in many branches it has reached such a degree that the fundamental principle of the present economic system, competition, is excluded, and has been replaced by monopoly. On the other hand the working class is becoming more and more organized, and the opinion is very generally held among working-men that the causes of material and intellectual poverty can be eliminated only by having the means of production held in common.

Supposing that this were actually realized, what would be the consequences as regards criminality? Let us take up this question for a moment. Although we can give only personal opinions as to the details of such a society, the general outlines can be traced with certainty.

The chief difference between a society based upon the community of the means of production and our own is that material poverty would be no longer known. Thus one great part of economic criminality (as also one part of infanticide) would be rendered impossible, and one of the greatest demoralizing forces of our present society would be eliminated. And then, in this way those social phenomena so productive of crime, prostitution and alcoholism, would lose one of their principal factors. Child labor and over-driving would no longer take place, and bad housing, the source of much physical and moral evil, would no longer exist.

With material poverty there would disappear also that intellectual poverty which weighs so heavily upon the proletariat; culture would no longer be the privilege of some, but a possession common to all. The consequences of this upon criminality would be very important, for we have seen that even in our present society with its numerous conflicts, the members of the propertied classes, who have often but a veneer of civilization, are almost never guilty of crimes of vengeance. There is the more reason to admit that in a society where interests were not opposed, and where civilization was universal, these crimes would be no longer present, especially since alcoholism also proceeds in large part from the intellectual poverty of the poorer classes. And what is true of crimes of vengeance, is equally true of sexual crimes in so far as they have the same etiology.

A large part of the economic criminality (and also prostitution to a certain extent) has its origin in the cupidity excited by the present economic environment. In a society based upon the community of the means of production, great contrasts of fortune would, like commercial capital, be lacking, and thus cupidity would find no food. These crimes will not totally disappear so long as there has not been a redistribution of property according to the maxim, "to each according to his needs," something that will probably be realized, but not in the immediate future.

The changes in the position of woman which are taking place in our present society, will lead, under this future mode of production, to her economic independence, and consequently to her social independence as well. It is accordingly probable that the criminality of woman will increase in comparison with that of man during the transition period. But the final result will be the disappearance of the harmful effects of the economic and social preponderance of man.

As to the education of children under these new conditions it is difficult to be definite. However, it is certain that the community will concern itself seriously with their welfare. It will see to it that the children whose parents cannot or will not be responsible for them, are well cared for. By acting in this way it will remove one of the most important causes of crime. There is no doubt that the community will exercise also a strict control over the education of children; it cannot be affirmed, however, that the time will come when the children of a number of parents will be brought up together by capable persons; this will depend principally upon the intensity that the social sentiments may attain.

As soon as the interests of all are no longer opposed to each other, as they are in our present society, there will no longer be a question either of politics ("a fortiori" of political *crimes*) or of militarism.

Such a society will not only remove the causes which now make men egoistic, but will awaken, on the contrary, a strong feeling of altruism. We have seen that this was already the case with the primitive peoples, where their economic interests were not in opposition. In a larger measure this will be realized under a mode of production in common, the interests of all being the same.

In such a society there can be no question of crime properly so called. The eminent criminologist, Manouvrier, in treating of the prevention of crime expresses himself thus: "The maxim to apply is, act so that every man shall always have more interest in being useful to his fellows than in harming them." It is precisely in a society where the community of the means of production has been realized that this maxim will obtain its complete application. There will be crimes committed by pathological individuals, but this will come rather within the sphere of the physician than that of the judge. And then we may even reach a state where these cases will decrease in large measure, since the social causes of degeneracy will disappear, and procreation by degenerates be checked through the increased knowledge of the laws of heredity and the increasing sense of moral responsibility.

"It is society that prepares the crime," says the true adage of Quetelet. For all those who have reached this conclusion, and are not insensible to the sufferings of humanity, this statement is sad, but contains a ground of hope. It is sad, because society punishes severely those who commit the crime which she has herself prepared. It contains a ground of hope, since it promises to humanity the possibility of some day delivering itself from one of its most terrible scourges.

White-Collar Criminality

EDWIN H. SUTHERLAND

This paper is concerned with crime in relation to business. The economists are well acquainted with business methods but not accustomed to consider them from the point of view of crime; many sociologists are well acquainted with crime but not accustomed to consider it as expressed in business. This paper is an attempt to integrate these two bodies of knowledge. More accurately stated, it is a comparison of crime in the upper or white-collar class, composed of respectable or at least respected business and professional men, and crime in the lower class, composed of persons of low socioeconomic

SOURCE: Edwin H. Sutherland, "White Collar Criminality," *American Sociological Review*, 5 (February, 1940), pp. 1–12. Reprinted by permission.

status. This comparison is made for the purpose of developing the theories of criminal behavior, not for the purpose of muckraking or of reforming anything except criminology.

The criminal statistics show unequivocally that crime, *as popularly conceived and officially measured*, has a high incidence in the lower class and a low incidence in the upper class; less than two percent of the persons committed to prisons in a year belong to the upper class. These statistics refer to criminals handled by the police, the criminal and juvenile courts, and the prisons, and to such crimes as murder, assault, burglary, robbery, larceny, sex offenses, and drunkenness, but exclude traffic violations.

The criminologists have used the case histories and criminal statistics derived from these agencies of criminal justice as their principal data. From them, they have derived general theories of criminal behavior. These theories are that, since crime is concentrated in the lower class, it is caused by poverty or by personal and social characteristics believed to be associated statistically with poverty, including feeblemindedness, psychopathic deviations, slum neighborhoods, and "deteriorated" families. This statement, of course, does not do justice to the qualifications and variations in the conventional theories of criminal behavior, but it presents correctly their central tendency.

The thesis of this paper is that the conception and explanations of crime which have just been described are misleading and incorrect, that crime is in fact not closely correlated with poverty or with the psychopathic and sociopathic conditions associated with poverty, and that an adequate explanation of criminal behavior must proceed along quite different lines. The conventional explanations are invalid principally because they are derived from biased samples. The samples are biased in that they have not included vast areas of criminal behavior of persons not in the lower class. One of these neglected areas is the criminal behavior of business and professional men, which will be analyzed in this paper.

The "robber barons" of the last half of the nineteenth century were white-collar criminals, as practically everyone now agrees. Their attitudes are illustrated by these statements: Colonel Vanderbilt asked, "You don't suppose you can run a railroad in accordance with the statutes, do you?" A. B. Stickney, a railroad president, said to sixteen other railroad presidents in the home of J. P. Morgan in 1890, "I have the utmost respect for you gentlemen, individually, but as railroad presidents I wouldn't trust you with my watch out of my sight." Charles Francis Adams said, "The difficulty in railroad management . . . lies in the covetousness, want of good faith, and low moral tone of railway managers, in the complete absence of any high standard of commerical honesty."

The present-day white-collar criminals, who are more suave and deceptive than the "robber barons," are represented by Krueger, Stavisky, Whitney, Mitchell, Foshay, Insull, the Van Sweringens, Musica-Coster, Fall, Sinclair, and many other merchant princes and captains of finance and industry, and by a host of lesser followers. Their criminality has been demonstrated again and again in the investigations of land offices, railways, insurance, munitions, banking, public utilities, stock exchanges, the oil industry, real estate, re-organization committees, receiverships, bankruptcies, and politics. Individual cases of such criminality are reported frequently, and in many periods more important crime news may be found on the financial pages of newspapers than on the front pages. White-collar criminality is found in every occupation, as can be discovered readily in casual conversation with a representative of an occupation by asking him, "What crooked practices are found in your occupation?"

White-collar criminality in business is expressed most frequently in the form of misrepresentation in financial statements of corporations, manipulation in the stock exchange, commercial bribery, bribery of public officials directly or indirectly in order to secure favorable contracts and legislation, misrepresentation in advertising and salesmanship, embezzlement and misapplication of funds, short weights and measures and misgrading of commodities, tax frauds, misapplication of funds in receiverships and bankruptcies. These are what Al Capone called "the legitimate rackets." These and many others are found in abundance in the business world.

In the medical profession, which is here used as an example because it is probably less criminalistic than some other professions, are found illegal sale of alcohol and narcotics, abortion, illegal services to underworld criminals, fraudulent reports and testimony in accident cases, extreme cases of unnecessary treatment, fake specialists, restriction of competition, and fee-splitting. Fee-splitting is a violation of a specific law in many states and a violation of the conditions of admission to the practice of medicine in all. The physician who participates in fee-splitting tends to send his patients to the surgeon who will give him the largest fee rather than to the surgeon who will do the best work. It has been reported that two thirds of the surgeons in New York City split fees, and that more than one half of the physicians in a central western city who answered a questionnaire on this point favored fee-splitting.

These varied types of white-collar crimes in business and the professions consist principally of violation of delegated or implied trust, and many of them can be reduced to two categories: misrepresentation of asset values and duplicity in the manipulation of power. The first is approximately the same as fraud or swindling; the second is similar to the double-cross. The latter is illustrated by the corporation director who, acting on inside information, purchases land which the corporation will need and sells it at a fantastic profit to his corporation. The principle of this duplicity is that the offender holds two antagonistic positions, one of which is a position of trust, which is violated, generally by misapplication of funds, in the interest of the other position. A football coach, permitted to referee a game in which his own team was playing, would illustrate this antagonism of positions. Such situations cannot be completely avoided in a complicated business structure, but many concerns make a practice of assuming such antagonistic functions and regularly violating the trust thus delegated to them. When compelled by law to make a separation of their functions, they make a nominal separation and continue by subterfuge to maintain the two positions.

An accurate statistical comparison of the crimes of the two classes is not available. The most extensive evidence regarding the nature and prevalence of white-collar criminality is found in the reports of the larger investigations to which reference was made. Because of its scattered character, that evidence is assumed rather than summarized here. A few statements will be presented, as illustrations rather than as proof of the prevalence of this criminality.

The Federal Trade Commission in 1920 reported that commercial bribery was a prevalent and common practice in many industries. In certain chain stores, the net shortage in weights was sufficient to pay 3.4 percent on the investment in those commodities. Of the cans of ether sold to the Army in 1923–1925, 70 percent were rejected because of impurities. In Indiana, during the summer of 1934, 40 percent of the ice cream samples tested in a routine manner by the Division of Public Health were in violation of law. The Comptroller of the Currency in 1908 reported that violations of law were found in 75 percent of the banks examined in a three months' period. Lie detector tests of all employees in several Chicago banks, supported in almost all cases by confessions, showed that 20 percent of them had stolen bank property. A public accountant estimated, in the period prior to the Securities and Exchange Commission, that 80 percent of the financial statements of corporations were misleading. James M. Beck said, "Diogenes would have been hard put to it to find an honest man in the Wall Street which I knew as a corporation lawyer" in (1916).

White-collar criminality in politics, which is generally recognized as fairly prevalent, has been used by some as a rough gauge by which to measure white-collar criminality in business. James A. Farley said, "The standards of conduct are as high among officeholders and politicians as they are in commercial life," and Cermak, while mayor of Chicago, said, "There is less graft in politics than in business." John Flynn wrote, "The average politician is the merest amateur in the gentle art of graft, compared with his brother in the field of business." And Walter Lippmann wrote, "Poor as they are, the standards of public life are so much more social than those of business that financiers who enter politics regard themselves as philanthropists."

These statements obviously do not give a precise measurement of the relative criminality of the white-collar class, but they are adequate evidence that crime is not so highly concentrated in the lower class as the usual statistics indicate. Also, these statements obviously do not mean that every business and professional man is a criminal, just as the usual theories do not mean that every man in the lower class is a criminal. On the other hand, the preceding statements refer in many cases to the leading corporations in America and are not restricted to the disreputable business and professional men who are called quacks, ambulance chasers, bucket-shop operators, dead-beats, and fly-by-night swindlers.[1]

The financial cost of white-collar crime is probably several times as great as the financial cost of all the crimes which are customarily regarded as the "crime problem." An officer of a chain grocery store in one year embezzled $600,000, which was six times as much as the annual losses from five hundred burglaries and robberies of the stores in that chain. Public enemies numbered one to six secured $130,000 by burglary and robbery in 1938, while the sum stolen by Krueger is estimated at $250,000,000, or nearly two thousand times as much. *The New York Times* in 1931 reported four cases of embezzlement in the United States with a loss of more than a million dollars each and a combined loss of nine million dollars. Although a million-dollar burglar or robber is practically unheard of, these million-dollar embezzlers are small-fry among white-collar criminals. The estimated loss to investors in one investment trust from 1929 to 1935 was $580,000,000, due primarily to the fact that 75 percent of the values in the portfolio were in securities of affiliated companies, although it advertised the importance of diversification in investments and its expert services in selecting safe securities. In Chicago, the claim was made six years ago that householders had lost $54,000,000 in two years during the administration of a city sealer who granted immunity from inspection to stores which provided Christmas baskets for his constituents.

The financial loss from white-collar crime, great as it is, is less important than the damage to social relations. White-collar crimes violate trust and therefore create distrust, which lowers social morale and produces social disorganization on a large scale. Other crimes produce relatively little effect on social institutions or social organization.

White-collar crime is real crime. It is not ordinarily called crime, and calling it by this name does not make it worse, just as refraining from calling it crime does not make it better than it otherwise would be. It is called crime here in order to bring it within the scope of criminology, which is justified because it is in violation of the criminal law. The crucial question in this analysis is the criterion of violation of the criminal law. Conviction in the criminal court, which is sometimes suggested as the criterion, is not adequate because a large proportion of those who commit crimes are not convicted in criminal courts. This criterion, therefore, needs to be supplemented. When it is supplemented, the criterion of the crimes of one class must be kept consistent in general terms with the criterion of the crimes of the other class.

---

[1] Perhaps it should be repeated that "white-collar" (upper) and "lower" classes merely designate persons of high and low socioeconomic status. Income and amount of money involved in the crime are not the sole criteria. Many persons of "low" socioeconomic status are "white-collar" criminals in the sense that they are well-dressed, well-educated, and have high incomes, but "white-collar" as used in this paper means "respected," "socially accepted and approved," "looked up to." Some people in this class may not be well-dressed or well-educated, nor have high incomes, although the "upper" usually exceed the "lower" classes in these respects as well as in social status.

The definition should not be the spirit of the law for white-collar crimes and the letter of the law for other crimes, or in other respects be more liberal for one class than for the other. Since this discussion is concerned with the conventional theories of the criminologists, the criterion of white-collar crime must be justified in terms of the procedures of those criminologists in dealing with other crimes. The criterion of white-collar crimes, as here proposed, supplements convictions in the criminal courts in four respects, in each of which the extension is justified because the criminologists who present the conventional theories of criminal behavior make the same extension in principle.

First, other agencies than the criminal court must be included, for the criminal court is not the only agency which makes official decisions regarding violations of the criminal law. The juvenile court, dealing largely with offenses of the children of the poor, in many states is not under the criminal jurisdiction. The criminologists have made much use of case histories and statistics of juvenile delinquents in constructing their theories of criminal behavior. This justifies the inclusion of agencies other than the criminal court which deal with white-collar offenses. The most important of these agencies are the administrative boards, bureaus, or commissions, and much of their work, although certainly not all, consists of cases which are in violation of the criminal law. The Federal Trade Commission recently ordered several automobile companies to stop advertising their interest rate on installment purchases as 6 percent, since it was actually 11½ percent. Also it filed complaint against *Good Housekeeping*, one of the Hearst publications, charging that its seals led the public to believe that all products bearing those seals had been tested in their laboratories, which was contrary to fact. Each of these involves a charge of dishonesty, which might have been tried in a criminal court as fraud. A large proportion of the cases before these boards should be included in the data of the criminologists. Failure to do so is a principal reason for the bias in their samples and the errors in their generalizations.

Second, for both classes, behavior which would have a reasonable expectancy of conviction if tried in a criminal court or substitute agency should be defined as criminal. In this respect, convictability rather than actual conviction should be the criterion of criminality. The criminologists would not hesitate to accept as data a verified case history of a person who was a criminal but had never been convicted. Similarly, it is justifiable to include white-collar criminals who have not been convicted, provided reliable evidence is available. Evidence regarding such cases appears in many civil suits, such as stockholders' suits and patent-infringement suits. These cases might have been referred to the criminal court but they were referred to the civil court because the injured party was more interested in securing damages than in seeing punishment inflicted. This also happens in embezzlement cases, regarding which surety companies have much evidence. In a short consecutive series of embezzlements known to a surety company,

90 percent were not prosecuted because prosecution would interfere with restitution or salvage. The evidence in cases of embezzlement is generally conclusive, and would probably have been sufficient to justify conviction in all of the cases in this series.

Third, behavior should be defined as criminal if conviction is avoided merely because of pressure which is brought to bear on the court or substitute agency. Gangsters and racketeers have been relatively immune in many cities because of their pressure on prospective witnesses and public officials, and professional thieves, such as pickpockets and confidence men who do not use strong-arm methods, are even more frequently immune. The conventional criminologists do not hesitate to include the life histories of such criminals as data, because they understand the generic relation of the pressures to the failure to convict. Similarly, white-collar criminals are relatively immune because of the class bias of the courts and the power of their class to influence the implementation and administration of the law. This class bias affects not merely present-day courts but to a much greater degree affected the earlier courts which established the precedents and rules of procedure of the present-day courts. Consequently, it is justifiable to interpret the actual or potential failures of conviction in the light of known facts regarding the pressures brought to bear on the agencies which deal with offenders.

Fourth, persons who are accessory to a crime should be included among white-collar criminals as they are among other criminals. When the Federal Bureau of Investigation deals with a case of kidnapping, it is not content with catching the offenders who carried away the victim; they may catch and the court may convict twenty-five other persons who assisted by secreting the victim, negotiating the ransom, or putting the ransom money into circulation. On the other hand, the prosecution of white-collar criminals frequently stops with one offender. Political graft almost always involves collusion between politicians and business men but prosecutions are generally limited to the politicians. Judge Manton was found guilty of accepting $664,000 in bribes, but the six or eight important commercial concerns that paid the bribes have not been prosecuted. Pendergast, the late boss of Kansas City, was convicted for failure to report as a part of his income $315,000 received in bribes from insurance companies but the insurance companies which paid the bribes have not been prosecuted. In an investigation of an embezzlement by the president of a bank, at least a dozen other violations of law which were related to this embezzlement and involved most of the other officers of the bank and the officers of the clearing house, were discovered but none of the others was prosecuted.

This analysis of the criterion of white-collar criminality results in the conclusion that a description of white-collar criminality in general terms will be also a description of the criminality of the lower class. The respects in which the crimes of the two classes differ are the incidentals rather than the essentials of criminality. They differ principally in the emplementation of the criminal laws which apply to them. The crimes of the lower class are handled by policemen, prosecutors, and judges, with penal sanctions in the form of fines, imprisonment, and death. The crimes of the upper class either result in no official action at all, or result in suits for damages in civil courts, or are handled by inspectors, and by administrative boards or commissions, with penal sanctions in the form of warnings, orders to cease and desist, occasionally the loss of a license, and only in extreme cases by fines or prison sentences. Thus, the white-collar criminals are segregated administratively from other criminals, and largely as a consequence of this are not regarded as real criminals by themselves, the general public, or the criminologists.

This difference in the implementation of the criminal law is due principally to the difference in the social position of the two types of offenders. Judge Woodward, when imposing sentence upon the officials of the H. O. Stone and Company, bankrupt real estate firm in Chicago, who had been convicted in 1933 of the use of the mails to defraud, said to them, "You are men of affairs, of experience, of refinement and culture, of excellent reputation and standing in the business and social world." That statement might be used as a general characterization of white-collar criminals for they are oriented basically to legitimate and respectable careers. Because of their social status they have a loud voice in determining what goes into the statutes and how the criminal law as it affects themselves is implemented and administered. This may be illustrated from the Pure Food and Drug Law. Between 1879 and 1906, 140 pure food and drug bills were presented in Congress and all failed because of the importance of the persons who would be affected. It took a highly dramatic performance by Dr. Wiley in 1906 to induce Congress to enact the law. That law, however, did not create a new crime, just as the federal Lindbergh kidnapping law did not create a new crime; it merely provided a more efficient implementation of a principle which had been formulated previously in state laws. When an amendment to this law, which would bring within the scope of its agents fraudulent statements made over the radio or in the press, was presented to Congress, the publishers and advertisers organized support and sent a lobby to Washington which successfully fought the amendment principally under the slogans of "freedom of the press" and "dangers of bureaucracy." This proposed amendment, also, would not have created a new crime, for the state laws already prohibited fraudulent statements over the radio or in the press; it would have implemented the law so it could have been enforced. Finally, the Administration has not been able to enforce the law as it has desired because of the pressures by the offenders against the law, sometimes brought to bear through the head of the Department of Agriculture, sometimes through congressmen who threaten cuts in the appropriation, and sometimes by others. The statement of Daniel Drew, a pious old fraud, describes the criminal law with some accuracy, "Law is like a cobweb; it's made for flies and the smaller kinds of insects, so to speak, but lets the big bumblebees break through. When technicalities of the law stood in my way, I have always been able to brush them aside easy as anything."

The preceding analysis should be regarded neither as an assertion that all efforts to influence legislation and its administration are reprehensible nor as a particularistic interpretation of the criminal law. It means only that the upper class has greater influence in moulding the criminal law and its administration to its own interests than does the lower class. The privileged position of white-collar criminals before the law results to a slight extent from bribery and political pressures, principally from the respect in which they are held and without special effort on their part. The most powerful group in medieval society secured relative immunity by "benefit of clergy," and now our most powerful groups secure relative immunity by "benefit of business or profession."

In contrast with the power of the white-collar criminals is the weakness of their victims. Consumers, investors, and stockholders are unorganized, lack technical knowledge, and cannot protect themselves. Daniel Drew, after taking a large sum of money by sharp practice from Vanderbilt in the Erie deal, concluded that it was a mistake to take money from a powerful man on the same level as himself and declared that in the future he would confine his efforts to outsiders, scattered all over the country, who wouldn't be able to organize and fight back. White-collar criminality flourishes at points where powerful business and professional men come in contact with persons who are weak. In this respect, it is similar to stealing candy from a baby. Many of the crimes of the lower class, on the other hand, are committed against persons of wealth and power in the form of burglary and robbery. Because of this difference in the comparative power of the victims, the white-collar criminals enjoy relative immunity.

Embezzlement is an interesting exception to white-collar criminality in this respect. Embezzlement is usually theft from an employer by an employee, and the employee is less capable of manipulating social and legal forces in his own interest than is the employer. As might have been expected, the laws regarding embezzlement were formulated long before laws for the protection of investors and consumers.

The theory that criminal behavior in general is due either to poverty or to the psychopathic and sociopathic conditions associated with poverty can now be shown to be invalid for three reasons. First, the generalization is based on a biased sample which omits almost entirely the behavior of white-collar criminals. The criminologists have restricted their data, for reasons of convenience and ignorance rather than of principle, largely to cases dealt with in criminal courts and juvenile courts, and these agencies are used principally for criminals from the lower economic strata. Consequently, their data are grossly biased from the point of view of the economic status of criminals and their generalization that criminality is closely associated with poverty is not justified.

Second, the generalization that criminality is closely associated with poverty obviously does not apply to white-collar criminals. With a small number of exceptions, they are not in poverty, were not reared in slums or badly deteriorated families, and are not feebleminded or psychopathic. They were seldom problem children in their earlier years and did not appear in juvenile courts or child guidance clinics. The proposition, derived from the data used by the conventional criminologists, that "the criminal of today was the problem child of yesterday" is seldom true of white-collar criminals. The idea that the causes of criminality are to be found almost exclusively in childhood similarly is fallacious. Even if poverty is extended to include the economic stresses which afflict business in a period of depression, it is not closely correlated with white-collar criminality. Probably at no time within fifty years have white-collar crimes in the field of investments and of corporate management been so extensive as during the boom period of the twenties.

Third, the conventional theories do not even explain lower class criminality. The sociopathic and psychopathic factors which have been emphasized doubtless have something to do with crime causation, but these factors have not been related to a general process which is found both in white-collar criminality and lower class criminality and therefore they do not explain the criminality of either class. They may explain the manner or method of crime—why lower class criminals commit burglary or robbery rather than false pretenses.

In view of these defects in the conventional theories, an hypothesis that will explain both white-collar criminality and lower class criminality is needed. For reasons of economy, simplicity, and logic, the hypothesis should apply to both classes, for this will make possible the analysis of causal factors freed from the encumbrances of the administrative devices which have led criminologists astray. Shaw and McKay and others, working exclusively in the field of lower class crime, have found the conventional theories inadequate to account for variations within the data of lower class crime and from that point of view have been working toward an explanation of crime in terms of a more general social process. Such efforts will be greatly aided by the procedure which has been described.

The hypothesis which is here suggested as a substitute for the conventional theories is that white-collar criminality, just as other systematic criminality, is learned; that it is learned in direct or indirect association with those who already practice the behavior; and that those who learn this criminal behavior are segregated from frequent and intimate contacts with law-abiding behavior. Whether a person becomes a criminal or not is determined largely by the comparative frequency and intimacy of his contacts with the two types of behavior. This may be called the process of differential association. It is a genetic explanation both of white-collar criminality and lower class criminality. Those who become white-collar criminals generally start their careers in good neighborhoods and good homes, graduate from colleges with some idealism, and with little selection on their part, get into particular business situations in which criminality is practically a folkway and are inducted into that system of behavior just as into any other folkway. The lower class criminals generally start their careers in deteriorated neighborhoods and families, find delinquents at hand from whom they acquire the attitudes toward, and techniques of, crime through association with delinquents and in partial segregation from law-abiding people. The essentials of the process are the same for the two classes of criminals. This is not entirely a process of assimilation, for inventions are frequently made, perhaps more frequently in white-collar crime than in lower class crime. The inventive geniuses for the lower class criminals are generally professional criminals, while the inventive geniuses for many kinds of white-collar crime are generally lawyers.

A second general process is social disorganization in the community. Differential association culminates in crime because the community is not organized solidly against that behavior. The law is pressing in one direction, and other forces are pressing in the opposite direction. In business, the "rules of the game" conflict with the legal rules. A business man who wants to obey the law is driven by his competitors to adopt their methods. This is well illustrated by the persistence of commercial bribery in spite of the strenuous efforts of business organizations to eliminate it. Groups and individuals are individuated; they are more concerned with their specialized group or individual interests than with the larger welfare. Consequently, it is not possible for the community to present a solid front in opposition to crime. The Better Business Bureaus and Crime Commissions, composed of business and professional men, attack burglary, robbery, and cheap swindles, but overlook the crimes of their own members. The forces which impinge on the lower class are similarly in conflict. Social disorganization affects the two classes in similar ways.

I have presented a brief and general description of white-collar criminality on a framework of argument regarding theories of criminal behavior. That argument, stripped of the description, may be stated in the following propositions:

1. White-collar criminality is real criminality, being in all cases in violation of the criminal law.

2. White-collar criminality differs from lower class criminality principally in an implementation of the criminal law which segregates white-collar criminals administratively from other criminals.

3. The theories of the criminologists that crime is due to poverty or to psychopathic and sociopathic conditions statistically associated with poverty are invalid because, first, they are derived from samples which are grossly biased with respect to socioeconomic status; second, they do not apply to the white-collar criminals; and third, they do not even explain the criminality of the lower class, since the factors are not related to a general process characteristic of all criminality.

4. A theory of criminal behavior which will explain both white-collar criminality and lower class criminality is needed.

5. An hypothesis of this nature is suggested in terms of differential association and social disorganization.

3. PSYCHOLOGISM

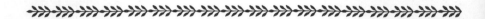

Crime and the Psychoanalyst

FRANZ ALEXANDER

The psychoanalytic study of unconscious psychic life leads to the conviction that every part of the human personality, which is socially adjusted, represents a later and comparatively labile product of a special evolution.

However, within the innermost nucleus of the personality, which is both quantitatively and dynamically much more powerful, it is impossible to differentiate normal from criminal impulses. The human being enters the world as a criminal, *i.e.*, socially not adjusted. During the first years of his life, the human individual preserves his criminality to the fullest degree. His actual social adjustment begins only at the time after the Œdipus complex is overcome. This happens during the so-called latency period which was described by Freud. This period begins between the ages of four and six, and ends at puberty. It is at this period that the development of the criminal begins to differentiate itself from that of the normal. The future normal individual succeeds (mostly in the latency period) in partly repressing his genuine criminal instinctual drives, and thus cuts them out of motor expression and partly in transforming them into socially acceptable striving; the future criminal more or less fails in carrying out this adjustment.

The criminal carries out in his actions his natural unbridled instinctual drives; he acts as the child would act if it only could. The repressed, and therefore unconscious criminality of the normal man finds a few socially harmless outlets, like the dream and phantasy life, neurotic symptoms and also some transitional forms of behavior which are less harmless, like duelling, boxing, bull fights and, occasionally, the free expression of one's criminality in war.

No better proof for the general criminality of mankind could be found than the proof which would be brought about by the daring experiment of depriving, say, the Spanish nation of its bull fights, the Americans of their boxing and football games, old Europe of its soldier game and the world of its

SOURCE: Reprinted with permission of the publisher from *The Criminal, the Judge and the Public* by Franz Alexander. Copyright 1931 by The Macmillan Company. Copyright 1956 by the Free Press, A Corporation. Pp. 34–41.

penal codes. The universal criminality of man of to-day demands violent, purely physical outlets; without them it would become transformed into a battle of all against all.

The only difference between the criminal and the normal individual is that the normal man partially controls his criminal drives and finds outlets for them in socially harmless activities. This power of controlling, and of the domestication of the primitive, unsocial tendencies is acquired by the individual as a result of education. In other words, criminality, generally speaking, is not a congenital defect but a defect in the bringing up; this statement does not cover certain borderline cases which should be considered separately. Our contention will become clearer if we could imagine that all the children of the world between the ages of two to six should suddenly become physically superior to the adult and were thus able to dominate the adult to the same degree as the adult dominates the child. These children, let us imagine further, would then set themselves to act out all their phantasies. These Gulliverian giant children dominating a world of dwarf-like adults would present a hundred-per-cent criminality in action.

The first drive in relation to the outside world which the newly born individual experiences is the drive to grasp, to dominate. This drive in its earliest expression appears in the form of the cannibalistic possession of the breast of the mother, a sort of a partial eating up of the mother. The psychic content of this drive on this level is known in the psychoanalytic theory of instinctual drives as the *oral-sadistic* phase of development of the individual. The pregenital sexuality of the suckling finds its satisfaction in the mouth activity while sucking the mother's breast, the nipple or the bottle or the thumb. In this phase one is naturally unable to find any trace of the future social attitude, *i.e.*, the tendency to consider the interests of others.

Disturbances in the normal functioning during this instinctual phase, particularly any educational mistake in the process of weaning, might influence the educability of the individual along the lines of social relationships. Individuals who at every frustration of a wish show a tendency to violent action, who react to any postponement of a pleasure with uncontrollable impatience, prove frequently to have been orally spoiled children; these individuals serve as a proof of how exceptionally long indulgence during the period of sucking reappears with a vengeance in an adult.[1] But weaning must inevitably come some day, and such spoiled babies respond to it with spiteful resistance; they do not want to give up a rightfully acquired habit. Abraham and Alexander[2] consider that the deepest roots of kleptomania are to be found in the history of this period.

The child finds itself compelled for the first time to submit to the wishes of the adult when it begins to be taught habits of cleanliness. At first the child experiences a definite pleasure in relation to its excretory functions; this

---

[1] Cf. Abraham—*Collected Papers*, London, 1927.
[2] Cf. Alexander—*Castration Complex and Character*, 1922.

pleasure consists either of holding back or expressing the excreta; this pleasure, as well as the coprophilic tendencies of the child, is considerably interfered with when the adult begins to present demands for orderliness, cleanliness, and propriety.

Interference with its primitive instinctual drives brings the child to the realization that its sovereignty is badly encroached upon; it becomes impossible for the child to utilize the excretory processes whenever and in whatever manner it wishes, and thus to derive pleasure from them whenever it wishes, in whatever manner and degree it wishes. One of the chief characteristics of this anal erotism is that it gives one a sense of power, a feeling that one's pleasures do not depend upon others; for, in contrast to breast or bottle, which can and are always taken away and therefore are connected with a feeling of insecurity, the excrements are products created by the child itself, and take the place of the breast or bottle as a source of pleasure. In other words, the source of oral pleasure is always in the hands of the adult, while the fecal masses, hidden within the body, are outside the reach of grown-ups who want to dominate.

The psychoanalytic literature has not yet considered with sufficient detail this strong drive for independence, the spite with which it is connected, and the high self-esteem of the anal phase of development. It was first recognized by Freud as stubbornness of the anal erotic; it is a sort of overcompensation for the sad experiences met with in the oral phase in which the child depended for pleasure on the whim of the mother.

However, sooner or later, the child learns to control and regulate its sphincter activity, because it is afraid of being censured and punished by the adults. The first crime which all humans, without exception, sooner or later commit is the violation of the prescription for cleanliness. Under the rule of this penal code of the nursery, man for the first time becomes acquainted with the punishment which the world metes out to individual transgressors. Ferenczi,[3] therefore, is right when he speaks of the "sphincter morality" as the beginning and foundation of adult human morality. As a prototype of certain refractory criminals who persist in their spiteful rejection of social demands, one can imagine a baby sitting on its little chamber pot persistently rejecting any demands coming from the outside; it sits in this sovereign position and feels superior to the grownups.

At the moment when the child begins to impose inhibitions on the demands of its own sphincter, it makes the first decisive step toward the adjustment to the outside world; at that moment it creates an inhibitory agency within its own personality, and this agency from now on demands from within what the outside world demanded heretofore. In other words, a definite part of the child's personality identifies itself with the demands of the person who is bringing it up. We thus deal here with an identification with a *demand;* i.e., a partial identification with a person; at a later phase the child will identify itself with an adult *person* as a whole instead of with a demand only.

---

[3] Ferenczi, *Psychoanalysis of Sexual Habits* in *Collected Papers.*

This education to cleanliness becomes a prototype for the future restrictions of instinctual life; a disturbance during this phase of development may naturally serve as a cause of a future disturbance in one's social adjustment.

The anal character traits which were described by Freud, Jones, and Abraham, in their exaggerated form present a number of anti-social and criminal characteristics.

The exaggerated, unsocial, stubborn bluntness of some violators of the law corresponds to the unyielding persistence of infantile anal spite. The characteristic self-centered stubbornness of the anal character acquires in the majority of criminals the form of proud, inaccessible spite, which is directed against all humanity.

In the course of the development of every child we find that its interests gradually broaden, and in addition to its relationship to its own physiological processes it tries to establish a relationship with the outer world. The instinctual drives in the phases of oral and anal development which were just mentioned were psychologically concerned with intake of food and its elimination; instinctual pleasure was derived from these two processes. However, in view of the fact that they begin to be directed toward objects of the outer world, they approach for the first time a psychological level of the adult individual. As is to be expected, the first objects of the outside world toward which the child's interest is directed are the immediate members of the family. Thus, the relationship of the child to father, mother, brothers and sisters, becomes the central problem of the future adult individual. The psychological management of these relationships on the part of the growing human being becomes definitely the decisive factor in the whole development and functioning of the adult person. After thirty years of therapeutic work and psychoanalytical research this point may be considered definitely proved. The way in which the child overcomes the conflicts arising from this situation determines whether it will develop into a healthy or sick individual, or whether his general behavior will be that of a socially adjusted person or that of a criminal. We should like to emphasize now, and we shall be able to prove later in these pages, that psychoneurosis and criminality are defects in one's social adjustment; they hardly differ from one another in their respective psychological contents; the differences are those of psychological dynamics. Both the neurotic and the criminal fell victims to their incapacity of finding a socially acceptable solution of the conflicts which the relationships to the various members of the family engendered. The neurotic expresses symbolically by means of his symptoms, which are socially innocuous, the same things which the criminal does by means of real actions. This important fact opens to us a promising method of study; we can understand the psychological content of a criminal act through the psychoanalysis of the neuroses.

We thus come to the fundamental problem as to which are the circumstances responsible for the fact that, in some individuals, the unconscious criminal phantasy finds it sufficient to come to expression in the substitution form of a neurotic symptom, while in other individuals it demands the motor

expression in the form of criminal acts. This problem requires the consideration of the economic and structural characteristics of the psychic apparatus;
it is a problem dealing with the relative strength of inhibitory psychic agencies as compared with the pressure coming from the undomesticated remnants
of our instinctual drives. We shall be able to throw light on the problem if
we consider the data acquired by psychoanalysis with regard to the structural
and dynamic development of the human personality.

It is self-evident that, in order to gain an understanding of criminality, we
shall have to investigate the process by means of which a socially adjusted
Ego develops out of a great homogeneous reservoir of instincts which originally were unsocial; this reservoir of instinctual drives is called the Id.

The two pregenital phases of adjustment which were described above,
oral and anal, are but preparatory to the first great necessity, which demands
that the object relationship to parents and siblings be transformed into relationships of a social nature.

Psychoanalysis and Crime

DAVID FELDMAN

Psychoanalysis is, of course, best known for its contributions to the understanding and treatment of mental disorders. Yet, almost from its inception,
psychoanalytic theory was conceived by Sigmund Freud as having equal
explanatory value in areas quite beyond what is usually considered the realm
of the psychopathological. And in accordance with this conception, psychoanalysts have, over the years, expanded their theoretical interests to include
very nearly every facet of the subject-matters treated in the social sciences
and arts.[1] But perhaps the most assiduously cultivated extracurricular interest for psychoanalysis has been the problem of criminal behavior. Indeed,
what may be called psychoanalytic criminology is already close to half a
century in age and remains still among the foremost influences in shaping
current programs of dealing with criminal and delinquent offenders. However, as has been the case in all of the behavioral disciplines, the fundamental
theoretical framework of psychoanalysis has received differential interpretations, resulting in the development of diverse psychoanalytic accounts of
criminality. In this survey of psychoanalytic criminology what follows, then,
is, first, a brief sketch of its underlying theoretical orientation and, second,

---

SOURCE: Prepared especially for this volume.

[1] See, e.g., the range of subject-matters covered in S. Lorand (ed.), *Psychoanalysis
Today* (New York, 1944) and in G. Roheim (ed.), *Psychoanalysis and the Social
Sciences*, (New York, 1947).

a consideration of some of the important recent trends in the various applications of that orientation.

Logically, psychoanalytic theory starts out with the commonplace, but crucial, assumption that all human behavior is motivated and, hence, goal-oriented or teleological in character. To begin with, this means that human behavior is functional, that it is undertaken to fulfill a given need or desire, and that it has consequences for other patterns of behavior. But since the same action can have many different purposes, it follows that neither the motives nor the functions of any given act can be ascertained by observing the overt action itself. This implies that, as a matter of general principle, a proper grasp of human behavior requires that this behavior be understood in terms of the subjective meanings and significances which the actor himself attaches to his action. This principle of subjective understanding now occupies a well-established, though not undisputed, position in contemporary sociological theory. But for psychoanalysis the situation is further complicated by its concept that the subjective meaning which an actor attaches to his action may be quite unconscious, so that the actor himself is consciously unaware of the functions he imputes to his own action. Thus, in addition to any manifest functions which an overt act may have for the actor, the same act can also have latent functions which, while of equal or more importance, remain unconscious.[2]

With respect to the problem of criminal behavior, this principle of motivational functionalism implies that a concentration of analysis on the manifest criminal act itself cannot hope to provide a proper etiological understanding of the crime. For like any other behavior, criminal behavior is a form of self-expression and what is intended to be expressed in the act of crime is not only unobservable in the act itself, but also may even be beyond the awareness of the criminal actor himself. So, for example, an overt criminal act of stealing may be undertaken for the attainment of purposes which are far removed from, and even contrary to, that of simple illegal aggrandizement; indeed, it may even be, as shall be seen in the sequel, that the criminal, in stealing, seeks not material gain by self-punishment. The etiological basis of a criminal act can, therefore, be understood only in terms of the functions, latent as well as manifest, which the act was intended to accomplish.[3]

---

[2] It is worth emphasizing that the distinction between manifest and latent functions, currently something of an issue in sociological discussion, was not imported for use in the present context. The distinction is actually very much a part of the psychoanalytic conception of motivation and was originated by Freud in his theory of dreams. In fact, it was Merton who popularized the notion in sociology and borrowed the terms from Freud. See R.K. Merton, *Social Theory and Social Structure* (Glencoe, Ill., rev. ed., 1957), p. 60 ff.

[3] The concept of motivational functionalism is most explicitly formulated in psychoanalytic criminology in W. Healy and A. Bronner, *New Light on Delinquency and Its Treatment* (New Haven, Conn., 1936). Today, of course, functionalism is highly fashionable, and it is no longer required to be a Freudian to think of crime in terms of its latent functions. See, e.g., A. K. Cohen, *Delinquent Boys* (Glencoe, Ill., 1955), which sets down a theory of the latent functions of gang delinquency.

But, of course, to know that a criminal act is functional and may have both manifest and latent functions is not yet to know anything about the specific causal determinants of that act. Accordingly, the methodological principle of motivational functionalism has to be supplemented with substantive concepts of the actual functions involved. Now crime, however it is defined, represents a behavioral violation of one or more social norms. Since the cognition of, and conformity to, social norms are resultants of the socialization process, it follows that the individual who engages in a pattern of criminal behavior has, in some sense, been defectively socialized or that the norms demanding his conformity are themselves, in some sense, defective. In either case, it also follows that prerequisite to a resolution of the problem of crime causation is a theoretical explication of the processes comprising the socialization of the individual. And such an analysis is precisely what constitutes the heart of the psychoanalytic conception of ego psychology.

In a gross way, it may be said that, as an analytic schema of the socialization process, psychoanalytic ego psychology revolves around, and reflects, the fact that the human individual, born into a family, group, and class, has in some way to come to terms with the operative norms which are arbitrarily imposed upon him as regulators of his behavior. Thus there is a certain tension built up within the individual as a result of the competing requirements of the social group and his own private and original impulses. In the Freudian view, these original impulses are part of the biological equipment of the individual and are essentially antisocial in nature, consisting of the sexual, aggressive, and destructive "instinct."[4] Left to his own devices, therefore, the individual would necessarily undertake actions which, in substance and aim, run counter to the normative demands of his social group. But since he is not allowed such license and is, moreover, for a long time after his birth, in a physical condition of total helplessness and dependency, thereby making him highly susceptible to both the danger of his environment and the threat of punishment, the individual has little choice in the matter and must find means of adapting himself to the "reality" of his situation. And he must do so because his needs for the support, protection, and acceptance of his family and group are far more urgent than are his needs to satisfy his antisocial drives.

However, one fundamental aspect of being born dependent and powerless is that the individual is, willy-nilly, subjected to an inexorable process of indoctrination in the group norms under a pedagogical technique consisting largely of a differential application of reward and punishment (love and rejection) and relying heavily on the individual's role-taking capacity. The individual manages his adaptation in primarily two ways: on the one hand,

---

[4] It should be noted that Freud's German term for "instinct" is "trieb," which, as Freudians are forever pointing out, does not have the connotations of rigidity and immutability associated with the English usage of "instinct." See, e.g., the discussion in O. Fenichel, *The Psychoanalytic Theory of Neurosis* (New York, 1945), pp. 12 f, 54 ff.

he resorts to reasoned calculations and compromises of what can and cannot be done, which of his original impulses he may seek to satisfy with impunity and which he must not act upon lest he suffer penalty. And, on the other hand, he incorporates and accepts for himself the group norms and evaluates his own impulses in their terms. This he does by means of identification, involving what Mead called "taking the role of the other," first with the immediate authority figures in his life, then with an expanding number of "significant others," and lastly with the social group as a whole representing the "generalized other."[5]

In short, there are three basic psychological processes operating within the individual comprising the original impulses, the mechanisms of adjustment, and the internalized group norms. Each of these processes tends to be in potential or active conflict with the others, and the individual is able to maintain a stable existence only to the extent that a viable "balance of power" obtains among them and functions to temper the conflicts and prevent an explosive eruption. And this balance, in turn, depends upon a minimally favorable equilibrium between the kinds and amounts of compensatory gratifications and enforced renunciations the individual experiences.[6]

Combining now the principle of motivational functionalism and the socialization schema of ego psychology, the basic etiological formula of psychoanalytic criminology becomes apparent; it simply states that criminality is undertaken as a means of maintaining psychic balance or as an effort to rectify a psychic balance which has been disrupted. On this general formula, a substantial consensus of opinion has been attained among psychoanalytic criminologists. At the same time, however, a considerable diversity of views has developed as to exactly what it is in the socialization of the individual which compels him to resort to crime and as to precisely how criminal behavior fulfills the function of helping retain psychic balance. In fact, there are at present at least five more or less contrasting psychoanalytic views available for consideration.

Among the first and still persistently maintained interpretations of the etiological formula is the view that criminality is a form of neurosis. The criminal is a person suffering from a neurotic illness which, in no fundamental way, differs from any of the other forms of neurotic phenomena. Psychodynamically, so it is held, the only difference between the common

---

[5] G.H. Mead, *Mind, Self, and Society* (Chicago, 1934), Chs. III and IV.

[6] In Freudian theory the three psychic processes are referred to as id, ego, and superego respectively. But, of course, these analytic categories entail a good deal more than has here been set down. The primary sources of ego psychology are S. Freud, *The Ego and The Id* (London, 1947) and S. Freud, *The Problem of Anxiety* (New York, 1936); less technical discussions are contained in S. Freud, *New Introductory Lectures on Psychoanalysis* (New York, 1933) and S. Freud, *An Outline of Psychoanalysis* (New York, 1936). The Freudian schema of socialization has been taken over practically intact by contemporary structural-functionalism in sociology and has already found expression in the textbook literature. See the interesting discussion in H.M. Johnson, *Sociology: A Systematic Introduction* (New York, 1960), Ch. 5.

symptomatic neurosis and criminal neurosis is merely that the latter is allo-
plastically manifested in overt acts, while the former finds expression in the
autoplastic symbolism of symptom formation. But exactly like the symptoms
of the symptomatic neurosis, the criminal acts of the criminal neurosis have
the function of providing neurotic gratifications and resolutions of unconscious conflicts over which the individual has partially lost control. Generally,
it is believed that the criminal neurotic suffers from a compulsive need for
punishment to alleviate intolerable guilt feelings stemming from unconscious, and poorly sublimated, incestuous strivings. Thus the criminal engages
in illegal activity so that he may be apprehended and penalized for his
crimes. From the subjective standpoint of the criminal, the real crime
demanding punishment is his incestuous wish; but by a form of neurotic
compromise, the punishment he receives for his overt crimes functions to
expiate his guilt and ameliorate the debilitating effects of his emotional
conflicts.[7]

A more recent, and contrasting, conception of the etiological formula holds
that, far from suffering guilt and needing punishment, the criminal feels no
guilt and strenuously avoids being subjected to penalty. On this view, the
criminal is an "antisocial character" who has been defectively socialized so
that he is unable to cope properly with the normative requirements of his
external situation. Realistically, every individual is frequently compelled to
postpone gratification of his needs or to modify them in a manner more
acceptable to his group and to himself. But the antisocial character, due to
certain deformities in his rearing, is chronically unable to orient his conduct
in accordance with the dictates of this "reality principle." He simply cannot
endure temporary frustrations and he cannot postpone the quest for satisfaction, and so he impulsively engages in antisocial, criminal behavior as a
means of seeking immediate gratification. Because the internalization of
social norms is, for the antisocial character, in a weakened state, he has no
strong internal guides to evaluate his actions; and because his mechanisms
of adjustment are poorly developed, he permits himself kinds of activities
which a properly socialized individual would not undertake. Basically, he
regards his behavior and his relationships to others sheerly in terms of
pleasure and penalty. If actions can provide pleasure without penalty he
will perform them, and if, upon misjudgment, he is penalized for these
actions, he does not react with remorse but with hatred and frustration at
having to put up with displeasure.[8]

A third, and extremely influential, interpretation of the etiological formula
is that criminal activity is undertaken as a means of obtaining substitutive

---

[7] An early and still influential statement of this view is F. Alexander and H. Staub,
The Criminal, The Judge, and the Public (Glencoe, Ill., rev. ed., 1956). The original
edition was published in translation in 1931.

[8] The concept of the antisocial character is most closely associated with K. Friedlander, *The Psychoanalytical Approach to Juvenile Delinquency* (New York, 1945);
a briefer statement is K. Friedlander, "Latent Delinquency and Ego Development," in
K.R. Eissler (ed.), *Searchlights on Delinquency* (New York, 1949).

and compensatory gratifications of needs and desires which would ordinarily be met and fulfilled within the network of familial relationships. These are the needs and desires which are fundamental in determining the nature of the individual's maturation and involve such matters as the inherent needs for security, recognition, acceptance, adequacy, status, and self-assertion. When the individual finds that these basic needs are frustrated in the inter-personal channels of his family environment, he inevitably experiences painful feelings of being thwarted and deprived. In these circumstances, it is a natural response for the individual to divert his activities into the illegal channels of delinquency and crime as a means of securing some substitute satisfactions and to pacify his frustrations. Where his family fails, the de-linquent gang can succeed in giving the individual the necessary sense of acceptance, recognition, and adequacy; and if the family cannot, or will not, allow outlets for the individual's expression of independence, self-assertion, and self-direction, he may wreak his vengeance and demonstrate his inner capacities to his own satisfaction in the act of crime. Criminality, therefore, is a consequence of a disturbance in the psychic balance and the criminal or delinquent is an emotionally frustrated and perturbed individual who unconsciously seeks in his offensive actions a resolution to his emotional problems in the form of compensatory satisfactions which have been denied him in his familial relationships.[9]

A quite recently developed fourth conception of the etiological formula is somewhat akin to the idea of the criminal as an antisocial character. How-ever, according to this newer view the deficiency within the criminal stems not from impoverished mechanisms of adjustment and internalized norms, but from the unconscious permissiveness of parental figures who are them-selves ambivalent towards the acceptance of the norms prohibiting criminal-ity. The delinquent or criminal, it is held, suffers from "superego lacunae," or unformed segments in his normative orientation; he may be fully oriented toward acceptance of most social norms, while toward some other norms he has not evolved an orientation of acceptance and conformity. These lacunae derive from similar defective normative orientations in his parents who unconsciously encourage criminal activities in their child as a means of obtaining vicarious gratifications for their own unconscious strivings. Thus the child, seeking the approbation of his parents, engages in delinquent acts because he believes that his delinquencies would be gratifying to them or because he rightly senses that such actions can be used as a weapon in his relations with his family.[10]

The concept of superego lacunae seems to hint slightly at a notion that the norms prohibiting criminal behavior are not strongly or consistently

---

[9] The most prominent statement of this position is W. Healy and A. Bronner, *op. cit.*, which has practically become a classic of psychoanalytic criminology.

[10] For an exposition of this view, see A.M. Johnson, "Sanctions for Superego Lacunae of Adolescents," in K.R. Eissler, *op. cit.*, and A.M. Johnson, "Juvenile Delinquency," in S. Arieti (ed.), *American Handbook of Psychiatry* (New York, 1959), Vol. I.

maintained as regulators of conduct; there is at least something of an implication that, aside from any psychological deficiencies within the criminal,
criminality may also ensue from the internalization of defective norms. This
implication has recently received some further development in yet a fifth
interpretation of the etiological formula which, in many respects, bears a
close resemblance to the theory of anomie currently so popular in sociological
circles.[11] According to this psychoanalytic conception of anomie, criminal
behavior occurs in the context of a social situation in which an extremely high
value is placed on the individual achievement of economic success, but
which, at the same time, stringently limits the legitimate means of obtaining
this goal. The value of individual initiative and success, it is maintained, is
an historical hangover from the period of the open frontier, when the
emphasis on personal effort and achievement was feasible economically and,
therefore, a natural ideological outgrowth of the prevailing conditions. Since
that period, however, the available opportunities for achieving success have
been progressively exhausted, and a heavy expenditure of individual initiative can no longer be expected to be rewarded by economic success. But
while the underlying socioeconomic conditions for achieving success have
changed, the ideological superstructure has been retained. In these circumstances, there must develop definite tensions for the individual who has been
socialized to incorporate the norms of personal initiative and achievement
and who finds himself placed socially in a situation of deprivation or poverty
where the legitimate exercise of these values can only lead to frustration and
failure. Yet this discrepancy between social structure and cultural norms
does not uniformly affect all individuals in like degree; it will, instead, have
its greatest psychological impact upon those individuals who are least
equipped psychically to undertake the unrewarding pursuit of success. Such
individuals who are, by nature, more passive, compliant, and dependent
than the average are trapped in an intolerable conflict with their internalization of the norms of personal achievement. Compelled to define their passivity
and dependency as personal weakness and incompetence, they will tend to
repress these qualities and, by the process of reaction-formation, overconform
to the social norms by adopting an excessively individualistic aggressiveness.
But barred from success by their social position and the social structure, this
exaggerated individualism will naturally find outlet in criminal behavior,
which serves the dual purpose of denying their unconscious dependency
while accruing material benefits. And so it is the social structure which generates tendencies towards criminality among select individuals who, as a
result of a combination of social position and psychic nature, are unable to
make the necessary adjustments.[12]

---

[11] The sociological theory of anomie was originally developed by Durkheim and
further extended by Merton. See R.K. Merton, *op. cit.*, Chs. IV and V.

[12] A clear statement of the psychoanalytic conception of anomie can be found in
F. Alexander, *Our Age of Unreason*, p. 301 ff. An earlier adumbration of this view
is F. Alexander and W. Healy, *The Roots of Crime* (New York, 1935).

Now looking over these variant interpretations of the same basic etiological formula, it is readily noted that they form something of a sequence ranging in scope from an exclusive emphasis on internal factors operating within the psychological constitution of the criminal to a fairly liberal concentration on external situational conditions confronting him. Partially, at least, this shift in perspective probably derives from the obvious vulnerability of the idea that all of the etiological sources of criminality are to be located in the personality of the criminal. Thus the notion of the neurotic criminal compulsively intent on self-punishment is plainly vitiated by the fact that most criminals seem to expend a great deal of energy and effort on escaping the clutches of the law and, on the whole, as is commonly acknowledged, are inordinately successful at it. Moreover, available evidence of the mental states of convicted criminals unmistakably points to the conclusion that the vastly major portion of them are simply not neurotic.[13] Again, the concept of the criminal as an antisocial character bent on obtaining immediate gratifications patently ignores the commonplace fact that criminality frequently demands much laborious training and planning of techniques and strategies, all of which belie the naive idea that the criminal is psychologically unable to endure temporary frustrations. And, indeed, if professional, organized, and white-collar crime are to be given their due, it must be acknowledged that much, if not most, criminality rather strongly adheres to the "reality principle" of Freudian theory.

Empirical considerations of this and other cognate sorts have, no doubt, persuaded many psychoanalytic criminologists to attempt an integration of sociological materials. Yet even the psychoanalytic conception of anomie, which probably comes as close to a distinctively sociological perspective as psychoanalysis has yet achieved, remains rooted in the idea that there must be something special and different about the personality of the criminal which induces him to behave in a criminal fashion. And while it cannot be said that criminological research has definitively disposed of this idea, evidence accumulated to date strongly suggests that the distribution of normality, pathology, and general personality traits among criminals is in approximately the same proportion as that found for the rest of the noncriminal population.[14] Thus it would seem that there is nothing in the criminal personality, apart from his criminality, to differentiate him from the noncriminal.

---

[13] See, e.g., the important study by W. Bromberg and C.B. Thompson, "The Relation of Psychosis, Mental Defect, and Personality Types to Crime," in *J. Crimin. Law & Criminology*, Vol. 28. Studying a random sample of close to ten thousand convicted criminals, Bromberg and Thompson found that 82.0 per cent were "average or normal."

[14] See the excellent review of research in this area by L.G. Lowrey, "Delinquent and Criminal Personalities," in J.M. Hunt (ed.), *Personality and the Behavior Disorders* (New York, 1944), Vol. II; see also K.F. Schuessler and D.R. Cressey, "Personality Characteristics of Criminals," in *Am. J. Socio.*, Vol. 55, and M.B. Clinard, "Criminological Research," in R.K. Merton, *et al.*, (eds.), *Sociology Today* (New York, 1959), p. 515 ff.

And if this is so, it must follow that criminality is not to be considered a function of the psychic state of the individual.

Nor has psychoanalytic criminology taken sufficient cognizance of the fact that the criminal does not spontaneously invent patterns of criminality. Criminal behavior, it hardly needs saying, is a social phenomenon, and a learning process has, therefore, to intervene between the personality of the criminal and his criminal actions. Typically, this learning process entails a wide assortment of techniques, ideas, and skills, all of which take time and practice to master and assimilate. Moreover, this learning process requires the individual's participation in the formation and maintenance of relationships with others who dispose of the necessary knowledge and put it to use. It is in the context of these relationships that the individual learns his criminality and adopts for himself distinctive criminalistic attitudes and precepts. Presumably, the experiences of such a learning process must have an effect on the personality of the individual undergoing them. Yet this reciprocating influence of criminal experience on the personality of the criminal appears to have received no consideration in psychoanalytic criminology. Indeed, all the interpretations of the basic etiological formula share this common implicit assumption that the personality differentials to which causal status is attributed are temporally antecedent to the individual's participation in criminal activity. Nevertheless, it is, at least, a plausible alternative possibility that such personality differentials are consequential precipitants of the individual's induction into criminality. And in failing to take this possibility into account, the entire structure of psychoanalytic criminology becomes vulnerable to the charge that it merely begs the question from the outset.

Social Disorganization and Individual Disorganization

HERBERT BLUMER

Very little systematic attention has been devoted to the interrelation of social disorganization and of individual disorder, as it is conceived by psychiatrists. Consequently, it is a welcome experience to receive the views, as they bear on this issue, of a set of distinguished psychiatrists. The contributions are of a high order of competence; to evaluate them from a sociological point of view is no easy task. While important differences exist between the

SOURCE: Reprinted from "Social Disorganization and Individual Disorganization," in *American Journal of Sociology*, 42:1 (May, 1937), by Herbert Blumer, by permission of the University of Chicago Press. Copyright, 1937, by the University of Chicago Press. Pp. 871–877.

views of the seven contributors, I believe there are four basic positions which they share more or less and which seem to comprise the psychiatric view of the problem at issue.

First, it is clear that the contributors (in varying degree) are inclined to view social disorganization as an extension of individual disorganization—as a projection, into the field of interpersonal relations, of the neurotic traits of disordered individuals. Individual disorganization and social disorganization tend to become generically alike under this view. Disorganized individuals, as participants in group life, are obviously in the position to express their dispositions inside of the texture of social relations; further, their neurotic behavior tends to induce neurotic behavior on the part of others. Viewed this way, social disorganization is the proliferation of individual disorganization; it has its genesis in the experiences of disordered individuals. This view serves nicely the interest of psychiatry for it permits one to attack the problem of social disorganization in terms of the knowledge gained through the study of individual disorder.

A recognition that this view is not ample enough to account for all social disorganization is readily given, in varying degree, by most of the contributors. A place is made for social disorganization which does not have its source in individual disorder. It is precisely at this point, however, that difficulty attends the psychiatric explanation, since this form of social disorganization does not seem to lend itself to interpretation by schemes formulated from the investigation of individual disorder. So far, then, as the area of psychiatric interpretation is concerned, it seems clear that social disorganization is viewed as being generic with individual disorganization.

Second, operating with this view, the contributions depict social disorganization as having the "unconsciously motivated" character that we are familiar with in the case of the neuroses. The interindividual behavior comprising social disorganization is essentially irrational, expressive of hidden and camouflaged impulses, and under the guidance of autistic or illusory images. The conduct of disordered individuals is under the sway of perspectives which have been distorted by earlier experiences which have induced the disorder; social disorganization is likewise associated with such distorted perspectives.

Third is the belief that the genesis of personal and, hence, of social disorganization is to be found in early childhood experience, especially as it takes place in the family milieu. These experiences which are so crucial and vital antedate, seemingly, the period at which the child orders its conduct by the intellectual or rational symbols of its culture. Further, the effects of such experiences are deep-seated and lasting, giving rise to an organization or pattern of life which shapes and determines subsequent experiences. Later experiences may act to intensify and bring to a crisis the disorganizing dispositions of the individual; they do not, seemingly, implant such dispositions.

Fourth is the belief that the elimination of social disorganization, as well as of personal disorganization, has to come through a form of child education. A program of child training, designed to prevent the experiences which establish impulses that would lead to subsequent individual disorder, becomes also the means of obviating the social disorganization which arises out of the same nexus. In a general sense, this is the type of solution to the problem of social disorganization that seems to be represented in the psychiatric position.

This scheme of four points is what I piece together out of the seven contributions as representing what I am taking the liberty of calling the "psychiatric" position. I frankly realize that it does not portray the individual variations among the contributions, and to this extent it cannot be regarded as doing justice to any one of them. Yet I feel that it does present a fair composite picture representative of what I detect to be the logic of the psychiatric position as it shapes itself in the symposium. It will serve, at any rate, as the means of stating certain observations, reflections, and inquiries bearing on the vital problem of the relation between personal and social disorganization.

Some helpful light on this problem is given by viewing social disorganization in collective terms. Organized social life seems to exist in the form of concerted behavior, i.e., the people who are in interdependent relations have their lines of activity so oriented that they fall into a concerted or co-ordinated arrangement. This seems to be the nature of orderly group life. Social disorganization is to be found in the disturbance of such concerted orientation but not in every such disturbance. For human group life is subject to constant reforming: crises emerge, new needs arise, and new situations have to be met. Every group has need of reorganizing its collective life in order to retain concertedness. Social disorganization, in any fundamental sense, prevails when a society in the face of disturbance loses the ability to re-establish concerted behavior. Such a society may be said to have lost orientation. This implies an absence of common objectives between individuals and groups of individuals, represented especially in conflicting values, which many sociologists have referred to as the "heart of social disorganization."

Viewed in this manner, it is well to stress that social disorganization may arise and persist without being an expression of personal disorganization. Through a variety of causes—communication, cultural contact, invention, redistribution of wealth, natural catastrophes—there may arise and flourish codes, philosophies, interpretations, aspirations, and convictions which are conflicting, contradictory, confused, and ambiguous. Competitive situations of different kinds may emerge without any adequate "rules of the game" to govern them. Conflicts may develop in religious circles, in the political arena, in moral relations, between age groups, in the family, between classes— conflicts which a given society is incapable, seemingly, of reconciling. It is quite unnecessary to think of such disorganization as emanating from the experiences of disordered individuals; for it may exist between the individuals who are not disorganized. If anything, the logical and temporal relation may be the reverse: social disorganization—individual disorganization. It is scarcely necessary to add that such social disorganization is not to be eliminated through a program of child training.

To admit that there may be social disorganization which does not arise out of the experience and conduct of disorganized individuals merely leaves us with the interesting and significant view that there is social disorganization which does have such a source. As suggested above, this view seems to be the heart of the psychiatric position. It deserves careful consideration, since it refers to at least one of the important facets of relation between personal and social disorganization.

First of all, may I express the view that neurotic or personally disordered individuals *may* carry on between them a collective life which is not disorganized, especially if their neurotic behavior is not severe. Their social life may not be at a level of high efficiency or wholesomeness, but it may be well under the influence of social discipline. This notion is not so improbable; for all of us, I imagine, are familiar with individuals who have at least slight evidence of what psychiatry would label as "neurotic" tendency, and who outwardly adhere to the rules and expectations of their group code. Their neurotic disposition is likely to lurk behind their overt social conduct, disordering, perhaps, their inner experience but not necessarily interfering with a capacity to carry on orderly and organized relations with their fellows.

Another observation leads me to believe that the neurotic makeup of individuals does not necessarily or inevitably lead to social disorganization, namely, the tendency for people under normal conditions to isolate socially an individual whose neurotic behavior becomes pronounced. I am not thinking of the extreme forms of such behavior, as, for example, the psychotic outbreak which in our society, at any rate, is likely to lead to some type of incarceration. I refer merely to those expressions which lead one's fellows to regard him as queer, unnatural, unreliable, or unsocial. If such conduct is not defined by the group in such a way as to elevate the individual into a special social position, the tendency, I think, is to encyst him and to this extent remove him from the web of social relations.

These observations do not invalidate the obvious fact that neurotic or disorganized individuals may contribute effectively to social disorganization. They do raise, however, the question as to the circumstances under which this is likely to occur. In answering the question, one must, I feel, attach considerable weight to the factor of social discipline. Where it is lax or ineffective, neurotic dispositions can break through and disorder the lives and conduct of others. This suggests that an already existing state of social disorganization forms an especially favorable situation to the expression of neurotic tendency at the expense of others. The absence of social disorganization, I feel, is a limiting condition to the free exercise of neurotic tendency in social relations.

The further question as to how far social disorganization may be augmented, intensified, or increased by individual disorganization is an interesting question, but one which I suspect to be unanswerable at present. It is clear that a neurotic individual who escapes the influence of social discipline may make the lives of some other people unpleasant, miserable, and perhaps even unbearable. It is further likely that such a person, if he happened to occupy some strategic social position, might be able to commit some action that might disturb considerably the organized life of a large segment of a population. However, I find it difficult to see how far such an individual could contribute directly to the confusion of social values or social objectives. This remains, however, an important problem.

Some consideration should be given to the opposite problem—the effect of social disorganization on personal makeup. The treatment given this problem by the contributed articles is rather slight and, on the whole, more implicit than explicit. It would seem, from the general character of the views expressed in the articles, that a place is made for the influence of social disorganization primarily in the setting of childhood experience. The family milieu, as it is stressed by most of the authors, and the general social environment, as it is implied by others, must be disordered to some extent to occasion in children the unfortunate experiences which result in neurotic traits. The detailed nature of this disordered condition is not made clear; it seems to consist primarily in actions which are of a forbidding character, which thwart the child's impulses, and which lead to wrong satisfactions and definitions. In turn, the conditions which might explain such conduct on the part of parents or elders are not given; the implication is merely that such conduct is itself neurotic in character.

Passing beyond the age of early childhood, it would seem that the subsequent role of social disorganization is merely that of occasioning distressing experiences which test the already established dispositions of the child. These experiences may bring such dispositions to a head but apparently do not implant such dispositions.

These views as to the influence passing from social disorganization to individual structure deserve comment. One thing that sociological studies do point to is the condition of individuals, seemingly well adjusted during childhood, who become quite disorganized under certain social conditions. I refer especially to the "marginal man" in the generic sense of that type. An individual who seems to have made normal social adjustments during the early part of his life may be placed in a situation where he is subject to conflicting social demands and appeals of a fundamental sort, and suffers distressing confusion as a result. But even more important than such social or cultural conflict is the acute and disturbing self-consciousness which such an individual may experience owing to the fact that his conception of himself is markedly disjointed from the actual social status which he occupies. His view of himself, as it is expressed in his hopes, in his ambitions, in the rights and claims which he believes to deserve social recognition, may be directly at variance with the social position he is forced to occupy. A disorganized personality may be the result. That distorted and neurotic emotional experiences appear at this point is true; I don't believe that the evidence warrants one to assume that they are merely the emergence of neurotic dispositions established in childhood. Conditions of great personal stress in adolescent or adult life may produce, and not merely test, dispositions leading to disorder.

A further point is suggested by sociological studies, namely, that in such instances personal disorganization need not have the character of the unconscious motivation that we have stressed for us in the case of neurosis. The individual may understand very well the reasons for his plight; the knowledge may even intensify his disappointment and distress. The closing of outlets may force him to abandon his hopes, ambitions, scheme of himself, and pattern of values. He may lose personal orientation.

These observations point to the need for further study of the relation between social and personal disorganization—study directed not so much to tracing the fate of neurotic tendencies established in childhood as to revealing the psychological character of a social structure and to showing the way in which this psychological structure, in the case of any social status, makes ingression into personal experience. We need to know the full implications of shared convictions and values; the nature of the semi-unwitting social rhythms which seem to constitute social support; and the nature of the psychological milieu as confusion enters these social values and social rhythms. We need to know the effect on self-conception and personal organization as the individual begins to respond to the disturbances in this psychological milieu. The desired knowledge requires collaborative efforts of psychiatrists and sociologists.

Value Congeries and Marital Counseling

DONALD CHARD MARSH
AND NORMAN D. HUMPHREY

What is the character of the boundaries within which "successful marital adjustment" occurs? The major underlying assumption of the typical marriage counselor appears to be that the best that can be done for a person "in trouble" is to aid him to be able better to bear the restrictions which middle class society and culture impose upon him. The boundaries, in short, appear to be middle class conventions, and success in marriage consists of conformity to them.

This also seems to be the verdict indicated by "objective research." Norman S. Hayner has derived a number of tentative conclusions drawn from the

SOURCE: Donald Chard Marsh and Norman D. Humphrey, "Value Congeries and Marital Counseling," *Marriage and Family Living* (February, 1953), pp. 28–32. Reprinted by permission.

literature of marriage research.[1] He indicates, among other things, that the longer the period of acquaintance the better are the chances for a happy marriage. Companionship is a better basis for a stable relationship than romantic love: emotional maturity, rather than chronological age. Certain specific personality characteristics are associated with happiness in marriage. Optimists, those who are not dominant, those who are neither neurotic nor self-sufficient, and the like, are types which make good marriage partners. For happiness in marriage, personality needs should gear into each other. But dissimilarity of customs, religious background, and the like, increase the risk of marital failure. While marriage problems center in the dynamic areas of sex, sex itself is secondary in import to personality factors in determining success of marriages. Occupations with small personal mobility and large impingements of social control are favorably associated with happiness in marriage. If both parents love their children, they provide a basis of emotional security for the children and for themselves.

From one perspective such materials would seem to add up to the fact that conformity to positive values of the middle class, to middle class virtue, makes for happiness, or success, in marriage. But what of psychological factors? The literature also abounds in statements that cases of marital maladjustment can usually be traced to such factors as "emotional immaturity" on the part of one or both of the partners. The basic cause of such immaturity is felt to lie primarily in the person, who sometimes is also regarded as the consequence of the impress of his own parents' immaturity upon him. Psychological factors are thus often regarded as primary and causal. But, from another view, the "maladjustment" is manifestly relevant to certain cultural norms which are rarely questioned, let alone highlighted in the equation. Such an arrangement of conceptions is of questionable validity, for it makes the psychological factors primary, and themselves productive of states of tension, when by another construction, it is the cultural standard (normally, middle class Protestant American morality, and more especially, virtue) which is the prime productive agent; and the so-called unhappiness and maladjustment, the psychological components, the actual consequence. As Dr. Jeurgen Ruesch, a psychiatrist, has noted, middle class American culture is the "core culture":

> The American culture . . . can be described as that culture which is represented by the lower middle class, composed of people of Anglo-Saxon descent and of Protestant religion. It is the core culture . . . [which] . . . set the cultural standards for the . . . country. All . . . immigrants were compelled to adapt to these standards. Public opinion in America is largely an expression of this core culture. We find it in novels, on the radio, in newspapers, public speeches and in the opinion of the man on the street.[2]

---

[1] "The Sociologist Views Marriage Problems," *Sociology and Social Research* 33: 20–24. September-October, 1948.

[2] "Social Technique, Social Status and Social Change in Illness," in C. Kluckhohn and H. A. Murray (editors) *Personality in Nature, Society and Culture* (New York: Knopf, 1948), pp. 126–127.

Certainly Mexican family organization, for example, and the culture it maintains, elicits different bases for "happiness" and "maladjustment" than those found in the United States. The question of the boundaries of successful marital adjustment devolves then, in part, into what is properly the independent, and what the dependent, variable: psychological make-up, or cultural standard.

Yet, almost all of the adjustment-in-marriage studies, including those predicting adjustment, show relationships between what, in effect, is adherence to conventional standards of the middle class, and so-called success in marriage. Indeed, it would be very surprising if conventional middle class persons, who were "well-adjusted," did not find themselves (or were not rated by friends) as correspondingly happy in their conventionalized states. To be unhappy would be to be "out-of-role" and the whole conditioning process would have gone for nought. But how adequate a criterion, except of conventionality, is a statement of happiness? As Erich Fromm has indicated: "What, for instance, do we know about the happiness of people in our culture? True enough many people would answer in a public opinion poll that they were happy because that is what a self-respecting citizen is supposed to feel."[3]

"Happiness" continues to be employed, however, as the criterion of success in marriage prediction, and as the major goal of the marriage counselor and client. To be sure, some criterion of success is necessary. But a criterion which would escape the endless circle of conventionality might be preferable and more useful. Much of the marriage prediction material appears to be measuring, scaling, and correlating several aspects of the same phenomenon. A piece of middle class conventionality is correlated with a part of adherence to the same morality; in effect with itself.

Emotional maturity (which is popularly indexed by the control of affect, in such forms as not exhibiting temper, inhibiting jealousy without manifest "projection," and the like) is also correlated with success in marriage. But what passes for "emotional maturity" is often simply adult middle class moral excellence. A highly conventional middle class person possesses much middle class virtue. Hence "becoming mature" and being indoctrinated with middle class morality, as they are utilized in the literature, are virtually the same thing.[4]

Kingsley Davis has long since demonstrated some of the relationships between the mental hygiene movement and the class structure.[5] C. Wright Mills has noted that the professional ideology of the social pathologists stems

---

[3] "Psychoanalytic Characterology and Its Application to the Understanding of Culture," in S. Stansfeld Sargent and Marian W. Smith, editors, *Culture and Personality* (New York: The Viking Fund, 1949), p. 9.

[4] As Ruesch notes, "In the lower class, where expression of anger is permitted, and where non-conformance and rebellion are sanctioned by class ideals there exist other means of expressing conflicts . . . [than by physical symptom formation]." *Op. cit.*, p. 124.

[5] "Mental Hygiene and the Class Structure," *Psychiatry*, 1:63 (Feb. 1938).

in part from their social origins and the values of their collective middle class mentalities.[6] Norton Springer indicates that middle class children tend to be better adjusted emotionally than children on lower rungs of the status scale. Springer found that children who come from middle class families make more satisfactory behavior adjustments than those who derive from a poor general social level. The latter indicate more maladjustment and undesirable personal characteristics. He feels that emotional stability is closely related to the general social status of the individual.[7]

One may raise the question as to whether measures of emotional stability, like measures of happiness in marriage, do not, at the same time, largely measure middle class morality, rather than scientific findings of an objective character. Because of the widespread use by marriage counselors of the findings of "objective studies," some of their assumptions and the implications for theory and for practice must be examined.

The change which has been underway for the past fifty years in American family culture (from the Burgess perspective as distinguished from Sorokin-Zimmerman viewpoint) has been that generally characterized as the movement from an institutionalized form to one understandable in terms of the central theme of companionship. While the stability of the companionship type of relationship depends upon strong interpersonal relations, the stability of the conventional type of family depended upon such things as gossip, mores, public opinion, and the like. Granted that there are still institutional aspects to the companionship type, and that there were companionship elements in the institutional family, it is nonetheless useful to treat the two types more or less as opposites. Most family counseling today, however, appears to be pointed toward the conventional family rather than toward the companionship relationship, and counseling invokes sanction from "objective" materials bearing on that somewhat anachronistic organization.

This situation gives rise to the question as to how a marriage counselor can deal with a problem situation deriving from conflicts in the area of strong interpersonal relations. In short, while counseling is supposed to be an application of scientific principles, in addition to being an art, how can it properly function when its major orientation is toward the mores of the conventional institutional family? There is certainly a basic unreality in regarding idealized middle class morality as the truly appropriate point of departure for all marriage problem phenomena even though such conventionality may be bolstered by findings of so-called objective studies.

Persons in trouble normally need some other standard imposed upon them than that which has been largely responsible for their "problem situation." It is almost notorious knowledge that relief for the guilt-ridden alcoholic can not derive from his knowledge of the actuarial tables on the "vice" of alcoholism, or from moral invocation to reform.

---

[6] "The Professional Ideology of Social Pathologists," *American Journal of Sociology*, 49:165–180 (September 1943).

[7] "Influence of General Social Status on the Emotional Stability of Children," *Journal of Genetic Psychology*, 53:321–327 (1938).

Under these circumstances what sort of "definition of the situation"[8] is appropriate to the marriage counselor? The research investigator, and consequently the marriage counselor, has in large degree come to the point where he is faced with the fact that success-in-marriage is what success-in-marriage predictions predict. While this position may be tenable "operationally," it is manifestly untenable from anything but a naive operational viewpoint. Such a question also requires something more than the trite answer that the situation must be defined on a "case to case basis." The definition of the situation has significance not only for marriage counseling, but also for American social science. For implicitly the counselor's definition of the situation also concerns itself with whether social scientific marriage prediction and analysis deal even with the American socio-cultural whole, or whether they are to limit their generalizations only to the plane of reference of the idealized morality of a single status grouping, which findings in turn it imposes on the totality of its materials.

Does the baseline from which "success" in marriage is determined need to be that of middle class morality and conventionality? Even within the American status structure there are other bases from which the data of the marriage counselors' "generalized other"[9] may be drawn. *The* family, for that matter even the *good* family, might conceivably be something quite different from the middle class conventional family.

Many persons in our society basically and ordinarily identify with "unconventional" subcultures. To be sure, some of these sub-cultures move in the direction of fulfilling personal sense satisfactions, rather than developing stable social relations. Other "deviant" relationships become quite stable. But it is with just such problems that the marriage counselor frequently must deal. The actuarial materials on happiness in these areas today do not exist.

A social segment in every metropolitan area, for example, works in downtown offices and shops and tends to find its sex partners, and to evolve stable social relationships, through associations developed in downtown bars. How significant are factors such as residential propinquity or church attendance for success in the companionship type of marriage derived from these groupings? Such persons, participating as they do in a greater variety of subcultures than conventional middle class persons, appear to be capable of much "multivalence." They consequently are able to emphasize one tradition and its dominant values in one circumstance, and a quite contrary tradition in another, without notable inner conflict, and with the several sets of values quite real and significant for adjustment to stable sex roles. Were the marriage counselor to define this situation with the criteria of middle class conven-

---

[8] See Edmund H. Volkart (ed.) *Social Behavior and Personality: Contributions of W. I. Thomas to Theory and Social Reserach* (New York: Social Science Research Council, 1951), pp. 80–81, for explication of this concept.

[9] This extension of the term "generalized other" derives from the discussion in George Herbert Mead, *Mind, Self and Society*, edited by Charles W. Morris (Chicago: U. of Chicago, 1934) pp. 154 ff.

tionality in judging problems and probabilities for success in such unions, he would tend to do scientific violence to an equivalent reality.[10]

The instruments developed for the actuarial prediction of success in marriage never take into account such common phenomena in American married life as the "phantom lover." The phantom lover performs all sorts of services, including the sex act, in such fashion that amazing "happiness" accrues to some women, and he is rarely matched by, unless he is imaginatively combined with, his "surrogate," the actual husband. Middle class morality does not countenance the existence of such a fantasy. It therefore never finds its way into the instrument from which predictive tables are derived.[11]

The problem faced by the marriage counselor is thus, from a scientific viewpoint, at least two fold. The marriage bond and family relationship may not always be adequately defined in terms of what *ought to be* from the viewpoint of middle class conventionality. And the counselor has little of an actual sort to guide him for other forms of relationship. He may even lack scepticism of the utility of his own values which a knowledge of cultural relativity potentially could give him.

Under the circumstances how much "scientific" education for marriage is feasible? As Willard Waller said some years ago: "Various 'educational' programs have been devised in order to promote better family life. Many such programs are definitely harmful, since their effect is merely to strengthen the existing mores and to accentuate the conflicts of persons unable to live within the mores. . . . Where such educational programs are based upon the scientific study of the family, and the possibility of changing mores instead of conforming the individual to them is not excluded, they may be helpful. . . ."[12]

Programs of education for marriage, and marriage counseling as a field, obviously need now to recognize, as social case work in part has come to recognize in the past ten years, that something other than the standards of middle class conventionality may be imposed on clients and students, and that success in marriage will have to be defined in terms of the several cultural traditions of the persons addressed. The areas of the "generalized other" must be examined until the most usual and tolerable locus of the person is determined.

---

[10] It would, however, be analogous to the case workers doing relief work early in the depression, who asked themselves what there was in clients' psychological make-ups which prevented them from getting employment.

[11] In view of the tendency toward homogamy in actual unions, and the tables indicating improbability for success the greater the discrepancy in cultural and religious background of mates, it would be interesting to determine the extent to which phantom lovers are of other ethnic and religious backgrounds.

[12] *The family: A Dynamic Interpretation* (New York: Cordon, 1938), pp. 600–601. Essentially the same conception is formulated in the revised edition of Waller's book, in which Chapter 25, "Proposed Changes in Family Designs," has been virtually rewritten in its entirety. See Willard Waller, *The Family: A Dynamic Interpretation* (rev. by Reuben Hill) (New York: Dryden, 1951), p. 570.

Without a broad exploration of the anthropological literature bearing on the variety of fulfillments of personality needs, at least the lesson of Freud's rather obvious dictum, that the illicit sex relationship of the lower class girl living on the ground floor of the Vienna apartment house will have quite different significance for *her* than the equivalent experience of her middle class counterpart on the second story, must be taken into account. Cultural tradition molds sex roles and marital difficulties and, for that matter, marital counseling. But marital counseling potentially could escape it.

4. SOCIAL PSYCHOLOGISM

The Primacy of Primary Groups

CHARLES H. COOLEY

By primary groups I mean those characterized by intimate face-to-face association and cooperation. They are primary in several senses, but chiefly in that they are fundamental in forming the social nature and ideals of the individual. The result of intimate association, psychologically, is a certain fusion of individuals in a common whole, so that one's very self, for many purposes at least, is the common life and purpose of the group. Perhaps the simplest way of describing this wholeness is by saying that it is a "we"; it involves the sort of sympathy and mutual identification for which "we" is the natural expression. One lives in the feeling of the whole and finds the chief aims of his will in that feeling.

It is not to be supposed that the unity of the primary group is one of mere harmony and love. It is always a differentiated and usually a competitive unity, admitting of self-assertion and various appropriate passions; but these passions are socialized by sympathy, and come, or tend to come, under the discipline of the common spirit. The individual will be ambitious, but the chief object of his ambition will be some desired place in the thought of the others, and he will feel allegiance to common standards of service and fair play. So the boy will dispute with his fellows a place on the team, but above such disputes will place the common glory of his class and school.

The most important spheres of this intimate association and cooperation—though by no means the only ones—are the family, the play-group of children, and the neighborhood or community group of elders. These are practically universal, belonging to all times and all stages of development; and are accordingly a chief basis of what is universal in human nature and human ideals. The best comparative studies of the family, such as those of Westermarck[1] or Howard,[2] show it to us as not only a universal institution, but as more alike the world over than the exaggeration of exceptional customs by an earlier school had led us to suppose. Nor can any one doubt the

---

SOURCE: Charles Horton Cooley, *Social Organization* (New York: Scribner, 1925), pp. 23–31.

[1] *The History of Human Marriage.*
[2] *A History of Matrimonial Institutions.*

general prevalence of play-groups among their elders. Such associations is clearly the nursery of human nature in the world about us, and there is no apparent reason to suppose that the case has anywhere or at any time been essentially different.

As regards play, I might, were it not a matter of common observation, multiply illustrations of the universality and spontaneity of the group discussion and cooperation to which it gives rise. The general fact is that children, especially boys after about their twelfth year, live in fellowships in which their sympathy, ambition and honor are engaged even more often than they are in the family. Most of us can recall examples of the endurance by boys of injustice and even cruelty, rather than appeal from their fellows to parents or teachers—as, for instance, in the hazing so prevalent at schools, and so difficult, for this very reason, to repress. And how elaborate the discussion, how cogent the public opinion, how hot the ambitions in these fellowships.

Nor is this facility of juvenile association, as is sometimes supposed, a trait peculiar to English and American boys; since experience among our immigrant population seems to show that the offspring of the more restrictive civilizations of the continent of Europe form self-governing play-groups with almost equal readiness. Thus Miss Jane Addams, after pointing out that the "gang" is almost universal, speaks of the interminable discussion which every detail of the gang's activity receives, remarking that "in these social folk-motes, so to speak, the young citizen learns to act upon his own determination."[3]

Of the neighborhood group it may be said, in general, that from the time men formed permanent settlements upon the land, down, at least to, the rise of modern industrial cities, it has played a main part in the primary, heart-to-heart life of the people. Among our Teutonic forefathers the village community was apparently the chief sphere of sympathy and mutual aid for the commons all through the "dark" and middle ages, and for many purposes it remains so in rural districts at the present day. In some countries we still find it with all its ancient vitality, notably in Russia, where the mir, or self-governing village group, is the main theatre of life, along with the family, for perhaps fifty millions of peasants.

In our own life the intimacy of the neighborhood has been broken up by the growth of an intricate mesh of wider contacts which leaves us strangers to people who live in the same house. And even in the country the same principle is at work, though less obviously, diminishing our economic and spiritual community with our neighbors. How far this change is a healthy development, and how far a disease, is perhaps still uncertain.

Besides these almost universal kinds of primary association, there are many others whose form depends upon the particular state of civilization; the only essential thing, as I have said, being a certain intimacy and fusion of personalities. In our own society, being little bound by place, people easily form clubs, fraternal societies and the like, based on congeniality, which may give

---

[3] *Newer Ideals of Peace*, 177.

rise to real intimacy. Many such relations are formed at school and college, and among men and women brought together in the first instance by their occupations—as workmen in the same trade, or the like. Where there is a little common interest and activity, kindness grows like weeds by the road-side.

But the fact that the family and neighborhood groups are ascendant in the open and plastic time of childhood makes them even now incomparably more influential than all the rest.

Primary groups are primary in the sense that they give the individual his earliest and completest experience of social unity, and also in the sense that they do not change in the same degree as more elaborate relations, but form a comparatively permanent source out of which the latter are ever springing. Of course they are not independent of the larger society, but to some extent reflect its spirit; as the Germany family and the German school bear somewhat distinctly the print of German militarism. But this, after all, is like the tide setting back into creeks, and does not commonly go very far. Among the German, and still more among the Russian, peasantry are found habits of free cooperation and discussion almost uninfluenced by the character of the state; and it is a familiar and well-supported view that the village commune, self-governing as regards local affairs and habituated to discussion, is a very widespread institution in settled communities, and the continuator of a similar autonomy previously existing in the clan. "It is a man who makes monarchies and establishes republics, but the commune seems to come directly from the hand of God."[4]

In our own cities the crowded tenements and the general economic and social confusion have sorely wounded the family and the neighborhood, but it is remarkable, in view of these conditions what vitality they show; and there is nothing upon which the conscience of the time is more determined than upon restoring them to health.

These groups, then, are springs of life, not only for the individual but for social institutions. They are only in part moulded by special traditions, and, in larger degree, express a universal nature. The religion or government of other civilizations may seem alien to us, but the children or the family group wear the common life, and with them we can always make ourselves at home.

By human nature, I suppose, we may understand those sentiments and impulses that are human in being superior to those of lower animals, and also in the sense that they belong to mankind at large, and not to any particular race or time. It means, particularly, sympathy and the innumerable sentiments into which sympathy enters, such as love, resentment, ambition, vanity, hero-worship, and the feeling of social right and wrong.[5]

Human nature in this sense is justly regarded as a comparatively permanent

---

[4] De Tocqueville, *Democracy in America*, vol. i, Chap. 5.
[5] These matters are expounded at some length in the writer's *Human Nature and the Social Order*.

element in society. Always and everywhere men seek honor and dread ridicule, defer to public opinion, cherish their goods and their children, and admire courage, generosity, and success. It is always safe to assume that people are and have been human.

It is true, no doubt, that there are differences of race capacity, so great that a large part of mankind are possibly incapable of any high kind of social organization. But these differences, like those among individuals of the same race, are subtle, depending upon some obscure intellectual deficiency, some want of vigor, or slackness of moral fibre, and do not involve unlikeness in the generic impulses of human nature. In these all races are very much alike. The more insight one gets into the life of savages, even those that are reckoned the lowest, the more human, the more like ourselves, they appear. Take for instance the natives of central Australia, as described by Spencer and Gillen,[6] tribes having no definite government or worship and scarcely able to count to five. They are generous to one another, emulous of virtue as they understand it, kind to their children and to the aged, and by no means harsh to women. Their faces as shown in the photographs are wholly human and many of them attractive.

And when we come to a comparison between different stages in the development of the same race, between ourselves, for instance, and the Teutonic tribes of the time of Caesar, the difference is neither in human nature nor in capacity, but in organization, in the range and complexity of relations, in the diverse expression of powers and passions essentially much the same.

There is no better proof of this generic likeness of human nature than in the ease and joy with which the modern man makes himself at home in literature depicting the most remote and varied phases of life—in Homer, in the Nibelung tales, in the Hebrew Scriptures, in the legends of the American Indians, in stories of frontier life, of soldiers and sailors, of criminals and tramps, and so on. The more penetratingly any phase of human life is studied the more an essential likeness to ourselves is revealed.

To return to primary groups: the view here maintained is that human nature is not something existing separately in the individual, but a *group-nature or primary phase of society,* a relatively simple and general condition of the social mind. It is something more, on the one hand, than the mere instinct that is born in us—though that enters into it—and something less, on the other, than the more elaborate development of ideas and sentiments that makes up institutions. It is the nature which is developed and expressed in those simple, face-to-face groups that are somewhat alike in all societies; groups of the family, the playground, and the neighborhood. In the essential similarity of these is to be found the basis, in experience, for similar ideas and sentiments in the human mind. In these, everywhere human nature comes into existence. Man does not have it at birth; he cannot acquire it except through fellowship, and it decays in isolation.

---

[6] *The Native Tribes of Central Australia.* Compare also Darwin's views and examples given in chap. 7 of his *Descent of Man.*

If this view does not recommend itself to commonsense I do not know that elaboration of it will be of much avail. It simply means the application at this point of the idea that society and individuals are inseparable phases of a common whole, so that wherever we find an individual fact we may look for a social fact to go with it. If there is a universal nature in persons there must be something universal in association to correspond to it.

What else can human nature be than a trait of primary groups? Surely not an attribute of the separate individual—supposing there were any such thing—since its typical characteristics, such as affection, ambition, vanity, and resentment, are inconceivable apart from society. If it belongs, then, to man in association, what kind or degree of association is required to develop it? Evidently nothing elaborate, because elaborate phases of society are transient and diverse, while human nature is comparatively stable and universal. In short the family and neighborhood life is essential to its genesis and nothing more is.

Here as everywhere in the study of society we must learn to see mankind in psychical wholes, rather than in artificial separation. We must see and feel the communal life of family and local groups as immediate facts, not as combinations of something else. And perhaps we shall do this best by recalling our own experience and extending it through sympathetic observation. What, in our life, is the family and the fellowship; what do we know of the we-feeling? Thought of this kind may help us to get a concrete perception of that primary group-nature of which everything social is the outgrowth.

The Secondary Nature of the Primary Group

BERNARD ROSENBERG
AND NORMAN D. HUMPHREY

In 1948 Edward Shils observed with some justice that American sociology tends to be "discontinuous." He meant that solidly established concepts are frequently forgotten and rediscovered a generation or two later, as if they had never been formulated in the first place.[1] Shils' most conspicuous case in point is the primary group, a term advanced by Charles Horton Cooley, who clearly stated, and perhaps overstated, its importance in 1909, only to have many of his sucessors neglect what he had highlighted. Much later,

SOURCE: Bernard Rosenberg and Norman D. Humphrey, "The Secondary Nature of the Primary Group," *Social Research*, 22:1 (Spring, 1955), pp. 25–38. Reprinted by permission.

[1] Edward Shils, *The Present State of American Sociology* (Glencoe, Illinois, 1948) p. 42.

researchers like Elton Mayo, Paul Lazarsfeld, and William F. Whyte learned independently and painstakingly what Cooley had known all along.

Shils' implication seems to be that American sociologists have engaged in restriction of output—that it would have been less wasteful to consult Cooley directly and thereby increase production while eliminating unnecessary expenditures of money and energy. It follows that Cooley's influence is intrinsically salutary. Such an assumption is warranted, however, only if we accept the validity of Cooley's thinking. And the burden of this paper is that, precisely because Cooley has been uncritically accepted or unwittingly duplicated, the renewed emphasis on primary-group relations has been seriously misleading. It is time to take another look at Cooley's "seminal" book, *Social Organization*.[2]

I

Cooley's *Social Organization* centers on the primary group, whose *all*-important and *wholly* benign character he takes for granted, as does a long succession of likeminded scholars. Here continuity may be found, but continuity is no end in itself, especially if it means perpetuation of an empirically inadmissible point of view.

The primary group may be defined in Cooley's own words (pp. 23–24): "By primary groups I mean those characterized by intimate face-to-face association and cooperation. . . . The most important spheres of this intimate association and cooperation—though by no means the only ones—are the family, the play-group of children, and the neighborhood or community group of elders. These are practically universal, belonging to all times and all stages of development; and are accordingly a chief basis of what is universal in human nature and human ideals."

This is an unexceptionable statement, which the contemporary social scientist might make even stronger by eliminating "practically" and simply postulating the universality of these spheres. But their primacy is another matter. They used to be the whole of man's social life; no other force supervened upon them. Then the small, isolated, relatively static, and simple society experienced enormous disruption, which nearly swept it away. In this upheaval the primary group did not disappear, but its monopoly was shattered. The term "secondary group," not to be found in Cooley's lexicon, became a point of entry for the exploration of entirely new phenomena.

If Max Weber seems relevant to us, it is precisely because he turned from the small group to those large impersonal forces that were routinizing and bureaucratizing our lives. Weber implicitly—in a kind of silent agony—and Cooley all too explicitly, bemoaned the change. Their common nostalgia for an irrecoverable past, coupled with the one's tough-mindedness and the

---

[2] Charles Horton Cooley, *Social Organization: A Study of the Larger Mind* (New York, 1909). Subsequent text references to Cooley are to this work.

other's tender-mindedness, led to totally different world views. Weber could transcend his feelings; Cooley could not.

These feelings permeate and vitiate Cooley's work. Even when he comes to grips with the modern world, they snatch it away from him. For example, he almost understood what was happening to the neighborhood, but recoiled in time to avert that illumination. Cooley wrote of the neighborhood (p. 25) that "from the time men formed settlements upon the land down to the rise of industrial cities" it has been paramount in "the primary heart-to-heart life of the people." He could even bring himself to state forcefully that all this had changed: "In our own life the intimacy of the neighborhood has been broken up by the growth of an intricate mesh of wider contacts which leaves us strangers to people who live in the same house" (p. 26). Any current statement to the same effect is but an echo of this one. Moreover, Cooley elaborated it by pointing to the proliferation of "wider contacts" which has reduced man's economic and spiritual community with his neighbors, not only in the city but in the country as well. How incongruous, then, for him to add (p. 26): "But the fact that the family and neighborhood groups are ascendant in the open and plastic time of childhood makes them even now incomparably more influential than all the rest."

Thus does Cooley avoid the distasteful reality he himself has depicted. We are strangers to people who live in the same house and yet they are incomparably more influential than any other group. The resolution of this paradox is presumably its reference to a relationship that obtains during the period of one's greatest plasticity. If so, it comes to this: that the agencies of socialization and enculturation are the agencies of socialization and enculturation.

Actually, the unchallengeable tautology cloaks a deeper confusion. Agencies of socialization transmit culture; they do not necessarily create it. Primary groups may be the nursery of a human nature whose shapes and contours they do not determine. A sacred society will use its neighborhoods in one way, a secular society in another. The child must always be socialized within a small group, but the norms it is obliged to "interiorize" have another and a larger locus. The child is plastic, and he is molded to a large extent by his family, his play group, and his neighbors, but all these take their essential character from courses external to them. In modern society this is true with respect to the indispensable norms governing such phenomena as language, which certainly do not originate in any primary group, and it is equally true with respect to all major prescriptions and proscriptions.

That it will not do to confound matrix and means can be illustrated analogically. To borrow a term from our technological age, we may speak of the primary group as a transmission belt or a conveyor belt. Mechanized production requires the use of some such belt in a factory, regardless of what is being manufactured. The belt operates no less efficiently in conveying arms than in conveying automobiles, at a slow pace than at a high one, under capitalism than under socialism. The belt is *eo ipso* a neutral object, which must be adjusted to work norms and end products impersonally thrust upon it.

What this means in human terms can be seen if we pursue a point made by Cooley. He observes (p. 26) that in some countries we still find the neighborhood in all its ancient vitality, notably in Russia, "where the mir, or self-government village group is the main theater of life, along with the family, for perhaps fifty millions of peasants." Less than half a century later there is no mir. In Soviet Russia agriculture has been collectivized, the peasant way of life has been transformed, and self-government has been obliterated. But the primary group has survived all shocks and dislocations. It remains indestructible, flourishing now to serve purposes wholly inimical to its immemorial function. The institutional belt, which needed to be broken and refashioned, is now stronger than ever. What it transmits is quite different.

Given such a highly symptomatic situation, one may legitimately inquire "How primary is the primary group?" According to Cooley (p. 27), primary groups are primary in the sense that they give the individual his earliest and fullest experience of social unity, and also in the sense that "they do not change in the same degree as more elaborate relations, but form a comparatively permanent source out of which others spring." However alien certain forms of religion and government may seem to us, families and children at play are always recognizable. Such groups are the "springs of life not only for the individual but for social institutions."

This kind of reasoning deserves closer inspection than it usually receives. If primary groups are comparatively permanent, how can they be the source out of which others spring when these "others" differ drastically from one another? How can Cooley's constants account for so many variables?

To assume that they do is doubly erroneous. In the first place, his analysis is reductivist: primary groups serve as a kind of substructure out of which such epiphenomenal institutions as government, literature, and religion arise. There is no more sense of institutional interplay here than in Marxism, perhaps less. In the second place, his scheme presupposes a relatively static substructure by means of which to explain an exceedingly dynamic superstructure. In this respect it is inferior to Marxism, whose substructure constantly shifts. Who can imagine Karl Marx analyzing capitalist ideology on the basis of handicraft production? Analyzing it solely on the basis of any economic system is indefensible. How much more so the basis of an obsolete system! But this is exactly what Cooley, in his own supposedly social terms, set out to do.

II

Cooley's social philosophy has fostered primary-group or, in its commonest form, familial determinism. At present social studies frequently remain fixed at this level. They may renounce the constancy of small groups, but not their centrality. It is almost as if there had been no movement from Gemein-

schaft to Gesellschaft, from status to contract, from kinship to territory. This
is most convenient for an anthropologist like W. Lloyd Warner, who is
accustomed to studying small communities and can therefore extract enough
from Yankee City to justify his grandiose conclusions about the Western
world.[3] Social psychology is committed to the study of small groups. Its practitioners, however, are not always satisfied with so limited a perspective.
Hence their penchant for reducing culture to interpersonal relations. In the
process, sociology loses its reason for being, and becomes social psychology, as
Leslie White has justifiably charged.[4] But this is far from the macroscopic
intention of those like Spencer and Tylor, who founded sociology in modern
Europe. Their purpose was to go beyond the individual to society in all its
multifariousness, not merely to the family, the neighborhood, and the artificially created group of students, but to the larger whole and to its laws.

The small group is more manipulatable, testable, and researchable than
the large group; the culture trait more than the culture pattern. This accounts,
in no small measure, for the intense fascination that small groups exercise
over experimenters and field workers, who are overawed by the complexity
of, let us say, contemporary American civilization. No one can gainsay their
scientific right to be preoccupied with smallness in a world grown large. Only
it is necessary to draw the line and insist that what they learn about small
groups applies just to small groups. No easy extrapolation from any number
of minuscule units will ever encompass the whole of human society.

Why not? All large groups, it may be held, are made up of smaller ones,
which may be so proportioned that, as George C. Homans has said, we can
get "all the way around" them.[5] The proposition has its charm. How pleasant
it would be if what was most readily apprehended also turned out to be most
relevant! It will scarcely help matters merely to assert the unpleasant fact
that this is not so. Homans himself taxes with a comparable error the em-
piricist who assumes that only quantitative data are significant. In *The
Human Group* Homans uses non-quantitative material drawn largely from
ethnology and industrial sociology, and appertaining exclusively to the small,
suitably manageable, and generally informal group; his stated objective (p.
3) is a "synthesis of the microcosm—that may be an attainable end."

But by what warrant other than the tradition of Cooley does Homans
conclude that small groups are a microcosm? Is there anything irreducible
about the small group? Why not a monad? Surely the individual can be
studied with greater thoroughness than any group, large or small. Rigorous
adherence to this position could produce only a restoration of Floyd Allport's
belief that all groups are unreal, that only the individual exists; or a reassertion of Emile Durkheim's anticipatory rejoinder that an individual is as
much an abstraction as the group, and as subject to subdivision; or involvement in an infinite regression.

---

[3] W. Lloyd Warner, *The Social Life of a Modern Community* (New Haven, 1941).
[4] Leslie A. White, *The Science of Culture* (New York, 1949), *passim*.
[5] George C. Homans, *The Human Group* (New York, 1950) p. 3.

Leaping from alleged microcosm to macrocosm has been a favorite pastime of voluntarist philosophers since antiquity, and most noticeably in our time since Heisenberg enunciated his principle of indeterminacy. Many a distinguished thinker has espoused the view that since molecular motion does not seem to be fully predictable, man must be a free agent. This judgment is made in spite of the physicist's warning that what holds for tiny particles of matter may not hold even for slightly larger particles. In short, whatever contingency obtains on a subatomic level has absolutely no bearing on the question of free will.

Similarly, what is true of small human aggregations is often quite untrue with respect to society at large. This can be understood without independent experimental verification. Consider what is perhaps Kurt Lewin's best known study: on the creation of authoritarian and democratic group atmospheres.[6] Lewin discovered that in a democratic group, which he created for experimental purposes, children were far more devoted to their leader than were other children in an authoritarian group. If replication of the experiment were to bear him out, it could be said that this was a uniformity of small-group behavior, although Lewin himself fluctuated between the idea that his results applied only to *this* group at *this* time and the idea that they applied to *all* groups. Clearly, if they do not apply even to other small groups, their scientific value is nil, and they cannot legitimately be applied to whole social orders. Commonsense observation is enough to indicate that in authoritarian cultures (Nazi Germany, Soviet Russia) the leader may be accorded more devotion, if not adoration, than is ever heaped on any democratic leader.

When we have to do with large-scale social phenomena it usually proves sterile to treat them as though they were overblown versions of a miniature reality. Abram Kardiner (and others) may start out to do this, but it is with the larger forces, such as technology and terrain, that he and they must deal in order to interpret many of their nonliterate cultures.[7] National Socialism can no more be understood as a byproduct of the structurally rather constant German family that Bolshevism can be understood as a byproduct of swaddling. This does not reduce the popularity of such theories; it simply invalidates them.

Revolutions require that the revolutionized state temporarily declare war on the family. Such action would be absurd if the family produced revolutionary ferment, if authoritarianism at home generated totalitarian revolution, if primary groups were the "springs of life not only for the individual but for social institutions." What Cooley did not realize is that primary groups may be sharply at variance with other more potent institutions. Implacable war had to be waged by Hitler and Stalin against the family because it was

---

[6] Kurt Lewin, Ronald Lippitt, and Ralph K. White, "Patterns of Aggressive Behavior in Experimentally Created 'Social Climates,'" in *Journal of Social Psychology*, vol. 10 (1939) pp. 271–99.

[7] Abram Kardiner, *The Psychological Frontiers of Society* (New York, 1945), and *The Individual and His Society* (New York, 1939).

the carrier of an old culture. If the ancient clan system in China proves durable, Mao Tse Tung must perforce fail in his efforts to communize the country. Once the old family system is pulverized, it can of course be reconstituted. The new family becomes a pliable and reliable instrument for the new society. This represents the capitulation of primary groups to powerful antagonists—to antagonists which it can hardly be said to have created.

Just as Cooley failed to see the possible conflict between state and family, in which the latter may be subdued, so he obscured the possible conflict between primary groups—even though he pointed out (pp. 24–25) that children live in fellowships which may engage their sympathy, ambition, and honor even more, at times, "than they are engaged in the family." As this suggests, there may be a certain rivalry for the allegiance of young people. Given the present rapidity of social change, youth culture may be seriously at odds with parent culture. The other-directed type delineated by David Riesman comes into prominence, and is ultimately more influenced by peers than by parents.[8] The gang will sometimes instil values that flatly contradict those of a feebler, but by no means extinct, primary group. This whole situation, in which roles are rendered ambiguous and moral directives are divergent, constitutes a social problem of whose existence Cooley showed no awareness. He touched only on the "universality and spontaneity of the group discussion and cooperation" to which play groups give rise.

Cooley's stress was on juvenile association as a trait not peculiar to English and American boys but common also among the offspring of "the more restrictive civilizations of Europe" (p. 27). He would certainly have been sobered by the youth movement of twentieth-century Germany, with their quota of bonafide youngsters plus the "perennial adolescents" who led them away from all traditional restraints and into Hitler's camp. These self-governing play groups, for all their spontaneity, group discussions, and cooperation, were not the bastions of democracy that Cooley conceived them to be. They were centers of antidemocratic infection, the Storm Troopers' headquarters, the training grounds for "independent" homosexuality. What would our mild Emersonian sage have said if confronted with such an everyday occurrence in Eastern Europe as the denunciation of parents—and their condemnation to death before a totalitarian tribunal—by children who have been alienated from them in state-sponsored "play groups"?

III

Cooley would have been shocked; and, if undeceived, he would have been obliged to abandon certain formulae that still seem attractive to his continuators. The illusion that primary groups are omnipotent can only serve to cripple social science. It has a peculiarly archaic quality when our culture, in

---

[8] David Riesman, *The Lonely Crowd* (New Haven, 1950); see particularly Chapters II, III, and IV.

point of fact, may be suffering from elephantiasis. A book like *Social Organization* dates itself in such a statement as this (p. 32), variations of which are still to be found in the literature: "Life in the primary groups gives rise to social ideals which, as they spring from similar experiences, have much in common throughout the human race."

This is part of Cooley's effort to establish a common human nature anchored in "those simple face-to-face groups that are somewhat alike in all societies" (p. 32). At roughly the same time William Graham Sumner, in his *Folkways* (1906), was stressing differences, and his emphasis achieved great popularity in the next generation. It culminated in a cultural relativism which has suddenly become unpalatable to the small-groupists, not a few of whom feel they have restored Cooley to his proper position. Nevertheless, it should be clear by now that man is compounded of likenesses *and* differences, and that whereas primary groups give rise to social ideals, social ideals also give rise to primary groups. All human associations are similar and dissimilar.

"Where," asked Cooley (p. 33), "do we get our notions of love, freedom, justice and the like which we are ever applying to social institutions? Not from abstract philosophy, surely, but from the actual life of simple and widespread forms of society like the family or the play group. In these relations mankind realizes itself and gratifies its primary needs in a fairly satisfactory manner." Suppose we invert all this. Does it ring any less true? Where do our notions of hate, slavery, and injustice originate? Not only from simple forms of society like the family, but from highly complex forms totally lacking in warmth and spontaneity, like those found among supine audiences passively exposed to mass manipulation. By his "selective inattention" to the seamy side of human nature, Cooley romanticized the primary group, where negative, no less than positive, traits are clearly in evidence. He also closed his eyes to the characteristic features of modern social life, in which mankind realizes itself but little and seldom gratifies its primary needs.

Cooley's purblind optimism is reflected in all his writings, and nowhere more so than in this passage (p. 33): "The ideal that grows up in familiar association is a part of human nature itself. In its most general form, it is that of a moral whole or community wherein individual minds are merged and the higher capacities of the members find total and adequate expression. Children and savages do not formulate any such ideal but they have it nevertheless; they see it; they see themselves and their fellows as indivisible and they desire this 'we' to be harmonious, happy and successful. And we come to feel that the same spirit should extend to our country, our world."

This is no doubt one side of the coin whose obverse side appears much more frequently in human affairs. "We" feelings produce centrifugal forces as abundantly as they produce centripetal forces, excluding the out group while embracing the in group. Sumner saw this clearly when he coined the term ethnocentrism. So did Giddings, another contemporary of Cooley's, who established a kind of dialectic between consciousness of kind and consciousness of others. The progression from tribal solidarity to universalism wrapped in moral sublimity may occur in rare spirits, but it is simply grotesque to speak of this and to ignore nationalism, irredentism, imperialism, regionalism, factionalism, indeed, the whole illimitable area of human conflict, as Cooley tended to do. He observed (p. 35) that "Moral unity admits and rewards strenuous ambition, but this ambition must either be for the success of the group or at least not inconsistent with it." The ideal of moral unity Cooley took to be the mother of all social ideals. His point in this connection was that what he called the normal self is molded in primary groups "to be a social self whose ambitions are formed by the common thought of the group" (p. 36). The grain of truth in this, as in almost all of Cooley's formulations, flowers into distortion.

Obviously there must be some bedrock of consensus in any society, else it ceases to exist. But Plato sensed a critical problem of the sort that Cooley could not perceive when, in *The Republic,* he proposed, for his elite, outright abolition of the family, whose members would thereby be freed of loyalties subsidiary to those of the state. Nor is Platonic wisdom necessary in order to see this matter in its true light. Any parent who is ideologically committed to the prosecution of a war, and nevertheless wishes to keep his son from serving in the armed forces, knows what this situation means. In its most extreme form, the close tie to a primary group produces disaffection from the overarching culture itself. No better proof of this can be offered than the subcultural segmentation of our own society. To the extent that a criminal is encased in the underworld, an underprivileged worker in the slums, a scholar in Academia, so far is he sealed off from the cohesive values of "average" men.

Cooley sought to bolster his conception of human nature by drawing upon data about primitive peoples. On this road there are two classic pitfalls, and Cooley escaped neither of them. One is the idealization of nonliterates, in which he freely indulged; the other is its opposite, the depreciation of nonliterates, from which he was unable to abstain. This is so despite Cooley's conviction that all men are essentially alike—for, along with that theme and clashing with it, there went a kind of social Darwinism.

Our species, as Cooley understood it in his Rousseauistic mood, is possessed of only the most virtuous qualities. Thus "in their crudest form such passions as lust, greed, revenge, the pride of power and the like are not distinctively human nature at all, but animal nature" (p. 36). The fact is that nothing could be more distinctively human than this brief catalogue of emotions which can be referred to other animals only anthropomorphically. Still, for Cooley, the passions are not humanized unless they come under the sway of primary-group ideals. All other ideals are animalistic by definition. "I know also that the most truculent behavior may be exalted into an ideal, like the ferocity of Samuel when he hewed Agag to pieces before the Lord. In general, there is always a morality of opposition, springing from the need of the sympathetic group to assert itself in the struggle for existence" (p. 37).

Even at present, Cooley admitted, this struggle more or less idealizes destructiveness and deceit in the conflicts of war, if not of commerce. But, he added, such traits are secondary, not ideals in the same primary and enduring sense that loyalty and kindness are: "Flourishing at certain stages of development because they are requisite under the prevailing conditions of destructive conflict, they are slowly abandoned or transformed when these conditions change. With the advance of civilization conflict itself is brought more and more under the control of those principles that prevail in primary groups and so far as this is the case, conduct which violates such principles ceases to have any value" (pp. 37–38). The sense of this passage seems to be that as the primary group recedes in importance it advances in importance. Progress consists in a diffusion of primary-group sentiments from primary-group culture, where they are less dominant, to civilization, where they are more dominant. This is romanticism of the sort one associates with Lévy-Bruhl or the unilinear evolutionists, who might have regarded whatever they did not like in man as vestigial savagery.

But the other Cooley had no stomach for this deflation of all that he had previously glorified. So he trapped himself, only a few pages later, in the other pitfall. Here primitive man becomes a Noble Savage once again. Cooley points to the authorities: Westermarck, on the kindness and altruism of uncivilized people, "Indeed their customs regarding mutual aid are often much more stringent than our own and this applies even to the lowliest savages"; Morgan reporting that "among the Iroquois kindness to the orphan, hospitality to all, and a common brotherhood are among the doctrines held up for acceptance by their religious instructors," and an Iroquois "would surrender his dinner to feed the hungry, vacate his bed to refresh the weary and give up his apparel to clothe the naked" (pp. 40–42).

There is no mention in this context of sacrification, headhunting, or cannibalism. Savages are given over to the gentler feelings; we have thought otherwise only because of our hostile contact with them. "Indeed," Cooley asserted (pp. 41–42), "a state of things, such as is found in our own cities, where want and plenty exist side by side without the latter feeling any compulsion to relieve the former is shocking and incomprehensible to many savages." In spite of this Cooley concluded, although the logic is incredible, that there is a "growing understanding of the unity of the human race" (p. 42), and an appropriate extension of sympathy and kindness. Within a page or two Cooley managed the head-on collision of Progress and Nostalgia, and remained completely unshaken, as if each actually ran smoothly on its own grooves. If there is brutality among savages, this is due to their struggle for existence; if there is much in the condition of our own cities that savages find shocking, this is due to the encroachment of modernity. In either case, things are getting better all the time.

This is a sample of Cooley's thinking. Even those who pay homage to it make certain reservations in the interests of consistency. They have thrown Progress overboard. Nostalgia remains. It can be seen in "the professional ideology of social pathologists"; in every dichotomy that begins with the ennoblement of "folk culture," whose purity is contrasted with the horrors of civilization; in almost all of social psychology; in the shrill supernaturalism of Arnold J. Toynbee and Pitirim A. Sorokin. It may well be that in this instance American sociology has been entirely too "continuous."

The Functions of Small-Group Research

LEWIS A. COSER

Research in *small groups* has grown tremendously in recent years. A specialized bibliography (12) indicates that not fewer than three times per week are now being "produced" while from 1930 to 1939 a total of two hundred ten times were published in this field; in the four-year period from 1950 to 1953 roughly as many small-group studies have appeared as in the whole twenty-year span from 1930 to 1950. For the forty years from 1890 to 1929 as many items are listed as are now published during a single year.

A recent issue of the *American Sociological Review* (1) was in its entirety devoted to small-group studies; a collection of small-group papers has proved to be a scientific best seller; (2) another collection is about to be published. One is led to agree with the editor of the aforementioned special issue of the *American Sociological Review* that small-group research has experienced in recent years a "runaway growth."

Sociologists are wont to direct their attention to the rise of new social movements, fashions or cults which arise in the society at large, but they have been rather reluctant to direct their efforts at an examination of similar phenomena within their own discipline. Yet such an analysis would seem to be both scientifically profitable and critically important. A science which does not employ its research tools for a self-critical analysis of its own structure and functions lays itself open to justified reproach.

Sociologists have been eager to study the growth of religious movements and to link their rise to specified functions that they perform for their practitioners. It is our purpose in the following pages to study in a similar way the rise of small-group analysis within the sociological discipline. For a sociologically sophisticated audience it should hardly be necessary to *stress that analysis of such a movement in no way aims to throw light upon the validity of its findings*. Just as the sociologist concerned with the analysis of religious phenomena is not making judgments as to the merits of specific religious

SOURCE: Lewis A. Coser, "The Functions of Small-Group Research," *Social Problems* 3:1 (July, 1955), pp. 1-6. Reprinted by permission.

views and attitudes, so the analyst of the rise of schools within a sc.. ntific discipline is not concerned with the validity of their results. Since small-group study claims to be part of the province of sociology, the validity of its *findings* should also come under the sociologists' scrutiny, but we are not concerned with this task here, important though it may be.

Small-group research has proceeded under the guidance of variant and divergent theoretical assumptions and it is fragmented into various "schools" which often seem to take little notice of each other. Under these conditions it is difficult to make valid generalizations about the whole "movement." We have therefore limited ourselves in the following to those small-group analysts who are primarily concerned with the laboratory study of small experimentally created groups. In order to further restrict our focus, we shall in the main be concerned with the contributions to the above-mentioned special issue of *The American Sociological Review*. It seems justified to concentrate on this publication since the editors of the official organ of the American Sociological Society apparently took these contributions to be representative of the work of sociological interest now going on in the small-group field.

The functional analysis of an item requires the description of the activity involved as well as the description of the participants in structural terms so as to locate them in their interconnected social statuses (8, p. 56).

Small-group research, to judge from the recent issue of the *American Sociological Review* (1), consists essentially of the observational study of small experimentally created groups. Most of these studies are carried on in larger universities with special laboratory facilities such as microphones, one-way vision screens, tape recorders, etc. Most of the. studies reported are carried out with college or high-school students as subjects: of eleven experimental studies reported, seven had college or high-school groups as their subjects and an additional study used twelve year old boys. Subjects usually are manipulated to create conditions for the testing of specific hypotheses as to the behavior in the experimental situation. To give just one example, in a study by Godfrey M. Hochbaum (4), it "was attempted to create four conditions in different individuals by first creating self-confidence regarding the task assigned to the experimental groups in about half the subjects, and feelings of inadequacy concerning the task in the other half. About half of the subjects in each of these two conditions were then made to conceive themselves as deviates." (4, p. 679.)

Moving now to the analysis of the status of those engaged in the behavior under scrutiny, what strikes one immediately is the relative youth of small-group analysts. The average age of the authors of the papers published in the recent issue of the *American Sociological Review* is in the low thirties. It thus differs significantly from the average age of the total membership of the American Sociological Society. Since it is usually between the ages of thirty and thirty-two that individuals enter the academic hierarchy (13, p. 58) as instructors, we can further assume that a high proportion of practitioners of small-group research are as yet occupying lower-staff statuses within the academy.

Having thus roughly located practitioners of small-group research within the social structure of the academic community in which their behavior is to be observed, we may now move to a tentative discussion of their motives.

As Logan Wilson and other observers have remarked, ascent on the academic ladder is marked by serious strains and anxieties. Among the main strains for the junior men in the academic hierarchy is the uncertainty as to criteria for advancement. The junior member is under pressure to "make good" and neither the wish for security nor the wish for recognition is adequately met (13, p. 63). The temporary insecurity for the individual may subserve positive functions for the university but it has serious dysfunctional consequences for the junior member involved. This is especially so in those major universities in which a high premium is put on the quantity of publication as a criterion for advancement. "Publish or perish" seems to be the unwritten maxim governing the advancement process (13, p. 201). Yet in the early years of an academic career the teaching activities of the junior members are likely to take a disproportionate amount of their time, thus impeding the necessary preparation for scholarly research. Also in those early years of a scholarly career, the young practitioner is not yet likely to have fully absorbed the available literature in his field and to have fully appropriated the theoretical inheritance of his discipline. Pressure to publish in a hurry is thus likely to lead to overzealous attempts to rush into print even though adequate preparation may as yet be lacking.

Furthermore, long established areas of investigation usually are preempted by senior members of the discipline so that entry into these areas of research is likely to involve prolonged periods of apprenticeship during which younger members attach themselves for a considerable time to senior members and slowly gain the recognition which enables them finally to stake out research claims of their own.

The pattern of sociological work in earlier periods was typically that of a researcher writing a book from library sources. But with the increasing complexity of sociological research in the more recent period, the refinement of method and the attendant growth of necessary apparatus, sociologists have found it more and more difficult to engage in research without considerable outside aid. The young scholar is not likely to have much access to such research funds and thus tends to be considerably hampered in his research activities; he generally is forced to attach himself to a "collaborative" project headed by a senior member who has access to different types of fund granting organizations.

Since library research is no longer prestigeful and work in a large-scale collaborative project headed by a senior member does not usually lead to rapid prestige, the junior member's access to the legitimate means for success within the academic structure is impeded. Under such conditions he is likely to be motivated to look for types of innovation which will allow him to attain the institutionally rewarded success by alternative means (8, p. 73).

Small-group research seems to be well suited for this purpose. Publication in this field need not be preceded by the kind of elaborate theoretical preparation that is requisite, although not always actually displayed, in more settled areas of investigation. The field is new and theoretical preparation, according to the standards applied within it, involves only an acquaintance with publications that have appeared within roughly the last fifteen years. Of the many hundred references in the special issue of the *American Sociological Review,* only seventeen referred to articles or books published before 1937! (1)

It might be said that analysis of small groups has, in fact, a very ancient history, going back, indeed, to classical Greek and Chinese philosophy, but this is irrelevant in our context since we are not concerned here with objective reality but with the ways the field has been defined by its practitioners. By *their* standards the writings of even the most recent forerunners of their movement, are judged irrelevant. Thus in the aforementioned bibliography of small-group work we note twenty-seven entries under Moreno, nineteen under Festinger, fifteen under Kurt Lewin, but only one under Freud. *The Polish Peasant* by W. I. Thomas and F. Znaniecki is not listed at all. (12)

Mention has already been made of the difficulties that await the young scholar who attempts to gain access to research funds and tools of research. But such conditions are not likely to prevail in the small-group field where the research apparatus is not as yet very elaborate. This is indeed a field on the frontier, where individuals can still stake out large claims of their own without being restricted by the settled jurisdictions prevailing in older territories. Since there are very few senior members now engaged in small-group research, younger members of the discipline can move ahead much faster, unencumbered by the many restrictions and controls which are likely to prevail in other areas of research.

As C. Wright Mills has observed, "The graduate school is often organized as a feudal system: the student trades his loyalty to one professor for protection against the other professors" (10, p. 130). But in a new field such feudal patterns have not yet been established; on the contrary, the pattern of organization may be compared to that of a band of pioneers linked by common rejection of the thought ways of the settled community, by contempt for the old and enthusiasm for the achievements of the members of the brotherhood. We already have commented upon the fact that small-group research, to judge from the evidence of bibliographies, seems to have little regard for work which is not contemporary or near-contemporary; we might add here that it is also characterized by in-group solidarity. When nine judges, mostly well-known small-group researchers, were asked by Strodtbeck and Hare to rate the most significant articles in the field since 1950, they chose twelve articles, five of which had been written by the judges themselves. These same judges considered the work of George Herbert Mead as "not important," felt it unnecessary to cite more than one work by Freud, did not list any work by Jean Piaget and mentioned only one article by Malinowski, which they judged "not important," while not only listing all the writings of the "in-group members" but even decorating them profusely with double and triple asterisks indicating that these were of the greatest importance. (12) We are reminded of Logan Wilson's description of cultism in the academic community: "As long as the cult thrives, particularism flourishes. Members of the in-group are favored by one another in book reviews; complimentary references are made only to the writings of authors with 'approved' points of view." (13, p. 209.)

In summary, while in the older areas of research the junior member remains for long periods a "marginal man" whose anticipatory socialization becomes dysfunctional for him since it leads him to become the victim of aspirations he cannot achieve, the relative openness of the structure within new areas of reseach may be said to be functional for the individual involved to the degree that it helps him to achieve the social status toward which he aspires (9, p. 88).

Though some technical paraphernalia for small-group research are relatively costly, these costs are generally borne by the university or fund-granting organizations and are still insignificant in comparison with field research. Moreover, where no special research equipment is available, the research design can be simplified so that less elaborate technical facilities can be used. Furthermore, many of the studies are conducted for clients in large-scale bureaucratic organizations which provide the requisite laboratory facilities: both the Air Force and the Navy possess their own small-group laboratories and so does the RAND Corporation. Two out of eleven studies reported in the *American Sociological Review* were conducted with Navy or Air Force subjects and four out of eleven were financed by Air Force or Navy grants.*

Subjects for small-group studies are easily available since, as has been noted, they can be taken from classes of college students or personnel of the armed forces. In small-group research the difficulties which stand in the way of field work are minimized. Expenses generally are much smaller than those involved in field work; difficulties in obtaining data are likewise minimized since the small-group researcher manufactures the data with which he operates through manipulation of subjects who are easily available and offer little resistance, being to a large extent students subordinated to their teachers or personnel of the armed forces subordinated to the clients of the researchers. It may be noted in passing that small-group researchers recently have turned their attention to techniques on how to improve manipulative devices so as to facilitate the process of recruiting college student "volunteers" for experiments. Thus Schachter and Hall (11) report that, among other things, recruitment of volunteers could be increased by requesting volunteers to raise their hands and having half the class pre-instructed to respond as if volunteering.

Not only does small-group research minimize expenditures of funds, it also

---

* Eight out of forty-one studies reported in the Cartwright and Zander volume (2) were likewise supported by grants from either the Navy or the Air Force.

minimizes expenditure of time. Results can be attained rather quickly and without the tantalizing expense of time that is so often involved in field work. While a community study or an interview program may involve several months or even years of work, a small experimental group study may only require several weeks or even days for its execution. There are no preliminary delays in which such preparatory work as sampling has to be undertaken since the sample to be studied *is* the universe.

In short, easy availability of subjects, minimization of expenses in money and time, and the frontier territory are all advantages which recommend such research to those members of the academic hierarchies who, for the reasons outlined above, are under pressure to produce "results" in a hurry.

Having examined some of the internal reasons which have made research in small groups attractive to its practitioners, we might now turn to the question why small group research seems to enjoy high prestige among non-practitioners.

In recent years higher prestige has accrued to quantifiable than to qualitative results in the social sciences and precision has been rated higher than significance (5, 7). Since findings in small-group research are typically reported in seemingly precise quantitative terms, often in mathematical formalization, they are well suited to bring prestige. In so far as sociologists as well as clients of sociology have been fascinated by natural science methods, the methodological asceticism and the seeming precision of small-group findings are likely to impress various decision-makers both inside and outside the academy. Surrounded as they are by the magic aura of "science," the products of such research seem more easily saleable than work using less precise methods and more complex sets of variables, many of which may not as yet be susceptible to quantification. Such precise formulations are likely to appeal to people who are not able to "take" the uncertainties and complexities arising in work in the uncontrolled world.

Karl Mannheim once remarked that "typical American studies start from questions in nowise connected with those problems which arouse our passions in everyday political and social struggle." (6, p. 191.) This remark may be applicable to much research carried on in America today but it eminently characterizes experimental small-group work. Research in this field seems indeed to be carried on under antiseptic conditions in which preoccupation with and contamination by the world at large are rigorously excluded. Such isolation from large-scale questions of import for political and social structure is a decided advantage for the practitioner. In an age of political insecurity and fear, the small group provides an area of research so far removed from the concrete issues of the day and at so high a level of abstraction that it may be considered entirely "safe." While the research in the field, especially in larger groups and organizations, is only too likely to encounter resistance and attack from vested interests or decision makers, while such research might find it hard to get support from foundations which are under Congressional or other scrutiny for their alleged orientation toward reform, small-group research is free from such dangers. Since it does not deal with specific variables operative in the real world outside of the laboratory, it is also not in danger of offending real susceptibilities. Yet it seems that much of small-group research, while conceived on a high level of abstraction is, in the selection of its problems, tied to the solution of immediate problems of various types of bureaucratic decision makers, whether Army, Navy, factory managers or welfare agencies. Small-group research appeals to those decision makers in large-scale organizations who need researchers who do not question or discuss the impact of the organizations' structures but who focus instead on small segments within these structures. The Navy, for example, is not likely to be interested in studies of the bureaucratization of decision making in top echelons or in the relation between the process of militarization and democratic values, but it may want to know more about conformity producing mechanisms. Mr. John R. P. French, a leading small-group expert, discussing field research, has formulated the problem with commendable frankness: "The dominant objective of industry is production and this objective cannot be subordinated to the research objectives of a field experiment. The freedom of the field experimenter is limited to those types of experiments which do not conflict with the goal of the organization with which he works. . . . It means that the researcher must be flexible in choosing appropriate problems, in a field setting. Most fundamentally, it means that he must render a service which helps the practioner to achieve his practical objectives." (3, p. 91.) Mr. Strodtbeck expresses the same idea somewhat differently when he writes: "The growth of social science research and the availability of agencies willing to invest resources in the solution of *their* (emphasis mine, L.A.C.) problem, are inseparably linked." (1, p. 652.)

While small-group research predisposes the practitioners to selective inattention to large-scale organizational problems and habitually keys its research to a high level of abstraction in which contamination with the problems of society is successfully minimized, it is, on the other hand, well suited to serve the decision maker in the practical problems that he encounters in administration. Just because this research operates on a high level of abstraction, it can easily be tailored according to the specifications of decision makers and clients. Moreover, since small-group researchers often, although not always, claim that results attained in groups of boy scouts or college students are valid beyond the juvenile universe and can be transferred to society at large, this may seem to the decision maker a convenient way of reaching macroscopic results with microscopic expenses.

In conclusion, we might ask whether channeling of a high proportion of personnel into small-group research does not have significantly dysfunctional consequences for the development of sociology as a discipline. The social functions of small-group research help determine its structure, including the recruitment of personnel, but the structure of small-group research also affects its function (8, pp. 80–81). The general research orientation of the small-group school enables its members to acquire a public among the managerial elites of American society and this orientation and public is likely to lead them to neglect crucial societal variables. To the extent that the recent vogue of small-group research leads to the neglect of problems of social structure in favor of preoccupation with the social psychology of adjustment, it may be said to have serious dysfunctional consequencies for the development of a mature science of society.

REFERENCES

1. *American Sociological Review,* 19 (December, 1954).
2. Cartwright, Dorwin and Zander, Alvin, Eds., *Group-Dynamics,* Evanston: Row, Peterson & Co., 1953.
3. French, John R. P., "Field Experiments: Changing Group Productivity," in *Experiments in Social Process,* Ed. Jas. G. Miller, New York: McGraw Hill, 1950.
4. Hochbaum, Godfrey M., "The Relation between Group Members' Self-Confidence and Their Reactions to Group Pressures to Uniformity," *American Sociological Review,* 19 (1954), 678-687.
5. Lee, Alfred McClung, "Individual and Organizational Research in Sociology," *American Sociological Review,* 16 (1951), 701-707.
6. Mannheim, Karl, *Essays on Sociology and Social Psychology,* New York: Oxford University Press, 1953.
7. Maslow, Abraham H., "Problem-centering vs. Means-centering in Science," *Philosophy of Science,* 13 (1946), 326-331.
8. Merton, Robert K., *Social Theory and Social Structure,* Glencoe: The Free Press, 1949.
9. Merton, Robert K. and Kitt, Alice S., "Contributions to the Theory of Reference Group Behavior," in *Continuities in Social Research,* Eds., Merton, Robert K. and Lazarsfeld, Paul F., Glencoe: The Free Press, 1950.
10. Mills, C. Wright, *White Collar,* New York: Oxford University Press, 1951.
11. Schachter S. and Hall R., "Group-Derived Restraints and Audience Participation," *Human Relations,* 5 (1952), 397-406.
12. Strodtbeck, Fred L. and Hare, A. Paul, "Bibliography of Small Group Research," *Sociometry,* 17 (1954), 107-178.
13. Wilson, Logan, *The Academic Man,* New York: Oxford University Press, 1942.

5. SOCIOLOGISM

The Professional Ideology of Social Pathologists

C. WRIGHT MILLS

An analysis of textbooks in the field of social disorganization reveals a common style of thought which is open to social imputation. By grasping the social orientation of this general perspective we can understand why thinkers in this field should select and handle problems in the manner in which they have.

By virtue of the mechanism of sales and distribution, textbooks tend to embody a content agreed upon by the academic group using them. In some cases texts have been written only after an informal poll was taken of professional opinion as to what should be included, and other texts are consulted in the writing of a new one. Since one test of their success is wide adoption, the very spread of the public for which they are written tends to insure a textbook tolerance of the commonplace. Although the conceptual framework of a pathologist's textbook is not usually significantly different from that of such monographs as he may write, this essay is not concerned with the "complete thought" or with the "intentions" of individual authors; it is a study of a professional ideology variously exhibited in a set of textbooks.[1]

SOURCE: Reprinted from "The Professional Ideology of Social Pathologists," in *American Journal of Sociology*, 49 (September, 1943), by C. Wright Mills by permission of the University of Chicago Press. Copyright, 1943 by C. Wright Mills.

[1] No attempt has been made to trace specific concepts to their intellectual origins. Only elements admitted into the more stable textbook formulations have come within my view: the aim is to grasp typical perspectives and key concepts. Hence, no one of the texts to be quoted exemplifies *all* the concepts analyzed; certain elements are not so visible in given texts as in others, and some elements are not evidenced in certain texts at all. In general, the documentary quotations which follow in footnotes are from the later editions of the following books: W. G. Beach and E. E. Walker, *American Social Problems* (1934); J. H. S. Bossard, (*a*) *Social Change and Social Problems* (1934) and (*b*) *Problems of Social Well-Being* (1927); C. H. Cooley, (*a*) *The Social Process* (1918), (*b*) *Human Nature and the Social Order* (1902, 1922), (*c*) *Social Organization* (1909); Edward T. Devine, (*a*) *The Normal Life* (1915, 1924), (*b*) *Progressive Social Action* (1933); R. C. Dexter, *Social Adjustment* (1927); G. S. Dow, *Society and Its Problems* (1920, 1929); M. A. Elliott and F. E. Merrill, *Social Disorganization* (1934, 1941); C. A. Ellwood, (*a*) *The Social Problem, a Constructive Analysis* (1915, 1919); (*b*) *Sociology and Modern Social Problems* (1910–35); H. P. Fairchild, *Out-*

Yet, because of its persistent importance in the development of American sociology and its supposed proximity to the social scene, "social pathology" seems an appropriate point of entry for the examination of the style of reflection and the social-historical basis of American sociology.

The level of abstraction which characterizes these texts is so low that often they seem to be empirically confused for lack of abstraction to knit them together.[2] They display bodies of meagerly connected facts, ranging from rape in rural districts to public housing, and intellectually sanction this low level of abstraction.[3] The "informational" character of social pathology is linked with a failure to consider total social structures. Collecting and dealing in a fragmentary way with scattered problems and facts of milieux, these books are not focused on larger stratifications or upon structured wholes. Such an omission may not be accounted for merely in terms of a general "theoretical weakness." Such structural analyses have been available; yet they have not been attended to or received into the tradition of this literature. American sociologists have often asserted an interest in the "correlation of the social sciences"; nevertheless, academic departmentalization may well have been instrumental in atomizing the problems which they have addressed.[4] Sociologists have always felt that "not many representatives of the older forms

---

line of Applied Sociology (1916, 1921); M. P. Follett, (*a*) *The New State* (1918), (*b*) *Creative Experience* (1924); James Ford, *Social Deviation* (1939); J. M. Gillette and J. M. Reinhardt, *Current Social Problems* (1933, 1937); J. L. Gillin, (*a*) *Poverty and Dependence* (1921, 1926, 1937), (*b*) *Social Pathology* (1933, 1939); J. L. Gillin, C. G. Dittmer, and R. J. Colbert, *Social Problems* (1928, 1932); E. C. Hayes, editor's introductions to texts in the "Lippincott Series"; W. J. Hayes and I. V. Shannon, *Visual Outline of Introductory Sociology* (1935); G. B. Mangold, *Social Pathology* (1932, 1934); H. A. Miller, *Races, Nations, and Classes* (1924); H. W. Odum, *Man's Quest for Social Guidance: The Study of Social Problems* (1927); Maurice Parmelee, *Poverty and Social Progress* (1916); H. A. Phelps, *Contemporary Social Problems* (1932, 1933, 1938); S. A. Queen and J. R. Gruener, *Social Pathology* (1940); S. A. Queen, W. B. Bodenhafer, and E. B. Harper, *Social Organization and Disorganization* (1935); C. M. Rosenquist, *Social Problems* (1940); U. G. Weatherly, *Social Progress* (1926).

[2] See Read Bain, "The Concept of Complexity," *Social Forces*, VIII, 222 and 369. K. Mannheim has called this type "isolating empiricism" ("German Sociology," *Politica*, February, 1934, p. 30).

[3] H. P. Fairchild, p. vii: "Dealing with applied sociology [this book] devotes itself to facts rather than to theories." James H. S. Bossard (*a*), p. xi: "In [*Problems of Social Well-Being*] an effort was made to consider chiefly in a factual vein, certain elements which seemed of basic importance. . . . ." G. P. Mangold, p. viii: "The author has tried to select that which [of factual material] best illustrates problems and practical situations."

The quotations in the footnotes are merely indications of what is usual. The imputations presented must be held against the reader's total experience with the literature under purview.

[4] In Germany the academic division of specialties prior to the rise of sociology channeled sociological work into a formal emphasis. In America a somewhat comparable situation led to a fragmentalization of empirical attention and especially to a channeling of work into "practical problems."

of social science are ready to admit that there is a function for sociology."[5] However, neither lack of theoretical ability nor restrictive channeling through departmentalization constitutes a full explanation of the low level of abstraction and the accompanying failure to consider larger problems of social structure.

If the members of an academic profession are recruited from similar social contexts and if their backgrounds and careers are relatively similar, there is a tendency for them to be uniformly set for some common perspective. The common conditions of their profession often seem more important in this connection than similarity of extraction. Within such a generally homogeneous group there tend to be fewer divergent points of view which would clash over the meaning of facts and thus give rise to interpretations on a more theoretical level.[6]

The relatively homogeneous extraction and similar careers of American pathologists is a possible factor in the low level of abstraction characterizing their work. All the authors considered[7] (except one, who was foreign born) were born in small towns, or on farms near small towns, three-fourths of which were in states not industrialized during the youth of the authors. The social circles and strata in which they have severally moved are quite homogeneous; all but five have participated in similar "reform" groups and "societies" of the professional and business classes. By virtue of their being college professors (all but three are known to have the Ph.D.), of the similar type of temporary positions (other than academic) which they have held, of the sameness of the "societies" to which they have belonged and of the social positions of the persons whom they have married, the assertion as regards general similarity of social extraction, career, and circles of contact seems justified.[8]

A further determinant of the level of abstraction and lack of explicit systematization (beyond which the mentality we are examining does not easily or typically go) is the immediate purpose and the type of public for

---

[5] A. W. Small, *American Journal of Sociology*, May, 1916, p. 785, citing an editorial in the *American Journal of Sociology*, 1907.

[6] Such "homogeneity" is not, however, the only condition under which some common style of thought is taken on by a group of thinkers. Compare the formal conception of "points of coincidence" advanced by H. H. Gerth in *Die sozialgeschichtliche Lage der burgerlichen Intelligenz um die Wende des 18 Jahrhunderts* (diss., Frankfurt A.M.) (V.D.I-Verlag, G.m.b.H. Berlin, N.W. 7). The entire question of the grounding of imputations in terms of social extraction and career-lines is an unfinished set of methodological issues. In this paper the major imputations advanced do *not* proceed upon career data as much as upon the social orientation implied by general perspectives and specific concepts, and by the selection of "problems."

[7] Information concerning twenty-four of the thirty-two authors was full enough to be considered. Five of the eight not considered were junior authors collaborating with persons who are included.

[8] The order of their respective experience has not been systematically considered. All career data on contemporary persons should be held tentatively: open to revision by knowledge not now publicly available.

which they have presumably written. They have been teachers and their specific public has been college students: this has influenced the content and direction of their intellectual endeavors.[9] Teaching is a task which requires a type of systematization to which the textbook answers. Most of the "systematic" or "theoretical" work in "social pathology" has been performed by teachers in textbooks for academic purposes.[10] The fact that sociology often won its academic right to existence in opposition to other departments may have increased the necessity for *textbook* systematization. Such systematization occurs in a context of presentation and of justification rather than within a context of discovery.[11] The textbook-writing and the academic profession of the writers thus figure in the character and function of systematic theory within the field.[12] Systematization of facts for the purpose of making them accessible to collegiate minds is one thing; systematization which is oriented toward crucial growing-points in a research process is quite another. An attempt to systematize on the level of the textbook makes for a taxonomic gathering of facts and a systematization of them under concepts that have already been logically defined.[13] The research possibilities of concepts are not as important as is the putting of the accumulated factual details into some sort of order.

But, even though the perspectives of these texts are usually not explicit, the

---

[9] See above. A. W. Small, p. 754: ". . . . the mental experience of the teacher-explorer in the course of arriving at the present outlook of sociologists . . . . has also been due to the fact that many of the advances in perception or expression have been in the course of attempts to meet students' minds at their precise point of outlook." See C. Wright Mills, "Language, Logic, and Culture," *American Sociological Review*, October, 1939, for mechanisms involved in such determinations of the thinker by his public.

[10] This statement, as is widely recognized, holds in a measure for all American sociology. Cf., e.g., Pitirim Sorokin, "Some Contrasts in Contemporary European and American Sociology," *Social Forces*, September, 1929, pp. 57–58. "In America sociology has grown as a child nursed by the universities and colleges. . . . . American literature in sociology has been composed largely out of textbooks."

[11] Cf. Hans Reichenbach, *Experience and Prediction*, chap. i. See P. Sorokin's comment, *op. cit.*, p. 59.

[12] J. L. Gillin (a), p. v: "My years of experience as a social worker and teacher have gone into the content and method of presentation." J. H. S. Bossard (a), p. 759: "In the preceding chapters, problems have been grouped on the basis of one underlying fact or condition. Obviously, this is an arbitrary procedure which can be justified only on the basis of pedagogical expedience"; p. xi: "The . . . . is the method followed. . . . . By way of defense, this seems simple and pedagogically preferable"; p. xii: "The decision to omit them was made . . . . second, because in an increasing number of colleges and universities, these particular fields are dealt with in separate courses."

[13] Cf. Fritz Mauthner, *Aristotle*, for the pedagogic character of the taxonomic logic of Aristotle. H. P. Fairchild, pp. 6–7: ". . . . the essential features of the scientific method . . . . are three in number. First, the accumulation of facts. . . . . Second, the arrangement or classification of these facts according to some predetermined logical basis of classification. . . . ." J. H. S. Bossard (a), p. 34: "It is the present contention that the scientific study of social problems which confines itself to mere description and classification serves a useful purpose."

facts selected for treatment are not "random." One way to grasp the perspective within which they do lie is to analyze the scope and character of their problems. What, then, are the selecting and organizing principles to be extracted from the range and content of these texts? What types of fact come within their field of attention?

The direction is definitely toward particular "practical problems"—problems of "everyday life."[14] The ideal of practicality, of not being "utopian," operated, in conjunction with other factors, as a polemic against the "philosophy of history" brought into American sociology by men trained in Germany; this polemic implemented the drive to lower levels of abstraction. A view of isolated and immediate problems as the "real" problems may well be characteristic of a society rapidly growing and expanding, as America was in the nineteenth century and, ideologically, in the early twentieth century. The depictive mode of speech and the heavy journalistic "survey" are intellectual concomitants of an expanding society in which new routines are rising and cities are being built.[15] Such an approach is then sanctioned with canons of what constitutes real knowledge; the practice of the detailed and complete empiricism of the survey is justified by an epistemology of gross description. These norms of adequate knowledge linger in an academic tradition to mold the work of its bearers. The emphasis upon fragmentary,[16] practical problems tends to atomize social objectives. The studies so informed are not

---

[14] M. A. Elliott, *American Sociological Review*, June, 1941, p. 317: "The only problems which need concern the sociologists' theories and research are the real, practical problems of everyday living." Queen and Gruener, p. 42: "[In contradistinction to scientific problems] social problems . . . . pertain directly to everyday life. . . . . Their concern is usually 'practical,' and often personal." J. H. S. Bossard (*a*), p. 32: "Frankly, applied sociology is utilitarian. It is concerned with practical problems and purposes." Gillette and Reinhardt, p. 22: "The study of social problems constitutes the heart of sociology as a science. . . . . Even so-called 'pure' sociology, or theoretical sociology, more and more devotes itself to these practical problems of society."

On the other hand, such writers as Ellwood, rising to a *very* high level of abstraction, conceive *formally* of "the social problem." C. A. Ellwood (*a*), pp. 13–14: "Some of us, at least, are beginning to perceive that the social problem is now, what it has been in all ages, namely, *the problem of the relations of men to one another*. It is the problem of human living together, and cannot be confined to any statement in economic, eugenic or other one-sided terms . . . . it is as broad as humanity and human nature. . . . . Such a statement [in terms of one set of factors] obscures the real nature of the problem, and may lead to dangerous, one-sided attempts at its solution." In terms of social and intellectual orientation, both ways of conceiving of "social problems" are similar in that neither is of a sort usable in collective action which proceeds against, rather than well within, more or less tolerated channels.

[15] See H. D. Lasswell, *Politics* (1936), p. 148; K. Mannheim, *op. cit.*, pp. 30–31; and *Ideology and Utopia*, pp. 228–29.

[16] Gillin, Dittmer, and Colbert, p. 44: "There are hudnreds of social problems, big and little." Queen and Gruener, p. 171: "We present here some of the problems of day by day living encountered by diabetics and cardiacs." J. H. S. Bossard (*a*), p. 33: "Certain particular social problems are coming to be reserved for applied sociology. Their selection has been determined less by logic or principle than by accident and historical development"; p. 44: "The more one deals with life's problems at first hand, the more one is impressed with their concreteness, their specificity, and their infinite variety." Gillette and Reinhardt, p. 14: "From almost any point of view there must

integrated into designs comprehensive enough to serve collective action, granted the power and intent to realize such action.

One of the pervasive ways of defining "problems" or of detecting "disorganization" is in terms of *deviation from norms*. The "norms" so used are usually held to be the standards of "society." Later we shall see to what type of society they are oriented. In the absence of studies of specific norms themselves this mode of problematization shifts the responsibility of "taking a stand" away from the thinker and gives a "democratic" rationale to his work.[17] Rationally, it would seem that those who accept this approach to "disorganization" would immediately examine these norms themselves. It is significant that, given their interest in reforming society, which is usually avowed, these writers typically assume the norms which they use and often tacitly sanction them.[18] There are few attempts to explain deviations from norms in terms of the norms themselves, and no rigorous facing of the implications of the fact that social transformations would involve shifts *in them*.

The easy way to meet the question of why norms are violated is in terms of biological impulses which break through "societal restrictions." A paste-pot eclectic psychology provides a rationale for this facile analysis.[19] Thus, more comprehensive problematization is blocked by a biological theory of social deviation. And the "explanation" of deviations can be put in terms of a requirement for more "socialization." "Socialization" is either undefined, used as a moral epithet, or implies norms which are themselves without definition. The focus on "the facts" takes no cognizance of the normative structures within which they lie.

The texts tend either to be "apolitical"[20] or to aspire to a "democratic"

---

be a large number of social problems today"; p. 15: "This book is a treatise on a large number of social problems. It does not claim to consider them all. It repeatedly recognizes the plurality of problems in its treatment of the great problems."

[17] C. M. Rosenquist, p. 19: ". . . . popular recognition of any social condition or process as bad, followed by any attempt to eliminate or cure it, serves as a criterion for its inclusion in a study of social problems. The writer merely accepts the judgment of public opinion. This is the method to be followed in this book." E. T. Devine (*a*), in Note to the Second Edition: "The object of Social Economy is that each shall be able to live as nearly as possible a normal life according to the standard of the period and the community."

[18] C. M. Rosenquist, p. 19: "Perhaps we may be on solid ground through a recognition of the capitalist system and its accompaniments as normal. We may then deal with its several parts, treating as problems those which do not function smoothly. This, it seems, is what the more reputable sociologist actually does." H. P. Fairchild, p. 59: ". . . . some of the social conditions which are the natural and consistent outcome of an individualistic-capitalistic organization of industry, and hence are to be considered as normal in modern societies." Examination of discussions of such items as poverty in most of the texts confirms this assertion. J. L. Gillin (*a*), p. 495: "For serious depressions carefully planned unemployment relief schemes should be formulated before the depression is felt."

[19] That is, an eclecticism that does not analyze in any adequate way the elements and theories which it seeks to combine. Cf. Reuter's critique, *American Journal of Sociology*, November, 1940, pp. 293–304.

[20] E. C. Hayes in the Introduction to H. A. Miller, p. x: "Not political action, the inadequacy of which Professor Eldridge (*Political Action*) has shown, nor revolution,

opportunism.[21] When the political sphere is discussed, its pathological phases are usually stated in terms of "the anti-social," or of "corruption," etc.[22] In another form the political is tacitly identified with the proper functioning of the current and unexamined political order; it is especially likely to be identified with a legal process or the administration of laws.[23] If the "norms" were examined, the investigator would perhaps be carried to see total structures of norms and to relate these to distributions of power. Such a structural point of sight is not usually achieved. The level of abstraction does not rise to permit examination of these normative structures themselves, or of why they come to be transgressed, or of their political implications. Instead, this literature discusses many kinds of apparently unrelated "situations."

About the time W. I. Thomas stated the vocabulary of the situational approach, a social worker was finding it congenial and useful. In M. E. Richmond's influential *Social Diagnosis* (1917) we gain a clue as to why pathologists tend to slip past structure to focus on isolated situations, why there is a tendency for problems to be considered as problems of individuals,[24] and why sequences of situations were not seen as linked into structures:

---

the pathological character of which Professor Sorokin has demonstrated, but social interaction, the causal efficiency of human relationships, is the predominant factor in securing both order and progress."

[21] J. H. S. Bossard (*a*), pp. 14–15: "The constructive approach . . . . may be summarized in one sentence: It is always possible to do something. . . . . Such an approach represents in welfare work that hopelessly incurable optimism which in political life we call democracy." Gillette and Reinhardt, pp. 16–17: "There are no certain rules to be followed step by step in the discovery of the solution. Our best recourse is to employ scientific methods rigidly at every step . . . . because of uncertain factors always present, we never can be sure that our conclusions are more than approximations of the truth. . . . . Since we cannot completely control their activities . . . . our cures must be partial and approximate." One type of link between democratic ideology and social pathology is shown in the following quotation, wherein a condition that deviates from the former is called pathological; the quotation also indicates a typical shying-away from all orders of domination other than that type legitimated traditionally, which is left open: H. A. Miller, p. 32: "When certain . . . . psycho-pathological conditions are found, we may postulate an abnormal relationship as a cause . . . . the particular form of pathology which is involved in our problem may be called the *oppression psychosis*. Oppression is the domination of one group by another." G. V. Price, reviewing Queen and Gruener, *Social Forces*, May, 1941, p. 566: "Without using the word democracy in the doctrinal sense the authors have shown what its utilities are in reducing pathologies."

[22] M. A. Elliott and F. Merrill, p. 28: "The pathological phases of the political process include such anti-social behavior as delinquency, crime, disorder, revolt, and revolution. Corrupt political activity is an important example of such malfunctioning."

[23] Note the identification of "political action" with legislation: Gillin, Dittmer, and Colbert, p. 94: "It is an American practice to attempt to solve any and every sort of social problem through political action. As a result, our statute-books are loaded with 'dead-letter' laws that are not enforced simply because public opinion does not respect them, nor does it feel responsible for them."

[24] J. L. Gillin (*a*), p. 13: "Experience shows that rehabilitation is possible only when each case of poverty or dependency is taken separately and its difficulties handled with strict regard for all the attendant circumstances. . . . . It must be done in terms of the individual, for . . . . it cannot be done *en masse*."

Social diagnosis . . . may be described as the attempt to make as exact a definition as possible of the situation and personality of a human being in some social
need—of his situation and personality, that is, in relation to the other human
beings upon whom he in any way depends or who depend upon him, and in
relation also to the social institutions of his community.[25]

This kind of formulation has been widely applied to isolated "problems"
addressed by sociologists.[26] And the "situational approach" has an affinity
with other elements which characterize their general perspective.[27]

Present institutions train several types of persons—such as judges and
social workers—to think in terms of "situations."[28] Their activities and mental
outlook are set within the existent norms of society; in their professional
work they tend to have an occupationally trained incapacity to rise above
series of "cases." It is in part through such concepts as "situation" and
through such methods as "the case approach"[29] that social pathologists have
been intellectually tied to social work with its occupational position and
political limitations. And, again, the similarity of origin and the probable
lack of any continuous "class experience" of the group of thinkers decrease
their chances to see social structures rather than a scatter of situations. The
mediums of experience and orientation through which they respectively view
society are too similar, too homogeneous, to permit the clash of diverse angles
which, through controversy, might lead to the construction of a whole.

The paramount fact of immigration in American culture, with each wave of
immigrants displacing the lower-class position of former waves and raising
the position of the earlier immigrants, also tends to obscure structural and
class positions.[30] Thus, instead of positional issues, pathologists typically see
problems in terms of an individual, such as an immigrant, "adjusting" to a
milieu[31] or being "assimilated" or Americanized. Instead of problems of class

---

[25] Richmond, p. 357; see also pp. 51 and 62.

[26] J. H. S. Bossard (a), p. 3: "Social problems consist of (a) a social situation,
(b) which are. . . . ." Gillette and Reinhardt, p. 15: "A social problem is a situation,
confronting a group. . . . ."

[27] J. H. S. Bossard (a), p. 57: ". . . . the emphasis in our social thinking upon the
situation as a unit of experience, as 'an aggregate of interactive and interdependent
factors of personality and circumstance,' is in essence a recognition of the idea of the
emergent. . . . . Queen recognizes the implications of the situational approach very
clearly in these words: 'For purposes of sociological analysis, a situation consists in
relationships between persons viewed as a cross section of human experience, constantly
changing. . . . . Thus we make of the concept "situation" an intellectual tool' "
(S. Queen, "Some Problems of the Situational Approach," *Social Forces*, June, 1931,
p. 481).

[28] See K. Mannheim, *Man and Society*, p. 305.

[29] Queen, Bodenhafer, and Harper, p. viii: Editor's Note by S. Eldridge: "The present volume . . . . features the case approach to social problems."

[30] Note the lack of structure in the conception of "class": Gillette and Reinhardt,
p. 177: "Viewing the matter historically, then, it appears that the chief cause of rigid
class systems of society with their attendant evils is the prolonged concentration of
wealth in the hands of a relatively few persons."

[31] See below, the concept of "adjustment."

structure involving immigration, the tendency has been to institute problems in terms of immigration involving the nationalist assimilation of individuals. The fact that some individuals have had opportunities to rise in the American hierarchy decreases the chance fully to see the ceilings of class. Under these conditions such structures are seen as fluctuating and unsubstantial and are likely to be explained not in terms of *class position* but in terms of *status attitudes.*[32]

Another element that tends to obviate an analytic view of structure is the emphasis upon the "processual" and "organic" character of society. In Cooley, whose influence on these books is decisive, one gets a highly formal, many-sided fluidity where "nothing is fixed or independent, everything is plastic and takes influence as well as gives it."[33] From the standpoint of political action, such a view may mean a reformism dealing with masses of detail and furthers a tendency to be apolitical. There can be no bases or points of entry for larger social action in a structureless flux. The view is buttressed epistemologically with an emotionalized animus against "particularism" and with the intense approval of the safe, if colorless, "multiple-factor" view of causation.[34] The liberal "multiple-factor" view does not lead to a conception of causation which would permit points of entry for broader types of action, especially political action.[35] No set of underlying structural shifts is given which might be open to manipulation, at key points, and which, like the fact of private property in a corporate economy, might be seen as efficacious in producing many "problems." If one fragmentalizes society into "factors," into elemental bits, naturally one will then need quite a few of them to account for something,[36] and one can never be sure they are all in.

---

[32] Gillin, Dittmer, and Colbert, p. 59: "The most fundamental cause of class and group conflict is the attitude of superiority on the part of one class, or group, toward another."

[33] *The Social Process*, pp. 44–45.

[34] Elliott and Merrill, p. 38: "One of the most significant concepts in the understanding of social problems is the idea of multiple causation."

[35] See above comments on political relevance. C. A. Ellwood (*b*) p. 324: "We may, perhaps, sum up this chapter by saying that it is evident that the cure of poverty is not to be sought merely in certain economic rearrangements, but in scientific control of the whole life process of human society. This means that in order to get rid of poverty, the defects in education in government, in religion and morality, in philanthropy, and even in physical heredity, must be got rid of. Of course, this can only be done when there is a scientific understanding of the conditions necessary for normal human social life."

[36] J. L. Gillin (*a*), pp. 51–128: ". . . . the modern theory of the causes of poverty has passed beyond any one-sided explanation to a many-sided theory." The following conditions of poverty and dependence are discussed: poor natural resources, adverse climate, adverse weather, insect pests, disasters, illness and diseases, physical inheritance, mental inheritance, adverse surroundings of children, death or disability of the earner, unemployment, lack of proper wages, traditions, customs, habits, advertising and instalment buying, fluctuations between costs of living and income, inequitable distribution of wealth and income, family marital relations, political conditions, unwise philanthropy, etc. After these discussions, *family cases* are presented as ". . . . studies in causation."

A formal emphasis upon "the whole" plus lack of total structural consideration plus a focus upon scattered situations does not make it easy to reform the status quo.

The "organic" orientation of liberalism has stressed all those social factors which tend to a harmonious balance of elements.[37] There is a minimization of chances for action in a social milieu where "there is always continuity with the past, and not only with any one element only of the past, but with the whole interacting organism of man."[38] In seeing everything social as continuous process, changes in pace and revolutionary dislocations are missed[39] or are taken as signs of the "pathological." The formality and the assumed unity implied by "the mores" also lower the chances to see social chasms and structural dislocations.

Typically, pathologists have not attempted to construct a structural whole. When, however, they do consider totalities, it is in terms of such concepts as "society," "the social order," or "the social organization," "the mores and institutions," and "American culture." Four things should be noted about their use of such terms: (*a*) The terms represent undifferentiated entities. Whatever they may indicate, it is systematically homogeneous. Uncritical use of such a term as "the" permits a writer the hidden assumption in politically crucial contexts of a homogeneous and harmonious whole.[40] The large texture of "the society" will take care of itself, it is somehow and in the long run harmonious,[41] it has a "strain toward consistency" running through it;[42] or, if not this, then only the co-operation of all is needed,[43] or perhaps even a right moral feeling is taken as a solution.[44] (*b*) In their formal emptiness these terms are commensurate with the low level of abstraction. Their *formality* facilitates the empirical concern with "everyday" problems of (com-

---

[37] Whereas many socialist theories have tended to overlook the elastic elements that do exist in a society. Cf. K. Mannheim, *Politica*, pp. 25–26.

[38] C. H. Cooley (*a*), p. 46.

[39] Max Lerner, *It Is Later than You Think*, pp. 14–15; and *Encyclopaedia of the Social Sciences*, article "Social Progress." See documentation and consequences below.

[40] Gillin, Dittmer, and Colbert, p. 11: "All this group life is nicely woven into a system that we call society. . . . ."

[41] *Ibid.*, p. 15: "But the aim of society is ever directed to the task of bringing uniform advantages to all." C. A. Ellwood (*b*), p. 395: "Social organization may refer to any condition or relation of the elements of a social group; but by social order we mean a settled and harmonious relation between the individuals or the parts of a society. The problem of social order is then the problem of harmonious adaptation among the individuals of the group. . . . ."

[42] It is significant that it was Sumner, with his tacit belief in "natural" order, who set forth the phrase and what it implies.

[43] Gillin, Dittmer, and Colbert, p. 13: "Since a community is made up of a number of neighborhoods, it is necessary that all cooperate in order to secure better schools, improved. . . . ."

[44] J. L. Gillin (*a*), p. 133: "Only as a passion for social righteousness takes the place of an imperative desire for selfish advantage . . . . will society do away with the conditions that now depress some classes of the population and exhalt others."

munity) milieu. (*c*) In addition to their "descriptive" use, such terms are used normatively. The "social" becomes a good term when it is used in ethical polemics against "individualism" or against such abstract moral qualities as "selfishness," lack of "altruism," or of "antisocial" sentiments.[45] "Social" is conceived as a "co-operative" "sharing" of something or as "conducive to the general welfare."[46] The late eighteenth-century use of "society" as against "state" by the rising bourgeoisie had already endowed "society" with a "democratic" tinge which this literature transmits. (*d*) There is a strong tendency for the term "society" to be practically assimilated to, or conceived largely in terms of, primary groups and small homogeneous communities. Such a conception typically characterizes the literature within our purview.[47] In explain-

---

[45] C. A. Ellwood (*b*), p. 84: ". . . . increasing altruism is necessary for the success of those more and more complex forms of cooperation which characterize higher civilization and upon which it depends." G. B. Mangold, p. 17: "Without the spirit of altruism society would be but a sorry exhibition of the collective humanity that we believe has been made in the image of God." Conversely, the "antisocial" is held to include certain abstract, moral traits of individuals. Elliott and Merrill, p. 43: "An analysis of the disorganization process suggests two types of anti-social forces: (1) the consciously directed anti-social forces and (2) the impersonal organic forces which are an outgrowth of the formalism discussed above . . . . to advance their own selfish ends. These men are thoroughly aware of their antisocial attitudes. Social values have no meaning for them. . . . . There has often been no socializing influence in the lives of those men. . . . . Cooperation, or 'mutual aid,' the implicit counterpart of effective social organization. . . . . Vice areas . . . . function because of human appetites, because individual desires are more deeply rooted than any sense of the social implications. . . . The prostitute exists only because she is a means to man's sensual pleasure and satiety"; p. 44: "Sin, vice, crime, corruption, all consciously directed anti-social forces, offer a primrose. . . . ." G. B. Mangold, p. 59: "Unsocial habits lead to poverty; particularly do they degrade poverty into dependency. Chief among these vices is intemperance. Before the advent of prohibition it was. . . . ." Queen, Bodenhafer, and Harper, p. 4: "When there is . . . . characterized by harmony, teamwork, understanding, approval, and the like, we may speak of organization. When the opposite is true and there is a . . . . marked by tension, conflict, or drifting apart, we may speak of disorganization."

[46] Gillin, Dittmer, and Colbert, p. 5: " 'The word [social] means conducive to the collective welfare, and thus becomes nearly equivalent to moral' [Cooley, *Human Nature and the Social Order*, p. 4] . . . . it is this . . . . meaning that comes closest to our interpretation . . . . —'conducive to the collective welfare'—relationships, and products of relationships that are believed to foster and promote *group life*, and to insure *group survival*."

[47] J. L. Gillin (*b*), p. 313: ". . . . personal relationships . . . . are the most important ties in the social organization. . . . ." C. A. Ellwood (*b*), pp. 3–4: "The tendency in the best sociological thinking is to emphasize the importance, for the understanding of our social life, of 'primary' or face-to-face groups"; p. 77: "Primary groups . . . . are of most interest sociologically, because they exhibit social life at its maximum intensity, and because they are the bearers of the most vital elements in social life, especially the traditions of civilization"; pp. 70–80: "The chief importance of primary groups is our social life, however, is that they . . . . furnish the 'patterns' which we attempt to realize in our social life in general"; pp. 84–85: "All human history has, from one point of view, been a struggle to transfer altruism and solidarity of the family to successively larger and larger groups of men"; pp. 90–91: "Primary, or face-to-face

ing it, we come upon an element that is highly important in understanding the total perspective.

The basis of "stability," "order," or "solidarity" is not typically analyzed in these books, but a conception of such a basis is implicitly used and sanctioned,[48] for some normative conception of a socially "healthy" and stable organization is involved in the determination of "pathological" conditions. "Pathological" behavior is not discerned in a *structural* sense (i.e., as incommensurate with an existent structural type) or in a *statistical* sense (i.e., as deviations from central tendencies). This is evidenced by the regular assertion that pathological conditions *abound* in the city.[49] If they *"abound"* therein, they cannot be "abnormal" in the statistical sense and are not likely to prevail in the structural sense. It may be proposed that the norms in terms of which "pathological" conditions are detected are "humanitarian ideals." But we must then ask for the social orientation of such ideals.[50] In this litera-

---

groups are the key to the understanding of our social life. . . . ." Gillin, Dittmer, Colbert, p. 282: ". . . . the home is probably our most fundamental social institution . . . ."; p. 285: "Anything that endangers the stability of the family endangers society." J. H. S. Bossard (*a*), p. 555: "Family life is the focal point of virtually all of our social problems."

[48] C. A. Ellwood (*b*), pp. 79–80: "The very ideal of social solidarity itself comes from the unity experienced in such [primary] groups." Elliott and Merrill, p. 581: "An ever-increasing number of persons living in the giant cities has become completely deracinated, cut off from all stable primary ties. They have lost not only their physical home, but often their spiritual home as well. Social disorganization breeds in these unattached masses of the urban proletariat. They furnish willing nuclei for robbery, brigandage, and revolution."

[49] J. L. Gillin (*b*), p. 411: "In the city we have a greater degree of disorganization in the sense in which we use that term"; p. 410: ". . . . in the simple and well-organized ties of country life . . . ."; p. 409: "Recreation in the country is largely homemade. . . . . In the city it is professional. . . . . The patterns of behavior . . . . are here again disorganized and new patterns have to be found." Gillette and Reinhardt, p. 116: "Cities exhibit all the social problems, save those peculiar to agricultural extractive pursuits." H. P. Fairchild, p. 304: "Since there are no *natural* facilities available to the majority of the *denizens* of cities for the gratification of the desire for dancing, it inevitably follows that provision is made on a commercial basis" (my italics). C. M. Rosenquist, p. 47: "The controls which were effective in the small, settled farm community no longer suffice in . . . . the city. To this fact may be traced many of the conditions we speak of as social problems. . . . . W. G. Beach and E. E. Walker, pp. 102–3: ". . . . men find their life interests and values in group membership and participation. The most influential groups are those which provide intimate, face-to-face relationships, as the family, the playground, the club, the neighborhood, and the small community. . . . . Any wholesome and satisfying life must provide for a continuation of such small groups and institutional forms. . . . . One of the most elusive and challenging problems arising from the growth of cities is that of preventing the complete disorganization of essential social groups. In the rural community. . . . ." J. H. S. Bossard (*a*), p. 113: "The marked trend of population to the city and the rapid rise of large urban centers, together with their reflex upon the rural regions, constitute the basis of virtually every problem to be discussed in this volume."

[50] This is what Waller does *not* do in his provocative discussion of "humanitarian" and "organizing mores" ("Social Problems and the Mores," *American Sociological Review*, December, 1936, pp. 922–33).

ture the operating criteria of the pathological are typically *rural* in orientation and extraction.[51]

Most of the "problems" considered arise because of the urban deterioration of certain values which can live genuinely only in a relatively homogeneous and primary rural milieu. The "problems" discussed typically concern urban behavior. When "rural problems" are discussed, they are conceived as due to encroaching urbanization.[52] The notion of disorganization is quite often merely the absence of that *type* of organization associated with the stuff of primary-group communities having Christian and Jeffersonian legitimations.[53]

Cooley, the local colorist of American sociology, was the chief publicist of this conception of normal organization. He held "the great historical task of mankind" to be the more effective and wider organization of that moral order and pattern of virtues developed in primary groups and communities.[54] Cooley took the idealists' absolute[55] and gave it the characteristics of an

[51] J. L. Gillin (*b*), p. 407: The home "developing as . . . . rural" is considered "disorganized" in the city; p. 409: "[In the city] it is only the rebel, unable and unwilling to adjust himself to machine and organization, who retains personal independence. . . . . The farmer, conscious that he lives by his own thinking . . . . responds to his environment with a feeling of independence—a normal response. The city worker has no keen perception of his dependence upon nature." Elliott and Merrill, p. 32: "However different their approach, the basic dilemma of civilization is the fundamental disparity of values and standards of universally accepted definitions of the situation."

[52] C. A. Ellwood (*b*), p. 281: "The reflex of the city problem is the rural problem." J. L. Gillen (*b*), p. 429: "[Urbanization] which has modified the solidarity of the rural family. . . . ." W. J. Hayes and I. V. Shannon, p. 22: "Contacts . . . . emancipate individuals from control of primary groups . . . . this leads to setting up personal norms of behavior instead of conforming to group standards." (Implies no conception of *urban* types of norms.)

[53] The intellectual consequences of the rural to urban drift are much wider than the perspectives noted in the literature of pathology. In more general American sociology the writings of a man like E. A. Ross are to be understood in terms of a reaction of those oriented to a farmer's democracy against the growth of big business, in its control of railroads, etc. Another division of American sociology in which America's rural past is *intellectually* evident is "rural sociology" itself. This field shows the positive side of the matter, for here the yearning for the values associated with rural simplicity and neighborliness is even more noticeable. In this literature a primary, rural heritage is taken as the source of "stability" and is conceived as the reservoir of "values." Such straddling concepts as "urban" function to limit recognition of the urban character of dominant contemporary social structures. In a historical sense we need not argue with these emphases: the underlying form of American democracy and religion, e.g., has drawn much from the dominance of a rural society. And a rapid urbanization may well be only a veneer upon masses of rurally oriented personalities. But the kind of structural stability in America which grew from rural patterns is historical. In the world today the kind of stability that can—indeed, in part has—emerged from the hunger for those primary contacts historically associated with ties of blood and closeness to soil is a streamlined variety.

[54] *Social Organization*, chap. v.

[55] G. H. Mead, "Cooley's Contribution to American Social Thought," *American Journal of Sociology*, XXXV, 701: "Cooley was Emersonian in finding the individual self in an oversoul." Cf. G. W. F. Hegel, *Lectures on the Philosophy of History* (London: Geo. Bell & Sons, 1884), especially pp. 39–44.

organic village; all the world should be an enlarged, Christian-democratic version of a rural village. He practically assimilated "society" to this primary-group community, and he blessed it emotionally and conceptually.[56] "There is reflected here," says T. V. Smith of Cooley—and what he says will hold for the typical social pathologist—"what is highly common in our culture, an ideal of intimacy short of which we do not rest satisfied where other people are concerned. Social distance is a dire fate, achieved with difficulty and lamented as highly unideal, not to say as immoral, in our Christian traditions. It is not enough to have saints; we must have 'communion' of the saints. In order to have social relations, we must nuzzle one another."[57]

The aim to preserve rurally oriented values and stabilities is indicated by the implicit model which operates to detect urban disorganization; it is also shown by the stress upon *community* welfare. The community is taken as a major unit, and often it sets the scope of concern and problematization.[58] It is also within the framework of ideally democratic communities that proposed solutions are to be worked out.[59] It should be noted that sometimes, although

---

[56] Note the common association of urban "impersonality" and "formalism" with "disorganization." Elliott and Merrill, p. 16: ". . . . lack of harmony between the various units of the social order is in a sense . . . . exemplified by the impersonal nature of the social organization and the consequent process of social disorganization . . . . [cf. C. H. Cooley, *Social Process*, pp. 3–29]"; p. 574: "There is a very close relationship between formalism and disorganization, although at first glance the two states appear to be opposite poles in the social process. They are in reality sequential steps in the same great movement of disorganization, which grows out of formalism. . . . ."

[57] *Beyond Conscience*, p. 111.

[58] C. A. Ellwood (*b*), p. 12: "All forms of association are of interest to the sociologist, though not all are of equal importance. The natural, genetic social groups, which we may call 'communities,' serve best to exhibit sociological problems. Through the study of such simple and primary groups as the family and the neighborhood group, for example, the problems of sociology can be much better attacked than through the study of society at large or association in general"; pp. 75–77: ". . . . natural groupings, such as the family, the neighborhood, the city, the state or province, and the nation. They may be, and usually are, called *communities*, since they are composed of individuals who carry on all phases of a common life. Voluntary, purposive associations always exist within some community, whether large or small. Groups which we call 'communities' are, therefore, more embracing, more stable, less artificial and specialized than purely voluntary groups. For this reason communities are of more interest to the sociologist than specialized voluntary groups, and sociology is in a peculiar sense a study of the problems of community life." J. H. S. Bossard (*a*), pp. 49–50: "Acceptance of the community as a definite unit in social work and in social theory has become general during the past fifteen years. American participation in the World War was an important factor in bringing this about, first because the community constituted the basic expression of that democratic spirit which the war engendered, and second, the community was seized upon by the various war-time activities and drives as the most effective unit for the mobilization of the spirit and resources of the nation."

[59] Gillin, Dittmer, and Colbert, p. 15: ". . . . *social work*, which means, scientifically developing and adjusting human relations in a way that will secure normal life to individuals and communities and encourage individual and community progress"; p. 47: ". . . . it is important to keep in mind that the central problem is that of adjusting our social life and our social institutions, so that, as individuals and as communities, we may use and enjoy the largest measure of civilization possible, and promote further

not typically or exclusively, solutions are conceived as dependent upon abstract moral traits or democratic surrogates of them, such as a "unanimous public will."[60]

"Cultural lag" is considered by many pathologists to be the concept with which many scattered problems may be detected and systematized. Whereas the approach by deviation from norms is oriented "ideologically" toward a rural type of order and stability, the cultural-lag model is tacitly oriented in a "utopian"[61] and progressive manner toward changing some areas of the culture or certain institutions so as to "integrate" them with the state of progressive technology.[62] We must analyze the use made by pathologists of "lag" rather than abstract formulations of it.[63]

Even though all the situations called "lags" *exist* in the present, their functional realities are referred back, away from the present. Evaluations are thus translated into a time sequence; cultural lag is an assertion of unequal "progress." It tells us what changes are "called for," what changes "ought" to have come about and didn't. In terms of various spheres of society it says what progress is, tells us how much we have had, ought to have had, didn't have, and when and where we didn't have it. The imputation of "lag" is complicated by the historical judgment in whose guise it is advanced and by the programmatic content being shoved into pseudo-objective phrases, as, for example, "called for."

It is not enough to recognize that the stating of problems in terms of cultural lag involves evaluations, however disguised. One must find the general loci of this kind of evaluation and then explain why just this form of evaluation has been so readily accepted and widely used by pathologists. The model in which institutions lag behind technology and science involves a positive evaluation of natural science and of orderly progressive change. Loosely, it derives from a liberal continuation of the enlightenment with its full rationalism, its messianic and now politically naïve admiration of physical science as a kind of thinking and activity, and with its concept of time as progress. This notion of progress was carried into American colleges by the once prevalent Scottish moral philosophy. From after the Civil War through the first

---

progress." M. P. Follett (*a*), Part III, has suggested that neighborhood groups be organized into political units. This would permit the expression of daily life and bring to the surface live needs that they may become the substance of politics. The neighborhood as a political unit would make possible friendly acquaintance; it would socialize people and would make for "the realization of oneness."

[60] J. L. Gillin (*b*), p. 97: "The 'liquor problem' is as acute in the United States today as it ever was in the past, perhaps even more so"; p. 101: "The solution must spring from an aroused and unanimous public will."

[61] Cf. K. Mannheim, *Ideology and Utopia*, for definitions of these terms.

[62] However, "lag" and "norms" are not unrelated: Queen, Bodenhafer, and Harper, p. 437: "Much of the discussion of cultural lags in the family assumes some kind of normal pattern which is commonly believed to have permanent validity because of the functions performed."

[63] See examples given in J. W. Woodard's "Critical Notes on the Cultural Lag Concept," *Social Forces*, March, 1934, p. 388.

two or three decades of the twentieth century the expanding business and middle classes were taking over instruments of production, political power, and social prestige; and many of the academic men of the generation were recruited from these rising strata and/or actively mingled with them. Notions of progress are congenial to those who are rising in the scale of position and income.

Those sociologists who think in terms of this model have not typically focused upon the conditions and interest groups underlying variant "rates of change" in different spheres. One might say that in terms of the rates of change at which sectors of culture *could* move, it is technology that is "lagging," for the specific reason of the control of patents, etc., by intrenched interests.[64] In contrast to the pathologists' use, Veblen's use of "lag, leak, and friction" is a structural analysis of industry versus business enterprise.[65] He focused on where "the lag" seemed to pinch; he attempted to show how the trained incapacity of legitimate businessmen acting within entrepreneurial canons would result in a commercial sabotage of production and efficiency in order to augment profits within a system of price and ownership. He did not like this "unworkman-like result," and he detailed its mechanism. In the pathologists' usage the conception has lost this specific and structural anchorage: it has been generalized and applied to everything fragmentarily. This generalization occurs with the aid of such blanket terms as "adaptive culture" and "material culture."[66] There is no specific focus for a program of action embodied in the application of such terms.

Another model in terms of which disorganizations are instituted is that of "social change" itself.[67] This model is not handled in any one typical way, but usually it carries the implicit assumption that human beings are "adjusted" satisfactorily to any social condition that has existed for a long time and that, when some aspect of social life changes, it may lead to a social problem.[68] The notion is oriented ideologically and yet participates in assumptions similar to those of cultural lag, which, indeed, might be considered a variant of it. Such a scheme for problematization buttresses and is buttressed by the idea of continuous process, commented on above; but here the slow,

---

[64] See, e.g., B. J. Stern's article in *Annals of the American Academy of Political and Social Science*, November, 1938.

[65] *The Engineers and the Price System; The Theory of Business Enterprise.*

[66] J. H. S. Bossard (*a*), p. 5: ". . . . as Ogburn put it [W. F. Ogburn, *Social Change* (1922)] to the extent that the adaptive culture has not kept pace with the material culture, the amount of social ill-being has increased relatively."

[67] J. L. Gillin (*b*), p. 416: "Social disorganization is a function of rapidly changing conditions in people's lives." W. J. Hayes and I. V. Shannon, p. 20: "Social disorganization is an abrupt break in the existing social arrangements or a serious alteration in the routine of group life causing maladjustment." H. W. Odum, p. 100: ". . . . if one reviews the general categories of social problems already listed in previous chapters, it must be clear that most of them or their present manifestations are due to or accentuated by the process of social change."

[68] The point is made and acutely discussed by Rosenquist, pp. 8–10.

"evolutionary" pace of change is taken explicitly as normal and organized,[69] whereas "discontinuity" is taken as problematic.[70] The orientation to "rural" types of organization should be recalled. In line with the stress on continuous process, the point where sanctioned order meets advisable change is not typically or structurally drawn.[71] A conception of "balance" is usual and sometimes is explicitly sanctioned.[72] The question, "Changes in what spheres induce disorganization?" is left open; the position taken is usually somewhere between extremes, both of which are held to be bad.[73] This comes out in the obvious fact that what a conservative calls *dis*organization, a radical might well call *re*organization. Without a construction of total social structures that are actually emerging, one remains caught between simple evaluations.

Besides deviation from norms, orientation to rural principles of stability, cultural lag, and social change, another conception in terms of which "problems" are typically discussed is that of adaptation or "adjustment" and their

---

[69] Gillin, Dittmer, and Colbert, p. 48: "Social life and its products require long periods of time to develop and ripen. . . . ." Gillette and Reinhardt, p. 13: "The larger proportion of social changes are small and simple, and resemble osmosis in the field of physics and organic life." This gradualism is related to the orientation to primary group relations and experiences and hence to the "sharing" conception of the social. E.g., Elliott and Merrill, p. 11: "Assimilation, on the other hand, is gradual and depends upon some degree of contact and communication, if there is to be any vital sharing of common experience (Cf. M. P. Follett, *Creative Experience*). . . . ."

[70] Gillette and Reinhardt, p. 30: ". . . . the need for thought about discontinuity in industry or education and about our dependence on proper training to keep society stabilized and progressive should be emphasized"; p. 21: "The habitual, daily, routine, conventional activities of life fortunately make up the greater part of life, most of the time. Often, however, they are broken across by social breakdowns, disturbances, and dislocations and the appearance of troublesome classes of persons." C. A. Ellwood (*a*), p. 230: ". . . . revolution is not a *normal* method of social change; . . . . it marks the breakdown of the normal means of social development; . . . . it is not inevitable, but may easily be avoided by plasticity in social institutions and in the mental attitudes of classes and individuals. . . . ."

[71] The notion of temporal contingency, at times extended to the point of historical irrationality, plays into the processual, nonstructural characteristics of the perspective; notice also its commensurability with the apolitical and one-thing-at-a-time reformism. Elliott and Merrill, p. 3: "Life is dynamic. Life is ceaseless, bewildering change, and man, armed though he is with the experience of the past, can never be certain of the future. He must recognize that the immediate present is a constantly changing frame of reference and that future problems are a matter of chance for which the past offers no sure panacea."

[72] E. C. Hayes' Editor's Introduction to U. G. Weatherly, p. xii: "Realization that progressive change is not likely to be less in the generation next to come . . . . and determination . . . . to promote progress, is the normal attitude for every person who is animated by generous loyalty and. . . . ." Weatherly, p. 138: "Both innovation and conservatism have their value, and the balance between them, which is an ideal attitude . . . ."; p. 380: "Discipline and liberation are not two antagonistic processes; they are complimentary parts of the same process, which is social equilibration. They illustrate the law of physics . . . . stability is reached only by a balance of forces."

[73] A. Ellwood (*a*), p. vii: "The aim of the book is to indicate the direction which our social thinking must take if we are to avoid revolution, on the one hand, and reactions, on the other."

opposites.[74] The pathological or disorganized is the maladjusted. This concept, as well as that of the "normal," is usually left empty of concrete, social content;[75] or its content is, in effect, a propaganda for conformity to those norms and traits ideally associated with small-town, middle-class milieux.[76] When it is an individual who is thought to be maladjusted, the "social type" within which he is maladjusted is not stated. Social and moral elements are masked by a quasi-biological meaning of the term "adaptation"[77] with an entourage of apparently socially bare terms like "existence" and "survival," which seem still to draw prestige from the vogue of evolutionism.[78] Both the quasi-biological and the structureless character of the concept "adjustment" tend, by formalization, to universalize the term, thus again obscuring specific social content. Use of "adjustment" accepts the goals and the means of smaller community milieux.[79] At the most, writers using these terms sug-

---

[74] H. P. Fairchild, p. 35: ". . . . it can be safely said that maladjustments are among the most numerous and important of all forms of abnormality, frequently being so extensive as to include entire social groups or classes."

[75] Gillin, Dittmer, and Colbert, p. 536: "All social problems grow out of *the* social problem—the problem of the adjustment of man to his universe, and of the social universe to man. The maladjustments in these relationships give us all our social problems. . . . ." H. P. Fairchild, p. 16: "While the word 'normal' carries a fairly definite and, for the most part, accurate implication to the mind of any intelligent person, it is nevertheless extremely difficult to define in concrete terms. . . . . As commonly used to convey a definite idea, the word 'normal' means that which is in harmony with the general make-up and organization of the object under discussion—that which is consistent with other normal factors."

[76] Elliott and Merrill, p. 17, correctly assert that in "Edward T. Divine's discussion of 'the normal life' the norm is the healthy and uneventful life cycle of the average middle-class man or woman. These persons are never subjected to the temptations of great wealth. Neither do they come in contact with poverty, crime, vice, and other unpleasantly sordid aspects of life [*The Normal Life*, pp. 5–8]. His discussion is thus a consideration of the 'normal standards' for the several ages of the bourgeoisie. . . . ."

[77] When it is so hidden; but note the heavily sentimental endowment the term may receive: R. C. Dexter, p. 408: ". . . . few of the present generation of little ones, and fewer still of the next, will never see the sun or the green grass because of the sins of their parents or the carelessness of their physician; and thanks to our increasing provision for free public education, more and more adapted to the needs of the individual child, thousands of boys and girls will become intelligent, responsible citizens, worthy of a free nation, instead of pawns for unscrupulous politicians. All this and much more is due to social adjustments, made by the unceasing effort and sacrifice of men and women who. . . . ."

[78] J. L. Gillin (*b*), p. 4: "Social pathology . . . . is the study of the social patterns and processes involved in man's failure to adjust himself and his institutions to the necessities of existence to the end that he may survive and satisfy the felt needs of his nature."

[79] J. L. Gillin (*b*), p. 8: "An individual who does not approximate these [socially approved] standards is said to be *unadjusted*. If he does not concern himself with living up to them, he is said to be demoralized or disorganized." R. C. Dexter, p. 407: "In this book the term Social Adjustment has been . . . . used as applying to . . . . the necessary task of smoothing-off the rough edges and softening the sledge-hammer blows of an indifferent social system. The term . . . . is practically synonymous with social adaptation—the fitting of man to his complete environment, physical and social alike. Until the present it has been the especially maladjusted individual or group who has received the service of 'straighteners.' " (Note *ideological* orientation of concept.)

gest techniques or means believed to be less disruptive than others to attain the goals that are given. They do not typically consider whether or not certain groups or individuals caught in economically underprivileged situations can possibly obtain the current goals without drastic shifts in the basic institutions which channel and promote them. The idea of adjustment seems to be most directly applicable to a social scene in which, on the one hand, there is a society and, on the other, an individual immigrant.[80] The immigrant then "adjusts" to the new environment. The "immigrant problem" was early in the pathologist's center of focus, and the concepts used in stating it may have been carried over as the bases for a model of experience and formulations of other "problems." *The Polish Peasant* (1918), which has had a very strong influence on the books under consideration, was empirically focused upon an immigrant group.

In approaching the notion of adjustment, one may analyze the specific illustrations of maladjustment that are given and from these instances infer a type of social person who in this literature is evaluated as "adjusted." The ideally adjusted man of the social pathologists is "socialized." This term seems to operate ethically as the opposite of "selfish;"[81] it implies that the adjusted man conforms to middle-class morality and motives and "participates" in the gradual progress of respectable institutions. If he is not a "joiner," he certainly gets around and into many community organizations.[82] If he is

---

[80] H. P. Fairchild, p. 34: "The other form of incompetence, which may be called 'maladjustment,' does not imply any lack on the part of the individual himself. . . . . The man is all right, but he is not in the right place. Our immigrants furnish abundant examples of this form of incompetence. . . . . But the foreigner is not by any means the sole example of maladjustment. Our modern life, particularly our modern city life, teems with cases of this sort." J. H. S. Bossard (*a*), p. 110 (under "The Immigrant's Problem of Adjustment"): "To most persons, life consists in large measure of habitual responses to the demands of a fairly fixed environment. When man changes his environment, new and perhaps untried responses are called for. New adjustments must be made, as we say." J. L. Gillin (*b*), p. 10: "Social pathology . . . . arises out of the maladjustment between the individual and the social structure." Elliott and Merrill, p. 22: "Just as an effective social organization implies a harmony between individual and social interests, so a disorganized social order must involve a conflict between individual and social points of view."

[81] Gillin, Dittmer, and Colbert, pp. 16–17: "By *socialization* we mean the directing of human motives toward giving to 'even the least' of the members of the social whole the benefits of cultural development. Socialization is thus practically the opposite to *aloofness, selfishness, greed, exploitation,* and *profiteering.* It causes the individual and the group to *feel* their *oneness* with the social whole. . . . . In brief, what society regards as *moral, i.e.,* good for the whole, becomes the aim of socialized individuals and groups. This being true, the improvement of society rests to a very large extent upon *moral progress.*"

[82] See Queen and Gruener, *Social Pathology: Obstacles to Social Participation.* These authors would deny this mode of statement, but such verbal denials must be tested against what they have done and the framework they have actually employed in defining pathologies. Their criterion of the pathological is correctly indicated in the subtitle of their book. Elliott and Merrill, p. 580: "There are various criteria by which the degree of individual participation may be measured roughly . . . . whether or not he votes at

socialized, the individual thinks of others and is kindly toward them. He does not brood or mope about but is somewhat extravert, eagerly participating in his community's institutions. His mother and father were not divorced, nor was his home ever broken. He is "successful"—at least in a modest way—since he is ambitious; but he does not speculate about matters too far above his means, lest he become "a fantasy thinker," and the little men don't scramble after the big money. The less abstract the traits and fulfilled "needs" of "the adjusted man" are, the more they gravitate toward the norms of independent middle-class persons verbally living out Protestant ideals in the small towns of America.[83]

A New Look at Mills' Critique

EMIL BEND AND
MARTIN VOGELFANGER

The study of social problems was one of the original areas of inquiry of American sociology, and an important impetus to its development. Today it

---

SOURCE: Prepared especially for this volume.

elections . . . . the individual's ownership of real or personal property . . . . the degree of specific interest in community activities may be roughly measured by the number and character of the institutions to which the individual belongs, as well as the voluntary community activities in which he participates. Communities in which there is a high percentage of individuals with a positive rating on the items listed above are logically those which are the most highly organized and efficient." (Note the character of the institutions, participation in which is defined as organized.)

[83] See above documentation; notice the Protestant ethical accent on *utility* and what it will do for one, apparently irrespective of social fact: Gillin, Dittmer, and Colbert, p. 106: "People who are useful, no matter what happens to be their race or color, come to be liked and respected. Consequently, the central aim of a sound educational program should be to teach people to be useful. (Hart, Hornell, *The Science of Social Relations*, 1927, pp. 521–524.)" In the following, note the norm of competitiveness: Elliott and Merrill, pp. 29–30: "Often, however, the individual cannot or will not compete. We then have the following pathological manifestations: '. . . . the *dependent* . . . . who is unable to compete; the *defective* . . . . who is, if not unable, at least handicapped in his efforts to compete. The *criminal*, on the other hand, ... who is perhaps unable, but at any rate refuses, to compete according to the rules which society lays down.' (Park and Burgess, *Introduction to the Science of Sociology*, p. 560)." Among the traits thought to characterize "the good life from the standpoint of the individual," Odum, pp. 50–51, cites: "patience," "specialized knowledge of some particular thing," "skill," "optimism," "love of work," "dynamic personality," "moderation," "trained will power," etc. Cf., in this connection, K. Davis, "Mental Hygiene and the Class Structure," *Psychiatry: Journal of the Biology and Pathology of Interpersonal Relations*, February, 1938, pp. 55–65.

is among the most frequently offered courses in the sociology curriculum.[1] One might guess that such a traditional and popular subject would be completely accepted within the field, and fairly well integrated with the theory it has produced. On the face of it, one might not except much controversy over such a "veteran crowd-pleaser"[2] as social problems. Yet controversy there is, for over the study of social problems, disorganization, pathology hover some of the persistent dilemmas of sociology. Published criticism of this area either explicitly or implicitly, but invariably, touches upon such basic issues as the boundaries and goals of sociology, the professional roles of sociologists, and public images of sociology. Behind every critique of the sociology of social problems reside questions in the sociology of knowledge. In some cases, these questions remain half-hidden; in others, they are prominently displayed. The latter is true of C. Wright Mills' widely quoted article, "The Professional Ideology of Social Pathologists."[3] Mills, whose paper is summarized below, wrote: "Because of its persistent importance in the development of American sociology, and its supposed proximity to the social scene, 'social pathology' seems an appropriate point of entry for the examination of the style of reflection and the social historical basis of American sociology."[4]

The criticism of social problems that has found its way into articles and book reviews in the professional journals falls into several classes. One contains the descriptions and/or denunciations of social problems as too distant from the mainstreams of contemporary sociology. One should examine the problems of society as one would any other sociologically relevant phenomena, as a means to the end of more and better facts and theories of social behavior. The foci of interest, modes of analysis, and underlying values in the field of social problems prevent its serving the above purpose. So runs this type of argument.

A second class of criticisms emphasizes the inability of the sociologists of social problems to solve, or perhaps even to perceive, the important problems of society. The field of social problems should apply the available resources of sociology toward the goal of understanding and ameliorating the conditions that trouble mankind. The foci of interest, and so on, of social problems prevent the achievement of that goal.

---

[1] The terminological smog is very heavy in this region. The field has been titled "social problems," "social disorganization," "social pathology," "social deviation," and still more. Although the different approaches vary in emphasis, they essentially cover the same ground, and fit into the same niches within sociology curricula. Since this paper is concerned with this whole sector of sociology, the terms shall be used interchangeably, except when otherwise noted.

[2] Podell, Vogelfanger, and Rogers, "Sociology in American Colleges: 15 Years Later," *American Sociological Review* (February, 1959). Of the 3763 undergraduate courses in the sample of 263 college catalogues, 13.9 per cent were categorized as "social problems" courses. It was noted that a number of courses dealing with social problems were placed in other categories for various reasons.

[3] *American Journal of Sociology*, 49 (September, 1943), pp. 165–80.

[4] *Ibid.*, p. 165.

The origins of such a classification can be traced to the very early days of American sociology, to Ward's distinction between "pure" and "applied" sociology, and to the many early references to societal or scientific problems versus social or ameliorative ones.

C. Wright Mills' critique, mentioned above, contains elements of both types of criticism. Mills examined a number of social problems books of the 1920's and 30's, and discovered great uniformities in the "typical perspectives and key concepts" of the field. He examined the life histories of the pathologists, and attributed the textbook uniformities to the overwhelming homogeniety in the social extraction, class, and career patterns of the authors. They were middle-class, rural-oriented individuals who interacted within academic and reform movement environments. The similarity in background, argued Mills, tended to lead to common unchallenged values which entered into the literature and were perpetuated.

The uniformities that Mills uncovered clustered about three points:

1. The nature of society, as seen by the pathologists.
2. The nature of social problems, as seen by the pathologists.
3. The criteria for the selection and organization of problems in textbooks utilized by the pathologists.

1. The model of social organization which the pathologists tended to adopt was that of the small town, blown up in scale. "The good society" was one where the intimacy and homogeniety of primary groups prevailed; where proper social change occurred in a slow and orderly fashion. The "good citizen" was one who joins and helps and is adjusted. Mills pointed to Cooley as one of the original architects of this model, through his emphasis on the "organic" (a harmonious balance of elements) and "processual" (continuous through time) nature of society.

2. Mills suggested that the concept of disorganization utilized by the pathologists quite often meant merely the absence of that type of organization described above. Social problems were often defined in terms of deviations by aggregates of individuals from the existing norms. They arise when numbers of individuals are unwilling or unable to conform to the status quo standards, as a result of encroaching urbanization, immigration, and soon. Norm violations were sometimes seen simply as biological impulses breaking through societal restrictions. This analysis was supported in Mills' remembered phrase, by "a paste-pot ecletic psychology."

In addition to the "deviation from norms" approach, another popular orientation to social problems centered about the concept of social change. The assumption in this type of analysis was that stability of any social pattern inevitably results in an adjustment to it, whereas change, except for the slow, orderly variety, invariably unlocks the Pandora's box of social problems. A frequent variant of the social change approach was that of culture lag, where social problems emerge out of the unequal rates of change of the different aspects of the culture.

The solutions to social problems served up by pathologists had as their major ingredient more and better socialization. In this way, individuals with problems could be adjusted or readjusted, and the repercussions of social change could be controlled more effectively.

3. The value uniformities which led to typical notions of social organization and disorganization also determined the principles for selecting and organizing problems in texts. For example, the method of presenting social problems was greatly influenced by the case-study approach of the social worker, in that problems selected leaned to the "practical problems of everyday life," problems of individuals in specific situations. The "situational approach" of W. I. Thomas contributed greatly to this mode of problems perception. The case-study approach plus the lack of any theory resulted in books that were "fragmentary collections of scattered problems and facts" selected in a non-random fashion, and characterized by an extremely low level of abstraction.

It has already been mentioned that Mills attributed the value patterns underlying pathology books primarily to the class origins and experiences of the authors. A second determining factor, present but less fully developed in Mills' analysis, is worth mentioning because of its revelance to our analysis of the contemporary social problems literature which comprises the major portion of this paper. This deals with the various academic pressures that have shaped the development of the social problems field. Almost everything written by sociologists about social problems has been in the form of textbooks, intended for student audiences. Mills commented on some results in the student-centered orientation: "[Textbook] systematization occurs in a context of presentation and justification rather than within a context of discovery."[5] And "Since one test of [textbook] success is wide adoption, the very spread of the public for which they are written tends to insure a textbook tolerance of the commonplace."[6]

What, according to Mills, have been the consequences of the middle-class, rural-oriented value uniformities shared by social pathologists?

First, they have been responsible for the lack of any sociological orientation in social problems writings. Mills' sample of pathologists exhibited an inability to focus upon the structural bases of society, to perceive the structural origins and interrelations of the individual conditions that have been described as social problems. This lack of theory has had the effect of supporting the acceptance of the existing norms as given and therefore good, and of portraying deviation as undesirable. Pathologists could not recognize that problems can emerge not only from deviation, but from conformity as well—conformity to conflicting or changing norms. Similarly, almost all stratificational aspects of social problems have been obscured by the lack of theory.

Second, the common values have prevented pathologists from attaining their avowed goal, the amelioration of problems, the reformation of the status quo. Mills insisted that the ways problems have been perceived and

---

[5] *Ibid.*, p. 167.
[6] *Ibid.*, p. 168.

analyzed, giving tacit and often open support to the status quo, made collective action oriented to their solution virtually impossible.

The above rough sketch does not do justice to the fullness and vigor of Mills' argument. With all its shortcomings, several of which Mills acknowledges in footnotes, we feel that it adequately describes a major portion of the output of American social pathologists of the post-World War I and pre-World War II period.

We would like to comment on a major problem inherent in the nonempirical type of analysis of which Mills' and the present paper are both examples. Mills does caution his readers that ". . . the aim is to grasp typical perspectives and key concepts. Hence no one of the texts . . . exemplifies *all* the concepts analyzed; certain elements are not so visible in given texts as in others, and some elements are not evidenced in certain texts at all."[7] After reading his article, one still imagines a fraternity of pathologists, befriending each other socially, and supporting each other ideologically. While it is beyond doubt that there existed a common core of values underlying the social problems literature, it must be noted that many pathologists were aware of the situation, and themselves critical of the consequences of such homogeneity. One can see this clearly in pathologists' book reviews of their "brethren's" works, or in the introductory remarks in a textbook, justifying the need for it to be published. Elliott and Merrill, whose very popular text is included in Mills' sample, wrote in 1933: "Courses in 'Social Problems' or 'Social Pathology' have been among the most popular offerings of academic sociology, yet there has seldom been any attempt to integrate the subject matter within a scheme of systematic sociology. For the most part, the approach to the conglomerate topics listed under these headings has been on a strictly common-sense level."[8]

It is interesting to see that Elliott and Merrill have, in turn, been found guilty of quite similar "textbook crimes."

The acceptance of Mills' description of the social problems literature does not commit us to accept his orientation to social pathology and pathologists. It is not difficult to see that the concepts and perspectives that Mills offers as replacements for the existing rural, middle-class oriented ones are themselves bound up in an ideology. Martindale, for example, in his excellent outline of past and present developments in the study of social problems in America, notes that "the one thing . . . all the critics—from Mills to Lemert, and many others in addition—are agreed upon is the presence of valuations in the theory of social disorganization. There is no question whatsoever about the fact that they are correct." Still, "the criticism is frequently marred . . . by the fact that the critic objects to *particular* evaluations rather than to the confusion of facts with values."[9]

The present paper focuses upon certain aspects of the modern body of

---

[7] *Ibid.*, p. 168.

[8] Mabel A. Elliot and Francis E. Merrill, *Social Disorganization* (New York: Harper, 1961), 4th ed., p. ix.

[9] Don Martindale, "Social Disorganization . . ." in Howard Becker and Alvin C. Boskoff, eds., *Modern Sociological Theory* (New York: Random House, 1961), p. 348.

writing of social pathologists. In common with Mills' article, it is not a systematic study. The content of the volumes in our sample has not been categorized or counted by formal techniques. The attempt has been to establish ideal types, which some existing works closely resemble, others, less so.

Let us stress that we are not interested in describing and evaluating the various approaches to social problems. This material can be found in the introductory chapters of a number of social problems textbooks. We are concerned with the present position and prospects of the field, much as Mills was 15 years ago. He asked the question, "What has the field of social problems to do with society?" The question underlying this paper is, "What has the field of social problems to do with sociology?" The values underlying that question are those of academic sociology.

We are interested in social pathology only because it has been generally recognized to be a subdivision of sociology,[10] because most such courses have been offered in sociology departments, and because much of the literature of the field has been produced by people with sociology degrees.

We make explicit the belief that the evaluation of any substantive segment or movement in sociology should be based on the answers to the following questions:

1. To what extent does segment or movement "X" utilize any of the theoretical schemes that are representative of modern sociological analysis?

2. To what extent does "X" contribute to the existing bodies of sociological facts and theories or point to possibly fruitful new directions in sociology?

About half a dozen different approaches to the study of the ills of society have been identified in the contemporary problems literature. As mentioned above, they are described in many pathology texts, as well as in the Martindale article.[11] We are interested in the ways the various approaches have been organized and presented to their readers. Three major organizational types can be distinguished. Beside differing in their structure, the types appear to differ in their authors' intentions, and in their attractiveness to various kinds of audiences. Although certain problems approaches have had an affinity for certain organizational types, the relationship is far from a consistent one.

The first type is the one most distant from the sociological center. As a matter of fact there is often not even the pretense of a sociological approach. This type has been called the "omnium gatherum," the collection of myriad, miscellaneous problems from Abortion to Zooerasty, with little or no attempt to relate them to a sociological framework, or, for that matter, to any frame-

---

[10] This, of course, refers to our "professional interest." In our other statuses, we can be interested or disinterested in the problems of society for a variety of different reasons.

[11] See, for example, Abbott P. Herman, *An Approach to Social Problems* (New York: Harper, 1949); Martin H. Neumeyer, *Social Problems and the Changing Society* (Princeton, N.J.: Van Nostrand, 1953); and Edwin H. Lemert, *Social Pathology* (New York: McGraw-Hill, 1951). Martindale noted the various approaches to social problems found in a number of the more important pathology textbooks.

work. The problems in this collection are held together by tradition and expectation alone. There is usually some minimal preliminary material, where mention may be made of several approaches to social problems. However, such material is decidedly prefatory to the major business at hand—the description of the many, many problems of society.

This type is often the third or fourth edition of a "best-seller," originally published in the 1920's or 1930's. There are a very few books that have changed little since then. Only the dates on charts and tables give them away as "modern" texts. It is common for this organizational type to have a "social problems" as opposed to a "disorganization" or "pathology" orientation. The various problems "readers," collections of articles and fragments of articles, fit neatly into this category.[12] Books of this type are produced simply to escort many college and junior college students along social problems paths well-travelled by "satisfied" student generations of the past.[13]

The second organizational type deserves more attention, because it attempts to do more, sociologically. In this volume one finds two sections: (1) a theoretical outline, which is intended to provide a basis for analyzing (2) the assortment of problems, comprising the major portion of the book. The theoretical material often bears resemblance to modern sociological theory; structural concepts are identified, the terminology is up to date, and so on. Invariably, however, the "analysis" of the problems in the second section turns out to be the standard descriptions of the standard problems. The theory rarely reaches the problems. Where it does reach, it appears to have been squeezed in, as a concession or an afterthought.

In this type of volume are reflected some of the "cross-pressures" experienced by present-day pathologists. Problems texts are no longer written by ex-social workers, ex-ministers located in sociology departments comprised of ex-ministers and ex-social workers. Contemporary pathologists have been trained as sociologists. One's professional self-image and relations within the academic department and within the profession are undoubtedly influences in determining what kind of book one should write. On the other horn of the dilemma are the other influences involved in the writing and selling of textbooks. It is known that in all but a few colleges and universities, presocial work, pre-education, pre-nursing and predomesticity students occupy most of the seats in sociology classes. It is also known that courses in social problems and in applied sociology have always been stellar attractions for these students. It is difficult for an author to remain unmoved by this information.

---

[12] Alfred McClung Lee and E. B. Lee, eds., *Social Problems in America*: A Source Book (New York: Holt, 1949). Lee and Lee, in their reader, combine excerpts from the works of famous sociological theorists, with those of journalists, clergymen, lawyers, government officials, and so on. The representatives of the other professions contribute little to the sociology of social problems.

[13] William W. Weaver, *Social Problems* (New York: Sloan Associates, 1951). As Weaver writes, "This book is submitted with few pretensions to erudition but with the earnest hope that it may be a useful guide for undergraduate students in their study of social problems."

If unimpressed he does remain, there is always his publisher to remind him. We know of no study of the influence of publishers on the ultimate content and form of texts. We feel that the odds in favor of rejection of the hypothesis of no association are great. The image of the "good book" held by those who purchase, print, design, and market manuscripts seems to be that of a text, similar to those that are known to have done well, with a new wrinkle or two to justify publication, and to provide copy for advertising.[14]

The type of book under discussion represents a way out of the pathologist's dilemma, containing as it does the little island of theory (the sociological imprimatur) separated from the vast archipelago of problems (for students and sales).

The last major organizational category contains the more serious efforts to present theories of disorganization, deviation, and others. In this type, the theoretical material is elaborately developed, sometimes taking up as much as half the volume. Problems are generally selected with a greater care for consistency than in the other types. This is achieved by narrowing the range of problems selected for analysis, because the specific theory can only handle certain kinds of problems.

Although attempts at theory-building are to be applauded and encouraged whenever they occur in the social problems area, we find that the actual theories leave much to be desired. They contain, at best, selected sociological elements. Some are theories of psychological more than sociological disorganization. Not one can be said to be a structural theory. One is disappointed by this lack more in this type of work than in the others. The others are completely devoid of *any* theory, but, when a sociologist works hard to present a theoretical system in a sociological work (thereby probably sacrificing junior college and schools of nursing adoptions), it is to be regretted that the result isn't sociology.

One did not have to read much between the lines of the above paragraphs to discover that, although writing of differences in the literature, we were implying that in a most important way the organizational types were more or less similar. The common feature of the sociology of social problems literature of today is its nonsociological, sometimes even antisociological, character.

This is not to suggest that the extreme simplifications, the unabashed moralizing, the exhortations to reform that characterized Mills' sample are to be found in the literature of today. A quarter of a century has elapsed since most of the volumes that Mills examined were published. Writings in pathology have not remained unaffected by the advances in sociology in those 25 years.

The important question is what lies behind the shiny, new exterior of up-to-date terminology, attempts at theories, and professed value neutrality that many modern works in social problems display. Have the old values been

---

[14] We do not wish to suggest that all publishers are anti-intellectual, or that all text-books contain only pap. We are dealing with types, rather than with individuals.

expunged, or do they still remain, in less extreme, less explicit form, but nonetheless present? The answer is "yes" and "no." Some of the standard concepts and usages of the 1920's and 1930's have gone completely out of sociological fashion and do not appear in modern problems literature. Other uniformities noted by Mills are still quite in evidence.

Two such examples are (1) the analysis of social problems as individual problems and (2) the nonrandom selection of social problems.

1. Many of the modern pathology primers contain a subdivision titled "personal or individual problems, crises, disorganizations." In this category fall the illnesses, addictions, vices, crimes, and the like.

The first critical question concerns the relevance of many of the individual problems to a sociological analysis. To be sure, such conditions as accidents, blindness, and mental deficiency affect many individuals in the population. But there are literally hundreds of potentially threatening conditions in man's environment, to which he attempts adjustment. The study of most of these conditions neither requires sociological theory nor contributes to it. Although members of the society may acknowledge the infirmities and handicaps and modify expectations in certain statuses; and deny participation in others. These are not sociological problems, for neither their causes, nor the reasons for their persistence, can be located within the structure of relationships that make up a human society.

Quite often the conditions singled out for consideration as social problems are simply those which affect the largest numbers of individuals. As one pathologist wrote: "One question often raised in the effort to locate and define problems, is, what is the number of people who are affected by them? . . . The assumption is that any problem is of major or minor significance in accordance with its incidence. Financial costs are used for the same purpose. The implication in the use of either implement is sound."[15]

A more serious deficiency in the literature revolves about those problems that could be structurally significant, and the ways in which they are treated. Variously labelled "group," "institutional," "family," "community," and so forth, they are with few exceptions analyzed as problems of individuals. One can illustrate this by considering the limited and unrewarding way "institution" might be used in the problems literature. An "institutional problem" is a condition that affects aggregates of individuals as they participate in an area of group life known to sociologists as an institution. The label serves only to indicate where in the society the problem is visible. Therefore divorce is a family problem, corruption and graft a political problem, unemployment an economic one. How is the "institutional problem" "analyzed" in the literature? Pathologists generally describe how many people are affected, how these rates have changed, and in what ways the problem is experienced by those affected and by others in the society. What brought the problem

---

[15] Harold A. Phelps and David Henderson, *Contemporary Social Problems*, 4th. ed. (Englewood Cliffs, N.J.: Prentice-Hall, 1952).

about (either "lags," "disorganizations," or "value conflicts," or any combination of the three), and perhaps, what can be done about it. In other words, the problems that are located in areas of the group life upon which modern sociological theory has been focused are "analyzed" in the same manner as the myriad ailments of mankind (physical, geographical, economic) with which the sociologist does not even pretend to be involved.

The simple message of this paper is that the fate of present-day sociological knowledge permits so much more than this to be done.

2. Almost every author will inform his readers that there are many social problems, both big and small. Of the large number of recognized problems, a handful can be thought of as the "G.O.P." (Grand Old Problems). Veritable universals are problems of physical and mental health, crime and delinquency, marriage and family problems, and problems of some kinds of minority groups. Also quite popular are some conditions that can be located in the economic institution—poverty, unemployment, and industrial relations, as well as population problems. Political and stratification problems (beside poverty) are two examples of those less frequently offered in the works of the pathologists.

There are several reasons why some problems are textbook universals, and others are rarely discussed. One is apparent from the following statement: ". . . Certain social problems have been central in the concept from the very beginning. A discussion of them is expected in books and courses on social problems, and this expectation has been respected."[16]

Another can be related to the criteria pathologists utilize in their definition of a social problem. We mentioned above that pathologists often define problems as conditions that affect aggregates of individuals. A very popular method of ascertaining which are the important problems of a society involves scrutinizing the population for the things that worry them, the conditions they would like to change. There are all sorts of evidence to support the position that Americans are generally not concerned with world or national issues. They worry about what is closest to them, what they experience most frequently—health, family, job. These, then, become the "universals," plus a few conditions which represent clear-cut and widely censured deviations from American norms and values.

Not only are certain problems rarely included in the literature, but one also finds that certain dimensions of the "acceptable" problems are ignored or barely noted. For example, the chapters on religion or religious minorities stress the discrimination against certain religions, the contributions of religious organizations towards amelioration of social problems, and so on. Rarely are the devisive consequences of religion in America discussed. The progress of the Negro is a popular theme in the chapters on minorities, but the consequences of progress, ranging up to mixed marriages, are hastily skipped over.

---

[16] Jessie Bernard, *Social Problems at Mid-Century* (New York: Holt, Rinehart, & Winston, 1957), p. 114.

In the ubiquitous chapter on health, syphillis, or whatever other interesting disease, is mentioned much more frequently than the A.M.A., although several recent texts have criticized developments in medical practice.

We have tried to point out, in the language of the pathologists, there exists a great "lag" between the developments in sociological theory and those in that branch of the field known as social problems, pathology, disorganization, deviation.

Let us review some of the factors that have contributed to this situation:

1. Most students who are enrolled in undergraduate courses in sociology are not especially interested in careers in sociology, nor in courses in sociological theory.

2. Since the size of the staff and the prestige of the department in many colleges are tied to the number of students enrolled, there are pressures to make available to students courses that will attract and satisfy. It is difficult to think of any other academic department that appears as concerned with what the student wants as is sociology. Perhaps the comparatively recent origins of sociology on the campus, and the widespread ignorance of it beyond the campus, help explain this.

3. Since it is not uncommon for authors to aspire to write books that sell, the literature geared to undergraduates tends to be lean on theory and rather overweight on the uncomplicated descriptive material that has been known to sell books.

4. The question of the role of the publisher in determining the content of the pathologists' literary output was raised in the body of the paper.

5. Since the study of social problems is so overwhelmingly an undergraduate proposition, the compulsion and the opportunity to do creative work, by either faculty or student body, are not very strong.

6. In many of the smaller colleges there are no conflicts between academic and applied sociology, as the former is barely to be seen. Social awareness and adjustment are the major educational aims of the social science program.

To criticize the field of social problems as we have done is neither novel nor difficult. What is harder to do, and therefore rarer, is to suggest how to infuse the problems field with significant theoretical content. Although the works of several important modern sociologists contain theories and theory fragments relating to disorganization and deviation, it remained for a recent article by A. K. Cohen[17] to provide a first step toward a rapprochement between sociological theory and social pathology. It is also to be noted as a hopeful sign that a recent issue of the *American Sociological Review* devoted most of its pages to theoretical papers in the sociology of deviation and of disorganization.

In spite of these first steps, it will be a long time before social problems offerings to undergraduates are reconstituted as truly sociological courses.

---

[17] Cohen, "The Study of Social Disorganization and Deviant Behavior," in Merton, Broom, and Cottrell, *Sociology Today*.

A less distant goal would be for some of the theoretical material to filter down into social pathology syllabi, and for some of the more blatantly non-sociological approaches to be transferred out of sociology departments and into some interdisciplinary artifact, such as "Problems of American Civilization" or "Problems of the Twentieth Century."

Ultimately, if we survive the "social problems" of the atomic era, we can look forward in this area to subdisciplines that are sociological, not through tradition and student expectations, but because of their ties to sociological theory and research. A sociology of deviation and one of disorganization would not only contribute to our scientific knowledge of the social behavior of man, but would also place powerful tools in the hands of those who by training and inclination are dedicated to the betterment of man's life.

Social Structure and Anomie

ROBERT K. MERTON

In competitive athletics, when the aim of victory is shorn of its institutional trappings and success in contests becomes construed as "winning the game" rather than "winning through circumscribed modes of activity," a premium is implicitly set upon the use of illegitimate but technically efficient means. The star of the opposing football team is surreptitiously slugged; the wrestler furtively incapacitates his opponent through ingenious but illicit techniques; university alumni covertly subsidize "students" whose talents are largely confined to the athletic field. The emphasis on the goal has so attenuated the satisfactions deriving from sheer participation in the competitive activity that these satisfactions are virtually confined to a successful outcome. Through the same process, tension generated by the desire to win in a poker game is relieved by successfully dealing oneself four aces, or, when the cult of success has become completely dominant, by sagaciously shuffling the cards in a game of solitaire. The faint twinge of uneasiness in the last instance and the surreptitious nature of public delicts indicate clearly that the institutional rules of the game *are known* to those who evade them, but that the emotional supports of these rules are largely vitiated by cultural exag-

SOURCE: Robert K. Merton, "Social Structure and Anomie," *American Sociological Review* (1938), pp. 672–82. Reprinted by permission.

EDITOR'S NOTE: This is an excerpt of the first published version of an article that has since become a classic of sociological literature. The interested reader should consult the revised and expanded version which appears in Robert K. Merton, *Social Theory and Social Structure* (Glencoe, Ill.: Free Press, 1959).

geration of the success-goal.[1] They are microcosmic images of the social macrocosm.

Of course, this process is not restricted to the realm of sport. The process whereby exaltation of the end generates a *literal demoralization,* i.e., a deinstitutionalization, of the means is one which characterizes many[2] groups in which the two phases of the social structure are not highly integrated. The extreme emphasis upon the accumulation of wealth as a symbol of success[3] in our own society militates against the completely effective control of institutionally regulated modes of acquiring a fortune.[4] Fraud, corruption, vice, crime, in short, the entire catalogue of proscribed behavior, becomes increasingly common when the emphasis on the *culturally induced* success-goal becomes divorced from a coordinated institutional emphasis. This observation is of crucial theoretical importance in examining the doctrine that antisocial behavior most frequently derives from biological drives breaking through the restraints imposed by society. The difference is one between a strictly utilitarian interpretation which conceives man's ends as random and an analysis which finds these ends deriving from the basic values of the culture.[5]

Our analysis can scarcely stop at this juncture. We must turn to other aspects of the social structure if we are to deal with the social genesis of the varying rates and types of deviate behavior characteristic of different societies. Thus far, we have sketched three ideal types of social orders constituted by distinctive patterns of relations between culture ends and means. Turning from these types of *culture patterning,* we find five logically possible, alternative modes of adjustment or adaptation *by individuals* within the

---

[1] It is unlikely that interiorized norms are completely eliminated. Whatever residuum persists will induce personality tensions and conflict. The process involves a certain degree of ambivalence. A manifest rejection of the institutional norms is coupled with some latent retention of their emotional correlates. "Guilt feelings," "sense of sin," "pangs of conscience" are obvious manifestations of this unrelieved tension; symbolic adherence to the nominally repudiated values of rationalizations constitute a more subtle variety of tensional release.

[2] "Many," and not all, unintegrated groups, for the reason already mentioned. In groups where the primary emphasis shifts to institutional means, i.e., when the range of alternatives is very limited, the outcome is a type of ritualism rather than anomie.

[3] Money has several peculiarities which render it particularly apt to become a symbol of prestige divorced from institutional controls. As Simmel emphasized, money is highly abstract and impersonal. However acquired, through fraud or institutionally, it can be used to purchase the same goods and services. The anonymity of metropolitan culture, in conjunction with this peculiarity of money, permits wealth, the sources of which may be unknown to the community in which the plutocrat lives, to serve as a symbol of status.

[4] The emphasis upon wealth as a success-symbol is possibly reflected in the use of the term "fortune" to refer to a stock of accumulated wealth. This meaning becomes common in the late sixteenth century (Spenser and Shakespeare). A similar usage of the the Latin *fortuna* comes into prominence during the first century B.C. Both these periods were marked by the rise to prestige and power of the "bourgeoisie."

[5] See Kingsley Davis, "Mental Hygiene and the Class Structure," *Psychiatry,* 1928, I, esp. 62–63; Talcott Parsons, *The Structure of Social Action,* 59–60, New York, 1937.

culture-bearing society or group.[6] These are schematically presented in the following table, where $(+)$ signifies "acceptance," $(-)$ signifies "elimination" and $(\pm)$ signifies "rejection and substitution of new goals and standards."

		CULTURE GOALS	INSTITUTIONALIZED MEANS
I.	Conformity	+	+
II.	Innovation	+	−
III.	Ritualism	−	+
IV.	Retreatism	−	−
V.	Rebellion*	±	±

* This fifth alternative is on a plane clearly different from that of the others. It represents a *transitional* response which seeks to *institutionalize* new procedures oriented toward revamped cultural goals shared by the members of the society. It thus involves efforts to *change* the existing structure rather than to perform accommodative actions *within* this structure, and introduces additional problems with which we are not at the moment concerned.

Our discussion of the relation between these alternative responses and other phases of the social structure must be prefaced by the observation that persons may shift from one alternative to another as they engage in different social activities. These categories refer to role adjustments in specific situations, not to personality *in toto*. To treat the development of this process in various spheres of conduct would introduce a complexity unmanageable within the confines of this paper. For this reason, we shall be concerned primarily with economic activity in the broad sense, "the production, exchange, distribution and consumption of goods and services" in our competitive society, wherein wealth has taken on a highly symbolic cast. Our task is to search out some of the factors which exert pressure upon individuals to engage in certain of these logically possible alternative responses. This choice, as we shall see, is far from random.

In every society, Adaptation I (conformity to both culture goals and means) is the most common and widely diffused. Were this not so, the stability and continuity of the society could not be maintained. The mesh of expectancies which constitutes every social order is sustained by the modal behavior of its members falling within the first category. Conventional role behavior oriented toward the basic values of the group is the rule rather than the exception. It is this fact alone which permits us to speak of a human aggregate as comprising a group or society.

Conversely, Adaptation IV (rejection of goals and means) is the least common. Persons who "adjust" (or maladjust) in this fashion are, strictly speaking, *in* the society but not *of* it. Sociologically, these constitute the true "aliens." Not sharing the common frame of orientation, they can be included within the societal population merely in a fictional sense. In this category

[6] This is a level intermediate between the two planes distinguished by Edward Sapir; namely, culture patterns and personal habit systems. See his "Contribution of Psychiatry to an Understanding of Behavior in Society," *Amer. J. Sociol.*, 1937, 42:862–70.

are *some* of the activities of psychotics, psychoneurotics, chronic autists, pariahs, outcasts, vagrants, vagabonds, tramps, chronic drunkards and drug addicts.[7] These have relinquished, in certain spheres of activity, the culturally defined goals, involving complete aim-inhibition in the polar case, and their adjustments are not in accord with institutional norms. This is not to say that in some cases the source of their behavioral adjustments is not in part the very social structure which they have in effect repudiated nor that their very existence within a social area does not constitute a problem for the socialized population.

This mode of "adjustment" occurs, as far as structural sources are concerned, when both the culture goals and institutionalized procedures have been assimilated thoroughly by the individual and imbued with affect and high positive value, but where those institutionalized procedures which promise a measure of successful attainment of the goals are not available to the individual. In such instances, there results a twofold mental conflict insofar as the moral obligation for adopting institutional means conflicts with the pressure to resort to illegitimate means (which may attain the goal) and inasmuch as the individual is shut off from means which are both legitimate *and* effective. The competitive order is maintained, but the frustrated and handicapped individual who cannot cope with this order drops out. Defeatism, quietism and resignation are manifested in escape mechanisms which ultimately lead the individual to "escape" from the requirements of the society. It is an expedient which arises from continued failure to attain the goal by legimate measures and from an inability to adopt the illegitimate route because of internalized prohibitions and institutionalized compulsives, *during which process the supreme value of the success-goal has as yet not been renounced.* The conflict is resolved by eliminating *both* precipitating elements, the goals and means. The escape is complete, the conflict is eliminated and the individual is asocialized.

Be it noted that where frustration derives from the inaccessibility of effec·tive institutional means for attaining economic or any other type of highly valued "success," that Adaptations II, III and V (innovation, ritualism and rebellion) are also possible. The result will be determined by the particular personality, and thus, the *particular* cultural background, involved. Inadequate socialization will result in the innovation response whereby the conflict and frustration are eliminated by reliquishing the institutional means and retaining the success-aspiration; an extreme assimilation of institutional demands will lead to ritualism wherein the goal is dropped as beyond one's reach but conformity to the mores persists; and rebellion occurs when emancipation

---

[7] Obviously, this is an elliptical statement. These individuals may maintain some orientation to the values of their particular differentiated groupings within the larger society or, in part, of the conventional society itself. Insofar as they do so, their conduct cannot be classified in the "passive rejection" category (IV). Nels Anderson's description of the behavior and attitudes of the bum, for example, can readily be recast in terms of our analytical scheme. See *The Hobo*, 93–98, *et passim*, Chicago, 1923.

from the reigning standards, due to frustration or to marginalist perspectives, leads to the attempt to introduce a "new social order."

Our major concern is with the illegitimacy adjustment. This involves the use of conventionally proscribed but frequently effective means of attaining at least the simulacrum of culturally defined success,—wealth, power, and the like. As we have seen, this adjustment occurs when the individual has assimilated the cultural emphasis on success without equally internalizing the morally prescribed norms governing means for its attainment. The question arises, Which phases of our social structure predispose toward this mode of adjustment? We may examine a concrete instance, effectively analyzed by Lohman,[8] which provides a clue to the answer. Lohman has shown that specialized areas of vice in the near north side of Chicago constitute a "normal" response to a situation where the cultural emphasis upon pecuniary success has been absorbed, but where there is little access to conventional and legitimate means for attaining such success. The conventional occupational opportunities of persons in this area are almost completely limited to manual labor. Given our cultural stigmatization of manual labor, and its correlate, the prestige of white collar work, it is clear that the result is a strain toward innovational practices. The limitation of opportunity to unskilled labor and the resultant low income can not compete *in terms of conventional standards of achievement* with the high income from organized vice.

For our purposes, this situation involves two important features. First, such antisocial behavior is in a sense "called forth" by certain conventional values of the culture *and* by the class structure involving differential access to the approved opportunities for legitimate, prestige-bearing pursuit of the culture goals. The lack of high integration between the means-and-end elements of the cultural pattern and the particular class structure combine to favor a heightened frequency of antisocial conduct in such groups. The second consideration is of equal significance. Recourse to the first of the alternative responses, legitimate effort, is limited by the fact that actual advance toward desired success-symbols through conventional channels is, despite our persisting open-class ideology,[9] relatively rare and difficult for those handicapped by little formal education and few economic resources. The dominant pressure of group standards of success is, therefore, on the gradual attenuation

---

[8] Joseph D. Lohman, "The Participant Observer in Community Studies," *Amer. Sociol. Rev.*, 1937, 2:890-98.

[9] The shifting historical role of this ideology is a profitable subject for exploration. The "office-boy-to-president" stereotype was once in approximate accord with the facts. Such vertical mobility was probably more common then than now, when the class structure is more rigid. (See the following note.) The ideology largely persists, however, possibly because it still performs a useful function for maintaining the *status quo*. For insofar as it is accepted by the "masses," it constitutes a useful sop for those who might rebel against the entire structure, were this consoling hope removed. This ideology now serves to lessen the probability of Adaptation V. In short, the role of this notion has changed from that of an approximately valid empirical theorem to that of an ideology, in Mannheim's sense.

of legitimate, but by and large ineffective, strivings and the increasing use of illegitimate, but more or less effective, expedients of vice and crime. The cultural demands made on persons in this situation are incompatible. On the one hand, they are asked to orient their conduct toward the prospect of accumulating wealth and on the other, they are largely denied effective opportunities to do so institutionally. The consequences of such structural inconsistency are psychopathological personality, and/or antisocial conduct, and/or revolutionary activities. The equilibrium between culturally designated means and ends becomes highly unstable with the progressive emphasis on attaining the prestige-laden ends by any means whatsoever. Within this context, Capone represents the triumph of amoral intelligence over morally prescribed "failure," when the channels of vertical mobility are closed or narrowed[10] *in a society which places a high premium on economic affluence and social ascent for all its members.*[11]

This last qualification is of primary importance. It suggests that other phases of the social structure besides the extreme emphasis on pecuniary success, must be considered if we are to understand the social sources of antisocial behavior. A high frequency of deviate behavior is not generated simply by "lack of opportunity" or by this exaggerated pecuniary emphasis. A comparatively rigidified class structure, a feudalistic or caste order, may limit such opportunities far beyond the point which obtains in our society today. It is only when a system of cultural values extols, virtually above all else, certain *common* symbols of success *for the population at large* while its social structure rigorously restricts or completely eliminates access to approved modes of acquiring these symbols *for a considerable part of the same population,* that antisocial behavior ensues on a considerable scale. In other words, our

---

[10] There is a growing body of evidence, though none of it is clearly conclusive, to the effect that our class structure is becoming rigidified and that vertical mobility is declining. Taussig and Joslyn found that American business leaders are being *increasingly* recruited from the upper ranks of our society. The Lynds have also found a "diminished chance to get ahead" for the working classes in Middletown. Manifestly, these objective changes are not alone significant; the individual's subjective evaluation of the situation is a major determinant of the response. The extent to which this change in opportunity for social mobility has been recognized by the least advantaged classes is still conjectural, although the Lynds present some suggestive materials. The writer suggests that a case in point is the increasing frequency of cartoons which observe in a tragi-comic vein that "my old man says everybody can't be President. He says if ya can get three days a week steady on W.P.A. work ya ain't doin' so bad either." See F. W. Taussig and C. S. Joslyn, *American Business Leaders,* New York, 1932; R. S. and H. M. Lynd, *Middletown in Transition,* 67 ff., chap. 12, New York, 1937.

[11] The role of the Negro in this respect is of considerable theoretical interest. Certain elements of the Negro population have assimilated the dominant caste's values of pecuniary success and social advancement, but they also recognize that social ascent is at present restricted to their own caste almost exclusively. The pressures upon the Negro which would otherwise derive from the structural inconsistencies we have noticed are hence not identical with those upon lower class whites. See Kingsley Davis, *op. cit.,* 63; John Dollard, *Caste and Class in a Southern Town,* 66 ff., New Haven, 1936; Donald Young, *American Minority Peoples,* 581, New York, 1932.

egalitarian ideology denies by implication the existence of noncompeting groups and individuals in the pursuit of pecuniary success. The same body of success-symbols is held to be desirable for all. These goals are held to *transcend class lines,* not to be bounded by them, yet the actual social organization is such that there exist class differentials in the accessibility of these *common* success-symbols. Frustration and thwarted aspiration lead to the search for avenues of escape from a culturally induced intolerable situation; or unrelieved ambition may eventuate in illicit attempts to acquire the dominant values.[12] The American stress on pecuniary success and ambitiousness for all thus invites exaggerated anxieties, hostilities, neuroses and antisocial behavior.

This theoretical analysis may go far toward explaining the varying correlations between crime and poverty.[13] Poverty is not an isolated variable. It is one in a complex of interdependent social and cultural variables. When viewed in such a context, it represents quite different states of affairs. Poverty as such, and consequent limitation of opportunity, are not sufficient to induce a conspicuously high rate of criminal behavior. Even the often mentioned "poverty in the midst of plenty" will not necessarily lead to this result. Only insofar as poverty and associated disadvantages in competition for the culture values approved for *all* members of the society is linked with the assimilation of a cultural emphasis on monetary accumulation as a symbol of success is antisocial conduct a "normal" outcome. Thus, poverty is less highly correlated with crime in southeastern Europe than in the United States. The possibilities of vertical mobility in these European areas would seem to be fewer than in this country, so that neither poverty *per se* nor its association with limited opportunity is sufficient to account for the varying correlations. It is only when the full configuration is considered, poverty, limited opportunity and a commonly shared system of success symbols, that we can explain the higher association between poverty and crime in our society than in others where rigidified class structure is coupled with *differential class symbols of achievement.*

In societies such as our own, then, the pressure of prestige-bearing success tends to eliminate the effective social constraint over means employed to this

---

[12] The psychical coordinates of these processes have been partly established by the experimental evidence concerning *Anspruchsniveaus* and levels of performance. See Kurt Lewin, *Vorsatz, Willie und Bedurfnis,* Berlin, 1926; N. F. Hoppe, "Erfolg und Misserfolg," *Psychol. Forschung,* 1930, 14:1–63; Jerome D. Frank, "Individual Differences in Certain Aspects of the Level of Aspiration," *Amer. J. Psychol.,* 1935, 47: 119–28.

[13] Standard criminology texts summarize the data in this field. Our scheme of analysis may serve to resolve some of the theoretical contradictions which P. A. Sorokin indicates. For example, "not everywhere nor always do the poor show a greater proportion of crime . . . many poor countries have had less crime than the richer countries . . . The [economic] improvement in the second half of the nineteenth century, and the beginning of the twentieth, has not been followed by a decrease of crime." See his *Contemporary Sociological Theories,* 560–61, New York, 1928. The crucial point is, however, that poverty has varying social significance in different social structures, as we shall see. Hence, one would not expect a linear correlation between crime and poverty.

end. "The-end-justifies-the-means" doctrine becomes a guiding tenet for action when the cultural structure unduly exalts the end and the social organization unduly limits possible recourse to approved means. Otherwise put, this notion and associated behavior reflect a lack of cultural coordination. In international relations, the effects of this lack of integration are notoriously apparent. An emphasis upon national power is not readily coordinated with an inept organization of legitimate, i.e., internationally defined and accepted, means for attaining this goal. The result is a tendency toward the abrogation of international law, treaties become scraps of paper, "undeclared warfare" serves as a technical evasion, the bombing of civilian populations is rationalized,[14] just as the same societal situation induces the same sway of illegitimacy among individuals.

The social order we have described necessarily produces this "strain toward dissolution." The pressure of such an order is upon outdoing one's competitors. The choice of means within the ambit of institutional control will persist as long as the sentiments supporting a competitive system, i.e., deriving from the possibility of outranking competitors and hence enjoying the favorable response of others, are distributed throughout the entire system of activities and are not confined merely to the final result. A stable social structure demands a balanced distribution of affect among its various segments. When there occurs a shift of emphasis from the satisfactions deriving from competition itself to almost exclusive concern with successful competition, the resultant stress leads to the breakdown of the regulatory structure.[15] With the resulting attenuation of the institutional imperatives, there occurs an approximation of the situation erroneously held by utilitarians to be typical of society generally wherein calculations of advantage and fear of punishment are the sole regulating agencies. In such situations, as Hobbes observed, force and fraud come to constitute the sole virtues in view of their relative efficiency in attaining goals,—which were for him, of course, not culturally derived.

It should be apparent that the foregoing discussion is not pitched on a moralistic plane. Whatever the sentiments of the writer or reader concerning the ethical desirability of coordinating the means-and-goals phases of the social structure, one must agree that lack of such coordination leads to anomie. Insofar as one of the most general functions of social organization is to provide a basis for calculability and regularity of behavior, it is increasingly limited in effectiveness as these elements of the structure become dissociated. At the extreme, predictability virtually disappears and what may be properly termed cultural chaos or anomie intervenes.

This statement, being brief, is also incomplete. It has not included an

---

[14] See M. W. Royse, *Aerial Bombardment and the International Regulation of War*, New York, 1928.

[15] Since our primary concern is with the socio-cultural aspects of this problem, the psychological correlates have been only implicitly considered. See Karen Horney, *The Neurotic Personality of Our Time*, New York, 1937, for a psychological discussion of this process.

exhaustive treatment of the various structural elements which predispose toward one rather than another of the alternative responses open to individuals; it has neglected, but not denied the relevance of, the factors determining the specific incidence of these responses; it has not enumerated the various concrete responses which are constituted by combinations of specific values of the analytical variables; it has omitted, or included only by implication, any consideration of the social functions performed by illicit responses; it has not tested the full explanatory power of the analytical scheme by examining a large number of group variations in the frequency of deviate and conformist behavior; it has not adequately dealt with rebellious conduct which seeks to refashion the social framework radically; it has not examined the relevance of cultural conflict for an analysis of culture-goal and institutional-means malintegration. It is suggested that these and related problems may be profitably analyzed by this scheme.

Deprivation as a Cause of Delinquency:
Economic or Moral?

BERNARD LANDER AND NATHAN LANDER

Robert K. Merton's essay on "Social Structure and Anomie" is undoubtedly one of the most significant and influential presentations of a theoretical formulation of the social sources of delinquency. Furthermore, his theories have served as bases for the development of important demonstration programs to combat delinquency. To Merton, "deviant behavior does not represent impulses of individuals breaking through social controls but, on the contrary, represents socially induced deviations—deviations which the culture and social organization conjoin to produce. In other words, social and cultural structures exert a definite pressure upon certain persons to engage in nonconforming rather than conforming conduct."[1]

The following hypotheses comprise major components of Merton's formulation:

1. A major aspect of the American culture is the high premium it places on economic affluence and success for *all*. "The road to fortune, like the public turnpike, is open to the children of the beggar and the de-

SOURCE: Excerpted by the authors from an unpublished manuscript entitled, "A Comparative and Cross-Cultural Study of Urban Delinquency in the United States," New York, National Council on Crime and Delinquency, 1962, pp. 39–53.

[1] In "New Perspectives for Research on Juvenile Delinquency," Children's Bureau Publication No. 356–1956.

scendents of kings." Americans are admonished to succeed. "The cultural manifest is clear: one must not quit, must not cease striving, must not lessen his goals." Merton maintains that this democratic ideology is equally pervasive in *all* strata of American society regardless of race or socioeconomic position. All Americans have a *moral mandate and right* to achieve an Horatio Alger dream.

2. The greatest pressure toward deviant behavior is exerted upon the lower strata including people holding manual labor and lesser white-collar jobs. Crime and delinquency constitute "normal responses to a situation where the cultural emphasis upon pecuniary success has been absorbed, but where there is little access to conventional and legitimate means for becoming successful."

3. Merton deals directly with the conflicting correlations between crime and poverty. A high frequency of crime and delinquency is not generated simply by lack of opportunity or exaggerated pecuniary emphasis. "Poverty as such, and consequent limitation of opportunity, are not sufficient to induce a high rate of criminal behavior. Even the often mentioned poverty in the midst of plenty will not necessarily lead to this result. . . . Thus poverty is less highly correlated with crime in Southeastern Europe than in the United States. The possibilities of vertical mobility in these European areas would seem to be fewer than in this country, so that neither poverty *per se* nor its association with limited opportunity is sufficient to account for the varying correlations. . . . It is only when a system of cultural values extols critically above all else, certain *common* success-goals *for the population at large* while the social structure rigorously restricts or completely closes access to approved modes of reaching these goals for a considerable part of the same population, that deviant behavior ensues on a large scale."

Thus, in Southeastern Europe the culture does not emphasize success-goals based upon pecuniary affluence as desirable and achievable by all strata of the population. Consequently, there is little delinquency even in the midst of abject poverty. In contrast, in the United States the ideology of individual success, the American dream, is so pervasive in and so much emphasized for *all* strata of society that it poses a problem of self-esteem for virtually *every* man. But in fact, the legitimate opportunities are unavailable or rigorously limited to many people, especially to those belonging to the working class. Consequently, the high frequency of crime and delinquency in these economically deprived social classes.

4. Merton implies that the rising trend of deviant behavior is understandable in view of "the growing evidence to the effect that our class structure is becoming rigidified and that vertical mobility is declining."

In this paper, we shall concentrate primarily on a critical review of Merton's theories because of their widespread acceptance as explanations for delinquency behavior and their importance as bases for the development of demonstration programs to combat delinquency.

We are concerned with the following questions:

1. Does the available data support Merton's major hypotheses?
2. Does Merton's theory of economic deprivation adequately account for the wide and significant variations in the delinquency rate among working class neighborhoods?
3. Does Merton's approach explain the large increases in juvenile crime in the United States and some European nations during the last decade?
4. Does Merton's paradigm adequately provide for the role of the family and child socialization practices in the etiology of delinquency?
5. Does Merton's use of the concept of social class require further analytic refinement?

THE LACK OF EMPIRICAL VERIFICATION

A review of the field reveals the paucity of the empirical data from which the theoretical formulations have been derived. In a large measure, they are based on a limited number of empirical studies—several of which are more than thirty years old—utilizing questionable research procedures. To our knowledge, we have no evidence that systematically relates the differential area delinquency rates to the differential feelings of economic or status deprivations.

THE PERVASIVENESS OF THE HORATIO ALGER MYTH

Ely Chinoy's study of *Automobile Workers and the American Dream* casts doubt upon the assumption that Americans of all strata have in fact internalized or seriously accepted the Horatio Alger myth. He questions whether the American dream of success has actually had much import upon the auto workers. "They do not aspire to the top level of business and industry; they want to become skilled workers, to gain promotion to supervision, to engage in small-scale farming, to open a retail store or a small service establishment of some kind.

"As soon as he leaves school, or even before, the working-class youth must come to terms with a world of limited opportunity where there are few chances. Lacking financial resources, he cannot look forward to the possibility of professional training, or even to four years of college which would widen his perspectives and increase his skills. He cannot step into a family business or acquire easily the funds with which to launch one of his own. As soon as his education ends, he must find some kind of job.

"The quick surrender by working-class youth to the difficulties they face is not necessarily forced or unwilling. Although they are encouraged to focus their aspirations into a long future and to make present sacrifices for the sake of eventual rewards, they are chiefly concerned with immediate gratifications. They may verbally profess to be concerned with occupational success and advancement (as did fourteen working-class boys who were interviewed), but they are likely to be more interested in 'having a good time' or 'having fun.' They want to 'go out' to have girl friends, to travel, to own a car or a motorcycle. When asked if 'fun' would be given up in order to take a job which might lead to advancement in the future, an eighteen-year-old boy about to graduate from high school answered: 'Do you want me to tell you the truth? I'd rather have fun.'

"Despite the fact that their aspirations are controlled by a relatively objective appraisal of what is possible rather than by the unreliable image of America projected by the tradition of opportunity, most workers do not explain their failure to rise in terms of forces beyond their control. . . . Instead they try to maintain their self-regard by redefining advancement to include the goals and interests with which they are actively concerned, by projecting their hopes and aspirations upon their children, and, to a lesser extent, by minimizing success and emphasizing alternative values."[2]

A recent unpublished doctoral dissertation by Martin G. Gold further tested the hypothesis that the discrepancy between occupational aspirations and expectations will provoke boys to delinquency. Gold reported that this hypothesis is not confirmed by evidence of greater discrepancies between occupational aspirations and expectations among delinquents; rather, these delinquents tend to have lower aspirations than nondelinquents and tend to be more confident of achieving their lower aspirations. His data also suggested that *anticipated failure to achieve prestigeful occupations is perceived by the boys as "personal failure and not the fault of the social system."*

THE NEGRO DELINQUENCY RATE

Many studies indicate that Negroes, especially in the South, are characterized by excessively high rates of delinquency and crime. We believe that it is a gross oversimplification of the problem to explain these high rates as a consequence of a disjunction between their acceptance of the American dream with the emphasis on egalitarian opportunities and pressure to succeed and the unavailability of adequate institutional means to achieve these success goals.

The Southern Negro lives in a social structure that is far more rigid than that of Southeastern Europe. It is also highly unlikely that Southern white culture fosters or supports these success-goals as available to or achievable by the Negro population.

---

[2] Ely Chinoy, *Automobile Workers and the American Dream* (Garden City, N.Y.: Doubleday, 1955).

John Dollard,[3] on the basis of his studies of the Southern Negro, reported that the lower-class Negro has surrendered the struggle to achieve higher social status. They do not care much whether they make money or not, and they do not experience any of the institutional pressures which produce an ambitious and aggressive attitude toward economic life.

SOCIAL CLASS MOBILITY

There is no evidence to support Merton's contention of a growing rigidity in the American class structure. Natalie Rogoff, on the basis of the Indianapolis mobility study, concluded that the total amount of vertical mobility had increased from 1910 to 1940. W. Lloyd Warner in 1947 supported the point of view that mobility in the United States is decreasing; in 1955, Warner changed his view and presented evidence to the effect that mobility has not decreased.

Bernard Barber, on the basis of his review of the literature in the field, found that "there has not been a trend toward less mobility, as has frequently been asserted recently. There may even have been slightly more mobility in the present than in the past. So far as rough measuring instruments permit a general statement, however, the safest tentative conclusion is that the amount of mobility has remained approximately the same over the last century. In any case, both now and in the past, the amount of mobility as a whole and mobility of the extreme kind have been enough to justify for Americans their institutionalized approval of an 'open-class' society."[4]

Furthermore, the researchers of the class distributions of income and wealth also suggest that "over the past quarter-century there has been a noticeable trend toward equalizing the distribution of personal income. The share accounted for by those at the top of the income hierarchy has been declining at the same time that the share taken by those at the bottom has been growing. The old maxim that the rich get richer as the poor get poorer, should be revised: the rich are getting rich less rapidly than the poor are getting less poor. This latter version is more cumbersome, but is also somewhat more accurate."[5]

Joseph A. Kahl,[6] summarizing the finding of Simon Kuznets and Herman P. Miller of the National Bureau of Economic Research, reported that:

The average real income (after adjustments for inflation) of the American people has been going up a great deal, approximately doubling in the first half of the century. The rise was not steady, however, for the rate of increase was fastest in the boom periods of the 1920's and the years since the end of the Second World War.

---

[3] John Dollard, *Class and Caste in a Southern Town* (New Haven, Conn.: Yale, 1947).

[4] Bernard Barber, *Social Stratification* (New York: Harcourt, 1957).

[5] Barber, *ibid.*

[6] Joseph A. Kahl, *The American Class Structure* (New York: Rinehart, 1957).

At the same time that per capita income increased on the average, income was being redistributed. The very rich actually lost ground during this period; the middle-income people gained, but the major gains were scored by the people at the bottom. In short, real income was going up for almost everybody, and inequalities in income among different groups were being markedly reduced, for the least affluent people were gaining ground much faster than the more affluent ones.

ECONOMIC DEPRIVATION AND VARIATIONS IN DELINQUENCY RATES

The second question we asked was, Does Merton's theory of economic deprivation adequately account for the wide and significant variations in the delinquency rate among working-class neighborhoods? A recent study of Norfolk, Virginia,[7] indicated that of the four census tracts characterized by the lowest median income and the greatest housing congestion only one ranked high in its ratio of juvenile delinquency. Census tract 48 ranked 17 in its juvenile delinquency rate; the other three census tracts—numbers 41, 42, and 53—ranked respectively 52, 49, and 45, in a total of 62 census tracts, which is far below the average juvenile delinquency rate and among the lowest delinquency rate areas of the entire city.

We also found wide variation in the prevalence of delinquency among working-class areas in Baltimore.[8] In many such neighborhoods we found disproportionately high delinquency rates. On the other hand in several poor neighborhoods we found a disproportionately low incidence of juvenile delinquency. For example, we noted several tracts characteriezd by striking economic deprivation—84 per cent or more of the homes were substandard, rentals of lower than $12.00 a month—with comparatively low delinquency rates. We found that a variety of statistical procedures indicated that delinquency is *fundamentally* related only to the *anomie* and not to the poor economic conditions of the tract.

The seeming association between delinquency and economic deprivation was a consequence of the fact that the areas of social instability were frequently the same as those that were economically depressed. But it is the anomie of an area rather than its economic characteristics that was fundamentally associated with the delinquency rate.

In an area characterized by normlessness or social instability, despite its high economic level, one would thus expect a high delinquency rate. On the other hand, one would predict a low delinquency rate for a stable community even though it were characterized by poverty, bad housing and over-crowding.

---

[7] "Juvenile Delinquency in Norfolk, Virginia," prepared for the Norfolk City Council by the United Communities Council of Social Agencies, 1959.

[8] Lander, *op. cit.*

THE DELINQUENCY RATE TREND

Cloward and Ohlin question the thesis advanced by Bloch and Neiderhoffer in *The Gang*[9] on the ground that "if delinquency rates are increasing, has there been a corresponding increase in the difficulties associated with the transition from adolescence to adulthood?"[10] We raise the same question of Merton.

The F.B.I. reported, in 1959, that juvenile crime has more than doubled since 1948 while the population of our young people has increased by approximately 30 per cent. On March 2, 1961, the Director of the F.B.I. reported "an alarming 12 per cent increase in serious crime in the United States over 1959. . . . Arrests of persons under 18 years of age continued their upward climb, rising 6 per cent in 1960 while adult arrests were only 2 per cent." Likewise, Robert M. MacIver found that, in New York City, both juvenile and adolescent crime has increased substantially during the past decade, increasing far out of proportion to the rise in youth population during the same period. During the past ten years there has been a striking rise in juvenile delinquency in the age group seven through fifteen years.

We do not know how *real* these increases are. A certain portion of the increases may reflect new administrative and reporting procedures, a growing public concern with the problem, and more frequent police use of court facilities. However, we believe that the evidence of dramatic increases in all regions of the United States and among all strata of the population and the increasing proportion of serious crime being committed by youths do suggest a rising trend in juvenile crime, even though we cannot be certain about its precise measure. Recent studies also suggest that these marked increases in delinquency rates affect all regions in the United States—rural and urban and all class strata.

What is the explanation for the dramatic rising trends in juvenile delinquency in cities of varying types, in rural areas, and among all strata of the American society? Is there any evidence of increases in feelings of deprivation? Have the available opportunities for employment or mobility been sharply reduced or limited in the recent decade or decades?

The United Nations reports that Sweden, the United States, and England have also experienced marked rises in delinquency since World War II. There have been no known changes in court or police procedures. Do the current theories provide an adequate explanation for this trend? Do we have any valid grounds for hypothesizing, for example, a rise in feelings of relative deprivation in Sweden since World War II? Why should Sweden, which has been a model welfare state, suffer from so marked a delinquency problem?

---

[9] Herbert Bloch, and Arthur Neiderhoffer, *The Gang* (New York: Philosophical Library, 1958).

[10] Richard A. Cloward, and Lloyd E. Ohlin, *Delinquency and Opportunity* (Glencoe, Ill.: Free Press, 1960).

THE ROLE OF THE FAMILY IN DELINQUENCY

Raymond F. Gould recently raised to Merton the question as to the relevance of research that emphasized the family as a unit of study. "As far as the literature I am familiar with goes, no use has been made of the family as a unit of research in this particular area—research which takes account of both psychological factors in the family and cultural relationships."[11] Merton responded, "I am unable to respond to your comment on the family as a particularly strategic social unit for dealing simultaneously with the social and cultural phases. For what the family is (what its cultural values are, what its social organization) is a reflection of changes in larger social structure, and not only of the family structure.[12]

We do not deny the impact of class position on the differential values, life styles, behavior, and family patterns of lower- and middle-class members. But we are not convinced that the life styles and family patterns are merely epiphenomenal consequences of one's class position. Is class position the only or primary determinant? How does class position relate to or compare in relative impact with other factors, such as ethnic background, religion, community stability, potential personalities, and aspirations? Are these factors to be considered only as epiphenomenal functions of class position; as intervening variables; or do they have independent validity in the understanding of the life styles and behavior of youths and adults?

Numerous studies suggest the independent significance of family patterns in the determination of the vulnerability of children to delinquency behavior. Merton oversimplifies the relationship of social class to the quality and nature of family relations.

A. P. Jephcott and M. P. Carter studied the 325 families residing in a high delinquency area. They allocated these families into three major types: (1) rough—72 families; (2) respectable—59 families; (3) medium—94 families. They differentiated these families in terms of their ability to plan for the future, participation in community organizations, and the nature of the parental ties with their children. The rough families contribute a disproportionate share of delinquency; children of medium families also sometimes adopt delinquency patterns but this is usually a *temporary phase* in their development; respectable families are characterized by little delinquency.

Sophia Robison summarizing these findings observed: "Jephcott, Carter, Mack, and Mays in England have challenged the accepted stereotype of family structure. They suggest that the presumed disorganization of family life in slum areas may be a middle-class fiction . . . what appears as a delinquent way of life to middle-class society is they suggest "normal" for the

---

[11] In *New Perspectives for Research on Juvenile Delinquency*, Children's Bureau Publication No. 356–1956.
[12] *Ibid.*

rough families who live side-by-side with respectable poor families who adhere to conventional middle-class behavior."[13]

The Gluecks'[14] findings also indicate that, within the same or similar social structures, differential patterns of family organization exist and that these, in turn, directly affect the probabilities of deviant behavior. The quality of the family life of delinquent children differs from that of nondelinquents regarding the relationship between parents, the cohesion of the family, parental ambitions for their children, parental standards of conduct, and their supervision of children. Since both sets of delinquent and nondelinquent children were carefully matched with reference to residence in underprivileged neighborhoods and the economic circumstances of their parents, we have here another striking evidence of how widely the patterns of family relations and life styles can range within the same social structure. The quality of the family is not merely a derivative of class position. It has independent validity in the understanding of differential delinquency rates. A theory of the determinants of delinquency which neglects the study of the family as a special unit of research is neglecting a crucial factor in the understanding of deviant behavior.

It is also relevant not to stress the narrowness of Merton's paradigm, which may lead to the neglect of vital areas of delinquency prevention programming. The Gluecks, Healy and Bronner, Ronald Lippitt, Richard Jenkins, August Aichorn, and others have documented the crucial importance of the quality of family life and the patterns of child socialization as significant factors in impulse control and the content and nature of adolescent behavior and self-conceptions. To overemphasize the raising of the occupational structure of youths and to neglect or to undervalue the importance of the family unit as a fulcrum for combatting delinquency, we believe represents a serious deficiency in an adequate action-program.

THE VAGUENESS OF THE WORKING-CLASS CONCEPT

The last question we raised regarding Merton's theories was if his use of the concept of social class require further analytic refinement.

Merton and Cohen describe the impact of the working-class; Ohlin refers to the impact of the lower class. Numerous studies suggest the vagueness of these concepts.

We have little agreement on the criteria of class membership. Different criteria have been used by different researchers to identify social classes. Among these are occupational prestige, residential area, class consciousnss, income, education, status feeling, community power, and life styles. There

---

[13] Sophia G. Robison, *Juvenile Delinquency* (New York: Holt, 1960).

[14] Sheldon Glueck, and Eleanor T. Glueck, *Unraveling Juvenile Delinquency* (Commonwealth Fund, 1950).

is no consensus among social scientists as to what criterion or combination of criteria delineate a social class. Neither Cohen, Merton, or Ohlin clarify their definitions of a social class or specify the nature of the criteria that describe the working class or lower class.

Arnold Rose observed: "It is legitimate under the canons of science to combine such variables as wealth, family background, education, and regard the combination as a new variable or concept such as class, provided: first, the constituent elements and the manner of their combination is made explicit; second, there is consistency in using the concept; and third, some reasonable way is devised for handling deviations from the correlations among the variables—to decide, for example, in what class a person shall be counted if he has high education but low income. Independent researchers who use the concept frequently do all three of these things, but they certainly do not do them in the same way. The result is that nearly everything can be shown to be related or not related to class in the United States."[15]

Landecker in his analysis of the class structure in Detroit studies the extent to which a given population strata could be given a "class" character. To what extent does a person's position occupationally correlate with his rank in the income, educational, ethnic-racial, and other rank systems? He found little class crystallization in the working class. Only in the upper social classes did class crystallization occur. Landecker concluded "If one wishes to determine the effects of class differences on other social phenomena, be they political ideologies or child-rearing practices, it will be advisable to collect one's data in class systems characterized by strong crystallization. Otherwise the findings may be inconclusive because the strata were too limited in class quality to yield significant class differences."[16]

We believe that the working-class concept requires considerable *specification* to make it a useful, analytic tool. We submit that at present it is an omnibus category encompassing the stable and frequently high-income skilled worker, the semiskilled worker, the worker in varied service trades, the unskilled, and the irregular worker. We are of the opinion that an analysis of the variations in delinquency rates between the stable skilled and semiskilled working class strata and the irregular and unskilled workers may be far more relevant and revealing than a comparison of the variations in delinquency rates, such as omnibus categories as middle-class and working-class groups. It is of interest to note that a recent analysis of social class differences in child rearing patterns found an overwhelming evidence that for economic behavior, class membership entails a wide range of other correlated differences. But it does not appear to be the case for socialization practices. Knowledge of class membership would neither permit one to make a safe prediction for small samples of individuals, nor to distinguish the causal processes

---

[15] Arnold Rose, "The Concept of Class in American Sociology," *Social Research* (Spring, 1958), vol. 25, no. 1.

[16] Werner S. Landecker, "Class Crystallization and Its Urban Pattern, *Social Research* (Autumn, 1960), vol. 27, no. 3.

responsible for the behavior. There is such an unsystemized collection of differences, and these differences overlap so much, that it is unlikely a significant *fundamentum divisiones* has been found. The members of the two groups are very much like one another.

ALTERNATIVE APPROACHES TO THE SOURCES OF DELINQUENCY

Durkheim primarily uses the concept of anomie to describe the deterioration of the belief systems; the distintegration of ability of the collective conscience to regulate society; the weakening of the cohesion and integration of a social group. To Durkheim the contemporary increase in the rate and toleration of crime is an index of the distintegration of the collective conscience. "Human passions stop only before a moral power they respect. If all *authority* of this kind is wanting, the law of the strongest prevails." Social cohesion is assured by a "community of beliefs and sentiments." But as man becomes mobile and normative patterns become more "unprecise and inconsistent," we face an increasing breakdown in the moral integration of our society and in its ability to discipline and regulate the behavior of the individual. In the conclusion to the *Division of Labor,* Durkheim described the anomie condition of our society: "Profound changes have been produced in the structure of our society in a very short time; they have been freed from the segmental type with a rapidity and in proportions such as never before seen in history. . . . Our faith has been troubled; tradition has lost its sway; individual judgment has been freed from collective judgment." "If anomie is an evil, it is above all because society suffers from it, being unable to live without cohesion and regulation." "Man is not governed by a material environment brutally imposed on him, but by a conscience superior to his own, the superiority of which he feels and accepts."[17]

In *Suicide,* Durkheim introduced a psychological aspect, and source of anomie; the disequilibrium between an individual's goal and the means available to him to achieve it. "Anomie, whether progressive or regressive, by allowing requirements to exceed appropriate limits, throws open the door to disillusionment and consequently to disappointment. . . . Passion, no longer recognizing bounds, has no goal left."[18]

Merton's theory stresses Durkheim's psychological description of anomie— the disequilibrium between goals and means. We believe that Durkheim's classic sociological analysis of the sources of anomie as reflecting a breakdown in the regulatory mechanism of society more adequately accounts for the area variations in delinquency and the rising trend in deviant behavior. We suggest that our mounting delinquency problems reflect the declining

---

[17] Emile Durkheim, *The Division of Labor in Society* (Glencoe, Ill.: Free Press, 1947).

[18] Emile Durkheim, *Suicide* (Glencoe, Ill.: Free Press, 1951).

stability and effectiveness of our traditional norms and social controls; the growing social disorganization of community life concomitant with population heterogeneity, spatial mobility, and culture conflicts; the decline of the stabilizing influence of the neighborhood and other primary associations; the failure of the family, school, and churches as effective transmission agencies for the moral values of the larger society.

If we were to polarize our positions, we would put it as follows: to Merton, the psychological consequences of *economic deprivation* are pivotal to the understanding of juvenile delinquency. For us, the social consequences of *moral deprivation* are decisive. We suggest that Merton has selected a minor component of Durkheim's analysis and has posited it as the major explanation of social pathology. We believe that Durkheim's classical definition of anomie—his stress on the deterioration of the moral code and belief systems as determinants of social pathology—should be restored to its central position.

Crime and Punishment in the Factory:
A Functional Analysis

J. BENSMAN AND I. GERVER

INTRODUCTION

This paper is a case study of the internal law of a particular organization,[1] specifically, rules of workmanship. For the sake of simplicity, the rules and their violations relevant to one instrument—the tap—are the subject of this study. This is because the study of the tap summarizes an entire area of the internal law of private organizations and their violation and enforcement, as embodied in rules of workmanship. One could also have selected their violations of workmanship rules, such as countersinking dimples, rolling of edges in fairing, stretching of metal skins, or greasing and waxing screw threads.

NOTE: Prepared especially for this volume.

[1] The research was carried out in an airplane factory employing 26,000 people in the New York metropolitan area. One of the authors was a participant observer from September, 1953, through September, 1954. He gathered his data in the daily course of work while working as an assembler on the aileron crew of the final wing line. No special research instruments were used; the ordinary activities of workers along the line were observed and noted as they occurred, and recorded daily. All aspects involved in the use of the tap were discussed in the context of the work situation when they were relevant and salient to the personnel involved, and without their realizing that they were objects of study.

The tap was selected as a major example because of its frequent usage and because it is the most serious violation of rules of workmanship.

While suggesting the engineering complexity of the data, our theoretical interest is in the social function of crime, particularly violations of private organizational law.

THE TAP AND ITS FUNCTIONS

The tap is a tool, an extremely hard steel screw, whose threads are slotted to allow for the disposal of the waste metal which it cuts away. It is sufficiently hard so that when it is inserted into a nut it can cut new threads over the original threads of the nut.

In wing assembly work, bolts or screws must be inserted in recessed nuts which are anchored to the wing in earlier processes of assembly. The bolt or screw must pass through a wing plate before reaching the nut. In the nature of the mass production process, alignments between nuts and plate-openings become distorted. Original allowable tolerances become magnified in later stages of assembly as the number of alignments which must be coordinated with each other increase with the increasing complexity of the assemblage. When the nut is not aligned with the hole, the tap can be used to cut, at a new angle, new threads in the nut for the purpose of bringing the nut and bolt into a new but not true alignment. If the tap is not used and the bolt is forced, the wing plate itself may be bent. Such new alignments, however, deviate from the specifications of the blueprint which is based upon true alignments at every stage of the assembly process. On the basis of engineering standards, true alignments are necessary at every stage in order to achieve maximum strength and a proper equilibrium of strains and stresses.

The use of the tap is the most serious crime of workmanship conceivable in the plant. A worker can be summarily fired for merely possessing a tap. However, it is estimated that at least one-half of the work force in a position to use a tap owns at least one. Every well-equipped senior mechanic owns four or five of different sizes, and every mechanic has access to and, if need be, uses them. In fact, the mass use of the tap represents a widespread violation of this most serious rule of workmanship.

The tap is defined as a criminal instrument, primarily because it destroys the effectiveness of stop nuts. Aviation nuts are specifically designed, so that, once tightened, a screw or bolt cannot back out of the nut under the impact of vibration in flight. Once a nut is tapped, however, it loses its holding power and at any time, after sufficient vibration, the screw or bolt can fall out and weaken the part it holds to the wing and the wing itself.

In addition, the use of a tap is an illegal method of concealing a structural defect. If the holes, for example, were properly drilled and the nuts were properly installed, the use of the tap would be unnecessary, since specifications calling for alignment would be fulfilled. Wherever a tap is used, there are indications of deviations from standards. Furthermore, such deviations make subsequent maintenance of the airplane difficult since maintenance mechanics have no records of such illegal deviations from specifications. Taps can be used in certain cases by special mechanics when such usage is authorized by engineers and when proper paper work supports such use. However, such authorization usually requires one to three days for approval.

The tap, then, is an illegal tool, the use or possession of which carries extreme sanctions in private organizational law, but which is simultaneously widely possessed and used despite its illegal status. The problem of such a pattern for the meaning of private organizational law is to account for the wide acceptance of a crime as a means of fulfilling work requirements within a private organization, the aircraft plant.

THE SOCIALIZATION OF THE WORKER

To most workers entering an aircraft plant the tap is an unknown instrument. Dies which thread bolts, that is, the process opposite to tapping, are relatively well known and are standard equipment of the plumbing trade. The new worker does not come into contact with the tap until he finds it impossible to align the holes in two skins. In desperation he turns to his more experienced partner. The experienced worker after trying legitimate techniques of lining up the holes will resort to the tap. While tapping the nut he gives the novice a lecture on the dangers of breaking a tap in the hole, and thereby leaving telltale evidence of its use.

For several weeks the older worker will not permit his inexperienced partner to use a tap when its use is required. If the novice demonstrates sufficient ability in other aspects of his work, he will be allowed to tap the hole under the supervision of a veteran worker. In order to enjoy his new found facility, the novice will begin to use the tap on his own, even when it is not necessary.

He may forego the easier illegal methods (which are also viewed as less serious crimes) of greasing and waxing bolts or enlarging the misaligned holes and indulge himself in the more pleasurable, challenging, and dangerous use of the tap. Sooner or later, he inevitably runs into difficulties for which he is technically unprepared to cope. When his partner is not available, he is forced to call upon the assistant foreman. If the situation requires it, the foreman will recommend the tap. If he has doubts about the worker's abilities, he may even tap the hole himself. In doing this, he risks censure of the union, because as a foreman he is not permitted to handle tools.

While the foreman taps the hole, he also gives a lecture on the proper and technically workmanlike ways of using the tap. The foreman goes on to warn the worker to make sure "not to get caught, to see that the coast is clear, to keep the tap well hidden when not in use, and to watch out for inspectors while using it." He always ends by cautioning the worker, "It's your own skin if you're caught."

When the worker feels that he is experienced and can use the tap with complete confidence, he usually buys his own, frequently displaying it to other workers and magnanimously lending it to those in need of it. He feels himself fully arrived when a two-star foreman or, even higher—an assistant general foreman—borrows his tap or asks him to perform the tapping. The worker has now established his identity and is known as an individual by the higher ups.

Once the "right" to use the tap is thus established, the indiscriminate use of it is frowned upon. A worker who uses a tap too often is considered to be a careless "botcher," but one who doesn't use the tap when it is necessary does not get his own work done on time.

AGENCIES OF LAW ENFORCEMENT

The enforcement of the plant rules of workmanship devolves upon three groups: foreman, plant quality control, and Air Force quality control. The ultimate and supreme authority resides in the latter group. The Air Force not only sets the blueprint specifications, but also, and more importantly, can reject a finished airplane as not meeting specifications.

Furthermore, the Air Force inspectors reinspect installations which have been previously "bought" by plant quality control. If these installations do not meet Air Force standards they are "crabbed," that is, rejected. When this happens, the plant inspectors who bought the installations are subject to "being written up." This means disciplinary action for unintentional negligence which may lead to suspensions, demotions, or, in extreme cases, loss of jobs.

There were only two Air Force inspectors to a shop at the time of these observations, so that it was almost impossible for Air Force inspectors to police an entire shop of over 2,000 men. As an Air Force inspector walks up the line, it is standard procedure for workers to nudge other workers in order to inform them of the approach of the "Gestapo." When tapping is essential and when it is known that Air Force inspectors are too near, guards of workers are posted to convey advance notice of this approach to anyone who is actively tapping. When the Air Force inspector is in the vicinity, workers who have a reputation for open or promiscuous use of the tap are instructed by the assistant foreman to "disappear."

Despite the Air Force inspectors' high authority and the severity of their standards, they are not sufficiently numerous to be considered the major policing agency for detecting and apprehending violators of the rules of workmanship. Plant quality control is the actual law enforcement agency in terms of the daily operations of surveillance. There are approximately 150 plant inspectors to a 2,000-man shop. They work along the assembly line along with the workers. In some cases, one inspector is attached to a specific work crew of an assistant foreman, but the inspector is in no way responsible to the assistant foreman. In other cases, a panel of inspectors is assigned to inspect the work done by a number of crews who are supervised by a two-star foreman. In this system, a call book which guarantees the equal rotation of the inspections is kept. When a worker has completed a job and requests an inspection, he enters his wing number and the requested inspection in the call book. The inspector, after completing an inspection, marks the job as completed and takes the next open inspection as indicated in the call book.

A result of either type of inspection setup is the free and intimate inter-mingling of inspectors and workers. In off moments, inspectors and workers gather together to "shoot the breeze and kill time." Inspectors may have long waiting periods before their next assignment. During such periods, they tend to fraternize with workers. This causes conflict between the role of "good egg" and the role of policeman. Another cause of leniency on the part of inspectors is intrinsic to the relationship between mechanics and themselves in circumstances not involving the tap. There is a sufficient amount of mechanical work which is not easily and immediately accessible to inspectors. In order for the inspector to complete his work and make sure that the work he "buys" will be acceptable to later inspectors, he must rely on the workman-ship of the mechanic. In brief, he must trust not only in the mechanic's workmanship, but more importantly he has to insure that the mechanic will not "louse him up." If the inspector gets the reputation of being a "heel," the mechanic is under no obligation to do a good job and thus protect the inspector.

Since the penalities for the use of the tap are so severe, no inspector feels comfortable about reporting a violation. A number of subterfuges are resorted to in an effort to diminish the potential conflict. There is a general under-standing that workers are not supposed to use a tap in the presence of plant inspectors. At various times, this understanding is made explicit. The inspector frequently tells the workers of his crew, "Now fellas, there's a big drive on taps. The Air Force just issued a special memo. For God's sakes, don't use a tap when I'm around."

At other times the verbalization comes from a worker. If a worker "has" to use a tap and the inspector is present, he will, if necessary, tell the inspector to "Get the hell outa here. I got work to do and can't do it while you're around." If the worker knows the inspector well, he may take out the tap, permitting the inspector to see it. The wise inspector responds to the gesture by leaving.

When there is an Air Force inspired drive against the tap, the inspectors will make the rounds and "lay the law down." "I want no more tapping around here. The next guy caught gets turned in. I can't cover you guys any more. If that s.o.b. foreman of yours insists on you doing it, tell him to do it himself. If you're caught, it's your skin not his. He's got to cover him-self, and he'll leave you holding the bag!"

For about three or four days thereafter, taps disappear from public view. The work slows down, and ultimately the inspectors forget to be zealous. A state of normal haphazard equilibrium is restored.

Another typical worker-inspector situation occurs when a mechanic is caught in the act of tapping, and the inspector does not look away. The inspector severely reprimands the mechanic, holds him in suspense as to whether or not he will turn him in, and then lets him go with a warning. This generally only happens to new workers. Occasionally, when a worker has a new inspector and no previously established trust relationship, the same situation may arise. In both cases, they are an integral part of the socialization of the worker to the plant, or rather to a specific phase of its operation.

THE ROLE OF THE FOREMAN

Another type of ceremonial escape from law enforcement through pseudo-law enforcement involves the foreman. In rare cases, an inspector will catch a worker using the tap, reprimand him, and turn him over to his foreman. The foreman then is forced to go through the procedure of reprimanding the errant worker. The foreman becomes serious and indignant, primarily because the worker let himself get caught. He gives the worker a tongue lashing, and he reminds him once again that he, as foreman, has to go to bat to save the worker's neck. He stresses that it is only because of *his* intervention that the worker will not lose his job.

The worker is obliged to accept the reprimand and to assume the countenance of a true penitent, even to the extent of promising that it won't happen again. Both the foreman and worker play these roles even though the worker tapped the nut at the specific request of the foreman. The most blatant violation of the mores in such a situation is when the worker grins and treats the whole thing as a comic interlude. When this happens, the foreman actually becomes enraged.

The public ritual therefore conceals an entirely different dimension of social functions involved in the use of the tap. The tap cannot be used without the active or passive collusion of the foreman. As noted, the foreman instructs the worker in its use, indicates when he wants it used, assists the worker in evading the plant rules, and, when the worker is caught, goes through the ritual of punishment. These role contradictions are intrinsic to the position of the foreman. His major responsibility is to keep production going. At the same time he is a representative of supervision, and is expected to encourage respect for company law. He is not primarily responsible for quality since this is the province of plant quality control, that is, inspection. He resolves the various conflicts in terms of the strongest and most persistent forms of pressures and rewards.

The work requirements of any particular foreman and his crew are determined by the production analysis section, another staff organization. Production analysis determines, on the basis of time studies, the number of men to be assigned to a specific crew, the locations of crews on the assembly line, and the cut-off points for work controlled by a particular foreman. Having done this, they determine the work load required of a foreman and keep production charts on completed work. As a moment's glance, top supervision can single out foremen who are not pulling their weight. In aviation assembly work, the work cycle for a particular team is relatively long (four to eight hours), and a foreman supervises relatively few work teams (usually three) doing the same job. Any obstacle which delays one team damages the foreman's production record in the immediately perceivable terms. Moreover, delay caused by the inability of one crew to complete its task prevents other crews working "up the line" from that crew. The foremen of these latter crews will complain to the two- or three-star foreman that they are being held up and that their production records will suffer because of another foreman's incompetence.

As a result of these considerations, the pressures "to get work out" are paramount for the foreman. Production records are the major consideration in supervisory mobility. All other considerations, for example, sociability, work-knowledge, personality, and so on are assumed to be measured by the production chart.

In this context, it is obvious that the foreman in permitting the use of the tap is compelled to violate some of the most important laws of the company and the Air Force. Crucial instances occur at times when the Air Force institutes stringent anti-tap enforcement measures. When key holes do not line up, it may be necessary to disassemble previous installations. The disassembling and reassembling may take a full eight hours before the previously reached work stage is again reached. The production chart for that eight-hour period will indicate that no work has been done. Use of the tap can prevent such delays, but the worker may refuse to tap a hole since he risks endangering his job. To get the work done, he therefore employs a whole rhetoric of veiled requests to get the worker to tap the misaligned nut. If the worker is adamant in refusing, the foreman will remind him of past favors, or plead, or promise future rewards.

If the requests, pleas, and promises do not produce results, the foreman may take the ultimate step of tapping the hole himself. He compounds the felony because he not only violates the rules of workmanship but also violates union rules which specifically state that no foreman can use a tool. To add insult to injury, the foreman furthermore has to borrow the tap in the midst of an anti-tap drive when taps are scarce.

From the viewpoint of maintaining production, the use of the tap is imperative to the functioning of the production organization, even though it is one of the most serious work crimes. This is recognized even at official levels, although only in indirect ways.

Taps, being made of hard steel, have the disadvantage of being brittle. If not handled carefully, they may break within the nut. This not only makes further work impossible but also makes for easier detection of the crime. To cope with such a problem, the tool crib is well equipped with a supply of tap extractors. Any worker can draw an appropriately sized tap extractor from the tool crib. All of these are official company property. He can do this even amidst the more severe anti-tap drives without the fear, or the danger, of punishment.

CRIME AND THE SOCIAL SYSTEM

Deviancy, in the sense that it implies a rejection of the norms of a social system or behavior outside of a system, is not a useful concept for analyzing this type of crime. Rather, the use of the tap is literally a major crime which is intrinsic to the system. The conception of a social system as a tightly knit series of interlocking functions, mutually supporting each other and contributing to the support and continuance of the system, is not at all applicable to an understanding of this case.

Crime as defined by the use of the tap (and the other crimes of workmanship subsumed under our discussion of the tap) supports, in its own way, the continuance of the system, just as the avoidance of the use of the tap contributes to the perfection of the system. The notion of deviancy as a residue of systemic analysis, that is, action not conforming to the demands of the system, or resulting in dysfunctions of the system, does not adequately describe the system. One reason for this inadequacy is that deviance, as thus understood, derives from a prior postulation of some primary but not specifically located end, which the analyst himself attributes to the system.

If one considers the actions called "deviant behavior" as intrinsic to the system, deviant behavior contributes to and supports the system just as does conformity, simply because the system is composed of its interrelated parts. From the standpoint of the past, any change is dysfunctional, that is, it represents a disruption of the system as it was. From the standpoint of the present, those same changes, when adopted, can be viewed as functions, since they become for the moment intrinsic parts of system.

In terms of the above analysis, the conceptualization of deviancy as functional or dysfunctional reduces to a semantic problem. Attributions of function and dysfunction are artifacts of the mode of analysis and are based upon the analyst's assumptions of ends for a system, rather than upon attributes of the actual collective behavior. The resolution of problems concerning the interrelations of specific social phenomena can best be performed by dealing with substantive data rather than at the level of the verbal pyrotechnics of formal model and deductive theory building. The real problems lie in relating specific data to concepts and not in the preoccupation with how concepts are abstractly related to each other.

However, verbal play is a less important concern than the problem of the imputation of ends. Ends are imputed to a system, and the functions of its structual elements are viewed as contributing to these ends and to the maintenance of this system. The problem for research is to *locate* and *specify* these ends. It is in principle, though not necessarily practice, fairly easy to locate and specify the ends of specific individuals as related to their social actions, but the ends of social systems and collectivities are much more difficult to locate. There is a prevalent tendency to succumb to an ever-present danger of selecting some one set of social ends as primary, and then to attribute them to the system as a whole. In such cases, the "objective world" becomes a projection of the personal values of the analyst, or the values of some group or individuals in the social system, to which the analyst is linked.

If these considerations are applied to our analysis of the tap, a whole new level of analysis is brought into focus.

Obviously profit-making through production is the major end of the company, that is, of its stock-holders, board of directors, officers, and supervisory staff. Even here, though there is a complex problem related to conflicts of ends, for example, between reinvestment and distribution of profits, expansion, and profit-taking. These are considerations which probably complicate the picture, but they are not treated here.

For the Air Force, the major official end is a high rate of production of high quality planes at low cost. Reducing costs and maintaining quality are secondary ends, or if one wishes so to describe it, means to the primary end of producing efficient aircraft. For the individual foreman, maintaining his job, gaining a promotion, or staying out of trouble may be his primary private ends. Maintaining or exceeding his production quota, while a major end for the "company" defined as a whole and as defined by the executives, is the means of attaining the private goals of the foreman.

Similarly, the primary ends of plant inspectors are to get along with workers, to avoid buying jobs which will be rejected in later inspection, and, in some cases, to achieve a supervisory position. Again the actions of inspectors in developing a mutual trust situation and in protecting themselves and workers in the tap situation represent a compromise between different private ends. Similarly, the ends of workers are to get their work done with a minimum of effort, to get along at least minimally with foremen and inspectors, to stay out of trouble, and to avoid being fired. The semisecret use of the tap, then, represents a compromise between these complexes of ends.

Taking these means-ends situations together, we find that what are means for one group are ends for another. In all cases, means and ends can be defined as either public or private attributes. Public ends are means to private ends, and private ends are, in some cases, limited by "public," that is, organizationally sanctioned, ends and means. In brief, the empirical situation is extremely complex, and not analyzable in a priori terms. The complex of public and private means and ends constitutes a specific research problem insofar as it accounts for an over-all operation of the organization.

In terms of the specific problem of the tap as an instrument, and its relationship to means and ends relationships within the organization, we find that use of taps is a private illegal means to publicly stated ends. But those ends to which the use of taps is oriented are, from both the standpoint of that abstraction "the company" and from the standpoint of its members, only one of a number of possible ends. It is the plurality of ends, which account for "deviant behavior" rather than the conflict between means and ends. A high rate of production is a major end, and quality is a necessary condition for the attainment of that end. Moreover, as individuals are distributed at different levels and in different lines of the organizational hierarchy, different ends become more salient to individuals occupying different positions. The relationship of means to ends at both the public and private levels is different (in fact is sometimes reversed) for individuals in different positions in the organization. The statement of "public ends" attached to the organization or the social system may then frequently be the ends of a limited number of particular and publicly accessible or visible positions in the system.

Thus, any theoretical model which accepts as an initial postulate the dominance of an ultimate end, and which conceptualizes disorganization as a conflict between means and ends, overlooks the possibility that conflicting means and ends are actually conflicts between the means to one end with the means to another.

Moreover, in any complex organization where plural ends are distributed in different ways among office holders, the conflict of ends and conflicts between means and ends are institutionalized as a conflict between various departments or segments in the organization. Thus, from the point of view of production supervision, quality control is a major obstacle to the achievement of its ends. From the standpoint of quality control, sloppy workmanship is a major crime which may result in sanctions applied to the inspector. The tolerance of the tap, of major measures of public crime, is a means by which workers, inspectors, and production supervisors attempt to achieve their respective ends in a manner which is mutually tolerable in a situation where they are forced to work together according to directives, which, if closely followed, would result in mutual frustration. For the worker, the inspector, and the foreman, the development of a satisfactory social environment, the minimization of conflict, and the development of tolerable social relations become a major end, among others, of the actors involved. Crime and the toleration of crime within the limits of avoiding sanctions, thus becomes a means to these social ends, as well as means to the publicly recognized ends of the organization.

As a result, a large part of behavior which is visible to an insider or to a sophisticated observer is "criminal," that is, it violates publicly stated norms. But since such behavior is accepted—in fact often stimulated, aided, and abetted by the effective on-the-spot authorities—the criminality of such behavior has limited consequences.

CONCLUSION

The resolution of the "means-end conflict" results in crime, but such crime often becomes fairly acceptable behavior and is stabilized as a permanent aspect of the organization. Crime becomes one of the major operational devices of the organization. As such, it is hard to consider it as a form of anomie. The use of the tap is neither an innovation, a form of rebellion, ritualism, nor retreatism. It is more aptly described as a permanent unofficial aspect of the organization. It is not an innovation since, for almost all of the personnel in the plant, the use of the tap in the plant precedes their knowledge of it. It is not rebellion since it is a means to a company end, a high production rate. It is neither a ritual nor a retreat since it is in some sense functional to all concerned. To most personnel, it is a crime only because there is an official ruling against its use and because there are a wide range of ceremonial forms of law enforcement and punishment. With respect to the Air Force, use of the tap still remains a serious crime. But in this area the wide range of cooperative behavior between workers, foremen, and plant inspectors combines to reduce the importance of Air Force law enforcement as a significant factor in the situation.

The ceremonial aspects of law enforcement are, however, of importance. These include secrecy in the use of the tap to avoid embarrassing the inspector, the reporting of tap violations by the inspector to the foreman who initially requested the use of the tap, the mock severity of the foreman in reprimanding the reported violator, and the penitence of the apprehended criminal before his judge, the foreman.

A form of institutional schizophrenia is the major result of the conflict of ends. Individuals act and think on at least two planes, the plane of public ideology and the plane of action. They shift from plane to plane, as required by their positions, their situations, and their means-ends estimations. In a sense, it is a form of double-think, and double-think is the major result of means-ends and ends-ends conflicts.

From the point of view of the actors involved, in the light of the double-think mechanism, the major definition of deviancy takes on another dimension. The major crime for the actors involved, is the lack of respect for the on-going social ceremonialism. The worker who allows an inspector to see him possessing or using a tap threatens the defences of the inspector, and is likely to be reprimanded for not being careful. He is likely to find it harder to "sell" his work to that inspector. The worker who casually mentions illegal workmanship to an inspector is told not to mention it. Finally, a worker who grins while being reprimanded for the use of the tap, is likely to be bawled out for his flippant attitude. The foreman is likely to threaten him with a withdrawal from the circle of protection given by the foreman to apprehended criminals.

Thus, lack of seriousness in adhering to the ceremonial forms of law violation is defined as a case of inappropriateness of affect and lack of reality orientation requiring serious forms of informal social control. A major crime, then, is the violation of the *rules* of criminal behavior.

The fact that tapping is a crime, a violation of an inoperative public ideology, does not mean that it is uncontrolled anomalous behavior. On the contrary, the very pervasiveness of the use of the tap, and its functional indispensability result in a relatively close control of tapping by supervisory authority.

The worker is taught the proper techniques of tapping, and he is taught the situations for which use of the tap is appropriate. Using the tap as a substitute for careful work or for less severely defined illegal techniques of work-manship are frowned upon.

The worker who uses the tap promiscuously is subject to a wide variety of informal controls. He is kidded and teased by other workers. Inspectors become sensitive to his action and his being caught. The foreman rides him unmercifully and tends to become more sensitive to all his faults of work-manship. If he persists in abusing the use of the tap, he ultimately gets transferred to another foreman who is short of men. The floating worker is presumed to be a botcher by the very fact of his being transferred.

Only rarely, however, are formal actions, which involve the possibility of dismissal, taken against the worker. This is because, in "writing-up" a worker for abusing the tap, the foreman would risk the danger of bringing the whole issue into the open. In punishing promiscuous tappers by official means, the foreman might risk losing opportunities to use the tap when he wants to. Also, in bringing serious charges against the deviant tapper, the foreman might find that other workers would be unduly hesitant to use the tap.

For these reasons, foremen and inspectors do not use the formal channels of law enforcement, but rely instead on informal controls. They limit use of the tap. In addition, such controls yield a new definition of crime and its function at the behavioral level. A "crime" is not a crime so long as its commission is controlled and directed by those in authority toward goals which they define as socially constructive. A violation of law is treated as a crime when it is not directed and controlled by those in authority or when it is used for exclusively private ends.

The kind, type, and frequency of crime is a function of the system of authority. The ranges of "socially permissible crime" and the degree and severity of punishment are determined by the ends and interests of those who are responsible for law enforcement. Severe law enforcement limits the freedom of leadership groups in attainment of their own ends. Loosening the fabric of law enforcement enables these groups to have greater freedom of action in the attainment of their ends but also permits a greater amount of crime at lower levels.

Evaluating Juvenile Delinquency Research

LOUISE G. HOWTON

Investigating juvenile delinquency is one of the best financed and most energetically pursued specialties in social research. Crimes and other socially

SOURCE: Prepared especially for this volume. References are to Barbara Wootton, *Social Science and Social Pathology* (New York: Macmillan, 1959).

impermissible acts committed by minors which bring them to the attention of the courts are highly visible and greatly regretted. Public opinion is understandably sensitive, in any society deeply committed to the value of children and the importance of protecting their welfare, to the reproof implied in a juvenile delinquency rate that rises year by year. Some respond by calling for sterner measures—a "get tough" attitude by the courts, less probation and more detention, even a return to corporal punishment in the schools. At the other extreme are those who blame society altogether and call for expanded treatment facilities, typically of the sort that rely on techniques of individual and group psychotherapy. The great liberal center responds by concluding that more research is needed in any event, and by making funds available.

Thus the specifics vary, but common to all sectors of public opinion is a sense of moral indignation and a will to act. The social scientist is provided with funds, encouragement, cooperation, plentiful and accessible records and, perhaps most important of all, a research problem that has theoretical as well as practical implications. With so many favoring circumstances one would expect to find empirically grounded knowledge of the subject to be well advanced. Examination reveals, however, that while the scale of the research effort is impressive, the findings are not. Too often they are so inconsistent as to nullify each other and bring us back practically to the zero point.

Criticism of large-scale criminological research has not been lacking in the American literature, but it remained for a British magistrate to do a critique systematic enough to be called definitive. Both as a judge sentencing youthful offenders and as a University District Head training social workers, Barbara Wootton became concerned about the failure of individual studies to be of much practical help. She undertook a systematic comparative evaluation, and found that they also fail as science. This is distressing enough but even worse, as she reports it, is that books on social work education and arguments used in court proceedings (taking this material as a source of relevant facts is one of the novel features of the book) present fashionable assumptions as if they were conclusions, and the findings of study X as if they were not called into question by study Y. This escalation of error damages both the rationality of practice and the prestige of science. At best, empirically established correlates of deviant behavior are presented loosely as causes and serve to confuse discourse; at worst, questionable ideas currently in vogue gain good repute and become incorporated into the policies and training doctrine of social agencies.

The portion of Wootton's critique which is summarized here systematically compares the findings of all the "competent" major empirical studies of "the causes and characteristic features of crime and delinquency." To qualify, the studies had to meet the following standards: inclusion of at least 200 subjects; collection and analysis of facts bearing on at least half of twelve factors hypothetically causative of delinquency; ample reporting of study design and research procedure; and detailed listing of results. These are stringent limitations. All journal articles were excluded as well as some well-known book length studies.

The twelve criminological hypotheses were chosen on the basis of their prevalence in the popular and professional literature concerned with the subject. They are listed below:

Twelve Factors Hypothetically Causative of Crime and Delinquency

1. Size of family
2. Presence of other criminals in family
3. Club membership
4. Church attendance
5. Employment record
6. Social status
7. Poverty
8. Mother employed outside the home
9. Truancy
10. Broken home
11. Health
12. Education attained

The analysis is exhaustive—hypothesis by hypothesis, twelve examinations of each of 21 studies. Despite the formidable investment of time and resources by the researchers (21 broad, careful projects in three countries over a period of four decades), basic limitations recur: noncomparable definitions, incommensurable features in research design, overinterpretation of findings, and unexplained anomalies in estimating significance.

The array of results bearing on each of the hypotheses is bewildering in its variety. This is apparent when one attempts the usual analytical summary in tabular form. For example, consider the hypothesis specifying *broken home* as a factor. Carr-Saunders finds that 28 per cent of delinquents, compared with 16 per cent of controls, come from broken homes. Trenaman's comparable figures are 57 per cent and 12 per cent, and Wilkins reports 22 per cent and 14 per cent. The Gluecks' figures are highest in both categories: 60.4 per cent and 34.2 per cent. This brief enumeration exhausts the studies which report figures for comparable categories; the others require special notation, such as that one includes handicapped and the other does not, or that one is limited to the provinces and the other to the metropolis. One researcher unaccountably reports information on only 823 out of his 1,000 cases, another divides the rates by boys and girls, another by age at which the break in social control occurs. This material is obviously not cumulative and cannot be directly compared with the percentage figures given above. One of the basic problems, clearly, is definition. Trenaman's is unusually broad, including cases classifiable as "homeless," "from broken homes," "had parents who were chronic invalids," or "parents absent for long periods." Gibb's figures are based on the institutionalization of a child as well as the loss of a parent to the home, including the very institutionalization of the child which led him to being included in the study in the first place.

The best summary that can be presented is that, for the British studies, broken homes as a factor ranges from 22 per cent to 57 per cent for the delinquents, and 11 per cent to 17 per cent for the controls. For the American studies, the corresponding ranges are 34 per cent to 62 per cent, and 14 per cent to 34 per cent, respectively. It is noteworthy that the control figures in the American studies can be larger than the delinquent figure in the British studies. Finally, the control figure in some of the American studies is not far from equality with the delinquent figure in others.

The cited range does not represent the results altogether fairly because of the omission of items that could not be scaled. However, there is reason to suspect even the most charitable tabulation. Shaw and McKay, for example, demonstrate a marked variation in the incidence of broken homes in various ethnic groups and a slighter one with regard to boys past seventeen years of age. This shows that in addition to the definitional problem of specifying criteria by which concepts are operationalized, there is the additional one of deciding what population is to be studied.

The foregoing is only a sampling, but it should serve to convey some sense of Miss Wootton's strategy and technique of critical evaluation. She sums up as follows:

All in all, therefore, this collection of studies, although chosen for its comparative methodological merit, produces only the most meagre, and dubiously supported generalizations. On the whole, it seems that offenders come from relatively large families. Not infrequently (according to some investigators very frequently) other members of the delinquents' (variously defined) families have also been in trouble with the law. Offenders are unlikely to be regular churchgoers, but the evidence as to whether club membership discourages delinquency is wildly contradictory. If they are of an age to be employed, they are likely to be classified as "poor" rather than "good" workers. Most of them come from the lower social classes, but again the evidence as to the extent to which they can be described as exceptionally poor is conflicting; nor is there any clear indication that their delinquency is associated with the employment of their mothers outside the home. Their health is probably no worse than that of other people, but many of them have earned poor reputations at school, though these may well be prejudiced by their teachers' knowledge of their delinquencies. In their schooldays they are quite likely to have truanted from school, and perhaps an unusually large proportion of them come from homes in which at some (frequently unspecified) time both parents were not, for whatever reason, living together; yet even on these points, the findings of some enquiries are negative. And beyond this we cannot go. (Pp. 134–35)

The studies are not without value, in Miss Wootton's opinion, although what they have achieved has been mostly incidental or by indirection. Most dramatically, perhaps, the results show that the assumptions still entrenched in the popular wisdom such as that poor health and working mothers cause delinquency are not substantiated. (The rate of incidence of working mothers in the families of delinquents and controls in the British studies shows a range of 4.6 per cent to 32 per cent and 7.4 per cent to 33 per cent, respectively, which is practically identical in level as well as range. A somewhat larger raw differential is found in the American studies, but it disappears when a correction is applied for social status. The same thing is true of health as a factor.) The earlier literature, especially, stresses the role of physiological and functional differences in causing deviant behavior, and some elaborate theories were spun out of poorly supported observations. What little evidence now remains of poor health in the offender group is easily accounted for as generally characteristic of the population from which it is drawn.

Wootton concludes that the type of research which assumes discoverable factors in the individual case characterizing a delinquent population has already contributed what little it can and should be abandoned. Juvenile delinquency as an all embracing category is too imprecise for research purposes. "In place of the quest for causes in the factorial sense, research needs to seek to achieve an understanding of the varieties of socialization—the ongoing life careers of young people with their frequent crises and turning points, their alternatives and choices and the patterns of the paths which develop." Research guided by short-term practical considerations, such as the needs of the magistrate in intelligently sentencing the offender, would be far more useful.

*   *   *

Analyzing child guidance literature over three historical periods, Martha Wolfenstein[1] concludes that while the image of the child has changed greatly there is not much evidence that he is better understood. Writing from a different perspective and generalizing from a different body of literature, Barbara Wootton finds a singular persistence in the image of the youthful offender: he is seen mechanically, as a collection of traits, or "factors." Different clusters of traits are emphasized in different decades by different researchers, but the variation is best understood as reflecting little more than the play of fashion. In social science research, too often the image changes without warrant or stays constant even when there is reason to question it.

If knowledge of the causes of juvenile delinquency is not ahead of what it was 40 years ago, it is not because researchers have been diligent in getting "the facts." The 21 studies constitute a record of diligence sadly misapplied. They show the futility of expecting the accumulation of facts to result automatically in the improvement of scientific knowledge. The line of inquiry assuming that what causes delinquency is something *in the individual* (psychological, biological) ought to be dropped; however, the demonstrated power of our cultural preconceptions to outride repeated failures to validate them is such that it will probably continue.

---

[1] Martha Wolfenstein, "Fun Morality: An Analysis of Recent American Child Training Literature," *Journal of Social Issues*, 7:4 (1951), pp. 15–25.

Part Two. EXTREME SITUATIONS

Political tyranny, the corruption of the rule of law, is as old as civil society. Still, its form and scope in the modern world is new. The tyrant of the past could not reach the whole population in an instant with his words and voice (and now his image), nor could he get back direct and reliable reports on the effect of his pronouncements and policies. Moreover, he could not mobilize the whole population—aside from being unable to reach it— if for no other reason than that he lacked economic room to manoeuver. The surplus of men and resources needed to sustain a large and permanent collective enterprise was not to be had. Without the means to reach and mobilize substantially everyone under one jurisdiction the specifically totalitarian form of tyranny is infeasible. The modern dictators, having such means, enjoy a whole new dimension of freedom to act; and, having outrun the ends for which conventional socio-political means have been used in the past, they have not been laggard in devising novel and up-to-date ones. Tyranny united with technology seeks nothing less than to remake the world or destroy it.

But totalitarianism, the specifically modern form of political tyranny, is nothing more than a particularly dramatic expression of certain features common to modern institutions generally—a kind of caricature of what is now the "normal." For example, it has become accepted statesmanlike rhetoric to include population categories ("our youth," "the aged," "farmers," etc.) among those things that can be called "our most important national resource." The fact that lumping people together with factories, forests, fisheries, mineral deposits, and the integrity of the dollar as things whose value lies in the use we can make of them passes without comment is not, in itself, evidence of a totalitarian mentality. But it does show a way of thinking about the world that reveals the bureaucratic quality of modern institutions—a quality of them that makes them susceptible to totalitarian deformation.[1]

The new political tyrants are not unique in relying on bureaucratic institu-

---

[1] This theme is basic to much of Karl Mannheim's later work. See especially Karl Mannheim, *Man and Society in An Age of Reconstruction*, New York: Harcourt, Brace, 1951, and *Freedom, Power, and Democratic Planning*, New York: Oxford University Press, 1950.

tions to achieve their goals. The regimes of all advanced nations do so, democracies and dictatorships alike. But bureaucracy is no mere mechanical contrivance, inanimate, lending all its power at the touch of a switch to whomever sits at the controls. It is more like a giant—a restless and cunning giant—than a machine. In offering means of unprecedented scope and power to realize human ends, it at the same time posits its *own* ends which, judged from the standpoint of traditional humane values, are of a ferocity hitherto unimaginable. Bureaucracy makes possible "thinking about the unthinkable" (to borrow the phrase of one of the foremost authorities on thermonuclear war)[2] by making it rational; and having made it possible, impelled by new insecurities grafted on to old national rivalries, it finally makes it necessary.

The materials reprinted in this Part bear in various ways on how this new set of means and ends of power in modern society place individuals in what have come to be called "extreme situations." In order to provide an analytical frame of reference we propose below a characterization or model of extreme situations sufficiently generalized to encompass the range of instances discussed in the reprinted materials.[3]

A SOCIOLOGICAL CONCEPTION OF EXTREME SITUATIONS

Bruno Bettelheim, a psychologist, is usually credited with introducing the term "extreme situations" into social science.[4] Suggestive as it is, however, his formulation unduly neglects social groups and institutions as significant factors in determining behavior. Drawing on his own experience and observations as an inmate of a Nazi concentration camp (Buchenwald), he sets out to account for individual differences in coping with an extremely hostile environment. The problem for the sociologist is rather different. What is of interest from the sociological standpoint is individual *similarities* rather than differences—the behavior common to a whole group and characteristic of it. This is what calls for explanation.

---

[2] Herman Kahn, *Thinking About the Unthinkable*, New York, 1963.

[3] It will be evident that we take as our theoretical point of departure Durkheim's conception of society as a moral order. Durkheim theorized that the individual's sense of values comes from "society itself." The "collective conscience," the body of norms and sentiments characteristic of a given society and to some extent peculiar to it, stands over and above the individual and constrains him in his conduct. This emphasis on society as a *moral* order is best understood in relation to its contrast conception: society as a *utilitarian* order, in which moral rules are reducible to (and ultimately derived from) enlightened self-interest. See especially Emile Durkheim, *The Elementary Forms of the Religious Life*, translated by J. W. Swain, Glencoe, Ill.: The Free Press, 1947, and *The Rules of Sociological Method*, translated by Sarah H. Solovay and John H. Mueller, Chicago, Ill.: University of Chicago Press, 1938.

[4] Bruno Bettelheim, "Individual and Mass Behavior in Extreme Situations," *Journal of Abnormal and Social Psychology*, 38 (1943), pp. 417–452.

The appropriate sociological research strategy is to attribute such similarities to the institutional character of the hostile environment, which then becomes the subject for investigation. Individual variations of behavior within a given group are considered deviant cases, to be explained as the consequences of variations in group affiliations and group structure. (The piece by Emil Luchterhand included below is illustrative of this approach.)

The numerous accounts of concentration camp survivors bear a notable common theme: when asked what hope kept them going they replied, in the words of one, "to come out alive *and unchanged.*" That very important proviso (one wants more than just to live) offers a clue to the direction our effort to reformulate and generalize the concept of extreme situations should take. Positing a universal wish to keep the self intact, to defend one's integrity, in the common phrase, we can characterize an extreme situation as one in which extraordinary pressure is brought to bear on the individual to accept a restructuring of his self.

To the extent that it is literally true (as our Western cultural heritage in principle demands) that the self-respecting individual guarantees, in some final encounter, to choose death over dishonor, it would seem that the limiting (ultimate) case on the continuum of extreme situations is not the one in which a threat to physical survival is carried out, but the one beyond it. That is, the threatened individual who commits an intolerably degrading act of acquiescence to preserve his life accepts a "fate worse than death"—a self altered and despised.

One can imagine all sorts of random circumstances that would constitute an extreme situation within the limits of the definition so far, which means that it needs to be tighter and sharper, more restrictive. Sociological analysis must be confined to characteristic regularities, social facts that are caused and therefore predictable, leaving to poets and philosophers the task of reflecting on how random concatenations of events reveal the condition of man.

What is it, then, that produces extreme situations? What characteristic of modern society, specifically, can account for the fact that extreme situations are no longer random and sporadic in their incidence but seem to be regular features of the social order?

Returning to the concentration camp literature, another thing that strikes us is that the survivors' descriptions of daily routine in the camps produces a shock of recognition. Bizarre as it seems, there is something about the plight of these victims of political terror that reminds us of experiences most Americans have had or know about from first-hand accounts. Jails, prisons, mental hospitals, military barracks, ships at sea, convents, monasteries, even boarding schools—all of these have some features in common with concentration camps. The sociologist Erving Goffman has recently characterized the genus: they are "total institutions."[5]

---

[5] Erving Goffman, *Asylums,* New York, Doubleday Anchor, 1961. See especially pp. 1–125.

The "totalness" of a total institution consists in the relation between the individual and the organized body of functionaries who form and carry out institutional policy, i.e., the officers. The "inmate" (using the term in a broadened sense) has much less privacy, and the functionary has much more freedom to intrude, than do their counterparts in more conventional relationships. This is true because (a) the inmate is completely dependent on the one institution and subject to its autocratic rules, and (b) the institution's mission is to *do something to* the inmate—to transform him, either as an end in itself (the patient, the offender), or else as a necessary means for making him into a useful instrument (the soldier, the sailor, the monk).

Total institutions, like extreme situations, are as old as history. Societies organized on any considerable scale have usually made provision for regular military units, forced labor camps, asylums and monasteries. But if there is nothing new about total institutions as a generic societal form, the same cannot be said of the specific form they have taken in the modern world, and, more especially, of the significance this new form has as a clue to the fundaments of the emerging social order. Just as extreme situations are no longer to be dismissed as random and sporadic in their incidence, we have the example of totalitarianism to remind us that total institutions are no longer things of the periphery—benign exceptions to an otherwise "healthy" state of affairs. In recent times the difference between total and non-total institutions seems to be one of degree, not kind; increasingly, as society becomes more and more bureaucratized, the individual feels powerless and "used" in all his institutional involvements.

The key to the totalness of institutions in modern society, and to the connection between total institutions and extreme situations, is to be found in the nature of the functionary-inmate relationship. *The more total the institution, the more specifically and completely bureaucratic is this relationship*. A total institution, in this reckoning, is nothing more than one which is comparatively (in the limiting case, completely) free from the restraints ordinarily imposed on functionaries by law and sentiment, and has molded its canons of procedure in accordance with the logic and spirit of bureaucracy to the maximum degree. This means that the rights and duties the individual has by virtue of being part of a political community are suspended.

The only rights and duties that count in a fully bureaucratized situation are those which are *functionally rational*: i.e., rights and duties derived from the requirements of the position the individual occupies in relation to the organizational mission. Since the inmate has no organizational function (he is there to be acted on rather than to act) he has no duties, *and no rights*. The functionary, on the other hand, has not only the right but the duty to abolish all considerations of law or sentiment in his relations with the inmate, and to deal with him as one would with a horse or a block of wood: to refashion it, use it, or destroy it, depending on circumstances and needs as they are defined by the institution.

This is, of course, to state the furthest logical possibility. In practice, the

total institutions Goffman describes are not able to carry functional rationalization this far. There are too many inhibiting factors—not only of the
formal, juridical sort, through which the state stands ready to protect the
civil rights of inmates, but also as a matter of custom. The tradition of respect
for the individual and the Kantian imperative that men ought to be treated
as ends, not means, is a powerful feature of the Western cultural heritage.
Unless countered, it can be expected to soften and "corrupt" bureaucratic
relationships with a leavening humanitarian sentiment. Nonetheless, we have
the example of the systematic destruction of the European Jews by the Nazis
to remind us that it *can* be countered. The gigantic extermination camp of
Auschwitz, and, to a lesser extent the German and Russian concentration
camps, closely approximate the pure conceptual model of an institution in
which functional rationality operates untrammeled. At Auschwitz, which had
the capacity to gas and burn 15,000 people a day, even the universally condemned but still human sentiments of cruelty and sadism could hardly be
said to exist in the bureaucracy.

It should be clear, now, that our leading proposition is this: *Total institutions produce extreme situations.* Moreover, the totalness of institutions in
modern society is a product of universal and pervasive bureaucratization. The
spirit of bureaucracy, its characteristic bent, is to transform people into
objects, objects into means, laws into rules of procedure, and all ends into
means to the one, penultimate end, which is the organizational mission.
Since they cannot be functionally rationalized, tradition and sentiment are
banned as irrelevant—except for the one sentiment which is functional, that
a man should conscientiously and efficiently carry out his assigned duty.[6]
The functionary finds it easier to do his job thoroughly and well if the inmate
with whom he deals is without power to mount a moral or legal claim against
him. Which is to say, a situation that is extreme for the inmate, as an inmate,
is ideal for the functionary, as a functionary.

Extreme situations, in this sociological reformulation, are those in which
the interaction between functionary and inmate is carried on without effective governance by societal norms. Since the situation is novel for both parties and is the result of an evolutionary process (bureaucratic functional
rationalization), we may say it is *de-normed*. Specifically, it is *de-moralized*
(humanitarian sentiment is ruled out) and *de-legalized* (law, in the form of
guarantees of civil rights, is ruled out). The process viewed comprehensively
may be called *denormatization*.

Six empirical instances of extreme situations, within the limits of this
broadened definition, are considered below. In each case we will now try to
establish the extent to which our conceptual model applies, and the sense
in which they may call extreme.

---

[6] For an elaboration of the thesis, see Hannah Arendt, *Eichman in Jerusalem: A
Report on the Banality of Evil.* New York: Viking, 1963.

SIX EMPIRICAL TYPES OF
EXTREME SITUATIONS

1. MENTAL HOSPITALIZATION. The hospitalized mental patient is only marginally subject to tolerated extralegal punishment or exploitation for private ends (such as sadistic amusement), and not at all to functionally rational destruction. Still, he is enmeshed in a profound threat to the self. His civil rights have been adjudicated and may be readjudicated at any time, and those on which he can effectively count are greatly diminished. (For example, his testimony may be discounted as a function of the illness for which he was committed.) The hospital as an institution is ordinarily isolated, and this gives the management and staff a comparatively free hand to set the scope of moral and legal propriety obtaining in their relation to inmates. They have the power to make their definition of social reality prevail.

Nor is the patient altogether free from realistic anxiety that he may be "destroyed" on functionally rational grounds. Lobotomy (surgical destruction of portions of the brain) was common a few years ago, and there is no question but that it was capable of producing permanent alterations in the self. Convulsive drugs and electric shock are still used in some hospitals. Whether or not these techniques will be entirely supplanted by the new tranquillizing drugs (it seems they may), it is still true, as Goffman and Krim remind us, that the values and attitudes the patient is implicitly asked to give up or accept as a condition of release from forcible confinement are in effect pressure to alter the self—a comparatively limited but nonetheless real form of destruction. It seems fair to conclude that extreme situations are a characteristic feature of hospitalization for mental illness regardless of specific treatment technique. The situation of the hospital inmate is certainly less extreme than that of his counterpart in a concentration camp, but the difference is neither qualitative nor decisive.

2. CONCENTRATION CAMPS. The original psychological approach to extreme situations stemmed from the experience of concentration camp inmates. Influenced, as it was, by Bruno Bettelheim's discussion,[7] the sociological model formulated above shows a relatively close fit with the facts of "life" in a concentration camp. But there are some anomalies.

To begin with, evidence of "legality" exists in the fact that guards were sporadically forbidden to mistreat inmates. Granting all possible elasticity to the operative conception of "mistreatment," there still seems to be law. But is there? The model of a total institution, it will be recalled, specifies three things: demoralization, delegalization, and functional rationalization. Were the SS guards forbidden on *moral* or *legal* grounds to mistreat inmates?

If the grounds were moral, there should be evidence of moral opprobrium

---

[7] Bruno Bettelheim, "Individual and Mass Behavior in Extreme Situations," *Journal of Abnormal and Social Psychology*, vol. 38 (October, 1943), pp. 417–452.

as a factor in the situation, and whatever there was would surely have been sensed by the inmates. But survivors testify that smaller, personalized acts were more keenly resented than occasional outright atrocities. Paradoxically, a considered slap in the face was more enraging than a random kick in the groin or two hours of pushups for a whole barracks in freezing mud. To qualify as morally significant, an act must call into question values which are generically human, not just those involving the safety of the person; it seems clear that when the typical SS man was inhibited at all, his grounds were not moral principle.

If the grounds were legal, there should be evidence that inmates could bring charges against the guards alleging violation of their civil rights. We are told that this occasionally took place, and in at least one instance the abuses complained of were halted. But the scarcity of such reports forces us to conclude that instances of this sort were most exceptional; they do not constitute evidence that inmates had even rudimentary civil rights. There was no rule of law in the concentration camp.

The fact that custodians were officially forbidden to mistreat their charges is more plausibly explained as evidence of functional rationality than of legality. It was not the "rights" of the inmates but the welfare of the SS as an organization that was at issue. It would have been contrary to its interests officially to permit its personnel to act as individuals in pursuit of purely private ends like sadistic gratification. The ultimately important (this is, functionally rational) thing was to forge the SS into an effective instrument and maintain it as such. It was functionally rational to look the other way when individual guards "irrationally" abused inmates, and even covertly to encourage such conduct as part of the hardening process for new recruits. But it would have been functionally irrational to permit them to forget that they were SS men, and under orders.

3. THE INEFFECTIVE STATE. A society which tolerates an ineffective set of institutions for securing justice and preserving order is divided, at war with itself. The individual citizen under such circumstances theoretically has the full complement of liberties guaranteed by civilized society, but in actuality they are more or less without effect. He is at the mercy of quasiofficial forces operating outside the law, either as vigilantes or guerrillas.

The Negro in the American rural South at first place has little in common with the inmate of a mental hospital or a concentration camp. His daily round of activities is not closely scrutinized, nor does society have plans for him. Simply by virtue of the looseness of the milieu he is not subject to daily harassment by guards or custodians, and if he does run the risk of being marked down in somebody's book as an "uppity Negro" there is no certainty that anything will be done about it. On the other hand, however, 100 years after emancipation the Negro is still denied full civil rights, and there are functionally rational grounds for this denial. Once it is assumed that Negroes must be kept from the seats of social power (ostensibly in order to prevent "mongrelization" through race mixing), the only power strong enough to nullify constitutional guarantees specifically providing for equality of access is the tightly organized, ever-vigilant local community. Passively or actively, it has to support a shadow-state, a state operating paradoxically outside the law, if the repression is to be effective.

Such a shadow-state is institutionalized vigilantism. Within its jurisdiction the Negro lives in the expectation that he may become at any moment an object of interest to its agencies; if he does, he can expect to be insulted, assaulted, jailed on trumped-up charges, denied due process of law in court, or even lynched—and all with relative impunity. He falls within a specially designated category in society, one that has the effect of freeing social functionaries from ordinary moral and legal limitations on the exercise of their discretion. Moreover, while they can and do use their freedom to exploit the Negro in his helplessness for private ends, legal and extralegal functionaries make it a matter of public duty to act effectively to "keep the nigger in his place." The situation of Negroes in the American South is significantly de-moralized and de-legalized, and functional rationality rather than simple corruption (which is functionally irrational) is the spirit of its structure. Thus it can be characterized as extreme within the limits of our definition.

The recent period of communal war in Algeria exemplifies the second type of shadow-state produced by the power vacuum of the ineffective state: the guerrilla underground. The essential difference between the two is that vigilantes seek to preserve the status quo while guerrillas seek to change it. Both make use of mass terror, although vigilantism has the advantage of operating in a context in which its techniques are already institutionalized. Guerrillas have to build up institutions of mass terror—which accounts in part for the comparatively greater savagery of their tactics.

In Algeria, the official agencies of society (the military forces, the police) initially failed to protect Europeans against terrorism by the Moslem FLN, and then failed to defend Moslems against counter-terrorism by the OAS, the European underground "Secret Army." The acts of terrorism in both cases were assaults by competing agencies of society—unofficially, of course, but still the rival underground organizations were acting for public, not private purposes—upon individuals just because they could be categorically identified as Moslems or Europeans. These actions were (presumptively) justified on functionally rational grounds as means to a socially necessary end: victory for the "right" and "just" cause. It is in the nature of underground warfare that a functionary "on business" must strike hard and run fast; neither of the rival underground organizations recognized moral or legal limitations on the scope of their "legitimate" discretion.

The situation of anyone caught in this crossfire is clearly extreme. It is de-moralized, de-legalized, and functionally rationalized. From the standpoint of a quasi-official agency of society (the guerrilla underground), the individual is an object to be manipulated or destroyed in the course of realizing an imperative social purpose, and not a human subject with inescapable moral and legal claims on it, precisely because it presumes to speak for the collectivity.

4. THE TOTALITARIAN STATE. Totalitarianism has been defined as the union of tyranny with (modern) technology. Governments which set themselves above the law are as old as civilization, but the ability of such regimes to stabilize and indefinitely extend their rule is as new as electronic communications and rational-legal bureaucracy. Totalitarianism is more than just old-fashioned tyranny by nontraditional means; its *purposes* are unprecedented as well. The new techniques have broadened the state's ability to act, and also the conception of what it should properly seek. The sheer technical possibilities for thoroughgoing social reorganization have become so compelling that the social good they point to has seemed, in time of crisis, to justify setting aside established immunities and guarantees to the individual. Once the social end becomes paramount, the individual is stripped of all but derivative value, value as means. If he cannot be "coercively persuaded"—"brainwashed"—to become a willing instrument, he may still find use as an *un*willing instrument: a scapegoat. Those whose social usefulness is questionable, on grounds of political unreliability or personal incapacity, may be classified as "objectively criminal" or "asocial." Both types are "surplus" and subject to "liquidation."

The totalitarian secret police is freed from all moral and legal restraint in dealing with individuals who fall into one of the "surplus" categories. A thoroughgoing functional rationality demands that nothing should stand in the way of ridding society of the threat posed by "objective criminals" (those thought to be predisposed to commit crimes against the state because of their class or "racial" identity) and the "waste" incurred in maintaining the "socially useless." (The secret police, like any other bureaucratic organization, needs these provisos in order to be able to act. Which things come first, and why? Is the proposed action worth what it will cost? Will pursuing it interfere with some other end? Determining costs and setting priorities requires relatively unambiguous criteria; this is as true of the totalitarian state as of any other organization in the modern world.)

The administrative designation of a certain category of persons as "objectively criminal" or "asocial" automatically places everyone so labelled in an extreme situation, as we have defined it. It has the immediate effect of stripping away the immunities conferred by citizenship; the situation so produced is de-legalized. Functional rationality, demanding a speedy and expeditious "solution," then, excludes all moral considerations as nonrational (for example, as "bourgeois sentimentality"); the situation becomes de-moralized as well.

When the categories "legitimately" subject to police terror are indefinitely broadened, as in the tendency of this institutional order, everyone is in an extreme situation. This is totalitarianism full-fledged: all moral and legal limitations on the state's freedom of action in relation to the individual become revocable privileges, capable at any moment of being set aside. Hannah

Arendt argues that a society so constituted has a built-in need for ever new categories of "surplus populations"—to be destroyed in the interest of what is called the common good.

5. GENOCIDE. Hilberg appropriately speaks of the *destruction* of the European Jews. Terms like "killing" or "murder" do not convey the meaning of genocide, because they have moral and legal overtones. For the Germans—like Adolph Eichmann—who planned and carried out this largest of all "actions"—there was no question of morality or legality. Only the end-in-view was relevant: the "cleansing" of Europe of what were officially taken to be vermin in human form. (The meaning of the "final solution to the Jewish question" to the Nazi bureaucrats who conducted the operation is best conveyed by their use of terms like "Judenfrei" and "Judenrein" to describe areas "free" or "cleansed" of Jews. If we take their repeated attestations at face value, they thought of themselves as engaged in a uniquely difficult and dangerous public health campaign. This is shown by their recognition of the danger that those who actually invented and implemented the techniques of extermination might deteriorate morally; they took extraordinary measures to sustain the myth that a conspiracy to commit mass murder, as judged by civilized society, was actually an heroic task.

Paradoxical as it sounds, and regardless of the horror and moral revulsion the destruction of the European Jews evokes in the civilized conscience, in the sociological sense the act was amoral and alegal. A Nazi functionary might act humanely or inhumanely, correctly (that is, dutifully) or incorrectly, in relation to an individual designated for transportation to the gas chambers, but *in the context of that relationship* he could not meaningfully commit an immoral or illegal act. An outsider (or an insider, for that matter) might judge an act to be immoral or criminal, but in doing so he would have to invoke norms of conduct simply not operative in that situation. A man cannot meaningfully commit a crime against a horse, for example, although he may act inhumanely; similarly, an SS man could not meaningfully commit a crime against a member of a "racial" or "asocial" category slated for extermination.

We have here, finally, the very essence of the extreme situation: the individual has neither a moral nor a legal claim on society. He is bereft and victimized, or simply destroyed. The totalitarian state abrogates the Hobbesian social contract; but, instead of a return to the war of all against all, there is the newly established war of all against one.

6. THERMONUCLEAR WAR. The situation of the soldier in combat affords one version of what we have called extreme situations: there is the individual being shot at for no other reason that that he is categorically identifiable (as "the enemy") by functionaries who know no restraint, moral or legal, in their efforts to kill him. They are governed solely by considerations of functional rationality. However, this is true only under certain conditions. "All's fair in love and war" needs some qualification, if it is to be accurately descriptive of the state of the norms. Civilized nations have always been quick to make propaganda capital out of atrocities allegedly committed

by their enemies, and the very idea of "atrocity" presupposes normative criteria capable of distinguishing between the atrocious and the nonatrocious. During any actual test of arms, functional rationality tends to be the supreme arbiter. But this is only one of many situations the soldier will encounter. Most of the time he is in uniform he is out of the enemy's reach. If he is reached and not killed but captured instead, as a prisoner of war he has all sorts of immunities (in principle) against immoral or illegal intrusions by enemy functionaries.

As social relationships are altered by the introduction of thermonuclear weapons, two sets of distinctions get blurred: between front and rear echelon troops, and between soldiers and civilians. This means, quite simply, that combatants now run no greater risk of getting killed than noncombatants. Everyone is within reach of enemy weapons, and everyone is a target. The effect of thermonuclear weapons and the tactics they demand is to transform what existentialists call the human condition into what we have been calling an extreme situation. The individual is an object of interest to wartime functionaries not for what he does but for what he is: part of a social category designated "the enemy." Moreover, he is "the enemy" in a new and dehumanized form. In the functionaries' decision to kill him or not to kill him, and how, is entirely an expression of functional rationality. Against those who have the power and may find it necessary (that is, rational) to annihilate him and his social type, he has no moral or legal claim.

Given the full development and diffusion of established weapons capabilities, every inhabitant of the globe will eventually find himself in this demoralized, de-legalized extreme situation.

SUMMARY AND CONCLUSIONS

To restate the main points of this discussion: an important share of human behavior in extreme situations can be imputed to norms and institutions, hence it is problematic for sociology as well as psychology;[8] the decisive characteristic of extreme situations in sociological perspective is that they have been denormatized—morality and legality have more and more been supplanted by functional rationality as *the* operative norm of conduct; extreme situations, in turn, are themselves the characteristic product of total institutions; finally, the fact that extreme situations can be demonstrated to occur outside the confines of total institutions is evidence that their spirit and structure tend to pervade modern society.

There are two conclusions to be drawn from this, one substantive, one programmatic.

The substantive conclusion concerns the nature of modern society and

---

[8] The differences between the sociological and psychological approaches to the study of concentration camps are discussed below, from the sociological point of view, by Emil Luchterhand. The uses and limitations of the psychological approach are exemplified in Hilde Bluhm's article.

bears closely on the theme of this book. In our review, we found that total institutions occur in nontotalitarian social structures, and extreme situations are not confined to total institutions. Does it not follow that the ultimate source of extreme situations must be located in society itself? If so, it makes little sense to continue looking for facts to support the view that institutional *breakdown* is the cause of the present crisis of world society. The closer we look the stronger is the evidence that the prime actors in the establishments and social enterprises that produce extreme situations cannot be described as criminals or madmen. Rather, they resemble the archetypal self-transcending hero (the dutiful functionary, the inspired fanatic) of our Western cultural heritage. It is not the failure of institutions that is the cause of our deepest trouble but their success.

The programmatic conclusion derives from this terrible paradox. Our civilization prides itself on unprecedented thoroughness in exploiting scientific technique, efficiency in organizing large numbers of people for cooperative enterprise, largeness of vision in the conception of welfare, and intensity of dedication to the ideal of duty in one's calling—work for the common good. And yet, it is just these virtues that made possible the destruction of the European Jews and now threatens the extinction of civilization through thermonuclear war.

What can be done? The social scientist's answer has to be—as always—more and better research, but of the sort that is all but impossible to organize and carry out on a large-scale, mechanized basis. The need specifically is for broad, comparative, and historical studies addressed to some of the prescient questions raised by Durkheim and Weber half a century ago. Self-knowledge, knowledge of what Weber called "this parcelling-out of the soul" produced by bureaucratization and massification, was never before so urgently needed. For example, we need to know why and how occupational psychosis—functional rationality—threatens to become the ethos of the new age. Unless we improve our understanding of such processes there will be little change to forestall them or blunt their tendency to produce extreme situations.

6. MENTAL HOSPITALS

The Insanity Bit

SEYMOUR KRIM

I was as wrong as you can be and still live to tell about it. In the summer of 1955, when I was 33, the thousand unacknowledged human (not literary!) pressures in my being exploded. I ran barefooted in the streets, spat at members of my family, exposed myself, was almost bodily thrown out of the house of a Nobel Prize-winning author, and believed God had ordained me to act out every conceivable human impulse without an ounce of hypocritical caution. I know today that my instinct was sound, but my reasoning was self-deceptive. It was not God who ordained me, but I who ordained God for my own understandable human purposes. I needed an excuse to force some sort of balance between my bulging inner life and my timid outer behaviour, and I chose the greatest and most comforting symbol of them all. He was my lance and my shield as I tore through the New York streets acting out the bitter rot of a world-full of frustrations that my human nature could no longer lock up. I was finally cornered on the 14th floor of the St. Regis Hotel by two frightened friends and another brother; and with the aid of handcuffs seriously-humorously clipped on by a couple of bobbies I was led off to Bellevue, convinced all along that I was right. I tolerated those who took me away with the kindly condescension of a fake Jesus.

From Bellevue I was soon transferred to a private laughing academy in Westchester and given insulin-shock treatments. No deep attempt was made to diagnose my "case"—except the superficial and inaccurate judgment that I had "hallucinated." Factually, this was not true; I did not have visual images of people or objects which were not there; I merely believed, with the beautiful relief of absolute justice which the soul of man finds when life becomes unbearable, that God had given me the right and the duty to do everything openly that I had secretly fantasied for years. But this distinction was not gone into by my judges and indifferent captors. They did not have the time, the patience, or even the interest because work in a flip-factory is determined by mathematics; you must find a common denominator of categoriza-

SOURCE: Seymour Krim, "The Insanity Bit," in Seymour Krim (ed.), *The Beats* (New York: Fawcett, 1960). Reprinted by permission.

tion and treatment in order to handle the battalions of miscellaneous humanity that are marched past your desk with high trumpets blowing in their minds.

Like all the other patients, I was considered beyond reasoning with and was treated like a child; not brutally, but efficiently, firmly and patronizingly. In the eyes of this enclosed world I had relinquished my rights as an adult human being. The causes for my explosion were not even superficially examined, nor was the cheek-pinching house psychiatrist—with a fresh flower in the button hole of his fresh daily suit—truly equipped to cope with it even if he had tried, which he did not. Private sanitariums and state institutions, I realized much later, were isolation chambers rather than hospitals in the usual sense; mechanical "cures" such as the one I underwent in a setup of unchallenged authority, like the Army or a humanitarian prison, slowly brought 75 per cent of the inmates down to a more temporarily modest view of reality. Within nine or ten weeks I too came down, humbled, ashamed, willing to stand up before the class and repeat the middle-class credo of limited expressiveness and the meaning of a dollar in order to get my discharge.

In three months' time I was out, shaken, completely alone, living in a cheap Broadway hotel-room (having been ashamed to go back to Greenwich Village) and going to a conventional Ph.D. psychologist (I had been to three medically-trained therapists in the preceding decade) as a sop to both my conscience and family. I had broken beyond the bounds of "reality"—a shorthand word which is used by the average psychiatrist for want of the more truthfully complex approach that must eventually accommodate our beings' increasing flights into higher altitudes—and come back to the position I was in before. But once again the causes that had flung me into my own sky continued to eat me up. Sexually unconfident, I went to whores, ate my meals alone, and forced myself to write a few pieces in that loneliest of places, a tiny blank hotel-room in the middle of nowhere. For the first time in my life the incentive to live, the isolation and frustration of my existence, grew dim; while the psychologist smiled and smoked his pipe—and did the well-adjusted, tweedy, urbane act behind his tastefully battered desk as he ladled out platitudes—I was saving up the sleeping bombs, and when I had enough to do the trick I burned the letters I had received through the years from the several men and women I had loved, destroyed my journal of 15 years' standing, and one carefully chosen night went to a hotel in Newark, N. J.

My plan was to take the pills and slowly conk out in the full bathtub, ultimately drowning like Thomas Heggen; if one missed the other would work. I splurged on a beautiful deathroom in a modernistic hotel, one that included a bathroom with the biggest tub in the house. But it was too small to fit my long body. The idea of not being able to drown and of surviving the pills afterwards, perhaps to become a burden or an invalid, began to scar what seemed like the paradise of suicide. I went instead to a Polish bar in downtown Newark, vaguely seeking the eternal anodynes of snatch and booze while I mentally played with my fate.

I found the booze, and saw a coarse, ignorant Polish girl do such a life-giving, saucy, raucous folk-dance (on the small dance-floor to the right of the bar) that I broke into loving sobs like prayers over my drink. The sun of life blazed from her into my grateful heart. I went back to the beautiful hotel-room, poured the pills down the toilet, and went to sleep. The next morning I returned to Manhattan a chastened man, shaking my head at how close I had come to non-being.

When I told my tale to Mr. Pipe, my psychologist, he speedily hustled me off to a legitimate head-doctor who doped me until a private ambulance came. Very much in my right and one and only mind but too paralyzed by drugs to move, I was once again taken on the long ride—this time to another hedge-trimmed bin in Long Island. I was helpless to protest, mainly because of the shame and guilt I felt for even contemplating suicide. Obviously I was not crazy, mad, psychotic, out of my mind, schizophrenic, paranoiac. I was simply a tormented man-kid who had never steeled himself to face the facts of life—who didn't know what it meant to have principles and live by them come grief or joy—and who thought that human worth and true independence comes as easily as it does in the movies we were all emotionally faked on. As a sputtering fiction-writer and fairly active literary critic, I had had occasional peaks of maturity and illumination; but as a man I was self-deceptive, self-indulgent, crying inwardly for the pleasures of a college-boy even while in my imagination I saw myself as another Ibsen or Dreiser. Ah, the extraordinary mismating of thoughts in the mind of the modern American literary romantic, as fantastic and truly unbelievable a stew of unrelated dreams as have ever been dreamt, believe me!

Once again I was on the human assembly-line: electric shock clubbed my good brain into needless unconsciousness (and I walked to my several executions like a brave little chappie instead of questioning them) and unquestioned Old Testament authority ruled our little club. Good-natured, but mostly cowlike and uneducated male orderlies carried out the orders from above; and apart from the mechanical treatment and the unimaginative grind of occupational therapy, each patient was left completely on his or her bewildered own, a sad and farcical sight when one considered the $125 per week that their frightened families were paying.

I saw now that nine-tenths of the people I was quartered with were not "insane" by any of the standards a normally intelligent person would use: the majority had lost confidence in their own ability to survive in the world outside, or their families were *afraid* of them and had palmed them off on "experts," but positively no serious effort was being made to equip them to become free and independent adults. This was their birthright—beyond country and society, indeed an almost religious obligation—but they were palliated with pills or jolted with shock, their often honest rage echoed back to them as a sign of their "illness." Some of them must have been "sick," you say. I answer: Who can not be conceived as such in a world so complex ("The truth is there is a truth on every side"—Richard Eberhart) that each group has its own method for judging manners, behaviour, ideas, and finally the worth of human values? What was more important was that I, a person from a hip milieu and with a completely opposite set of values, could see their so-called sickness with the human sensibility that an immersion in literature and experience had given to me—rather than as a clinical manifestation. When I later recognized the objective provinciality of many psychiatrists in precisely the humanistic areas that could cover the actions of the majority of the inmates without finding it "psychotic," I realized that the independent thinker and artist today must learn to be resolute towards a subtle, socially powerful god-father who often drips paternalism: namely, the newly-enthroned psychiatric minority that has elevated itself to a dangerous position of "authority" in the crucial issues of mind, personality, and sanity.

I now began to fight persistently—but still with shakiness—for my release; my life was my own; it did not belong to the cliches of the salesman-aggressive, well-barbered, Jewish refugee (my brother, my enemy!) house psychiatrist or to my smiling, betweeded nonentity of a psychologist, who paid me diplomatically inscrutable visits like a Japanese ambassador. Even if I had been or if there were such a reality as a "raving maniac"—which, perhaps childishly, I implore the over-imaginative, zeitgeist-vulnerable reader to believe is an impossible conception today—I would and should have fought for my release. What the institution-spared layman does not realize is that a sensitive and multiple-reacting human being remains the same everywhere, including a sanitarium, and such an environment can duplicate the injustice or vulgarity which drove your person there in the first place. By this I mean that a mental hospital is not an asylum or a sanctuary in the old-fashioned sense: it is just a roped-off side-street of modern existence, rife with as many contradictions, half-truths and lousy architecture as life itself.

Both of the sanitariums I was in were comparable to Grossinger's, in that they took in only financially comfortable, conventionally middle-class, non-intellectual people. By every human standard my being there was life's sarcastic answer to whatever romantic ideas I had about justice. Since the age of 19 I had deliberately led an existence of experimentation, pursuit of truth, bohemianism, and non-commercialism: fate's punishment for my green naivete was for me to recover my supposed mental health in this atmosphere of uncriticizable authority, air-conditioned by just the whiffs of truth that are perfumed and bland, and based on a pillar of middle-class propriety with the cut-throat reality of money underneath. Could I accept my former life, which had produced some good work, as a lie to myself— which the house-psychiatrist wanted me to do (in effect) in his one psychotherapeutic pass at me (he left me alone after this)? I could not and never would: not only for myself but for the great principles and accomplishments of others, both living and dead, which had been my guide throughout my adult life. I might fail—but why go on having an identity at all if in a crisis you will throw away not only your past years, but the moral achievements of rare souls who have shared in your emotional and intellectual experience and whose own contributions to existence are also at stake?

When I heard this second house-psychiatrist literally equate sanity with the current cliches of adjustment and describe Greenwich Village as a "psychotic community," I saw with clarity that *insanity* and *psychosis* can no longer be respected as meaningful definitions—but are used by limited individuals in positions of social power to describe ways of behaving and thinking that are alien, threatening, and *obscure* to them. (A year later when I took a psychiatrist friend of mine to the San Remo, she told me with a straight face that it reminded her of the "admission ward in Bellevue," where she had interned. This was her analogy on the basis of accurate but limited experience, that increasing chasm which separates intelligent people from understanding each other. I realized with a sense of almost incommunicable hopelessness that the gap between her and the well-known poet with whom I had had a beer at the Remo two weeks before was tremendous, and that between these two poles of intelligence the neutral person—who could see the logic of each —was being mashed up with doubt and conflict. The poet was at home, or at least the heat was off, there; while the psychiatrist felt alien and had made a contemptuous psycho-sociological generalization. There was little bond of shared values and therefore genuine communication between both of these intelligent and honest human beings, each of whom contributed to my life.)

To finish with my four months in the sanitarium: I argued and reasoned for the basic right to the insecurity of freedom, and finally a good friend did the dirty in-fighting of getting me out. Had I to do it over again, I believe I would now have the guts to threaten such an institution or psychologist with a law suit, ugly as such a procedure can be to a person already vulnerable with the hash-marks of one legally defined "psychotic episode" and the contemplation of the criminal act of suicide. But I had been—as so many of Jack Kerouac's subterraneans are when faced with the machinery of official society—milk and sawdust when, in such situations, you must be iron and stone in spite of your own frailty. It is not that the present-day authorities of mental life want to railroad anyone, as in your Grade C horror movie; it is merely that as one grows older it becomes clear that there are almost unremediable differences between people in the total outlook towards life.

Mine had hardened as a result of my experiences, and I realized it was better to die out in the world, if need be, than be deprived of the necessity to confront existence behind the cheap authority of a lock and key. The majority of people who stay in mental institutions for any length of time do not want to return to the uncertain conditions outside the walls: which in our time spells out to emotionally anarchic, multi-dimenisonal, brain-trying, anxiety-loaded, and—O hear me mortality, from the year one!—ultimate and divine life.

The Moral Career of the Mental Patient: The Inpatient Phase

ERVING GOFFMAN

The last step in the prepatient's career can involve his realization—justified or not—that he has been deserted by society and turned out of relationships by those closest to him. Interestingly enough, the patient, especially a first admission, may manage to keep himself from coming to the end of this trail, even though in fact he is now in a locked mental-hospital ward. On entering the hospital, he may very strongly feel the desire not to be known to anyone as a person who could possibly be reduced to these present circumstances, or as a person who conducted himself in the way he did prior to commitment. Consequently, he may avoid talking to anyone, may stay by himself when possible, and may even be "out of contact" or "manic" so as to avoid ratifying any interaction that presses a politely reciprocal role upon him and opens him up to what he has become in the eyes of others. When the next-of-relation makes an effort to visit, he may be rejected by mutism, or by the patient's refusal to enter the visiting room, these strategies sometimes suggesting that the patient still clings to a remnant of relatedness to those who made up his past, and is protecting this remnant from the final destructiveness of dealing with the new people that they have become.[1]

Usually the patient comes to give up this taxing effort at anonymity, at not-hereness, and begins to present himself for conventional social interaction to the hospital community. Thereafter he withdraws only in special ways—by always using his nickname, by signing his contribution to the patient weekly with his initial only, or by using the innocuous "cover" address tactfully provided by some hospitals; or he withdraws only at special times, when, say, a flock of nursing students makes a passing tour of the ward, or when, paroled to the hospital grounds, he suddenly sees he is about to cross the path of a civilian he happens to know from home. Sometimes this making of oneself available is called "settling down" by the attendants. It marks a new

SOURCE: Erving Goffman "The Moral Career of the Mental Patient," *Psychiatry*, 22 (1959), pp. 123–142. Copyright by The William Alanson White Psychiatric Foundation, Inc. Reprinted by special permission of The William Alanson White Psychiatric Foundation, Inc.

[1] The inmate's initial strategy of holding himself aloof from ratifying contact may partly account for the relative lack of group formation among inmates in public mental hospitals, a connection that has been suggested to me by William R. Smith. The desire to avoid personal bonds that would give licence to the asking of biographical questions could also be a factor. In mental hospitals, of course, as in prisoner camps, the staff may consciously break up incipient group formation in order to avoid collective rebellious action and other ward disturbances.

stand openly taken and supported by the patient, and resembles the "coming-out" process that occurs in other groupings.[2]

Once the prepatient begins to settle down, the main outlines of his fate tend to follow those of a whole class of segregated establishments—jails, concentration camps, monasteries, work camps, and so on—in which the inmate spends the whole round of life on the grounds, and marches through his regimented day in the immediate company of a group of persons of his own institutional status.

Like the neophyte in many of these total institutions, the new inpatient finds himself cleanly stripped of many of his accustomed affirmations, satisfactions, and defenses, and is subjected to a rather full set of mortifying experiences: restriction of free movement, communal living, diffuse authority of a whole echelon of people, and so on. Here one begins to learn about the extent to which a conception of oneself can be sustained when the usual setting of supports for it are suddenly removed.

While undergoing these humbling moral experiences, the inpatient learns to orient himself in terms of the "ward system."[3] In public mental hospitals this usually consists of a series of graded living arrangements built around wards, administrative units called services, and parole statuses. The "worst" level often involves nothing but wooden benches to sit on, some quite indifferent food, and a small piece of room to sleep in. The "best" level may involve a room of one's own, ground and town privileges, contacts with staff that are relatively undamaging, and what is seen as good food and ample recreational facilities. For disobeying the pervasive house rules, the inmate will receive stringent punishments expressed in terms of loss of privileges; for obedience he will eventually be allowed to acquire some of the minor satisfactions he took for granted on the outside.

The institutionalization of these radically different levels of living throws light on the implications for self of social settings. And this in turn affirms that the self arises not merely out of its possessor's interactions with significant others, but also out of the arrangements that are evolved in an organization for its members.

There are some settings that the person easily discounts as an expression or

---

[2] A comparable coming out occurs in the homosexual world, when a person finally comes frankly to present himself to a "gay" gathering not as a tourist but as someone who is "available." See Evelyn Hooker, "A Preliminary Analysis of Group Behavior of Homosexuals," *Journal of Psychology*, XLII (1956), pp. 217–25; see especially p. 221. A good fictionalized treatment may be found in James Baldwin's *Giovanni's Room* (New York: Dial, 1956), pp. 41–57. A familiar instance of the coming-out process is no doubt to be found among prepubertal children at the moment one of these actors sidles *back* into a room that had been left in an angered huff and injured *amour propre*. The phrase itself presumably derives from a *rite-de-passage* ceremony once arranged by upper-class mothers for their daughters. Interestingly enough, in large mental hospitals the patient sometimes symbolizes a complete coming out by his first active participation in the hospital-wide patient dance.

[3] A good description of the ward system may be found in Ivan Belknap, *Human Problems of a State Mental Hospital* (New York: McGraw-Hill, 1956), ch. ix, especially p. 164.

extension of him. When a tourist goes slumming, he may take pleasure in the situation not because it is a reflection of him but because it so assuredly is not. There are other settings, such as living rooms, which the person manages on his own and employs to influence in a favorable direction other persons' views of him. And there are still other settings, such as a work place, which express the employee's occupational status, but over which he has no final control, this being exerted, however tactfully, by his employer. Mental hospitals provide an extreme instance of this latter possibility. And this is due not merely to their uniquely degraded living levels, but also to the unique way in which significance for self is made explicit to the patient, piercingly, persistently, and thoroughly. Once lodged on a given ward, the patient is firmly instructed that the restrictions and deprivations he encounters are not due to such blind forces as tradition or economy—and hence dissociable from self—but are intentional parts of his treatment, part of his need at the time, and therefore an expression of the state that his self has fallen to. Having every reason to initiate requests for better conditions, he is told that when the staff feel he is "able to manage" or will be "comfortable with" a higher ward level, then appropriate action will be taken. In short, assignment to a given ward is presented not as a reward or punishment, but as an expression of his general level of social functioning, his status as a person. Given the fact that the worst ward levels provide a round of life that inpatients with organic brain damage can easily manage, and that these quite limited human beings are present to prove it, one can appreciate some of the mirroring effects of the hospital.[4]

The ward system, then, is an extreme instance of how the physical facts of an establishment can be explicitly employed to frame the conception a person takes of himself. In addition, the official psychiatric mandate of mental hospitals gives rise to even more direct, even more blatant, attacks upon the inmate's view of himself. The more "medical" and the more progressive a mental hospital is—the more it attempts to be therapeutic and not merely custodial—the more he may be confronted by high-ranking staff arguing that his past has been a failure, that the cause of this has been within himself, that his attitude to life is wrong, and that if he wants to be a person he will have to change his way of dealing with people and his conceptions of himself. Often the moral value of these verbal assaults will be brought home to him by requiring him to practice taking this psychiatric view of himself in arranged confessional periods, whether in private sessions or group psychotherapy.

Now a general point may be made about the moral career of inpatients which has bearing on many moral careers. Given the stage that any person

---

[4] Here is one way in which mental hospitals can be worse than concentration camps and prisons as places in which to "do" time; in the latter, self-insulation from the symbolic implications of the settings may be easier. In fact, self-insulation from hospital settings may be so difficult that patients have to employ devices for this which staff interpret as psychotic symptoms.

has reached in a career, one typically finds that he constructs an image of his life course—past, present, and future—which selects, abstracts, and distorts in such a way as to provide him with a view of himself that he can usefully expound in current situations. Quite generally, the person's line concerning self defensively brings him into appropriate alignment with the basic values of his society, and so may be called an apologia. If the person can manage to present a view of his current situation which shows the operation of favorable personal qualities in the past and a favorable destiny awaiting him, it may be called a success story. If the facts of a person's past and present are extremely dismal, then about the best he can do is to show that he is not responsible for what has become of him, and the term sad tale is appropriate. Interestingly enough, the more the person's past forces him out of apparent alignment with central moral values, the more often he seems compelled to tell his sad tale in any company in which he finds himself. Perhaps he partly responds to the need he feels in others of not having their sense of proper life courses affronted. In any case, it is among convicts, "winos," and prostitutes that one seems to obtain sad tales the most readily.[5] It is the vicissitudes of the mental patient's sad tale that I want to consider now.

In the mental hospital, the setting and the house rules press home to the patient that he is, after all, a mental case who has suffered some kind of social collapse on the outside, having failed in some over-all way, and that here he is of little social weight, being hardly capable of acting like a full-fledged person at all. These humiliations are likely to be most keenly felt by middle-class patients, since their previous condition of life little immunizes them against such affronts, but all patients feel some downgrading. Just as any normal member of his outside subculture would do, the patient often responds to this situation by attempting to assert a sad tale proving that he is not "sick," that the "little trouble" he did get into was really somebody else's fault, that his past life course had some honor and rectitude, and that the hospital

---

[5] In regard to convicts, see Anthony Heckstall-Smith, *Eighteen Months* (London: Allan Wingate, 1954), pp. 52–53. For "winos" see the discussion in Howard G. Bain, "A Sociological Analysis of the Chicago Skid-Row Lifeway" (Unpublished M.A. thesis, Department of Sociology, University of Chicago, September 1950), especially "The Rationale of the Skid-Row Drinking Group," pp. 141–46. Bain's neglected thesis is a useful source of material on moral careers.

Apparently one of the occupational hazards of prostitution is that clients and other professional contacts sometimes persist in expressing sympathy by asking for a defensible dramatic explanation for the fall from grace. In having to bother to have a sad tale ready, perhaps the prostitute is more to be pitied than damned. Good examples of prostitute sad tales may be found in Henry Mayhew, *London Labour and the London Poor*, Vol. IV, *Those That Will Not Work* (London: Charles Griffin and Co., 1862), pp. 210–72. For a contemporary source, see *Women of the Streets*, edited by C. H. Rolph (London: Secker and Warburg, 1955), especially p. 6: *"Almost always, however, after a few comments on the police, the girl would begin to explain how it was that she was in the life, usually in terms of self-justification. . . ."* Lately, of course, the psychological expert has helped out the profession in the construction of wholly remarkable sad tales. See, for example, Harold Greenwald, *The Call Girl* (New York: Ballantine Books, 1958).

is therefore unjust in forcing the status of mental patient upon him. This self-respecting tendency is heavily institutionalized within the patient society where opening social contacts typically involve the participants' volunteering information about their current ward location and length of stay so far, but not the reasons for their stay—such interaction being conducted in the manner of small talk on the outside.[6] With greater familiarity, each patient usually volunteers relatively acceptable reasons for his hospitalization, at the same time accepting without open immediate question the lines offered by other patients. Such stories as the following are given and overtly accepted.

I was going to night school to get a M.A. degree, and holding down a job in addition, and the load got too much for me.

The others here are sick mentally but I'm suffering from a bad nervous system and that is what is giving me these phobias.

I got here by mistake because of a diabetes diagnosis, and I'll leave in a couple of days. [The patient had been in seven weeks.]

I failed as a child, and later with my wife I reached out for dependency.

My trouble is that I can't work. That's what I'm in for. I had two jobs with a good home and all the money I wanted.[7]

The patient sometimes reinforces these stories by an optimistic definition of his occupational status. A man who managed to obtain an audition as a radio announcer styles himself a radio announcer; another who worked for some months as a copy boy and was then given a job as a reporter on a large trade journal, but fired after three weeks, defines himself as a reporter.

A whole social role in the patient community may be constructed on the basis of these reciprocally sustained fictions. For these face-to-face niceties tend to be qualified by behind-the-back gossip that comes only a degree closer to the "objective" facts. Here, of course, one can see a classic social function of informal networks of equals: they serve as one another's audience for self-supporting tales—tales that are somewhat more solid than pure fantasy and somewhat thinner than the facts.

But the patient's apologia is called forth in a unique setting, for few settings could be so destructive of self-stories except, of course, those stories already constructed along psychiatric lines. And this destructiveness rests on more than the official sheet of paper which attests that the patient is of unsound mind, a danger to himself and others—an attestation, incidentally, which seems to cut deeply into the patient's pride, and into the possibility of his having any.

---

[6] A similar self-protecting rule has been observed in prisons. Thus, Alfred Hassler, *Diary of a Self-Made Convict* (Chicago: Regnery, 1954), p. 76, in describing a conversation with a fellow prisoner: *"He didn't say much about why he was sentenced, and I didn't ask him, that being the accepted behavior in prison."* A novelistic version for the mental hospital may be found in J. Kerkhoff, *How Thin the Veil: A Newspaperman's Story of His Own Mental Crack-up and Recovery* (New York: Greenberg, 1952), p. 27.

[7] From the writer's field notes of informal interaction with patients, transcribed as nearly verbatim as he was able.

Certainly the degrading conditions of the hospital setting belie many of the self-stories that are presented by patients, and the very fact of being in the mental hospital is evidence against these tales. And of course there is not always sufficient patient solidarity to prevent patient discrediting patient, just as there is not always a sufficient number of "professionalized" attendants to prevent attendant discrediting patient. As one patient informant repeatedly suggested to a fellow patient: "If you're so smart, how come you got your ass in here?"

The mental-hospital setting, however, is more treacherous still. Staff have much to gain through discreditings of the patient's story—whatever the felt reason for such discreditings. If the custodial faction in the hospital is to succeed in managing his daily round without complaint or trouble from him, then it will prove useful to be able to point out to him that the claims about himself upon which he rationalizes his demands are false, that he is not what he is claiming to be, and that in fact he is a failure as a person. If the psychiatric faction is to impress upon him its views about his personal make-up, then they must be able to show in detail how their version of his past and their version of his character hold up much better than his own.[8] If both the custodial and psychiatric factions are to get him to co-operate in the various psychiatric treatments, then it will prove useful to disabuse him of his view of their purposes, and cause him to appreciate that they know what they are doing, and are doing what is best for him. In brief, the difficulties caused by a patient are closely tied to his version of what has been happening to him, and if co-operation is to be secured, it helps if this version is discredited. The patient must "insightfully" come to take, or affect to take, the hospital's view of himself.

The staff also have ideal means—in addition to the mirroring effect of the setting—for denying the inmate's rationalizations. Current psychiatric doctrine defines mental disorder as something that can have its roots in the patient's earliest years, show its signs throughout the course of his life, and invade almost every sector of his current activity. No segment of his past or present need be defined, then, as beyond the jurisdiction and mandate of psychiatric assessment. Mental hospitals bureaucratically institutionalize this extremely wide mandate by formally basing their treatment of the patient upon his diagnosis and hence upon the psychiatric view of his past.

The case record is an important expression of this mandate. This dossier is apparently not regularly used, however, to record occasions when the patient

---

[8] The process of examining a person psychiatrically and then altering or reducing his status in consequence is known in hospital and prison parlance as bugging, the assumption being that once you come to the attention of the testers you either will automatically be labeled crazy or the process of testing itself will make you crazy. Thus psychiatric staff are sometimes seen not as discovering whether you are sick, but as making you sick; and "Don't bug me, man" can mean, "Don't pester me to the point where I'll get upset." Sheldon Messinger has suggested to me that this meaning of bugging is related to the other colloquial meaning, of wiring a room with a secret microphone to collect information usable for discrediting the speaker.

showed capacity to cope honorably and effectively with difficult life situations. Nor is the case record typically used to provide a rough average or sampling of his past conduct. One of its purposes is to show the ways in which the patient is "sick" and the reasons why it was right to commit him and is right currently to keep him committed; and this is done by extracting from his whole life course a list of those incidents that have or might have had "symptomatic" significance.[9] The misadventures of his parents or siblings that might suggest a "taint" may be cited. Early acts in which the patient appeared to have shown bad judgment or emotional disturbance will be recorded. Occasions when he acted in a way which the layman would consider immoral, sexually perverted, weak-willed, childish, ill-considered, impulsive, and crazy may be described. Misbehaviors which someone saw as the last straw, as cause for immediate action, are likely to be reported in detail. In addition, the record will describe his state on arrival at the hospital—and this is not likely to be a time of tranquillity and ease for him. The record may also report the false line taken by the patient in answering embarrassing questions, showing him as someone who makes claims that are obviously contrary to the facts:

Claims she lives with oldest daughter or with sisters only when sick and in need of care; otherwise with husband, he himself says not for twelve years.

Contrary to the reports from the personnel, he says he no longer bangs on the floor or cries in the morning.

. . . conceals fact that she had her organs removed, claims she is still menstruating.

At first she denied having had premarital sexual experience, but when asked about Jim she said she had forgotten about it 'cause it had been unpleasant.[10]

Where contrary facts are not known by the recorder, their presence is often left scrupulously an open question:

The patient denied any heterosexual experiences nor could one trick her into admitting that she had ever been pregnant or into any kind of sexual indulgence, denying masturbation as well.

Even with considerable pressure she was unwilling to engage in any projection of paranoid mechanisms.

No psychotic content could be elicited at this time.[11]

---

[9] While many kinds of organization maintain records of their members, in almost all of these some socially significant attributes can only be included indirectly, being officially irrelevant. But since mental hospitals have a legitimate claim to deal with the "whole" person, they need officially recognize no limits to what they consider relevant, a sociologically interesting licence. It is an odd historical fact that persons concerned with promoting civil liberties in other areas of life tend to favor giving the psychiatrist complete discretionary power over the patient. Apparently it is felt that the more power possessed by medically qualified administrators and therapists, the better the interests of the patients will be served. Patients, to my knowledge, have not been polled on this matter.

[10] Verbatim transcriptions of hospital case-record material.

[11] Verbatim transcriptions of hospital case-record material.

And if in no more factual way, discrediting statements often appear in descriptions given of the patient's general social manner in the hospital:

When interviewed, he was bland, apparently self-assured, and sprinkles high-sounding generalizations freely throughout his verbal productions.

Armed with a rather neat appearance and natty little Hitlerian mustache this 45 year old man who has spent the last five or more years of his life in the hospital, is making a very successful hospital adjustment living within the role of a rather gay liver and jim-dandy type of fellow who is not only quite superior to his fellow patients in intellectual respects but who is also quite a man with women. His speech is sprayed with many multi-syllabled words which he generally uses in good context, but if he talks long enough on any subject it soon becomes apparent that he is so completely lost in this verbal diarrhea as to make what he says almost completely worthless.[12]

The events recorded in the case history are, then, just the sort that a layman would consider scandalous, defamatory, and discrediting. I think it is fair to say that all levels of mental-hospital staff fail, in general, to deal with this material with the moral neutrality claimed for medical statements and psychiatric diagnosis, but instead participate, by intonation and gesture if by no other means, in the lay reaction to these acts. This will occur in staff-patient encounters as well as in staff encounters at which no patient is present.

In some mental hospitals, access to the case record is technically restricted to medical and higher nursing levels, but even here informal access or relayed information is often available to lower staff levels.[13] In addition, ward personnel are felt to have a right to know those aspects of the patient's past conduct which, embedded in the reputation he develops, purportedly make it possible to manage him with greater benefit to himself and less risk to others. Further, all staff levels typically have access to the nursing notes kept on the ward, which chart the daily course of each patient's disease, and hence his conduct, providing for the near present the sort of information the case record supplies for his past.

I think that most of the information gathered in case records is quite true, although it might seem also to be true that almost anyone's life course could

---

[12] Verbatim transcriptions of hospital case-record material.

[13] However, some mental hospitals do have a "hot file" of selected records which can be taken out only by special permission. These may be records of patients who work as administration-office messengers and might otherwise snatch glances at their own files; of inmates who had elite status in the environing community; and of inmates who may take legal action against the hospital and hence have a special reason to maneuver access to their records. Some hospitals even have a "hot-hot file," kept in the superintendent's office. In addition, the patient's professional title, especially if it is a medical one, is sometimes purposely omitted from his file card. All of these exceptions to the general rule for handling information show, of course, the institution's realization of some of the implications of keeping mental-hospital records. For a further example, see Harold Taxel, "Authority Structure in a Mental Hospital Ward" (Unpublished M.A. thesis, Department of Sociology, University of Chicago, 1953), pp. 11–12.

yield up enough denigrating facts to provide grounds for the record's justification of commitment. In any case, I am not concerned here with questioning the desirability of maintaining case records, or the motives of staff in
keeping them. The point is that, these facts about him being true, the patient
is certainly not relieved from the normal cultural pressure to conceal them,
and is perhaps all the more threatened by knowing that they are neatly
available, and that he has no control over who gets to learn them.[14] A manly
looking youth who responds to military induction by running away from the
barracks and hiding himself in a hotel-room clothes closet, to be found there,
crying, by his mother; a woman who travels from Utah to Washington to
warn the President of impending doom; a man who disrobes before three
young girls; a boy who locks his sister out of the house, striking out two
of her teeth when she tries to come back in through the window—each of
these persons has done something he will have very obvious reasons to conceal from others, and very good reason to tell lies about.

The formal and informal patterns of communication linking staff members
tend to amplify the disclosive work done by the case record. A discreditable
act that the patient performs during one part of the day's routine in one part
of the hospital community is likely to be reported back to those who supervise other areas of his life where he implicitly takes the stand that he is not
the sort of person who could act that way.

Of significance here, as in some other social establishments, is the increasingly common practice of all-level staff conferences, where staff air their views
of patients and develop collective agreement concerning the line that the
patient is trying to take and the line that should be taken to him. A patient
who develops a "personal" relation with an attendant, or manages to make
an attendant anxious by eloquent and persistent accusations of malpractice,
can be put back into his place by means of the staff meeting, where the
attendant is given warning or assurance that the patient is "sick." Since the

---

[14] This is the problem of "information control" that many groups suffer from in
varying degrees. See Goffman, "Discrepant Roles," in *The Presentation of Self in
Everyday Life* (New York: Anchor Books, 1959), ch. iv, pp. 141–166. A suggestion
of this problem in relation to case records in prisons is given by James Peck in his
story, "The Ship that Never Hit Port," in *Prison Etiquette*, edited by Holley Cantine
and Dachine Rainer (Bearsville, N.Y.: Retort Press, 1950), p. 66:

*"The hacks of course hold all the aces in dealing with any prisoner because they can
always write him up for inevitable punishment. Every infraction of the rules is noted
in the prisoner's jacket, a folder which records all the details of the man's life before
and during imprisonment. There are general reports written by the work detail screw,
the cell block screw, or some other screw who may have overheard a conversation. Tales
pumped from stoolpigeons are also included.*

*"Any letter which interests the authorities goes into the jacket. The mail censor may
make a photostatic copy of a prisoner's entire letter, or merely copy a passage. Or he
may pass the letter on to the warden. Often an inmate called out by the warden or
parole officer is confronted with something he wrote so long ago he had forgot all
about it. It might be about his personal life or his political views—a fragment of
thought that the prison authorities felt was dangerous and filed for later use."*

differential image of himself that a person usually meets from those of various levels around him comes here to be unified behind the scenes into a common approach, the patient may find himself faced with a kind of collusion against him—albeit one sincerely thought to be for his own ultimate welfare.

In addition, the formal transfer of the patient from one ward or service to another is likely to be accompanied by an informal description of his characteristics, this being felt to facilitate the work of the employee who is newly responsible for him.

Finally, at the most informal of levels, the lunchtime and coffee-break small talk of staff often turns upon the latest doings of the patient, the gossip level of any social establishment being here intensified by the assumption that everything about him is in some way the proper business of the hospital employee. Theoretically there seems to be no reason why such gossip should not build up the subject instead of tear him down, unless one claims that talk about those not present will always tend to be critical in order to maintain the integrity and prestige of the circle in which the talking occurs. And so, even when the impulse if the speakers seems kindly and generous, the implication of their talk is typically that the patient is not a complete person. For example, a conscientious group therapist, sympathetic with patients, once admitted to his coffee companions:

I've had about three group disrupters, one man in particular—a lawyer [*sotto voce*] James Wilson—very bright—who just made things miserable for me, but I would always tell him to get on the stage and do something. Well, I was getting desperate and then I bumped into his therapist, who said that right now behind the man's bluff and front he needed the group very much and that it probably meant more to him than anything else he was getting out of the hospital—he just needed the support. Well, that made me feel altogether different about him. He's out now.

In general, then, mental hospitals systematically provide for circulation about each patient the kind of information that the patient is likely to try to hide. And in various degrees of detail this information is used daily to puncture his claims. At the admission and diagnostic conferences, he will be asked questions to which he must give wrong answers in order to maintain his self-respect, and then the true answer may be shot back at him. An attendant whom he tells a version of his past and his reason for being in the hospital may smile disbelievingly, or say, "That's not the way I heard it," in line with the practical psychiatry of bringing the patient down to reality. When he accosts a physician or nurse on the ward and presents his claims for more privileges or for discharge, this may be countered by a question which he cannot answer truthfully without calling up a time in his past when he acted disgracefully. When he gives his view of his situation during group psychotherapy, the therapist, taking the role of interrogator, may attempt to disabuse him of his face-saving interpretations and encourage an interpretation suggesting that it is he himself who is to blame and who must change. When he claims to staff or fellow patients that he is well and has never been really sick, someone may give him graphic details of how, only one month ago, he was prancing around like a girl, or claiming that he was God, or declining to talk or eat, or putting gum in his hair.

Each time the staff deflates the patient's claims, his sense of what a person ought to be and the rules of peer-group social intercourse press him to reconstruct his stories; and each time he does this, the custodial and psychiatric interests of the staff may lead them to discredit these tales again.

Behind these verbally instigated ups and downs of the self is an institutional base that rocks just as precariously. Contrary to popular opinion, the "ward system" insures a great amount of internal social mobility in mental hospitals, especially during the inmate's first year. During that time he is likely to have altered his service once, his ward three or four times, and his parole status several times; and he is likely to have experienced moves in bad as well as good directions. Each of these moves involves a very drastic alteration in level of living and in available materials out of which to build a self-confirming round of activities, an alteration equivalent in scope, say, to a move up or down a class in the wider class system. Moreover, fellow inmates with whom he has partially identified himself will similarly be moving, but in different directions and at different rates, thus reflecting feelings of social change to the person even when he does not experience them directly.

As previously implied, the doctrines of psychiatry can reinforce the social fluctuations of the ward system. Thus there is a current psychiatric view that the ward system is a kind of social hothouse in which patients start as social infants and end up, within the year, on convalescent wards as resocialized adults. This view adds considerably to the weight and pride that staff can attach to their work, and necessitates a certain amount of blindness, especially at higher staff levels, to other ways of viewing the ward system, such as a method for disciplining unruly persons through punishment and reward. In any case, this resocialization perspective tends to overstress the extent to which those on the worst wards are incapable of socialized conduct and the extent to which those on the best wards are ready and willing to play the social game. Because the ward system is something more than a resocialization chamber, inmates find many reasons for "messing up" or getting into trouble, and many occasions, then, for demotion to less privileged ward positions. These demotions may be officially interpreted as psychiatric relapses or moral backsliding, thus protecting the resocialization view of the hospital; these interpretations, by implication, translate a mere infraction of rules and consequent demotion into a fundamental expression of the status of the culprit's self. Correspondingly, promotions, which may come about because of ward population pressure, the need for a "working patient," or for other psychiatrically irrelevant reasons, may be built up into something claimed to be profoundly expressive of the patient's whole self. The patient himself may be expected by staff to make a personal effort to "get well," in something less than a year, and hence may be constantly reminded to think in terms of the self's success and failure.[15]

In such contexts inmates can discover that deflations in moral status are not so bad as they had imagined. After all, infractions which lead to these demotions cannot be accompanied by legal sanctions or by reduction to the status of mental patient, since these conditions already prevail. Further, no past or current delict seems to be horrendous enough in itself to excommunicate a patient from the patient community, and hence failures at right living lose some of their stigmatizing meaning.[16] And finally, in accepting the hospital's version of his fall from grace, the patient can set himself up in the business of "straightening up," and make claims of sympathy, privileges, and indulgence from the staff in order to foster this.

Learning to live under conditions of imminent exposure and wide fluctuation in regard, with little control over the granting or withholding of this regard, is an important step in the socialization of the patient, a step that tells something important about what it is like to be an inmate in a mental hospital. Having one's past mistakes and present progress under constant moral review seems to make for a special adaptation consisting of a less than moral attitude to ego ideals. One's shortcomings and successes become too central and fluctuating an issue in life to allow the usual commitment of concern for other persons' views of them. It is not very practicable to try to sustain solid claims about oneself. The inmate tends to learn that degradations and reconstructions of the self need not be given too much weight, at the same time learning that staff and inmates are ready to view an inflation or deflation of a self with some indifference. He learns that a defensible picture of self can be seen as something outside oneself that can be constructed, lost, and rebuilt, all with great speed and some equanimity. He learns about the viability of taking up a standpoint—and hence a self—that is outside the one which the hospital can give and take away from him.

The setting, then, seems to engender a kind of cosmopolitan sophistication, a kind of civic apathy. In this unserious yet oddly exaggerated moral context building up a self or having it destroyed becomes something of a shameless game, and learning to view this process as a game seems to make for some demoralization, the game being such a fundamental one. In the hospital, then, the inmate can learn that the self is not a fortress, but rather a small open city; he can become weary of having to show pleasure when held by troops of his own, and weary of having to show displeasure when held by the enemy. Once he learns what it is like to be defined by society as not having a viable self, this threatening definition—the threat that helps attach people to the self society accords them—is weakened. The patient seems to gain a new plateau when he learns that he can survive while acting in a way that society sees as destructive of him.

A few illustrations of this moral loosening and moral fatigue might be

---

[15] For this and other suggestions, I am indebted to Charlotte Green Schwartz.
[16] See "The Underlife of a Public Institution," this book, fn. 167.

given. In state mental hospitals currently a kind of "marriage moratorium" appears to be accepted by patients and more or less condoned by staff. Some informal peer-group pressure may be brought against a patient who "plays around" with more than one hospital partner at a time, but little negative sanction seems to be attached to taking up, in a temporarily steady way, with a member of the opposite sex, even though both partners are known to be married, to have children, and even to be regularly visited by these outsiders. In short, there is licence in mental hospitals to begin courting all over again, with the understanding, however, that nothing very permanent or serious can come of this. Like shipboard or vacation romances, these entanglements attest to the way in which the hospital is cut off from the outside community, becoming a world of its own, operated for the benefit of its own citizens. And certainly this moratorium is an expression of the alienation and hostility that patients feel for those on the outside to whom they were closely related. But, in addition, one has evidence of the loosening effects of living in a world within a world, under conditions which make it difficult to give full seriousness to either of them.

The second illustration concerns the ward system. On the worst ward level, discreditings seem to occur the most frequently, in part because of lack of facilities, in part through the mockery and sarcasm that seem to be the occupational norm of social control for the attendants and nurses who administer these places. At the same time, the paucity of equipment and rights means that not much self can be built up. The patient finds himself constantly toppled, therefore, but with very little distance to fall. A kind of jaunty gallows humor seems to develop in some of these wards, with considerable freedom to stand up to the staff and return insult for insult. While these patients can be punished, they cannot, for example, be easily slighted, for they are accorded as a matter of course few of the niceties that people must enjoy before they can suffer subtle abuse. Like prostitutes in connection with sex, inmates on these wards have very little reputation or rights to lose and can therefore take certain liberties. As the person moves up the ward system, he can manage more and more to avoid incidents which discredit his claim to be a human being, and acquire more and more of the varied ingredients of self-respect; yet when eventually he does get toppled— and he does—there is a much farther distance to fall. For instance, the privileged patient lives in a world wider than the ward, containing recreation workers who, on request, can dole out cake, cards, table-tennis balls, tickets to the movies, and writing materials. But in the absence of the social control of payment which is typically exerted by a recipient on the outside, the patient runs the risk that even a warmhearted functionary may, on occasion, tell him to wait until she has finished an informal chat, or teasingly ask why he wants what he has asked for, or respond with a dead pause and a cold look of appraisal.

Moving up and down the ward system means, then, not only a shift in self-constructive equipment, a shift in reflected status, but also a change in the calculus of risks. Appreciation of risks to his self-conception is part of everyone's moral experience, but an appreciation that a given risk level is itself merely a social arrangement is a rarer kind of experience, and one that seems to help to disenchant the person who undergoes it.

A third instance of moral loosening has to do with the conditions that are often associated with the release of the inpatient. Often he leaves under the supervision and jurisdiction of his next-of-relation or of a specially selected and specially watchful employer. If he misbehaves while under their auspices, they can quickly obtain his readmission. He therefore finds himself under the special power of persons who ordinarily would not have this kind of power over him, and about whom, moreover, he may have had prior cause to feel quite bitter. In order to get out of the hospital, however, he may conceal his displeasure in this arrangement, and, at least until safely off the hospital rolls, act out a willingness to accept this kind of custody. These discharge procedures, then, provide a built-in lesson in overtly taking a role without the usual covert commitments, and seem further to separate the person from the worlds that others take seriously.

The moral career of a person of a given social category involves a standard sequence of changes in his way of conceiving of selves, including, importantly, his own. These half-buried lines of development can be followed by studying his moral experiences—that is, happenings which mark a turning point in the way in which the person views the world—although the particularities of this view may be difficult to establish. And note can be taken of overt tacks or strategies—that is, stands that he effectively takes before specifiable others, whatever the hidden and variable nature of his inward attachment to these presentations. By taking note of moral experiences and overt personal stands, one can obtain a relatively objective tracing of relatively subjective matters.

Each moral career, and behind this, each self, occurs within the confines of an institutional system, whether a social establishment such as a mental hospital or a complex of personal and professional relationships. The self, then, can be seen as something that resides in the arrangements prevailing in a social system for its members. The self in this sense is not a property of the person to whom it is attributed, but dwells rather in the pattern of social control that is exerted in connection with the person by himself and those around him. This special kind of institutional arrangement does not so much support the self as constitute it.

In this paper, two of these institutional arrangements have been considered, by pointing to what happens to the person when these rulings are weakened. The first concerns the felt loyalty of his next-of-relation. The prepatient's self is described as a function of the way in which three roles are related, arising and declining in the kinds of affiliation that occur between the next-of-relation and the mediators. The second concerns the protection required by the person for the version of himself which he presents to others, and the way in which the withdrawal of this protection can form a systematic, if unintended, aspect of the working of an establishment. I want to stress that these are only two kinds of institutional rulings from which a self emerges for the participant; others, not considered in this paper, are equally important.

In the usual cycle of adult socialization one expects to find alienation and mortification followed by a new set of beliefs about the world and a new way of conceiving of selves. In the case of the mental-hospital patient, this rebirth does sometimes occur, taking the form of a strong belief in the psychiatric perspective, or, briefly at least, a devotion to the social cause of better treatment for mental patients. The moral career of the mental patient has unique interest, however; it can illustrate the possibility that in casting off the raiments of the old self—or in having this cover torn away—the person need not seek a new robe and a new audience before which to cower. Instead he can learn, at least for a time, to practise before all groups the amoral arts of shamelessness.

Medical Model and Mental Hospitalization

ERVING GOFFMAN

Next I want to suggest that, compared to a medical hospital or garage, a mental hospital is ill-equipped to be a place where the classic repair cycle occurs. In state mental hospitals, and to a greater extent in private and veterans' hospitals, opportunity for observing the patient is available, but staff are often too busy to record anything but acts of disobedience. Even when staff time is available for this work, the patient's conduct on the ward can hardly be taken as a sample of his conduct off it: some conduct felt to be unacceptable on the outside does not occur here (especially when this conduct was a response to disliked persons in the patient's home environment), and other forms of misconduct overlay the old in response to the inmate's current involuntary situation. A refraction of conduct thus occurs, the walls of the institution acting like a thick and faulted prism. Unless one argues for the validity of testing persons under this particular kind of stress, the ward would seem to be the worst possible place for a server's observations.

Similarly, even where diagnostic conferences are held in regard to each patient, the effort of these meetings can be directed to agreeing on which of the legally required labels will be affixed to the case-record statement; and the timing of these meetings may have little to do with the presence or absence of an accumulation of data to act upon.

SOURCE: From *Asylums* by Erving Goffman. Copyright © 1961 by Erving Goffman. Reprinted by permission of Doubleday & Company, Inc.

What is true of the difficulties of diagnosis in mental hospitals is even more true of treatment. As already suggested, the problem of easing the patient's attitude to the world is confused and exacerbated by the problem of easing his attitude to involuntary hospitalization. In any case, the treatment given in mental hospitals is not likely to be specific to the disorder, as it is, in general, in a medical hospital, garage, or radio repair shop; instead if treatment is given at all, a cycle of therapies tends to be given across the board to a whole entering class of patients, with the medical work-up being used more to learn if there are counterindications for the standard treatments than to find indications for them.

At the same time, the patient's life is regulated and ordered according to a disciplinarian system developed for the management by a small staff of a large number of involuntary inmates. In this system the attendant is likely to be the key staff person, informing the patient of the punishments and rewards that are to regulate his life and arranging for medical authorization for such privileges and punishments. Quiet, obedient behavior leads to the patient's promotion in the ward system; obstreperous, untidy behavior to demotion. Interestingly enough, it is when the patient finds himself willing to improve his social conduct that the attendant is likely to bring him to the attention of the doctor as both worthy of consideration and able to profit from it, so that, as Ivan Belknap has described, the patient often gets a doctor's attention when he least needs it.[1]

The period in the mental hospital is a difficult one for the patient to

---

[1] Belknap, *op. cit.*, p. 144. I would like to add that since mental patients are persons who on the outside declined to respond to efforts at social control, there is a question of how social control can be achieved on the inside. I believe that it is achieved largely through the "ward system," the means of control that has slowly evolved in modern mental hospitals. The key, I feel, is a system of wards graded for degree of allowable misbehavior and degree of discomfort and deprivation prevalent in them. Whatever the level of the new patient's misbehavior, then, a ward can be found for him in which this conduct is routinely dealt with and to a degree allowed. In effect, by accepting the life conditions on these wards, the patient is allowed to continue his misbehavior, except that now he does not particularly bother anyone by it, since it is routinely handled, if not accepted, on the ward. When he requests some improvement in his lot he is then, in effect, made to say "uncle," made to state verbally that he is ready to mend his ways. When he gives in verbally he is likely to be allowed an improvement in life conditions. Should he then again misbehave in the old way, and persist in this, he is lectured and returned to his previous conditions. If instead of backsliding he states his willingness to behave even better, and retains this line for a suitable length of time, he is advanced further within the quick-discharge cycle through which most first admissions are moved up and out within a year. A point then is often reached where the patient is entrusted to a kinsman, either for walks on the hospital grounds or for town expeditions, the kinsman now being transformed into someone who has the incarcerating establishment and the law to reinforce the threat: "Be good or else I'll send you back." What we find here (and do not on the outside) is a very model of what psychologists might call a learning situation—all hinged on the process of an admitted giving-in. For this reason, patient morale on the rebellious wards seems stronger and healthier than on the discharge wards, where there is a slight air of persons having sold out to get out.

assimilate to the medical model. A very standard complaint is: "Nothing is being done with me—I'm just left to sit." And corresponding to this difficulty is the fact that current official psychiatric treatment for functional disorders does not, in itself, provide a probability of success great enough easily to justify the practice of institutional psychiatry as an expert service occupation, as here defined, especially since the probability that hospitalization will damage the life chances of the individual is, as already suggested, positive and high.

The problem, however, is not merely that of a low probability of successful service but, for some patients, a question of the validity of applying the whole service frame of reference in the first place.

First, we must see that the discreteness of the entity in which the disorder exists is questionable. True, in cases that are organic in character, the patient encloses within himself the world in which the damage is felt and the world in which repairs, if possible, can be made. This is not so in instances of functional psychosis. In so far as the patient's symptomatic behavior is an integral part of his interpersonal situation, the server would have to import this whole situation into the hospital in order to observe the patient's difficulty and to treat it. Instead of there being a relatively benign and passive environment and an isolated point of trouble, the figure and ground of usual service conceptions merge into one, the patient's interpersonal environment being inseparable from the trouble he is experiencing. Theoretically, it might of course be possible for a slight therapeutic change in the patient to have a benign circular effect on his environment when he gets sent back to it, and it might be possible to arrange to return him to a new environment, but in practice the patient is usually returned, when he is discharged, back into the system of which his psychotic response is a natural part.

But there is a still more fundamental issue, which hinges on the applicability of the concept of "pathology." Ordinarily the pathology which first draws attention to the patient's condition is conduct that is "inappropriate in the situation." But the decision as to whether a given act is appropriate or inappropriate must often necessarily be a lay decision, simply because we have no technical mapping of the various behavioral subcultures in our society, let alone the standards of conduct prevailing in each of them. Diagnostic decisions, except for extreme symptoms, can become ethnocentric, the server judging from his own culture's point of view individuals' conduct that can really be judged only from the perspective of the group from which they derive. Further, since inappropriate behavior is typically behavior that someone does not like and finds extremely troublesome, decisions concerning it tend to be political, in the sense of expressing the special interests of some particular faction or person rather than interests that can be said to be above the concerns of any particular grouping, as in the case of physical pathology.[2]

---

[2] See T. S. Szasz, "Psychiatry, Ethics, and the Criminal Law," *Columbia Law Review*, LVIII (1958), p. 188.

For the patient, the application of the pathology concept to his conduct can have effects that are incompatible with the service ideal. In so far as he feels he has acted inappropriately at all, he may see his action as part of the normal social world of intention, responsibility, and culpability—much like the initial lay perception of his troublesome conduct. To have one's behavior defined as involuntary, non-responsible, and non-culpable may be helpful in some cases, but this none the less involves a technical schema, not a social one, and ideally ought to disqualify the patient for any participation in the service relation even while qualifying him as an object of service. Szasz's description can be cited here:

More precisely, according to the common-sense definition, mental health is the ability to play whatever the game of social living might consist of and to play it well. Conversely, to refuse to play, or to play badly, means that the person is mentally ill. The question may now be raised as to what are the differences, if any, between social non-conformity (or deviation) and mental illness. Leaving technical psychiatric considerations aside for the moment, I shall argue that the difference between these two notions—as expressed for example by the statements "He is wrong" and "He is mentally ill"—does not necessarily lie in any observable *facts* to which they point, but may consist only of a difference in our *attitudes* toward our subject. If we take him *seriously,* consider him to have human rights and dignities, and look upon him as more or less our equal—we then speak of disagreements, deviations, fights, crimes, perhaps even of treason. Should we feel, however, that we cannot communicate with him, that he is somehow "basically" different from us, we shall then be inclined to consider him no longer as an equal but rather as an inferior (rarely, superior) person; and we then speak of him as being crazy, mentally ill, insane, psychotic, immature, and so forth.[3]

We should not overestimate this problem, however, because, in fact, there is no great danger in mental hospitals of having one's acts consistently defined in a neutral technical frame of reference. In medicine it is possible to act as if there were no right or wrong streptococci, merely dangerous ones. In psychiatry there is a formal effort to act as if the issue is treatment, not moral judgment, but this is not consistently maintained. Ethical neutrality is indeed difficult to sustain in psychiatry, because the patient's disorder is intrinsically related to his acting in a way that causes offense to witnesses. Further, the standard way of dealing with such offenses in our society is to sanction the offender, negatively and correctively. Our whole society operates on this assumption in every item and detail of life, and without some functional equivalent it is hard to see how we could maintain a social order without it.

It is understandable, then, that even occasions set aside to demonstrate that professional non-moralistic psychotherapy is taking place in the institu-

---

[3] T. S. Szasz, "Politics and Mental Health," *American Journal of Psychiatry,* CXV (1958), p. 509. See also his "Psychiatric Expert Testimony—Its Covert Meaning & Social Function," *Psychiatry,* XX (1957), p. 315, and "Some Observations on the Relationship between Psychiatry and the Law," *A.M.A. Archives of Neurology and Psychiatry,* LXXV (1956), pp. 297–315.

tion will be invaded by a moralistic perspective, albeit a modified one. It is understandable that a large part of psychotherapy consists of holding the sins of the patient up to him and getting him to see the error of his ways. And in a sense, I do not see how it can or should be otherwise. The interesting point here is that psychiatric staff are in a position neither to forego the fiction of neutrality nor actually to sustain it.

When applied to the mental hospital, the service model leads to a very characteristic ambivalence of action on the part of staff. Psychiatric doctrine requires ethical neutrality in dealing with patients, for what others see as misbehavior the staff must see as pathology. The law even underwrites this position, a mental patient having the privilege of committing crimes without having to face legal action. And yet, in the actual management of patients, ideals of proper conduct must be held up as desirable, infractions inveighed against, and the patient treated as a "responsible" person, that is, one capable of a personal effort to behave himself. Psychiatric staff share with policemen the peculiar occupational task of hectoring and moralizing adults; the necessity of submitting to these lectures is one of the consequences of committing acts against the community's social order.

7. MASS TERROR, I:
CONCENTRATION CAMPS

Daily Routine in Buchenwald

EUGENE KOGON

The camp was awakened by whistles, in the summer between four and five o'clock, in the winter between six and seven o'clock. Half an hour was allotted to washing, dressing, breakfasting and bed-making, sometimes an impossible job within that period.

A number of camps insisted on morning calisthenics, performed winter and summer at break-neck pace for half an hour before the regular rising time. They consisted mostly of everlasting push-ups in the snow and muck. Because of numerous fatal cases of pneumonia, this practice never persisted for very long.

Breakfast consisted of a piece of bread from the ration issued for the day and a pint of thin soup or so-called "coffee," without either milk or sugar. The bread ration was issued at different times to different barracks. Those who had got it at night and had immediately eaten it up had no bread for breakfast.

Next came morning roll call. On a signal the prisoners from each barracks fell in on the camp street and marched eight abreast to the roll-call area. Thousands of zebra-striped figures of misery, marching under the glare of the floodlights in the haze of dawn, column after column—no one who has ever witnessed it is likely to forget the sight.

Each barracks had its own assigned place in the roll-call area. The entire strength of the camp was counted, and this roll call usually took an hour, until it was light enough to start work. Morning roll call was not as important as its evening counterpart, still to be discussed, for little change was likely to take place overnight—deaths during the night were reported ahead of time from the prisoner hospital. After roll call came a thunderous com-

SOURCE: Reprinted from *The Theory and Practice of Hell* by Eugene Kogon, by permission of Farrar, Straus & Company, Inc. Published in 1950 by Farrar, Straus & Company, Inc. Also reprinted by permission of Martin Secker & Warburg Limited, London.

mand from the Roll Call Officer over the public-address system, addressed to the army of shorn men: "Caps off!" and "Caps on!" This was the morning salute for the Officer-in-Charge. If it was not executed smartly enough, it had to be repeated again and again, to the accompaniment of such comment at this: "You god-damned ass-holes, if you're too lazy to ventilate your filthy pates, I'll make you practice till the juice boils in your tails, you sons of bitches!"

Now came the dreaded call: "Prisoners under orders to the gatehouse!" It affected all those who had received a slip from the Orderly Room the night before. In Buchenwald six numbered signs were mounted at the wall of the left wing of the gatehouse. There the prisoners had to await the nameless terror about to engulf them. When they had painfully come to learn which number meant a summons before the Political Department, and which indicated more harmless matters—records, signatures, notarizations, etc.—the assignment of the numbers would be suddenly changed. The prisoners often had to wait for hours, haunted by uncertainty. If their families had only known the fear they could engender by routine inquiries and business matters! It was impossible to evade such a summons, and the waiting prisoners were at the mercy of the SS men who always loitered near the gatehouse.

Often prisoners so summoned were not given notice the night before at all. Their numbers were simply called out at the end of morning roll call and they were ordered to report to such-and-such a sign. I can state from personal experience that such an unexpected announcement of one's number was like a stab in the heart, regardless of what was involved.

The next command was "Labor details—fall in!" There was a wild milling about, as the prisoners moved to their assigned assembly points with all possible speed. The camp band, in the winter-time scarcely able to move its fingers, played merry tunes as the columns moved out five abreast. At the gatehouse caps had to be snatched off again, hands placed at the trouser seams. The details then marched off in double time, the prisoners compelled to sing.

Work continued until late afternoon, with half an hour for lunch, out in the open. For a long time the prisoners were not permitted to carry bread with them. Under an alternate plan, the details marched back into camp at noon, for half an hour or three-quarters, to bolt down their lunch. This hot meal, the only one all day, generally consisted of a single dish—a quart of soup or broth, often very thin and devoid of nourishment. The work schedule differed from camp to camp, but by and large it followed the schemes here described.

In the winter work ended around five o'clock, in the summer, around eight—between March and November the time was periodically shifted by half-hour intervals. At the conclusion of the work day the prisoners were marched back to camp, past the band, again ordered to play sprightly tunes. Then came evening roll call.

In every camp this head count was the terror of the prisoners. After a hard day's work, when ordinary men look forward to well-deserved rest, they had to stand in ranks for hours on end, regardless of rain or storm or icy cold, until the SS had tallied its slaves and established that none had escaped during the day. The preliminary work for these roll calls often had to be done by prisoner clerks, since few SS men were capable of making an accurate tabulation. The prisoners always endeavored to avoid the slightest error, especially in counting the numerous inmates on "permanent detail," whose work brooked no interruption and who therefore never appeared in line, though they were, of course, counted. Any slip, even though not a man was missing, was likely to result in hours of checking and delay, depriving the exhausted prisoners of the last shreds of leisure. So long as the number of prisoners to be accounted for did not exceed 5,000 to 7,000, any absence was quickly noted. It was a different matter when the number swelled to 20,000, to say nothing of 50,000. A great many non-German inmates looked on this roll call as just another form of Prussian drill, to be evaded whenever possible. On many occasiones a shirker would simply sleep away roll call in some hiding place, while tens of thousands of his fellows stood in stupor and agony until the culprit was found. (His would be an unenviable lot—

PENAL LABOR

The idea has occurred to me that if one wanted to crush, to annihilate a man utterly, to inflict on him the most terrible of punishments so that the most ferocious murderer would shudder at it and dread it beforehand, one need only give him work of an absolutely, completely useless and irrational character. . . . [If the convict laborer] had to pour water from one vessel into another and back, over and over again, to pound sand, to move a heap of earth from one place to another and back again—I believe the convict would hang himself in a few days or would commit a thousand crimes, preferring rather to die than endure such humiliation, shame and torture. Of course such a punishment would become a torture, a form of vengeance, and would be senseless, as it would achieve no rational object. But as something of such torture, senseless, humiliation and shame is an inevitable element in all forced labour, penal labour is incomparably more painful than any free labour—just because it is forced.

SOURCE: Fyodor Dostoyevsky, *The House of the Dead,* trans. by Constance Garnett (New York: Dell, 1959), pp. 48–49.

---

no one took pity on him!) If a single prisoner was absent, hundreds of names and numbers from various barracks had to be called out—Polish names, Russian names, French names that could be pronounced only with the aid of interpreters. The SS men would lose their tempers, bellow, and let their fists and boots fly. Few roll calls took less than an hour and a half.

Whenever a prisoner actually escaped, the whole camp was kept on its feet until he was recaptured, often a matter of many hours. Guards were kept posted around the entire camp area during roll call, to insure that no prisoner could lurk about the headquarters area. The search within this guard line was the job of the Senior Block Inmates, the Barracks Orderlies, the Prisoner Foremen and the Camp Police. Successful escapes drew such savage punishment upon the entire camp, especially in the early years, that the political prisoners renounced even the attempt until the final months. Then a few escapes, undertaken with the approval of the underground leadership, proved necessary in order to establish contact with the approaching Allies.

During evening roll call on December 14, 1938, two convicts turned up missing at Buchenwald. The temperature was 5° above zero and the prisoners were thinly clad—but they had to stand in the roll-call area for nineteen hours. Twenty-five had frozen to death by morning; by noon the number had risen to more than seventy.

During the fall of 1939 there was another occasion when the entire camp was kept standing for eighteen hours on end, because two convicts had hidden in the pigsty. Oh, it is easy enough to write about now—standing like that, after a full day's work, throughout the night and until next noon, without food! The cold death figures can be set down—but not the permanent damage suffered by hundreds who later perished of the after effects. What a relief when the war in the air forced even the SS to black out, when the floodlights could no longer be turned on! From that time onward, roll call simply had to be called off after a certain period, whether there were any absences or not. In the complete blackout the SS would have lost control of the camp, would have had good reason for fear in its own ranks.

From time to time the Block Leaders were ordered to "frisk" the inmates during roll call. Pockets had to be emptied and the contents were examined by the SS, a process during which as a rule much money and tobacco simply disappeared. One Sunday in February (!) 1938, the prisoners were compelled to stand stripped to the skin for three hours on such an occasion. The wife of Commandant Koch, in company with the wives of four other SS officers, came to the wire fence to gloat at the sight of the naked figures.

Roll call was a time for many special tortures. Often, following the head count, the command would be heard, "All Jews, remain behind"—to sing over and over again deep into the night the vile jingles known as the "Jew song":

> For years we wreaked deceit upon the nation,
> No fraud too great for us, no scheme too dark.
> All that we did was cheat and lie and swindle,
> Whether with dollar or with pound or with mark.

It ended with the following verses:

> But now at last the Germans know our nature
> And barbed wire hides us safely out of sight.
> Traducers of the people, we were fearful
> To face the truth that felled us overnight.

And now, with mournful crooked Jewish noses,
We find that hate and discord were in vain.
An end to thievery, to food aplenty.
Too late, we say, again and yet again.

This choice product of Nazi culture was the work of one of the "asocials" who sought to insinuate himself into the favor of the SS. Rödl, a man who could hardly be described as very discriminating, had the Jews sing it twice and then even he had enough. He forbade it. It was Officers-in-Charge Florstedt and Plaul, vicious anti-Semites, who restored it to Nazi honors. An especially popular procedure for entertaining visitors to the camps was to have the Jews line up in the roll-call area to the left of the tower and sing the vile tune.

Everyone had to appear for roll call, whether alive or dead, whether shaken by fever or beaten to a bloody pulp. The only exceptions were inmates on permanent details, and those in the prisoner hospital. The bodies of men who had died during the day, either in the barracks or at work, had to be dragged to the roll-call area. During particularly virulent sieges, there were always dozens of dying and dead laid in neat "rank and file" beyond the block formations, to answer the final roll call. For the SS exacted order and discipline down to the last breath. Not until after roll call could the dying be taken to the hospital, the dead to the morgue.

Once evening roll call was over, with the commands of "Caps off!" and "Caps on!" there usually followed another command: "Left face!"—and the public punishments, yet to be discussed in a separate chapter, were meted out. Or one of the Officers-in-Charge might call for a song. It might be raining or storming. The prisoners might scarcely be able to keep to their feet. All the more reason for exacting a song, as much as possible at odds with the situation—once, three times, five times in succession—"I saw a little bird flying," or "Something stirs in the forest." Most of the camps had songs of their own, written and composed by prisoners, on command. Some of these have become widely known, notably "The Peat-Bog Soldiers" and "The Buchenwald Song."

It might have been thought that once the final "Fall out!" had sounded the day's torments were over and the prisoners could sit down to eat and rest at leisure. But often they returned to the barracks, only to be confronted by the results of the inspection conducted during the day by the Block Leaders— lockers overturned, their contents scattered in every direction. The search for one's mess kit often led to savage clashes among the prisoners, driven beyond the limits of human endurance.

When the prisoners worked through the day, the main meal was issued at night. Of course it was cold by the time a protracted roll call was completed. The remaining ration, when issued at night, consisted of bread, a dab of margarine, and a bit of sausage or possibly a spoonful of cottage cheese. At any moment during "dinner" the Barracks Orderly might suddenly sing out: "Attention! B-wing of Barrack X reporting! One hundred and thirty-five prisoners at mess!" Some SS sergeant had conceived the notion to pay a visit. Not yet through the door, he would bellow: "Get under the tables, you swine!" Benches would be overturned, mess gear clatter to the floor. Still, there were always a few left over who, try as they might, could not find room under the tables and became the particular whipping boys. There were many variations on this tune. A Block Leader might simply order a barracks cleared during the meal, having the prisoners execute some senseless command, such as standing on their heads in the snow. To execute a headstand is not the easiest thing, even for a youngster. But even the aged and decrepit had to do it as a matter of course, just as they might have to double-time endlessly around the barracks. Any hesitation drew kicks and beatings. Even when nothing whatever happened in the barracks after roll call, the prisoners were obsessed by the fear that lightning might strike at any moment.

If roll call had been concluded with reasonable dispatch, work had to be continued for several hours deep into the night by certain prisoner groups. The rest might stroll about the camp streets, in front of the barracks, in the washrooms or toilets—unless they preferred to retire immediately. When taps sounded—between eight and ten o'clock, according to season—everyone except those on detail had to be indoors, half an hour later in bed.

Prisoners were permitted to wear only their shirts while sleeping, even in the deep of winter, when the barracks grew bitter cold and the damp stone walls often coated with ice at the windows and corners. Block Leaders frequently conducted night inspections, ordering all the inmates in a barracks to line up beside the beds or even outdoors, in order to catch those who might be wearing an additional garment. Whoever was found in socks or underwear could expect merciless punishment. On occasion an entire barracks was chased around the block for as much as an hour, barefoot and dressed only in shirts.

These nocturnal invasions did not occur regularly. They came from time to time, at irregular intervals, unexpectedly, generally when the Block Leaders were drunk. But they *could* happen at any moment. The threat was ever-present. Mercifully, the prisoners were far too exhausted to brood on the danger. For a few short hours each night sleep spread its balm over the misery. Only the aged, the fretful, the sick, the sleepless, lay awake in a torment of worry, awaiting the ordeal of another day.

How Did They Survive? Mechanisms of Defense in Nazi Concentration Camps

HILDE O. BLUHM

Death in a Nazi concentration camp requires no explanation. Survival does. Detailed knowledge of the techniques of torture and extermination has made us "understand" the outcome of nine to ten million dead. What bewilders us are the survivors. Through the flogging and the shooting, the cold and the hunger, the sixteen hours working day and the epidemics, through individual tortures and mass murder, thousands of them lived for years, three, five, eight years, and longer. What was it that enabled them to survive? Death reached out for them ever so often. How did their urge to live win over the wish to die? What kept them from suicide and insanity?

Some of the survivors have begun to speak. In books and articles they have tried to communicate an experience which "is impossible to communicate"—as one of them put it (9).

The following study is based on twelve such autobiographical accounts.[1] They have been written by authors of greatly different background: among them a German poet (Wiechert), an Austrian economist (Kautsky), a French professor of philosophy (Rousset), a Polish-Jewish businessman (Szalet), a British officer (Burney), two psychologists (Bettelheim and Frankl), two journalists (Karst and Kalmar), a Polish girl student (Szmaglewska). The authors include political and non-political prisoners, Germans and non-Germans, men and one woman; the terms of their imprisonment range from several months to seven years.

The character of the books is as different as the background of their authors. There are grim accusations, such as Kalmar's *Zeit ohne Gnade* ("Time without Mercy") and Karst's *Beasts of the Earth;* there is Wiechert's *Forest of the Dead,*—a poetic story which is like a stream of never ending sadness; there is Kautsky's *Teufel und Verdammte* ("The Devil and the Damned")—actually a comprehensive sociology of the concentration camp, written in a highly detached and scholarly way; there is, furthermore, Szalet's *Experiment E,* a detailed and realistic report of facts, and Bettelheim's revealing psychological analysis *My Life in a Concentration Camp.*

Apart from the books on which this study is based, other biographical reports on concentration camps have been written and still more are coming out. They may add to the insight to be gained from our selection; the essence

SOURCE: Hilde O. Bluhm, "How Did They Survive? Mechanisms of Defense in Nazi Concentration Camps," *American Journal of Psychotherapy*, 2 (1948), pp. 3-32. Reprinted by permission.

[1] For a complete list see Bibliography.

of this insight, however, does not depend on the completeness of the underlying material.

The topic of this study is the mental mechanisms of survival, i.e., the
mechanisms of defense developed by the ego in order to protect the individual
from physical death and mental disintegration. But this prevalence of psychological interest must not make us overlook the great number of other
circumstances on which survival in a concentration camp has depended, circumstances which have little to do with mental phenomena of the type
mentioned. There was, first of all, the factor of physical stamina: the sick,
the old, and the weak were those most likely to perish; there was also the
difference in locality and time: in some camps, the food, housing, working,
and hygienic conditions were much worse than in others, and it also happened that in the same camp periods of deterioration alternated with periods
of improvement. Likewise significant was the kind of work to which the
inmate had been assigned: Wiechert, for instance, seems to owe his life to
the fact that he was transferred from working in a quarry to mending stock-
ings. Of greatest importance was, furthermore, the official classification of
the prisoner. The camp was a rather complicated setup of many divisions
and sub-divisions, and every prisoner belonged to several official categories.[2]
As far as living conditions were concerned, it made all the difference,
whether the internee was a German or a non-German, an "Aryan" or a Jew.

In general, German "Aryans" fared best. Their barracks were not as
crowded and not as dirty as the quarters of others; their food was supplemented by extra-rations; discipline was not so rigid. Next came foreign
nations (members of resistance movements, saboteurs, prisoners of war).
Jews, of course, fared worst, and among them the Polish Jews always got
the worst of the worst.

The influence of these classifications has been emphasized by Kautsky.
Looking back at seven years imprisonment in various concentration camps,
he feels that two circumstances decided the outcome of his struggle for
survival. They were the "aryanization" granted to him after a few years, and
the material support he received from his Social-Democratic comrades; they
often shared their food with him when he still was classified as a Jew.

To a certain extent, the racial and national classification was tied up with
another determinant of survival; that was the "social position" of the prisoner
in the camp. The camps were, in fact, run by prisoners. The masters, the
SS, reserved for themselves only the key positions; all other functions were
transferred to inmates. This organization resulted in a kind of camp-hierarchy
consisting of an "aristocracy" as well as a "middle class," both made up by
promoted prisoners. The camp-seniors, the *capos* (heads) of the kitchen, the
clothing and tool magazine, the postoffice, the workshops etc., constituted

---

[2] Apart from the large "racial" and national groups, there was a great number of
special categories, such as "the politicals," "the criminals," "the homosexuals" (im-
prisoned for having offended the law), "Jehovah's Witnesses" (a religious sect), and
numerous others.

the aristocracy. It consisted almost exclusively of German Aryans. During the first period of the Hitler regime, the middle class, that is, the room capos, certain guards, foremen, clerks, cooks, nurses, workers in the workshops, and others, was also made up by German Aryans only. Later on, foreigners, too, and, in exceptional cases, even Jews were promoted to such positions.

The promoted prisoner enjoyed many privileges. He had enough to eat, drink, and smoke; he had all the clothing he wanted; his quarters were clean and roomy; his work was easy, control by superiors negligible. During a period when Jews housed in their emergency quarters died out within four to six months, mortality in the upper strata of prisoners was zero, and in the middle class hardly above the average of the age group concerned (8).

Yet—factors such as that of location and time, classification and social position, or any planned action *per se,* could, at any moment be put out of commission by one great unpredictable force that ruled over life and death of the inmates. It was the anarchic *power of accident.* If a person happened to lie next to the door through which a group of drunken SS-men entered, he may have been tramped or kicked to death, while his neighbor suffered no harm. If a prisoner met a guard who asked him to walk closer to the wire and he did it, he may have been shot; if he refused to do it, he may have been shot as well. If a man was strung up on a tree, a troop leader who happened to pass him, may have taken his cigarette and burned a hole in the face of the wretch. Such incidents occurred on countless occasions.

This anarchic power of accident, of the unexpected, of terror,[3] not only ruled over the inmate's life and death in a physical sense, but was perhaps the strongest force in the mental dynamics of concentration camp life.

Autobiographical reports are seldom revelations of depth-psychology. Conscious and unconscious censorship keeps authors from "confessing" certain facts, from noticing others, and even more, from recognizing underlying mechanisms and motives. In our books, these limitations seem to have been not quite as narrow as in many other self-representations. We shall understand later that the emergency situation in which they were conceived had already torn down certain emotional barriers which, otherwise, might have stood in the way of cognition and communication. Still, conscious and unconscious censorship remains effective. It prevents the disclosure of certain facts and interrelationships which would come out in individual analysis. There were, e.g., types who experienced a great relief of guilt feelings through the "punishments" in concentration camps. Reactions of this kind, if they reach consciousness at all, will hardly be confessed in autobiographical publications—except in cases where masochistic exhibitionism strives for gratification through rejection by the public. Yet the subject of this study is neither the abnormal personality nor the specific network of individual involvements. We are rather interested in the so called "normal" and the "typical." We are

---

[3] Unexpected action causing "fright" is an essential element of terror. An excellent analysis of the mental effects of terror in general has been given by Leo Lowenthal in his article, *Terror's Atomization of Man,* Commentary, New York, January, 1946.

looking for an answer to a socio-psychological problem: *Which were the mental effects produced in a great number of people by an emergency which lasted for years? Did the mass of prisoners develop typical reactions which were essential for their survival?*

Of such reactions our books give ample evidence.

TRAUMA AND ESTRANGEMENT

The average prisoner experienced the initial incidents of concentration

---

FROM THE PREFACE TO
UNDER TWO DICTATORS

From 1935 to 1937 . . . [my husband and I] both worked in Moscow as translators. During those two years we were already political outcasts and really prisoners in all but name. Our every movement was watched and everything we said in public was noted. In April, 1937, he was finally arrested by the N.K.V.D., the Soviet Secret Police, now the M.V.D., but better known as the G.P.U., by which initials I propose to refer to it. In June, 1938, my turn came. In 1940, after imprisonment in Moscow and in a Soviet concentration camp in Siberia, I was handed over to the German Gestapo during the period of the Russo-German friendship pact. I then spent five further years in the notorious German concentration camp at Ravensbrueck.

This book is the plain story of my experiences at the hands of both Russian and German secret police. . . .

SOURCE: Margarete Buber, *Under Two Dictators*, Trans. by Edward Fitzgerald (New York: Dodd, 1949) pp. xi, xii.

camp life as a severe trauma. This statement seems to be almost too obvious. However, the term "trauma" has an individual connotation, and its use in a socio-psychological sense requires special explanation.

An incident is called traumatic if it subjects the mind to a strong increase of stimulation within a short period of time—with the effect that this stimulation cannot be assimilated or elaborated by normal means. Whether or not assimilation is actually achieved, depends on the predisposition of the individual concerned. Some persons experience even a slight change in external conditions as traumatic, while others are able to take severe blows without developing a severe disturbance. Yet, every individual has his "breaking point," and exceptionally powerful incidents are likely to have a traumatic effect on everybody.[4]

Life in a concentration camp was filled with such incidents. In the con-

---

[4] On the concept of trauma see S. Freud's *A General Introduction to Psychoanalysis*, New York, 1943, p. 243, and O. Fenichel's *The Psychoanalytic Theory of Neurosis*, New York, 1943, p. 117/8.

text of this study we are, therefore, entitled to speak of "traumatic experience" as a reaction produced by similar stimuli in a great number of people. Thus, the traumatic experiences as well as the ensuing defense measures of the ego can be looked upon as typical phenomena. The traumatic character of the initial experience is brought out by several authors. Some of them stress that the first days were the hardest of all, although later torments often were more severe. "It was the suddenness, the ceaselessness of the terror which made it so hard to bear," says Szalet (p. 37). "Ceaselessness" points at the essential condition of a traumatic experience; it achieves "the strong increase of stimulation within a short period of time," and the "suddenness," i.e., the unexpectedness of an incident is likely to increase its traumatic effect. Other authors emphasize the moment of unexpectedness by speaking of "the initial shock" or the "shocks of the initial period."

This initial shock acted, from the beginning, as a principle of selection between those who were, virtually, fit for survival, and those who were not. The latter, unable to cope with the threats of the outer world or with their counter-aggressive impulses, "annihilated" either reality or themselves. By far the greatest number of suicides and outbreaks of psychosis occurred during the first few weeks of imprisonment. Kautsky recalls dozens of cases of insanity among newcomers. Reactions of grave melancholia also were frequent. Such cases used to end in suicide or in death occasioned by an otherwise trifling incident (pp. 182 and 283). Karst holds that the "prisoner's life expectation rose rapidly after he had survived half-a-year in the camp" (p. 130).

In most cases the urge for self-preservation won. To assist it in its struggle, additional mental energies had to be called up. That means, they had to be withdrawn from other, non-vital, functions, particularly from those which maintained the contact with the outer world. By such shifting of energies from the world of objects to the self, the ego not only succeeded in checking the excess of stimulation aroused by the initial experiences; it also protected itself from future dangers of a similar kind. The special mechanisms of defense developed for this purpose manifest themselves also in the books published.

Wiechert observed a strange change in his emotions, which he describes in the following way: "It was the sensation of an ever growing coldness that spread gradually from deep within until it filled his entire being.[5] It was as if the life he had lived up to now, and his world, were freezing to numbness in this chill. As though he was gazing through a thick sheet of ice at very distant things. And in that distance moved the noiseless and unreal spirits of his past; the people he had loved, his books, his hopes and plans . . . he felt a crack running through God's image, a crack that would not ever heal" (p. 63). Kalmar in a similar picture speaks of the coldness which took possession of him and which remained in him "through the burning summers . . . through the fires of the crematorium which consumed the bodies

---

[5] Wiechert uses the impersonal "he" instead of "I."

of my comrades . . . it was the numb coldness of an arctic solitude" (p. 32).
Frankl observes: "After the first shock, the prisoner glides into the second
stage, that of relative apathy. He begins to kill his feelings, such as the
burning longing for his home, the disgust of dirt . . . soon one can look on
quietly while others are beaten; the suffering, the sick, the dying don't touch
the heart any more" (p. 30). A fellow-prisoner advised Wiechert, "You must
not see nor hear . . . you must go through this like a stone . . . here one who
suffers with the rest must break" (p. 78). On the transportation to the camp,
when the whole arsenal of "initiation-techniques" was practiced on the
prisoners, Bettelheim noticed that his emotions became "extremely detached."
He started to "watch" things. So did his comrades. They felt: "It cannot be
true. Such things don't happen."

All these descriptions show that various blocking mechanisms were put
in motion in order to protect the individual from further traumatic experiences. There was the attempt to bar new external stimuli by obstructing
apperceptive functions ("you must not see nor hear"), there was the coldness, the feeling of inner estrangement which permeated the traumatized
personality. Closely associated with this "emotional frigidity" was the impression that the objects of the outer world, too, became shadowy, unreal,
estranged. In many cases, external and internal estrangement[6] seem to have
joined to guard the ego from being flooded by new excitation. Persons in
which this lack of feelings prevailed were soon able to "see and to hear"
again, they even felt urged to "watch" their own and their fellow-prisoners'
behavior. Their affects were replaced by self-observation.

Protective blocking mechanisms thus finally established a sort of "mental
emergency regime" under which the ego was able to function without breaking down. It was characterized by feelings of estrangement, especially lack
of emotions, and by a strong tendency toward self-observation. This syndrome resembles a state of mind which we know as *depersonalization*. In the
state of depersonalization, Nunberg points out, the ego perceives, but the
reality of the perception is not recognized by another part of the ego. ("It
cannot be true, such things don't happen.")

Much like in other cases communicated in analytical literature, the ego
of the prisoners refused to accept the estrangement it was subjected to. It,
therefore, turned the experiences connected with the loss of its feelings into
an object of its intellectual interests. As a secondary symptom, depersonalization thus produced the urge for *self-observation*. By turning its inner development into an object of investigation, the ego makes the first attempt to restore
its contact with the world of objects from which it had withdrawn under
the impact of the initial trauma. This interpretation is all the more intelligible,
as self-observation always includes also the tendency to observe others. We
can understand ourselves only if we understand others and vice versa. Reik[7]

---

[6] Paul Federn makes this distinction.
[7] In several respects this analysis is based on ideas expressed by Reik (19).

compares the appearance of self-observation in depersonalization to the out-break of a fever which is a symptom of physical illness and, at the same time, an attempt on the part of the body to regain health.

In the case of our authors, the healthy component of self-observation was strengthened by an additional and most essential factor. Luckier than their less articulate comrades, they were privileged by the relieving gift of *self-expression*. The close association of depersonalization, self-observation and self-expression, comes forth in several of their reports. A twofold correlation established itself between self-observation and self-expression. The urge to observe not only generated, or increased, the wish for expression, but also the opposite was true: the wish for expression increased the tendency to observe. Szalet, for instance, decided one day to write down his experiences in camp. From that moment on "a strange mood took possession of me, a mixture of despair, fear, and boundless curiosity. So must an explorer feel who has fallen in the power of a cannibal tribe. . . . Sometimes I felt like a man studying the effects of a dangerous and perhaps deadly serum on him-self and on those around him" (p. 137). Bettelheim felt that he was split into two persons, one that observed, and one that was experiencing the things which happened. He asked himself whether he was going insane. At the same time, he saw peculiar changes occurring in some of his previously normal fellow-prisoners. They turned into pathological liars, or were unable to restrain themselves. "How can I protect myself against becoming as they are?" he asked himself. And he decided that first of all, he had to find out what had happened to them and to him. Thus he embarked on a sort of inquiry. He started to question his comrades about their thoughts, their emo-tions, their dreams. He called this occupation a particular type of defense, based on his background and interest and developed to protect his person-ality from disintegration. In fact, Bettelheim had this type of defense in common with all our authors, or rather with all those who were able to turn the urge for self-observation, which they experienced passively, into active self-expression. This ability was a reassurance that the therapeutic com-ponent of the "fever" would predominate over the element of disease.

That an internee chose concentration camp life as an object for his self-expression was not an indispensable prerequisite of such therapeutic effects. There may have been prisoners who elaborated on a book about birds or about mountain climbing. The minds of others may have been busy with the drawing of a picture representing a woman or a street scene in Venice. No doubt, these forms of self-expression would have also been helpful in "turning the tide"; they, too, would have shown that part of the energies which had been withdrawn from reality had returned to the world of objects; but only to a fancied world. Those, however, who embarked on a study about the concentration camp proper, turned toward that very reality which had threatened to overpower them; and they rendered this reality into an object of their "creation." This turn from a passive suffering to an active undertaking indicated that the ego was regaining control. The association between self-observation and self-expression became a most successful mechanism of survival.

The blocking mechanisms evoked by the initial shock produced one of the most striking phenomena of concentration camp life. Our authors unanimously agree that for the mass of inmates a *sex problem* did not exist. This observation contradicts all we know about the doings in other institutions where persons of the same sex are forced to live together, as, for instance, in ordinary prisons, in soldiers' camps, and the like. Kautsky holds that 90% of the concentration camp inmates felt no sexual need (p. 195). Billinger was present when a group of internees discussed the sensational experience that they had no erections any more. In his opinion, this phenomenon was caused by "the heavy spiritual burden" rather than by malnutrition and overwork (p. 173). Kautsky shares this view. In contrast to Frankl who stresses the factor of malnutrition (p. 46), he recalls that the stopping of sexual feelings was observed during his first stay in Dauchau when the inmates concerned were sufficiently fed. He puts the main emphasis on what he terms "mental pressure."

The stopping of sexual needs in men had a counterpart in women. Bloch (13), who studied some five hundred Jewish women after their liberation, reports that their menstruation had ceased in the camp. It was restored under the influence of rest, care, appropriate diet, and relief from fear. It seems, though, that the cessation of menstruation in women was not as common a phenomenon[8] as was the stopping of the sexual urge in men, a condition experienced by the overwhelming majority of inmates; and since it began as early as in the first period of imprisonment and was largely independent of hunger and overwork, one may conclude that its main driving force was the traumatic shock. The dynamics were those effective in the impairment of other functions: Sexual energies, like other libidinal energies, were withdrawn in order to rescue the ego from an overpowering excitation. The ego, frustrated by the outer world to an almost unbearable extent, abandoned its genital claims as it abandoned other forms of object libido. Fenichel, Reik, Dreyfuss, a.o., have analyzed such processes in detail. Dreyfuss mentions also the frequent occurrence of impotence after shell shock (15).

Whenever a person is subject to a severe trauma, he is liable to undergo two complementary experiences. He experiences the "Omni-potence" of fate and, at the same time, his own "Im-potence."

Although our authors agree with each other about the role of the sexual problem, some doubts may still exist. We have heard so much about sexual perversions in Nazi concentration camps that we wonder if sexual strivings were really blocked. Did they not, at least to some extent, shift in the direction of the inmates own sex—in a similar way as in ordinary prisons and soldiers camps? Homosexuality was widely spread, indeed, but primarily among the masters of the camps, the SS-men. As far as prisoners were con-

---

[8] This conclusion can—indirectly—be drawn from Szmaglewska's book.

cerned, it was practiced almost exclusively by the upper strata and by some old-timers, but not by the group of common men. The "prominents," of course, used to look for their objects among the common prisoners, particularly the young ones, and they found them with ease. The promise of extra food and clothing, of protection from hard labor and mistreatment, seldom failed to have the desired effect. Kautsky recalls "undescribable orgies" in which such "pleasure boys" were induced to participate. The result was extreme deprivation of the youth whose age was often below maturity. In Buchenwald, for instance, the youngest prisoner was, according to Kautsky, twelve years of age, according to Burney, eight.

The cessation of sexual strivings in the mass of prisoners, which resembled a reversion to patterns of the pre-puberty state of latency, persisted throughout the entire period of imprisonment. So did the phenomenon of estrangement, the second effect of the blocking activity of the ego, which followed the initial shock. One may ask if the perseverance of these disturbances was due to the first experiences only. Was the original trauma so powerful that its effects lasted for years? Or was the natural tendency of the ego to restore its normal ways of functioning checked by new incidents?

Both assumptions are equally permissible. As mentioned before, the power of a trauma depends on two factors, on its "density," i.e., the amount of excitation it arouses within a short unit of time, and on the degree of unexpectedness with which it occurs.

The presence of the first criterion can hardly be disputed. The "initiation techniques" applied by the Nazis on the transportation to the camp or during the first days in the camp, were a concentrated selection from their large repertory of brutal practices. They included all kinds of physical and mental tribulations, such as being subject to hunger and thirst; to fatigue and dirt; to being kicked and beaten; to defiling and to cursing oneself and one's family, one's nation and political party, one's ideals and one's God.

As to the second criterion, the unexpectedness, the question might be considered moot. Did not at least Jews and active anti-Nazis know what was in store for them? Were they not rather in the state of constant preparedness? They were—and they were not. For years, many a Jew was used to finding all sorts of rationalizations to prove to himself that he, personally, was in no danger: He was a "veteran from world war I," one whom nobody would hurt; or he was "too old" to be of interest for the extermination policy of the Nazis; or there existed a high ranking official whose life he had once saved, who would now protect him.

However, even after all these illusions had broken down, and people were mentally prepared for their deportation, they were not spared the shock. Expectation failed to fulfill its protective function; for what actually happened, was "beyond expectation."

Measured by both criteria, density and unexpectedness, the initial trauma was, thus, exceedingly strong. Even if it had not been followed by other appalling incidents, its assimilation would have required a considerable period of time. Yet appalling incidents did follow in abundance, involving the danger of ever new traumata. Much like in the beginning, this danger was increased by unexpectedness. The prisoner never knew what would happen to him in the next minute. Although ill treatment, or torture, or death, were expected constantly—in most instances they did occur unexpectedly. The individual was always prepared, and—was never prepared. Under the anarchic rule of accident, preparedness was rendered futile. The permanent danger of additional shocks, together with the lasting effects of the initial trauma, prevented the ego from restoring its normal ways of functioning and made it retain its protective "coat of ice."

When Bettelheim conducted his inquiry, he wondered why the greatest shocks did not appear in the dreams of prisoners. This absence of a reaction which could be anticipated, seems to be related to the special circumstances of concentration-camp life. "Repetition in dreams" is a common means of the ego to elaborate a trauma in order to restore normal conditions. In the inmates of concentration camps, however, the tendency of the ego to return to its normal state was obliterated by the efforts to avoid additional shocks. As long as repetitions of the trauma in reality were imminent, repetition in dreams was deprived of its meaning.

REGRESSIVE PHENOMENA AND THE "BARRIERS" OF CULTURE

The protection granted to the individual by the defense mechanism of estrangement was certainly not complete, but without it, many a prisoner who did survive, might have been defeated in his struggle for self-preservation. In the long run, further modes of physical and psychic adjustment to the camp situation had to be developed.

With the modes of physical adaptation we do not have to deal here at length. Enough to mention that they produced a curious insensibility toward injuries and dangers which under normal circumstances might have been pernicious. Kautsky observed that persons running a fever of 104 degrees were walking around in the cold of the winter for days, and recovered. Certain types of disease, such as rheumatism and some nervous conditions seemed to disappear completely. And Frankl found the condition of gums in the inmates better than they had ever been before, despite the poor vitamin contents of the food

Psychic adjustment, the topic of this study, has been determined by some basic facts of mental functioning. No human being can live without pleasure. If it is to survive, its "pleasure instincts" (14)—"sexual instincts" in the terminology of Freud—have to be satisfied as well as its urge for self-preservation. Through the so called "sublimation," direct instinctual gratification can, to a certain extent, be replaced by spiritual enjoyment. However, in an average individual the capacity for sublimation is limited; and if the normal "adult" ways of gratification are obstructed, the instincts tend to turn back for satisfaction to pleasure sources of the childhood period; they "reoccupy" formerly abandoned positions of enjoyment by way of "regression." The tendency to regress is the stronger, the weaker the adult ego, and the more the instincts have remained "fixated" on gratifications which prevailed in early stages of their development.

Regression was, of course, what the Nazis aimed at—unless complete extermination was intended; regression to a state of child-like dependence in which the prisoners would become helpless instruments in their masters' hands. This was the so-called "educational purpose" of the concentration camps.

Under the living conditions of the internees, even infantile satisfactions were frequently out of reach, or they could be acquired only by means against which culture has erected strong prohibitions. Such prohibitions, internalized in the individual as "super-ego-demands," establish the standard of values to which it adheres; in part they also join with biological reactions and assume an almost instinctual character. The most outstanding representatives of such quasi-instinctual inhibitive reactions are the feelings of *disgust and shame*. These primitive "agents of culture" were a favorite target for the attacks which the sadism of the Nazis launched against the adult ego of the prisoners. Such attacks—if they succeeded—would not only promote regression to very early levels; they would also expose the victim to severe internal conflicts. The more the cultural barriers had themselves assumed instinctual character, the more painful were the assaults upon them. Enforced breakdown of these barriers was capable of bringing the prisoner near to mental disintegration. The greater the tensions he had to suffer, the more intense was the enjoyment of his tormentors.

Nothing seemed better fit to provide such enjoyments than the primary functions of life: the intake and elimination of food. Since both, the urge for self-preservation and the urge for pleasure, depend for their satisfaction on these functions, they offered a chance to hit the fundamental needs of the individual simultaneously from two sides. No wonder that the camp masters developed a whole arsenal of oral- and anal-sadistic techniques.

Their *anal-sadistic practices* ranged from the common system of enforcing strict toilet regulations to monstrous and diabolic tortures. Karst emphasizes the effect of the toilet regulations. "Because of the cold," he says, "people had cystic catarrhs, and constantly had to let water. . . . Since the elder people could not contain themselves, they let water into their clothing" (p. 66). Szalet also mentions "bladder-sufferers" who wet their clothes and filled the air with the reek of urine and ammonia fumes. Many wet their neighbours as well, and this led to outbursts of resentment. "It was an infernal atmosphere," he adds. "We felt abandoned, ashamed, and degraded" (p. 63). Wiechert expresses similar feelings: "Filth degrades the innermost being of man" (p. 17). Karst reports an incident which discloses the anal- and oral-sadistic tendencies of the tormentors at the same time. "The SS-men

asked the prisoners with simulated sympathy if anyone was thirsty, and
when a poor wretch dared say 'yes,' his neighbor was ordered to urinate 'into
the mouth of the swine' " (p. 111). A similar occurrence is recorded by
Szalet. Once several of his comrades had secretly slipped into the toilet and
were discovered there. Severe punishment followed. At first, they had to
sing, turn around in circles, and insult their countrymen. The next day they
were vehemently beaten and rolled about on the urine-covered floor. Then
they were ordered to drink out of toilet bowls. The men could not bring
themselves to obey; they only pretended to. But the "block leaders forced
their heads deep into the bowls until they were covered with excrement. At
that they almost went out of their minds—that was why their screams had
sounded so demented" (p. 42). When an epidemic of dysentery broke out in
the Sachsenhausen camp, the same author reports, the worst cases were
ordered to sleep in the toilet room. The bowls were often so full that their
contents overflowed. Among the very sick was a well-known old professor
from the University of Warsaw. One night, Szalet found him lying in the
toilet room, the face smeared with excrement, the hands covered with slime.
He asked for a piece of paper. By chance Szalet possessed a whole newspaper
which he gave him. The old man was deeply grateful. "I am so happy," he
said. "I will never forget it." Szalet adds: "An old newspaper had become
the supreme blessing for a man who a few months before had been the pride
of Polish scholarship. . . . I ran back—my sobs were like screams" (p. 211).

The "mildest" among the scourges described here were the toilet regulations, although they actually were a source of constant suffering. Even where
physical reasons did not make it altogether impossible to comply with such
rules, their observance required a considerable amount of energy. In quite
a number of cases, the inhibitions of disgust and shame were not strong
enough to prevent an individual from a return to childhood reactions, and
manifest symptoms of regression occurred. People did not retain themselves;
men who were allowed to get up at night and ease their needs, did not do it;
they fell back to bed-wetting instead. Kautsky stresses the psychogenic character of many such occurrences, and it is open to question which of the
"bladder sufferers" mentioned by Karst and Szalet were really organic cases.

In calling these reactions regressive we are well aware that people who
live under extraordinary conditions, such as soldiers in war or explorers in
uncivilized regions, are able to give up their habitual standards of cleanliness
without deeper disturbance; yet only up to certain limits. These limits are
determined by the area within which the demands of disgust and shame are
flexible, that is, shaped by history, by the patterns of a particular civilization,
or by social standards. Cleanliness habits in the field of urination and defeca-
tion, however, are not within this range of flexibility; they are enforced by
any culture at an early stage of training, they are part of the process of
acculturation. Their neglect means return to the instinctual behavior of early
childhood. Kautsky felt distinctly the regressive character not only of the
particular phenomenon of enuresis, but of the growing indifference towards
dirt in general. He blames for it a factor he calls the "lack of self-restraint"

and stresses the importance of keeping up the "sense of cleanliness." He noticed that individuals who became negligent, stopped washing themselves, etc., were particularly liable to disintegration (p. 183/4).

In the direction of disintegration worked the monstrous anal-sadistic tortures reported above. Only infants have not yet developed a disgust toward their own excrements; certain psychotics, too, may play with their feces and even eat them; however, the normal adult of our civilization shares the disgust toward the contact with his excrements with members of tribes who live on the lowest levels of culture. This disgust seems to be a demarkation line, the transgression of which can produce effects much more devastating than the appearance of more or less isolated regressive symptoms. It means regression of the major part of the personality to the narcissisic stage of infancy, a dissolution of the ego into the state of insanity. Szalet understood instinctively that the prisoners "almost" went out of their minds when they had to drink the contents of toilet bowls. Much as death did at other times, in such moments, insanity reached out for them. But they screamed. They were able to keep up their feelings of disgust, of shame, of degradation.

All these considerations are based on the assumption that mental illness can, in principle, be induced by exogenic causes. We are well aware that this is only half of the truth, and that external factors do not become effective unless their influence is warranted by individual predisposition. However, few people would become ill only on account of their predisposition, were it not for the additional injurious experiences to which life has exposed them.

It is true that any torture the prisoners were subjected to was an additional "injurious experience." It appears, however, that particularly perilous were the violent attacks against the earliest inhibitions imposed by culture on instincts which are buried deep in the unconscious layers of the human mind.

The masters of the camp were not only possessed by their open anal-sadistic strivings; they had also developed reaction-formations against them. The result was that, on the one hand, they tried to destroy the demands of disgust and shame which were part of the adult ego of the prisoners; on the other hand, they increased these demands to a paradoxical extent. The inmates who had to endure "orgies" of dirt, were also subjected to orders of ridiculously meticulous *cleanliness.* Certain rules were so extreme that they contributed to destroy normal standards of cleanliness rather than uphold them. One favored subject of such orders were the boots. Szalet recalls a capo who found out that the prisoners dirtied the barrack with their clay-smeared boots when they returned from work. Thus, they had to take off their boots and to wade in excrement when they went to the toilet (p. 273). Karst reports that the boots had to be polished three times a day. "We used to say that our souls dropped into our soles" (p. 117/8). When a certain SS-man noticed a speck on a prisoner's boots, he had the guilty tied to a tree (p. 131). Kautsky mentions that not only the shoes had to be clean and shiny, the soles had to be shiny to. He once saw an inspector scratching with a nail-file under the nail of a sole—to find whether there was a grain of sand (p. 217).

Both Karst and Kautsky recall the orders concerning cupboards, closets, towels, toothbrushes, beds, etc. Towels and toothbrushes had always to be spotlessly clean. In order to comply with these requirements, the men did not touch them. For actual use, they carried a rag and a second toothbrush in their pockets.—The beds had not to be "made," they had to be "built." The bedspreads, as far as they existed, had to be turned in along their square pattern in a strictly straight line; blankets and pillows had to be arranged according to a fixed rite. Any failure to do so was punished severely. It happened quite often that a prisoner who was not up to this kind of job hired one of his more skilled comrades as a "bed-builder." The fee was five to six mark a month. Kautsky saw a man sleeping on the floor next to his bed,— he did not want to destroy the precious structure. Whenever an inspection was due the following day, two men used to sleep in the same bad, so that only half of the "buildings" had to be restored in the morning (p. 218).

The obstacles which civilization has put in the way of instinct satisfaction through childhood pleasures are of different strength. Undisguised gratification of oral strivings is permitted to a greater extent than are manifest anal enjoyments. The man who is disappointed in love and takes to excessive eating, is a case in point. He may be able to enjoy the pleasures of orality without being disturbed by inhibitions. Where malnutrition, even starvation, prevailed, there was little chance for gratifications of this kind. But the concentration camp inmates were not only deprived of such sources of substitute pleasure; the sources of pleasure were turned into sources of pain instead; for the sadistic practices applied by the camp masters in the sphere of *orality* were not more restrained than the anal-sadistic techniques we have just exposed.

The following are a few examples:

Szalet and his comrades were lying in their room in stench and thirst. Paul, the room-senior, came in. "Who wants water?" he asked. One prisoner said, "I." He was beaten up fiercely. Paul asked again, and nobody dared to say anything. So he took a bucket and threw its contents into the room. The men greedily licked the drops which had fallen on their arms and clothes (p. 41).

Another incident: After the men had just started to eat, an overseer suddenly announced that the time was up for the roll call. He made the prisoners pour their soup into the toilets, so that the majority went hungry. In fact, there was still half-an-hour left. They stood around, not knowing what to do (p. 234).

One of the most diabolic oral tortures was the notorious "bread game." The block-leader "would throw bread into the corner of the room, and we would pounce on it like a pack of famished hounds. Then he threw more bread into the opposite corner. The human knot on the floor untied itself and lunged towards the other corner. We hurled each other aside, trampled and kicked each other. And all the time the room rang with bellows of laughter." Szalet stresses the suffering from bitter shame and degradation brought upon the prisoners by this infliction (p. 145). Rousset pictures a similar scene. "Franz, the camp senior, tosses the bread into the middle of the aisle . . . two bodies hurl themselves on the bread. Then, like a cascade plunging into a gulf, a furious pell-mell of flaring fists and thrashing feet. Bellies groan: 'Bread!' . . . Franz and the Kammercapo throw themselves upon the the pile . . . blackjacks rise and fall . . . three men still clutch the bread, beside themselves with greed. . . . Franz laughs wholeheartedly— . . . he had felt the need for entertainment" (p. 147).

Such incidents caused the prisoner nothing but pain. The degradation he had to suffer was not accompanied by instinctual gratification: hunger was not satisfied—let alone the strivings for oral enjoyment. The need for pleasure, deprived of almost all objects in the sphere of reality, took refuge in the last resort of the poor and defeated, in *fantasy.* All authors emphasize the endless discussions on food among the inmates. Much like the shipwrecked in a raft, they exchanged memories of the splendid meals they had had in the past; they fancied what they would eat on the day of their liberation; they worked out elaborate menus; they discussed recipes; they talked on and on, for hours, unable to stop, it was like a compulsion. A camp-jargon called such conversations "stomach masturbation" (Frankl, p. 43), unconsciously hitting the autoerotic nature of this pleasure in which the real object was replaced by fantasy.

The dreams of the prisoners, too, revolved mainly around oral satisfactions. Bettelheim and Frankl who questioned their comrades found that their dreams had hardly any sexual contents in the narrower sense; instead, their topics were bread, pies, cigarettes, or a warm bath. Wiechert reports: From the day on when he was prohibited to drink a drop of water during the hardest work in the burning sun, "visions of the spring in his yard at home ran through his dreams day and night" (p. 71).

The role played by fantasy in the pursuit of oral satisfaction adopted extraordinary forms. The behavior of the prisoners as pictured in the following scene reminds one almost of psychotic reactions. On Christmas, Szalet reports, an extra allotment of a whole loaf of bread was distributed in the block. "Only a few withdrew with their bread to a distant corner, like dogs with particularly juicy bones, and did not emerge until the last crumb had vanished. Most of the comrades simply could not make up their mind to eat. They eyed the bread lovingly, cradled it in their arms, walked with it to and fro as if they were having a private talk with their precious treasure . . . they wanted to enjoy it as long as possible. . . . The thought that they must eat it up at once, and that their dreams would soon end in a full belly, seemed unbearable. . . . Only after repeated urgings from Karl (the room senior) did they sit down and eat their bread, dutifully and without pleasure . . ." (p. 185).

These prisoners, in their search for satisfaction, had taken refuge in fantasy to such an extent that they almost gave up the contact with reality. The men hesitated to exchange the rich and never ending pleasures of fantasy for a poor and passing "real" gratification. As long as they held the loaf of bread in their arms, it still was the beloved object of their dreams; it embodied the enjoyments of tomorrow and of the day after tomorrow, of a life without suffering from unfulfilled needs. Eating the bread meant destruction of this symbol of a future of plenty, meant brief pleasure followed by disappointment and by the necessity to withdraw anew to the abode of fantasy.

Although fantasy might have supplied substitute gratification to the frustrated strivings for pleasure—it could not satisfy the urge for physical self-preservation. Hunger and thirst demanded direct and "real" satisfaction. Whenever these needs became urgent enough, they were capable of overthrowing almost all obstacles which the superego demands put in the way of their fulfillment—from the subtler requests of conscience to the most primitive impositions of disgust and shame.

The extremest break-down which these primitive barriers of culture suffered in the sphere of orality, expressed itself in the appearance of *cannibalism.* Cannibalism was not observed in all camps described by our authors. Kautsky found no evidence of it, but he does not exclude its possibility. Frankl mentions the outbreak of cannibalism in one camp without giving further details. Rousset, however, recalls some striking incidents. In the camp Neuengamme, one day a human jawbone was discovered in the soup. Investigations revealed that the kitchen-capo together with the capo of the crematorium had sold the meat, which was intended for the kitchen, to civilians and had fed the prisoners on cadavers. "After all, dead flesh is meat," remarks Rousset, and he is ready to "wager that many a man regretted that X ever made this discovery" (p. 123). According to the same author, three cases of cannibalism occurred in the camp Woebbelin when hunger was rampant. To prevent further incidents of this kind, a guard had to be set up around the morgue (p. 160). And finally, after Germany's defeat, when near Hannover all the capos and foreman were massacred, . . . "the Russians ate the thigh of Gaertner, the revoltingly brutal capo of D" (p. 165).

However, these were exceptional cases, indeed. In average individuals the break-down of cultural inhibitions referred to the sphere of *moral values* rather than to regulations of human behaviour of the most primitive character.

To what extent moral standards can be destroyed by the urge for self-preservation, is confessed by a cultured British woman, previously noted for her generosity and humanitarian interests. She says: "I decided I wanted to live. Nothing else counted. I would have stolen from husband, child, parent, in order to accomplish this . . . I . . . devoted every fiber of my being to those things which would make that possible. Every day . . . I had an objective: stealing a sweater, bargain for a blanket . . . for an extra-bowl of soup . . . , do something that I could survive . . . I would remain close to those who were too far gone or too weak to eat their meagre ration of Ersatz-Kaffe or soup, and instead of pressing them to eat so that they might exist, I would eagerly take it from them and wolf it down, if they gave the slightest evidence that the effort for them was too great."[9] Similar experiences are reported by others. Kautsky, e.g., recalls situations in which the prisoners snatched bread from the hands of their comrades and tore clothes and blankets away from the bodies of the weak (p. 172).

However, the most striking collapse of moral values occurred in a group of inmates who did not have to struggle for the necessities of life, namely in the privileged group of functionaries. Among them were individuals who completely abandoned their own moral standards and took over the values of the Nazis instead. They went so far as to inflict the most cruel tortures on their fellow-prisoners, imitating the techniques of their SS-masters. Much like these, they enjoyed playing the "bread game," they prohibited other prisoners to relieve themselves or to drink a drop of water, they made their comrades pour their food into the toilet and go hungry, they beat them to death at work, and let them perish in filth and disease.

The highest ranking inmate was the camp-senior. According to Kautsky, the gulf between him and the mass of inmates was infinitely greater than that between a powerful capitalist or statesman in a democracy and an unemployed who has to spend his nights on a park bench. This is the picture he gives of the camp-senior in Auschwitz-Bunau: "He could eat and drink to his heart's delight. He had his meals especially cooked; . . . clothes, underwear, shoes—as many and as beautiful as he wanted; for what, after all, did the Jews in the gas chambers die? Women—the camp bordello or the thousands of girls in Buna supplied all material desired. Art—the camp orchestra with first rate players was at his disposal, among them the first violinist of the Berlin opera and graduates from the Vienna school of music; painters and artists complied with all his wishes; a theatre group had to follow his orders. . . . To deal with his sicknesses, the real and the imagined ones, specialists from all countries could be put into action: a Polish surgeon, a French expert in internal medicine, a Hungarian eye-specialist, a German earman." Finally, he was permitted to do "something that no capitalist or statesman could do. . . . Without fear of punishment he was able to live out his sadistic impulses, beat human beings to death, until his lust was satisfied" (p. 168/9).

Some authors felt distinctly that, in most cases, the brutal behavior of the prisoner-superiors involved an element of fear. In their opinion, the prominents were afraid to lose their privileged position, unless they showed extreme austerity. This interpretation reveals only a part of the truth. In fact, quite a few capos and foremen did treat their comrades with kindliness, whenever they felt sure that no Nazi supervisor was around. It appears rather that the fear which instigated atrocities of this type was of a much deeper and less conscious nature than was presumed by our writers. It has been substantiated that certain individuals try to protect themselves against severe anxieties through an *identification with their aggressor.* This defense mechanism is

---

[9] Quoted by Bloch a.o.

particularly frequent in children. Anna Freud reports about a little girl who advised her younger brother on how to get rid of his fear for ghosts. "There is no need to be afraid in the hall," she said. "You just have to pretend that you're the ghost who might meet you" (17). Forenczi's little Arpad crowed like a cock and imitated its behavior in order to alleviate his fear the cock might bite off his penis (16). "By impersonating the aggressor, assuming his attitudes or imitating his aggression, the child transform himself from the person who is threatened into the person who makes the threat" (17).

After having given so much consideration to the working of regressive tendencies in the inmates of concentration camps, we may understand that weak egos, which a priori were susceptible to regression, developed reactions particularly characteristic of children. Even the partial protection through feelings of estrangement could not save the prisoners from anxieties inevitably associated with the rule of accident and terror. Through identification with the tormentor, the prominents tried to free themselves from such anxieties and to gain security. For losing one's self in a powerful enemy, being "eaten up" by him, means overcoming one's own helplessness and participating in his omnipotence.

The wish for identification with the aggressor has been observed also in adults. In some illustrative case reports, Clara Thompson stresses the vicious circle put in motion by this defense-mechanism (21). The stronger the need for identification, the more a person loses himself in his omnipotent enemy—the more helpless he becomes. The more helpless he feels, the stronger the identification, and—we may add—the more likely it is that he tries even to surpass the aggressiveness of his aggressor. This may explain the almost unbelievable phenomenon that prisoner-superiors sometimes acted more brutally than did members of the SS.

Kautsky holds that most of the prominents (and even of the SS-men) committed their brutalities with a distinctly bad conscience. The old ego-ideals and their underlying identifications apparently were still in existence. They conflicted with the attempts of the regressed part of the ego to make new identifications which were strictly opposed to those of the past. It seems that not seldom the prominents tried to overcome ensuing guilt-feelings by a very common reaction: they projected the guilt they felt onto the objects of their aggression, and fell upon them in the resulting fits of rage. These were, of course, followed by increased guilt feelings which promoted new projections and more aggression—another vicious circle, sometimes broken only by the death of the tormented tormentors, inflicted upon them by the hands of their victims.

Identification with the aggressor represented the final stage of passive adaptation. It was a means of defense of a rather paradoxical nature: survival through surrender; protection against the fear of the enemy—by becoming part of him; overcoming helplessness—by regressing to childish dependence.

It is an appalling fact that this was the course taken by quite a number of internees in concentration camps, by members of various nationalities, by political and non-political prisoners, by men and by women. Yet—compared with the total of the interned, their number was small; and before drawing any general conclusions from such occurrences, we will have to learn to what extent this complete defeat of all previous ego-ideals in one group was offset by the achievements of counter-regressive forces in other groups.

SUBLIMATION

One of the first attempts to overcome the predicaments of the concentration camp by means of sublimation had been made by our authors when they started to write their books, or at least to conceive them.

Indulgence in pleasant memories of the past, enjoyment of nature, discussions on all kinds of spiritual topics, and sometimes even extraordinary moral accomplishments—all these were immaterial satisfactions with which the inmates took refuge. Most authors emphasize that their sense of beauty, their love of nature, was not destroyed in the camp. Szmaglewska gives particularly impressive descriptions of such enjoyments. She recalls, for instance, the pathetic picture of women sitting on the edge of the camp and looking on a meadow behind the wire where a yellow iris opened its petals. "Sometimes it grew quite dark and the women are still sitting there. A deep silence flows from the fields and the meadows and takes these miserables into its possession. They lose the precious hours of sleep, but gain peace of mind which let them live through the day with determination, perhaps even with cheerfulness" (p. 193). Kautsky holds that "there was no better means against hunger than discussions on Goethe and Mozart, on mountain climbing and swimming, on beautiful Paris or Geneva, on Caesar or the French revolution"; and he remembers with pride the grotesque sight of the "latrine commando" in Buchenwald discussing such topics with the greatest of ardor while carrying the feces cask from one latrine to the other (p. 185). Frankl recalls a lecture he gave one evening when everybody was in a desperate mood. He spoke about the meaning of life and of suffering, and afterwards people thanked him with tears in their eyes (p. 91). Moral values, too, were not completely lost in the camp. Next to instances of utmost recklessness as recorded above, all authors remember deeds which proved to them that kindness, courage, and consideration for others had not perished altogether. Kalmar reports that one of his fellow-prisoners risked his life to bring him some wine when he lay sick in the camp hospital. He even hails the inmates for their "unconditional comradeship" (p. 15). Kautsky, in his more sober way, holds that, on the one hand, nobody was ready to practice comradeship, on the other hand, nobody would have survived without it. He, too, emphasizes that testimonies of a genuine humaneness were to be found in all camps, in members of all nations, in all groups of prisoners (p. 175 and 179).

However, the power of such spiritual forces was inevitably enfeebled. When fatigue, physical pain, hunger, the suffering from filth and vermin surpassed certain limits, instinctual needs could no longer be satisfied by immaterial objects. These limits certainly differed from individual to individual. However, here again the concentration camp turned individual phenomena into typical ones: in innumerable situations the pressure of primitive urges was so great that nobody was able to cope with it by way of sublimation.

There was one spiritual force left which might have held its ground in such extreme situations; this force was religion. How did it fare in the Inferno of the Nazi concentration camp? A most intensely religious personality among our authors is Wiechert. His faith, however, did not stand this test. In peaceful moments he was still able to feel that the world was God's creation. The view of the glowing evening clouds made his exclaim, "Oh, how beauteous is Thy world, Father!" But, the very next minute, when an old man close to him was tortured, he cried out: "No, no Father any longer beyond the stars and golden clouds!" (p. 85). Most revealing are the few sentences in which shortly before he was released from the camp he sums up his feelings. Says he: "Just once the veil was lifted from ultimate things, and J. (i.e., Wiechert) had looked behind the veil. 'No man shall see the face of the Lord and live' was written in the Bible. But if this is Jehovah's face, then it was better to erase his name and to replace it with a simpler one, a name without glory or love; that of a man or of one of the beasts of the Revelation" (p. 126). And finally, when he left the camp, "from everywhere they waved to him, stealthily, and almost with their eyes alone. 'God be with you! God be with you!' had been the cry of the convicts in Dostojewsky's *House of the Dead*. But here they could not say 'God be with you.' God had forsaken them and died" (p. 129).

These are desperate and rebellious words expressing the defeat of religion rather than the inability of human beings to live up to its demands. They touch upon an issue connected with the very essence of faith and distinguishing it from all other spiritual values, namely, the question of ultimate responsibility for the affairs of this world. This question inevitably preys on the mind of any religious person in situations of utmost affliction. Two opposite answers have been given by the desperate inmates of concentration camps; one by those Jews who, when driven to the gas-chambers, loudly repeated psalms of penitence or confessed their sins. They put the blame for their inflictions on themselves. Others, in the same situation, imprecated God (20). They felt like Wiechert who held God responsible. God had permitted such conditions to arise; he had failed to fulfill his promises; instead of protecting his children, he delivered them to the destructive forces of man. Feeling that there was only once choice left, either to submit unconditionally to those "unscrutable ways of the Lord," or to revolt, the disappointed son revolted against the deceitful father and pronounced him dead.

There occurred also other types of "religious rebellion." Kautsky recalls a Protestant minister who from the bunker where he was detained, loudly addressed the prisoners outside, condemning injustice and terror and stirring up resistance. Needless to say he did not survive. Great moral strength based on religious convictions was exhibited by members of the sect of "Jehovah's Witnesses." The Nazis offered them release from the camp under the condition that they abandoned their doctrine and entered the army. Almost all of them refused. Our authors, while on the one hand, praising the attitude of these men, on the other hand, emphasize their narrowness and rigidity. Says Wiechert: "All their faces seemed stamped by the same narrowness, the same compulsions, and the same prophetic promise. Faces of which J. could well imagine that they would look on expressionless while all heretics were roasting over a slow fire into damnation everlasting" (p. 98).

Our books do not contain much about the "silent consolation" religion may have brought to the believer, although we find occasional remarks on impressive services or moods of deep devotion. The scantiness of such observations may be attributable to the fact that several of our authors had no close relationship towards religion—if any.

They were inclined to follow an earthy father rather than a father "beyond the clouds" (Wiechert). If we adopt the view that a group leader, and even a group-ideal, represents a father substitute,—then we must admit that those father figures who were the formative forces of *political groupings* exercised a remarkable influence on the inmates of concentration camps.

Belonging to a political group whose ideology was strictly opposed to Nazism, taking part in its secret activities in the camp, managing to keep up the connection with group members outside the camp—these were some of the most important object relations the prisoner was able to maintain. Such activities allowed a certain amount of emotional discharge in a socially approved way, thereby strengthening the anti-regressive tendencies in the individual and increasing its chances to act in harmony with its old ego-ideals. Most authors stress the fact that within the framework of such political groups, comradeship, solidarity, and discipline were maintained to a remarkable extent. The more successful the group comrades outside the camp were in their active struggle against the Nazis, the greater was this moral influence. We may perhaps say, the more powerful the father with whom the individual had identified itself through "love," the smaller the temptation to make new identifications caused by fear. Ardent anti-Communists, such as Karst who is a convinced Catholic, emphasize the comradely spirit within the Communist group (p. 89). Kautsky, himself an old and faithful Social-Democrat and enemy of Communism, shares this view, and praises also the moral standard of his group, especially the readiness of its members to assist each other in the struggle for survival. He holds that the clandestine preparations for action after Hitler's expected defeat, were an eminent source of inner strength for members of all political groups during the last year of imprisonment; and he recalls with pride the surprise of the American liberators when "among mountains of corpses, in barracks crowded with the dying and the starving, they found men, full of will power, with unbroken spirit, alive with hatred against fascism and with the burning wish to serve the idea of freedom" (p. 181).

HOW DID THEY SURVIVE?

When Bettelheim asked himself what his and his comrades' main problem was in the camp all the time, he would say: to come out alive and unchanged. He tried "to safeguard his ego in such a way that, if by any good luck he should regain liberty, he would be approximately the same person he was when deprived of liberty" (p. 19).

The preceding study has emphasized the changes to which the ego of the prisoners was subjected while they stayed in the camp: the internal and external estrangement; regressions to infantile ways of instinct satisfaction; abandonment of moral demands to the extent where the ego gave up itself in order to be preserved. Did, thus, the survivors accomplish only a part of their essential endeavor? Did they come out alive but not unchanged?

The sparing information given by our authors on their experiences after their liberation allows only some preliminary considerations.

The reports show that a certain period of time elapsed before the ego relinquished the protective mechanisms it had developed during camp life.

Frankl felt that, at first, the most urgent physical needs had to be satisfied. "One starts to eat—for hours, for days, through half the night," he says. Then . . . "one talks, without stopping, like under a compulsion" (p. 124). One day, the ice melts, emotions awaken, one begins to feel—freedom.

Kalmar describes his return home to his wife. "My heart was so cold that I felt the blood congealing under my nails. The response to tenderness did not work any more, it had been repressed too long to answer the first call." So, he and his wife talked in more or less "empty phrases";—the same kind of phrases they had used in the letters they had been allowed to exchange twice a month, for seven years. "Thank you that you have waited for me," he said. "Thank you for having come back," she replied. Then silence followed, and some of the obstructed sources broke open. But Kalmar was not yet back home. Entering his room, he noticed a mask of his father—the person he had loved more than any other man, and who had died while the son was in the camp. At the time when the news of his death arrived, Kalmar felt nothing. Now, looking at the silent mask of the dead, "a crack ran through the iron wall which had protected me against the merciless realities of the camp. The blood flowed back into the coldness of my lonely heart, and flooded over the empty craters of a pathless desert" (p. 26).

It appears that the restoration of affects, the reversion of the feelings of estrangement were among the first symptoms of a return to mental health. To what extent, and at what time, the other ego changes were revoked, we hardly know. Did the cultured British woman regain in full the moral standards she had abandoned? Did all those whose instincts had taken recourse to the primitive satisfactions of childhood find back to their previous ways of enjoyment? In which ways and to what degree? The answer to these questions may depend on various factors—such as, for example, on the individual's need for a belated mastery of the traumata it had suffered, on its way to comply with this need, and on the opportunities to fulfill it. Some people were capable of a slow and gradual elaboration of their experiences, others strived for a violent discharge of the counter-aggressive impulses which they had repressed for so long a time. Frankl recalls one of his good comrades shouting: "I want this hand to be cut off unless it will be stained with blood the day I will leave the camp" (p. 124). In some cases, as in the massacre of the capos reported by Rousset, such wishes materialized, in most cases they did not. Kautsky praises the restraint which political leadership imposed on the masses after liberation. It is hard to say whether aggressive impulses which thereby remained pent up, are still liable to eruptions—perhaps at the wrong moment and against the wrong objects. This seems to be a danger at which a prominent leader of the present Germany hinted, when he said that the Germans suffered from "a prevented revolution."[10]

Our study has dealt with extreme reactions produced by extreme frustrations and with attempts to overcome them. In this struggle, weak egos sometimes followed the temptations of dark and forgotten instincts which belong to the animal heritage of man. The average prisoner, though abandoning his normal standards of values to a large extent, still refused to be pulled into an abyss which—uncovered by the sadism of the Nazis—was about to swallow the very foundations of civilization and society.

Our authors repeatedly expressed the feeling that they had sunk to the level of animals. This strikes only a part of the truth. Like animals they suffered from hunger, from thirst and from physical pain. Like human beings, however, they suffered from shame, disgust, degradation. Like animals they were the prey of want and of fear. Like human beings they clung to the demands of culture which exposed them to grave conflicts. Sometimes these conflicts reached into the depths of the mind far remote from the layers a human being ever touches under normal circumstances of living.

From the occurrences we have dealt with, quite contrary conclusions may be drawn. One may be horrified by the most extreme reactions, such as the brutal behavior towards the sick and the dying, or the cruelties of the prisoner-functionaries, or the—hardly conceivable—appearance of cannibalism. "How thin are the layers of culture," one may say, "if such things can happen!" But one may just as well form the opposite opinion—as did some of our authors, among them Kautsky. He feels by no means pessimistic about mankind, having observed that even under the most horrible conditions of the concentration camp, compassion, friendship, and humaneness were not completely absent. He holds that the destructive forces in society can be mastered, once social and political achievements will have freed man from want and fear.

Any judgment depends on the gauge one applies. If measured by the

---

[10] Dr. Kurt Schumacher, head of Germany's Social Democratic Party, in a speech in October 1947.

standards which we are used to taking for granted as long as we are not confronted with extreme tribulations, the power of resistance sustained by the socalled "cultured personality" may be set down as rather insignificant. And yet, the same power of resistance may command full respect, if we consider the overwhelming force of the opposing instincts to which all living creatures are subjected. And finally, we must not forget that this study was dealing with the survivors only. Many of those who did not survive, outside as well as inside the camps, perished because of their unconquerable will to maintain their standards of values at any price. It was this will that forced them into actions for which—they knew well—they had to pay with their lives. The examples of moral strength among the survivors as well as among the dead, entitle even the sceptic to at least one modest conclusion: that the never ending efforts of man to derive gratification from "Civilization and its Discontents" have not been entirely in vain.

BIBLIOGRAPHY

A. *List of Autobiographical Works on Which This Study Was Based*

1. Bettelheim, Bruno, *My Life in Nazi Concentration Camps*; Haldeman, Julius; Girard, Kan. (no publishing date).
2. Billinger, Karl, *Fatherland*. New York, 1935.
3. Burney, Christopher, *The Dungeon Democracy*. New York, 1946.
4. Federn, Ernst, "Essai sur la psychologie de la terreur," in *Synthèses*, Revue Mensuelle Internationale. Bruxelles, 1946, No. 7 and 8.
5. Frankl, Victor E., *Ein Psycholog erlebt das Konzentrationslager* (A Psychologist Experiences the Concentration Camp). Vienna, 1946.
6. Kalmar, Rudolf, *Zeit ohne Gnade* (Time without Mercy). Vienna, 1946.
7. Karst, George M., *The Beasts of the Earth*. New York, 1942.
8. Kautsky, Benedikt, *Teufel und Verdammte* (The Devil and the Damned). Zurich, 1946.
9. Rousset, David, *The Other Kingdom*. New York, 1947.
10. Szalet, Leon, *Experiment E*. New York, 1945.
11. Szmaglewska, Seweryna, *Smoke over Birkenau*. New York, 1947.
12. Wiechert, Ernst, *Forest of the Dead*. New York, 1947.

B. *Other References*

13. Bloch, Herbert A., "The Personality of Inmates of Concentration Camps," *American Journ. of Sociology*, January, 1947.
14. Brun, Rudolf, *Allgem. Neurosenlehre*. Basel, 1946.
15. Dreyfuss, Daniel, *Zur Theorie der traumatischen Neurose*, Int. Zeitschr. f. Psychoanalyse, 1941, Vol. 26.
16. Ferenczi, S., "Ein kleiner Hahnemann" (A Little Rooster-Man), *Bausteine z. Psychoan.*, Zurich, Vienna, 1927.

17. Freud, Anna, *The Ego and the Mechanisms of Defense*. New York, 1946.
18. Uunberg, Herman, *Allg. Neurosenlehre*. Bern, Berlin, 1932.
19. Reik, Theodor, *Wie man Psychologe wird* (How to Become a Psychologist), Vienna, 1927.
20. Syrkin, Marie, *Blessed Is the Match*. New York, 1947.
21. Thompson, Clara, "Identification with the Enemy and Loss of the Sense of Self," *Psychoanalyt. Quarterly*, 1940.

Survival in the Concentration Camp: An Individual or a Group Phenomenon?

EMIL LUCHTERHAND

It is the emergence of a prisoner social system, even under the smoke-pall of the crematoria and outdoor pyres and pits, which Bettelheim[1] neglects. Perhaps because of the time-and-place limitations of his own experience, he misses the subtlety and complexity of many kinds of relationships in the camps. In this, he is not alone. The fellowship of error includes, among others, the sociologist Herbert Bloch. He interviewed survivors informally at several locations after liberation. Projecting from his knowledge of prisoner relationships in American penal institutions, Bloch published an article in the *American Journal of Sociology* early in 1947 in which he characterized the camps as "modern feral communities."[2] The phrase caught on and is memorialized in various speculative writings on the camps in this country.

The peculiarities of American theory and discussion of the camps, as contrasted with most of the European work, stem from two main sources. *First*, there were gross reporting errors as well as the difficulty of making sense of the strange world of the camps. *Second*, at the war's end, there was quick publication of poorly grounded theories. These tended to support the familiar theses of Bettelheim published in his very widely quoted and reprinted article of 1943. *Third*, and this is a point made by the sociologist, Paul Foreman, in an article in *Social Forces* in May, 1959—"early American discussions are conforming and tend to seal off major sociological interests."

Special criticism has been directed against Bettelheim despite the truly noteworthy contributions which he has made. It is not simply that his main

SOURCE: Prepared especially for this volume.

[1] Bruno Bettelheim, "Individual and Mass Behavior in Extreme Situations," *Journal of Abnormal and Social Psychology*, 1943, 38, pp. 417–452; also, *The Informed Heart* (Glencoe, Ill.: Free Press, 1960).

[2] Herbert A. Bloch, "The Personality of Inmates of Concentration Camps," *American Journal of Sociology* (January, 1947).

theses conflict sharply at crucial points with Kogon, Kautsky, Frankl, Rousset, Cohen, and many other competent prisoner observers with longer and later imprisonment experience than Bettelheim; it is also because Bettelheim is so zealous about his errors. If it makes sense to study the camps, then research must face the curiously persistent and narrow enthusiasm for Bettelheim's theses in American social psychology. This acceptance, reinforced by Bloch's claims, tend to close out the study of prisoner behavior and social system, and of the rise and fall of the Nazi camps. Yet, since the camp system is the most distinctive product of the Nazi movement and government, the study of that system bears fatefully on historical interpretations of the Third Reich—its rise and its fall.

A word now on how the Bettelheim book as a whole bears on the tasks of research on the Nazi camps. It would be incorrect to treat this work as though it was a new study of the camps. However, since *The Informed Heart* incorporates a comprehensive restatement of his earlier theory of prisoner behavior, it is reasonable to expect him to avail himself of the personal accounts of other survivors and relevant research to make up for the time, place, and situational limits on his own observations. It is disappointing to note that he seems to have made no use of the scholarly work in European and American journals, and very little use of prisoner accounts. There are four footnote references to Kogon, two of them misleading, and an *ad hominem* attack on his *Der SS Staat*.[3] There is one incidental reference each to the first-hand reports of Benedikt Kautsky, Odd Nansen, Alexander Mitscherlich and Fred Mielke, David Rousset, Miklos Nyiszli, Edgar Kupfer, Olga Lengyel, and Ernst Federn. That is all. This neglect of other sources is the more unfortunate in that almost all of the camp literature appeared after Bettelheim first published his theory, early in 1943.

It is also disappointing that Bettelheim (in *The Informed Heart*) dismisses consideration of prisoner behavior in the extermination camps as "offering less of psychological interest" than behavior in other camps. It is no less disappointing that he ignores completely prisoner behavior during the last year of the camp system. This period and the much longer one of the developed camp underground, with its national and international camp committees, is omitted entirely. It is also disappointing that he fails to deal with the evidence of a generally low incidence of suicides and of mental disorder. All these omissions have a critical bearing on the Bettelheim theory. . . .

---

[3] Translated as *The Theory and Practice of Hell*.

8. MASS TERROR, II:
THE STATE AND THE
CITIZEN

The Plague of Terror in Oran

ROBERT C. DOTY

ORAN, ALGERIA—The last act of the Algerian tragedy probably will be played out in the streets of this fear-stricken city. It is here that the terrorist Secret Army, drawing support from the 200,000 Europeans who share Oran with a like number of Moslems, is likely to make its last desperate stand for a "French Algeria" against the Moslem-dominated independent state to which both France and the Moslem majority are committed.

Viewed from Paris, the advent of that independent Moslem Algeria seems to be the inevitable consequence of an irreversible current of history and those who would stand in its way seem to be criminals and fools.

Here in Oran, the criminals and fools take on faces and names. The juggernaut of history is moving in the same direction and just as irreversibly as it seems to move in Paris. But here it ceases to be an abstraction, and the people being crushed beneath the wheels are visible. And their protest—even when expressed in criminal folly—becomes understandable.

For here, as in all the crises of history, it is the little people who are paying the price. It is the *petit blanc*—the poor white—the European cab or bus driver, the factory hand, the clerk, the stevedore—who will be lost in a Moslem-ruled Algeria.

The business man, the professional, even the big landowner will have something necessary and useful to offer the new Algeria, and place will be made for them. If it is not, or if the place does not suit them, they will have the material and intellectual resources to permit them to re-establish themselves in France or elsewhere.

Not so the poor whites. In Oran at least two-thirds of them are of Spanish

---

SOURCE: Robert C. Doty, "The Plague of Terror in Oran," *The New York Times Magazine* (May 13, 1962). Reprinted by permission.

rather than French origin—the Lopezes and Mendozas who used to send Communist deputies to represent them in the French National Assembly. It was these same, unstable Mediterraneans who swung Right with Marshal Pétain and General Giraud during the war, veered Left during the Fourth Republic and, today, have enlisted in what observers identify as a movement Fascist in spirit. In each case, it was their interpretation of their own self-interest—the interest of a "French Algeria"—rather than an ideology that motivated them. In each case the movement that enlisted their mercurial allegiance seemed, at the moment, to offer the best hope for continuity of the society they knew.

For them, the pressure of Moslem competition for their unskilled or semi-skilled jobs will be overwhelming. Even if they could keep their jobs, the social balance will change humiliatingly for them. The fact of being light-skinned, Christian and European no longer will bring privilege and protection.

They will face the choice of joining the Moslems in an undifferentiated proletariat or lower middle class or of packing up and going to France, a country many of them have never seen and with which they feel little real identification, despite their current passionate and violent efforts to remain "French."

Their desperation before these prospects has taken on the ugly visage of murder and blind, unreasoning hatred for the forces—notably President de Gaulle—they link with their fate. Their once-pleasant, sun-filled and ebullient Mediterranean city has become a place of waking nightmare.

*   *   *

The scene: The city lies in a rough semicircle, its base along the cliffs and beaches of the sea front. At the center, from the soaring luxury apartments along the waterfront, the European quarter makes a smaller semicircle, cross-hatched with several broad avenues, tree-filled squares and the narrower side streets where live the *petits blancs*.

Around this inner European enclave are the Moslem and European suburbs, once blending one into another through mixed quarters in between, now rigidly segregated by barbed-wire entanglements and troops to keep the two communities from each other's throats. To the west rise the dominating and wooded residential heights of *Les Planteurs,* mainly a Moslem quarter, capped by an old Spanish fort and chapel. Below, in the old port, scores of pleasure craft—sail and power—ride at moorings, but few of their owners today have the time or inclination to take them out for week-end cruises as in the past.

Dotting the horizon in such working-class suburbs as Gambetta, Saint-Eugène, Lamur and Lyautey are gleaming white ten- and twenty-story *cités* —low-rent housing projects of the European workers. In the principal Moslem quarter, the so-called *Ville Nouvelle* (New City), the houses are mostly two- and three-story structures of an earlier era, teeming with Oran's share of the Moslem population "explosion" that has complicated Algeria's already grave demographic problem.

* * *

The situation: Throughout most of the seven-year long Moslem rebellion, the 200,000 Europeans and 200,000 Moslems lived here with relatively less violence than in other parts of Algeria. Never did Oran experience the paroxysms of Moslem terrorism that afflicted Algiers, for example, in 1956 and 1957.

But with President de Gaulle's offer of self-determination for Algeria in September, 1959, and as that prospect took on substance in subsequent negotiations, tension rose as the Moslems saw in it a promise—the Europeans, a threat—of independence. Intercommunity clashes broke out last fall and gangs of young thugs from each side began hunting out and lynching isolated members of the other community.

The Oran police, all, or almost all, recruited locally, were clearly partisan and unwilling to interfere with the *ratonnades* (rat hunts) by the Europeans. Army and gendarmerie forces were in insufficient strength to replace the local police.

Into the power vacuum rushed the Secret Army, led by the fugitives from the abortive Army mutiny of April, 1961, and led locally by former Air Force General Edmond Jouhaud, recently captured, tried and sentenced to death in Paris. With the Secret Army in complete command of the European city—challenged only occasionally in major sorties by Government forces from their fortified enclaves—the division between the Moslems and Europeans became total.

Within the Moslem quarters the law was that of the rebel National Liberation Front, its young leaders battling to prevent the Moslem masses from responding to Secret Army provocations by attacks in force on the European city. This was precisely what the Secret Army extremists sought to bring about, in the belief that, in a battle between Moslem and European masses, the Army, key to control of Algeria, would be led by racial solidarity to defend the Europeans and fire on the Moslems.

Such an event would end hopes of putting into effect the cease-fire, and political settlement, looking toward Algerian independence in amicable cooperation with France, that was negotiated between France and the Moslem Rebel Provisional Government at Evian-les-Bains in March.

* * *

The results: Imagine a city of 400,000 inhabitants without effective police and with authority exercised by a secret society whose aim is the overthrow of constituted authority and whose method is murder. Imagine that several thousand of the young men between 15 and 25 years of age—including all of the potential delinquents—carry pistols and believe they have a patriotic excuse for using them.

Their "legitimate" prey includes all Moslems who come within pistol range and any European suspected of dissent from Secret Army aims and methods or of sympathy for the official policy of his Government in Paris.

The result, as it reveals itself in Oran, is something close to anarchy.

* * *

Noon—Place des Victoires—an oblong public square in the heart of Oran —two or three sidewalk cafes swarming with youths and men—bright sunlight on the square, deep shadow under the trees and in the colonnaded arcades. This is the listening post and gathering place of Oran's Secret Army.

A middle-aged Moslem rides through the *place* on a bicycle. He can be there only through ignorance: perhaps a man from the peaceful countryside; or desperation: an errand important enough for him to warrant the risk.

A pistol shot cracks from under the arcade. The Moslem sprawls to the street, his bicycle clattering in the gutter. The man pulls himself to the sidewalk, blood streaming from a head wound. Somehow he claws himself erect, takes one or two blind, staggering steps, his hands outstretched before him, then plunges face downward. The crowd, including a few women, watches his death impassively. In the center of the street lies his dusty red *chéchia*— skull cap.

In a little while a city ambulance will come to take the body to the overstocked morgue. End of incident—one of about twelve similar ones that day.

Footnotes: (1) A dozen people, at least, saw the killer but nobody knows him. Nobody would know him, even if ever again murders in the streets were to be investigated.

(2) For those who like their violence neat and tidy, it may be remarked that there is some likelihood that the killer was the brother, son or cousin of a European killed during the seven-year-long Moslem terror. In other words, one murder plus one murder equals either an even score or a loss of two, depending on how you look at it.

* * *

Warm, velvety night in the Place de la Bastille, in the silence of the first hours after the 9 P. M. curfew. Suddenly, the shutters of a fourth-floor window are thrown back with a clatter and a woman's voice, near hysteria, screams. *"Assassins! Assassins! Ils l'ont condamné à mort!"*

Everyone else has heard the radio broadcast, too—Jouhaud, the Oran-born Secret Army general, has been condemned to death by a high military tribunal.

Within minutes the insistent rhythm—three short, two long—*Al-gérie Fran-çaise!*—is beaten out on anything that will make noise, from a saucepan to a piece of corrugated iron. Hundreds descend into the street in defiance of the curfew and soon an excited mob is chanting: "Free Jouhaud!"

Two nights later, heralded by bursts of firing into the air, the scene is repeated, jubilantly this time, on the rumor—false—spread by the Secret Army itself, that Jouhaud has escaped.

* * *

Late afternoon—heavy firing by automatic weapons and occasionally the serious flat crack of a 37-mm. turret gun from an armored car. Somewhere near the Place Jouty and Place des Victoires. A cheer goes up from the crowd as an incendiary grenade makes a torch of a personnel carrier that brought Republican Security Guards to the scene.

Groups of excited youths stop a British radio correspondent half a dozen times. They think his portable tape recorder is a camera capable of gathering pictorial evidence against those attacking the security forces.

At a corner there is a long, glistening wet patch on the pavement. A drunken youth is capering with a Security Guard helmet on his head. It takes a minute or two to make the connection. The long, glistening wet patch on the pavement was made as they dragged away the original wearer of the helmet.

After taking their losses—six killed and a dozen wounded—the Security Guards bring up reinforcements. A heavy machine gun begins to spray half-inch slugs along the street and the crowd scatters in panic under the archways.

Fifty yards away, in the next street, women are filling their string market bags with the makings of the evening meal.

The next day a heavy-shouldered dark young man—at a guess, a Secret Army second lieutenant—proudly conducts journalists over the scene and shows the corner from which his section brought the troops under fire.

* * *

Mid-morning: Another fight between Secret Army commandos and soldiers in the working class suburb of Gambetta.

Gendarmes, their faces showing the fear and strain of scanning each of several hundred silent, hostile windows whence anonymous shots can kill them, crouch in the open turrets of armored cars, fingering the triggers of .50-caliber machine guns.

Inside a twenty-story workers' building, tenants gather in interior hallways while the firing goes on outside. Heads shown incautiously above the roof parapet bring a spatter of shots. A burly youth guiding visitors is lightly touched in the leg by a spent ricochet and chooses to make of it an excuse to go dramatically berserk.

While comrades restrain him, he rants: "You will see—you Americans—when it is too late! You are letting another Budapest happen here!"

* * *

The evening before, a young Australian girl, widow of a French Gaullist "liberal," shot down by the Secret Army in his own doorway that day, told the story between deep, shuddering intakes of breath that served to fight down her sobs.

"Naturally, you were upset," says the bland-faced apologist for the Secret Army over coffee the next morning. "But you don't understand what is going on here. That young man knew he was doomed from the moment he set out to defend de Gaulle. It's very hard on his wife, of course, but these people are fighting for their lives.

"How do they expect to save things? Well, I suppose the only hope is to overthrow de Gaulle. Another Government in France would listen to the Europeans here. De Gaulle is letting them slide down the drain because, during the war, the people here preferred Pétain and then Giraud to de Gaulle, and he has never forgiven them."

* * *

The garbage piles up in the streets because the Moslems who used to man the collection trucks dare not report for work.

The body of a European nurse who persisted in entering the Moslem quarter to serve in one of the improvised hospitals there is found with a bullet in the back of her neck.

The doctors of Oran protest against atrocities attributed to the security forces in their dealings with the Oran populace. They worry, too, over the garbage in the streets and reports of increases in the number and boldness of the rats. (The late Albert Camus, Oran's most illustrious writer, once wrote an interestingly apposite allegorical novel about this city—"The Plague.")

In the fortified Château-Neuf—the headquarters of the besieged Government authority—General Joseph Katz, the tough, devoted, uncompromisingly republican military commander, ponders his situation. With the troops he has he can master a riot—but only by using firepower to mow down the rioters. He lacks the numerical strength to reestablish control and keep a riot from beginning.

With the rest of the world, he wonders whether his repeated demands for reinforcements will be acted upon in Algiers and Paris in time to avert the worst.

[THE INEFFECTIVE STATE, II]

Unlawful Police Violence

UNITED STATES COMMISSION ON CIVIL RIGHTS

The Commission's study of the administration of justice concentrates on police brutality—the use of unlawful violence—against Negroes. Complaints and litigation suggest four subdivisions of the problem. The first involves the

SOURCE: United States Commission on Civil Rights, *Justice*, Report No. 5, 1961. (Washington, D.C.: U. S. Government Printing Office, 1961).

use of racially motivated brutality to enforce subordination or segregation. The second, a not altogether separate category, entails violence as a punishment. The third relates to coerced confessions. The last and largest entails the almost casual, or spontaneous, use of force in arrests. Only the first category necessarily involves racial discrimination. In the others it may, or may not, be present, but Negroes are the victims with disproportionate frequency.

In the text of this chapter the Commission briefly describes the alleged facts in 11 typical cases of police brutality. They are presented in the belief that they contribute to an understanding of the problem. The allegations of misconduct are supported in several cases by criminal convictions[1] or findings by impartial agencies; in others, by sworn testimony, affidavits from eye witnesses, or by staff field investigations. In no case has the Commission determined conclusively whether the complainants or the officers were correct in their statements. This is the function of a court. The Commission is of the opinion, however, that the allegations appeared substantial enough to justify discussion in this study.

Most citizens do not look upon policemen with fear. Indeed, the law officer's badge has become a symbol worthy of much respect. There is good reason for this. Many citizens call upon policemen for aid in any emergency. And it is the policeman who must enforce the criminal law. The extent of the burden on this country's approximately 200,000 policemen[2] is demonstrated by the 1,861,300 serious offenses reported in 1960.[3] In carrying out their vital mission policemen sometimes face extreme danger. The Federal Bureau of Investigation recently reported:[4]

> During 1959, 49 police employees were killed in line of duty, . . . pointing up the hazardous nature of the occupation and devotion to duty of these dedicated men. In 1960, 48 police lost their lives.

Moreover, in 1960 a total of 9,621 assaults on American policemen were reported to the FBI. This amounts to a rate of 6.3 assaults for every 100 police officers in the country.[5] The Commission's study of denials of rights to citizens by some policemen should be viewed in the context of the difficult and dangerous job that policemen are required to perform.

---

[1] In two of the incidents described in the text the officers were convicted in a Federal civil rights prosecution—the *Screws* case *infra*, at 6 and the *Clark* case *infra*, at 14. Since the Civil Rights Section of the Department of Justice became a Division in December 1957, it has obtained police brutality convictions from juries in four cases, while in two cases the defendant officers entered pleas of *nolo contendere*. See ch. 4 at 66 *infra*. In none of these cases were the victims known to be minority group members, except in the *Clark* case wherein the victim was a Canadian born Indian.

[2] Federal Bureau of Investigation, *Uniform Crime Reports—1960* at 105 (1961). The total for 3,779 cities with a total population of 103,493,753 is 195,109, which figure includes civilian employees.

[3] *Id.* at 1.

[4] *Id.* at 19 and 104.

[5] *Id.* at 106.

PATTERNS OF POLICE BRUTALITY
Enforcement of segregation or subordinate status

THE KILLING OF A NEGRO IN GEORGIA: 1943.—In the early morning of January 30, 1943, Manley Poteat responded to a call for an ambulance at the jail in Newton, Baker County, Georgia. He explained in sworn testimony later that he found an "unconscious" man crawling around in a pool of blood on the floor of a cell.[6] The man was a young Negro, Bobby Hall, a skilled mechanic who was married and had one child. He was taken to a hospital in Albany, 22 miles away, where he died approximately 1 hour after his arrival. When Walter Poteat, Manley's father, embalmed the body, he observed that it had been brutally beaten.[7]

The authorities in Albany, which is not in Baker County, were notified and saw the body; photographs were made; and the matter soon came to public attention. Sheriff Claude M. Screws—and the other officers—who beat and killed Hall were later prosecuted by the Federal Government for violation of an 1866 statute that makes it a Federal crime for an officer of the law to interfere with the constitutional rights of any person.[8] In beating and killing young Hall without justification, a Federal grand jury in Macon charged, the sheriff had deprived the victim of a number of constitutional rights including the right not to be subjected to punishment except after a fair trial and the right to equal protection of the laws. Screws was convicted, and eventually appealed to the Supreme Court, challenging the constitutionality of the statute. In the landmark decision of *Screws* v. *United States*,[9] the Supreme Court in 1945 upheld the statute, construed it strictly, and overturned the conviction because it had not been established that in killing Bobby Hall, Screws had intended to deprive him of a constitutional right.[10] Screws was later tried again under the standard set forth by the Supreme Court and acquitted.[11]

While this example of police brutality took place almost two decades ago it is still a classic case. Recent complaints coming to the attention of this Commission contain allegations that bear a striking similarity to it. For this reason the case will be described in detail.

Sheriff Screws testified at his first trial that the trouble began late that

---

[6] Record, p. 109, *Screws* v. *United States*, 325 U.S. 91 (1945).

[7] *Id.* at 114.

[8] 14 Stat. 27 (1866), 18 U.S.C. sec. 242 (1958).

[9] *Screws* v. *United States*, *supra*, note 6.

[10] A full discussion of the statute, the *Screws* case, and other aspects of the enforcement of the Civil Rights Acts are found in ch. 4 *infra*.

[11] *United States* v. *Screws*, Crim. No. 1300, M.D. Ga., Nov. 1, 1945.

January evening in 1943 when he asked night patrolman Frank E. Jones and Deputy Sheriff Jim Bob Kelley to serve a warrant of arrest on Bobby Hall for theft of a tire. The two men brought the Negro back to Newton in the Sheriff's car. Screws continued:[12]

I opened the door and I said, "All right, Bobby, get out" and I noticed he wasn't in any hurry to get out but when he, when I did see him come out, I saw something coming out ahead of him like that (indicating) and I discovered it was a gun; and he said, "You damn white sons"—and that is all I remember what he said. By that time I knocked the gun up like that and the gun fired off right over my head; and when it did he was on the ground by then and me and Kelley and Jones ran in to him and we all were scuffling and I was beating him about the face and head with my fist. I knew Jones had a blackjack and I told him to hit him and he hit him a lick or two and he didn't seem to weaken and I said, "Hit him again!" When he fell to the ground, we didn't hit him on the ground.

*   *   *

At no time when I saw the deceased or Bobby Hall did he have any handcuffs on him.

The only colored prosecution witness who observed a crucial part of this event was Mrs. Annie Pearl Hall, the wife of the victim. She contradicted, in part, one vital item in the defendant's case: Mrs. Hall stated after the victim left their home under arrest, "they were handcuffing him when I went to the door."[13] All three of the officers said that he had never been handcuffed and was, therefore, able to grab the shotgun from the front seat of the car and attack them with it.

While there are many similarities between this case and others in Commission files, there is one major difference. A number of white people observed the beating of Bobby Hall and events connected with it—and appeared at the trial as witnesses. Their stories supported one another and directly contradicted that of Screws. The testimony of these witnesses may be summarized as follows: Screws and his companions had threatened to get a "nigger" that night; they took Hall to an open area in the center of town near the public pump; the three men beat him to the ground and continued for 15 to 30 minutes to pound him with a heavy object—which was later found to be a 2-pound metal blackjack; the victim was handcuffed during all of these proceedings; after the beating the shotgun was fired once—not by the unconscious victim but apparently by one of the officers for some unknown reason.[14]

One of the white eyewitnesses who appeared at the trial and swore to these

---

[12] Record, *supra*, note 6, at 171.

[13] *Id.* at 60.

[14] This description is based primarily on the testimony of these white eyewitnesses: Mr. A. B. Edwards (*id.* at 79–82), Mrs. A. B. Ledbetter (*id.* at 83–85), Mr. A. B. Ledbetter (*id.* at 85–89), Mrs. Mabel Burke (*id.* at 105–106), and Mrs. Ollie Jernigan (*id.* at 89–92).

facts was Mrs. Ollie Jernigan. Her husband, J. H. Jernigan, did not see the incident, but he testified that he was walking through town one day and Sheriff Screws called him over to his car where the following conversation took place:[15]

"Herschell, you know those FBI men are down here investigating that case?" He said, "Well, I understand that your wife saw it." I told him "Yes." He says, "Well, you know we have always been friends and I want us to continue to be friends." I told him, "Well, I hoped we could."

The dynamics of combined prejudice and violence in this case are suggested in the testimony of James P. Willingham, a white man, who said that shortly after the killing he had a talk with his friend, Officer Frank Jones:[16]

[H]e told me that the Negro had a mighty good pistol and they had taken it away from him and the Negro acted so damn smart and went before the Court in some way trying to make them give it back to him . . . and that they went out there that night with a warrant and arrested him and handcuffed him and brought him to town and the Negro put up some kind of talk about wanting to give bond or something to that effect and they beat hell out of him; then, that when they got him up to the well they whipped him some more and he died shortly afterwards. He said the Negro attempted to shoot them at the well; said the Negro attempted to shoot them at the well with a shotgun and said he hit him with a blackjack pretty hard and I asked him about how in the world did the Negro try to shoot you and you had him handcuffed and he said well we finished him off and that is all.

Bobby Hall apparently was considered a somewhat "uppity" Negro. Evidence produced at the trial indicated that the tire theft charge was a sham for, as suggested in the Willingham testimony, Hall's major "crime" was to challenge the power of the sheriff to confiscate his pistol. Bobby Hall was not accused of any crime in connection with the weapon. He needed it, he claimed, for protection. In attempting to exercise not his civil rights but his property rights, Hall contacted a lawyer and even went before a local grand jury. But he did not recover his pistol.[17] And, while he never challenged the system of segregation, he was something of a leader among Negroes.[18]

No State or local action was taken against the alleged offenders. Prosecution by the State—which has the power to impose the supreme penalty—may be blocked in cases of this type by the fact that the potential defendant is the person who must start up the machinery of the criminal law. While the district solicitor general in the *Screws* case had formal power to prose-

---

[15] *Id.* at 93.

[16] *Id.* at 120.

[17] *Id.* at 67–68.

[18] Special Agent Marcus B. Calhoun of the FBI office testified at the trial that, "Mr. Screws . . . told me that he had had trouble with Bobby Hall, that he seemed to be a leader or denominated himself as such and that when a Negro got in trouble with the law that he, Bobby Hall, would advise him as to what action he should take." Record, *supra*, note 6, at 78.

cute, he reportedly felt "helpless in the matter" because he had "to rely upon the sheriff and policemen of the various counties of his circuit for investigation."[19] In the absence of an investigation and a complaint from Sheriff Screws, or by another police officer implicating Screws, no prosecution was commenced. In police brutality cases where the potential defendant is not the *chief* law enforcement officer of the county, there is a greater possibility of criminal or disciplinary action by local authorities. But even in such situations, local action against officers of the law is not common.[20]

Neither Screws nor any of his associates was ever punished. They experienced the difficulty and expense of months of litigation but a second Federal jury acquitted them. The episode did not seriously tarnish the reputation of Claude M. Screws. In 1958 he ran for the State Senate and was elected.

THE KILLING OF A NEGRO IN GEORGIA: 1958.—The town of Dawson in Terrell County, Ga. is approximately 30 miles south of Newton. There on April 20, 1958, James Brazier, a Negro in his thirties, suffered a beating at the hands of officers of the law (from which he later died)—in circumstances similar to those in the *Screws* case.[21]

According to the police account, the incident started in the early evening of Sunday, April 20, 1958, when Dawson Police Officer "X" arrested James Brazier's father on a charge of driving under the influence of alcohol. When the elder Brazier resisted, he was subdued by a blackjack. James Brazier protested and, according to the policemen, threatened the officer who later returned with Officer "Y" and arrested the younger Brazier, allegedly with a warrant, for interfering with an arrest. He resisted violently and was subdued with a blackjack. Shortly thereafter he was taken to jail and examined by a local physician who found no serious injury.[22]

Brazier died 5 days later at a hospital in Columbus, Ga. from brain damage and a fractured skull. He had four to six bruised spots on his scalp from a blunt instrument which apparently also caused the skull fracture.[23] The police claimed that Brazier was hit only once or twice at the time of the arrest.

---

[19] Information from the Department of Justice, as quoted in Carr, *Federal Protection of Civil Rights* 107 (1947).

[20] See ch. 6 at 79 *infra*.

[21] The description of the Brazier case is largely based on evidence gathered in an investigation by Commission representatives in late August, 1960 and incorporated into a Commission document entitled *Report on Field Investigation In Terrell County, Georgia*. Four Negro eyewitnesses to various parts of the Brazier incident were interviewed and statements taken from them. In addition, statements were received from other Negro eyewitnesses who were not then available to be interviewed. Four white people were interviewed regarding the case.

In addition to the Brazier incident other cases in Terrell County involving alleged Police brutality to Negroes were investigated on this field trip. The evidence supporting complaints in these cases was not as strong as that in the Brazier case.

[22] *Id.* at 10–12.

[23] This information comes from the Certificate of Death of James Brazier and from an interview with a doctor who attended the victim at the Columbus Medical Center, *Report on Field Investigation in Terrell County, Georgia, supra*, note 21, at 18.

In a sworn statement to Commission representatives Mrs. Hattie Bell Brazier, the widow of the victim, claimed that this affair had actually started months earlier. Mrs. Brazier explained that she and her husband had purchased a new Chevrolet in 1956—and another in 1958.[24] In November of 1957 James Brazier had been arrested on a speeding charge. According to Mrs. Brazier, her husband told her that Dawson Officer "Y" took him to jail, and that:[25]

"When I first entered the door of the jail, ["Y"] hit me on the back of the head and knocked me down and said, 'You smart son-of-a-bitch, I been wanting to get my hands on you for a long time.' I said, 'Why you want me for?' ["Y"] said, 'You is a nigger who is buying new cars and we can't hardly live. I'll get you yet.' "

Officer "Y" then allegedly hit Brazier several more times, put his foot on the small of the prostrate Negro's back (Mrs. Brazier said she saw the footprints there later), and warned him, "You'd better not say a damn thing about it or I'll stomp your damn brains out." After his release from jail, Brazier was bleeding from his ear and vomiting blood. From this time in the fall of 1957 until the second incident in April of 1958, James Brazier was under the care of a local white doctor because of these injuries. Officer "X", the policeman who accompanied "Y" during the arrest in April 1958, also allegedly made a remark about the new car at some time previous to the fatal incident.[26] It appears that James Brazier of Terrell County, like Bobby Hall of Baker County, was considered an "uppity" Negro.

The story of the fatal incident in 1958 as told by Mrs. Brazier and several other colored witnesses contradicts the account given by the officers. In her affidavit Mrs. Brazier stated that her husband had been beaten brutally by the arresting officers in full view of numerous colored people, including herself and her four children. No warrant was presented by the officers, nor was any paper observed in their hands. The officers, she said, simply ran out of their car and roughly grabbed her husband. While pulling him toward the police car, "Y" beat him repeatedly with a blackjack. Mrs. Brazier's affidavit continued:[27]

---

[24] Affidavit of Mrs. Hattie Bell Brazier, and *Report on Field Investigation In Terrell County, Georgia, supra*, note 21, at 14. Although their hourly wages were not high, Mrs. Brazier explained, she had three jobs and her late husband, two. They sometimes worked at menial tasks from early morning until late night. This allowed them to purchase the automobiles. Interview With Mrs. Hattie Bell Brazier, Albany, Ga., August 23, 1960.

[25] Affidavit of Mrs. Hattie Bell Brazier, and *Report on Field Investigation in Terrell County, Georgia, supra*, note 21, at 12–13.

[26] Earlier in the Spring of 1958 Mrs. Brazier alleged that Officer "X" saw the Brazier's new car and asked them how they managed to purchase it. James Brazier replied flippantly, "I works for what I gets." And "X" countered in a threatening tone, "You'll never remember paying for it." Mrs. Brazier said that this took place in her presence, and it is set out in her affidavit and in *Report on Field Investigation In Terrell County, Georgia, supra*, note 21, at 14.

[27] Affidavit of Mrs. Hattie Bell Brazier and *Report on Field Investigation in Terrell County, Georgia, supra*, note 21, at 15.

["Y"] then said, "You smart son-of-a-bitch, I told you I would get you." James said, "What do you want to hurt me for? I ain't done nothing. I got a heap of little chillun. [sic]." ["Y"] said, "I don't give a goddamn how many children you got, you're going away from here" . . .["Y"] pulled out his pistol and stuck it against James' stomach and said, "I oughta blow your goddamn brains out."

Then these events allegedly occurred: James Brazier's 10-year-old son pleaded with the officers to stop beating his father and was knocked to the ground by "Y";[28] the victim was thrown onto the floor of the police car with his legs dangling outside; "Y" kicked him twice in the groin; slammed the car door on his legs; threw a hat full of sand into his bloody face, and drove off.[29]

When Brazier reached the jail, he was bloody but conscious and apparently not seriously injured by the beating he had received. Yet, when he was taken to court the next morning, he was virtually unconscious. The question that arises is whether Brazier was beaten during the interval between his arrival in jail at approximately 7 p.m. and his appearance in court at approximately 9 a.m. the next day. There is evidence that he was. It comes from several witnesses, one of whom has since died[30] and may be identified —Marvin Goshay, a Negro who was 23 years of age when he signed an affidavit on August 24, 1960 during an interview with Commission representatives in Albany, Ga. Goshay was in jail on a charge of assault and battery when Brazier was incarcerated. The story, as Goshay saw it, is as follows: When James Brazier was brought into the jail he was fully dressed in suit, shirt, tie, and shoes. He talked coherently to Goshay (describing his arrest consistently with Mrs. Brazier's later testimony). Several hours later —probably around midnight—he was ordered out of the cell by Officers "X" and "Y". "They took Brazier out again," Goshay stated in his affidavit. "He asked them to wait because he wanted to put on his shoes. The police said, 'You won't need no shoes.'" This was the last time that Goshay saw him that night. Goshay next saw Brazier on the following morning. His affidavit continued:

He had on pants, a torn undershirt, no coat, no tie, no white shirt. The last time I saw him, he had on a blue suit, white shirt, and tie. He looked worse on his head than when I saw him also . . . it was beaten worse than when I first saw him. On his back were about four long marks about a foot long. They looked reddish and bruised. His head was bleeding. We had to carry [him] to the car because he couldn't walk. He was slobbering at the mouth. When we got to the

---

[28] Affidavit of Mrs. Hattie Belle Brazier, Affidavit of James Brazier, Jr. (aged 10), and *Report on Field Investigation in Terrell County, Georgia, supra,* note 21, at 16. Mrs. Brazier explained in a subsequent interview that the shock of this incident brought on a nervous condition in James, Jr., and forced her to send the boy to live with his grandmother in the North. Interview with Mrs. Hattie Bell Brazier, Albany, Ga., August 23, 1960.

[29] In addition to the affidavit of Mrs. Brazier this story is supported by several colored eyewitnesses interviewed by Commission representatives in Georgia. *Report on Field Investigation in Terrell County, Georgia, supra,* note 21, at 16.

[30] See note 35, *infra.*

POLICE VIOLENCE

. . . in the front rank, a little ahead. They were crossing the bridge. They were walking on cobbles on a badlylighted street under an elevated structure. Trains roared overhead. "Only a few blocks from Charlestown jail," a voice yelled.

This time the cops were using their clubs. There was the clatter of the horses' hoofs on the cobbles and the whack thud whack thud of the clubs. And way off the jangle jangle of patrolwagons. Mary was terribly scared. A big truck was bearing down on her. She jumped to one side out of the way behind one of the girder supports. Two cops had hold of her. She clung to the grimy girder. A cop was cracking her on the hand with his club. She wasn't much hurt, she was in a patrolwagon, she'd lost her hat and her hair had come down. She caught herself thinking that she ought to have her hair bobbed if she was going to do much of this sort of thing.

"Anybody know where Don Stevens is?"

Don's voice came a little shakily from the blackness in front. "That you, Mary?"

"How are you, Don?"

*   *   *

Much I thought of you when I was lying in the death house—the singing, the kind tender voices of the children from the playground where there was all the life and the joy of liberty—just one step from the wall that contains the buried agony of three buried souls. It would remind me so often of you and of your sister and I wish I could see you every moment, but I feel better that you will not come to the death house so that you could not see the horrible picture of three living in agony waiting to be electrocuted.

The Camera Eye (50)

they have clubbed us off the streets   they are stronger   they are rich   they hire and fire the politicians the newspapereditors the old judges the small men with reputations the collegepresidents the wardheelers (listen businessmen collegepresidents judges   America will not forget her betrayers) they hire the men with guns   the uniforms the policecars the patrolwagons

all right you have won   you will kill the brave men our friends tonight

there is nothing left to do   we are beaten   we the beaten crowd together in these old dingy schoolrooms on Salem Street   shuffle up and down the gritty creaking stairs sit hunched with bowed heads on benches and hear the old words of the haters of oppression   made new in sweat and agony tonight

our work is over   the scribbled phrases   the nights typing releases the smell of the printshop the sharp reek of newprinted leaflets the rush for Western Union stringing words into wires the search for stinging words to make you feel who are your oppressors America

America our nation has been beaten by strangers who have turned our language inside out who have taken the clean words our fathers spoke and made them slimy and foul

their hired men sit on the judge's bench they sit back . . .

car. James, who was dazed but not completely out, didn't know enough to get in the car. Mr. ["Z"—a Dawson police officer] said if he didn't get in, he'd beat him with his blackjack.

More than a year after Brazier's death Sheriff Z. T. Mathews of Terrell County allegedly made the following statement to Mrs. Brazier:[31]

I oughta slap your damn brains out. A nigger like you I feel like slapping them out. You niggers set around here and look at television and go up North and come back and do to white folks here like the niggers up North do, but you ain't gonna do it. I'm gonna carry the South's orders out like it oughta be done.

Also, Sheriff Mathews told reporter Robert E. Lee Baker, "You know, Cap, . . . there's nothing like fear to keep niggers in line. I'm talking about 'outlaw' niggers."[32]

No local disciplinary or criminal action was taken against any of the officers involved. The attitude of local authorities toward police was protective in this and several other cases of alleged brutality that occurred within a brief period in Dawson. Indeed, there was indignation when Negroes claimed they were "living in an atmosphere of fear."[33] As in the *Screws* case the Department of Justice was sufficiently impressed with the results of an FBI investigation to authorize Civil Rights Acts prosecutions. From August 4 to 8, 1958, the local United States Attorney presented witnesses to a Federal grand jury in Macon and requested indictments in five cases of alleged police brutality against policemen "X," "Y," and another Dawson officer.[34] The grand jury returned no indictments.[35]

---

[31] Affidavit of Mrs. Hattie Bell Brazier, and *Report on Field Investigation in Terrell County, Georgia, supra,* note 21, at 20. Mayor James Griggs Raines of Dawson reported in an interview with two Commission representatives that he felt that Sheriff Mathews was a bad influence on Dawson policemen. "In my opinion the Sheriff, Mathews, is unfit and has violated the Civil Rights Acts. I've seen him beat a pregnant Negro woman. He's unfit to hold office. You can quote me," the Mayor stated. *Id.* at 40.

[32] Washington Post, June 8, 1958, p. A–12.

[33] Atlanta Constitution, June 9, 1958, pp. 1–5; June 10, 1958, pp. 1, 8.

[34] The Government contended that the officers had violated 18 U.S.C. sec. 242 because by these acts of brutality they had "under color of law" interfered with the constitutional rights of the victims.

[35] Although Marvin Goshay was subpenaed by the Federal Government to testify before the grand jury sitting in Macon, he did not appear. In his sworn statement to a Commission representative Goshay explained that shortly after he received the subpena, Officer "Y" found him walking on the street in Dawson and ordered him to jail. When the Negro asked why he was being incarcerated, "Y" replied, "You just need to be in jail." The young man was kept prisoner for 1 week, during which time the Federal grand jury met and refused indictments. One week later, "Officer ["Y"] came in and told me I could go on home," Goshay explained. "I never was brought to . . . court during this time. I just stayed in jail. I can only guess, although no one ever told me, that the only reason I was locked up was because they didn't want me to go to Macon." Goshay was slated to be a witness in a pending Federal civil suit for $177,000 brought by Mrs. Brazier against Officer "Y" and others. On March 14, 1961, Marvin Goshay was found dead—apparently of asphyxiation—in a Dawson undertaking parlor. An FBI investigation failed to uncover evidence of foul play.

In the 15 years between the death of Bobby Hall and the death of James Brazier the world had changed in many ways. But in Terrell and Baker, as in some other rural southern counties,[36] the economy, the social system, and racial attitudes remained virtually what they had been. James Griggs Raines who owns many of the buildings in Dawson and has been its Mayor, explained in a 1960 interview that, "This is a feudalistic system. But I don't know if, or how, it will be changed."[37] Few Negroes vote in these counties and in most ways they are deprived and subordinate. Officers of the law sometimes enforce this status by illegal or violent methods.[38]

Not long after Brazier died, police officer "Y" was promoted to Chief of the Dawson Police Department. Z. T. Mathews at this writing is still sheriff of Terrell County.

The Hall and Brazier cases are more dramatic than most, partly because they resulted in death. But the Commission has reviewed complaints and reports of similar incidents. Reports of some of the most heinous of these have come to the Commission from the Mississippi State Advisory Committee which says that it has received "many and at times almost unbelievable reports of atrocities and brutalities" perpetrated by law enforcement officials.[39] As

---

[36] Those rural, southern counties which have a high percentage of nonwhites in their population are the subject of a separate and detailed analysis in this report. See part III, *supra*.

[37] *Report on Field Investigation in Terrell County, Georgia, supra*, note 21, at 5.

[38] In addition to the Brazier case, there are recent cases containing similar allegations in the files of the Commission. Some of these have been referred to the Department of Justice for possible prosecutive action.

[39] Report of the Mississippi Advisory Committee to the Commission on Civil Rights, *The 50 States Report* 315, 317 (1961). The following two cases, which came to the attention of the Commission from sources other than the Mississippi Advisory Committee, are illustrative of reports from that State.

On August 9, 1958, about midday, Theodore R. Nash was stopped by a deputy sheriff 5 miles north of Winona, Miss., on a charge of reckless driving. In the car with Nash were his wife, Geraldine, his daughter, Pearlie Mae Boatman, and four small children under 6 years of age—all Negroes. Nash was a native of Mississippi but had lived in Milwaukee, Wis., since 1950. When this incident occurred, he and his family were on a vacation trip. The Nashes reported to the Commission that the following events took place: The deputy sheriff roughly ordered Nash to the nearby office of a justice of the peace. While outside the office, an altercation developed. The officer allegedly kicked Mrs. Nash, because she protested that they had not been speeding; and the justice of the peace is allged to have struck her on the side of the head with his fist and to have dragged her along by her arms and hair because Mrs. Nash replied "No"—without adding a "Sir"—to a question from the justice. At one point the officer cocked his pistol and threatened Mr. Nash: "I just wish you would make any kind of an attempt, I would blow your damn brains out here in the street, and I wouldn't have anything to do except to write out a statement that you are tempting the law, and there won't be nothing done about it."

When the babies in the car stated to cry, the officer told Nash's daughter, "If you don't quiet them, I'll take this pistol handle and beat their damn brains out into the seats and there won't be enough of them left to try to bury." Mrs. Nash was placed in jail but was soon released after fines of $19 (for resisting arrest) and $34 (for reckless driving) were paid on the spot. The officers then told the family to "Get out of here—

with many other current complaints, these are now under investigation by the Department of Justice and for that reason will not be considered here.

Some of the worst complaints of police brutality have included allegations that the officers involved expressed some racial motive for their conduct. The extensive violence found in the Hall and Brazier cases, for example, is rarely seen in incidents where there is no element of racial hate.

Punishment

A student said the Batista police were so sadistic, once the policemen put you in a scout car, you had your judge and jury, trial and punishment before you get out.

My most embarrassing moment came when a student asked me did the police in Detroit beat people. What could I say?[40]

The primary motivation for police brutality in the cases discussed above and in similar ones seem to have been a desire to "keep the Negro in his place." Cases of similar misconduct often occur—in many parts of the Nation —that appear to have been motivated by a desire to *punish* for reasons other

---

and don't be caught in here any more" on pain of death. "They told us that they were going to stop us northern niggers from coming down there. They said these niggers get up here in the northern state[s] around these damn rich Jews, saying 'Yes' and 'No' and think that they can come down there in Mississippi doing the same thing, but before they would take that they would kill every nigger that comes down here and kill them and nothing would be done whether they were in the right or wrong. They said they make the laws and they break them as they see fit to do."

This information comes from (1) an affidavit executed by Theodore Nash on October 4, 1958, and (2) a statement given to a Commission representative on January 27, 1961, by Mr. Nash, Mrs. Nash, and Pearlie Mae Boatman, their daughter. This case was investigated by the Department of Justice. No prosecution was authorized because no corroboration beyond the story told by the Nash family regarding the violence was available. The officers alleged that Mrs. Nash attacked them and had to be subdued. Interview with Civil Rights Division attorney.

In early April 1961, a wire service photograph appeared in newspapers and magazines across the county. Life, April 7, 1961, p. 30. It showed policemen in Jackson, Miss., armed with clubs moving into a crowd of retreating, well-dressed Negroes. A German Shepherd dog on a leash had leaped upon a Negro and seemed about to bite his arm. The man was later identified to the Commission as Reverend S. Leon Whitney, the Pastor of the Farish Street Baptist Church and one of the most prominent Negro clergymen in Jackson. He suffered a severe laceration of his arm from the dog's attack. Other Negroes in the crowd also suffered injuries including an elderly man, W. R. Wren, whose arm was broken. The incident started when a group of Negroes applauded nine Negro students who were going into court to be tried in connection with Mississippi's first sit-in demonstration which had occurred in a public library. The applauding Negroes did not commit or threaten violence. After driving them away with clubs and dogs, the officers returned and *asked* a nearby crowd of approximately 70 white persons to disperse. United Press International dispatch as reported in the N.Y. Times, March 30, 1961, p. 19.

[40] *Detroit Hearings* 433 (attributed to a Negro columnist in the Statement of Judge Victor J. Baum).

than violation of local segregation customs.[41] A few examples are described in this section.

Policemen and comparable officials have absolutely no authority to punish anyone. Police may use whatever force is necessary to defend themselves and perform their public duties—beyond that they act illegally.[42] As the Wickersham Commission wrote three decades ago, "their fight against lawless men, if waged by forbidden means, is degraded almost to the level of a struggle between two law-breaking gangs."[43]

---

[41] In five of the six successful police brutality prosecutions under section 242 by the Civil Rights Division, Department of Justice since January 1, 1958, the officers apparently were primarily motivated by a desire to punish for other than racial reasons. In only one of these five cases—the *Clark* case, described at 14, *infra*—was the victim known to be a minority group member; and in that case this did not appear to be a major factor. The facts in the other four "punishment" cases are as follows: (This information comes from interviews with Civil Rights Division attorneys and from the indicated annual Reports of the Attorney General.)

In *United States* v. *Koch*, Crim. No. 18,850, E.D. Ill., June 17, 1958, complaints were made to the Department of Justice alleging that prisoners of the St. Clair County Jail in East St. Louis, Ill., had been subjected to sadistic punishment for such offenses as violation of jail rules. Three deputy sheriffs were indicted and on June 17, 1958, pled guilty. See *Annual Report of the Attorney General of the United States for the Fiscal Year Ended June 30, 1958* at 177–78, and ch. 4, note 194, *infra*.

In *United States* v. *Saxon*, Crim. No. Cp. 2091, M.D. Ala., June 11, 1958, the sheriff of Coosa County, Ala., was charged with having beaten two men with his fists and a blackjack at a filling station in Goodwater, Ala. The sheriff, H. Pierce Saxon, was reportedly annoyed at a remark one of the men made concerning Saxon's bright headlights. A Federal grand jury indicted Saxon on September 11, 1957, but trial in November 1957 resulted in a hung jury. On July 11, 1958, Sheriff Saxon entered a plea of *nolo contendere* (no contest). See *Annual Report of the Attorney General of the United States For The Fiscal Year Ended June 30, 1958* at 177, and ch. 4, note 194, *infra*.

In *United States* v. *Barber*, Crim. No. 1428, M.D. Ga., Mar. 18, 1959, a police officer of Nashville, Ga., was convicted on evidence that he had beaten John Lester Teal, the manager of a Valdosta jewelry store. Barber, while off duty and in plain clothes, had beaten Teal because he had insulted Barber's daughter in the course of an attempted repossession of a ring. As the beating was taking place, another officer, Hancock, arrived but did nothing to stop it. At the station house later Hancock allegedly held Teal while Barber beat him again. Hancock was tried but acquitted. Barber was convicted on March 18, 1959. See *Report of the Attorney General Of the United States for the Fiscal Year Ended June 30, 1959* at 187, and ch. 4, note 193, *infra*.

In *United States* v. *Payne*, Crim. No. 55,788, N.D. Ga., Mar. 25, 1959, the evidence indicates that Herbert C. Payne, a police officer of the town of Lyerly, Ga., incited a mob to beat the victim on two separate occasions. The victim was known as the town drunk, a ne'er-do-well, and had a reputation for beating his children. The announced purpose of the attacks was to force him to leave town. Payne and a nonofficial member of the mob were indicted under section 242 and under 18 U.S.C. sec. 371 for conspiracy to violate section 242. Payne was convicted on March 25, 1959, under the conspiracy charge. See *Annual Report of the Attorney General of the United States For the Fiscal Year Ended June 30, 1959* at 188, and ch. 4, note 193, *infra*.

[42] See discussion of "Force Permissible" in Orfield, *Criminal Procedure From Arrest to Appeal* 26–27 (1947).

[43] National Commission on Law Observance and Enforcement, *Report on Lawlessness in Law Enforcement* 190 (1931).

``GENTLEMEN COPS DON'T SOLVE CRIMES'': DE-
TROIT, 1959.—A fight between eight Negro boys and several policemen
took place in Detroit on the evening of September 10, 1959. There was a
direct conflict in the stories of the policemen and the youths as to the cause of
this eruption, but it is undisputed that four of the policemen were injured
and sent to a hospital for treatment.

When Thaddeus Steel, one of the boys involved, arrived at the police
station, a white reporter from the Detroit Free Press observed his reception
and reported as follows:[44]

A 16-year-old boy, arrested for hitting a policeman with a chair, was beaten
and kicked by at least four patrolmen Thursday night after he was a prisoner in
the Vernor Station garage.

*   *   *

Steel was brought into the police garage in a scout car, closely followed by
three other cars filled with police.

He sat in the back seat of the car. His face showed pain. There was a patrolman sitting next to him.

As the car halted, the patrolman left the car and yanked Steel from it by the
neck. Another patrolman raced up.

"Is this him?" he shouted.

Then he threw a fist into Steel's face.

A second patrolman pushed that assailant aside and sank his fist into Steel's
stomach.

Steel fell to the garage floor, moaning.

*   *   *

The newsmen stood outside the open door of the garage.

One of the policemen saw them and shouted:

"Lower that door!"

But all were too busy slugging Steel, now prone on the floor.

Thy dragged him to the side and the onlookers could see only patrolmen kick-
ing and slugging at him.

"Lower that door!" shouted one again.

Two detectives had entered the other side of the garage and strode grimly
across to the newsmen. Their expressions softened as they reached them.

"Gentlemen cops don't solve crimes," one of the detectives said.

The patrolmen picked Steel up and rushed him into the station. The detectives
turned and walked away.

*   *   *

Inspector Leslie Caldwell, commander of the station, is on furlough.

Lt. Raymond Glinski, acting inspector at Vernor, said, "We can't use kid
gloves on gang fighters."

"When policemen are sent to the hospital, we don't want to tap the hoodlums
who hurt them on the shoulder and send them home," he said.

"After all, four policemen were hit seriously enough by juveniles to be admitted and the juvenile was released from Receiving Hospital without treatment."

Glinski said he did not want to condone beating of prisoners.

---

[44] Detroit Free Press, Sept. 10, 1959, pp. 1, 3.

"But, after all, when it's a question of a policeman going to the hospital or a hood, I think both should go," he said.

After an investigation, Detroit Police Commissioner Herbert W. Hart decided to take no action against the police officers and announced that "no evidence to substantiate charges of police brutality" had been found.[45] "As far as I am concerned, it is a closed issue," he added.[46] When asked by the Detroit Free Press for amplification regarding the eyewitness story of its reporter, Commissioner Hart said that he did "not disbelieve" it.[47] The newspaper editorialized, "The facts stated in our story were accurate."[48] But the editor admitted that the reporter could identify only one detective who was present at the beating.

Wayne County Prosecutor Samuel H. Olsen also ordered an investigation but did not prosecute because the alleged assailants could not be identified.[49] The Federal Government did not prosecute under the Civil Rights Acts. Several of the older Negroes were prosecuted by the State and convicted of conspiracy to commit assault and battery. Thaddeus Steel and the other juveniles were released after a hearing on similar charges by the juvenile court. . . .

POLICE BRUTALITY AND THE CONSTITUTION

In whatever category they may fall most instances of unlawful police violence involve the deprivation of rights guaranteed by the Federal Constitution. Police brutality is ordinarily treated as a violation of due process.[50] Like other matters involving constitutional rights, however, such misconduct may involve not only denials of due process but of equal protection as well. It is upon the latter, of course, that the Commission's jurisdiction depends.[51] The extent to which the two constitutional provisions overlap depends in part upon the way the equal protection clause is interpreted. In a narrow view, the latter prohibits only deliberate discrimination against a person on the basis of his membership in a racial or other minority group.[52] Thus, for instance, it would apply only to brutality directed against a Negro because he is a Negro. A broader interpretation would apply the equal protection

[45] Detroit Free Press, Sept. 13, 1959, p. A–1. The testimony of Commissioner Hart of this incident is found in *Detroit Hearings* 392–93.

[46] Detroit Free Press, *supra*, note 45.

[47] *Ibid.*

[48] *Ibid.*

[49] Prosecutor Olsen's description of his investigation of this incident is found in *Detroit Hearings* 502–503.

[50] See, e.g., *Screws v. United States*, 325 U.S. 91 (1945).

[51] See ch. 1 at 2, *supra*.

[52] This view was set forth as *dictum* in the *Slaughterhouse Cases*, 83 U.S. (16 Wall.) 36 at 81 (1873). Later cases (see notes 106 and 107 *infra*) definitely give a far broader meaning to the equal protection clause.

provision in any case where a person is deliberately denied the enjoyment of a right (such as the right to be protected from physical harm while in the custody of the police)[53] that is commonly afforded others in like circumstances.[54] This view would make it applicable to instances of police brutality where there was in fact improper treatment, whether or not it was deliberately directed against the victim on account of his minority status. Thus as a practical matter, under this view, every act of police brutality would appear to constitute a denial of equal protection, since the police do not in fact brutalize all persons whom they arrest or hold in custody. As a matter of policy the Commission's studies are confined to cases involving members of minority groups—so that they fall far short of the outer limits of the broader interpretation.

EXTENT AND EFFECTS

The Commission's studies indicate that police brutality in the United States today is a serious[55] and continuing problem in many parts of the country. Whether in the country as a whole it is increasing or decreasing is not clear. There seems to have been no marked overall abatement in recent years, although improvements have been reported in particular areas—such as Atlanta and Chicago.[56]

The most comprehensive statistics available on police brutality were compiled by Commission staff members from complaints that have come to the

---

[53] *Catlette* v. *United States*, 132 F. 2d 902, 906–907 (4th Cir. 1943).

[54] *Lynch* v. *United States*, 189 F. 2d 476, 479 (5th Cir. 1951), *cert. denied*, 342 U.S. 831 (1951).

[55] The seriousness of the problem of police brutality in quantitative terms is documented by the cases described in this Report; by many similar reports in Commission files not included in this Report; by the many complaints received by the Department of Justice, see app. VII, tables 2 and 3; and by the opinion of Department of Justice officials that many acts of brutality are not reported to officials due to apathy, fear, or ignorance, see ch. 4 at 58, *infra*. In qualitative terms the problem must be considered serious because any act of unlawful violence, especially by an official, is harmful to our society. The effect of such acts on the Negro community is described in Willis Ward's testimony, p. 27, infra. The seriousness of this situation is also suggested by this excerpt from a recent study by Bullock entitled *The Houston Murder Problem* 80–81 (1961):

> Negroes also have a "Bully" image of Houston's policemen. Whenever one hears about the police descending upon a group of Negroes, there is always raised this question: "How many heads were whupped?" The reasons for this attitude grow out of the spread of reports concerning instances of police brutality.
>
> * * *
>
> Gradually and insidiously, these reports seep into the minds of Negroes and reinforce ugly images about all of Houston's policemen. Therefore, when Negroes are asked what they think of policing in Houston, their response is a series of negative attitudes that are heavily laden with disrespect. We asked this question of more than five hundred (500) people, and we got attitudinal patterns that were generally negative.

[56] See ch. 6 at 82 and 87, *infra*.

attention of the Department of Justice. These statistics, presented in the accompanying table, do not include all cases of alleged police brutality that occurred during the period in question, for as indicated below,[57] not all incidents come to the attention of the Department. The Department, none-theless, receives notice of more such incidents than any other agency. Of course, not all the complaints that are received are valid by any means.[58] Yet they do provide at least a rough measure of the outlines of the problem.

TABLE 1. *Allegations of Police Brutality by Race of Victim*
(Matters received by the Department of Justice, January 1, 1958 to June 30, 1960)

	TOTAL	NEGRO AND OTHER MINORITY*	WHITE	UNKNOWN
National totals	1,328	461	506	361
	Per cent	*Per cent*	*Per cent*	*Per cent*
	100	35	38	27
Northern and Western States	433	117	193	123
	Per cent	*Per cent*	*Per cent*	*Per cent*
	100	27	44.6	28.4
Southern States	895	344	313	238
	Per cent	*Per cent*	*Per cent*	*Per cent*
	100	38.4	35	26.6

* Includes 24 cases of other minority group victims: Indian, 12; Mexican, 10; Mixed, 1; and other, 1.

The statistics suggest that Negroes feel the brunt of official brutality pro-portionately more than any other group in American society. As Table 1

[57] See ch. 4 at 57–58, *infra.*
[58] Harold R. Tyler, Jr., former Assistant Attorney General in charge of the Civil Rights Division, wrote the Commission on October 18, 1961, in this connection:

As most lawyers are aware, there has been an increasing tendency over the years for defendants and their counsel in criminal cases, particularly those of the common law variety, to raise by way of defensive matter the issue of coercion or improper treat-ment at the hands of the police. I feel that this phenomenon has some impact upon the nature, number, and type of complaints received by the Department of Justice. Further, Department attorneys must keep this in mind when evaluating complaints. The Department cannot be expected to prosecute complaints which are motivated by a desire on the part of the complainants to "use" the Government to raise defen-sive matters collaterally, even in those situations where the facts *prima facie* might support a Section 242 prosecution. Then, too, the Government should not be ex-pected to litigate, at least in most instances, those complaints of criminal defendants which necessarily will be aired before the courts in the complainants' own cases. Other ramifications of this point are too detailed for profitable discussion here, but the point remains that this tendency on the part of criminal case defendants, though not susceptible to statistical evaluation, is often a real problem in evaluating and acting upon complaints.

shows, among the complaints of police brutality received by the Department in the two and one half year period ending June 30, 1960, the alleged victims were Negroes (who constitute approximately 10 per cent of the total population) in 35 per cent of the cases and whites in 38 per cent of the cases; in 27 per cent of the cases the race of the victim was unknown.

In terms of regions, approximately two out of every three complaints over the last few years (as seen in Table 1), and probably over the last 20 years,[59] originated in the 17 Southern States and the District of Columbia. This may indicate that police brutality is more prevalent in the South than in other regions of the country. But this is by no means certain, for these statistics may be evidence merely of a greater tendency of non-southern victims to complain to local rather than to Federal authorities.

A review of the cases and complaints from all sources suggests that brutality is largely confined to State and local police or prison forces. Several Department of Justice officials stated that while complaints do come in against Federal civilian police officers or prison guards, they are quite rare. The Wickersham Commission in 1931 also found that police brutality is almost exclusively confined to State and local agencies.[60]

Illegal violence by officers of the law casts a cloud of suspicion over the entire system of American justice. It violates highly valued constitutional rights, and may produce a pervading fear regarding the security of the person. Brutality against a few Negroes may cause many of them to distrust all police officers. This is unfortunate not only for Negroes but also for the police and the entire community. Criminal investigations rely to a great extent on information supplied by private persons. The job of crime control becomes vastly more difficult when a whole segment of the community is wary of any contact with the police. Mr. Willis Ward, a former assistant county prosecutor, testified regarding the relationship between Negro distrust of the police and the problems of crime solution at the Commission's Detroit Hearing:[61]

It is said that there are four crimes currently in the papers today, heinous crimes, involving murder and robbery, and from what we read in the paper it would appear that the suspects are colored citizens. It would appear that perhaps in this city the people most apt to know who did it might be colored people, but the thing that shudders me is: As much as the good colored people as well as the white people want criminals apprehended and brought to justice, that if a person knows or has reason to believe it would help us to locate these culprits the chances are, 99 chances out of a hundred, if he complains he will be treated more as a suspect than as a citizen attempting to reduce crime in the city of Detroit.

---

[59] See app. VII, table 3.
[60] Referring to brutality connected with the third degree, the Wickersham Commission wrote that there was "little evidence of the practice among Federal officials." National Commission on Law Observance and Enforcement, *op. cit. supra*, note 43 at 4.
[61] *Detroit Hearings* 381.

SUMMARY

Police brutality—the unnecessary use of violence to enforce the mores of segregation, to punish, and to coerce confessions—is a serious problem in the United States. Much of it occurs when an ill-trained or prejudiced policeman first comes in contact with a suspect. Yet, many policemen have demonstrated that it is possible to perform their duty effectively without resorting to unlawful violence which creates suspicions about the fairness of the American system of criminal justice.

[THE TOTALITARIAN STATE, I]

The Totalitarian Secret Police

HANNAH ARENDT

Up to now we know only two authentic forms of totalitarian domination: the dictatorship of National Socialism after 1938, and the dictatorship of Bolshevism since 1930. These forms of domination differ basically from other kinds of dictatorial, despotic or tyrannical rule; and even though they have developed, with a certain continuity, from party dictatorships, their essentially totalitarian features are new and cannot be derived from one-party systems. The goal of one-party systems is not only to seize the government administration but, by filling all offices with party members, to achieve a complete amalgamation of state and party, so that after the seizure of power the party becomes a kind of propaganda organization for the government. This system is "total" only in a negative sense, namely, in that the ruling party will tolerate no other parties, no opposition and no freedom of political opinion. Once a party dictatorship has come to power, it leaves the original power relationship between state and party intact; the government and the army exercise the same power as before, and the "revolution" consists only in the fact that all government positions are now occupied by party members. In all these cases the power of the party rests on a monopoly guaranteed by the state and the party no longer possesses its own power center.

The revolution initiated by the totalitarian movements after they have

SOURCE: Hannah Arendt, *The Origins of Totalitarianism,* copyright 1951 by Hannah Arendt; Second Enlarged Edition copyright 1958 by Hannah Arendt (New York: The World Publishing Company (Meridian Books): U.S.A. and Canadian market) (London: George Allen & Unwin Ltd.: world, excluding U.S.A. and Canadian, market). By permission of the author and publishers.

seized power is of a considerably more radical nature. From the start, they consciously strive to maintain the essential differences between state and movement and to prevent the "revolutionary" institutions of the movement from being absorbed by the government.[1] The problem of seizing the state machine without amalgamating with it is solved by permitting only those party members whose importance for the movement is secondary to rise in the state hierarchy. All real power is vested in the institutions of the movement, and outside the state and military apparatuses. It is inside the movement, which remains the center of action of the country, that all decisions are made; the official civil services are often not even informed of what is going on, and party members with the ambition to rise to the rank of ministers have in all cases paid for such "bourgeois" wishes with the loss of their influence on the movement and of the confidence of its leaders.

Totalitarianism in power uses the state as its outward façade, to represent the country in the nontotalitarian world. As such, the totalitarian state is the logical heir of the totalitarian movement from which it borrows its organizational structure. Totalitarian rulers deal with nontotalitarian governments in the same way they dealt with parliamentary parties or intraparty factions before their rise to power and, though on an enlarged international scene, are again faced with the double problem of shielding the fictitious world of the movement (or the totalitarian country) from the impact of factuality and of presenting a semblance of normality and common sense to the normal outside world.

Above the state and behind the façades of ostensible power, in a maze of multiplied offices, underlying all shifts of authority and in a chaos of inefficiency, lies the power nucleus of the country, the superefficient and supercompetent services of the secret police.[2] The emphasis on the police as the sole organ of power, and the corresponding neglect of the seemingly greater power arsenal of the army, which is characteristic of all totalitarian regimes, can still be partially explained by the totalitarian aspiration to world rule and its conscious abolition of the distinction between a foreign country and a home country, between foreign and domestic affairs. The military forces, trained to fight a foreign aggressor, have always been a dubious instrument for civil-war purposes; even under totalitarian conditions they find it diffi-

---

[1] Hitler frequently commented on the relationship between state and party, and always emphasized that not the state, but the race, or the "united folk community," was of primary importance (cf. the afore-quoted speech, reprinted as annex to the *Tischgespräche*). In his speech at the Nuremberg Parteitag of 1935, he gave this theory its most succinct expression: "It is not the state that commands us, but we who command the state." It is self-evident that, in practice, such powers of command are possible only if the institutions of the party remain independent from those of the state.

[2] Otto Gauweiler, *Rechseinrichtungen und Rechtsaufgaben der Bewegung*, 1939, notes expressly that Himmler's special position as Reichsfuehrer-SS and head of the German police rested on the fact that the police administration had achieved "a genuine unity of party and state" which was not even attempted anywhere else in the government.

cult to regard their own people with the eyes of a foreign conqueror.[3] More important in this respect, however, is that their value becomes dubious even in time of war. Since the totalitarian ruler conducts his policies on the assumption of an eventual world government, he treats the victims of his aggression as though they were rebels, guilty of high treason, and consequently prefers to rule occupied territories with police, and not with military forces.

Even before the movement seizes power, it possesses a secret police and spy service with branches in various countries. Later its agents receive more money and authority than the regular military intelligence service and are frequently the secret chiefs of embassies and consulates abroad.[4] Its main tasks consist in forming fifth columns, directing the branches of the movement, influencing the domestic policies of the respective countries, and generally preparing for the time when the totalitarian ruler—after overthrow of the government or military victory—can openly feel at home. In other words, the international branches of the secret police are the transmission belts which constantly transform the ostensibly foreign policy of the totalitarian state into the potentially domestic business of the totalitarian movement.

These functions, however, which the secret police fulfill in order to prepare the totalitarian utopia of world rule, are secondary to those required for the present realization of the totalitarian fiction in one country. The dominant role of the secret police in the domestic politics of totalitarian countries has naturally contributed much to the common misconception of totalitarianism. All despotisms rely heavily on secret services and feel more threatened by their own than by any foreign people. However, this analogy between totalitarianism and despotism holds only for the first stages of totalitarian rule, when there is still a political opposition. In this as in other respects totalitarianism takes advantage of, and gives conscious support to, nontotalitarian misconceptions, no matter how uncomplimentary they may be. Himmler, in his famous speech to the Reichswehr staff in 1937, assumed the role of an ordinary tyrant when he explained the constant expansion of the police forces by assuming the existence of a "fourth theater in case of war, internal Germany."[5] Similarly, Stalin at almost the same moment half succeeded in convincing the old Bolshevik guard, whose "confessions" he needed, of a war threat against the Soviet Union and, consequently, an emergency in which the country must remain united even behind a despot. The most striking aspect of these statements was that both were made after all political

---

[3] During the peasant revolts of the twenties in Russia, Voroshilov allegedly refused the support of the Red Army; this led to the introduction of special divisions of the GPU for punitive expeditions. See Anton Ciliga, *The Russian Enigma*, London, 1940, p. 45.

[4] In 1935, the Gestapo agents abroad received 20 million marks while the regular espionage service of the Reichswehr had to get along with a budget of 8 million. See Pierre Dehillotte, *Gestapo*, Paris, 1940, p. 11.

[5] See *Nazi Conspiracy*, U.S. Government, Washington, D. C., 1946, IV, 616 ff.

opposition had been extinguished, that the secret services were expanded when actually no opponents were left to be spied upon. When war came, Himmler neither needed nor used his SS troops in Germany itself, except for the running of concentration camps and policing of foreign slave labor; the bulk of the armed SS served at the Eastern front where they were used for "special assignments"—usually mass murder—and the enforcement of policy which frequently ran counter to the military as well as the Nazi civilian hierarchy. Like the secret police of the Soviet Union, the SS formations usually arrived after the military forces had pacified the conquered territory and had dealt with outright political opposition.

In the first stages of a totalitarian regime, however, the secret police and the party's elite formations still play a role similar to that in other forms of dictatorship and the well-known terror regimes of the past; and the excessive cruelty of their methods is unparalleled only in the history of modern Western countries. The first stage of ferreting out secret enemies and hunting down former opponents is usually combined with drafting the entire population into front organizations and re-educating old party members for voluntary espionage services, so that the rather dubious sympathies of the drafted sympathizers need not worry the specially trained cadres of the police. It is during this stage that a neighbor gradually becomes a more dangerous enemy to one who happens to harbor "dangerous thoughts" than are the officially appointed police agents. The end of the first stage comes with the liquidation of open and secret resistance in any organized form; it can be set at about 1935 in Germany and approximately 1930 in Soviet Russia.

Only after the extermination of real enemies has been completed and the hunt for "objective enemies" begun does terror become the actual content of totalitarian regimes. Under the pretext of building socialism in one country, or using a given territory as a laboratory for a revolutionary experiment, or realizing the *Volksgemeinschaft,* the second claim of totalitarianism, the claim to total domination, is carried out. And although theoretically total domination is possible only under the conditions of world rule, the totalitarian regimes have proved that this part of the totalitarian utopia can be realized almost to perfection, because it is temporarily independent of defeat or victory. Thus Hitler could rejoice even in the midst of military setbacks over the extermination of Jews and the establishment of death factories; no matter what the final outcome, without the war it would never have been possible "to burn the bridges" and to realize some of the goals of the totalitarian government.[6]

The elite formations of the Nazi movement and the "cadres" of the Bolshevik movement serve the goal of total domination rather than the security

---

[6] This is supported by Hitler's statements during the war, quoted by Goebbels (*The Goebbels Diaries,* ed. Louis P. Lochner, 1948) to the effect that "the war had made possible for us the solution of a whole series of problems that could never have been solved in normal times," and that, no matter how the war turned out, "the Jews will certainly be the losers" (p. 314).

of the regime in power. Just as the totalitarian claim to world rule is only in appearance the same as imperialist expansion, so the claim to total domination only *seems* familiar to the student of despotism. If the chief difference between totalitarian and imperialist expansion is that the former recognizes no difference between a home and a foreign country, then the chief difference between a despotic and a totalitarian secret police is that the latter does not hunt secret thoughts and does not use the old method of secret services, the method of provocation.[7]

Since the totalitarian secret police begins its career after the pacification of the country, it always appears entirely superfluous to all outside observers —or, on the contrary, misleads them into thinking that there is some secret resistance.[8] The superfluousness of secret services is nothing new; they have always been haunted by the need to prove their usefulness and keep their jobs after their original task had been completed. The methods used for this purpose have made the study of the history of revolutions a rather difficult enterprise. It appears, for example, that there was not a single anti-government action under the reign of Louis Napoleon which had not been inspired by the police itself.[9] Similarly, the role of secret agents in all revolutionary parties in Czarist Russia strongly suggests that without their "inspiring" provocative actions the course of the Russian revolutionary movement would have been far less successful.[10] Provocation, in other words, helped as much to maintain the continuity of tradition as it did to disrupt time and again the organization of the revolution.

---

[7] Maurice Laporte, *Histoire de l'Okhrana*, Paris, 1935, rightly called the method of provocation "the foundation stone" of the secret police (p. 19).

In Soviet Russia, provocation, far from being the secret weapon of the secret police, has been used as the widely propagandized public method of the regime to gauge the temper of public opinion. The reluctance of the population to avail itself of the periodically recurring invitations to criticize or react to "liberal" interludes in the terror regime shows that such gestures are understood as provocation on a mass scale. Provocation has indeed become the totalitarian version of public opinion polls.

[8] Interesting in this respect are the attempts made by Nazi civil servants in Germany to reduce the competence and the personnel of the Gestapo on the ground that Nazification of the country had been achieved, so that Himmler, who on the contrary wanted to expand the secret services at this moment (around 1934), had to exaggerate the danger coming from the "internal enemies." See *Nazi Conspiracy*, II, 259; V, 205; III, 547.

[9] See Jean Gallier-Boissière, *Mysteries of the French Secret Police*, 1938, p. 234.

[10] It seems, after all, no accident that the foundation of the Okhrana in 1880 ushered in a period of unsurpassed revolutionary activities in Russia. In order to prove its usefulness, it had occasionally to organize murders, and its agents "served despite themselves the ideas of those whom they denounced. . . . If a pamphlet was distributed by a police agent or if the execution of a minister was organized by an Azev—the result was the same" (M. Laporte, *op. cit.*, p. 25). The more important executions moreover seem to have been police jobs—Stolypin and von Plehve. Decisive for the revolutionary tradition was the fact that in times of calm the police agents had to "stir up anew the energies and stimulate the zeal" of the revolutionaries (*ibid.*, p. 71).

See also Bertram D. Wolfe, *Three Who Made a Revolution: Lenin, Trotsky, Stalin*, 1948, who calls this phenomenon "Police Socialism."

A PREMONITION OF TOTALITARIANISM

Then—this is all what you say—new economic relations will be established, all ready-made and worked out with mathematical exactitude, so that every possible question will vanish in the twinkling of an eye, simply because every possible answer to it will be provided. Then the "Palace of Crystal" will be built. Then . . . In fact, those will be halcyon days. Of course there is no guaranteeing (this is my comment) that it will not be, for instance, frightfully dull then (for what will one have to do when everything will be calculated and tabulated?), but on the other hand everything will be extraordinarily rational. Of course boredom may lead you to anything. It is boredom sets one sticking golden pins into people, but all that would not matter. What is bad (this is my comment again) is that I dare say people will be thankful for the gold pins then. Man is stupid, you know, phenomenally stupid; or rather he is not at all stupid, but he is so ungrateful that you could not find another like him in all creation. I, for instance, would not be in the least surprised if all of a sudden, apropos of nothing, in the midst of general prosperity a gentleman with an ignoble, or rather with a reactionary and ironical, countenance were to arise and putting his arms akimbo, say to us all: "I say, gentlemen, hadn't we better kick over the whole show and scatter rationalism to the winds, simply to send these logarithms to the devil, and to enable us to live once more at our own sweet foolish will!" That again would not matter; but what is annoying is that he would be sure to find followers—such is the nature of man. And all that for the most foolish reason, which, one would think, was hardly worth mentioning. that is, that man everywhere and at all times, whoever he may be, has prefered to act as he chose and not in the least as his reason and advantage dictated. And one may choose what is contrary to one's own interests, and sometimes one *positively ought* (that is my idea). One's own free unfettered choice, one's own caprice—however wild it may be, one's own fancy worked up at times to frenzy—is that very "most advantageous advantage" which we have overlooked, which comes under no classification and against which all systems and theories are continually being shattered to atoms. And how do these wiseacres know that man wants a normal, a virtuous choice? What has made them conceive that man must want a rationally advantageous choice? What man wants is simply *independent* choice, whatever that independence may cost and wherever it may lead. And choice, of course, the devil only knows what choice. . . .

SOURCE: Fyodor Dostoyevsky *Notes from Underground*, Trans. by Constance Garnett (New York, 1960).

This dubious role of provocation might have been one reason why the totalitarian rulers discarded it. Provocation, moreover, is clearly necessary only on the assumption that suspicion is not sufficient for arrest and punishment. None of the totalitarian rulers, of course, ever dreamed of conditions in which he would have to resort to provocation in order to trap somebody he thought to be an enemy. More important than these technical considerations is the fact that totalitarianism defined its enemies ideologically before it seized power, so that categories of the "suspects" were not established through police information. Thus the Jews in Nazi Germany or the descendants of the former ruling classes in Soviet Russia were not really suspected of any hostile action; they had been declared "objective" enemies of the regime in accordance with its ideology.

The chief difference between the despotic and the totalitarian secret police lies in the difference between the "suspect" and the "objective enemy." The latter is defined by the policy of the government and not by his own desire to overthrow it.[11] He is never an individual whose dangerous thoughts must be provoked or whose past justifies suspicion, but a "carrier of tendencies" like the carrier of a disease.[12] Practically speaking, the totalitarian ruler proceeds like a man who persistently insults another man until everybody knows that the latter is his enemy, so that he can, with some plausibility, go and kill him in self-defense. This certainly is a little crude, but it works—as everybody will know who ever watched how certain successful careerists eliminate competitors.

The introduction of the notion of "objective enemy" is much more decisive for the functioning of totalitarian regimes than the ideological definition of the respective categories. If it were only a matter of hating Jews or bourgeois, the totalitarian regimes could, after the commission of one gigantic crime, return, as it were, to the rules of normal life and government. As we know, the opposite is the case. The category of objective enemies outlives the first ideologically determined foes of the movement; new objective enemies are discovered according to changing circumstances: the Nazis, foreseeing the completion of Jewish extermination, had already taken the necessary preliminary steps for the liquidation of the Polish people, while Hitler even planned the decimation of certain categories of Germans;[13] the Bolsheviks, having started with descendants of the former ruling classes, directed their

---

[11] Hans Frank, who later became Governor General of Poland, made a typical differentiation between a person "dangerous to the State" and a person who is "hostile to the State." The former implies an objective quality which is independent of will and behavior; the political police of the Nazis is concerned not just with actions hostile to the state but with "all attempts—no matter what their aim—which in their effects endanger the State." See *Deutsches Verwaltungsrecht*, pp. 420–430. Translation quoted from *Nazi Conspiracy*, IV, 881 ff.—In the words of Maunz, *op. cit.*, p. 44: "By eliminating dangerous persons, the security measure . . . means to ward off a state of danger to the national community, independently of any offense that may have been committed by these persons. [It is a question of] warding off an *objective* danger."

[12] R. Hoehn, a Nazi jurist and member of the SS, said in an obituary on Reinhard Heydrich, who prior to his rule of Czechoslovakia had been one of the closest collaborators with Himmler: He regarded his opponents "not as individuals but as carriers of tendencies endangering the state and therefore beyond the pale of the national community." In *Deutsche Allgemeine Zeitung* of June 6, 1942; quoted from E. Kohn-Bramstedt, *Dictatorship and Political Police*, London, 1945.

[13] As early as 1941, during a staff meeting in Hitler's headquarters, it was proposed to impose upon the Polish population those regulations by which the Jews had been prepared for the extermination camps: change of names if these were of German

full terror against the kulaks (in the early thirties), who in turn were followed by Russians of Polish origin (between 1936 and 1938), the Tartars
and the Vulga Germans during the war, former prisoners of war and units
of the occupational forces of the Red Army after the war, and Russian Jewry
after the establishment of a Jewish state. The choice of such categories is
never entirely arbitrary; since they are publicized and used for propaganda
purposes of the movement abroad, they must appear plausible as possible
enemies; the choice of a particular category may even be due to certain
propaganda needs of the movement at large—as for instance the sudden entirely unprecedented emergence of governmental antisemitism in the Soviet
Union, which may be calculated to win sympathies for the Soviet Union in
the European satellite countries. The show trials which require subjective
confessions of guilt from "objectively" identified enemies are meant for these
purposes; they can best be staged with those who have received a totalitarian
indoctrination that enables them "subjectively" to understand their own
"objective" harmfulness and to confess "for the sake of the cause."[14] The
concept of the "objective opponent," whose identity changes according to the
prevailing circumstances—so that, as soon as one category is liquidated, war
may be declared on another—corresponds exactly to the factual situation
reiterated time and again by totalitarian rulers: namely, that their regime is
not a government in any traditional sense, but a *movement*, whose advance
constantly meets with new obstacles that have to be eliminated. So far as one
may speak at all of any legal thinking within the totalitarian system, the
"objective opponent" is its central idea.

Closely connected with this transformation of the suspect into the objective enemy is the change of position of the secret police in the totalitarian

---

origin; death sentences for sexual intercourse between Germans and Poles (*Rassen-
schande*); obligation to wear a P-sign in Germany similar to the Yellow Star for Jews.
See *Nazi Conspiracy*, VIII, 237 ff., and Hans Frank's diary in *Trial, op. cit.*, XXIX,
683. Naturally, the Poles themselves soon began to worry about what would happen to
them when the Nazis had finished the extermination of the Jews (*Nazi Conspiracy*,
IV, 916). [Nor were the Germans themselves exempt.] Hitler contemplated during the
war the introduction of a National Health Bill: "After national X-ray examination, the
Fuehrer is to be given a list of sick persons, particularly those with lung and heart
diseases. On the basis of the new Reich Health Law . . . these families will no longer
be able to remain among the public and can no longer be allowed to produce children.
What will happen to these families will be the subject of further orders of the Fuehrer."
It does not need much imagination to guess what these further orders would have
been. The number of people no longer allowed "to remain among the public" would
have formed a considerable portion of the German population (*Nazi Conspiracy*,
VI, 175).

[14] F. Beck and W. Godin, *Russian Purge and the Extraction of Confession* (1951),
p. 87. Beck and Godin speak of the "objective characteristics" which invited arrest in
the USSR; among them was membership in the NKVD (p. 153). Subjective insight
into the objective necessity of arrest and confession could most easily be achieved with
former members of the secret police. In the words of an ex-NKVD agent: My superiors
know me and my work well enough, and if the party and the NKVD now require me
to confess to such things they must have good reasons for what they are doing. My
duty as a loyal Soviet citizen is not to withhold the confession required of me"
(*ibid.*, p. 231).

state. The secret services have rightly been called a state within the state, and this not only in despotisms but also under constitutional or semiconstitutional governments. The mere possession of secret information has always given this branch a decisive superiority over all other branches of the civil services and constituted an open threat to members of the government.[15] The totalitarian police, on the contrary, is totally subject to the will of the Leader, who alone can decide who the next potential enemy will be and who, as Stalin did, can also single out cadres of the secret police for liquidation. Since the police are no longer permitted to use provocation, they have been deprived of the only available means of perpetuating themselves independently of the government and have become entirely dependent on the higher authorities for the safeguarding of their jobs. Like the army in a nontotalitarian state, the police in totalitarian countries merely execute political policy and have lost all the prerogatives which they held under despotic bureaucracies.[16]

The task of the totalitarian police is not to discover crimes, but to be on hand when the government decides to arrest a certain category of the population. Their chief political distinction is that they alone are in the confidence of the highest authority and know which political line will be enforced. This does not apply only to matters of high policy, such as the liquidation of a whole class or ethnic group (only the cadres of the GPU knew the actual goal of the Soviet government in the early thirties and only the SS formations knew that the Jews were to be exterminated in the early forties); the point about everyday life under totalitarian conditions is that only the agents of the NKVD in an industrial enterprise are informed of what Moscow wants when it orders, for instance, a speed-up in the fabrication of pipes—whether it simply wants more pipes, or to ruin the director of the factory, or to liquidate the whole management, or to abolish this particular factory, or, finally, to have this order repeated all over the nation so that a new purge can begin.

One of the reasons for the duplication of secret services whose agents are unknown to each other is that total domination needs the most extreme flexibility: to use our example, Moscow may not yet know, when it gives its order for pipes, whether it wants pipes—which are always needed—or a purge. Multiplication of secret services makes last-minute changes possible, so that one branch may be preparing to bestow the Order of Lenin on the director of the factory while another makes arrangements for his arrest. The efficiency of the police consists in the fact that such contradictory assignments can be prepared simultaneously.

---

[15] Well known is the situation in France where ministers lived in constant fear of the secret *"dossiers"* of the police. For the situation in Czarist Russia, see Laporte, *op. cit.*, pp. 22–23: "Eventually the Okhrana will wield a power far superior to the power of the more regular authorities. . . . The Okhrana . . . will inform the Czar only of what it chooses to."

[16] "Unlike the Okhrana, which had been a state within a state, the GPU is a department of the Soviet government; . . . and its activities are much less independent" (Roger N. Baldwin, "Political Police," in *Encyclopedia of Social Sciences*).

Under totalitarian, as under other regimes, the secret police has a monopoly on certain vital information. But the kind of knowledge that can be possessed only by the police has undergone an important change: the police are no longer concerned with knowing what is going on in the heads of future victims (most of the time they ignore who these victims will be), and the police have become the trustees of the greatest state secrets. This automatically means a great improvement in prestige and position, even though it is accompanied by a definite loss of real power. The secret services no longer know anything that the Leader does not know better; in terms of power, they have sunk to the level of the executioner.

From a legal point of view, even more interesting than the change from the suspect to the objective enemy is the totalitarian replacement of the suspected offense by the possible crime. The possible crime is no more subjective than the objective enemy. While the suspect is arrested because he is thought to be capable of committing a crime that more or less fits his personality (or his suspected personality),[17] the totalitarian version of the possible crime is based on the logical anticipation of objective developments. The Moscow Trials of the old Bolshevik guard and the chiefs of the Red Army were classic examples of punishment for possible crimes. Behind the fantastic, fabricated charges one can easily detect the following logical calculation: developments in the Soviet Union might lead to a crisis, a crisis might lead to the overthrow of Stalin's dictatorship, this might weaken the country's military force and possibly bring about a situation in which the new government would have to sign a truce or even conclude an alliance with Hitler. Whereupon Stalin proceeded to declare that a plot for the overthrow of the government and a conspiracy with Hitler existed.[18] Against these

---

[17] Typical of the concept of the suspect is the following story related by C. Pobyedonostzev in *L'Autocratie Russe: Mémoires politiques, correspondance officiele et documents inédits . . . 1881–1894*, Paris, 1927: General Cherevin of the Okhrana is asked, because the opposing party has hired a Jewish lawyer, to intervene in favor of a lady who is about to lose a lawsuit. Says the General: "The same night I ordered the arrest of this cursed Jew and held him as a so-called politically suspect person. . . . After all, could I treat in the same manner friends and a dirty Jew who may be innocent today but who was guilty yesterday or will be guilty tomorrow?"

[18] The charges in the Moscow Trials "were based . . . on a grotesquely brutalized and distorting anticipation of possible developments. [Stalin's] reasoning probably developed along the following lines: they may want to overthrow me in a crisis—I shall charge them with having made the attempt. . . . A change of government may weaken Russia's fighting capacity; and if they succeed, they may be compelled to sign a truce with Hitler, and perhaps even agree to a cession of territory. . . . I shall accuse them of having entered already into a treacherous alliance with Germany and ceded Soviet territory." This is I. Deutscher's brilliant explanation of the Moscow Trials in *Stalin: A Political Biography* (New York and London, 1949), p. 377.

A good example of the Nazi version of the possible crime can be found in Hans Frank, *op. cit.*: "A complete catalogue of attempts 'dangerous to the State' can never be drawn up because it can never be foreseen what may endanger the leadership and the people some time in the future." (Translation quoted from *Nazi Conspiracy*, IV, 881.)

"objective," though entirely improbable, possibilities stood only "subjective" factors, such as the trustworthiness of the accused, their fatigue, their inability to understand what was going on, their firm conviction that without Stalin everything would be lost, their sincere hatred of Fascism—that is, a number of factual details which naturally lacked the consistency of the fictitious, logical, possible crime. Totalitarianism's central assumption that everything is possible thus leads through consistent elimination of all factual restraints to the absurd and terrible consequence that every crime the rulers can conceive of must be punished, regardless of whether or not it has been committed. The possible crime, like the objective enemy, is of course beyond the competence of the police, who can neither discover, invent, nor provoke it. Here again the secret services depend entirely upon the political authorities. Their independence as a state within the state is gone.

Only in one respect does the totalitarian secret police still resemble closely the secret services of nontotalitarian countries. The secret police has traditionally, *i.e.*, since Fouché, profited from its victims and has augmented the official state-authorized budget from certain unorthodox sources simply by assuming a position of partnership in activities it was supposed to suppress, such as gambling and prostitution.[19] These illegal methods of financing itself, ranging from friendly acceptance of bribes to outright blackmail, were a prominent factor in freeing the secret services from the public authorities and strengthened their position as a state within the state. It is curious to see that the financing of police activities with income from its victims has survived all other changes. In Soviet Russia, the NKVD is almost entirely dependent upon the exploitation of slave labor which, indeed, seems to yield no other profit and to serve no other purpose but the financing of the huge secret apparatus.[20] Himmler first financed his SS troops, who were the cadres of the Nazi secret police, through the confiscation of Jewish property; he then concluded an agreement with Darré, the Minister of Agriculture, by which Himmler received the several hundred million marks which Darré earned annually by buying agricultural commodities cheaply abroad and selling them at fixed prices in Germany.[21] This source of regular income disappeared of course during the war; Albert Speer, the successor of Todt and the greatest employer of manpower in Germany after 1942, proposed a similar deal to Himmler in 1942; if Himmler agreed to release from SS authority the imported slave laborers whose work had been remarkably inefficient,

---

[19] The criminal methods of the secret police are of course no monopoly of the French tradition. In Austria, for example, the feared political police under Maria Theresa was organized by Kaunitz from the cadres of the so-called "chastity commissars" who used to live by blackmail. See Moritz Bermann, *Maria Theresa und Kaiser Joseph II*, Vienna-Leipzig, 1881. I owe this reference to Robert Pick.

[20] That the huge police organization is paid with profits from slave labor is certain; surprising is that the police budget seems not even entirely covered by it; Kravchenko, (Victor Kravchenko, *I Chose Freedom* [New York, 1946]), mentions special taxes, imposed by the NKVD on convicted citizens who continue to live and work in freedom.

[21] See Fritz Thyssen, *I Paid Hitler*, London, 1941.

the Speer organization would give him a certain percentage of the profits for the SS.[22] To such more or less regular sources of income, Himmler added the old blackmail methods of secret services in times of financial crisis: in their communities SS units formed groups of "Friends of the SS" who had to "volunteer" the necessary funds for the needs of the local SS men.[23] (It is noteworthy that in its various financial operations the Nazi secret police did not exploit its prisoners. Except in the last years of the war, when the use of human material in the concentration camps was no longer determined by Himmler alone, work in the camps "had no rational purpose except that of increasing the burden and torture of the unfortunate prisoners."[24]

However, these financial irregularities are the sole, and not very important, traces of the secret police tradition. They are possible because of the general contempt of totalitarian regimes for economic and financial matters, so that methods which under normal conditions would be illegal, and would distinguish the secret police from other more respectable departments of the administration, no longer indicate that we are dealing here with a department which enjoys independence, is not controlled by other authorities, lives in an atmosphere of irregularity, nonrespectability, and insecurity. The position of the totalitarian secret police, on the contrary, has been completely stabilized, and its services are wholly integrated in the administration. Not only is the organization *not* beyond the pale of the law, but, rather, it is the embodiment of the law, and its respectability is above suspicion. It no longer organizes murders on its own initiative, no longer provokes offenses against state and society, and it sternly proceeds against all forms of bribery, blackmail and irregular financial gains. The moral lecture, coupled with very tangible threats, that Himmler could permit himself to deliver to his men in the middle of the war—"We had the moral right . . . to wipe out this [Jewish] people bent on wiping us out, but we do not have the right to enrich ourselves in any manner whatsoever, be it by a fur coat, a watch, a single mark, or a cigarette"[25]—strikes a note that one would look for in vain

---

[22] See *Nazi Conspiracy*, I, 916–917.—The economic activity of the SS was consolidated in a central office for economic and administrative affairs. To the Treasury and Internal Revenue, the SS declared its financial assets as "party property earmarked for special purposes" (letter of May 5, 1943, quoted from M. Wolfson, *Uebersicht der Gliederung verbrecherischer Nazi-Organisationen. Omgus*, December, 1947).

[23] See Kohn-Bramstedt, *Dictatorship and Political Police* (London, 1945), p. 112. The blackmail motive is clearly revealed if we consider that this kind of fund-raising was always organized by local SS units in the localities where they were stationed. See *Der Weg der SS*, issued by the *SS-Hauptamt-Schulungsamt* (undated), p. 14.

[24] *Ibid.*, p. 124.—Certain compromises in this respect were made for those requirements pertaining to the maintenance of the camps and the personal needs of the SS. See Wolfson, *op. cit.*, letter of September 19, 1941, from Oswald Pohl, head of the WVH (*Wirtschafts-und Verwaltungs-Hauptamt*) to the Reichskommissar for price control. It seems that all these economic activities in the concentration camps developed only during the war and under the pressure of acute labor shortage.

[25] Himmler's speech of October, 1943, at Posen, *International Military Trials*, Nuremberg, 1945–46, Vol. 29, p. 146.

in the history of the secret police. If it still is concerned with "dangerous thoughts," they are hardly ones which the suspected persons know to be dangerous; the regimentation of all intellectual and artistic life demands a constant re-establishment and revision of standards which naturally is accompanied by repeated eliminations of intellectuals whose "dangerous thoughts" usually consist in certain ideas that were still entirely orthodox the day before. While, therefore, its police function in the accepted meaning of the word has become superfluous, the economic function of the secret police, sometimes thought to have replaced the first, is even more dubious. It is undeniable, to be sure, that the NKVD periodically rounds up a percentage of the Soviet population and sends them into camps which are known under the flattering misnomer of forced-labor camps;[26] yet although it is quite possible that this is the Soviet Union's way of solving its unemployment problem, it is also generally known that the output in those camps is infinitely lower than that of ordinary Soviet labor and hardly suffices to pay the expenses of the police apparatus.

Neither dubious nor superfluous is the political function of the secret police, the "best organized and the most efficient" of all government departments,[27] in the power apparatus of the totalitarian regime. It constitutes the true executive branch of the government through which all orders are transmitted. Through the net of secret agents, the totalitarian ruler has created for himself a directly executive transmission belt which, in distinction to the onion-like structure of the ostensible hierarchy, is completely severed and isolated from all other institutions.[28] In this sense, the secret police agents are

---

[26] "Bek Bulat (the pen name of a former Soviet professor) has been able to study documents of the North Caucasian NKVD. From these documents it was obvious that in June, 1937, when the great purge was at its apex, the government prescribed the local NKVDs to have a certain percentage of the population arrested. . . . The percentage varied from one province to the other, reaching 5 per cent in the least loyal areas. The average for the whole of the Soviet Union was about 3 per cent." Reported by David J. Dallin in *The New Leader*, January 8, 1949.—Beck and Godin, *op. cit.*, p. 239, arrive at a slightly divergent and quite plausible assumption, according to which "arrests were planned as follows: The NKVD files covered practically the whole population, and everyone was classified in a category. Thus statistics were available in every town showing how many former Whites, members of opposing parties, etc., were living in them. All incriminating material collected . . . and gathered from prisoners' confessions was also entered in the files, and each person's card was marked to show how dangerous he was considered; this depending on the amount of suspicious or incriminating material appearing in his file. As the statistics were regularly reported to higher authorities, it was possible to arrange a purge at any moment, with full knowledge of the exact number of persons in each category."

[27] Baldwin, *op. cit.*

[28] The Russian secret-police cadres were as much at the "personal disposal" of Stalin as the SS Shock Troops (*Verfügungstruppen*) were at the personal disposal of Hitler. Both, even if they are called to serve with the military forces in time of war, live under their own special jurisdiction. The special "marriage laws" which served to segregate the SS from the rest of the population, were the first and most fundamental regulations which Himmler introduced when he took over the reorganization of the SS. Even prior to Himmler's marriage laws, in 1927, the SS was instructed by official

the only openly ruling class in totalitarian countries and their standards and scale of values permeate the entire texture of totalitarian society.

From this viewpoint, it may not be too surprising that certain peculiar qualities of the secret police are general qualities of totalitarian society rather than peculiarities of the totalitarian secret police. The category of the suspect thus embraces under totalitarian conditions the total population; every thought that deviates from the officially prescribed and permanently changing line is already suspect, no matter in which field of human activity is occurs. Simply because of their capacity to think, human beings are suspects by definition, and this suspicion cannot be diverted by exemplary behavior, for the human capacity to think is also a capacity to change one's mind. Since, moreover, it is impossible ever to know beyond doubt another man's heart— torture in this context is only the desperate and eternally futile attempt to achieve what cannot be achieved—suspicion can no longer be allayed if neither a community of values nor the predictabilities of self-interest exist as social (as distinguished from merely psychological) realities. Mutual suspicion, therefore, permeates all social relationships in totalitarian countries and creates an all-pervasive atmosphere even outside the special purview of the secret police. . . .

[THE TOTALITARIAN STATE, II]

"Thought Reform" in Communist China

ROBERT J. LIFTON

I had the opportunity to study this process ["thought reform"] in Hong Kong over a period of seventeen months, working with twenty-five Westerners who had been in Chinese prisons,[1] and with fifteen Chinese intellectuals who had undergone the type of process I am going to describe.

decree "never [to participate] in discussions at membership meetings" (*Der Weg der SS, op. cit.*). The same conduct is reported about the members of the NKVD, who kept deliberately to themselves and above all did not associate with other sections of the party aristocracy (Beck and Godin, *op. cit.*, p. 163).

SOURCE: Robert J. Lifton, "Methods of Forceful Indoctrination: Psychiatric Aspects of Chinese Communist Thought Reform," in Maurice R. Stein, Arthur J. Vidich, and David Manning White (eds.), *Identity and Anxiety in Mass Society* (New York: Group for the Advancement of Psychiatry, Inc., 1960), pp. 480–92. Reprinted by permission.

[1] R. J. Lifton, "Thought Reform of Western Civilians in Chinese Communist Prisons," *Psychiatry*, XIX (1956), pp. 173–95. R. J. Lifton, "Chinese Communist Thought Reform: The Assault Upon Identity and Belief," presented before the American Psychiatric Association, May, 1956.

Although I could occasionally conduct interviews in English, where the subject had been exposed to a Westernized education (generally in mission-endowed institutions), I usually worked through interpreters. That set up a very complicated three-way communication system, which I won't discuss now. I found that it was very important to work with a subject over a long period of time, and the most meaningful data that I was able to obtain came through working with people for over a year. There is a very simple reason for this. It is a Chinese—and East Asian—cultural trait to say what one thinks the listener wants to hear, as a form of politeness and propriety. So I would first encounter many cliché anti-Communist statements; one could only get into the real areas of conflict when there developed a meaningful and trusting relationship, and when the subject could realize that I wanted to know about his true feelings.

Who attends a revolutionary college? Students are drawn from many divergent sources: former Nationalist officials and affiliates, teachers who had been associated with the old regime, Communist cadres who had demonstrated significant "errors" in their work or thoughts, party members who had spent long periods of time in Nationalist areas, students returning from the West, and finally, arbitrarily selected groups of university instructors or recent graduates. Many in these groups came in response to thinly veiled coercion—the strong "suggestion" that they attend; but others actively sought admission on a voluntary basis, in order to try to fit in with the requirements of the new regime, or at least to find out what was expected of them.

The college itself is tightly organized along Communist principles of "democratic centralism." One center may contain as many as 4,000 students, subdivided into sections of about 1,000 each, then into classes of 100 to 200 each, and finally into six- to ten-man groups. The president of the institution may be a well-known scholar serving as a figurehead; technically below him in rank are a vice-president and the section heads, who are likely to be Communist party members, and exert the real authority at the center. Under their supervision are the class-heads, each of whom works with three special cadres.

These cadres, usually long-standing and dedicated party workers, play a central role in the thought reform process: they are the connecting link between the faculty and the students, and it is they who perform the day-to-day leg work of the reform process. The three cadres of each class may be designated according to function: the executive cadre, concerned essentially with courses of study; the organizing cadre, most intimately involved with the structure and function of the small group and the attitudes of the individual students who make them up; and the advisory cadre—the only one of the three who may be a woman—offering counsel on personal and ideological "problems" which come up during this arduous experience.

I have divided the "thought reform" process into three stages, referring to the successive psychological climates which are created. These are my subdivisions, but I believe that they are very much in keeping with the Communist view of their own process: first, the Great Togetherness—the stage

of Group Identification; second, the Closing in the Milieu—the stage of
Emotional Conflict; and third, Submission and Rebirth—the Final Confession.

THE GREAT TOGETHERNESS—
GROUP IDENTIFICATION

New students approach the course with a varying mixture of curiosity,
enthusiasm, and apprehension. When a group of them arrives, their first
impression is likely to be a favorable one. They encounter an atmosphere
which is austere, but friendly—an open area of low-slung wooden buildings
(frequently converted from military barracks) which serve as living quarters
and class rooms—old students and cadres greeting them warmly, showing
them around, speaking glowingly of the virtues of the revolutionary college,
of the Communist movement, of the new hope for the future. Then, after
a warm welcoming speech by the president of the college, they are organized
into ten-man study groups. And for a period of from a few days to two weeks
they are told to "just get to know each other."

Students are surprised by this free and enthusiastic atmosphere: some
among the older ones may remain wary, but most are caught up in a feeling
of camaraderie. Within the small groups they vent their widely shared hostility towards the old regime—an important stimulus to the thought reform
process. There is a frank exchange of feeling and ideas, past and present, as
they discuss their background experiences, and hopes and fears for the
future. There is an air of optimism, a feeling of being in the same boat, a
high *esprit de corps*.

Let me illustrate this with a few sentences quoted directly from one of
my subjects:

Everyone felt a bit strange at first, but we soon realized that we were all in the
same position. We all began to talk freely and spontaneously; we introduced ourselves to each other, and talked about our past life and family background. . . .
The Revolutionary College seemed to be a place which brought together young
people from all over with a great deal in common. We ate, slept, and talked together, all of us eager to make new friends. I had very warm feelings towards
the group, and towards the school. . . . I felt that I was being treated well in a
very free atmosphere. I was happy and thought that I was on my way to a new
life.

Next, through a series of "thought mobilization" lectures and discussions,
the philosophy and rationale of the program are impressed upon the individual student: the "old society" was evil and corrupt; this was so because it
was dominated by the "exploiting classes"—the landowners and the bourgeoisie; most intellectuals come from these "exploiting classes" (or from the
closely related *petite bourgeoisie*) and therefore retain "evil remnants" of
their origins and of the old regime; each must now rid himself of these

"ideological poisons" in order to become a "new man" in the "new society." In this way, he is told, the "ideology of all classes" can be brought into harmony with the changing "objective material conditions."[2]

Also quoted invariably is a highly significant speech of Mao Tse-tung, the chairman of the Communist party in China:

> . . . our object in exposing errors and criticizing shortcomings is like that of a doctor in curing a disease. The entire purpose is to save the person, not to cure him to death. If a man has appendicitis, the doctor performs an operation and the man is saved. If a person who commits an error, no matter how great, does not bring his disease to an incurable state by concealing it and persisting in his error, and in addition if he is genuinely and honestly willing to be cured, willing to make corrections, we will welcome him so that his disease may be cured and he can become a good comrade. It is certainly not possible to solve the problem by one flurry of blows for the sake of a moment's satisfaction. We cannot adopt a brash attitude towards diseases of thought and politics, but must have an attitude of saving men by curing their diseases. This is the correct and effective method.[3]

This illustrates the tone with which thought reform is presented to the student. What we see as a coercive set of manipulations, they put forth as a *morally uplighting, harmonizing, and therapeutic experience.*

Then the formal courses begin—the first usually entitled the History of the Development of Society (to be later followed by Lenin—the State, Materialistic Dialectics, History of the Chinese Revolution, Theory of the New Democracy, and Field Study—visits to old Communist workshops and industrial centers). The subject matter is introduced by a two- to six-hour lecture delivered by a leading Communist theorist. This is followed by the interminable *hsueh hsi* or study sessions within the six- to ten-man group, where the real work of thought reform takes place. Discussion of the lecture material is led by the group leader who has been elected by its members— usually because of his superior knowledge of Marxism. At this point he encourages a spirited exchange of all views, and takes no side when there is a disagreement. The other students realize that the group leader is making daily reports to a cadre or to the class head, but the full significance of these is not yet appreciated; they may be viewed as simply a necessary organizational procedure. Most students retain a feeling of pulling together towards a common goal in a group crusading spirit.

THE CLOSING IN OF THE MILIEU— THE PERIOD OF EMOTIONAL CONFLICT

About four to six weeks from the beginning of thought reform—at about the time of the completion of the first course—a change begins to develop in

---

[2] Ssu-Ch'i Ai, "On Problems of Ideological Reform," *Hsueh Hsi,* III (January 1, 1951).

[3] C. Brandt, B. Schwartz, and J. K. Fairbank, "Correcting Unorthodox Tendencies in Learning, the Party, and Literature and Art," in *A Documentary History of Chinese Communism* (1954), p. 392.

the atmosphere. With the submission of the first "thought summary" (these must be prepared after each course) there is a shift in emphasis from the intellectual and ideological to the personal and the emotional. The student begins to find that he, rather than the Communist doctrine, is the object of study. A pattern of criticism, self-criticism, and confession develops—pursued with increasing intensity throughout the remainder of the course.

Now the group leader is no longer "neutral"; acting upon instructions from above, he begins to "lean to one side," to support the "progressive elements"; to apply stronger pressures in the direction of reform. He and the "activists" who begin to emerge, take the lead in setting the tone for the group. The descriptions of the past and the present attitudes which the student so freely gave during the first few weeks of the course now come back to haunt him. Not only his ideas, but his underlying motivations are carefully scrutinized. Failure to achieve the correct "materialistic viewpoint," "proletarian standpoint," and "dialectical methodology," is pointed out, and the causes for this deficiency are carefully analyzed.

Criticisms cover every phase of past and present thought and behavior; they not only "nip in the bud" the slightest show of unorthodoxy or nonconformity, but they also point up "false progressives"—students who outwardly express the "correct" views without true depth of feeling. Group members are constantly on the lookout for indications in others of lack of real emotional involvement in the process. Each must demonstrate the genuineness of his reform through continuous personal enthusiasm, and active participation in the criticism of fellow students. In this way he can avoid being rebuked for "failure to combine theory with practice."

Standard criticisms repeatedly driven home include: "individualism"—placing personal interests above those of "the people"—probably the most emphasized of all; "subjectivism"—applying a personal viewpoint to a problem rather than a "scientific" Marxist approach; "objectivism"—undue detachment, viewing oneself "above class distinction," or "posing as a spectator of the new China"; "sentimentalism"—allowing one's attachment to family or friends to interfere with reform needs, therefore "carrying about an ideological burden" (usually associated with reluctance to denounce family members or friends allegedly associated with the "exploiting classes"). And in addition: "deviationism," "opportunism," "dogmatism," "reflecting exploiting class ideology," "overly technical viewpoints," "bureaucratism," "individual heroism," "revisionism," "departmentalism," "sectarianism," "idealism," and "pro-American outlook."

The student is required to accept these criticisms gratefully when they are offered. But more than this, he is expected to both anticipate and expand upon them, through the even more important device of *self-criticism*. He must correctly analyze his own thoughts and actions, and review his past life—family, educational, and social—in order to uncover the source of his difficulties. And the resulting "insights" are always expressed within the Communist jargon—corrupt "ruling class" and "bourgeois" influences, derived from his specific class origin.

The criticism and self-criticism process is also extended into every aspect of daily life, always with a highly moralistic tone. Under attack here are the "bourgeois" or "ruling class" characteristics of pride, conceit, greed, competitiveness, dishonesty, boastfulness, and rudeness. Relationships with the opposite sex are discussed and evaluated solely in terms of their effects upon the individual's progress in reform. Where a "backward" girl friend is thought to be impeding his progress, a student may be advised to break off a liaison; but if both are "progressive," or if one is thought to be aiding the other's progress, the relationship will be condoned. Sexual contacts are, on the whole, discouraged, as it is felt that they drain energies from the thought-reform process.

The student must, within the small group, *confess* all of the "evils" of his past life. Political and moral considerations here become inextricably merged; especially emphasized are any "reactionary" affiliations with the old regime or with its student organizations. Each student develops a "running confession," supplemented by material from his self-criticisms and "thought summaries"; its content becomes widely known to students, cadres, and class heads, and it serves as a continuous indicator of his progress in reform.

Most are caught up in the universal confession compulsion which sweeps the environment: students vie to outdo each other in the frankness, completeness, and luridness of their individual confessions; one group challenges another to match its collective confessions; personal confession is the major topic of discussion at small group meetings, large student gatherings, informal talks with cadres, and in articles in wall newspapers. Everywhere one encounters the question: "Have you made your full confession?"

Confession tensions are brought to a head through a mass, pre-arranged, revival-like gathering where a student with a particularly evil past is given the opportunity to redeem himself. Before hundreds or even thousands, of fellow students, he presents a lurid description of his past sins: political work with the Nationalists, anti-Communist activities, stealing money from his company, violating his neighbor's daughter. He expresses relief at "washing away all of my sins," and gratitude towards the Government for allowing him to "become a new man."

As the months pass, "progressives" and "activists" take increasing leadership, aided by group manipulations by cadres and class heads. Where a group leader is not sufficiently effective, if his reports to the class head are not considered satisfactory, or where there is a general "lagging behind" in a particular group, a reshuffling of groups is engineered from above. The weak group becomes reinforced by the addition of one or two "activists," and the former group leader, in his new group, is reduced to the level of an ordinary student. Although group leaders may still be elected by students, these shifts can insure that this position is always held by one considered "progressive" and "reliable."

At the same time, "backward elements"—students with suspicious backgrounds, whose confessions are not considered thorough enough, who do not demonstrate adequate enthusiasm in reforming themselves and criticizing others, whose attitudes are found wanting—are singled out for further attention. Such a student becomes the target for relentless criticism in his group; and during odd hours he is approached by other students and cadres in attempts to persuade him to mend his ways. Should he fail to respond, friendliness gives way to veiled threats, and he may be called in to receive an official admonition from a class head. As a last resort, he may be subjected to the ultimate humility of a mass "struggle" meeting: in ritualistic form, he is publicly denounced by faculty members, cadres, and fellow students, his deficiencies reiterated and laid bare. It becomes quite clear that his future in Communist China is indeed precarious, and the ceremony serves as a grim warning for other students of questionable standing.

In response to all of these pressures, no student can avoid experiencing some degree of fear, anxiety, and conflict. Each is disturbed over what he may be hiding, worried about how he may come out of this ordeal. Some, recalling either stories they have heard or personal experiences, find revived in their minds images of the extreme measures used by the Communists in dealing with their enemies. All are extremely fearful of the consequences of being considered a "reactionary."

I can again illustrate this through the feelings expressed by another one of my subjects:

Towards the middle of the semester the intensity of my anti-Communist thoughts greatly increased. I developed a terrible fear that these thoughts would come out and be known to all, but I was determined to prevent this. I tried to appear calm but I was in great inner turmoil. I knew that if I kept quiet no one would know the secret which I had not confessed. But people were always talking about secrets. In small group meetings or large confession meetings, everyone would say that it was wrong to keep secrets, that one had to confess everything. Sometimes a cadre or a student would mention secrets during a casual talk, and I would feel very disturbed. Or at large meetings someone would get up and say, "There are still some students in the University who remain 'anti-organization.'" I knew that no one else was thinking specifically of me, but I couldn't help feeling very upset. The secret was always something that was trying to escape from me.

Students who show signs of emotional disturbance are encouraged to seek help by talking over their "thought problem" with the advisory cadre, in order to resolve whatever conflicts exist. Many experience psychosomatic expressions of their problems—fatigue, insomnia, loss of appetite, vague aches and pains, or gastrointestinal symptoms. Should they take their complaints to the college doctor, they are apt to encounter a reform-oriented and psychosomatically sophisticated reply: "There is nothing wrong with your body. It must be your thoughts that are sick. You will feel better when you have solved your problems and completed your reform." And indeed, most students are in a state of painful inner tension; relief is badly needed.

SUBMISSION AND "REBIRTH" —
THE FINAL CONFESSION

The last stage—that of the over-all thought summary or final confession—supplies each student with a means of resolving his conflicts. It is ushered in by a mass meeting at which high Communist officials and faculty members emphasize the importance of the final thought summary as the crystallization of the entire course. Group sessions over the next two or three days are devoted exclusively to discussions of the form this summary is to take. It is to be a life history, beginning two generations back and extending through the reform experience. It must, with candor and thoroughness, describe the historical development of one's thoughts, and the relationships of these to actions. It is also to include a detailed analysis of the personal effects of thought reform.

The summary may be from five to twenty-five thousand Chinese characters (roughly equivalent numerically to English words) and require about ten days of preparation. Each student then must read his summary to the group, where he is subjected to more prolonged and penetrating criticism. He may be kept under fire for several days of detailed discussion and painful revision, as every group member is considered responsible for the approval of each confession presented, and all may even have to place their signature upon it.

The confession is the student's final opportunity to bring out anything he has previously held back, as well as to elaborate upon everything he has already said. It always includes a detailed analysis of class origin. And in almost every case, its central feature is the denunciation of the father, both as a symbol of the exploiting classes, and as an individual. The student usually finds the recitation of his father's personal, political, and economic abuses to be the most painful part of his entire thought reform. He may require endless prodding, persuasion, and indirect threats before he is able to take this crucial step. But he has little choice and he almost invariably complies.

The confession ends with an emphasis of personal liabilities which still remain, attitudes in need of further reform, and the solemn resolve to continue attempts at self-improvement and to serve the regime devotedly in the future. When his confession is approved, the student experiences great emotional relief. He has weathered the thought reform ordeal, renounced his past, and established an organic bond between himself and the Government. His confession will accompany him throughout his future career as a permanent part of his personal record. It is his symbolic submission to the regime, and at the same time his expression of individual rebirth into the Chinese Communist community. . . .

9. GENOCIDE

Auschwitz: A Transport Arrives

TADEUSZ BOROWSKI

PROLOGUE, OR ANTICIPATION OF THE "TRANSPORT"

Greeks are sitting around us, moving their jaws voraciously like huge inhuman insects, greedily eating moldy clods of bread. They are uneasy; they don't know what they'll be doing. Rails and planks worry them. They don't like heavy hauling.

"Was wir arbeiten?" they ask.

"Niks. Transport kommen, alles Krematorium, compris?"

"Alles verstehen," they answer in crematorium esperanto. They calm down; they won't be loading rails on trucks, or carrying planks.

ACT I, OR THE ARRIVAL OF THE "TRANSPORT"

A striped crowd lay near the tracks in the long strips of shade. It breathed heavily and unevenly, spoke lazily in its own tongues and gazed indifferently

---

SOURCE: Reprinted from *The Captive Mind* by Czeslaw Milosz, by permission of Alfred A. Knopf, Inc. Copyright 1951, 1953 by Czeslaw Milosz. Also, by permission of Martin Secker & Warburg Ltd., London. (From a story by Tadeusz Borowski. The adapted version reprinted here first appeared in English translation, attributed to an anonymous Polish author, in Czeslaw Milosz, *The Captive Mind*, trans. by Jane Zielenko. Its authorship became known to English-speaking readers when the complete story, "This Way for the Gas," trans. by Barbara Vedder, appeared in *Commentary* (July, 1962), pp. 39–47.

EDITORS' NOTE: This is a fictional account of actual events, written by an eyewitness and participant. Czeslaw Milosz introduces it in these words: "In the abundant literature of atrocity of the twentieth century, one rarely finds an account written from the point of view of an accessory to the crime. Authors are usually ashamed of this role. But collaboration is an empty word as applied to a concentration camp. The machine is impersonal; responsibility shifts from those who carry out orders to those higher, always higher. . . . [This story] should, I believe, be included in all anthologies of literature dealing with the lot of men in totalitarian society, if such anthologies are compiled." His judgment carries weight; it is that of one who has lived under and knows intimately the totalitarianism of Communist Poland as well as Nazi Germany.

at the majestic people in green uniform, at the green of the trees, near and unattainable, at the steeple of a distant little church which at that moment was tolling a late angelus.

"The transport is coming," someone said, and everyone stood up in expectation. Freight cars appeared around the curve as the train backed in. The trainman standing in the caboose leaned out, waved his hand, whistled. The locomotive screeched, wheezèd and the train trundled slowly along the station. Behind the tiny barred windows one could see human faces, pale, crumpled, disheveled, as if they were sleepy—frightened women, and men who, exotically, had hair. They passed slowly, gazing at the station in silence. Then something started to boil inside the wagons and to beat against their wooden walls.

"Water! Air!" Despairing, hollow cries burst out.

Human faces pressed to the windows, lips desperately gasping for air sucked in a few gulps, vanished; others struggled into their place, then they too vanished. The shrieks and moans grew steadily louder.

ACT II, OR THE SEGREGATION (A FEW SCENES WILL SUFFICE)

Here comes a woman walking briskly, hurrying almost imperceptibly yet feverishly. A small child with the plump, rosy face of a cherub runs after her, fails to catch up, stretches out its hands, crying, "Mama, mama!"

"Woman, take this child in your arms!"

"Sir, it isn't my child, it isn't mine!" the woman shouts hysterically, and runs away covering her face with her hands. She wants to hide; she wants to reach those who won't leave in a truck, who will leave on foot, who will live. She is young, healthy, pretty, she wants to live.

But the child runs after her, pleading at the top of its voice, "Mama, mama, don't run away!"

"It's not mine, not mine, not . . . !"

Until Andrej, the sailor from Sevastopol, overtook her. His eyes were troubled by vodka and the heat. He reached her, knocked her off her feet with a single powerful blow and, as she fell, caught her by the hair and dragged her up again. His face was distorted with fury.

"Why you lousy fucking Jew-bitch! Jebit twoju mat'! You'd run away from your own child! I'll show you, you whore!" He grabbed her in the middle, one paw throttling her throat which wanted to shout, and flung her into the truck like a heavy sack of grain.

"Here! Take this with you, you slut!" And he threw her child at her feet.

"Gut gemacht. That's how one should punish unnatural mothers," said an SS man standing near the van.

A pair of people fall to the ground entangled in a desperate embrace. He digs his fingers into her flesh convulsively, tears at her clothes with his teeth.

She screams hysterically, curses, blasphemes until, stifled by a boot, she chokes and falls silent. They split them apart like a tree; and herd them into the car like animals.

Others are carrying a young girl with a missing leg; they hold her by her arms and by her one remaining leg. Tears are streaking down her face as she whispers sadly, "Please, please, it hurts, it hurts . . ." They heave her into a truck, among the corpses. She will be burned alive, together with them.

ACT III, OR THE CONVERSATION OF THE WITNESSES

A cool and starry evening falls. We are lying on the tracks. It is infinitely silent. Anemic lamps burn on high poles behind the circles of light.

"Did you exchange shoes?" Henri asks me.

"No."

"Why not?"

"Man, I have enough, absolutely enough!"

"Already? After the first transport? Just think, me—since Christmas maybe a million people have passed through my hands. The worst are the transports from Paris: a man always meets friends."

"And what do you say to them?"

"That they're going to take a bath, and that we'll meet later in the camp. What would you say?"

EPILOGUE (MANY TRAINS CAME TO AUSCHWITZ THAT EVENING. THE TRANSPORT TOTALED 15,000 PEOPLE)

As we return to the camp, the stars begin to fade, the sky becomes ever more translucent and lifts above us, the night grows light. A clear, hot day announces itself.

From the crematoriums, broad columns of smoke rise steadily and merge above into a gigantic, black river that turns exceedingly slowly in the sky over Birkenau and disappears beyond the forests, in the direction of Trzebinia. The transport is already burning.

We pass an SS squad, moving with mechanized weapons to relieve the guard. They march evenly, shoulder to shoulder, one mass, one will.

"Und Morgen die ganze Welt . . ." they sing at the top of their lungs.

The Destruction of the European Jews

RAUL HILBERG

1. THE PERPETRATORS

The Germans killed five million Jews. A process of such magnitude does not come from the void; to be brought to a conclusion in such dimensions an administrative undertaking must have meaning to its perpetrators. To Adolf Hitler and his followers the destruction of the Jews had meaning. To these men, the act was worthwhile in itself. It could not be questioned. It had to be done. When half of Europe lay conquered at Germany's feet, the uniqueness of the opportunity became compelling. The chance could not be missed. At that moment the German bureaucrat beckoned to his Faustian fate. The scope of human experience was to be widened as never before. Inevitably, at this point the German machine of destruction had to attempt the ultimate, for when a generation seeks to accomplish more than its scientific and artistic heritage has equipped it for, its path to fulfilment lies only in destruction. The process of creation is tedious and long; destruction alone is both swift and lasting.

Let us point out at once that the Germans have not been the only ones in history who have had a reason to embark upon a destructive course of action. When we examine the world historical scene, we may note that many times, in many countries, bureaucracies have launched the opening phases of a destruction process. Even now, in the Union of South Africa and elsewhere specialists are selecting, exploiting, and concentrating new victims. Very often, seemingly harmless bureaucratic activities—such as the definition of a particular group and the exclusion of its members from office—contain the seeds of administrative continuity. Potentially, these measures are steppingstones to a killing operation, but as a rule insurmountable barriers from without and within arrest and disrupt the destructive development. Externally, the opposition of the victims may bring the process to a halt; internally, administrative and psychological obstacles may bar the way. The discriminatory systems of many countries are the leftovers of such disrupted destruction processes.

The German destruction of the Jews was not interrupted. That is its crucial, decisive characteristic. At the threshold of the killing phase the flow of administrative measures continued unchecked. Technocratic and moral obstacles were overcome. An unprecedented killing operation was inaugu-

SOURCE: Raul Hilberg, *The Destruction of the European Jews* (Chicago: Quadrangle, 1961), pp. 639–69. Reprinted by permission.

EDITORS' NOTE: All footnotes have been preserved. Unless otherwise noted, page references are to *The Destruction of the European Jews*.

rated, and with the beginning of this operation the Germans demonstrated once and for all how quickly even large groups, numbering in the millions, could be annihilated.

How was this done?

The Destructive Expansion

The German destructive effort may be likened to a three-dimensional structure which was expanding in all three directions. In one direction we can see an alignment of agency after agency in a machinery of destruction. In another direction we note the development, step by step, of the destruction process. In the third we can observe an attempt to set up multiple processes aimed at new victims and pointing to a destruction, group by group, of all human beings within the German reach.

Let us examine first the horizontal expansion at the base: the growth of the machinery of destruction. We know that as the process unfolded, its requirements became more complex and its fulfilment involved an ever larger number of agencies, party offices, business enterprises, and military commands. The destruction of the Jews was a total process, comparable in its diversity to a modern war, a mobilization, or a national reconstruction.

An administrative process of such range cannot be carried out by a single agency, even if it is a trained and specialized body like the Gestapo or a commissariat for Jewish affairs, for when a process cuts into every phase of human life, it must ultimately feed upon the resources of the entire organized community. That is why we found among the perpetrators the highly differentiated technicians of the armament inspectorates, the remote officials of the Postal Ministry, and—in the all-important operation of furnishing records for determination of descent—the membership of an aloof and withdrawn Christian clergy. The machinery of destruction, then, was structurally no different from organized German society as a whole; the difference was only one of function. The machinery of destruction *was* the organized community in one of its special roles.

As the apparatus expanded, its potential increased—the wider the base, the farther the reach. When the machine was finished, so was the process. But now we may ask: What determined the order of involvement? What determined the sequence of steps? We know that the bureaucracy had no master plan, no basic blueprint, no clear-cut view even of its actions. How, then, was the process regulated? What was the key to the operation?

A destruction process has an inherent pattern. There is only one way in which a scattered group can effectively be destroyed. Three steps are organic in the operation:

Definition
|
Concentration (or seizure)
|
Annihilation

FACT SHEET ON GENOCIDE

united nations
work for human rights

A clearly written account of United Nations achievements during ten years toward the promotion and protection of human rights throughout the world. It provides informati

MEANING OF GENOCIDE

The cornerstone of all human rights is the right to exist. Yet, since time immemorial, entire groups of people — racial, religious, national — were put to destruction either by ruthless governments or by groups blinded by hatred and intolerance. For these victims, guarantees of free speech were meaningless, while their torturers were cutting out their tongues. The guarantees of free worship by national constitutions meant nothing while their churches were razed through organized fury. Millions of Christians were slaughtered in the Balkans; more than a mi

of Maronites were levelled

Iraq. Out of 80,000 Hereros

extermination campaign led

million Jews under Nazi o

This is genocide — the d

linguistic and political grou

THE CRIME
OF GENOCIDE

REPORT
OF THE
INTERNATIONAL LAW
COMMISSION

COVERING ITS SECOND SESSION
5 JUNE — 29 JULY 1950

GENERAL ASSEMBLY
OFFICIAL RECORDS: FIFTH SESSION
SUPPLEMENT No. 12 (A/1316)

UNITED   NATIONS

FACT SHEET
ON
GENOCIDE

REPORT OF THE
AD HOC COMMITTEE
ON GENOCIDE
5 April to 10 May 1948

This is the invariant structure of the basic process, for no group can be killed without a concentration or seizure of the victims, and no victims can be segregated before the perpetrator knows who belongs to the group.

There are, of course, additional steps in a modern destructive undertaking. These added steps are not required for the annihilation of the victim, but they are dictated by conisderations of cost and economy. These are expropriations. In the destruction of the Jews expropriatory measures were introduced after every organic step. Thus dismissals and Aryanizations came after the definition; exploitation and starvation measures followed concentration; and the confiscation of personal belongings was incidental to the killing operation. In its completed form a destruction process in a modern society will consequently be structured as shown in the accompanying chart.

The sequence of steps in a destruction process is thus determined. If there is an attempt to inflict maximum injury upon a group of people, it is therefore inevitable that a bureaucracy—no matter how decentralized its apparatus or how unplanned its activities—should push its victims through these stages. This is a twofold destructive expansion: the growth of the machine of destruction and the development of the destruction process. Today we know of a destructive expansion upon still another plane: as the machine was thrown into high gear and as the process accelerated toward its goal, German hostility became more generalized. The Jewish target became too narrow. More targets had to be added. This development is of the utmost importance, for it casts a revealing light upon the perpetrators' fundamental aim.

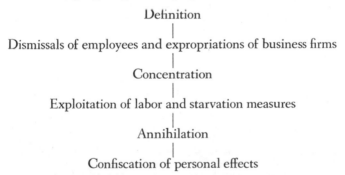

Definition
|
Dismissals of employees and expropriations of business firms
|
Concentration
|
Exploitation of labor and starvation measures
|
Annihilation
|
Confiscation of personal effects

If a group seeks merely the destruction of hostile institutions, the limit of its most drastic action would be drawn with the complete destruction of the bearers of the institutions. The Germans, however, did not draw the line with the destruction of Jewry. They attacked still other victims, some of whom were thought to be like Jews, some of whom were quite unlike Jews, and some of whom were Germans. The Nazi destruction process was, in short, not aimed at institutions; it was aimed at people. The Jews were only the first victims of the German bureaucracy; they were only the first caught in its path. That they should have been chosen first is not accidental—historical precedents, both administrative and conceptual, determined the selection of the people which for centuries had been the standby victim of recurring destructions. No other group could fill this role so well. None was so vulnerable. But the choice could not be confined to the Jews. Three illustrations will make this more clear.

Example I. The destruction process engulfed a group which was classified as a parasitical people leading a parasitical life: the Gypsies.[1] There were 34,000 to 40,000 Gypsies in the Reich. In accordance with a Himmler directive the Criminal Police were empowered to seize all persons who looked like Gypsies or who wandered around in "Gypsie-like" manner. Those who were seized were classified as follows:

Z   Full Gypsy (Zigeuner)
ZM+   Gypsy *Mischling*, predominantly Gypsy
ZM   Gypsy *Mischling* with equal Gypsy and German "blood-shares" (*Blutsanteile*)
ZM—   Gypsy *Mischling*, predominantly German
NZ   Free of Gypsy blood (*Nicht Zigeuner*)

The victims in the first three categories were subjected to special wage regulations, taxes, and movement restrictions. Special provisions were made for "privileged Gypsy mixed marriages," etc.[2] In the 1940's the Germans went one step further: mobile units of the Security Police in Russia killed roving Gypsies;[3] the military commander in Serbia concentrated Gypsies and shot them;[4] and in Auschwitz several thousand Gypsies were gassed.[5]

Example II. The Poles in the territories incorporated by the Reich were in a rather precarious position. It had been planned to shove them into the

---

[1] In the past the Gypsies had been linked to the Jews in popular belief as well as scholarly investigation. A seventeenth-century German writer, Johann Christof Wagenseil, wrote a thesis to prove that "the very first Gypsies were Jews who stemmed from Germany [*die allerersten Ziegeiner sind aus Teutschland gebürtige Juden gewesen*]." Wagenseil, *Der Meister-Singer Holdseligen Kunst* (in the introduction), printed 1697. The Nazis were no so sure of the Gypsy origins; however, it was thought that there was some racial affinity to the Jews. Two agencies were engaged in research on the subject: the *Reichszentrale zur Bekämpfung des Zigeunerwesens* and *Rassenhygienische Forschungsstelle* of the *Reichsgesundheitsamt*. H. Küppers, "Die Beschäftigung von Zigeunern," *Reichsarbeitsblatt*, V (March 25, 1942), 177, reprinted in *Die Judenfrage (Vertrauliche Beilage*), April 15, 1942, pp. 30–31.

[2] Küppers in *Reichsarbeitsblatt*, V, 177. Circular decree by Sauckel, June 24, 1942, in *Ministerialblatt des Reichs- und Preussischen Ministeriums des Innern*, July 22, 1942, p. 1488.

[3] See p. 241n.

[4] See pp. 438, 439–40, 441n., 442.

[5] Lengyel, *Five Chimneys*, pp. 68, 112–13, 121. The Gypsies had been brought to Auschwitz from the Reich-Protektorat area, Poland, France, and Hungary. A Gypsy transport was also brought to Lodz. See pp. 142–44. Gypsies were concentrated in a number of camps. Note reference to Lackenbach (Austria) in letter by Deputy Gauleiter Gerland of Niederdonau to Himmler, August 24, 1942, NO–39. In the Orleans area (France), Jaregeau had 600 Gypsies. Oberstabsarzt Sonntag to *Chef, Militärbezirk A* (Glt. von der Lippe), October 2, 1942, NOKW–1516. In general, see also Dora E. Yates, "Hitler and the Gypsies—The Fate of Europe's Oldest Aryans," *Commentary*, November, 1949, pp. 455–59.

Generalgouvernement, while the incorporated provinces to the west were to have become purely German. But that program, like the forced emigration of the Jews from Europe, collapsed. In the back of some people's minds a "territorial solution" now loomed for these Poles. On May 27, 1941, an interministerial conference took place under the chairmanship of Staatssekretär Conti of the Interior Ministry. The subject of discussion was the reduction of the Polish population in the incorporated territories. The following proposals were entertained: (1) no Pole to be allowed to marry before the age of twenty-five; (2) no permission to be granted unless the marriage was economically sound; (3) a tax on illegitimate births; (4) sterilization following illegitimate birth; (5) no tax exemptions for dependents; and (6) permission to submit to abortion to be granted upon application of the expectant mother.[6]

One year later, on May 1, 1942, Gauleiter Greiser of the incorporated Wartheland reported to Himmler that the "special treatment" of 100,000 Jews in his *Gau* would be completed in another two or three months. Greiser then proceeded in the same paragraph to request Himmler's permission for the use of the experienced (*eingearbeiteten*) *Sonderkommando* at Kulmhof in order to liberate the *Gau* from still another danger which threatened "with each passing week to assume catastrophic proportions." Greiser had in his province 35,000 tubercular Poles. He wanted to kill them.[7] The suggestion was passed on to health expert Blome (Conti's deputy) who wanted to refer the matter to Hitler. Months passed without a decision. Finally Greiser expressed his disappointment to Himmler. "I for my person do not believe that the Fuhrer has to be bothered with this question again, especially since he told me only during our last conversation, with reference to the Jews, that I may deal with those in any way I pleased."[8]

Example III. In consequence of an agreement between Himmler and Justice Minister Thierack, so-called asocials were transferred from prisons to concentration camps. On November 16, 1944, after the transfer of the "asocials" had largely been completed, the judiciary met to discuss a weird subject: ugliness. The phrase on the agenda was "gallery of outwardly asocial prisoners [*Museum äusserlich asozialer Gefangener*]." The summary of that conference states:

> During various visits to the penitentiaries, prisoners have always been observed who—because of their bodily characteristics—hardly deserve the designation human [*Mensch*]; they look like miscarriages of hell [*Missgeburten der Hölle*]. Such prisoners should be photographed. It is planned that they too shall be eliminated [*auszuschalten*]. Crime and sentence are irrelevant. Only such photographs should be submitted which clearly show the deformity.[9]

---

[6] Reich Chancellery memorandum, May 27, 1941, NG–844.

[7] Greiser to Himmler, May 1, 1942, NO–246. Greiser was also *Reichsstatthalter.*

[8] Greiser to Himmler, November 21, 1942, NO–249. The Poles were ultimately spared.

[9] *Generalstaatsanwalt* (chief prosecutor), *Oberlandesgericht Bamberg,* to Generalstaatsanwalt Helm in Munich, November 29, 1944, enclosing summary of conference held under the chairmanship of Ministerialdirektor Engert on November 16, 1944, NG–1546.

The Obstacles

We have talked so far about a destructive expansion which is unparalleled in history. An entire bureaucratic network was involved in these operations; a destruction process was brought to its final conclusion; and a veritable target series was established in a first attempt at unlimited destruction. The German bureaucracy, however, did not always move with unencumbered ease. From time to time barriers appeared on the horizon and caused momentary pauses. Most of these stoppages were occasioned by those ordinary difficulties which are encountered by every bureaucracy in every administrative operation: procurement difficulties, shortages, mixups, misunderstandings, and all the other annoyances of the daily bureaucratic process. We shall not be concerned with these occurrences here. But some of the hesitations and interruptions were the products of extraordinary administrative and psychological obstacles. These blocks were peculiar to the destruction process alone, and they must therefore claim our special attention.

ADMINISTRATIVE PROBLEMS.—The destruction of the Jews was not a gainful operation. It imposed a strain upon the administrative machine and its facilities. In a wider sense it became a burden which rested upon Germany as a whole.

One of the most striking facts about the German apparatus was the sparseness of its personnel, particularly in those regions outside the Reich where most of the victims had to be destroyed. Moreover, that limited manpower was preoccupied with a bewildering variety of administrative undertakings; upon close examination the machinery of destruction turns out to have been a loose organization of part-timers. There were at most a handful of bureaucrats who could devote all their time to anti-Jewish activities. There were the "experts" on Jewish affairs in the ministries, the mobile killing units of the RSHA, the commanders of the killing centers. But even an expert like Eichmann had two jobs: the deportation of Jews and the resettlement of ethnic Germans; the mobile killing units had to shoot Jews, Gypsies, commissars, and partisans alike; while a camp commander like Höss was host to an industrial concentration next to his gas chambers.

In the totality of the administrative process the destruction of the Jews presented itself as an additional task to a bureaucratic machine already overburdened and strained to the utmost by war preparations and by war itself. To grasp this fact, we need think only of the railroads or of the armies which moved east into Russia.[10] The German administration, however, was not deterred by the pressures of other assignments; it never resorted to pretenses, like the Italians, it never took token measures, like the Hungarians, it never

---

[10] "In the Reich only the most vitally important transports are run." Präsident Emrich in traffic conference held on December 9, 1942, in Paris; summary, dated December 12, 1942, in Wi/I 2.10. As for the military in Russia, see chapter on mobile killing operations, *passim*.

procrastinated, like the Bulgarians. The German bureaucrats worked efficiently, in haste, and with a sense of urgency. Unlike their collaborators, the Germans never did the minimum. They always did the maximum.

Indeed, there were moments when an agency's eagerness to participate in the decision-making led to bureaucratic competition and rivalry. Such a contest was in the offing when Unterstaatssekretär Luther concluded an agreement with the RSHA to preserve the Foreign Office's power to negotiate with Axis satellites in Jewish matters.[11] Again, within the SS itself, a jealous struggle was waged between two technocrats of destruction, Obersturmbann-führer Höss and Kriminalkommissar Wirth, over the replacement of carbon monoxide with Zyklon B in the killing centers.[12] We have observed this bureaucratic warfare also in the attempt of the judiciary to conserve its jurisdiction in Jewish affairs. When that attempt was finally given up, Justice Minister Thierack wrote to his friend Bormann:

> I intend to turn over criminal jurisdiction against Poles, Russians, Jews, and Gypsies to the *Reichsführer-SS*. In doing so, I base myself on the principle that the administration of justice can make only a small contribution to the extermination of these peoples.[13]

This letter reveals an almost melancholy tone. The judiciary had done its utmost; it was no longer needed.

The bureaucrats did not spare themselves; neither could they spare the economy. Just how expensive was the destruction of the Jews? What were the effects of this cost? Table 1 reveals the financial aspects of the operations.[14]

Upon analysis of Table 1, we observe two important trends: with the progress of the destruction process, gains declined; on the other hand, expenditures tended to increase. Looking at the table horizontally, we thereupon discover that in the preliminary phase (above the dividing line) financial gains, public or private, far outweighed expenses, but that in the killing phase (below the dividing line) receipts no longer balanced losses. Let us examine the cost of this killing phase a little more closely.

Receipts (last three items in the left column) were meager. This is explained by the fact that in occupied and satellite territories the Germans did not engage in extensive confiscations. In the interest of a "final solution" in these areas the German perpetrators had to leave most of the Jewish property to their non-German collaborators.[15]

Losses, however, were high. How do we explain those figures? Direct

---

[11] See pp. 289–90.

[12] See pp. 571–72.

[13] See pp. 295–96.

[14] Aryanization differentials, Reich property tax, and confiscations under the 11th Ordinance listed in letter from *Restverwaltung des ehemaligen Reichsfinanzministeriums* to Allied Control Commission, November 14, 1946, NG–4906. For other statistics, see this book, *passim*.

[15] See p. 354.

expenditures (here estimated in the hundreds of millions) were comparatively small. They represent a remarkable attempt at economizing. We have seen how sparingly personnel were used, both in the killing units and in the killing centers. The deportation trains (*Sonderzüge*) were made up of freight cars, and several thousand Jews could be transported in one train. The killing centers were extraordinarily cheap, notwithstanding Speer's complaint that Himmler was using scarce building materials too extravagantly. The installa-

TABLE I . *The Cost of Destroying the Jews*

RECEIPTS, GAINS, SAVINGS	EXPENDITURES AND LOSSES
Net profits to industry from purchase and liquidations of Jewish enterprises: ca. one-fourth to one-half of value of Jewish business property in Reich-Protektorat area. These profits probably amounted to billions of reichsmark.	Loss of markets abroad in consequence of buyers' resistance and boycott: no estimates.
Aryanization differentials paid by companies to Reich: 49,000,000 reichsmark.	
Reich Flight Tax: 900,000,000 reichsmark.	
Reich Property Tax (fine): 1,127,000,000 reichsmark.	
Wage differentials and other industry savings as result of employment of Jewish labor: probably in tens of millions.	
Wage differentials, special income tax, and other wage savings accruing to Reich: probably in tens of millions.	Direct expenditures for *a.* personnel and overhead (prior to killing phase)
Confiscations under the eleventh ordinance (securities and bonds): 186,000,000 reichsmark.	*b.* personnel and overhead (in killing operations) *c.* Transport *d.* Camp installations (in hundreds of millions)
Confiscations under the eleventh ordinance and other measures (not including securities and bonds): 592,000,000 reichsmark.	Extraordinary direct expense for razing of Warsaw ghetto: 150,000,000 reichsmark.
Miscellaneous confiscations not booked by Finance Ministry in above figures: possibly hundreds of millions.	Loss of Jewish production in consequence of the "final solution": ca. 3,000,000,000 reichsmark.

tions were built with camp labor, and the inmates were housed in huge barracks with no light and no modern toilet facilities. The investment in gas chambers and ovens was not very great, either. Why all this economizing? The answer is simple. In all these cases savings did not reduce efficiency; they might even have promoted the smooth implementation of bureaucratic measures. The destruction process was oriented not to cost but to efficiency. Not money but time was of the essence.

This point is even more sharply illustrated when we examine the next two items. The razing of the Warsaw ghetto ruins after the battle of April–May, 1943, was a Himmler project for which the Finance Ministry received a bill in the amount of 150,000,000 reichsmark.[16] Himmler felt that a park should obliterate the site of the ghetto, lest Warsaw grow back to its former size.

The last item in the expense column—the loss of Jewish war production—is a glaring illustration of the triumph of speed over cost. Himmler never made any pretense that for him the destruction of the Jews had priority even over armaments. When he was overwhelmed with arguments in favor of the war effort, Himmler had only this reply: "The argument of war production, which nowadays in Germany is the favorite reason for opposing anything at all, I do not recognize in the first place.[17] In the measured language of the Ministry for Eastern Occupied Territories, the priority of the destruction process was phrased as follows: "Economic questions should not be considered in the solution of the Jewish question."[18] Let us now explore the consequences entailed by the loss of the Jewish labor force.

The war economy lost the aggregate value of those products which two or three million workers in Germany and in the occupied countries could produce in two or three years. This loss was total because the destruction process had removed the Jewish labor force without replacement from going concerns. This does not imply that in individual plants or warehouses Jews were not replaced; it does mean that in the total production picture the loss of Jewish labor could never be made up, in spite of all labor recruitment drives by Plenipotentiary for Labor Allocation Sauckel, for in 1944 the shortage of workers had reached a total of not less than 4,000,000.

What was the value of that lost production? In military terms the loss cannot be calculated, but in monetary terms it is possible to make some estimates. Economy Minister Funk estimated after the war that the total value of war production in Germany, from 1941 through 1943, was 260 billion reichsmark. The amount produced in the occupied territories he estimated (for the same period) at 90 billion marks.[19] If we consider that in Germany about 0.5 per cent of the labor force engaged in war production was Jewish, and

---

[16] See p. 327.
[17] In his pronouncements, *passim*.
[18] See p. 247.
[19] Testimony by Funk, *Trial of the Major War Criminals*, XIII, 129–30.

that in the occupied territories about 2 per cent were Jews, the value of
Jewish war production lost is approximately 3 billion reichsmark. This figure
swamps the entire income derived from the destruction process after the "final
solution" had started, and it proves that whenever it was not efficient to be
thrifty, the implementation of the operations could be extravagant in the
extreme.

P S Y C H O L O G I C A L   P R O B L E M S .—The most important problems of
the destruction process were not administrative but psychological. The very
conception of the drastic "final solution" was dependent on the ability of the
perpetrators to cope with weighty psychological obstacles and impediments.
The psychological blocks differed from the administrative difficulties in one
important respect: an administrative problem could be solved and eliminated;
the psychological difficulties had to be dealt with continuously. They were
held in check but never removed. Commanders in the field were ever watchful for symptoms of psychological disintegration. In the fall of 1941 Higher
SS and Police Leader Russia Center von dem Bach shook Himmler with the
remark:

Look at the eyes of the men of this *Kommando,* how deeply shaken they are.
These men are finished [*fertig*] for the rest of their lives. What kind of followers
are we training here? Either neurotics or savages [*Entweder Nervenkranke oder
Rohlinge*]![20]

Von dem Bach was not only an important participant in killing operations.
He was also an acute observer. With this remark he pointed to the basic
psychological problem of the German bureaucracy: the German administration had to make determined efforts to prevent the breakdown of its men
into either "savages" or "neurotics." This was essentially a dual task—one
part disciplinary, the other moral.

The disciplinary problem was understood clearly. The bureaucrats were
fully aware of the dangers of plundering, torture, orgies, and atrocities. Such
behavior was first of all wasteful from an administrative point of view, for the
destruction process was an organized undertaking which had room only for
organized tasks. Moreover, "excesses" attracted attention to aspects of the
destruction process which had to remain secret. Such were the activities of
Brigadeführer Dirlewanger, whose rumored attempts to make human soap
drew the attention of the public to the killing centers.

Indeed, atrocities could bring the entire "noble" work into disrepute. What
was wasteful administratively was dangerous psychologically. Loose behavior
was an abuse of the machine, and a debauched administration could disintegrate. That was why the German administration had a certain preference
for quick, blow-type (*schlagartige*) action. Maximum destructive effect was
to be achieved with minimum destructive effort. The personnel of the machinery of destruction were not supposed to look to the right or to the

---

[20] See p. 218.

left; they were not allowed to have either personal motives or personal gains. An elaborate discipline was introduced into the machine of destruction.

The first and most important rule of conduct of this discipline was the principle that all Jewish property belonged to the Reich. So far as Himmler was concerned, the enforcement of that rule was a success. In 1943 he told his Gruppenführer:

The riches which they [the Jews] owned we have taken from them. I have given strict orders, which Obergruppenführer Pohl has carried out, that this wealth should naturally [*selbstverständlich*] be delivered to the Reich. We have taken nothing. Individuals who have transgressed are being punished in accordance with an order which I gave in the beginning and which threatened that anyone who takes just one mark is a condemned man. A number of SS men—not many—have transgressed against that order, and they will be condemned to death mercilessly. We had the moral right vis-à-vis *our* people to annihilate [*umzubringen*] *this* people which wanted to annihilate us. But we have no right to take a single fur, a single watch, a single mark, a single cigarette, or anything whatever. We don't want in the end, just because we have exterminated a germ, to be infected by that germ and die from it. I will not stand by while a slight infection forms. Whenever such an infected spot appears, we will burn it out. But on the whole we can say that we have fulfilled this heavy task with love for our people, and we have not been damaged in the innermost of our being, our soul, our character.[21]

There is, of course, considerable evidence that more than a few individuals "transgressed" against the discipline of the destruction process. No estimate can be formed of the extent to which transport *Kommandos*, killing units, the ghetto and killing center personnel, and even *Kommando* 1005—the grave-destruction *Kommando*—filled their pockets with the belongings of the dead. Moreover, we should note that Himmler's rule dealt only with *unauthorized* takings by participating personnel in the field. It did not deal with *authorized* distributions to the participants.

The essence of corruption is to reward people on the basis of their proximity to the loot—in a corrupt system, the tax collectors become rich. In the course of the destruction process many distributions were made to the closest participants. We need remind ourselves only of the Finance Ministry's appropriation of fine furniture during the deportations of Jews from Germany, the distribution of better apartments to civil servants, the cuts taken by the railways, SS and Police, and postal service in the allocation of the furniture of the Dutch, Belgian, and French Jews, the "gifts" of watches and "Christmas presents" to SS-men and their families. The destruction process had its own built-in corruption. Only unauthorized corruption was forbidden.

The second way in which the Germans sought to avoid damage to "the soul" was in the prohibition of unauthorized killings. A sharp line was drawn between killings pursuant to order and killings induced by desire. In the

[21] Speech by Himmler at *Gruppenführer* meeting at Poznan, October 4, 1943, PS–1919.

former case a man was thought to have overcome the "weaknesses" of "Christian morality;"[22] in the latter case he was overcome by his baseness. That was why in the occupied USSR both the army and the civil administration sought to restrain their personnel from joining the shooting parties on the killing sites.

Perhaps the best illustration of the official attitude is to be found in an advisory opinion by a judge on Himmler's Personal Staff, Obersturmbann-führer Bender. Bender dealt with procedure to be followed in the case of unauthorized killings of Jews by SS personnel. He concluded that if purely political motives prompted the killing, if the act was an expression of idealism, no punishment was necessary unless the maintenance of order required disciplinary action or prosecution. However, if selfish, sadistic, or sexual motives were found, punishment was to be imposed for murder or for manslaughter, in accordance with the facts.[23]

The German disciplinary system is most discernible in the mode of the killing operation. At the conclusion of the destruction process Hitler remarked in his testament that the Jewish "criminals" had "atoned" for their "guilt" by "humane means."[24] The "humaneness" of the destruction process was an important factor in its success. It must be emphasized, of course, that this "humaneness" was evolved not for the benefit of the victims but for the welfare of the perpetrators. Time and again, attempts were made to reduce opportunities for "excesses" and *Schweinereien* of all sorts. Much research was expended for the development of devices and methods which arrested propensities for uncontrolled behavior and which lightened, at the same time, the crushing psychological burden on the killers. The construction of gas vans and of gas chambers, the employment of Ukrainian, Lithuanian, and Latvian auxiliaries to kill Jewish women and children, the use of Jews for the burial and burning of bodies—all these were efforts in the same direction. Efficiency was the real aim of all this "humaneness."

So far as Himmler was concerned, his SS and Police had weathered the destruction process. In October, 1943, when he addressed his top commanders, he said to them:

Most of you know what it means when 100 corpses lie there, or when 500 corpses lie there, or when 1000 corpses lie there. To have gone through this and —apart from a few exceptions caused by human weakness—to have remained decent, that has made us great. That is a page of glory in our history which has never been written and which is never to be written. . . .[25]

However, the descent into savagery was not nearly so important a factor in the destruction process as the feeling of growing uneasiness that pervaded the bureaucracy from the lowest strata to the highest. That uneasiness was

[22] See p. 603.
[23] Memorandum by OStubaf. Bender, October 22, 1942, NO-1744.
[24] See p. 635.
[25] Himmler speech, October 4, 1943, PS-1919.

the product of moral scruples—the lingering effect of two thousand years of Western morality and ethics. A Western bureaucracy had never before faced such a chasm between moral precepts and administrative action; an administrative machine had never been burdened with such a drastic task. In a sense, the task of destroying the Jews put the German bureaucracy to a supreme test. The German technocrats solved also that problem and passed also this test.

To grasp the full significance of what these men did, we have to understand that we are not dealing with individuals who had their own separate moral standards. The bureaucrats who were drawn into the destruction process were not different in their moral makeup from the rest of the population. The German perpetrator was not a special kind of German. What we have to say here about his morality applies not to him specially but to Germany as a whole. How do we know this?

We know that the very nature of administrative planning, of the jurisdictional structure, and of the budgetary system precluded the special selection and special training of personnel. Even the killing units and the killing centers did not obtain professional killers. Every lawyer in the RSHA was presumed to be suitable for leadership in the mobile killing units; every finance expert of the WVHA was considered a natural choice for service in a death camp. In other words, all necessary operations were accomplished with whatever personnel were at hand. However one may wish to draw the line of active participation, the machinery of destruction was a remarkable cross-section of the German population. Every profession, every skill, and every social status was represented in it. We know that in a totalitarian state the formation of an opposition movement outside the bureaucracy is next to impossible; however, if there is very serious opposition in the population, if there are insurmountable psychological obstacles to a course of action, such impediments reveal themselves *within* the bureaucratic apparatus. We know what such barriers will do, for they emerged clearly in the Italian Fascist state. Again and again the Italian generals and consuls, prefects and police inspectors, refused to co-operate in the deportations. The destruction process in Italy and the Italian-controlled areas was carried out against unremitting Italian opposition. No such opposition is to be found in the German area. No obstruction stopped the German machine of destruction. No moral problem proved insurmountable. When all participating personnel were put to the test, there were very few lingerers and almost no deserters. The old moral order did not break through anywhere along the line. That is a phenomenon of the greatest magnitude.

Just how did the German bureaucracy overcome its moral scruples? We know that it was something of a struggle; we know also that the struggle was won only with the employment of the most complex psychological tools fashioned during centuries of German cultural development. Fundamentally, the psychological defense arsenal consisted of two parts: the repressive mechanism and the system of rationalizations.

First of all, the bureaucracy wanted to hide its deeds, it wanted to conceal the destruction process, not only from all outsiders but also from the censuring gaze of its own conscience. The repression proceeded through five stages. The first was secrecy.

As we might expect, every effort was made to hide the ultimate aim of the destruction process from Axis partners and from the Jews. Inquiries such as Hungarian Prime Minister Kallay put to the Foreign Office about the disappearance of European Jewry,[26] or questions which foreign journalists in Kiev asked army authorities about mass shootings,[27] could obviously not be answered. Rumors which could spread like wildfire had to be smothered. "Plastic" evidence, such as "souvenir" photographs of killings, mass graves, and the wounded Jews who had risen from their graves, had to be destroyed.[28] All these efforts were an administrative necessity. However, beyond that, they were necessary also for psychological reasons. The extreme care with which the machinery of destruction, and particularly the SS and Police, guarded the secrecy of its operations betrayed uncertainty, worry, and anxiety. In May, 1944, the RSHA complained to the Justice Ministry that the *Landgericht* in Vienna was making too many inquiries to elicit the whereabouts of deported Jews for the purpose of rendering decisions in proceedings involving proof of descent (*Abstammungsverfahren*). The *Landgericht* had been told repeatedly, said the complaint, that no information could be given about deportees, but the court had persisted in making inquiries. Quite apart from the fact that the "Jews" (that is, the persons seeking clarification of their status) had been given plenty of time to clear questions about their descent, these people were only trying to hide their ancestry, anyway, in order to remove themselves from the effect of "Security Police measures" (*sicherheitspolizeiliche Massnahmen*). For these reasons, and because of more pressing war work, the Security Police could not furnish replies, etc. etc.[29]

Thus the first stage in the repression was to shut off the supply of information from all those who did not have to know it. Whoever did not participate was not supposed to know. The second stage was to make sure that whoever knew would participate.

There was nothing so irksome as the realization that someone was watching over one's shoulder, that someone would be free to talk and accuse because he was not himself involved. This fear was the origin of what Leo Alexander has called the "blood kit,"[30] the irresistible force that drew every official "observer" into the destruction process. The "blood kit" explains why so many office chiefs of the RSHA were assigned to mobile killing units and why

---

[26] See p. 522.
[27] See p. 212.
[28] See pp. 246, 249–50.
[29] RSHA to Justice Ministry, May 3, 1944, NG–900.
[30] Leo Alexander, "War Crimes and Their Motivation," *Journal of Criminal Law and Criminology*, XXXIX (September–October, 1948), 298–326.

staff officers with the killing units were ordered to participate in the killing operations.[31] The "blood kit" also explains why Unterstaatssekretär Luther of the Foreign Office's *Abteilung Deutschland* insisted that the Political Division countersign all instructions to embassies and legations for the deportation of Jews.[32] Finally, the "blood kit" explains the significant words spoken by Generalgouverneur Frank at the conclusion of a police conference in Krakow:

> We want to remember that we are, all of us assembled here, on Mr. Roosevelt's war-criminals list. I have the honor of occupying first place on that list. We are therefore, so to speak, accomplices in a world-historical sense.[33]

The third stage in the process of repression was the prohibition of criticism. Public protests by outsiders were extremely rare; the criticisms were expressed, if at all, in mutterings on the rumor circuit. It is sometimes hard, even to distinguish between expressions of sensationalism and real criticism, for often the two were mixed. One example of such mixed reactions is to be found in the circulation of rumors in Germany about the mobile killing operations in Russia. The Party Chancellery, in confidential instructions to its regional machinery, attempted to combat these rumors. Most of the reports, the chancellery stated, were "distorted" and "exaggerated." "It is conceivable," the circular continued, "that not all of our people—especially people who have no conception of the Bolshevik terror—can understand sufficiently the necessity for these measures." In their very nature, "these problems," which were sometimes "very difficult," could be solved "in the interest of the security of our people" only with "ruthless severity."[34]

In the German documents we found a singular example of a genuine public protest: A Catholic priest named Lichtenberg, prayed for the Jews in open services at St. Hedwig's Cathedral in Berlin. He prayed not only for baptized Jews but for all the Jewish victims. Placed in custody, he pronounced himself a foe of National Socialism and declared that he wanted to share the fate of the Jews in the East, in order to pray for them there. Released from prison, Lichtenberg died on the way to a concentration camp.[35]

Within the bureaucracy we find a few more examples of criticism, though again it was very seldom outspoken protest. Of course, it was permissible to criticize measures from the viewpoint of German welfare. We have seen the unbelievable amount of discussion about the *Mischlinge* and Jews in mixed marriages—that is, persons against whom action could not be taken without hurting Germans. Again, we have noted the voluminous correspondence, dealing with the adverse effects of anti-Jewish measures on the war effort. Once in a while it was permissible even to mention the harmful

---

[31] See p. 215.
[32] See p. 350.
[33] See p. 332.
[34] See p. 300.
[35] See pp. 299–300.

psychological effects of killings on the perpetrators, but a sharp line was drawn between such criticisms and the implication that the destruction process itself was intrinsically wrong.

A Director of the Reichsbank, Wilhelm, overstepped the line when he cautioned his chief, Puhl, not to visit concentration camps and when he announced his refusal to participate in the distribution of Jewish belongings with the words: "The Reichsbank is not a dealer in second-hand goods."[36] Generalkommissar Kube of White Russia violated the injunction against moral condemnations by making accusations against the KDS in White Russia, Strauch. Kube implied that Jews—at least those Jews who had come from Germany ("from our own cultural level")—were human beings and that Strauch and his killers were maniacs and sadists who had satisfied their sexual lust during shootings. Strauch did not take kindly to such criticism. In a complaint against Kube he wrote that "it was regrettable that we, in addition to having to perform this nasty job, were also made the target of mud-slinging."[37] In the Interior Ministry the expert on Jewish affairs, Ministrialrat Lösener, was disturbed by reports of killings which had occurred in Riga; he began to put questions to his chief, Staatssekretär Stuckart, and requested a transfer. After a while a colleague asked Lösener to stop pestering the Staatssekretär, for Stuckart's position was difficult enough.[38]

On the highest level, the following story was told by Gauleiter Schirach's secretary: While Schirach's wife was staying in a hotel in Amsterdam, she watched a roundup of Jews at night. The Jewish women "screamed terribly." Mrs. Schirach's nerves were so much on edge that she decided to tell her husband about it. The *Gauleiter* advised her to tell the story to Hitler himself, since the Führer would not tolerate such "abuses" (*Missstände*). During their next visit to Hitler Mrs. Schirach told the story. Hitler listened "ungraciously," interrupting several times and telling her not to be so sentimental. Everyone present found the exchange between Hitler and Mrs. Schirach "very embarrassing" (*äusserst peinlich*). The conversation broke down, no one spoke, and Mr. and Mrs. Schirach left the room. The Schirachs departed the next day without saying good-bye.[39]

In its fourth stage and repressive mechanism eliminated the destruction process as a subject of social conversation. Among the closest participants it was considered bad form to talk about the killings. This is what Himmler had to say on the subject in his speech of October 4, 1943:

I want to mention here very candidly a particularly difficult chapter. Among us it should be mentioned once, quite openly, but in public we will never talk about it. Just as little as we hesitated on June 30, 1934, to do our duty and to put

---

[36] See p. 617.

[37] See p. 253.

[38] Affidavit by Lösener, February 24, 1948, NG–1944–A.

[39] Affidavit by Maria Höpken, January 19, 1946, Schirach–3. Affiant was not a witness but claims that the identical story was told to her on separate occasions by Schirach and his wife.

comrades who had transgressed [the brown shirts] to the wall, so little have we talked about it and will ever talk about it. It was with us, thank God, an inborn gift of tactfulness, that we have never conversed about this matter, never spoken about it. Every one of us was horrified, and yet every one of us knew that we would do it again if it were ordered and if it were necessary.

I am referring to the evacuation of the Jews, to the extermination of the Jewish people. . . .[40]

This, then, was the reason why that particular "page of glory" was never to be written. There are some things that can be done only so long as they are not discussed, for once they are discussed they can no longer be done.

We know, of course, that among those who were not quite so close to the killing operations the sensations of the destruction process were irresistible. The rumor network was spread all over Axis Europe. One Foreign Office official stationed in Rome mentions that he discussed details of the killings with at least thirty of his colleagues.[41] But the urge to talk was not so deep in men who were heavily involved in the destruction process. Höss, the Auschwitz commander, says that he never spoke about his job even to his wife. She found out about what he was doing because of an inadvertent remark by a family friend. Gauleiter Bracht.[42] The Treblinka guard, Hirtreiter, never spoke of his task at all.[43]

The fifth and final stage of the repressing process was to omit mention of "killings" or "killing installations" even in the secret correspondence in which such operations had to be reported. The reader of these reports is immediately struck by their camouflage vocabulary: *Endlösung der Judenfrage* ("final solution of the Jewish question"), *Lösungsmöglichkeiten* ("solution possibilities"), *Sonderbehandlung* (or SB–"special treatment"), *Evakuierung* ("evacuation"), *Aussiedlung* (same), *Umsiedlung* (same), *Spezialeinrichtungen* ("special installations"), *durchgeschleusst* ("dragged through"), and many others.

There is one exchange of correspondence in which knowing officials carried the game of pretense to the point of distortion and outright falsification: In 1943 the Foreign Office inquired whether it would be possible to exchange 30,000 Baltic and White Russian Jews for Reich Germans in Allied countries. The Foreign Office representative in Riga replied that he had discussed the matter with the Security Police commander in charge; the BdS had felt that the "interned" Jews could not be sent away for "weighty Security Police reasons." As was known (*bekanntlich*), a large number of Jews had been "done away with" in "spontaneous actions." In some places these actions had resulted in "almost total extermination" (*fast völlige Ausmerzung*). A removal of the remaining Jews would therefore give rise to "anti-German

---

[40] Himmler speech, October 4, 1943, PS–1919.
[41] Affidavit by Vortragender Legationsrat Dr. Ulrich Dörtenbach, May 13, 1947, NG–1535.
[42] See pp. 621–22.
[43] See p. 622.

atrocity propaganda," etc.[44] Thus even in 1943 an internal secret letter could claim that the Jews in the East had all been victims of pogroms.

A particularly revealing example of disassociation may also be found in a private letter written by a sergeant of the Rural Police to a police general. The sergeant, at the head of 23 German gendarmes and 500 Ukrainian auxiliary policemen, had killed masses of Jews in the Kamenets Podolski area. These are excerpts from his letter.

Naturally we are cleaning up considerably, especially among the Jews. . . .
I have a cozy apartment in a former children's asylum. One bedroom and a living room with all of the accessories. Practically nothing is missing. Naturally, the wife and the children. You will understand me. My Dieter and the little Liese write often, after their fashion. One could weep sometimes. It is not good to be a friend of children as I was. I hope that the war, and with it the time of service in the East, soon ends.[45]

The process of repression was continuous, but it was never completed. The killing of the Jews could not be hidden completely, either from the outside world or from the inner self; therefore the bureaucracy was not spared an open encounter with its conscience. It had to pit argument against argument and philosophy against philosophy. Laboriously, and with great effort, the bureaucracy had to justify its activities.

Psychological justification is called rationalization. The Germans employed two kinds of rationalizations. The first was an attempt to justify the destruction process as a whole; it was designed to explain why the Jews had to be destroyed. It was focused on the Jew. The other explanations served only to justify individual participation in the destruction process: a signature on a piece of paper or the squeeze of a trigger. They were focused entirely on the perpetrator. Let us consider first the broad rationalizations which encompassed the whole destruction process. In the formation of these justifications old conceptions about the Jew—reinforced and expanded by new propaganda —played an important role. Precisely how did German propaganda function in this process?

The Germans had two kinds of propaganda. One was designed to produce action. It exhorted people to do things, for instance, to come to a mass meeting, to boycott Jewish goods, or to kill Jews. This type of propaganda— the command propaganda—does not concern us here since it was confined, on the whole, to the incitement of boycotts and pogroms, the so-called *Einzelaktionen*. But the Germans also engaged in a campaign which consisted of a series of statements, for example, allegations which implied that the Jew was bad. This propaganda had a very important place in the arsenal of psychological defense mechanisms.

The function of declarative propaganda is to act as a storehouse which

---

[44] Windecker to Foreign Office, April 5, 1943, NG–2652.
[45] Meister der Gendarmerie Fritz Jacob to OGruf. Rudolf Querner, May 5, 1942, NO–5654.

may be drawn upon according to need. The statement "the Jew is bad" is taken from the storehouse and is converted in the perpetrator's mind into a complete rationalization: "I kill the Jew because the Jew is bad." To understand the function of this propaganda is to realize why it was continued until the very end of the war, and, surreptitiously, even after the end of the war. Propaganda was needed to combat doubts and guilt feelings wherever they arose—whether inside or outside the bureaucracy—and whenever they arose —before or after the perpetration of the acts.

In fact, we find that in April, 1943, after the deportations of the Jews from the Reich had largely been completed, the press was ordered to deal with the Jewish question continuously and without letup.[46] In order to build up a storehouse the propaganda had to be turned out on a huge scale. "Research institutes" were formed,[47] doctoral dissertations were written,[48] and volumes of propaganda literature were printed by every conceivable agency. At times this activity even led to bureaucratic competition. Thus Unterstaatssekretär Luther of the Foreign Office had to assure Obergruppenführer Berger of the SS-Main Office that the Foreign Office's pamphlet *Das russische Tor ist aufgestossen* (*"The Russian Gate is Thrown Open"*) in no way competed with Berger's masterpiece *Der Untermensch* (*"The Subhuman"*).[49]

What did all this propaganda accomplish? How was the Jew portrayed in this unending flow of leaflets and pamphlets, books and speeches? How did the propaganda image of the Jew serve to justify the destruction process?

First of all, the German map drew a picture of an international Jewry ruling the world and plotting the destruction of Germany and German life. "If international-finance Jewry," said Adolf Hitler in 1939, "inside and outside of Europe should succeed in plunging the nations into another world war, then the result will not be the Bolshevization of the earth and, with it, the victory of the Jews, but the annihilation of the Jewish race in Europe."[50] In 1944 Himmler said to his commanders: "This was the most frightening order which an organization could receive—the order to solve the Jewish question," but if the Jews had still been in the rear, the front line could not have been held, and if any of the commanders were moved to pity, they had only to think of the bombing terror, "which after all is organized in the last analysis by the Jews."[51]

The theory of world Jewish rule and of the incessant Jewish plot against the German people penetrated into all offices. It became interwoven with foreign policy and sometimes led to preposterous results. Thus the conviction grew that foreign statesmen who were not very friendly toward Germany

---

[46] Instructions by Reich Press Chief, April 29, 1943, NG–4705.

[47] Notably, the Institut zur Erforschung der Judenfrage in Frankfurt, under Dr. Klaus Schickert. Steengracht to Rosenberg, January 22, 1944, NG–1689.

[48] Dr. Hans Praesent, "Neuere deutsche Doktorarbeiten über das Judentum," *Die Judenfrage*, November 15, 1943, pp. 351–53.

[49] Luther to Berger, June 22, 1942, NG–3304.

[50] See p. 257.

[51] Himmler speech, June 21, 1944, NG–4977.

were Jews, part-Jews, married to Jews, or somehow dominated by Jews. Streicher did not hesitate to state publicly that he had it on good Italian authority that the Pope had Jewish blood.[52] Similarly, Staatssekretär Weizsäcker of the Foreign Office once questioned the British chargé d'affaires about the percentage of "Aryan" blood in Mr. Rublee, an American on a mission in behalf of refugees.[53]

This type of reasoning was also applied in reverse. If a power was friendly, it was believed to be free of Jewish rule. In March 1940, after Ribbentrop had succeeded in establishing friendly relations with Russia, he assured Mussolini and Ciano that Stalin had given up the idea of world revolution. The Soviet administration had been purged of Jews. Even Kaganovich (the Jewish Politbureau member) looked rather like a Georgian.[54]

The claim of Jewish world rule was to be established irrefutably in a show trial. Toward the end of 1941 the Propaganda Ministry, the Foreign Office, and the Justice Ministry laid plans for the trial of Herschel Grynzpan, the man who had assassinated a German Embassy official (vom Rath) in Paris in 1938.[55] The trial was to prove that Grynzpan's deed was part of a "fundamental plan by international Jewry to drive the world into a war with National Socialist Germany,"[56] but it was never held, because the Justice Ministry in its eagerness had made the fatal mistake of adding homosexuality to the indictment. At the last moment, it was feared that Grynzpan might reveal "the alleged homosexual relations of Gesandtschaftsrat vom Rath." And so the whole scheme was dropped.[57]

When Germany began to lose the war at Stalingrad, the propaganda machine sought to make up in sheer volume of endless repetition for the "proof" it had failed to obtain in the ill-fated Grynzpan trial. The Jew was now the principal foe, the creator of capitalism and Communism, the sinister

---

[52] Memorandum by Ribbentrop, November 18, 1938, on the Italian protest in the Streicher affair, *Documents on German Foreign Policy 1918–1945*, Ser. D, IV, 524–25. The pontiff in question was the "temperamental Pope," Pius XI, not the "diplomatic Pope," Pius XII.

[53] Weizsäcker to Wörmann, Dg. Pol., trade and legal divisions, *Referat Deutschland* (Aschmann), November 7, 1938, NG–4686. The British diplomat replied that he didn't think Rublee had any Jewish blood.

[54] Summary of conference between Ribbentrop, Mussolini, and Ciano, May 10, 1940, PS–2835.

[55] Ministerialrat Diewerge (Propaganda Ministry) to Gesandter Dr. Krümmer (Foreign Office), December 22, 1941, NG–971. Krümmer to Foreign Office press division, January 2, 1942, NG–971. Summary of interministerial conference, January 23, 1942, NG–973. Rintelen to Weizsäcker, April 5, 1942, NG–179. Krümmer via Luther to Weizsäcker, April 7, 1942, NG–179. Schlegelberger to Göbbels, April 10, 1942, NG–973. Memorandum by Diewerge, April 11, 1942, NG–971.

[56] Rintelen to Weizsäcker, quoting Ribbentrop's views, April 2, 1942, NG–179.

[57] Summary of Grynzpan conference, January 23, 1942, NG–973. Louis P. Lochner (ed.), *The Goebbels Diaries*, entries for February 11, 1942, and April 5, 1942, pp. 78, 161. After the trial was dropped, Grynzpan was kept "on ice." He was discovered in 1957, living quietly in Paris. Kurt R. Grossmann, "Herschel Gruenspan lebt!" *Auf bau* (New York), May 10, 1957, pp. 1, 5–6.

force behind the entire Allied war effort, the organizer of the "terror raids," and, finally, the all-powerful enemy capable of wiping Germany off the map. By February 5, 1943, the press had to be cautioned not to "over-estimate the power of the Jews"[58] On the same day, however, the following instructions were issued:

> Stress: If we lose this war, we do not fall into the hands of some other states but will all be annihilated by world Jewry. Jewry firmly decided [*fest entschlossen*] to exterminate all Germans. International law and international custom will be no protection against the Jewish will for total annihilation [*totaler Vernichtungswille der Juden*].[59]

How was this theory applied to justify specific operations? The "Jewish conspiracy" was used over and over again. We find the theory in the correspondence of the German Foreign Office, which pressed for deportations in Axis countries on the ground that the Jews were a security risk.[60] The Jews were the spies, the enemy agents. They could not be permitted to stay in coastal areas because in the event of Allied landings they would attack the defending garrisons from the rear. The Jews were the inciters of revolt; that was why they had to be deported from Slovakia in 1944. The Jews were the organizers of the partisan war, the "middle men" between the Red Army and the partisan field command; that was why they could not be permitted to remain alive in partisan-threatened areas. The Jews were the saboteurs and assassins; that was why the army chose them as hostages in Russia, Serbia, and France.[61] The Jews were plotting the destruction of Germany; and that was why they had to be destroyed. In Himmler's words: "We had the moral right vis-à-vis our people to annihilate this people which wanted to annihilate us." In the minds of the perpetrators, therefore, this theory turned the destruction process into a kind of preventive war.

However, the Jews were portrayed not only as a world conspiracy but also as a criminal people. This is the definition of the Jews, as furnished in instructions to the German press:

> Stress: In the case of the Jews there are not merely a few criminals (as in every other people), but all of Jewry rose from criminal roots, and in its very nature it is criminal. The Jews are no people like other people, but a pseudo-people welded together by hereditary criminality [*eine zu einem Scheinvolk zusammengeschlossene Erbkriminalität*]. . . . The annihilation of Jewry is no loss to humanity, but just as useful as capital punishment or protective custody against other criminals.[62]

And this is what Streicher had to say:

---

[58] *Zeitschriften Dienst* (Propaganda Ministry), February 5, 1943, NG–4715.
[59] *Deutscher Wochendienst*, February 5, 1943, NG–4714.
[60] See pp. 415, 548.
[61] See pp. 198, 436–41, 404.
[62] *Deutscher Wochendienst*, April 2, 1943, NG–4713.

Look at the path which the Jewish people has traversed for millenia: Everywhere murder; everywhere mass murder![63]

A Nazi researcher Helmut Schramm, collected all the legends of Jewish ritual murder.[64] The book was an immediate success with Himmler. "Of the book *The Jewish Ritual Murders,*" he wrote to Kaltenbrunner, "I have ordered a large number. I am distributing it down to *Standartenführer* [SS-colonel]. I am sending you several hundred copies so that you can distribute them to your *Einsatzkommandos,* and above all to the men who are busy with the Jewish question."[65] *The Ritual Murders* was a collection of stories about alleged tortures of Christian children. Actually, hundreds of thousands of Jewish children were being killed in the destruction process. Perhaps, that is why *The Ritual Murders* became so important. In fact, Himmler was so enthusiastic about the book that he ordered Kaltenbrunner to start investigations of "ritual murders" in Roumania, Hungary, and Bulgaria; he also suggested that Security Police people be put to work tracing British court records and police descriptions of missing children, "so that we can report in our radio broadcasts to England that in the town of XY a child is missing and that it is probably another case of Jewish ritual murder."[66]

How the theory of Jewish criminality was applied in practice may be seen in the choice of some of the expressions in the reports of killing operations, such as the term "execution" (in German, *hingerichtet, exekutiert, Vollzugstätigkeit*). In correspondence dealing with the administration of the personal belongings taken from dead Jews, the WVHA used the cover designation "utilization of the property of the Jewish thieves [*Verwertung des jüdischen Hehler- und Diebesgutes*]."[67]

A very striking example of how the theory invaded German thinking is furnished in the format of portions of two reports by the army's Secret Field Police in occupied Russia:[68]

Punishable offenses by members of the population:

Espionage	1
Theft of ammunition	1
Suspected Jews (*Judenverdacht*)	3
Moving about with arms (*Freischärlerei*)	11
Theft	2
Jews	2

---

[63] Speech by Streicher during dedication of Wilhelm Gustloff Bridge in Nuremburg, September, 1937, M–4. Gustloff, the AO *Landesgruppenleiter* in Switzerland, had been assassinated by a Jew

[64] Helmut Schramm, *Der judische Ritualmord—Eine historische Untersuchung* (Berlin, 1943).

[65] Himmler to Kaltenbrunner, May 19, 1943, NG–4589.

[66] *Ibid.*

[67] See p. 614.

[68] GFP Group 722 to 207th Security Division Ic, February 23, 1943, NOKW–2210. GFP Group 722 to 207th Security Division Ic, March 25, 1943, NOKW–2158.

In the culmination of this theory to *be* a Jew was a punishable offense (*strafbare Handlung*); thus it was the function of the rationalization of criminality to turn the destruction process into a kind of judicial proceeding.

There was a third rationalization which was focused on the Jew: the conception of the Jew as a lower form of life. Generalgouverneur Frank was given to the use of such phrases as "Jews and lice." In a speech delivered on December 19, 1940, he pointed out that relatives of military personnel surely were sympathizing with men stationed in Poland, a country "which is so full of lice and Jews." But the situation was not so bad, he continued, though of course he could not rid the country of all lice and Jews in a year.[69] On July 19, 1943, the chief of the *Generalgouvernement* Health Division reported during a meeting that the typhus epidemic was subsiding. Frank remarked in this connection that the "removal" (*Beseitigung*) of the "Jewish element" had undoubtedly contributed to better health (*Gesundung*) in Europe. He meant this not only in the literal sense but also politically: the re-establishment of sound living conditions (*gesunder Lebensverhältnisse*) on the European continent.[70]

In a similar vein Foreign Office Press Chief Schmidt once declared during a visit to Slovakia, "The Jewish question is no question of humanity, and it is no question of religion; it is solely a question of political hygiene" (*eine Frage der politischen Hygiene*).[71]

In the terminology of the killing operations the conception of Jews as vermin is again quite noticeable. Dr. Stahlecker, the commander of *Einsatzgruppe A*, called the pogroms conducted by the Lithuanians "self-cleansing actions" (*Selbstreiningungsaktionen*). In another report we find the phrase "cleansing-of-Jews actions" (*Judensäuberungsaktionen*). Himmler spoke of "extermination" (*Ausrottung*). Many times, the bureaucracy used the word *Entjudung*; this expression, which was used not only in connection with killings but also with reference to Aryanizations of property, means to *rid* something of Jews.[72] Again, we discover the term *judenrein*, which in exact translation means "clean of Jews." Finally, in the most drastic application of this theory, a German fumigation company, the Deutsche Gesellschaft für Schädlingsbekämpfung, was drawn into the killing operations by furnishing one of its lethal products for the gassing of a million Jews. Thus the destruction process was also turned into a "cleansing operation."

In addition to the rationalizations which were used to justify the whole undertaking as a war against "international Jewry," as a judicial proceeding against "Jewish criminality," or simply as a "hygienic" process against "Jewish

---

[69] Speech by Frank to men of guard battalion, December 19, 1940, Frank diary, PS–2233.

[70] Summary of *Generalgouvernement* health conference, July 9, 1943, Frank diary, PS–2233.

[71] See p. 471.

[72] Compare Entlausung ("ridding of lice") and Entwesung ("ridding of vermin," or "fumigation").

vermin," there were also those rationalizations which were fashioned in order to enable the individual bureaucrat to justify his individual task in the destruction process. It must be kept in mind that most of the participants did not fire rifles at Jewish children or pour gas into gas chambers. A good many, of course, also had to perform these very "hard" tasks, but most of the administrators, and most of the clerks did not see the final, drastic link in these measures of destruction.

Most bureaucrats composed memoranda, drew up blueprints, signed correspondence, talked on the telephone, and participated in conferences. They could destroy a whole people while sitting at their desks. Except for inspection tours, which were not obligatory, they never had to see "100 bodies lie there, or 500, or 1000." However, these men were not stupid; they realized the connection between their paper work and the heaps of corpses in the East. And they realized, also, the shortcomings of those rationalizations which placed all evil on the Jew and all good on the German. That was why they were compelled to justify their individual activities. Their justifications contain the implicit admission that the paper work was to go on, regardless of the actual plans of world Jewry and regardless of the actual behavior of the Jews who were about to be killed. We can divide the rationalizations focused on the perpetrator into five categories.

The first rationalization was the oldest, the simplest, and therefore the most effective: the doctrine of superior orders. First and foremost there was discipline. First and foremost there was duty. No matter what objections there might be, orders were given to be obeyed. A clear order was like absolution; armed with such an order, a perpetrator felt that he could pass his responsibility and his conscience upward. When Himmler addressed a killing party in Minsk, he told his men that they need not worry. Their consciences were in no way impaired, for they were soldiers who had to carry out every order unconditionally.[73]

Every bureaucrat knows, of course, that open defiance of orders is serious business, but he also knows that there are many ingenious ways of evading orders. In fact, the opportunities for evasion and hesitation increase as one ascends in the hierarchy. Even in Nazi Germany orders were disobeyed, and they were disobeyed even in Jewish matters. We have mentioned the statement of Reichsbankdirektor Wilhelm, who would not participate in the distribution of "second-hand goods." Nothing happened to him. A member of the RSHA, Sturmbannführer Hartl, simply refused to take over an *Einsatzkommando* in Russia. Nothing happened to this man, either.[74] Even Generalkommissar Kube, who had actually frustrated a killing operation in Minsk and who had otherwise expressed himself in strong language, was only warned.

The bureaucrat clung to his orders not so much because he feared his

---

[73] See pp. 218–19.
[74] Affidavit by Albert Hartl, October 9, 1947, NO–5384.

superior (with whom he was often on good terms) but because he feared his own conscience. The many requests for "authorization"—whether for permission to mark Jews with a star or to kill them—demonstrate the true nature of these orders. When they did not exist, the bureaucrats had to invent them.

The second rationalization was the administrator's insistence that he did not act out of personal vindictiveness. In the mind of the bureaucrat duty was an assigned path; it was his "fate." The German bureaucrat made a sharp distinction between duty and personal feelings; he insisted that he did not "hate" Jews, and sometimes he even went out of his way to perform "good deeds" for Jewish friends and acquaintances. When the trials of war criminals started, there was hardly a defendant who could not produce evidence that he had helped some half-Jewish physics professor, or that he had used his influence to permit a Jewish symphony conductor to conduct a little while longer, or that he had intervened on behalf of some couple in mixed marriage in connection with an apartment. While these courtesies were petty in comparison with the destructive conceptions which these men were implementing concurrently, the "good deeds" performed an important psychological function. They separated "duty" from personal feelings. They preserved a sense of "decency." The destroyer of the Jews was no "anti-Semite."

Staatssekretär Keppler of the Office of the Four-Year Plan was interrogated after the war as follows:

QUESTION [by Dr. Kempner of the prosecuting staff]: Tell me, Mr. Keppler, why were you so terribly against the Jews? Did you know the Jews?

ANSWER: I had nothing against the Jews.

QUESTION: I am asking for the reason. You were no friend of the Jews?

ANSWER: Jews came to me. Warburg invited me. Later Jews looked me up in the Reich Chancellery and asked me to join the board of directors of the Deutsche Bank.

QUESTION: When were you supposed to join the board of directors?

ANSWER: I didn't want to; it was in 1934, they wanted to give me a written assurance that I would be a director in half a year. If I had been such a hater of Jews, they would not have approached me.

QUESTION: But you transferred capital from Jews into Aryan hands.

ANSWER: Not often. I know the one case of Simson-Suhl. Also the Skoda-Wetzler Works in Vienna. But it turned out that was no Jewish enterprise.

Keppler was then asked whether he had not favored the "disappearance" of the Jews from Germany. The Staatssekretär fell back on Warburg, with whom he had once had an "interesting discussion." The interrogator broke in with the remark that "now we do not want to talk about anti-Semitism but about the final solution of the Jewish question." In that connection, Keppler was asked whether he had heard of Lublin. The *Staatssekretär* admitted hesitantly that he had heard of Lublin and offered the explanation that he was "deeply touched by this matter" (*dass mich das furchtbar peinlich berührt*). What did Keppler do when he was touched like this? "It was

very unpleasant for me, but after all it was not even in my sphere of jurisdiction."[75]

Another defendant in a war-crimes trial, the former commander in Norway, Generaloberst von Falkenhorst, offered the following explanation for
his order to remove Jews from Soviet prisoner-of-war battalions in his area.
Falkenhorst pointed out that, to begin with, there were no Jews among these
prisoners, for the selection had already taken place in Germany (i.e., the
Jewish prisoners had already been shot as they were shuttled through the
Reich). The order was consequently "entirely superfluous and might just as
well not have been included. It was thoughtlessly included by the officer of
my staff who was working on it, from the instructions sent to us, and I overlooked it." The general then continued:

For the rest it may be inferred from this that the Jewish question played as
infamous a part in Norway as elsewhere, and that I and the Army were supposed
to have been particularly anti-semitic.

Against this suspicion I can only adduce the following: First, that in Scandi-
navian countries there are only very few Jews. These few are hardly ever in evidence. The sum total in Norway was only about 350. [Actual figure, 2000.] A
negligible number among two or three million Norwegians. These [Jews] were
collected by [Reichskommissar] Terboven and according to orders despatched to
Germany by steamship. In this manner the Jewish problem in Norway was
practically solved [i.e., by deportation to Auschwitz].

As regards myself, I made at this time an application to Terboven at the request
of the Swedish Consul, General Westring, in Oslo, who did not much like
visiting Terboven, for the release of a Jew of Swedish nationality and of his
family with permission to leave the country, gladly and, as a matter of course,
fulfilling the Consul's wish to facilitate the return of these people to Stockholm.

If I had been a rabid anti-semite I could, without further ado, have refused
this request, for the matter did not concern me in the slightest.

On the one hand, however, I wanted to help the Swedish Consul, and, on the
other hand, I have nothing against the Jews. I have read and heard their writings
and compositions with interest, and their achievements in the field of science are
worthy of the highest respect. I have met many fine and honorable people among
them.[76]

How widespread the practice of "good deeds" must have been may be
gauged from the following remark by Heinrich Himmler:

And then they come, our 80,000,000 good Germans, and each one has his
decent Jew. It is clear, the others are swine [*Schweine*], but this one is a first-class
Jew. Of all those who speak thus, no one has seen it, no one has gone through
it.[77]

But even if Himmler regarded these interventions as expressions of misplaced

---

[75] Interrogation by Kempner of Keppler, August 20, 1947, NG–3041.

[76] Affidavit by von Falkenhorst, July 6, 1946, in *Trial of Nikolaus von Falkenhorst*
(London, 1949), p. 25.

[77] Speech by Himmler, October 4, 1943, PS–1919.

humanity, they were necessary tools in the attempt to crystallize one of the important justifications for bureaucratic action—duty. Only after a man had done "everything humanly possible" could he devote himself to his destructive activity in peace.

The third justification was the rationalization that one's own activity was not criminal, that the next fellow's action was the criminal act. The Ministerialrat who was signing papers could console himself with the thought that he did not do the shooting. But that was not enough. He had to be sure that *if* he were ordered to shoot, he would not follow orders but would draw the line right then and there.

The following exchange took place during a war-crimes trial. A Foreign Office official, Albrecht von Kessel, was asked by defense counsel (Dr. Becker) to explain the meaning of "final solution."

INTELLECTUAL PREPARATION FOR GENOCIDE

It was in recognition of the cultural importance of the Jews that the Nazis almost immediately after achieving power sought to combat them intellectually. Quite early they established a special Jewish-research division in their Reichsinstitut für Geschichte des neuen Deutschlands in Munich. This was followed by the Institut zur Erforschung der Judenfrage in Frankfort, the directorship of which was entrusted to the leading ideologist of the Nazi movement, Alfred Rosenberg. The Institut worked hard to assemble a library of Judaica and Hebraica which could be used for attacking the Jewish people and its religion. After confiscating many German and French collections, including the Rothschild archives and the library of the Alliance Israélite Universelle, the Frankfort institution brought together by 1941 some 350,000 volumes which could serve to support whatever distortions of the Jewish past were dictated by the Nazi ideology. Even the vulgar antisemite Julius Streicher, who needed no "scholarly" evidence for his pornographic attacks on the Jews, assembled a substantial collection of Hebraica, most of which is now in New York, on which he employed a number of so-called experts to find passages usable in his anti-Jewish propaganda. With the spread of the New Order, the Germans saw to it that similar institutes for the study of "the Jewish question" were also established in Paris, where it was affiliated with the Department of Jewish Affairs, and in Lodz. The Institut für deutsche Ostarbeit, founded in Cracow in 1940, likewise concerned itself with Jewish matters, as did a special professorship in Jewish history and languages attached to the newly established University of Poznan in 1941. Under Nazi prompting, Italy made available in 1942 research facilities for the study of race and Jewish matters at the universities of Florence, Bologna, Milan, and Trieste.

SOURCE: Salo Baron, *European Jewry Before and After Hitler* (New York: American Jewish Committee, 1962), pp. 37–38.

ANSWER: This expression "final solution" was used with various meanings. In 1936 "final solution" meant merely that all Jews should leave Germany. And, of course, it was true that they were to be robbed; that wasn't very nice, but it wasn't criminal.

JUDGE MAGUIRE: Was that an accurate translation?

DR. BECKER: I did not check on the translation. Please repeat the sentence.

ANSWER: I said it was not criminal; it was not nice, but it was not criminal. That is what I said. One didn't want to take their life; one merely wanted to take money away from them. That was all.[78]

The most important characteristic of this dividing line was that it could be *shifted* when the need arose. To illustrate: Once there was a Protestant pastor by the name of Ernst Biberstein. After several years of ministering to his congregation, he moved into the Church Ministry; from that agency he came to another office which was also interested in church matters—the Reich Security Main Office. That agency assigned him to head a local Gestapo office. Finally he became the chief of *Einsatzkommando* 6 in southern Russia. As commander of the *Kommando*, Biberstein killed two or three thousand people. These people, in his opinion, had forfeited the right to live under the rules of war. Asked if there were Jews among his victims, he replied: "It is very difficult to determine that. Also, I was told at that time that wherever there were Armenians, there were not so many Jews."[79] To Biberstein the moral dividing line was like the receding horizon. He walked toward it, but he could never reach it.

Among the participants in the destruction process there were very few who did not shift the line when they had to cross the threshold. One reason why the person of Generalkommissar Kube is so important is that he had a firm line beyond which he could not pass. The line was arbitrary, and very advanced. He sacrificed the Russian Jews and fought desperately only for the German Jews in his area. But the line was fixed. It was not movable, it was not imaginary, it was not self-deceptive. We have indicated that the destruction process was autonomous, that it could not be stopped internally; the adjustable moral standard was one of the principal tools in the maintenance of this autonomy.

There was a fourth rationalization which implicitly took cognizance of the fact that all shifting lines are unreal. It was a rationalization of more sophisticated people and was built on simple premise. No man alone can build a bridge. No man alone can destroy the Jews. The participant in the destruction process was always in company. Among his superiors he could always find those who were doing more than he; among his subordinates he could always find those who were ready to take his place. No matter where he looked, he was one among thousands. His own importance was diminished, and he felt that he was replaceable, perhaps even dispensable.

In such reflective moments the bureaucrat quieted his conscience with

---

[78] Testimony by Albrecht von Kessel, Case No. 11, tr. pp. 9514–15.

[79] Interrogation of Biberstein, June 29, 1947, NO–4997.

the thought that he was part of a tide and that there was very little a drop of water could do in such a wave. When Werner von Tippelskirch, a Foreign Office official, was interrogated after the war, he pointed out that he had never protested against the killing of Jews in Russia because he had been "powerless." His superiors, Erdmannsdorff, Wörmann, and Weizsäcker, had also been "powerless." All of them had waited for a "change of regime." Asked by Prosecutor Kempner whether it was right to wait for a change of regime "and in the meantime send thousands of people to their death," von Tippelskirch replied, "A difficult question."[80]

The fifth rationalization was the most sophisticated of all. It was also a last-ditch psychological defense, suited particularly to those who saw through the self-deception of superior orders, impersonal duty, the shifting moral standard, and the argument of powerlessness. It was a rationalization also for those whose drastic activity or high position placed them out of reach of orders, duty, moral dividing lines, and helplessness. It was the jungle theory.

Oswald Spengler once explained this theory in the following words: "War is the primeval policy of all living things, and this to the extent that in the deepest sense combat and life are identical, for when the will to fight is extinguished, so is life itself."[81] Himmler remembered this theory when he addressed the mobile killing personnel at Minsk. He told them to look at nature: wherever they would look, they would find combat. They would find it among animals and among plants. Whoever tired of the fight went under.[82]

From this philosophy Hitler himself drew strength in moments of meditation. Once at the dinner table, when he thought about the destruction of the Jews, he remarked with stark simplicity: "One must not have mercy with people who are determined by fate to perish [*Man dürfe kein Mitleid mit Leuten haben, denen das Schicksal bestimmt habe, zugrunde zu gehen*]."[83]

2. THE VICTIMS

So far we have pointed out how the Germans overcame their administrative and psychological obstacles; we have dealt with the internal problems of the bureaucratic machine. But the internal technocratic and moral conflicts do not fully explain what happened. In a destruction process the perpetrators do not play the only role; the process is shaped by the victims, too. It is the interaction of perpetrators and victims that is "fate." We must therefore discuss the reactions of the Jewish community and analyze the role of the Jews in their own destruction.

[80] Interrogation by Kempner of Werner von Tippelskirch, August 29, 1947, NG–2801.

[81] Oswald Spengler, *Der Untergang des Abendlandes* (Munich, 1923), II, 545–46.

[82] See p. 219.

[83] Henry Picker (ed.), *Hitler's Tischgespräche im Führerhauptquartier 1941–1942* (Bonn, 1951), entry for April 2, 1942, p. 227. The entries are summaries by Picker of "Hitler's remarks at the dinner table."

When confronted by force, a group can react in five ways: by resistance, by an attempt to alleviate or nullify the threat (the undoing reaction), by evasion, by paralysis, or by compliance. Let us consider each in turn.

The reaction pattern of the Jews is characterized by almost complete lack of resistance. In marked contrast to German propaganda, the documentary evidence of Jewish resistance, overt or submerged, is very slight. On a European-wide scale the Jews had no resistance organization, no blueprint for armed action, no plan even for psychological warfare. They were completely unprepared. In the words of Anti-Partisan Chief and Higher SS and Police Leader Russia Center von dem Bach, who observed the Jews and killed them from 1941 to the end:

Thus the misfortune came about. . . . I am the only living witness but I must say the truth. Contrary to the opinion of the National Socialists that the Jews were a highly organized group, the appalling fact was that they had no organization whatsoever. The mass of the Jewish people were taken completely by surprise. They did not know at all what to do; they had no directives or slogans as to how they should act. That is the greatest lie of anti-Semitism because it gives the lie to the old slogan that the Jews are conspiring to dominate the world and that they are so highly organized. In reality they had no organization of their own at all, not even an information service. If they had had some sort of organization, these people could have been saved by the millions; but instead they were taken completely by surprise. Never before has a people gone as unsuspectingly to its disaster. Nothing was prepared. Absolutely nothing. It was not so, as the anti-Semites say, that they were friendly to the Soviets. That is the most appalling misconception of all. The Jews in the old Poland, who were never communistic in their sympathies, were, throughout the area of the river Bug eastward, more afraid of Bolshevism than of the Nazis. This was insanity. They could have been saved. There were people among them who had much to lose, business people; they didn't want to leave. In addition there was love of home and their old experience with pogroms in Russia. After the first anti-Jewish actions of the Germans, they thought now the wave was over and so they walked back to their undoing.[84]

The Jews were not oriented toward resistance. They took up resistance only in a few cases, locally, and at the last moment. Measured in German casualties, Jewish armed opposition shrinks into insignificance. The most important engagement was fought in the Warsaw ghetto (16 dead and 85 wounded on the German side, including collaborators).[85] In Galicia sporadic resistance resulted in some loses to SS and Police Leader Katzmann (8 dead, 12 wounded).[86] In addition, there were clashes between Jewish partisans and German forces in other parts of the East, and occasional acts of resistance by small groups and individuals in the ghettos and killing centers. It is doubtful that the Germans and their collaborators lost more than a few hundred

---

[84] Von dem Bach made this statement to Leo Alexander, who quoted it in his article "War Crimes and Their Motivation," *Journal of Criminal Law and Criminology*, XXXIX, 315.

[85] See p. 326.

[86] See pp. 317, 327.

men, dead and wounded, in the course of the destruction process. The number of men who dropped out because of disease, nervous breakdowns, or court martial proceedings was probably greater. The Jewish resistance effort could not seriously impede or retard the progress of destructive operations. The Germans brushed that resistance aside as a minor obstacle, and in the totality of the destruction process it was of no consequence.

The second reaction was the attempt to avert the full force of the German destructive measures. This attempt was carried out in three forms. One was the petition—the appeal. By appealing, the Jews sought to transfer the struggle from a physical to an intellectual and moral plane. If only the fate of the Jews could be resolved with arguments rather than with physical resources and physical combat—so Jewry reasoned—there would be nothing to fear. In a petition by Rabbi Kaplan to French Commissioner Xavier Vallat this Jewish mentality becomes absolutely clear. Among other things, the Rabbi pointed out that a pagan or an atheist had the right to defame Judaism, but in the case of a Christian, did not such an attitude appear "spiritually illogical as well as ungrateful?" To prove his point, Kaplan supplied many learned quotations.[87] The letter is as though it were not written in the twentieth century. It is reminiscent of the time toward the close of the Middle Ages when Jewish rabbis used to dispute with representatives of the Church over the relative merits of the two religions.

Yet in various forms, some more eloquent than others, the Jews appealed and petitioned wherever and whenever the threat of concentration and deportation struck them: in the Reich, in Poland, in Russia, in France, in the Balkan countries, and in Hungary.[88] Everywhere the Jews pitted words against rifles, dialectics against force, and everywhere they lost. The reliance upon petitions became so great that internal struggles developed over the formulation and timing of the appeals.

When the petition system is unsuccessful, when an appeals fails to save the whole group, there is a tendency to appeal for part of the group. In the minds of the drafters, these appeals therefore become life-and-death matters. Whoever is excluded is given up. We may cite as an example the conflict in the Vienna Jewish community over the petitioning for exemptions from deportations. At the end of 1941, when the community organization (*Kultusgemeinde*) made an "agreement" with the Gestapo about "exempt" categories, the head of the Jewish war invalids, who had been left out of the "negotiations," accused the deportation expert of the *Kultusgemeinde* of "sacrificing" the disabled veterans.[89] Later on, when the war invalids were pressed to the wall, the leaders of the veterans' organization discussed the advisability of presenting an independent petition. One of the war-invalid chiefs remarked, "Fundamentally, I am of the opinion that we cannot afford a war with the *Kultusgemeinde*." Another commented: "The *Hauptsturm-*

---

[87] See pp. 398–99.
[88] See pp. 280, 150, 248, 398–99, 400, 481, 494–95, 503, 541–42.
[89] See pp. 279–80.

führer will say to himself 'These are Jews, and those are Jews. Let them fight among themselves. Why should I worry about that?' He [the *SS-Hauptsturmführer*] will eventually drop us in this matter [*Er wird uns in dieser Frage eventuell fallen lassen*]." Thereupon the head of the war veterans said, "My answer is that in such an eventuality it will be time to disband our organization."[90]

Sometimes the Jews appealed not with words but with personal gifts; they attempted to bribe individual Germans. But these attempts were also largely unsuccessful: the German officials accepted the gifts but these Germans were not bought.[91] Even the few Jewish girls who offered themselves to policemen on the eve of ghetto-clearing operations were killed on the next day.[92] The bribery *did* worry Himmler, but it had no effect on the progress of the operations.

There was a second way in which the Jews tried to avert disaster: by judicious compliance with orders, and sometimes by anticipatory compliance with orders not yet issued. The most conspicuous example of anticipatory compliance was the decision of the Jewish community leaders in Poland to organize a forced labor system.[93] Another anticipatory move was made by the Jewish leadership in Kislovodsk (Caucasus), where, in full awareness of the German threat, the *Judenrat* confiscated all Jewish valuables—including gold, silver, carpets, and clothing—and handed the property to the German commander.[94] A third example of anticipatory compliance may be found in the minutes of a discussion held in the Shavel *Judenrat* (in Latvia) on March 24, 1943. The *Judenrat* had been asked three times whether any births had occurred in the ghetto, and each time it had denied that there were any births. Now, however, the Jewish leadership was confronted with twenty pregnancies. It decided to use persuasion and, if need be, threats on the women to submit to abortions. One woman was in her eighth month; the *Judenrat* decided that in this case a doctor would induce premature birth and that a nurse would kill the child (A doctor objected to doing the job himself.) The nurse would be told to proceed in such a way that she would not know the nature of her act.[95]

In one respect this Jewish co-operation created administrative problems within the machinery of destruction. The zeal with which the Jews applied themselves to the German war effort accentuated the differences of interests which paired industry and the armament inspectorates against the SS and Police, but these differences were ultimately resolved to the disadvantage of the Jews. And insofar as the Jews co-operated in other ways, the attempts

[90] See pp. 281–82.
[91] See pp. 162, 529.
[92] See pp. 248–49.
[93] See p. 163.
[94] Protocol by Prof. P. A. Ostankov and others, July 5, 1943, USSR–1 A (2–4).
[95] Minutes of the Shavel *Judenrat*, March 24, 1943, found by the Red Army and turned over to the Soviet Extraordinary State Commission, in Jewish Black Book Committee, *The Black Book* (New York, 1946), pp. 331–33.

at forestalling not only availed nothing but actually fitted into German plans. Playing into German hands, they speeded the process of destruction.

The third alleviation attempt may be noted in the system of relief and salvage, from the elaborate social services of the ghetto communities to the primitive "organization" in the killing centers.[96] The relief system was basically the product of a calculation of time, the hope or expectation that the liberation would come before the destruction process could consume itself. We know, simply by counting the relative handful of survivors, that this attempt failed also.

The basic reactions to force are fundamentally different from each other. Resistance is opposition to the perpetrator. Nullification or alleviation is opposition to the administrative enactment. In the third reaction, evasion, the victim tries to remove himself from the effects of force by fleeing or hiding. The phenomenon of flight is most difficult to analyze. We know that the emigration of approximately 350,000 Jews from Germany and German-occupied Czechoslovakia before the war was forced. In many cases the emigrating Jews had been deprived of their livelihood, and they reacted to the consequences of anti-Jewish measures rather than in anticipation of disaster. The flight of the Belgian and Parisian Jews in 1940 and the evacuation of Soviet Jews a year later was compounded with mass migrations of non-Jews. Here again, the flight was not a pure reaction to the threat of the destruction process but also a reaction to the war. We know that only a few thousand Jews escaped from the ghettos of Poland and Russia, that only a few hundred Jews hid out in the large cities of Berlin, Vienna, and Warsaw, that only a handful of Jews escaped from camps. Von dem Bach mentions that in Russia there was an unguarded escape route to the Pripet Marshes, but few Jews availed themselves of the opportunity.[97] In the main, the Jews looked upon flight with a sense of futility; the great majority of those who did not escape early did not escape at all.

There were instances when in the mind of the victim, the difficulties of resistance, undoing, or evasion were just as great as the problems of automatic compliance; in such instances the futility of all alternatives became utterly clear, and the victim was paralyzed. Paralysis occurred only in moments of crisis. During ghetto-clearing operations many Jewish families were unable to fight, unable to petition, unable to flee, and also unable to move to the concentration point to get it over with. They waited for the raiding parties in their homes, frozen and helpless. Sometimes the same paralytic reaction struck Jews who walked up to a killing site and for the first time gazed into a mass grave half-filled with the bloodied corpses of those who had preceded them.

The fifth reaction was automatic compliance. Much has been said and much has been written about the *Judenräte*, the informers, the Jewish police,

---

[96] To "organize" in a camp meant to take a bit of food or some item of clothing wherever it could be found.

[97] Statement by von dem Bach in *Aufbau* (New York), September 6, 1946, p. 40.

the *Kapos*—in short, all those persons who deliberately and as a matter of policy co-operated with the Germans. But these collaborators do not interest us so much as the masses of Jews who reacted to every German order by complying with it automatically. To understand the administrative significance of this compliance, we have to see the destruction process as a composite of two kinds of German measures: those which perpetrated something upon the Jews and involved only action by Germans, such as the drafting of decrees, the running of deportation trains, shooting, or gassing, and those which required the Jews to do something, for instance, the decrees or orders requiring them to register their property, obtain identification papers, report at a designated place for labor or deportation or shooting, submit lists of persons, pay fines, deliver up property, publish German instructions, dig their own graves, and so on. The successful execution of these latter measures depended on action by the Jews. Only when one realizes how large a part of the destruction process consisted of the fulfilment of these measures can one begin to appraise the role of Jews in their own destruction.

If, therefore, we look at the whole Jewish reaction pattern, we notice that in its two salient features it is an attempt to avert action and, failing that, automatic compliance with orders. Why is this so? Why did the Jews act in this way? The Jews attempted to tame the Germans as one would attempt to tame a wild beast. They avoided "provocations" and complied instantly with decrees and orders. They hoped that somehow the German drive would spend itself.

This hope was founded on a two-thousand-year-old experience. In exile the Jews had always been in a minority; they had always been in danger; but they had learned that they could avert danger and survive destruction by placating and appeasing their enemies. Even in ancient Persia an appeal by Queen Esther was more effective than the mobilization of an army. Armed resistance in the face of overwhelming force could end only in disaster.

Thus, over a period of centuries the Jews had learned that in order to survive they had to refrain from resistance. Time and again they were attacked; they endured the Crusades, the Cossack uprisings, and the Czarist persecution. There were many casualties in these times of stress, but always the Jewish community emerged once again like a rock from a receding tidal wave. The Jews had never really been annihilated. After surveying the damage, the survivors had always proclaimed in affirmation of their strategy the triumphant slogan, "The Jewish people lives [*Am Yisrael Chaj*]." This experience was so ingrained in the Jewish consciousness as to achieve the force of law. The Jewish people could not be annihilated.

Only in 1941, 1942, and 1943 did the Jewish leadership realize that, unlike the pogroms of past centuries, the modern machine-like destruction process would engulf European Jewry. But the realization came too late. A two-thousand-year-old lesson could not be unlearned; the Jews could not make the switch. They were helpless.

Let us not suppose, however, that compliance was easy. If it was difficult for the Germans to kill, it was harder still for the Jews to die. Compliance is a course of action which becomes increasingly drastic in a destruction process. It is one thing to comply with an order to register property but quite another to obey orders in front of a grave. The two actions *are* part of the same habit—the Jews who registered their property were also the ones who lined up to be killed. The Jews who lined up on a killing site were the ones who had registered their property. Yet these two activities are very different in their effects. Submission is altogether more burdensome in its last stages than in its beginning, for as one goes on, more and more is lost. Finally, in the supreme moment of crisis the primeval tendency to resist aggression breaks to the surface; resistance then becomes an obstacle to compliance, just as compliance is an obstacle to resistance. In the Jewish case the co-operation reaction was the stronger one until the end. The Jews consequently dealt with their resistance in much the same way as the Germans dealt with their consciences.

The major obstructions faced by the Jews in their course of submission were never physical ones. No major administrative encumbrances were encountered by the surrendering victims. Only a resistance organization with sufficient power to interfere with surrender can erect such obstructions. This kind of resistance organization could not be formed, and this kind of organized resistance could therefore not occur. However, there were significant psychological blocks on the path to capitulation, blocks which revealed themselves clearly in the victims' repressions and rationalizations.

People do not easily accept the fact that they are going to be killed; if they have the know-how to resist, they will defend themselves as best they can. If, on the other hand, they have unlearned the art of resistance, they will repress their knowledge of the true situation and will attempt to go on as though life could not change. The Jews could not resist. In complying with German orders they therefore tried, to the utmost of their ability, to ignore all evidence of danger and to forget all intimation of death. They pretended that nothing unusual was happening to them, and that belief became so crucial that they did anything to perpetuate it.

One is struck by the fact that the Germans repeatedly employed very crude deceptions and ruses. The Jews were bluffed with "registrations" and "resettlements," with "baths" and "inhalations." At each stage of the destruction process the victims thought that they were going through the last stage. And so it appears that one of the most gigantic hoaxes in world history was perpetrated on five million people noted for their intellect. But were these people really fooled? Or did they deliberately fool themselves?

We have evidence that even in the absence of misleading promises the Jewish victims managed to repress their awareness of catastrophe and to substitute for that knowledge a mere illusion. In survivors' accounts we find long descriptions of the elaborate educational programs for the children, and one survivor tells us that in the closing days of the Kaunas ghetto the slogan of the victims was "life for an hour is also life [*A sho gelebt is oich gelebt*]."[98]

[98] Samuel Gringauz, "The Ghetto as an Experiment in Jewish Social Organization," *Jewish Social Studies*, XI (1949), 17.

The Jews, in short, did not always have to be deceived; they were capable of deceiving themselves; the Jewish repressive mechanism could work independently and automatically. In the minutes of the Vienna Jewish war invalids' conferences we discover the same significant absence of direct references to death and killing centers that we have already noted in German correspondence. The Jewish documents abound with such roundabout expressions as "favored transport" (meaning Theresienstadt transport), "I see black," "to tempt fate," "final act of the drama," etc.[99] The direct word is lacking.

Moreover, the attempt to repress unbearable thoughts was characteristic not only of the ghetto community but of the killing center itself. In Auschwitz the inmates employed a special terminology of their own for killing operations: a crematory was called a "bakery"; a man who could no longer work—and who was therefore destined for the gas chamber—was designated a "Moslem"; and the depot holding the belongings of the gassed was named "Canada."[100] These, it must be emphasized, are not Nazi terms; they are expressions by the victims. They are the counterparts of the Nazi vocabulary, and, like the German euphemisms, they were designed to blot out visions of death.

There were moments, of course, when the issue could not be evaded, when forgetting was no longer effective. In such moments of crisis the victims, like the perpetrators, resorted to rationalizations. The Jews, too, had to justify their actions. It is interesting to note how the two principal rationalizations emerged directly from the repressive pattern.

The Germans were notably successful in deporting Jews by stages, for always those who remained behind could reason that it was necessary to sacrifice the few in order to save the many. The operation of that psychology may be observed in the Vienna Jewish community, which concluded a deportation "agreement" with the Gestapo, with the "understanding" that six categories of Jews would not be deported.[101] Again, the Warsaw ghetto Jews argued in favor of co-operation and against resistance on the ground that the Germans would deport sixty thousand Jews but not hundreds of thousands.[102] The bisection phenomenon occurred also in Salonika, where the Jewish leadership co-operated with the German deportation agencies upon the assurance that only "Communist" elements from the poor sections would be deported, while the "middle class" would be left alone.[103] That fatal arithmetic was also applied in Vilna, where *Judenrat* chief Gens declared:

---

[99] See pp. 278–82.

[100] On "bakery," see Lengyel, *Five Chimneys*, p. 22. On "Moslem" (*Muselmann*), see report by commander's office, Auschwitz III, May 5, 1944, NI–11019. On "Canada," see Sehn, "Oswiecim," in *German Crimes in Poland*, p. 41.

[101] See pp. 279–80.

[102] See pp. 318–20.

[103] See pp. 445–46.

"With a hundred victims I save a thousand people. With a thousand I save ten thousand."[104]

In situations where compliance with death orders could no longer be rationalized as a life-saving measure there was still one more justification: the argument that with rigid, instantaneous compliance unnecessary suffering was eliminated, unnecessary pain avoided, the necessary torture reduced. The entire Jewish community, and particularly the Jewish leadership, now concentrated all its efforts in one direction—to make the ordeal bearable, to make death easy.

This effort is reflected in the letter which the Jewish Council in Budapest sent to the Hungarian Interior Minister on the eve of the deportations: "We emphatically declare that we do not seek this audience in order to lodge complaints about the merit of the measures adopted, but merely ask that they be carried out in a humane spirit."[105]

The effort is also illustrated in the following statement, which the chief of the Reich Association of the Jews in Germany, Rabbi Leo Baeck, made after the war:

I made it a principle to accept no appointments from the Nazis and to do nothing which might help them. But later, when the question arose whether Jewish orderlies should help pick up Jews for deportation, I took the position that it would be better for them to do it, because they could at least be more gentle and helpful than the Gestapo and make the ordeal easier. It was scarcely in our power to oppose the order effectively.[106]

When Baeck was in Theresienstadt, an engineer who had escaped from Auschwitz informed him about the gassings. Baeck decided not to pass on this information to anyone in the ghetto city because "living in the expectation of death by gassing would only be the harder."[107]

The supreme test of the compliance reaction came in front of the grave; yet here, too, the Jews managed to console themselves. From one of the numerous German eyewitness reports comes the following typical passage:

The father was holding the hand of a boy about ten years old and was speaking to him softly; the boy was fighting his tears. The father pointed to the sky, stroked his head, and seemed to explain something to him. . . . I remember a girl, slim and with black hair, who passed close to me, pointed to herself, and said, "Twenty-three." . . . The people, completely naked, went down some steps which were cut in the clay wall of the pit and clambered over the heads of the people lying there, to the place where the SS-man directed them. Then they lay down in front of the dead or injured people; some caressed those who were still alive and spoke to them in a low voice. Then I heard a series of shots.[108]

---

[104] Philip Friedman, "Two 'Saviors' Who Failed," *Commentary*, December, 1958, p. 487.

[105] See pp. 541–42.

[106] Leo Baeck in Eric H. Boehm (ed.), *We survived* (New Haven, 1949), p. 288.

[107] *Ibid.*, pp. 292–93.

[108] Affidavit by Hermann Friedrich Graebe, November 10, 1945, PS–2992.

The German annihilation of the European Jews was the world's first completed destruction process. For the first time in the history of Western civilization the perpetrators had overcome all administrative and moral obstacles to a killing operation. For the first time, also, the Jewish victims—caught in the strait jacket of their history—plunged themselves physically and psychologically into catastrophe. The destruction of the Jews was thus no accident. When in the early days of 1933 the first civil servant wrote the first definition of a "non-Aryan" into a civil service ordinance, the fate of European Jewry was sealed.

Comment on Hilberg

H. R. TREVOR-ROPER

This is a forbidding book.* It is nearly 800 pages long. The pages are double-columned. It has nearly a hundred statistical tables. It is written in an austere style, without literary grace or emotion. And it deals with a subject of which, this year, we have already heard a great deal. I hardly thought, on taking it up, that I should be unable to put it down: that having postponed the reading of it till a time of leisure, I should then have read it through, almost without interruption, and quite without skipping, to the end. For this is not merely a compilation or a recapitulation of the now documented facts. It is not yet another chronicle of horrors. It is a careful, analytic, three-dimensional study of a social and political experience unique in history: an experience which no one could believe possible till it had happened and whose real significance still bewilders us. Superficial minds may be satisfied by superficial explanations; the partisans and the apologists may exchange their well-worn arguments or rationalizations; but still it must perplex any thinking person that one of the most highly civilized countries of Europe, in the full light and freedom of the 20th century, should, without protest and without hitch, deliberately and scientifically murder millions of people against whom nothing could be proved except the religion of their grandparents; and that it should do this in full knowledge of the cost which it must entail, not only to its own national psychology but also, even more obviously, to its own economy and its own war potential in the midst of a desperate war.

SOURCE: H. R. Trevor-Roper, "Nazi Bureaucrats and Jewish Leaders," *Commentary* (April, 1962), pp. 351–356. Copyright by the American Jewish Committee. Reprinted by permission.

* Book referred to is *The Destruction of the European Jews* by Raul Hilberg (Chicago: Quadrangle, 1961).

The Germans themselves have a simple explanation. These atrocities, they tell us, were exclusively the work of the Nazi party and, within that party, of a few men whom all now conveniently disown. At the time no one else knew, or could know. Rigorous means were adopted to insure secrecy, and the revelation of those secrets, after 1945, was a terrible shock to the entire German people.

However one may seek to excuse the Germans, no rational man can accept this argument. It is perfectly true that the policy of destroying the European Jews, and the will which carried that policy through, was Hitler's. Without Hitler, the holocaust would not have happened. It is also true that the details of the extermination camps (though not of the mass shootings by the *Einsatzkommandos*) were shrouded, as far as possible, in secrecy. An elaborate myth was spread that the European Jews were merely being transported to "the East" and "resettled" there; and extraordinary, costly refinements were devised in order to keep up this pretense. For instance, as Mr. Hilberg shows, the whole institution of the concentration camp at Theresienstadt, which involved a huge administrative upheaval, was simply a device to give plausibility to the myth of "resettlement." But the fact remains that by the summer of 1942, only six months after the organization of the "Final Solution," the general fact—that European Jewry was being deported to the East for mass annihilation in gas chambers—was well known. The whole of Poland, and all the Germans stationed there, knew it. The German Army knew it: while ostentatiously looking the other way, it supplied men, material, and encouragement for so useful a job. The German Foreign Office knew it and—behind the habitual euphemisms—actively forwarded the work. So did the Finance Ministry, which handled the spoils, and the business corporations, which used the labor and the waste products (and incidentally acquired an SS mentality in the process). All these bodies, by their complicity, not only assisted the program: they also gave it its peculiar bureaucratic, military, economic character. By 1942, it is perfectly clear, any German who asked himself certain questions knew what the answer must be. Therefore those questions were not asked. The anodyne formulas were used, the grave conferences were held, the minutes and orders were signed, and, with the unavowed complicity of the whole nation, the unmentioned, unmentionable work went on. For five million men cannot be scientifically and secretly detached from the community, transported, murdered, and destroyed without trace, by a small professional group only. The mere technical process requires national involvement. So does the psychological process without which such a technical process cannot be carried out.

The great interest of Mr. Hilberg's book is that he has faced this total problem. He is not content to chronicle or to exclaim. While keeping to a narrative form, he has studied the social problem analytically: his narrative carries along with it a profound social content. That is why I call it "three-dimensional." It reveals, methodically, fully, and clearly, the development of both the technical and the psychological process; the machinery and the mentality whereby one whole society sought to isolate and destroy another which, for centuries, had lived in its midst.

Essentially, the process began with a reversal. In the century before Hitler the Jews of Western Europe had been gradually assimilated. From being a separate group they had become part of the native society. This change was not merely factual: it was legal. But from the moment of Hitler's accession to power, the German bureaucracy, hardly waiting for the politicians to command it, began a systematic reversal of the law. The first step was to define the Jews; for it is impossible (as the earlier German anti-Semites had admitted) to strike at a social group until one knows exactly who belongs to that group. The officials of the Ministry of the Interior gradually worked out a definition. Then the persons defined as Jews had to be detached from the machinery which would be used against them: otherwise it could not be used effectively. So that machinery, the bureaucracy itself, hastened to purge itself. Then. came expropriation. The destined victims, cut off from the sources of power, were systematically impoverished. At this point the German business world joined hands with the bureaucracy. First "voluntary," then forcible "Aryanization," followed by penal taxation, transferred the wealth and economic power of the Jews to the German banks, German big business, and the German Finance Ministry. Having been deprived by these processes of the means of resistance, the Jews were next physically segregated and concentrated. Drawn into the city by the logic of events, they were forced, by legal and economic pressure, into real or national ghettos. Marked with new names, labeled with yellow stars, they were subjected to separate regulation and to an internal administration of their own, charged to enforce it. Thus isolated, thus exposed, the victims awaited their fate. As far as the rest of German society was concerned they could, if a place of reception could be found, be deported. They could equally, if no such place was available, be liquidated.

In all this process undoubtedly it was the Nazi party which gave the signal but it was the German bureaucracy in the widest sense—that is, not only the civil servants but the army and the business world—which made it possible. Again and again Mr. Hilberg makes this clear. Between party and bureaucracy there were occasional differences. They differed, for instance, in their attitude to *Mischlinge,* half-Jews. But in general they worked hand-in-glove, and often it was the bureaucracy which was the driving force. The main difference was in method. The bureaucracy did not like *Einzelaktionen* —violent outbreaks, pogroms, spectacular (and costly) episodes like the famous *Kristallnacht* of November 1938. It wanted persecution to be systematic, orderly, official, following a recognizable, predictable, well-considered procedure. Once that bureaucratic procedure had been devised, agreement was complete and the party became, in a sense, a part of it. Once the persecution had turned to mass murder, the bureaucracy was relieved to know that there was a "department" responsible for the last, most disagreeable stages. So the SS *Einsatzkommandos* in Russia found that their work was "surprisingly welcome" to the army, which positively urged them on to dispatch this work quickly. They were even approached by army officers with additional requests: could they not, while they were about it, clean out some billets for the troops by murdering a few thousand Poles or Russians, or relieve the pressure by disposing of invalid Soviet prisoners of war? The eagerness with which the bureaucracy made use of the SS for their common purpose is well-illustrated by the action of the Minister of Justice who, in September 1942—i.e. after the Final Solution had been launched—spontaneously renounced his criminal jurisdiction over Poles, Russians, Jews, and Gypsies to Himmler. "In doing so," he explained, "I stand on the principle that the administration of justice can make only a small contribution to the extermination of these peoples."

With minor differences, the same method which had proved effective in Germany was applied throughout continental Europe. Here the army, there the Foreign Office made it possible. In 1941, when the decision was taken to liquidate instead of merely to deport the Jews, the basic machinery did not change. Nor did the attitude of those who manned it. The same respectable officials—a Weizsäcker, a Steengracht—passed on the orders, signed the minutes, negotiated the surrenders, refused to hear the protests. It was a dirty business, everyone agreed—even the SS agreed to that. But those anodyne phrases prevented a brutal confrontation with the facts; it was bad form—contrary to the German "inborn gift of tactfulness"—to discuss the details; and anyway everyone was involved in it. The involvement was deliberate: it was a form of self-defense. And once a man was involved, there was the justification. To critics, one could plead superior orders (though often such orders were solicited rather than imposed); to one's self, one could plead the infinitesimal personal share in a vast national act; and anyway that act, it was dogmatically declared, was necessary: a bitter necessity, which later generations might not appreciate (therefore the evidence must be concealed), but which the present generation did not doubt.

Here indeed we come to the central problem. For one thing which emerges clearly from Mr. Hilberg's study is that the Germans persuaded themselves that the extermination of the Jews was a necessity. Those who positively organized the extermination saw themselves as idealists, and they were anxious that this idealism, which enabled them to carry out a hideous task, should not be sullied by sadism or corruption. They must show that their action was materially and psychologically disinterested. . . .

But . . . there are always two parties to destruction: the destroyers and the destroyed. During the Eichmann trial in Israel a question constantly asked by younger Israelis was: But why was there no resistance? After all, the Jews were not a few scattered people, easily rounded up by overwhelming force. They were numerous and intelligent. They far outnumbered their captors and their guards. They were millions, rounded up and slaughtered by thousands. At Auschwitz the ratio of prisoners to guards varied from 20 to 1 to 35 to 1. And yet they went like sheep to the slaughter. The Germans themselves, who have long staggered the world by their bovine docility, were amazed. The Jews meekly accepted every successive order which rendered them impotent, they queued up for the deportation trains, they dutifully dug their graves and knelt down to be shot and tumble into them, they filed into the gas chambers. Resistance was negligible, German casualties almost nil. The last-minute resistance of the Warsaw Ghetto was a heroic exception. It was also the exception which proves the rule: for it was carried out by a revolution inside the Jewish community. Had the Jewish community preserved its old internal organization, the Warsaw Ghetto would have been evacuated as easily, and its members gassed as quietly, as all the other ghettos of Poland.

For when the Germans had done their worst, we cannot escape the fact that the Jews of Europe, obedient to their leaders and to their own habits of mind, collaborated in their own destruction. Again and again this fact emerges from Mr. Hilberg's narrative. It is his most surprising revelation, and it will probably be the least welcome to his readers. But it is inescapable. For two thousand years, as he says, the Jews had been unlearning the habit of resistance, and in the end they could not, without a revolution, recover it. For two thousand years they had believed that by yielding and compromise they would survive the spasmodic pogroms and expulsions which were their fate. Their habits, their institutions, their responses were conditioned by that belief. And so, in the end, they yielded and compromised even with a society which was resolved that they should not survive, whose persecution was not spasmodic but systematic, sustained, final. . . .

It is against this background that the revolt of the Warsaw Ghetto is so significant. Futile though it proved to be, it was, in Jewish history, "literally a revolution; for after two-thousand years of a policy of submission the wheel had been turned and once again Jews were using force." Moreover, we may add, it is a revolution which has continued. Today, as never before since the days of Bar Kochba, there are two Jewries: the Jewry of the Dispersion, continuing the inveterate traditions of the Dispersion, and the Jewry of Israel, resuming, after a long interruption, the traditions of military, nationalist resistance. This division, like Israel itself, was born out of the Nazi period, and in this year it has revealed itself, appropriately, in the division of opinion over the trial of Eichmann. Once again, the Jews of the Dispersion urge compliance, compromise, oblivion. But the Jews of Israel, the activist heirs of the Warsaw rebels, hold a different view. They go back to Bar Kochba, or to those Zealots of Judea who, as Mr. Hilberg notes, were fighting their Roman conquerors when the "dispersed" Jews of Alexandria "had already unlearned the art of revolt." Not the least of the contributions which Mr. Hilberg has made to history and sociology in this impressive work is his illumination of this great gulf between those who continued and those who sought to reverse a long-successful but, in its latest and perhaps unique encounter with the German bureaucracy, ultimately disastrous tradition.

10. THERMONUCLEAR WAR

Hiroshima Diary

MICHIHIKO HACHIYA

6 AUGUST 1945

The hour was early; the morning still, warm, and beautiful. Shimmering leaves, reflecting sunlight from a cloudless sky, made a pleasant contrast with shadows in my garden as I gazed absently through wide-flung doors opening to the south.

Clad in drawers and undershirt, I was sprawled on the living room floor exhausted because I had just spent a sleepless night on duty as an air warden in my hospital.

Suddenly, a strong flash of light startled me—and then another. So well does one recall little things that I remember vividly how a stone lantern in the garden became brilliantly lit and I debated whether this light was caused by a magnesium flare or sparks from a passing trolley.

Garden shadows disappeared. The view where a moment before all had been so bright and sunny was now dark and hazy. Through swirling dust I could barely discern a wooden column that had supported one corner of my house. It was leaning crazily and the roof sagged dangerously.

Moving instinctively, I tried to escape, but rubble and fallen timbers barred the way. By picking my way cautiously I managed to reach the *roka* and stepped down into my garden. A profound weakness overcame me, so I stopped to regain my strength. To my surprise I discovered that I was completely naked. How odd! Where were my drawers and undershirt?

What had happened?

All over the right side of my body I was cut and bleeding. A large splinter was protruding from a mangled wound in my thigh, and something warm trickled into my mouth. My cheek was torn, I discovered as I felt it gingerly, with the lower lip laid wide open. Embedded in my neck was a sizable fragment of glass which I matter-of-factly dislodged, and with the detachment of one stunned and shocked I studied it and my blood-stained hand.

Where was my wife?

SOURCE: Michihiko Hachiya, *Hiroshima Diary* (Chapel Hill, N.C.: U. of N.C., 1955). Reprinted by permission.

Suddenly thoroughly alarmed, I began to yell for her: "Yaeko-san! Yaeko-san! Where are you?"

Blood began to spurt. Had my carotid artery been cut? Would I bleed to death? Frightened and irrational, I called out again: "It's a five-hundred-ton bomb! Yaeko-san, where are you? A five-hundred-ton bomb has fallen!"

Yaeko-san, pale and frightened, her clothes torn and blood-stained, emerged from the ruins of our house holding her elbow. Seeing her, I was reassured. My own panic assuaged, I tried to reassure her.

"We'll be all right," I exclaimed. "Only let's get out of here as fast as we can."

She nodded, and I motioned for her to follow me.

The shortest path to the street lay through the house next door so through the house we went—running, stumbling, falling, and then running again until in headlong flight we tripped over something and fell sprawling into the street. Getting to my feet, I discovered that I had tripped over a man's head.

"Excuse me! Excuse me, please!" I cried hysterically.

There was no answer. The man was dead. The head had belonged to a young officer whose body was crushed beneath a massive gate.

We stood in the street, uncertain and afraid, until a house across from us began to sway and then with a rending motion fell almost at our feet. Our own house began to sway, and in a minute it, too, collapsed in a cloud of dust. Other buildings caved in or toppled. Fires sprang up and whipped by a vicious wind began to spread.

It finally dawned on us that we could not stay there in the street, so we turned our steps toward the hospital.[1] Our home was gone; we were wounded and needed treatment; and after all, it was my duty to be with my staff. This latter was an irrational thought—what good could I be to anyone, hurt as I was.

We started out, but after twenty or thirty steps I had to stop. My breath became short, my heart pounded, and my legs gave way under me. An overpowering thirst seized me and I begged Yaeko-san to find me some water. But there was no water to be found. After a little my strength somewhat returned and we were able to go on.

I was still naked, and although I did not feel the least bit of shame, I was disturbed to realize that modesty had deserted me. On rounding a corner we came upon a soldier standing idly in the street. He had a towel draped across his shoulder, and I asked if he would give it to me to cover my nakedness. The soldier surrendered the towel quite willingly but said not a word. A little later I lost the towel, and Yaeko-san took off her apron and tied it around my loins.

Our progress towards the hospital was interminably slow, until finally, my legs, stiff from drying blood, refused to carry me farther. The strength, even the will, to go on deserted me, so I told my wife, who was almost as badly hurt

---

[1] Dr. Hachiya's home was only a few hundred meters from the hospital.

as I, to go on alone. This she objected to, but there was no choice. She had to go ahead and try to find someone to come back for me.

Yaeko-san looked into my face for a moment, and then, without saying a word, turned away and began running towards the hospital. Once, she looked back and waved and in a moment she was swallowed up in the gloom. It was quite dark now, and with my wife gone, a feeling of dreadful loneliness overcame me.

I must have gone out of my head lying there in the road because the next thing I recall was discovering that the clot on my thigh had been dislodged and blood was again spurting from the wound. I pressed my hand to the bleeding area and after a while the bleeding stopped and I felt better.

Could I go on?

I tried. It was all a nightmare—my wounds, the darkness, the road ahead. My movements were ever so slow; only my mind was running at top speed.

In time I came to an open space where the houses had been removed to make a fire lane. Through the dim light I could make out ahead of me the hazy outlines of the Communications Bureau's big concrete building, and beyond it the hospital. My spirits rose because I knew that now some one would find me; and if I should die, at least my body would be found.

I paused to rest. Gradually things around me came into focus. There were the shadowy forms of people, some of whom looked like walking ghosts. Others moved as though in pain, like scarecrows, their arms held out from their bodies with forearms and hands dangling. These people puzzled me until I suddenly realized that they had been burned and were holding their arms out to prevent the painful friction of raw surfaces rubbing together. A naked woman carrying a naked baby came into view. I averted my gaze. Perhaps they had been in the bath. But then I saw a naked man, and it occurred to me that, like myself, some strange thing had deprived them of their clothes. An old woman lay near me with an expression of suffering on her face; but she made no sound. Indeed, one thing was common to everyone I saw—complete silence.

All who could were moving in the direction of the hospital. I joined in the dismal parade when my strength was somewhat recovered, and at last reached the gates of the Communications Bureau.

Familiar surroundings, familiar faces. There was Mr. Iguchi and Mr. Yoshihiro and my old friend, Mr. Sera, the head of the business office. They hastened to give me a hand, their expressions of pleasure changing to alarm when they saw that I was hurt. I was too happy to see them to share their concern.

No time was lost over greetings. They eased me onto a stretcher and carried me into the Communications Building, ignoring my protest that I could walk. Later, I learned that the hospital was so overrun that the Communications Bureau had to be used as an emergency hospital. The rooms and corridors were crowded with people, many of whom I recognized as neighbors. To me it seemed that the whole community was there.

My friends passed me through an open window into a janitor's room recently converted to an emergency first-aid station. The room was a shambles; fallen plaster, broken furniture, and debris littered the floor; the walls were cracked; and a heavy steel window casement was twisted and almost wrenched from its seating. What a place to dress the wounds of the injured.

To my great surprise who should appear but my private nurse, Miss Kado, and Mr. Mizoguchi, and old Mrs. Saeki. Miss Kado set about examining my wounds without speaking a word. No one spoke. I asked for a shirt and pajamas. They got them for me, but still no one spoke. Why was everyone so quiet?

Miss Kado finished the examination, and in a moment it felt as if my chest was on fire. She had begun to paint my wounds with iodine and no amount of entreaty would make her stop. With no alternative but to endure the iodine, I tried to divert myself by looking out the window.

The hospital lay directly opposite with part of the roof and the third floor sunroom in plain view, and as I looked up, I witnessed a sight which made me forget my smarting wounds. Smoke was pouring out of the sunroom windows. The hospital was afire!

"Fire!" I shouted. "Fire! Fire! The hospital is on fire!"

My friends looked up. It was true. The hospital *was* on fire.

The alarm was given and from all sides people took up the cry. The high-pitched voice of Mr. Sera, the business officer, rose above the others, and it seemed as if his was the first voice I had heard that day. The uncanny still-ness was broken. Our little world was now in pandemonium.

I remember that Dr. Sasada, chief of the Pediatric Service, came in and tried to reassure me, but I could scarcely hear him above the din. I heard Dr. Hinoi's voice and then Dr. Koyama's. Both were shouting orders to evacu-ate the hospital and with such vigor that it sounded as though the sheer strength of their voices could hasten those who were slow to obey.

The sky became bright as flames from the hospital mounted. Soon the Bureau was threatened and Mr. Sera gave the order to evacuate. My stretcher was moved into a rear garden and placed beneath an old cherry tree. Other patients limped into the garden or were carried until soon the entire area became so crowded that only the very ill had room to lie down. No one talked, and the ominous silence was relieved only by a subdued rustle among so many people, restless, in pain, anxious, and afraid, waiting for something else to happen.

The sky filled with black smoke and glowing sparks. Flames rose and the heat set currents of air in motion. Updrafts became so violent that sheets of zinc roofing were hurled aloft and released, humming and twirling, in erratic flight. Pieces of flaming wood soared and fell like fiery swallows. While I was trying to beat out the flames, a hot ember seared my ankle. It was all I could do to keep from being burned alive.

The Bureau started to burn, and window after window became a square of flame until the whole structure was converted into a crackling, hissing inferno.

Scorching winds howled around us, whipping dust and ashes into our eyes and up our noses. Our mouths became dry, our throats raw and sore from the biting smoke pulled into our lungs. Coughing was uncontrollable. We would have moved back, but a group of wooden barracks behind us caught fire and began to burn like tinder.

The heat finally became too intense to endure, and we were left no choice but to abandon the garden. Those who could fled; those who could not perished. Had it not been for my devoted friends, I would have died, but again, they came to the rescue and carried my stretcher to the main gate on the other side of the Bureau.

Here, a small group of people were already clustered, and here I found my wife. Dr. Sasada and Miss Kado joined us.

Fires sprang up on every side as violent winds fanned flames from one building to another. Soon, we were surrounded. The ground we held in front of the Communications Bureau became an oasis in a desert of fire. As the flames came closer the heat became more intense, and if someone in our group had not had the presence of mind to drench us with water[2] from a fire hose, I doubt if anyone could have survived.

Hot as it was, I began to shiver. The drenching was too much. My heart pounded; things began to whirl until all before me blurred.

"*Kurushii*," I murmured weakly. "I am done."

The sound of voices reached my ears as though from a great distance and finally became louder as if close at hand. I opened my eyes; Dr. Sasada was feeling my pulse. What had happened? Miss Kado gave me an injection. My strength gradually returned. I must have fainted.

Huge raindrops began to fall. Some thought a thunderstorm was beginning and would extinguish the fires. But these drops were capricious. A few fell and then a few more and that was all the rain we saw.[3]

The first floor of the Bureau was now ablaze and flames were spreading rapidly towards our little oasis by the gate. Right then, I could hardly understand the situation, much less do anything about it.

An iron window frame, loosened by fire, crashed to the ground behind us. A ball of fire whizzed by me, setting my clothes ablaze. They drenched me with water again. From then on I am confused as to what happened.

I do remember Dr. Hinoi because of the pain, the pain I felt when he jerked me to my feet. I remember being moved or rather dragged, and my whole spirit rebelling against the torment I was made to endure.

My next memory is of an open area. The fires must have receded. I was alive. My friends had somehow managed to rescue me again.

A head popped out of an air-raid dugout, and I heard the unmistakable

---

[2] The water mains entered the city from the north and since the Communications Bureau was in the northern edge of the city, its water supply was not destroyed.

[3] There were many reports of a scanty rainfall over the city after the bombing. The drops were described as large and dirty, and some claimed that they were laden with radioactive dust.

voice of old Mrs. Saeki: "Cheer up, doctor! Everything will be all right. The
north side is burnt out. We have nothing further to fear from the fire."

I might have been her son, the way the old lady calmed and reassured me.
And indeed, she was right. The entire northern side of the city was com-
pletely burned. The sky was still dark, but whether it was evening or midday
I could not tell. It might even have been the next day. Time had no meaning.
What I had experienced might have been crowded into a moment or been
endured through the monotony of eternity.

Smoke was still rising from the second floor of the hospital, but the fire
had stopped. There was nothing left to burn, I thought; but later I learned
that the first floor of the hospital had escaped destruction largely through the
courageous efforts of Dr. Koyama and Dr. Hinoi.

The streets were deserted except for the dead. Some looked as if they had
been frozen by death while in the full action of flight; others lay sprawled as
though some giant had flung them to their death from a great height.

Hiroshima was no longer a city, but a burnt-over prairie. To the east and
to the west everything was flattened. The distant mountains seemed nearer
than I could ever remember. The hills of Ushita and the woods of Nigitsu
loomed out of the haze and smoke like the nose and eyes on a face. How
small Hiroshima was with its houses gone.

The wind changed and the sky again darkened with smoke.

Suddenly, I heard someone shout: "Planes! Enemy planes!"

Could that be possible after what had already happened? What was there
left to bomb? My thoughts were interrupted by the sound of a familiar name.

A nurse calling Dr. Katsube.

"It is Dr. Katsube! It's him!" shouted old Mrs. Saeki, a happy ring to her
voice. "Dr. Katsube has come!"

It was Dr. Katsube, our head surgeon, but he seemed completely unaware
of us as he hurried past, making a straight line for the hospital. Enemy planes
were forgotten, so great was our happiness that Dr. Katsube had been spared
to return to us.

Before I could protest, my friends were carrying me into the hospital. The
distance was only a hundred meters, but it was enough to cause my heart to
pound and make me sick and faint.

I recall the hard table and the pain when my face and lip were sutured,
but I have no recollection of the forty or more other wounds Dr. Katsube
closed before night.

They removed me to an adjoining room, and I remember feeling relaxed
and sleepy. The sun had gone down, leaving a dark red sky. The red flames
of the burning city had scorched the heavens. I gazed at the sky until sleep
overtook me.

Is This Our Life?

BERNARD ROSENBERG

All men are equal, only some are more equal than others. By the same token, man's situation is always extreme, only sometimes it is more extreme. If we ever thought that, although human beings were individually mortal, the species itself was immortal, even this illusion has been shattered and taken from us.

This reflection is probably to be found on a subliminal level everywhere in the world, and it is brought to the foreground of our consciousness by a book like Michihiko Hachiyas' *Hiroshima Diary.*

Juding from some of the reviews, *Hiroshima Diary* is being used rather widely as an anodyne to what might otherwise be guilt feelings. Dr. Hachiya, himself a victim—with no fewer than one hundred and fifty separate little wounds—absolves America for having dropped the bomb. No survivor of Nagasaki has so far thanked us for the second, more destructive and even less justified explosion. Actually, about Nagasaki there is nothing but silence; perhaps some sense of residual guilt lies behind the absence of a Nagasaki Diary.

If so, the American will have to look far to find it. He will surely have to look beyond the memoirs of Harry Truman, who has reaffirmed his conviction that we had to use the bombs, not by dropping them first, let us say, on a desert island and thus advertising their power, but just as they were used. Rexford Tugwell has remembered that "When Harry S. Truman had to decide whether the United States should produce H bombs, he was acting as our surrogate. We were and are in it with him. That he had to do it for us does not entitle us to blame him—not unless we can honestly say we would have decided differently." One wishes that there were even a little more depth to Truman so that by now, at least, he could realize the awesomeness of his initial decision. But apart from that, today we are all equally implicated. This is the burden our frail ethic must bear. Is it not obscene that so many should shrug off the whole matter and that some should even find solace in Dr. Hachiya's searing description?

His book reads like a highly contrived allegory with Dr. Hachiya as Everyman. The diarist reports bad nocturnal dreams—which are no worse than the real experiences he has just had. One envelopes the other until we have been drawn into a phantasmagoric but unendurably real world. The Western reader cannot but be reminded of Franz Kafka. With only a trifling change

SOURCE: Bernard Rosenberg, "Is This Our Life?" A Review of Michihiko Hachiya, *Hiroshima Diary. Dissent* (Summer, 1957), vol. iv, no. 3. Reprinted by permission.

of the symptoms that are noted, the following passage from Kafka's prophetic story, "A Country Doctor," could as easily have come from this journal:

Yes, now I see that the boy is really sick. In his right side, near the hip, he has a wound as big as a dinner plate. In many shades of pink, darker beneath the surface, lighter at the edges, scabby, unevenly congealed with blood, it is as wide open as a mine pit. I see that from a distance. Close up there is still another obstacle. It is enough to make one whistle. Rosy worms, the thickness and length of my finger, spattered with blood, with little white heads and innumerable legs, crawl around in the wound, held fast in the putrefaction.

This flight of the "diseased imagination" is qualitatively no different from what Dr. Hachiya saw minutes after the people of Hiroshima were incinerated. Bodies that were burned and swollen, sheets of skin peeled away from their tissues as they glistened with ugly secretions; blood-stained pus; human beings without eyes, noses, or mouths, who looked as if their ears had melted off. Nevertheless, to be featureless, faceless, was perhaps less merciful a fate than to be headless. "Getting to my feet, I discovered that I had tripped over a man's head. 'Excuse me, excuse me, please,' I cried hysterically. There was no answer. The man was dead. The head had belonged to a young officer whose body was crushed beneath a massive gate." Where does *wahrheit* end and *dichtung* begin?

Dr. Hachiya's purity of style and economy of expression are also reminiscent of Kafka, although they no doubt stem from such poetic forms as the *haiku* in which he is well versed. This man must be regarded as an artist: he agonizes over the esthetic adequacy of a medical report, and afterwards, regrets that he ever rushed into print with his manuscript. When, therefore, Dr. Hachiya compares the creatures around him with scarecrows, dry codfish, or rats, we know how carefully he has selected his metaphor. And, again, the vision of man transformed into an inanimate object or a ravening beast or a paltry insect establishes a transcendent affinity between the Czech novelist and the Japanese physician. Could anyone else have recorded the question asked by a certain Mr. Hirohata who witnessed what survivors in and around Hiroshima called the *pika* or flash-boom? "Doctor," asked Mr. Hirohata, *"a human being who has been roasted becomes quite small, doesn't he?"*

The clinical definition of trauma is a state that results from an overwhelming experience, such as birth or death, which is greater than the psyche's ability to absorb it. Those who were close to the hypocenter in Hiroshima on August 6, 1945 and did not look away as a parachute laden with one bomb fell lazily to earth, simply had their eyes burnt out. The rest of us here and there were traumatized. As a direct result of that unassimilable shock, most men would now be spiritually at home in an Antarctic "whiteout." This climatological phenomenon was described the other day by an Associated Press correspondent as he touched upon one of several hazards connected with a forthcoming international geo-physical expedition:

In a "white-out" the sun's rays slant through snow clouds to create a great white void. The horizon disappears and there is no way to tell right from left, up from down. Men become dizzy and have difficulty standing. It is as if they were suspended inside a bale of cotton.

We are morally and politically, if not spatially, disoriented in just this fashion. Shall we belabor the fool who does not know which way is up when no man can tell for sure, any more than he can distinguish between left and right from one end of a small world to another? The first A bomb produced a huge cloud that rose angrily over Hiroshima "and, on both sides of the main cloud beautiful smaller clouds spread out like a golden screen," says one witness who adds, "I have never seen anything so magnificent in my life." When we are gripped by the universal madness, slaughter and beauty seem logically conjoined. From inside our bales of cotton such a combination produces no great sense of incongruity. The violence of art and the art of violence have frequently been noted in Japanese culture. However, it remained for America to fuse them in one apocalyptic moment of gorgeous annhilation.

In extreme situations, which are a series of traumata bombarding the nervous system, men rapidly lose their special sensitiveness. Dr. Hachiya leaves no doubt that he is a devout and compassionate soul. Still, as the Atomic Age reached its second day, he had already begun to castigate himself for his inhumanity. "In two days I had become at home in this environment of chaos and despair." When there is nothing but sorrow, pain and horror all around us, our emotions are bound to be coarsened, dulled and finally, blunted altogether. If the medical doctor, presumably inured to death and suffering, experiences such a reaction, how much more certain it is to dehumanize the layman.

Bruno Bettelheim has written of long-time political prisoners in Dachau who, under sufficient duress but without the current brain-washing, tended to accept Nazi ideology. They even emulated the SS. A few years ago Harold Orlansky gave us an unforgettable picture of his own brutalization and that of his fellow attendants assigned to work in a mental hospital. We know how a number of inordinately ethical C.O.'s, when subjected to a systematic semi-starvation at the University of Minnesota, took to stealing and lost interest in their outside obligations. (August 15: "After supper, Mr. Mizoguchi, Miss Kado, old Mrs. Saeki and I lingered in the dining room. I learned people were looting the supply dump at the engineering corps. Vandals even came with carts and hauled away everything they could carry. Some of the supplies we received this morning had already been stolen out of the hospital. Hiroshima was becoming a wicked town.") There were even some Jews in the Warsaw ghetto who capitalized on the misery of their fellows—till they too were reduced to inorganic matter.

From the madhouse, the concentration camp, the death factory, the experimental laboratory, and the ruins of a radioactive city, the same hypotheses are regularly validated. Any unduly extreme situation converts men, victims and perpetrators alike, into sub-men, a new species whose life expectancy is not very great.

For acres and acres the city was like a desert except for the scattered piles of brick and roof tile. I had to revise my meaning of the word to describe what I saw. Devastation may be a better word, but really, I know of no word or words to describe the view from my twisted iron bed in the fire-gutted ward of the Communication Hospital.

Finally, there is no vocabulary suited to describe the unutterable. In what language shall we represent Miss Yama, half of whose body was so scorched that she reminded Dr. Hachiya of a dirty plaster doll tossed on a trash heap? Or Dr. Hasada whose badly swollen face looked like a glazed bun sprinkled with white powder? Or Miss Susukida with features twisted into what appeared to be a comic mask?

We can only recoil from the thought of such disfiguration. Last year the Hiroshima Maidens were brought to America: they are here to have their faces lifted so that they may become presentable once more. The young ladies were exhibited over television but only behind screens and in silhouette. The program, which provided an air of absolute fantasticality, was called "This Is Your Life." Heaven help us, this *is* our life.

A Hypothetical Thermonuclear Strike

LEIBA BROWN AND RUTH LEEDS

Instants after the bombs exploded at the earth's surface at each of the 224 target locations, balls of fire formed, emitting highly destructive thermal radiation. Nuclear reactions causing the explosions were accompanied by damaging radiation, much of which remained as part of the fall-out. Minutes after the explosion, a destructive shock wave formed in the air, moving

SOURCE: Leiba Brown and Ruth Leeds, "What the Bombs Can Do," in Amitai Etzioni, *The Hard Way to Peace* (New York: Collier Books, 1962), pp. 270–275. Reprinted by permission.

EDITORS' NOTE: Based on testimony by military and scientific experts who were asked by a Congressional committee to describe the effects of a possible attack. It was assumed that enemy bombs (atomic and thermonuclear) with explosive force equivalent to 1,500 megatons of TNT were dropped on 71 urban areas within the continental United States, plus 153 other strategic targets, on October 17, 1958. Casualties, as calculated, totalled 70 million—23 million killed instantly, 28 million wounded who later died of their injuries, and 19 million wounded who recovered. (Joint Committee on Atomic Energy, Congress of the United States, *Biological and Environmental Effects of Nuclear War* [Washington, D.C.: U.S. Government Printing Office, 1959]).

rapidly away from the fireballs and leveling everything in its path. The fireballs excavated highly radioactive craters where they came to rest, and, as if they possessed a magic wand, all they touched vaporized.

EFFECTS ON PHYSICAL STRUCTURES

BLAST DAMAGE. Throughout the country, a quarter of the homes—11,800,000 dwelling units—were completely demolished. Another eight million were badly damaged but could be made habitable again with major repairs. Still another 500,000 buildings sustained light damage. In buildings where total destruction had not reaped its toll, the shock wave broke gas lines and fuel tanks, upset stoves and furnaces, and short-circuited wiring, so that severe fire damage also resulted from the blast.

Thriving cities were reduced to rubble within seconds. When a ten-megaton bomb exploded in New York at Rockefeller Center, all buildings without steel supports, within a radius of seven and a half miles collapsed completely. Multistory brick apartment houses were mowed down. Wood-frame houses and stores within a nine-mile radius fell like the proverbial house of cards. Bridges within a three-and-a-half-mile zone were destroyed and, within ten miles, telephone and power lines were out of commission. In short, most buildings and communication and transportation networks, so vital for survival and evacuation, were demolished.

EFFECTS OF THERMAL RADIATION. The heat emitted by the fireball ignited most combustible materials within the destruction zone (up to twenty-five miles for a ten-megaton bomb). Any accessible paper, trash, window curtains, awnings and leaves caught fire immediately. Flames spread rapidly through the crowded wholesale districts and the slums. In some areas, depending on local weather and terrain, "fire storms" raged with unconquerable fury through woods and towns.

EFFECTS OF THE CRATER. Where the fireball touched the earth, it sucked up all beneath it, leaving a cavernous hole. All underground shelters, subways and other subterranean installations within the quarter-mile radius of the crater were destroyed, for the crater at its deepest was 240 feet.

EFFECTS OF FALL-OUT. Many buildings that were left standing were contaminated by radiation and thereby rendered temporarily useless for human purposes. The radioactive fall-out affected about thirteen million homes, making them uninhabitable for at least two months.

The physical damage caused by the attack, although far-reaching in its impact, did not turn the United States into the utter wasteland it became in Nevil Shute's *On the Beach*. Roughly one-third of the homes were still intact, and many of the roads could be used for travel. But our economic, political, cultural, religious, and medical centers, as well as our communications system, were ruined.

EFFECTS ON MAN

Casualties caused by the impact of the air shock waves could not be isolated from deaths and injuries by fire and radiation. The blast directly hit persons close to ground zero, inflicting serious injury to lungs, stomach, intestines, eardrums, and the central nervous system. These same persons were also the most likely to be hit by flying debris, trapped by fire, or buried by collapsing buildings. Within a seven-mile radius of a ten-megaton burst, the secondary effects of blast accounted for many deaths.

THERMAL EFFECTS. Within a twenty-five mile radius of ground zero, any survivor who was out of doors when the bomb exploded sustained second-degree flash burns on his exposed skin. The thermal radiation ignited his clothing as well, causing severe flame burns. While the fire storms raged, many were trapped in burning buildings, suffocating from the inhalation of acrid fumes.

RADIATION EFFECTS. Nuclear radiation is measured in rems. A rem is that amount of radiation required to produce a biological effect equivalent to that of one roentgen of x-ray. A single dosage of up to 220 rems will cause nausea and vomiting for about a day, but it is not fatal. If a population is exposed to a dosage of 270 to 330 rems, about 20 per cent of the group will die within two to six weeks following exposure. The remaining 80 per cent will recover, following a three-month bout with radiation sickness. With a dosage of 550 rems or more, chances of survival are very slim, and recovery takes about six months for those few who do survive. A dosage of 1000 rems is virtually lethal.

The number of rems released in a nuclear explosion is determined by its location (air, surface, or underground) its tonnage, and its "cleanliness." The so-called clean nuclear warheads do not release enough energy to explode the highly destructive element, Uranium 238, but they do explode other elements that yield radioactive particles of Carbon 14 and Strontium 90. The "dirty" bombs, on the other hand, have the capacity to unleash Uranium 238. Once exploded, U-238 releases additional energy and an immense quantity of exceedingly poisonous fall-out. Thus, a "dirty" ten-megaton bomb gives off enough rems to kill a man within 140 miles of ground zero if he remains outside for thirty-six hours. The fifteen-megaton "superbomb" tested at Bikini in 1954 contained U-238, and its fall-out was responsible for the radiation sickness of the Japanese fishermen eighty miles from the test site. (Although the Congressional report on which our account is based did not state explicitly whether clean or dirty bombs were used, the weight of current reputable information suggests that most of the weapons tested, if not all, were dirty bombs. The report's fall-out statistics hold only for dirty bombs.)

The bombs the United States is likely to be bombed with will probably not be "clean," because Russia—as far as we know—does not know how to produce "clean" bombs, and the West refused to tell her how to "clean" them.

Initial nuclear radiation effects. Each ten-megaton explosion instantaneously released 700 rem, covering a two-mile radius from ground zero. All unsheltered and unshielded persons within this area received a lethal dose of radiation. But anyone this close to ground zero was equally likely to succumb to blast or fire.

Local fall-out effects. Local fall-out is caused by those radioactive particles which descend to earth within several hundred miles of ground zero and within a few days of the explosion. Its damaging effects are greatly influenced by local weather, altitude, and terrain, and must be calculated separately for each region of the country.

Regardless of local conditions, the effects of fall-out were not felt immediately. The unsheltered and unshielded persons within 150 miles downwind from ground zero and within twenty-five miles of the crosswinds around the crater received at least 450 rems within forty-eight hours. These were the persons most likely to die or to be seriously ill for many months. But those who were able to spend the few days following the explosion indoors or could leave the areas vulnerable to fall-out had a good chance for survival, and, if taken ill, had a relatively quick recovery.

Worldwide fall-out. The effect of worldwide fall-out cannot be calculated precisely even for a specific set of conditions, with place, time, weather, altitude, terrain, density of buildings, and the like held constant. We do know that worldwide fall-out leads to additional deaths by increasing a person's long-term susceptibility to such diseases as cancer. Long after the nuclear attack, then, the survivors continue to be exposed to additional radiation, which would eventually shorten the lives of some of them.

Genetic effects. Approximately four out of 100 babies presently are born with defects, some of which were caused by damaged genes. To prevent an increase in the present 4 per cent rate of defective births, each person's gonads should sustain less than ten roentgens of radiation during his first thirty years of life, and no more than ten roentgens during each succeeding decade. Should radiation dosages increase on a mass scale, so that every American receives the ten-roentgen limit, the rate of defective births would increase by four per thousand in the first generation and by four per hundred in future generations.

The amount of cumulative radiation experienced by each of the survivors of the October 17 nuclear attack was about 250 to 500 roentgens. If we assume that genetically defective births increase at the same rate as the increase in exposure to radiation, then the rate of defective births would increase by at least 25 per cent. Furthermore, the genes damaged by fall-out would continue to be inherited by the next twenty to forty generations, carrying the curse of fall-out from generation to generation until we are remembered only as the children-torturer generation.

HOW FAR AWAY IS "SAFE"?

When we played hide-and-seek as children, the closer to base we hid, the easier it was to come home safely. But in a nuclear bombardment, as the figures in Table 1 indicate, "safe" is relatively far from ground zero.

TABLE 1 . *The Distance to Safe Territory*
Figures are estimates, calculated on the basis
of weather conditions for October 17, 1958

	DISTANCE FROM GROUND ZERO	
EFFECT	ONE MEGATON	TEN MEGATONS
Inanimate objects		
Crater (dry soil)	Radius 650 feet	Radius 1250 feet
	Depth 140 feet	Depth 240 feet
Brick apartment houses collapse	Radius 3 miles	Radius 7 miles
Ignition of light kindling materials	Radius 9 miles	Radius 25 miles
Man		
Blast injury (flying debris)	Radius 3 miles	Radius 7 miles
	Area 28 square miles	Area 150 square miles
Second degree burns on bare skin	Radius 9 miles	Radius 25 miles
	Area 250 square miles	Area 2000 square miles
Initial nuclear radiation (700 rem)	Radius 1½ miles	Radius 2 miles
	Area 7 square miles	Area 12½ square miles
Fallout: 15 knot winds (450 rem in 48 hours), no shielding	40 miles downwind	150 miles downwind
	5 miles crosswinds	25 miles crosswinds
	Area 200 square miles	Area 2500 square miles

Let us suppose Rockefeller Center was ground zero for a ten-megaton bomb. To be safe from initial nuclear radiation, one would have to be at least as far downtown as the garment district, or as far uptown as the Museum of Natural History, or as far across town as the other side of the East River. To escape falling buildings and flying debris, one would have to be at least as far as the Bronx Zoo, the Statue of Liberty, or Forest Hills. To be spared second-degree burns, one would have to be as distant as Jones Beach or Greenwich, Connecticut. For safety from local fall-out, one would have to be in Rutland, Vermont, or Fort Ticonderoga, New York, to the north, or Lewistown, Pennsylvania, to the west, or the Atlantic Ocean to the east. One would not be safe south of New York, for then one would suffer the effects of the bombs dropped on Philadelphia, Baltimore, and Washington, D. C.

If one were in Rutland, Lewistown, or Ticonderoga, one would probably escape direct personal injury. The likelihood of getting radiation sickness from local fall-out is comparatively slight. Moreover, if one's home is in one of these towns, it will be untouched by blast or fire. But a "safe" distance from ground zero by no means assures immunity from the effects of nuclear war. The lucky people live in one of those towns not hit, out of the blow of the fall-out carrying winds, and are not on a business trip or vacation in a target area when the bombs come. That is, such persons' bone structure and tissues will not suffer, but they will still never be the same again. Less fortunate relatives—perhaps brothers, sisters, parents—will have perished in a thermonuclear cloud; many millions of one's fellow citizens will have vanished; America will be lying in ruins. Actually, a survivor might not consider himself lucky at all.

EDITORS' EPILOGUE: What happens when the bombs get bigger? Under certain conditions, as the authors point out, a 100 mt bomb (only half again as powerful as the one the Russians exploded over Siberia in 1961) could set off a fire storm capable of engulfing 11,000 square miles, an area larger than the state of Vermont. Aside from thermal and blast effects—and 100 mt is by no means the technological upper limit on size—radiation yield could be greatly stepped up by building the completely feasible "dirty" bomb (with a shell of cobalt, sodium oxide, or similar substances), or the as yet-undeveloped neutron bomb. And delivery systems are constantly being improved: the newer missiles are larger, less vulnerable, and more reliable than earlier generations, and they require less reaction time. Above all, of course, not only are *their* numbers increasing, but the number of political sovereignties that possess bombs and the means of delivering them is almost certain to increase. Terrible as it was, the hypothetical attack described above is based on assumptions long since obsolete.

Fallout: I Feel It in My Bones

ISAAC ASIMOV

The presidential campaign of 1956 introduced a new word to the American public: *strontium-90*. And ever since then, the sound of the word has been growing louder and louder.

What exactly is strontium-90? Or, to begin with, what exactly is strontium?

SOURCE: Isaac Asimov, "I Feel It in My Bones," *Fantasy and Science Fiction*, 13:6 (December, 1957). Copyright © 1957 by Mercury Press, Inc. Reprinted by permission from the December, 1957, issue of *The Magazine of Fantasy and Science Fiction*.

EDITORS' NOTE: Except for minor deletions (made by the author) this is the original article. The fact that it first appeared six years ago should be borne in mind by the reader. However, in our judgment, the essentials of the argument are as valid today as they were then.

Strontium is a chemical element first isolated in 1808. In the century and a half since then, strontium has the rather odd distinction of having remained one of the most nearly useless elements in the entire list.

Strontium nitrate, when heated in a flame, gives that flame a bright red color, so that it is used in railroad flares and in fireworks. Strontium oxide has a minor application in sugar-refining and strontium bromide and strontium iodide have very limited medical uses. That about exhausts the list.

But strontium has one fatal property which all chemists knew about from the beginning but which no chemist ever suspected (until this decade) would have such awesome consequences for the human race.

Strontium, you see, has chemical properties that are very similar to the more familiar and infinitely more useful element, calcium. The strontium atom is a little over twice as heavy as the calcium atom but that is the only difference worth mentioning. Almost anything the calcium atom will do, the strontium atom, in more lumbering fashion, will also do.

Living creatures have learned to utilize calcium compounds in a number of ways. Calcium is an indispensable factor in the clotting of blood and in the cement that keeps cells glued together. The bones of all vertebrates (including man) are made up chiefly of calcium phosphate. The shells of molluscs and of birds' eggs are calcium carbonate.

Presumably, living things might have learned to use strontium compounds as easily and have done about as well, except that there seems no point to it. Strontium atoms occur in the soil and ocean much less commonly than do calcium atoms. In fact, in the Earth's crust generally there is only one strontium atom for every four hundred calcium atoms. Why bother looking for that one strontium when there are four hundred calciums available?[1]

So strontium is not necessary to life and is not found in living tissue except as an accidental contaminant.

In fact, no chemistry textbook, except the largest and most comprehensive, ever devoted more than a paragraph to strontium; and a paragraph is all it was worth.

That is, until 1944.

Now for the "90" part of strontium-90. Every strontium atom has in its nucleus exactly 38 protons, no more and no less. In addition, the nucleus contains a certain number of neutrons. The neutron number, however, is not fixed, but varies from atom to atom. Some strontium atoms contain 46 neutrons in their nucleus, some contain 48, some 49 and some 50. If we count in the 38 protons present in each case, it means that some strontium

---

[1] And yet just to show that it can be done and that old Mother Nature is still the best science fiction writer of them all, there is a species of shellfish in the Great Lakes (so I am told) that fashions its shell out of strontium carbonate. Why it should go to the bother of sieving the rare strontium out of the waters and how it manages to latch on to it, to the exclusion of the so-similar calcium, no one knows.

atoms have a total of 84 particles in the nucleus, some 86, some 87 and some 88.

To distinguish these varieties of strontium atoms, the nuclear chemist speaks of strontium-84, strontium-86, strontium-87 and strontium-88.[2] To the ordinary chemist, however, these varieties (called *isotopes*) are strictly yawn-worthy. The four strontium isotopes are practically identical in chemical behavior. All four are equally useless.

Only these four strontium isotopes exist in nature. Nuclear chemists, however, by bombarding atoms with speeding sub-atomic particles have managed to put together strontium atoms with anywhere from 43 to 59 neutrons.

None of these additional strontium isotopes, these man-made varieties, are stable. The nucleus of one of these artificial isotopes will, even if left strictly alone, explode in various ways and emit particles. In doing so, it changes its nuclear composition to some stable arrangement of protons and neutrons. Then, and only then, does the atom quiet down, and when it does so, it is no longer strontium of any variety.

Now strontium-90 is one of the man-made strontium isotopes. Its nucleus contains 38 protons and 52 neutrons. (38 + 52 = 90) One of the ways in which this isotope may be man-made is through man-arranged uranium fission.

A uranium-235 atom, when struck by a neutron under the proper conditions, breaks approximately in half. It doesn't always break in exactly the same way, so that up to 170 different isotopes are formed in the process with anywhere from 72 to 161 particles in their nuclei. One of these isotopes is strontium-90 and, as a matter of fact, it is one of the more frequent isotopes formed, making up about 5 per cent of the total.

All the isotopes so formed, the *fission fragments*, including strontium-90, are unstable. All emit energetic particles, changing their atomic identity as they do so.

As long as the subject of uranium fission has arisen, let's follow it up. It will lead us back to strontium-90; you can be sure of that.

The explosion of a nuclear bomb presents the population in the vicinity with three kinds of immediate danger, and the population of the Earth generally with a fourth kind of delayed danger. The three immediate dangers are 1) blast, 2) heat, and 3) radiation.

Blast and heat are the familiar accompaniments of ordinary bombs, but are much magnified in nuclear bombs. The radiation is something newer and uglier. It consists of x-rays and gamma rays speeding outward from the explosion, shouldering their way through any living tissue that they strike and often disrupting vital chemical processes in doing so. If disruption is

---

[2] Every sample of strontium or its compounds contains some of each of these varieties. Out of every 10,000 strontium atoms chosen at random, the inquiring chemist would find 8,256 strontium-88 atoms, 987 strontium-86 atoms, 702 strontium-87 atoms and 55 strontium-84 atoms.

sufficient, *radiation sickness* is the result and, in extreme cases, death. It depends on the dose.

However, the burst of dangerous radiation that accompanies a nuclear bomb explosion lasts only a minute or so.

That leaves the fourth danger, the delayed danger, the great danger.

The unstable (*i.e.*, *radioactive*) fission fragments formed by an exploding nuclear bomb are blown up into the atmosphere by the familiar fireball and mushroom cloud we have all seen on television or in photographs. Eventually, the fragments come to Earth again and it is this settling back of fission fragments that is called *fallout*.

There are three types of fallout, depending on the size of the bomb and its position when exploded. If a nuclear bomb is exploded at ground level, the fission fragments are all bound up with relatively large particles of soil and settle back to Earth speedily, and usually within a hundred miles of the blast. This is *local fallout*.

A bomb exploded in the air will, if it is a small one in the *kiloton* range (that is, equivalent in explosive force to a mere thousand tons or so of dynamite), send its radioactive debris into the lower atmosphere (the *troposphere*) unmixed with soil particles. The prevailing westerly winds will carry it eastward for hundreds or even thousands of miles and it will settle out within one or two months, mainly in the latitude in which the bomb was originally exploded. This is the *tropospheric fallout*.

A large bomb exploded in the air, one in the *megaton range* (that is, equivalent in explosive force to a million tons or more of dynamite), will send radioactive material still higher. The stratosphere will be reached. Once in the stratosphere, the fission fragments will remain there for years, being carried by the jet streams to all corners of the Earth and slowly, little by little, coming to Earth again—everywhere. This is the *stratospheric fallout*.[3]

Now what are the dangers of fallout?

The radioactive fission fragments produced in a nuclear explosion become stable by emitting very energetic electrons from the nucleus (and sometimes gamma rays as well). The collision of those electrons with living tissue can produce radiation sickness and, depending on the dose, death.

The danger of a particular type of unstable atom depends upon the force with which those electrons are sprayed outward and the number being emitted in a given time.

---

[3] There has been talk of developing "clean" H-bombs; that is, H-bombs that will, on explosion, yield a non-radioactive fallout.

Hydrogen fusion itself does not result in any radioactivity to speak of. However, in order to get hydrogen atoms to fuse to helium, they must first be heated to millions of degrees Centigrade. The way that is done is to use a uranium fission bomb to produce the heat and act as a trigger for the hydrogen fusion bomb. It is from the exploding fission bomb that radioactive fragments are derived.

To reduce the radioactivity, we must figure out a way to reduce the size of the uranium fission bomb trigger. Better still, a method might be devised for reaching the required temperatures by some means other than uranium fission. (Alternate methods do exist in theory.)

Some atoms are very unstable and break down rapidly; some are less unstable and breakdown rather slowly. The measure of the instability of a particular type of atom is its *half-life*; that is, the time it takes for half the atoms in a quantity of a particular type to break down.

All things being equal, a heap of atoms with short half-lives spray more electrons (or other particles or radiation) into the surrounding space than does a similar heap of atoms with long half-lives. Thus, it would seem that a short-lived atom would be more likely to cause radiation sickness than would a long-lived atom.

So it would . . . at first.

The very energy and enthusiasm with which short-lived atoms break up means that after a while none or practically none is left. Atoms with half-lives of only a few seconds (which includes many of the fission fragments) are gone with the fireball and so can do no damage to anyone not so close to the explosion as to be consumed by blast and heat at once.

Even atoms that have half-lives of a few days or weeks can have only local effects. They are gone by the time tropospheric fallout comes to Earth. The electrons have been expended harmlessly several miles up and it is the stable descendants of those atoms that settle down.

But there are also long-lived atoms among the fission fragments and these must also be considered. Their radiations are weaker and they are less dangerous than the short-lived atoms to begin with. But the long-lived atoms hang around. An atom with a half-life of six weeks, say, will still be around in fair quantities when the tropospheric fallout comes to Earth. An atom with a half-life of ten years will linger in dangerous amounts when even the stratospheric fallout comes to Earth. An atom with a half-life of thirty years will not only be around when the stratospheric fallout comes down, but will be still with us in annoying quantity a century after it comes down.

If the half-life were *too* long, say, a few thousand years, the radiation effects would last enormously long but would be so weak as to constitute little if any danger.

This is the way it works out, then:

(1) Fission fragments with *very short* half-lives are extremely intense radiators but are not dangerous because they don't last long. (Not dangerous, that is, to mankind as a whole.)

(2) Fission fragments with *very long* half-lives last a long time but are not dangerous because they are very weak radiators.

(3) Fission fragments with *intermediate* half-lives are strong enough radiators to be dangerous and last long enough to be dangerous, too.

It is the third category that we must worry about.

There are just two types of fission fragments that fit neatly into category three. These are cesium-137 and strontium-90. And of these two, strontium-90 is by far the more dangerous, for several reasons.

Cesium-137 and strontium-90 have about equal half-lives (30 years for cesium-137 and 28 years for strontium-90) so that one might think they were equally dangerous. A cesium-137 atom, however, breaks down by emitting one electron, becoming in this fashion a stable atom of barium-137.

A strontinum-90 atom, on the other hand, breaks down by emitting *two* electrons, becoming in this fashion a stable atom of zirconium-90. The double dose of strontium-90 electrons is even worse than it sounds since the strontium-90 electrons are individually more energetic than the cesium-137 electrons and can therefore do more damage.[4]

Secondly, if cesium-137 happens to get into the body (where, being right in the center of things, it can do the most damage), it doesn't stay there long. Cesium atoms do not occur naturally in the body and the body has no use for them.

To be sure, cesium atoms bear a strong chemical resemblance to the much smaller sodium and potassium atoms (which do occur in the body and are necessary to its functioning) but these related atoms undergo rapid turnover. That is, they are taken in and eliminated by the body fairly rapidly so that while sizable amounts of sodium and potassium are always in the body, any particular sodium or potassium atom doesn't stay in the body very long.

Therefore, even if the cesium-137 tried to get by on its relationship to sodium and potassium, it wouldn't linger in the body. The level of cesium-137 in the body at any particular moment would remain very low; so low that the danger of the speeding electrons it emits would be virtually zero.

How different for strontium-90. Here is where the similarity to calcium is devastating. There is a turnover of calcium in the body, too, just as in the case of sodium or potassium. However, 99.5 per cent of the body's relatively large supply of calcium (which may be as much as 3 pounds or more) is in the bones. Bone is a sluggish tissue and while turnover of atoms in it exists, it is very slow. A particular calcium atom in bone may remain there a long time, even years.

The method by which strontium-90 gets into the body is simple enough. To begin with, the strontium-90 settles onto the soil along with the rest of the fallout. Vegetation growing in the soil absorbs the strontium-90 along with

---

[4] A still more damaging isotope that many of us have heard of is *cobalt-60*. The cobalt-60 atom emits only a single electron in breaking to the stable nickel-60 atom. However, its half-life is 5.3 years so that a quantity of cobalt-60 would be emitting just over 2½ times as many electrons as would a similar quantity of strontium-90. This, perhaps, does not sound *too* bad, especially when you consider that the cobalt-60 electrons are less energetic than the strontium-90 electrons.

But cobalt-60 does something that strontium-90 does not do. Cobalt-60 emits gamma rays in addition to electrons, and unusually energetic gamma rays at that. Gamma rays are much more penetrating and can do much more damage than the speeding electrons could.

Fortunately, cobalt-60 is *not* among the fission fragments of ordinary nuclear explosions. However, the grisly suggestion has already been made that a nuclear bomb can be encased in matter that would, under the intense radioactive bombardment of the concentrated fission fragments formed in the first moments of nuclear explosion, be converted to cobalt-60. This would then be spread far and wide in a "super-dirty" fallout.

the calcium it is really after. Animals (including man, of course) which eat the vegetation then take up the strontium-90 along with the calcium they are really after.[5]

When strontium-90 enters the body, the chemical mechanisms of the body make little distinction between it and the very similar calcium. It, too, is deposited in the bones.

And there the strontium-90 atoms remain for years.

And there the strontium-90 atoms accumulate.

Until twenty years ago, strontium-90 existed nowhere on Earth, except perhaps in exceedingly small quantities in the special equipment of a few nuclear physicists. Until twenty years ago, no creature on Earth, in all the long history of life, had any strontium-90 at all in its bones.

Today strontium-90 exists everywhere. An estimated total of 400 pounds of it is spread out over the surface of the Earth while another 1000 pounds is still floating about in the stratosphere.

Of course, this is pretty thin spreading in actual fact and to talk about quantities of strontium-90 in individual human beings, scientists find it convenient to use a much smaller unit of weight than the pound. They use the *Sunshine Unit*, which they abbreviate S.U. (This is so called because the AEC studies of fallout were termed "Project Sunshine.")

One micromicrocurie of strontium-90 for every gram of calcium in one's body is what is meant by 1 S.U. The *curie* is a unit not of mass but of radiation. It was originally defined as the radiation given off by a gram of radium in equilibrium with its emanation (radon). (A gram is about one twenty-eighth of an ounce.) It is now more generally calculated as meaning 37 billion disintegrations per second.

A *micromicrocurie* is one one-trillionth of a curie, or 2.12 disintegrations per minute. This number of disintegrations would result from 45 million atoms of strontium-90.

The body of the average adult male contains 1400 grams of calcium. So a man with 1 S.U. (which, I should add, nobody has reached yet) would have 63 billion atoms of strontium-90, or one two-trillionth of an ounce. Because the S.U. is a unit of radiation-mass ratio, it should be clear that a child, with less mass, can have a smaller amount of strontium-90 than a man but a higher S.U. figure. (And children also acquire strontium-90 more readily, because they deposit calcium in their growing bones more rapidly than adults do.)

Now then, every adult human being on Earth today contains about 0.1 to 0.2 S.U. of strontium-90 scattered throughout the bones of his body.

---

[5] Actually, the major source of calcium in the American diet is milk and cheese. It is therefore also the major source of strontium-90 in the diet. The cow picks up strontium-90 from the grass it eats and pumps the radioactive atoms into the milk along with the calcium that belongs there. The milk industry is as concerned these days about public fears of strontium-90 as is the tobacco industry about its fears of lung cancer.

Children have as much as 0.5 S.U. (Much the same goes for any animal with bones, by the way, not just humans.)

Furthermore, the quantity of strontium-90 in bones must increase, even if all nuclear bomb testing stopped today. There is still the thousand pounds of strontium-90 in the stratosphere that is slowly settling out.

As the body absorbs more strontium-90, a point will be reached where the strontium-90 in the bones will be excreted or will break down at a rate just equal to that at which new strontium-90 is being absorbed. In this way, an equilibrium will be attained.

If no more nuclear bomb testing takes place, this equilibrium will be reached (it is estimated) in about 5 to 10 years and bones will then contain 2 to 3 S.U. If, however, nuclear testing continues at the present rate of about 10 megatons per year, then the equilibrium (it is estimated) won't be reached for fifty or sixty years and bones will then contain somewhere between 16 and 40 S.U. of strontium-90.

All right, so we have less than half an S.U. of strontium-90 in our bones right now. How bad is that?

In some ways, it might seem to be not bad at all. After all, we are exposed continuously to all sorts of energetic radiation and speeding sub-atomic particles just by virtue of being on Earth. When these other radiations are measured in Sunshine Units, the term first devised for measuring strontium-90 absorption, the meaning of 1 S.U. is "the amount of radiation you would get from the equivalent quantity (defined above) of strontium-90."

For instance, the soil is slightly radioactive.[6] If you live in a building, you will pick up the equivalent of 17 S.U. a year more than the amount you would pick up if you lived in a frame house, because brick has higher natural radioactivity than wood has. If your town is a mile high in altitude you will collect the equivalent of 8 S.U. more per year than if you lived at sea-level, because of the additional bombardment of cosmic rays. All in all, the average man picks up a total of 50 S.U. per year from all sources.

Well, then what's another few tenths of an S.U.? Why worry?

The worry, it seems, is in the *location* of the strontium-90 and the fact that it stays put in that location. Radiation and particles from all other natural sources bombard the body from outside (or from a moving position inside) in random fashion. Few significant hits are made (It's like shooting blindfold at a few flies buzzing about in Grand Central Station.)

The strontium-90, however, concentrates all its fire in the region of the bones and the bones have a particularly sensitive spot. The red blood cells

---

[6] The radioactivity of the soil is not just because it contains a scattering of uranium and thorium. Every bit of the soil contains the very common element, potassium, and one of the potassium isotopes, potassium-40, is weakly radioactive. A carbon isotope, carbon-14, is formed in small quantities in the atmosphere by cosmic ray action, and it is radioactive. Both potassium-40 and carbon-14 are in our bodies from birth to death as a consequence.

and some of the white blood cells are formed in the marrow of certain bones and the continuous bombardment of the marrow by high-speed electrons could result in knocking the cell-forming mechanisms awry.

One form of awry-ness will produce the disease known as *leukemia,* a kind of cancer of the blood in which the bone marrow is forming excessive quantities of immature white blood cells. The condition gets progressively worse as these useless white blood cells crowd out the necessary red blood cells and death follows inevitably. As far as we know today, the condition is incurable.

Now it is known that radiation, in general, will cause leukemia. Radiologists (that is, doctors who specialize in x-ray therapy and such things) have an incidence of leukemia ten times that of other doctors.

In 1954, 10,000 people died in the United States of leukemia. Dr. Edward Lewis of California Institute of Technology estimates that about 1000 of these cases were caused by the effects of the general radiation of our environment. (What caused the other 9000? Ha, don't we wish we knew.)

But, were any of the deaths caused by the strontium-90 blasting away at the bone marrow at point-blank range?

That is where the major disagreement among experts lies. Some say strontium-90 has already caused leukemia and some say not. The arguments depend on whether a *threshold of action* does or does not exist.

What do we mean by a threshold of action?

Suppose we have a brick resting on the sidewalk. Push it very gently. Nothing happens. The force of your push is insufficient to overcome the frictional forces between brick and cement.

Push the brick harder. Still nothing. Push it still harder. Ah—now it begins to move.

It takes a certain minimum push to make the brick move at all. After that minimum has been reached, the harder you push the faster the brick moves, but as long as you don't reach the minimum, the brick doesn't move at all. The minimum push required to move the brick is the threshold of action.

The moving-the-brick-on-cement case is an example of an action with a pronounced threshold of action. Suppose, instead, you had a billiard ball on a perfectly smooth glassy surface. The lightest push will set it rolling. You couldn't push it so lightly as not to make it move. (Of course, an exceedingly light push will cause it to roll exceedingly slowly.)

All right, then, consider electrons bombarding the bone marrow. If there is a sizable threshold to this action, it means that as long as there are fewer electrons than a certain minimum, there will be no effect at all on the bone marrow. Only when total electron energy raises itself above that minimum will action start and leukemia become a possibility.

AVERAGE AGE AT DEATH

Physicians having no known contact with radiation.	65.7 years
Specialists having some exposure to radiation (dermatologists, urologists, etc.)	63.3 years
Radiologists	60.5 years
U.S. Population over 25 years of age	65.6 years

SOURCE: "Summary Report of the Committee on Pathologic Effects," p. 35, in National Academy of Sciences-National Research Council, *The Biological Effects of Atomic Radiation* (Washington, D.C., 1956), pp. 33–43.

The National Academy of Sciences Committee on Internal Emitters has suggested that a quantity of strontium-90 as high as 100 S.U. may represent such a threshold. If this were the case, then strontium-90 is not endangering human beings now and won't be even if H-bomb testing were continued at the present rate.

Ah, but is 100 S.U. the threshold? Actually, it may be simply a plausible (or, perhaps, wishful-thinking) guess. There are a number of scientists who seem convinced that there is a very low threshold of action to the strontium-90 effect.

If that were so then strontium-90 is a killer right now. If 1000 people died of leukemia in 1954 as a result of the 50 S.U. they picked up from natural radioactivity, then the 0.5 S.U. (maximum) of strontium-90 in the bones now may have caused 1 per cent of those deaths. That would mean that strontium-90 was killing 10 Americans a year with leukemia. (Exactly which particular American would die would depend on which particular American had the unlucky hit scored upon the proper points in the proper cells by the speeding electrons. It's a kind of huge shooting gallery with ourselves the ducks.)

From a cold-blooded and objective standpoint, 10 deaths a year may not seem much of a price to pay for the possible good that may be derived from H-bomb research. Even a rise to 800 deaths a year as the strontium-90 level reaches as high as 40 S.U. may not seem excessive. After all, the pleasure car kills some 40,000 Americans a year.

Unfortunately, we don't know that the leukemia effect is necessarily one of simple direct proportion.

Thus, to bring up an analogy, a concentration of carbon monoxide in the air of less than 0.01 per cent is harmless. No effect and no symptoms. We are below the threshold of action.

A concentration of 0.05 per cent of carbon monoxide will, however, give you a headache within an hour. A concentration of 0.1 per cent will give you a worse headache and a concentration of 0.2 per cent a still worse headache. Raise it to 0.3 per cent, however, and it's no longer a question of the headache getting still worse. You're dead.

Now, then, as strontium-90 goes up in concentration, is it just a question of the leukemia incidence rising with it in direct proportion, or is there a point which is another boundary line, another threshold of action, beyond which everybody gets leukemia? If so where is it?

No one knows about that either.[7]

Now why should there be this disagreement about the thresholds of action of strontium-90 and leukemia?

One reason lies in the difficulty of conducting long-term experiments on human beings in a matter of this sort. (It is always difficult to tell for sure how far animal experiments might apply.)

The logical thing would be to take a large number of human beings and subject them to carefully graded doses of radiation or feed them carefully measured quantities of strontium-90, observe them for fifty years or so and note how many develop leukemia—running appropriate controls, of course.

Well, who's going to volunteer for such an experiment? Or conduct one? Not I. Not anybody.

A lot of the information upon which scientists are depending goes back to the cases of the few unfortunate women who got radium poisoning back in the twenties while working on radium-dial watches (and pointing the brushes they used with their lips, if I remember correctly). The radium, which is another member of the calcium family, also got stored in the bones. Those studies seem to show a quite high threshold of action, but the number of cases were few and the experimental methods of handling radioactive data were primitive, then. It would be unsafe to rely on those data.

So we're left uncertain, with a very poor gamble on our hands. At best, we break even; no harm done. At worst, we may lose everything; literally everything. . . .

---

[7] An even more subtle danger to the human race than leukemia is the question of mutations. It is known that radiation causes mutations and that increasing the intensity of radiation increases the number of mutations and that most mutations are for the worst. And as far as mutations are concerned, most authorities are agreed that there is no threshold to speak of. So it is quite conceivable that the human race has been done tremendous damage already that may not show up in all its ugliness for several generations.

Theses for the Atomic Age

GUNTHER ANDERS

1 . HIROSHIMA AS WORLD CONDITION : On August 6, 1945, the Day of Hiroshima, a New Age began: the age in which at any given moment we have the power to transform any given place on our planet, and even our planet itself, into a Hiroshima. On that day we became, at least "modo negativo," omnipotent; but since, on the other hand, we can be wiped out at any given moment, we also became totally impotent. However long this age may last, even if it should last forever, it is "The Last Age": for there is no possibility that its "differentia specifica," the possibility of our self-extinction, can ever end—but by the end itself.

2 . THE TIME OF THE END VERSUS THE END OF TIME : Thus, by its very nature, this age is a "respite," and our "mode of being" in this age must be defined as "not yet being non-existing," "not quite yet being non-existing." Thus the basic moral question of former times must be radically reformulated: instead of asking *"How* should we live?" we now must ask *"Will* we live?" For us, who are "not yet non-existing" in this Age of Respite, there is but one answer: although at any moment The Time of the End could turn into The End of Time, we must do everything in our power to make The End Time endless. Since we believe in the possibility of The End of Time, we are Apocalyptics, but since we fight against this man-made Apocalypse, we are—and this has never existed before—"Anti-Apocalyptics."

3 . NOT ATOMIC WEAPONS IN THE POLITICAL SITU- ATION, BUT POLITICAL ACTIONS IN THE ATOMIC SITUATION : Although it sounds absolutely plausible, it is misleading to say that atomic weapons exist in our political situation. This statement has to be turned upside down in order to become true. As the situation today is determined and defined exclusively by the existence of "atomic weapons," we have to state: political actions and developments are taking place within the atomic situation.

4 . NOT WEAPON, BUT ENEMY : What we are fighting is not this or that enemy who could be attacked or liquidated by atomic means, but

SOURCE: Günther Anders, "Theses for the Atomic Age," *The Massachusetts Review* (Spring, 1962), pp. 493–505. Reprinted by permission.

EDITORS' NOTE: In February, 1959, at the Free University of Berlin, Günther Anders conducted a two-day seminar on "The Moral Implications of the Atomic Age." At its conclusion, the students asked Anders for a short text which could serve them as a basis for further discussion. Anders dictated these "theses," which later appeared as "Thesen zum Atomzeitalter," *Berliner Hefte* (1960), pp. 16–22. The translation here printed is by Mr. Anders.

the atomic situation as such. Since this enemy is the enemy of all people, those who, up to now, had considered each other to be enemies, have now to become allies against the common menace. Peace actions from which we exclude those with whom we wish to live in peace amount to hypocrisy, self-righteousness and a waste of time.

5 . TO THREATEN WITH ATOMIC WEAPONS IS TO-TALITARIAN : A pet theory broad enough to be embraced by subtle philosophers as well as by brutal politicians, by Jaspers as well as by Strauss, runs: "If it were not for our ability to threaten with total annihilation, we would be unable to hold the totalitarian menace in check." This is a sham argument for the following reasons: (1) The atom bomb *has* been used, although those who used it were not in danger of falling victim to a totalitarian power. (2) This argument is a fossil from the "ancient" days of atomic monopoly and has become suicidal today. (3) The catchword "totalitarian" is taken from a political situation which not only *has* already fundamentally changed, but will continue to change; atomic war, on the other hand, excludes all chance of such a change. (4) By threatening with atomic war, thus with liquidation, we cannot help being totalitarian; for this threat amounts to blackmail and transforms our globe into one vast concentration camp from which there is no way out. Thus, whoever bases the legitimacy of this extreme deprivation of freedom upon the alleged interests of freedom is a hypocrite.

6 . EXPANSION OF OUR HORIZON : Since radioactive clouds do not bother about milestones, national boundaries or curtains, distances are abolished. Thus in this Time of the End everybody is in deadly reach of everybody else. If we do not wish to lag behind the effects of our products—to do so would be not only a deadly shame but a shameful death—we have to try to widen our horizon of responsibility until it equals that horizon within which we can destroy everybody and be destroyed by everybody—in short, till it becomes global. Any distinction between near and far, neighbors and foreigners, has become invalid; today we are all "proximi."

7 . ''THE UNITED GENERATIONS'' : Not only our horizon of space must be widened, but also that of time. Since acts committed today (test explosions, for instance) affect future generations just as perniciously as our own, the future belongs within the scope of our present. "The future has already begun"[1]—since tomorrow's thunder belongs to today's lightning. The distinction between the generations of today and of tomorrow has become meaningless; we can even speak of a *League of Generations* to which our grandchildren belong, just as automatically as we ourselves. They are our *"neighbors in time."* By setting fire to *our* house, we cannot help but make the flames leap over into the cities of the future, and the not-yet-built homes of the not-yet-born generations will fall to ashes together with our

---

[1] This formula is taken from the title of Robert Jungk's book, *Die Zukunft hat schon begonnen.*

homes. Even our ancestors are full-fledged members of this League: for by dying we would make them die, too—a second time, so to speak; and after this second death everything would be as if they had never been.

8 . NOTHINGNESS — THE EFFECT OF THE NOT-IMAG- INED NOTHINGNESS : The apocalyptic danger is all the more menacing because we are unable to picture the immensity of such a catastrophe. It is difficult enough to visualize someone as not-being, a beloved friend as dead; but compared with the task our fantasy has to fulfil now, it is child's play. For what we have to visualize today is not the not-being of something particular within a framework, the existence of which can be taken for granted, but the nonexistence of this framework itself, of the world as a whole, at least of the world as mankind. Such "total abstraction" (which, as a mental performance, would correspond to our performance of total destruction) surpasses the capacity of our natural power of imagination: "Transcendence of the Negative." But since, as "homines fabri," we are capable of actually producing nothingness, we cannot surrender to the fact of our limited capacity of imagination: the attempt, at least, must be made to visualize this nothingness.

9 . ''WE ARE INVERTED UTOPIANS'' : The basic dilemma of our age is that, "We are smaller than ourselves," incapable of mentally realizing the realities which we ourselves have produced. Therefore we might call ourselves "inverted Utopians": while ordinary Utopians are unable to actually produce what they are able to visualize, we are unable to visualize what we are actually producing.

10 . ''THE PROMETHEAN DISCREPANCY'' [2] : This in- verted Utopianism is not simply one fact among many, but the outstanding one, for it defines the moral situation of man today. The dualism to which we are sentenced is no longer that of spirit against flesh or of duty against inclina- tion, is neither Christian nor Kantian, but that of our capacity to produce as opposed to our power to imagine.

11 . THE SUPRA-LIMINAL : Not only has imagination ceased to live up to production, but feeling has ceased to live up to responsibility. It may still be possible to imagine or to repent the murdering of one fellow man, or even to shoulder responsibility for it; but to picture the liquidation of one hundred thousand fellow men definitely surpasses our power of imagination. The greater the possible effect of our actions, the less are we able to visualize it, to repent of it or to feel responsible for it; the wider the gap, the weaker the brake-mechanism. To do away with one hundred thou- sand people by pressing a button is incomparably easier than to slay one individual. The "subliminal," the stimulus too small to produce any reaction, is recognized in psychology; more significant, however, though never seen, let alone analyzed, is the "supra-liminal": the stimulus too big to produce any reaction or to activate any brake-mechanism.

---

[2] The elaboration of this category is given in the author's *Die Antiquiertheit des Menschen*, 3rd ed. (Munich: C. H. Beck, 1961), pp. 21–95.

THE DOOMSDAY MACHINE

Assume that for, say, $10 billion we could build a device whose only function is to destroy all human life. The device is protected from enemy action (perhaps by being thousands of feet underground) and then connected to a computer which is in turn connected, by a reliable communication system, to hundreds of sensory devices all over the United States. The computer would then be programmed so that if, say, five nuclear bombs exploded over the United States, the device would be triggered and the earth destroyed. . . . [The mechanism used would most likely not involve the breaking up of the earth, but the creation of really large amounts of radioactivity or the causing of major climatic changes or, less likely, the extreme use of thermal effects.] . . . If Khrushchev should order an attack, both Khrushchev and the Soviet population would be automatically and efficiently annihilated.

SOURCE: Herman Kahn, *On Thermonuclear War* (Princeton, N.J.: Princeton U. P., 1961), p. 145. Reprinted by permission.

EDITORS' NOTE: Mr. Kahn does not advocate the kind of strategy that would call for the building of a Doomsday Machine, nor does he think it likely in any event that one will be built. His aim, as he says, is to clarify current thinking on the subject. It is of interest to the general reader, nevertheless, to know that it is neither infeasible nor irrational (given assumptions widely and seriously held) to threaten to destroy all life on earth.

1 2 . S E N S E S D I S T O R T S E N S E . F A N T A S Y I S R E A L - I S T I C : Since our pragmatic life horizon (sec. 6), the one within which we can reach and be reached, has become limitless, we must try to visualize this limitlessness, although by trying to do so we would evidently violate the "natural narrowness" of our imagination. Although insufficient by its very nature, there is nothing other than imagination which could be considered as an organon of truth. Certainly not perception. Perception is a "false witness," in a far more radical sense than Greek philosophy meant when warning against it. For the senses are myopic, their horizon is "senselessly" narrow. It is not in the wide land of imagination that escapists of today like to hide, but in the ivory tower of perception.[3]

1 3 . T H E C O U R A G E T O F E A R : When speaking of the "imagining of nothingness," the act meant is not identical with what psychology imagines to be imagination, for I speak of fear, which *is* the imagining of nothingness "in concreto." Therefore we can improve the formulations of the last paragraphs by saying: it is our capacity to fear which is too small and which does not correspond to the magnitude of today's danger. As a matter of fact, nothing is more deceitful than to say, "We live in the Age of Anxiety

---

[3] No wonder that we feel uneasy in front of those normal pictures which are painted according to the conventional rules of perspective. Though realistic in the ordinary sense of the word, they are actually utterly unrealistic since they ignore the limitless horizon of today's world.

anyway." This slogan is not a statement but a tool manufactured by the fellow travellers of those who wish to prevent us from becoming really afraid, of those who are afraid that we once may produce the fear commensurate to the magnitude of the real danger. On the contrary, we are living in the Age of Inability to Fear. Our imperative: "Expand the capacity of your imagination," means, in concreto: "Increase your capacity of fear." Therefore: don't fear fear, have the courage to be frightened,[4] and to frighten others, too. Frighten thy neighbor as thyself. This fear, of course, must be of a special kind: 1) a fearless fear, since it excludes fearing those who might deride us as cowards, 2) a stirring fear, since it should drive us into the streets instead of under cover, 3) a loving fear, not fear *of* the danger ahead but *for* the generations to come.

14. PRODUCTIVE FRUSTRATION: Time and again our efforts to comply with the imperative, "Widen your capacity to fear and make it commensurate with the immensity of the effects of your activities," will be frustrated. It is even possible that our efforts will make no progress whatsoever. But even this failure should not intimidate us; repeated frustration does not refute the need for repeating the effort. On the contrary, every new failure bears fruit, for it makes us vigilant against our initiating further actions whose effects transcend our capacity to fear.

15. ''DISPLACED DISTANCE'': If we combine our statement about the abolition of distances (sec. 6) with that about the Promethean discrepancy (sec. 10)—and only this combination makes the picture of our situation complete—we reach the following result: the "abolition" of time and space distances does not amount to abolition of distances altogether, for today we are confronted with the daily increasing distance between production and imagination.

16. END OF THE COMPARATIVE: Our products and their effects surpass not only the maximum size of what we are able to visualize or to feel, but even the size of what we are able to *use*. It is common knowledge that our production and supply often exceed our demand and produce the need for the production of new needs and new demands. But this is not all: today we have reached the situation in which products are manufactured which simply contradict the very concept of need, products which simply *cannot* be needed, which are too big in an absolute sense. In this stage our own products are being domesticated as if they were forces of nature. Today's efforts to produce so-called "clean weapons" are attempts of a unique kind: for what man is now trying is to increase the quality of his products by decreasing their effects.

If the number and the possible performance of the already existing stock of weapons are sufficient to reach the absurd aim of the annihilation of mankind, then today's increase in production is even more absurd and proves that the producers do not understand at all what they are actually doing. The

---

[4] It is not Roosevelt's "Freedom *from* Fear" for which we have to strive, but the Freedom *to* fear.

comparative, the principle of progress and competition, has lost its sense. *Death is the boundary line of the comparative: one cannot be deader than dead and one cannot be made deader than dead.*

17. APPEAL TO COMPETENCE PROVES MORAL IN-COMPETENCE: We have no reason to presuppose (as, for instance, Jaspers does) that those in power are better able to imagine the immensity of the danger or that they realize the imperatives of the atomic age better than we ordinary "morituri." This presupposition is even irresponsible. And it would be far more justified to suspect them of having not even the slightest inkling of what is at stake. We have only to think of Adenauer, who dared to berate eighteen of the greatest physicists of today, telling them that they are incompetent in the "field of atomic armament and atomic weapons questions," and that they should talk shop instead and not "meddle" with those issues. It is precisely by using these vocables that he and his kind demonstrate their moral incompetence. For there is no more final and no more fatal proof of moral blindness than to deal with the Apocalypse as if it were a "special field," and to believe that rank is identical with the monopoly to decide the "to be or not to be" of mankind. Some of those who stress competence are doing so solely in order to disguise the anti-democratic elements of their monopoly. By no means should we be taken in by this camouflage. After all, we are living in allegedly democratic states. If the word "Democracy" has any sense at all, then it means that precisely the province *beyond* our professional competence should concern us, that we are not only entitled, but obliged—not as specialists but as citizens and human beings—to participate in deciding about the affairs of the "res publica." Since, after all, we *are* the "res publica," the reproach that we are "meddling" amounts to the ridiculous accusation that we are interfering with our own business. There has never been and will never be an affair more "publica" than today's decision about our survival. By renouncing "interference," we not only fail to fulfill our democratic duties, but we risk our collective suicide.

18. ABOLITION OF "ACTION": The possible annihilation of mankind seems to be an "action." Therefore those who contribute to it seem to be "acting." They are not. Why not? Because there is hardly anything left which, by a behaviorist, could be classified as "acting." For activities which formerly had occurred *as* actions and were meant and understood as such by the acting subjects themselves, now have been replaced by other variants of activity: (1) by working, (2) by "triggering."

(*1*) *Work: Substitute for Action:* The employees in Hitler's death factories did, so to speak, "nothing," thought they had done nothing, because they had done "nothing but work." By "nothing but work" I mean that kind of performance (generally considered to be the natural and only type of operation today) in which the *eidos* of the end-product remains invisible to the operator—no, does not even matter to him—no, is not even supposed to matter to him—no, ultimately is not even permitted to matter to him. Typical of today's work is its seeming moral neutrality; *non olet;* no work-goal, however evil, can defile the worker. Nearly all jobs assigned to and performed by man today now are understood as belonging to this universally accepted and monocratic type of operation. Work—the camouflaged form of action. This camouflage exempts even the mass murderer from his guilt, since, according to today's standards, the worker is not only "freed" from responsibility for his work, but he simply *cannot* be made guilty by his work.

Consequence: once we have realized that today's fatal equation runs, "All action is work," we have to have the courage to invert it and to formulate: "*All work is action.*"

(2) *"Triggering"—Substitute for Work:* What is true of work applies even more to "triggering," for in triggering, the specific characteristics of work— effort and consciousness of effort—are diminished, if not nullified. Triggering —the camouflaged form of work. As a matter of fact, there exists hardly anything today which cannot be achieved through triggering. It can even happen that one first push of a button sets in motion a whole chain of secondary triggerings—till the end-result—never intended, never imagined, by the first button-pusher—consists of millions of corpses. Seen behavioristically, such a manipulation would be considered neither work nor action. Although seemingly no one would have done anything, this "doing nothing" would actually produce annihilation and nothingness. No button-pusher (if such a minimum-operator is still required at all) feels *that* he is acting. And since the scene of the act and the scene of the suffering no longer coincide, since cause and effect are torn apart, no one can perceive what he is doing—"*schizotopia*" by analogy with "schizophrenia."

Evident again (see above): only he who continuously tries to visualize the effect of his doings, however far away in space or in time the scene of his effects may be, has the chance of truth; perception "falls short."

This variant of camouflage is unique. While formerly it had always been the aim of camouflaging to prevent the prospective victim from recognizing the danger, or to protect the doer from the enemy, now camouflaging is meant to prevent the doer himself from recognizing what he is doing. Therefore today's doer is also a victim. Eatherly[5] belongs to those whom he has destroyed.

19. THE DECEITFUL FORM OF TODAY'S LIE: The examples of camouflage teach us something about the present-day type of lie. For today the lie no longer needs to dress itself in the costume of an assertion; ideologies are no longer required. Victorious today is that type of lie which prevents us from even suspecting that it *could* be a lie; and this victory has become possible because today lying no longer needs to assume the disguise of assertions. For whereas until now, in "honest hypocrisy," lies had pretended to be truths, they now are camouflaging themselves in a completely different costume.

(1) Instead of appearing in the form of assertions, they now appear in that of naked *individual words* which, although seemingly saying nothing,

---

[5] See *Burning Conscience, The Case of the Hiroshima Pilot, Claude Eatherly, Told in His Letters to Günther Anders* (New York: Monthly Review, 1962).

secretly already contain their deceitful predicate. Example: since the term "atomic weapon" makes us believe that what it designates may be classified as a weapon, it already *is* an assertion, and as such a lie.[6]

(2) Instead of appearing in the form of false assertions, they appear in that of *falsified reality.* Example: once an action appears in the disguise of "work," its action-character becomes invisible; and so much so that it no longer reveals, not even to the doer himself, that ultimately he is acting; and thus the worker, although working conscientiously, enjoys the chance of renouncing conscience with a clean conscience.

(3) Instead of appearing in the form of false assertions, lies appear in that of *things.* In the last example it is still man who is active, although he misinterprets his acting as working. But even this minimum can disappear—and this, the supreme triumph of lying, has already begun. For during the last decade action has shifted (of course through human action) from the province of man to another region: to that of machines and instruments. These have become, so to speak, "incarnated" or "reified actions." Example: through the mere fact of its existence, the atom bomb is an uninterrupted blackmailing—and that blackmailing has to be classified as an "action" is, after all, indisputable. Since we have shifted our activities and responsibilities to the system of our products, we believe ourselves able to keep our hands clean, to remain "decent people." But it is, of course, just this surrender of responsibility that is the climax of irresponsibility.

This, then, is our absurd situation: in the very moment in which we have become capable of the most monstrous action, the destruction of the world, "actions" seem to have disappeared. Since the mere existence of our products already proves to be action, the trivial question, how we should use our products for action (whether, for instance, for deterrence), is an almost fraudulent one, since this question obscures the fact that the products, by their mere existence, already *have* acted.

2 0 . N O T   R E I F I C A T I O N   B U T   P S E U D O - P E R S O N A L I Z A -
T I O N : One cannot adequately interpret the phenomenon by giving it the Marxian label of "reification," for this term designates exclusively the fact that man is reduced to a thing-function. We are stressing, however, the fact that the qualities and functions taken away from man by his reification are now becoming qualities and functions of the products themselves, that they transform themselves into pseudo-persons, since, through their mere existence, they are acting. This second phenomenon has been ignored by philosophy, although it is impossible to understand our situation without seeing both sides of the process simultaneously.

---

[6] For a discussion of why the atomic bomb cannot be classified as a weapon, see the author's *Die Antiquiertheit des Menschen*, 247 ff., *Der Mann auf der Brücke* (Munich: C. H. Beck, 1959), 95 ff., and *Off limits für das Gewissen* (Rowohlt, 1961), 30 (English edition: London: Weidenfeld and Nicolson, 1962, p. 15). The main argument runs: a weapon is a means. Means are defined by dissolving in their ends, ends by their surviving the means. This cannot be applied to atomic weapons, since there is no end which could survive the use of weapons and no end conceivable which could justify such an absurd means.

2 1 . T H E   M A X I M S   O F   P S E U D O - P E R S O N S :   These pseudo-persons have rigid principles of their own. The principle of "atomic weapons," for example, is pure nihilism, because, if they could speak, they would say: "Whatever we destroy, it's all the same to us." In them, nihilism has reached its climax and has become naked "Annihilism."[7]

Since action has shifted from man to work and products, examination of our conscience today cannot confine itself to listening to the voice of our heart. It is far more important to listen to the mute voice of our products in order to know their principles and maxims—in other words, the "shift" has to be reversed and revoked. Therefore, today's imperative runs: have and use only those things, the inherent maxims of which could become your own maxims and thus the maxims of a general law.

2 2 . M A C A B R E   A B O L I T I O N   O F   H A T R E D :   If (sec. 18) the scene of action and the scene of suffering are torn apart—if the suffering does not occur at the place of the act, if acting becomes acting without visible effect, if suffering becomes suffering without identifiable cause—hatred disappears, although in a totally delusive way.

Atomic war will be waged with less hatred than any war before: attacker and victims will not hate each other since they will not see each other. There is nothing more macabre than this disappearance of hatred which, of course, has nothing to do with peacefulness or love. It is striking how rarely, and with how little hatred, Hiroshima victims mention those who have caused their suffering. This, however, does not mean that hatred will play no part in the next war: since it will be considered indispensable for psychological warfare, the production of hatred will, no doubt, be organized. In order to nourish what a perverted age calls "morale," identifiable and visible objects of hatred will be exhibited, in emergency cases invented —"Jews" of all kinds. Since hatred can bloom only if the objects of hatred are visible and can fall into the hater's hand, it will be the domestic scene from which one will choose scapegoats. Since the targets of this artificially manufactured hatred and the target of the military attacks will be totally different, the war mentality will become actually schizophrenic.

I have published these words in order to prevent them from becoming true. If we do not stubbornly keep in mind the strong probability of the disaster, and if we do not act accordingly, we will be unable to find a way out. There is nothing more frightful than to be right.—And if some, paralyzed by the gloomy likelihood of the catastrophe, have already lost courage, they still have a chance to prove their love of man by heeding the cynical maxim: "Let's go on working as though we had the right to hope. Our despair is none of our business."

---

[7] Even this climax of nihilism has been surpassed, for the principle of the neutron bomb would run: "Whomever we destroy, it's all the same to us. The world of objects, however, has to remain sacrosanct. *Products should not kill other products.*" As a matter of fact, this is the most radical perversion of moral principles which has ever existed.

"A MODEST PROPOSAL"

To the Editor of The Washington Post:

I address myself to the Eminences and the Serenities. I make them a Modest Proposal. Let our children go.

A nuclear war, which day by day seems more likely may very well end human life. But suppose, more cheerfully, that only the people of the Northern Hemisphere are exterminated; that in the Southern Hemisphere it will still be possible, some how, for some persons to survive. Why should we not transport our young children to these regions as a refuge? The merits and advantages of the Proposal are obvious and many as well as of the highest importance.

For first, as I cannot conceive any sane person capable of human feeling would challenge, the war to come, if war comes, is not the children's concern. Our quarrels, our bitterness, our hatreds, our fears do not possess them. Our heroes and our devils are not theirs. They have barely begun their lives, they are not ready to end them for Causes. They are too innocent and foolish to realize that death is preferable to life under alien creeds. I recall a story which Carl Sandburg told of a little girl, perhaps his granddaughter, who, after hearing his description of a battle of the Civil War, observed, "Suppose they gave a war and no one came." There is no reason to suppose that children, unless forced, would come to our war.

Secondly, the conduct of the war would be so much less Burdensome if the children were removed. It would be unnecessary to yield to niceties, to observe amenities, to nurse the sick, to shield the weak, to spare the infirm. With the children gone, without the distractions and temptations of their cries and complaints, we could give ourselves over completely to the serious business at hand. There would be many fewer mouths to feed, less need for water and air and bandages and whole blood. Children are notoriously subject to epidemic diseases; thus a prolific source of infection would be eliminated.

The savings in money alone would be immense, and would not only pay to transport the children and maintain them until they could fend for themselves, but would leave a handsome margin for use in vigorous prosecution of the war. I have made a rough calculation for U. S. children which bears on the point. Say we take many of the children from the ages of two to twelve—the younger are too frail, the older are more stable and could be useful to us at home—then we shall have about 25 million to transport and keep. For this purpose, allow $1000 a head. The total is $25 billion, a sum well under half our annual military appropriation. Surely this is not too much to spend, considering the advantages to be gained.

Thirdly, we rid ourselves once for all of the Incubus of a shelter program. What a relief no longer to have to pretend! What a comfort simply to face the facts! No sensible person, even among scientists, believes in the efficacy of shelters. Down one goes to the well-stocked, cozy hole. Then what? There is the gentle patter of fallout on the roof; one is shielded from the blast; the light of a thousand suns (or is it now a million suns?) does not penetrate. The Lares and Penates are there. The family is snug. Father is pedalling the air-pump. Mother is preparing a tuna-fish casserole. The radio is on. Splendid. But when does one come up and what is there to come up to? Anarchy? Cannibalism? The living dead? Bloated corpses? Troublesome questions. And even more troublesome is the effect of fire and heat,

"A MODEST PROPOSAL" (*cont.*)

a subject which none of the experts and no one in the Establishment has seen fit to discuss. I lay this omission, of course, to delicate feelings. It would, I believe, undermine morale to be reminded of the fire storms over Tokyo, Hamburg, Dresden, where a mere few thousands of tons of high explosives produced atmospheric convulsions.

Now with weapons, each of which may yield the equivalent of ten, or fifty, or 100 million tons of high explosives, the fire storm produced by a single bomb will, I am reliably informed by an article in Scientific American, vaporize the structures and burn off the vegetation of an area of at least 15,000 square miles. Even in a deep shelter the occupants will be quickly barbecued. What a dreadful thing to contemplate. It is enough to make cowards of us all. The necrophiles, the bitter ones, the incandescent patriots, those among the aged and ailing who take comfort in the thought that their demise will coincide with that of mankind: these endorse the view that shelters will give shelter. But secretly they laugh at our innocence. We must not encourage them. If we are to die for the Cause, let us not cheapen and betray the sacrifice: Away with the shelters, and all will become clear.

Fourthly, there is the grave moral issue of suicide. The law forbids it to the individual. On a national scale, however, is it apparently acceptable. Do we not, after all, make the law? Thus we may write its exceptions. Still, the question nags us, can we require the suicide of those who have no voice in the making of the laws, viz children? It is a fine point, and none would venture to say how our leaders would feel compelled to decide it. My Proposal disencumbers them of this obligation.

Fifthly, there must be many who, like myself, have a Weakness for children. In format and freshness they are much preferable to the larger editions, their parents. Children are unwrinkled, unwarped. They are healthy. They smell nice. They are not cynical. They suppose life to be an end in itself. Properly nourished, watered and cared for, they grow up. When grown they can breed. The dead do not breed. Quite recently the eminent geneticist Herman Muller described a scheme for setting up large-scale sperm banks. Sperm could be stored indefinitely; it could be classified according to the characteristics of the males who produced it. Human evolution would thus, in a sense, come under man's own control. Yet the scheme presupposes the continuance of women. It is my impression that sperm by itself will yield no fruit. Here again the Proposal is vindicated; for there will be female as well as male children: instead of storing germ plasm we will be storing the young themselves and thus assure the future.

For the moment I have said enough. I am anxious that Wise men consider my Proposal. Is it Feasible? (Less feasible, say than a journey to the planets?) Is it visionary? (More visionary than the preservation of Freedom by a nuclear war?) Is it too Costly? Is there yet time to execute it—in part at least if not in whole? Could it be made a matter of International Cooperation? Is a country without children worth living in? Perhaps not. In that case some better course must be found. Let the Wise men define it.

JAMES R. NEWMAN
Chevy Chase, Md.
Sept. 20, 1961.

SOURCE: *The Washington Post* (Monday, Sept. 25, 1961). Reprinted by permission.

Part Three. ENDEMIC CONDITIONS

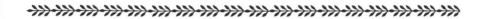

Americans tend to assume that social problems are easily solved. Once there is agreement among competent observers that a certain state of affairs in society is undesirable, it is only necessary to ask: of what cause is this an effect? Once "the" cause is found, through scientific research, the next step is to summon the experts to devise a solution. Then there only remains the task of educating the public and the policy makers on what, specifically, is to be done and how. At this point, it is just a question of mechanics—so goes the assumption.

It is amply evident, however, from a long history of aborted efforts, that solving social problems involves more than "just a question of mechanics." Problems such as urban rapid transit were solved on paper thirty years ago, and yet they are still very much with us. Some of these "old" problems are even worse now than when solutions were first devised, and new ones keep coming up. Why is this? Is it lack of technical knowledge? Lack of public education on the need? Lack of will and civic spirit? Opposition by powerful reactionary forces with a stake in keeping social problems unsolved? One can answer "yes" item by item, but the "yesses" disappointingly add up to the prescription as before: (1) more and better research, (2) more and better information to the public, (3) more and better reformist agitation. This strategy has fallen short of its promise in the past, and there is not much reason to hope that it will suddenly become effective in the future.

In this Part we will examine materials illustrative of a revised conception of social problems (again following Durkheim) as they reflect conditions inherent in society itself. If social problems are thought of as something more than minor kinks in the social machinery, as symptoms, rather, of a deep-seated pathology, the potential uses and inescapable limitations of science when applied to socially meliorative ends may be clarified.

ENDEMIC CONDITIONS: A DEFINITION AND A FRAME OF REFERENCE

Every known and imaginable human society has certain features in common with all others: some sort of family system, some sort of occupational and political organization, some sort of religion. Since the specific institutional forms vary, however, it is possible to speak *comparatively* of social conditions. A description of conditions in society X implicitly invokes conditions in society Y as the basis for comparison, or, more generally, social conditions in all other societies considered in terms of their characteristic features.

It is also possible to speak *normatively* of social conditions. In both instances, "social conditions" are visible to the observer only to the extent that specific institutional forms and processes differ from what he expects. But there is a difference between expectations based on knowledge of what is and expectations based on opinions of what ought to be. The first is comparative, and the second normative. Social conditions within a given type of society which are substantially universal in their incidence, which can be judged pathological, and which are native to the species, are *endemic*. Endemic conditions underlie and give rise to "social problems," as conventionally defined, and occur in all societies which are constitutionally of the same type—such as those that are urbanized and industrialized to a significant extent. This is the locus of our present interest.

The advantage of defining the subject matter of social pathology in this fashion is that it affords insight into why experience has shown the solving of social problems to be more than "just mechanics." If the conditions which give rise to social problems are endemic (universal and persistent), this is *prima facie* evidence that they are linked to the generic constitution of society. Before rushing to the conclusion that nothing can be done to improve matters, however, the nature of the linkage should be examined.

In Durkheim's conception society is a moral entity standing over and above the individual. It provides him with his moral and ethical standards, and is so constituted that he is rewarded for conforming and punished for deviating from them. But the individual must do more than simply refuse choices that are morally and legally disallowed; he must also choose means instrumentally effective in achieving the goals already set. And his goals, of course, are also a product of his socialization. They, too, come from society. This means that society normatively requires the individual to act effectively as well as correctly. Again, the structure of institutions is such that "achievement" is rewarded and "failure" punished.

Thus there are two constraints operating upon the individual: the demand for normative correctness and the demand for instrumental effectiveness. Both are distributed with a certain randomness, however. The content of normative correctness is partly a matter of varying situational definitions (what I feel incumbent upon me, in my situation, is not necessarily the same as what you feel incumbent upon you, in your situation), and instrumental effectiveness is always a function of the availability of means, knowledge of their availability, and the skill necessary to use them. It is this looseness of structure in the moral and intellectual environment, together with unevenness in the distribution of skills and resources, that immediately tests the mettle of the individual and finally creates problems for the collectivity. When we find these problems clustering empirically (as do those common to all industrialized societies, for example), we can speak of their roots as endemic conditions with pathogenic significance.

CRIME AND MENTAL ILLNESS

Crime is functional, Durkheim asserts (p. 359), in the sense that it is an understandable consequence of a given set of societal institutions and cultural values. (As Daniel Bell [p. 377] points out, crime in America is "an American way of life.") The rates may be abnormally high or low, the forms may be conventional or innovative, but a society without crime is not imaginable as a realistic possibility. Moreover, each society has the amount of crime and the kind of crime it "deserves." Our own society is one committed to the pragmatic credo that "results count," as is shown by the fact that not a few of our national heroes were "white collar criminals" and proud of it. We judge them, in William James' terms, by their "fruits, not by their roots." There is some evidence of historical decline of crime in political office, but corruption has been and still is endemic and epidemic on municipal, state, and federal levels of government. The market for illegal goods and services (narcotics, gambling, prostitution, stolen merchandise) continues, and racketeering and thievery—business enterprise by other means—remain significant national and international industries. In the social sense, crime is an occupation, a vocation that one learns and to which one becomes morally committed. Cressey (p. 396) describes the learning experience and points out that it is extraordinarily difficult to change mature criminals. Crime is functional in that people end up enacting roles negatively sanctioned by society, yet at the same time implied in the structure of institutions and values it selectively fosters.

However, the self-employed professional thief and the career man of organized crime do not exhaust the Durkheimian category of functional deviance. In addition to the fairly rational deviant, there is another, far larger category: those whose character and personality disorders compel them either to commit antisocial acts or to fail to perform the minimum of self-care that society defines as necessary if they are to be let alone. These are the compulsive deviants. Their "resources" are inadequate, and they come to the attention of official agencies, generally police, because of their dramatic and symptomatic delinquencies.

The more fortunate of these misfits find patterned though deviant roles as consumers, producers, or purveyors of illegal goods and services. These are the gamblers, prostitutes, drug addicts, alcoholics, panhandlers, pimps, pushers, and steerers of the tenderloin districts of big cities. Homosexuals provide a particularly instructive instance of patterned deviance. (While quite a few of the tenderloin "characters" are homosexuals—this is especially true of prostitutes—homosexuals as such do not form an enclave within the organized underworld. It would be more accurate to say that they have their own underworld, one which cuts across and through the better known under-

world and upperworld, lower class and upper class, bohemia and suburb.)
Toward homosexuals and other compulsive deviants society adopts a mildly
disapproving, passively tolerant attitude unless their need drives them to
commit "hard" crimes. Those who are so driven comprise the second, less
fortunate category of compulsive deviants. What is society to do—treat them
as wards, as sick people in need of care and treatment, or as criminals who
must be relentlessly suppressed? This question is discussed by Charles
Winick (p. 401), in the case of narcotics addiction.

Our selection from the Midtown Study of mental illness in New York
City provides essential perspective for interpreting deviant behavior caused
by character and personality disturbance. Moreover, it provides the strongest
possible evidence that crime and other forms of deviance are functional. If
the mental health of nearly one-quarter of the population of the metropolis
can be called "impaired," it should cause no dismay to learn that high crime
rates are endemic and substantial.

SEGREGATION AND SOCIAL RELATIONS

Segregation is a social problem to those who wish to speak responsibly
for the conscience of American society, that is, for its ultimate values. But
segregationists as well as desegregationists offer themselves as reasonable
spokesmen for society's conscience; the difference is that they locate the
"social problem" not in the existence of racial discrimination but in the dissatisfaction with it which, as they see it, is stirred up by liberal critics. Ordinary people in the unaffected majority are not likely to see segregation as a
social problem, since if it touches their interests at all it does so tangentially
in contexts that often remind them that they have a stake in its perpetuation.
Nor do ordinary people in the affected minority see segregation as a social
problem. For them it is a question of right, not expediency; of justice, not
"health." To call segregation a "social problem" implies that there is a moral
issue to be debated, facts to be ascertained, a policy to be chosen. The
minority group member knows of no unresolved moral issue, and no scarcity
of facts or knowledge. From his point of view it is "their" problem, not
"ours."

This normative dissensus is a basic, if sometimes implicit, theme of the
various materials collected and reprinted in Chapter 12. The resultant failure
in communication is evident in the personal documents, including the case
of interracial marriage and James Baldwin's (p. 423) observations on Negro-
Jewish relations in Harlem. The man-in-the-middle, the marginal man, feels
the impress of both sets of conflicting norms. His anguish reminds us that
while whole societies can tolerate a certain amount of normative inconsistency,
those who occupy points of stressful intersection within them are wracked
and torn. "Being of two minds," a characteristic product of segregation, is
again evident in Seeman's (p. 425) analysis of the intellectual perspective
that corresponds to a minority (Jewish) status. Antonovsky introduces yet
another dimension, the striving for success that ironically makes economic

and social interest a factor in keeping the barriers to mobility where they are. Minority group members are by no means exempt from reading the calculus of self-interest as dictating a "sensible" and "moderate" decision on the question of agitation for change. Finally, in reviewing Abrams' study of housing, Rosenberg (p. 438) raises the question of values again in pointing out some destructive consequences of the Northern-style pattern of residential segregation.

WORK AND LEISURE

It can be argued on Durkheimian premises that the poor, like the criminal and the deviant element, we will always have with us (despite very real possibilities for meliorative action). This is no less true of the disfranchised minorities. In the short run, at least, society has shown that it can and will sustain such endemic pathological conditions. But can it tolerate a chronic unemployment rate of 6 per cent, 10 per cent, 20 per cent, 30 per cent, or even more? (Who knows how much "technological displacement" there may be if the current pump-priming tenth of the Gross National Product going for armaments is greatly reduced?) The key problem for nineteenth-century industrializing societies was to bring about the civic reintegration of the ex-peasant who had become an industrial worker, to find a place for him in the polity. The industrially mature, automated societies of the immediate future may find that their problem is to reintegrate the ex-worker who has become unemployable. Being poor is bad enough, but in a society which places all but supreme emphasis on having work to do, being unemployed is even worse. Swados' (p. 443) portrait of miners without work is illustrative.

But what of the effects of automation on the meaning of the work one has? Men seek not only to work but to work meaningfully; beyond work they seek to live meaningfully—to participate in the public life, and at the same time engage in satisfying private activities. Terms like "satisfying" and "meaningful participation" remind us that men and women are dependent on society for their moral as well as their physical sustenance, and in leisure as well as at work. As Faunce's (p. 446) study shows, automation threatens to deny the worker the satisfaction not only of organizing and pacing his work —many have already lost that on the assembly line—but of working cooperatively in a group.

One quite probable consequence of increasing automation is a reduction in the work week. Desirable as it may be, this is no real palliative. The social values which are built into the character of working class Americans inordinately stress "vocational virtue." Not surprisingly, as Ben Seligman (p. 463) points out, it is precisely the reliable, hard-working type who "moonlights" a second job once his regular work week is reduced much below 40 hours. The man who really can enjoy his leisure is thus deprived of the means to do so, while the work-oriented blue collar man finds himself with more gadgets but less leisure than he had before.

KNOWLEDGE: LIMITATIONS ON ITS PRODUCTION AND USE

The definition of a social problem in the first place—the analytical specification of its character and scope—is made by the specialized man of knowledge, whether he follows or leads a consensus on the matter. Once the definition is made, facts must be gathered and appraised and means devised for "solving" it. If the diagnosis of the social ailment and the prescription of a remedy are to stand the test of critical scrutiny, both must be found technically competent by the relevant community of scientific specialists. In a democratic society, to recognize the existence of a social problem is to generate a demand for corrective social action. Each of these phases requires the past production and present services of knowledgeable specialists.

But if knowledge and the services of men who know how to interpret it, extend it, and apply it are demanded by society, at the same time the activities and products of the man of knowledge are morally unsettling. Moore and Tumin (p. 516) show that knowledge is sometimes dysfunctional, from society's standpoint, and Rosenberg (p. 527) reinterprets Samuel Stouffer's sanguine findings on the level and quality of knowledge in use by the public to draw conclusions which are much less comforting.

Society is a moral entity, and the sacred character of social values is automatically threatened by the secular spirit of inquiry. Weber argues forcefully that the calling of the man of knowledge requires him to be ethically neutral while "at work," so to speak. Nothing can be held sacred, nothing is beyond the reach of his inquiry. But as a matter of institutional practice all sorts of limitations are placed on the freedom of science, especially of social science. In the universities, as Veblen shows, the emphasis on vocationalism is an understandable consequence of a system in which the governing boards are mostly composed of businessmen. Similarly, and to a degree that would have appalled even Veblen, Bennis (p. 508) describes the work of scientists in research institutes supported by foundations; he finds them almost obsessively concerned with the fact that the kind of research pursued this year can be expected to have consequences for the size of the grant awarded next year. Some projects "sell" better than others. So progress in science is again dependent on the judgments and preferences of lay governing boards. The sense of powerlessness, of dependence, and the lowered self-esteem that comes from knowing that one's vital interests are decided by groups socially remote from oneself and hardly in sympathy with one's goals, are dramatically manifested in Seeman's (p. 494) findings that the intellectuals in his sample unconsciously think of themselves as members of a minority group.

POLITICS: PARTICIPATION AND DEMOCRATIC INSTITUTIONS

Voting and in other ways participating in the democratic political process are both expressive and instrumental in their meaning. The mere act of voting (or contributing, or writing, or demonstrating) is a way of expressing social solidarity, and the stand one takes is a way of expressing care about the future moral constitution of the collectivity. Again, normative factors are predominant. But political activity is also a rational way of selecting means in relations to some predetermined end. Voting—or, more commonly, taking direct measures to influence voters, candidates, or officials—becomes an instrument in the realization of some quite private objective, possibly, such as power or money. There's the rub in a democracy: society demands of the individual that he act both correctly and effectively. Given the incompleteness of structure and the inconsistency of the moral environment, "correctness" means different things to different people as they are variously situated. Given the variable distribution of political resources and the skills to use them, differences in situation once more affect one's ability to achieve.

Riesman and Glazer (p. 535) discuss the meaning of political apathy in terms which are not hard to translate into our frame of reference. Using affect and competence as axes, they construct a typology specifying three types of apathetics: "indignants," "inside dopesters," and "indifferents." Their incidence is hypothesized to be a function of such variables as social class and degree of urbanism. Apathetic-indignants are found mostly in the small town middle class, apathetic-inside-dopesters in the urban upper middle class, and apathetic-indifferents in both urban and rural lower classes. Now, affect and competence are roughly equivalent, respectively, to normative orientation and instrumental orientation. The analytical gain from making this translation is that political apathy is shown to be a form of deviant behavior analogous, respectively, to compulsive antisocial behavior (indignants), rational crime (inside dopesters), and the total withdrawal of mental illness (indifferents).

To consider political apathy from the perspective of social pathology is to invite a charge of parochial bias. We have tried to correct for this possibility by including material from two quite different analyses of political participation. Banfield points out, in effect, that what would be considered apathy in the United States is taken for granted in Great Britain. The masses are not expected, nor are they encouraged, to participate in local government. Lipset (p. 559) characterizes the whole of the Western world as having entered a "post-political" phase, and implicitly sees this as a normal and desirable development. To him "apathy" is no problem; in fact, in the emerging nations a little more of it might be a good thing.

11.   CRIME AND MENTAL
ILLNESS

Juvenile Crime as a Meaningful Act: The Koslow Case

HARRY SLOCHOWER

. . . On the night of August 19, 1954, Koslow and three other Brooklyn boys met and talked vaguely of what to do. Walking aimlessly, they came across Willard Menter, a Negro, sleeping on a park bench. Koslow held a lit match to his soles, then pulling Menter up told him to come along. The group walked to a pier near the Williamsburg Bridge in Brooklyn. There, Mittman, Koslow's buddy, hit Menter and when the Negro ducked Koslow's follow-up punch, he fell into the water where he was left to drown.

What made a deep impression on me when I read Marya Mannes' account in *The Reporter* (January 27, 1955), as well as Dr. Fredrick Wertham's book about Frank Santana in *The Circle of Guilt* (New York, 1956) was that the acts of these boys were carried out in a mechanical, passionless manner which brought them no catharsis. Koslow was not after Menter's money. This particular Negro meant nothing to him, nor was he an adversary against whom such "victory" could bring glory. Dostoyevsky's Raskolnikov in *Crime And Punishment* has some cause for personal resentment against the woman with whom he had pawned his watch; so has Richard Wright's Bigger Thomas, in *Native Son,* who feels affronted by his social status among the whites. In Koslow's and Santana's case, we find no similar personal motive. Why then did they kill? Koslow told Dr. Wertham: "I'm a fascist and a white supremacist. Everybody is really. That's all the talk you hear around anyway. . . . Violence? It's everywhere. All I'm interested in is violence—destruction—death."

And Frank Santana: "War pictures, gangsters, crime. . . . People are killed in all the pictures."[1]

One of the motivations for delinquent behavior is the desire to assume a

---

SOURCE: Prepared especially for this volume.

[1] Clinical data indicate that antisocial behavior is invited, fostered, and approved by parents whose children carry out their own forbidden drives. See S. A. Szurek, A. Johnson, E. I. Falstein: "Collaborative Psychiatric Treatment of Parent-Child Problems," *American Journal of Orthopsychiatry,* vol. XII (July, 1942); A. Johnson in *Searchlight on Delinquency,* ed. by K. R. Eissler (New York, 1949).

hero role to compensate for the feeling that they don't belong. Among the insignia the gangs adopt are Supermen, Panthers, Dragons, Tarzans, Enchanters, Devils, Rebels. Of the delinquents who have come to my attention, Jack Koslow comes closest to a distorted figure of a mythic hero, suggested by his intense interest in Greek mythology.

Jack was a highly gifted boy with an IQ of 135 when he was nine years old. He was in a class of "gifted children" and made high school in three years. He did not suffer economic privation, came from a fairly stable home, although he hated his father for beating him. Despite these relatively favorable circumstances, Jack became a drifter, went from job to job, finding fault with everybody. From June, 1954, on, he was unemployed and became "a bum."

When Koslow was asked to characterize his method, he said: "Just hit or miss. . . . He looks at you out of one eye. It's disgusting. It incites me to hit him." Was Koslow's disgust with being looked at out of one eye disgust with an aspect of himself? Was his war against bums a war against his own hated identity as a bum? He said of the murder: "I had to do it to preserve my individuality," a formulation strikingly similar to Dostoyevsky's Raskolnikov who killed to prove himself ("to have the daring"). And when the Negro fell into the water, Koslow cried out: "Now, we're all murderers." Here, he expressed not only the need to socialize his guilt, but also to confess himself a murderer. His self-assertion was also self-accusation which invited retaliation. He, a Jewish boy, cried "Heil Hitler," and said that he loved the Nazis. We are reminded of Freud's tenet that criminality comes from a sense of guilt and is an unconscious desire to be apprehended. The delinquent identifies himself with the very authority against which he rebels, fears his own drives, and seeks punishment. Frank Santana voiced this idea when he told Dr. Wertham that the creeps "made the person who die rise up again and kill the guy who killed." Here . . . [they] sense that their behavior is, in part, the internalization of the very ruling symbols against which it is directed.

Crime and Conformity

E M I L E   D U R K H E I M

If there is any fact whose pathological character appears incontestable, that fact is crime. All criminologists are agreed on this point. Although they explain this pathology differently, they are unanimous in recognizing it. But

SOURCE: Reprinted with permission of The Free Press of Glencoe from *Rules of Sociological Method* by Emile Durkheim. Copyright 1938 by The University of Chicago.

let us see if this problem does not demand a more extended consideration.

We shall apply the foregoing rules. Crime is present not only in the majority of societies of one particular species but in all societies of all types. There is no society that is not confronted with the problem of criminality. Its form changes; the acts thus characterized are not the same everywhere; but, everywhere and always, there have been men who have behaved in such a way as to draw upon themselves penal repression. If, in proportion as societies pass from the lower to the higher types, the rate of criminality, i.e., the relation between the yearly number of crimes and the population, tended to decline, it might be believed that crime, while still normal, is tending to lose this character of normality. But we have no reason to believe that such a regression is substantiated. Many facts would seem rather to indicate a movement in the opposite direction. From the beginning of the [nineteenth] century, statistics enable us to follow the course of criminality. It has everywhere increased. In France the increase is nearly 300 per cent. There is, then, no phenomenon that presents more indisputably all the symptoms of normality, since it appears closely connected with the conditions of all collective life. To make of crime a form of social morbidity would be to admit that morbidity is not something accidental, but, on the contrary, that in certain cases it grows out of the fundamental constitution of the living organism; it would result in wiping out all distinction between the physiological and the pathological. No doubt it is possible that crime itself will have abnormal forms, as, for example, when its rate is unusually high. This excess is, indeed, undoubtedly morbid in nature. What is normal, simply, is the existence of criminality, provided that it attains and does not exceed, for each social type, a certain level, which it is perhaps not impossible to fix in conformity with the preceding rules.[1]

Here we are, then, in the presence of a conclusion in appearance quite pathological. Let us make no mistake. To classify crime among the phenomena of normal sociology is not to say merely that it is an inevitable, although regrettable, phenomenon, due to the incorrigible wickedness of men; it is to affirm that it is a factor in public health, an integral part of all healthy societies. This result is, at first glance, surprising enough to have puzzled even ourselves for a long time. Once this first surprise has been overcome, however, it is not difficult to find reasons explaining this normality and at the same time confirming it.

In the first place crime is normal because a society exempt from it is utterly impossible. Crime, we have shown elsewhere, consists of an act that offends certain very strong collective sentiments. In a society in which criminal acts are no longer committed, the sentiments they offend would have to be found

---

[1] From the fact that crime is a phenomenon of normal sociology, it does not follow that the criminal is an individual normally constituted from the biological and psychological points of view. The two questions are independent of each other. This independence will be better understood when we have shown, later on, the difference between psychological and sociological facts.

without exception in all individual consciousnesses, and they must be found to exist with the same degree as sentiments contrary to them. Assuming that this condition could actually be realized, crime would not thereby disappear; it would only change its form, for the very cause which would thus dry up the sources of criminality would immediately open up new ones.

Indeed, for the collective sentiments which are protected by the penal law of a people at a specified moment of its history to take possession of the public conscience or for them to acquire a stronger hold where they have an insufficient grip, they must acquire an intensity greater than that which they had hitherto had. The community as a whole must experience them more vividly, for it can acquire from no other source the greater force necessary to control these individuals who formerly were the most refractory. For murderers to disappear, the horror of bloodshed must become greater in those social strata from which murderers are recruited; but, first it must become greater throughout the entire society. Moreover, the very absence of crime would directly contribute to produce this horror; because any sentiment seems much more respectable when it is always and uniformly respected.

One easily overlooks the consideration that these strong states of the common consciousness cannot be thus reinforced without reinforcing at the same time the more feeble states, whose violation previously gave birth to mere infraction of convention—since the weaker ones are only the prolongation, the attenuated form, of the stronger. Thus robbery and simple bad taste injure the same single altruistic sentiment, the respect for that which is another's. However, this same sentiment is less grievously offended by bad taste than by robbery; and since, in addition, the average consciousness has not sufficient intensity to react keenly to the bad taste, it is treated with greater tolerance. That is why the person guilty of bad taste is merely blamed, whereas the thief is punished. But, if this sentiment grows stronger, to the point of silencing in all consciousnesses the inclination which disposes man to steal, he will become more sensitive to the offenses which, until then, touched him but lightly. He will react against them, then, with more energy; they will be the object of greater opprobrium, which will transform certain of them from the simple moral faults that they were and give them the quality of crimes. For example, improper contracts, or contracts improperly executed, which only incur public blame or civil damages, will become offenses in law.

Imagine a society of saints, a perfect cloister of exemplary individuals. Crimes, properly so called, will there be unknown; but faults which appear venial to the layman will create there the same scandal that the ordinary offense does in ordinary consciousness. If, then, this society has the power to judge and punish, it will define these acts as criminal and will treat them as such. For the same reason, the perfect and upright man judges his smallest failings with a severity that the majority reserve for acts more truly in the nature of an offense. Formerly, acts of violence against persons were more frequent than they are today, because respect for individual dignity was less strong. As this has increased, these crimes have become more rare; and also, many acts violating this sentiment have been introduced into the penal law which were not included there in primitive times.[2]

In order to exhaust all the hypotheses logically possible, it will perhaps be asked why this unanimity does not extend to all collective sentiments without exception. Why should not even the most feeble sentiment gather enough energy to prevent all dissent? The moral consciousness of the society would be present in its entirety in all the individuals, with a vitality sufficient to prevent all acts offending it—the purely conventional faults as well as the crimes. But a uniformity so universal and absolute is utterly impossible; for the immediately physical milieu in which each one of us is placed, the hereditary antecedents, and the social influences vary from one individual to the next, and consequently diversify consciousness. It is impossible for all to be alike, if only because each one has his own organism and that these organisms occupy different areas in space. That is why, even among the lower peoples, where individual originality is very little developed, it nevertheless does exist.

Thus, since there cannot be a society in which the individuals do not differ more or less from the collective type, it is also inevitable that, among these divergencies, there are some with a criminal character. What confers this character upon them is not the intrinsic quality of a given act but that definition which the collective conscience lends them. If the collective conscience is stronger, if it has enough authority practically to suppress these divergences, it will also be more sensitive, more exacting; and, reacting against the slightest deviations with the energy it otherwise displays only against more considerable infractions, it will attribute to them the same gravity as formerly to crimes. In other words, it will designate them as criminals.

Crime is, then, necessary; it is bound up with the fundamental conditions of all social life, and by that very fact it is useful, because these conditions of which it is a part are themselves indispensable to the normal evolution of morality and law.

Indeed, it is no longer possible today to dispute the fact that law and morality vary from one social type to the next, nor that they change within the same type if the conditions of life are modified. But, in order that these transformations may be possible, the collective sentiments at the basis of morality must not be hostile to change, and consequently must have but moderate energy. If they were too strong, they would no longer be plastic. Every pattern is an obstacle to new patterns, to the extent that the first pattern is inflexible. The better a structure is articulated, the more it offers a healthy resistance to all modification; and this is equally true of functional, as of anatomical, organization. If there were no crimes, this condition could not have been fulfilled; for such a hypothesis presupposes that collective

---

[2] Calumny, insults, slander, fraud, etc.

sentiments have arrived at a degree of intensity unexampled in history. Nothing is good indefinitely and to an unlimited extent. The authority which the moral conscience enjoys must not be excessive; otherwise no one would dare criticize it, and it would too easily congeal into an immutable form. To make progress, individual originality must be able to express itself. In order that the originality of the idealist whose dreams transcend his century may find expression, it is necessary that the originality of the criminal, who is below the level of his time, shall also be possible. One does not occur without the other.

Nor is this all. Aside from this indirect utility, it happens that crime itself plays a useful role in this evolution. Crime implies not only that the way remains open to necessary changes but that in certain cases it directly prepares these changes. Where crime exists, collective sentiments are sufficiently flexible to take on a new form, and crime sometimes helps to determine the form they will take. How many times, indeed, it is only an anticipation of future morality—a step toward what will be! According to Athenian law, Socrates was a criminal, and his condemnation was no more than just. However, his crime, namely, the independence of his thought, rendered a service not only to humanity but to his country. It served to prepare a new morality and faith which the Athenians needed, since the traditions by which they had lived until then were no longer in harmony with the current conditions of life. Nor is the case of Socrates unique; it is reproduced periodically in history. It would never have been possible to establish the freedom of thought we now enjoy if the regulations prohibiting it had not been violated before being solemnly abrogated. At that time, however, the violation was a crime, since it was an offense against sentiments still very keen in the average conscience. And yet this crime was useful as a prelude to reforms which daily became more necessary. Liberal philosophy had as its precursors the heretics of all kinds who were justly punished by secular authorities during the entire course of the Middle Ages and until the eve of modern times.

From this point of view the fundamental facts of criminality present themselves to us in an entirely new light. Contrary to current ideas, the criminal no longer seems a totally unsociable being, a sort of parasitic element, a strange and unassimilable body, introduced into the midst of society.[3] On the contrary, he plays a definite role in social life. Crime, for its part, must no longer be conceived as an evil that cannot be too much suppressed. There is no occasion for self-congratulation when the crime rate drops noticeably below the average level, for we may be certain that this apparent progress is associated with some social disorder. Thus, the number of assault cases never falls so low as in times of want.[4] With the drop in the crime rate, and as a

---

[3] We have ourselves committed the error of speaking thus of the criminal, because of a failure to apply our rule (*Division du travail social*, pp. 395–96).

[4] Although crime is a fact of normal sociology, it does not follow that we must not abhor it. Pain itself has nothing desirable about it; the individual dislikes it as society does crime, and yet it is a function of normal physiology. Not only is it necessarily

reaction to it, comes a revision, or the need of a revision in the theory of punishment. If, indeed, crime is a disease, its punishment is its remedy and cannot be otherwise conceived; thus, all the discussions it arouses bear on the point of determining what the punishment must be in order to fulfil this role of remedy. If crime is not pathological at all, the object of punishment cannot be to cure it, and its true function must be sought elsewhere.

Mental Health in the Metropolis

LEO SROLE, THOMAS S. LANGNER,
STANLEY T. MICHAEL, MARVIN K. OPLER,
AND THOMAS A. C. RENNIE

HOME SURVEY SAMPLE:
MENTAL HEALTH DISTRIBUTIONS

With this review of the main technical features of the Home Interview Survey, we can now turn to the sample of 1,600 Midtown adults for a first report on their standing within the gradient classification of symptom formation.[1]

In Table 7 we see that roughly 1 in 5 (18.5%) respondents were viewed by the team psychiatrists as free of other than inconsequential symptoms and can be regarded as essentially Well.

The Mild and Moderate categories are the most populous strata (36.3 and 21.8%, respectively), together holding a 58.1% majority of the Midtown sample. It will be remembered that these represent people who to all appear-

---

derived from the very constitution of every living organism, but it plays a useful role in life, for which reason it cannot be replaced. It would, then, be a singular distortion of our thought to present it as an apology for crime. We would not even think of protesting against such an interpretation, did we not know to what strange accusations and misunderstandings one exposes oneself when one undertakes to study moral facts objectively and to speak of them in a different language from that of the layman.

SOURCE: From *Mental Health in the Metropolis: The Midtown Study*, vol. 1, by Leo Srole, *et al.* Copyright 1962. McGraw-Hill Book Company, Inc. Reprinted by permission. Pp. 138–145.

[1] This is the number of respondents who were finally interviewed, with the results reported and discussed below. (A probability sample of 1,911 was drawn from the 110,000 persons 21 to 59 years of age estimated to reside within a delimited area of midtown Manhattan. The figure 1,660 includes those who could be reached and agreed to cooperate by giving information.) Each respondent was interviewed in his home. The interviews required about two hours, and covered such topics as life history, social functioning, and sociocultural environment as well as psychophysiological symptoms. Summaries of each interview protocol were then prepared, and two psychiatrists, working independently, rated the mental health of each respondent.

TABLE 7. *Home Survey Sample (Age 20–59)*

Respondent's Distribution on Symptom-formation
Classification of Mental Health

Well	18.5%
Mild symptom formation	36.3
Moderate symptom formation	21.8
Marked symptom formation	13.2
Severe symptom formation	7.5
Incapacitated	2.7
Impaired*	23.4
N = 100%	(1,660)

* Marked, Severe, and Incapacitated combined.

TYPES OF SYMPTOMATIC INDICATORS OF MENTAL ILLNESS

Functional	*Psychological*	*Physiological*
breathing	worry	sweats
eating	nervousness	nausea
sleeping	inertia	weakness

How can the presence and intensity of mental illness be inferred from responses to an administered questionnaire? The findings of epidemiological research are based in part on answers to questions drawn from "symptom in ventories" such as the NSA (Neuropsychiatric Screening Adjunct) and MMPI (Minnesota Multiphasic Personality Inventory). Most of the eighteen items (out of a total of over a hundred) reported by the authors of *Mental Health in the Metropolis* to constitute a "core series of 'psycho-physiologic manifestations of emotional disturbance'" (see pp. 42, 43) fall into the categories laid out above. Authorities generally agree that the MMPI and NSA are reliable and valid discriminators between persons who are mentally ill in the clinical sense—patients—and controls. What is less certain is that two psychiatrists, working with summaries of data only (mainly limited to verbal responses in structured questions) taken in a nonclinical setting by nonmedical interviewers, have produced a convincing, six-step rating of the mental health of the metropolis.

EDITORS' NOTE: For discussion and comment on methodological aspects of the Midtown study, see the review by August Hollingshead in the *American Sociological Review*, 27:6 (December, 1962), pp. 864–866. Edgar Z. Friedenberg's observations on the possible class bias introduced by taking verbal responses at face value are also noteworthy. See his review in *Commentary*, 34:6 (December, 1962), pp. 545–547.

ances are performing their adult responsibilities passably or better, although they carry significant loads of pathology-denoting symptoms. It seems, therefore, that these subclinical strata define the most frequent conditions in the Midtown population, and probably in the inclusive Manhattan white population as well. Whether these are also the most prevalent mental health conditions in more comprehensive segments of the American people is a question rather beyond the capabilities of our data to answer.

Although separately they are the least populated, the three Impaired categories add up to a sizable 23.4% slice of the Midtown respondents. Had we also sampled Midtown's absentee mental hospital patients in the 20 to 59 age range, they would have raised the Incapacitated category (by 0.5%) to 3.2% and the Impaired proportion to 23.9%. Applying the necessary margin for sampling error, we estimate with 95% confidence that in the Midtown population universe the mental morbidity rate stands in a range between 21.9 and 25.9%. Next, on the basis of our earlier indication that this estimate probably involves an error of understatement, it seems likely that the true rate stands closer to the high point in this range.

With the particular kinds of respondent data that were secured, the symptom-formation classification could be readily applied by the Study's psychiatrists. For reasons already discussed, such confidence could not be extended to classification of sample respondents in terms of the established psychiatric nomenclature. Nonetheless, at the beginning of the evaluation process the ultimate workability of the symptom-formation mode of classification was still uncertain. In short, it entailed an unknown risk of losing invaluable, irreplaceable time. As a form of insurance, therefore, Rennie instructed the evaluating psychiatrists to apply as best they could a second, supplementary classification system, designated as the *gross typology*. This involved nosological categories familiar in psychiatry, but their qualification with the term *probable* (more strictly speaking, *possible*) reflects the recognition that they were based on a very large leverage of psychiatric impression and intuition based on a fulcrum of data not designed for this purpose. With the utility of the symptom-severity rating system subsequently established, the reserve use of the gross typology scheme is obviated in this volume. However we yield one exception at this point, for whatever suggestive value there may be in sensing the diverse make-up of the impaired group as delineated under the symptom-formation mode of classification. Thus, analysis of the gross typology composition of the sample's 389 Impaired respondents suggests that about 1 in 20 (5.7%) falls in the probable organic (damage or deficiency) type, 1 in 4 (26.5%) in the probable psychotic type, and the remaining two-thirds (67.8%) in the probable neurotic or probable personality disorder types. Of course, the latter two types are concentrated most heavily in the Marked category of symptom formation.

MENTAL MORBIDITY RATES AND CRITERIA IN OTHER STUDIES

The 23.4% impairment rate found in the noninstitutional, in-residence sample population of Midtown may be viewed by some students as staggering in magnitude, or of dubious credibility.

We must address ourselves to such skepticism as potentially justifiable. Specifically, the credibility of the finding may be questioned on two different planes. On one level, the question may imply that the morbidity rate reported is beyond serious technical reproach, but the study population in its loading of mental pathology may be an extreme, local deviant on the American scene. On another level, the study population may not be grossly atypical, but the Midtown psychiatrists' criterion of mental morbidity could be faulty in its excessive breadth.

To get purchase on the first level, a nationwide study of mental health applying the Midtown classification of symptom formation, is lacking to us. However, the Midtown interview instrument included a series of "signs and symptoms" questions that had previously been used in the development of the Army's Neuro-psychiatric Screening Adjunct questionnaire. Toward this development in 1944, a cross-section control sample of 3,501 white enlisted men on active duty, with no overseas service (and almost entirely between the ages of 18 and 36), anonymously filled out the experimental questionnaire. Compared to the Midtown sample, this sample was of course more homogeneous in age, sex, and socioeconomic status, more heterogeneous in rural-urban and regional origins, and in general more representative of the white population in the nation at large.

Despite these differences, if Midtown adults in mental health respects are an atypical population we would expect them to show consistently larger frequencies of specific pathognomic signs than did the Army sample. For purposes of this comparison we have confined ourselves to the 18 symptom questions that were used in both studies with identical wordings. Only in two of these items did the Midtown sample appreciably exceed the Army's frequencies of "symptom positive" answers. On eight questions, it was the Army sample that exceeded Midtown's in this respect. And in eight other items, the two samples were more or less identical in their replies. Particularly significant in the latter series was the query: "Are you ever bothered by nervousness?" "Yes, often" rejoinders were given by 17% of the Army men and by 18% of the Midtown respondents.

Nothing can be extracted from this limited analysis to support the inference that the Midtown population is any more deviant than the comparison population of relatively selected,[2] able-bodied, young, white enlisted men. A lesser but related clue may be offered by the 2,252 New Yorkers who applied for treatment to a new, unopened, low-cost psychiatric clinic. Scattered through the five boroughs, they comprised a city-wide rate of 26 per 100,000 population. Midtowners among these applicants represented an area rate of 23 per 100,000. In this expressed need for psychiatric help, Midtown hardly appears atypical of New York City at large.

---

[2] *Selected* here refers to the fact that obvious physical and mental misfits had already been in largest part screened out. On the other hand, it should not be overlooked that the military environment is at a considerable sociological distance from the family and community settings of these ex-civilians.

A second basis for questioning the magnitude of the Midtown impairment rate can turn on the possibility that the criterion of mental morbidity it reflects was stretched beyond resemblance to clinical realities. Rennie's calibration of the Midtown impaired categories to the out-patients and hospital patients in his metropolitan experience lessens this specific possibility.

The skeptics can insist, nonetheless, that the Midtown morbidity rate is out of line with previous knowledge, drawn principally from studies of patients. Even more to their case, they can point to two other studies involving professional evaluation of mental health in a large metropolitan sample and producing morbidity rates patently well below that of Midtown's in both cases. One of these was the investigation in Baltimore conducted by the Commission on Chronic Illness.[3] The other was the wartime study of Selective Service examinees in the Boston induction station, as reported by Hyde and Kingsley.[4]

To meet such evidence it is possible, of course, to marshal counter-indications, e.g., the various estimates that 10 to 50% of patients seen by general practitioners and internists are "psychiatric cases."[5] Or there is the morbidity rate of 32% uncovered in a Salt Lake City sample of 175 households, by methods exemplifying rather less than the most advanced standards of sampling.[6]

Even if these rates were defensible, however, they would still be irrelevant to the challenge offered the Midtown Study by the Baltimore and Boston investigations, to which we must now detour for careful examination.

The Baltimore investigation consisted of three different research operations, the only one of pertinence here being that designated the *clinical evaluation*. Focused on a broad spectrum of chronic and acute somatic illnesses, and also mental disorder, this particular operation started with a drawn sample of 1,292 persons in an age range defined as reaching from "under 15 to over 65." Of these, 809 individuals, or 62.6% all told, appeared in clinic for (1) a battery of laboratory tests and (2) thorough physical examinations by one of a staff of 31 physicians, internists in the main. From this sample of participating examinees a "weighted" estimate of 10.9% was derived as the prevalence rate for mental disorder.[7] This figure has not only been extrapolated to the city of Baltimore and quoted in Federal publications

---

[3] This has been fully reported, authors undesignated, in *Chronic Illness in a Large City: The Baltimore Study* (1957).

[4] "Studies in Medical Sociology: The Relation of Mental Disorders to Population Density," *New Engl. J. Med.*, vol. 23, no. 17 (Oct. 26, 1944), pp. 571–577.

[5] *Third Annual Report*, Joint Commission on Mental Illness and Health (1958), p. 11.

[6] N. J. Cole, C. H. Branch, and O. M. Shaw, "Mental Illness: A Survey Assessment of Community Rates, Attitudes and Adjustments," *A.M.A. Arch. Neurol. Psychiat.*, vol. 77 (Apr. 17, 1957), pp. 393–398.

[7] Such cases were classified in one of four categories, namely: (1) psychoses; (2) psychoneuroses; (3) psychophysiologic, autonomic, and visceral disorders; and (4) other mental, psychoneurotic, and personality disorders.

addressed to the general public, but in a variety of publications has also been projected on the American population at large.

The basic fact that need concern us here is that between the reported Baltimore mental disorder frequency of 10.9% and Midtown's 23.4% impairment rate stretches a seemingly unbridgeable gulf. Before we accept this difference as lending credence to views that the Midtown Study's criterion of mental morbidity was overextended, we must first determine whether the two studies are comparable in other relevant respects.

First, the studied populations are far from demographic comparability, but this can be partially corrected by isolating the segment of the Baltimore sample that most nearly matches the Midtown respondents, at least in race and age composition. The closest Baltimore age approximation reported in the source volume[8] is the 15 to 64 age range, where the morbidity frequency is 14%. We are not told the disorder rate for examined sample people of this age span who are white, numbering 371 individuals. However, we are told that for the whites of all ages the morbidity rate is almost three-fourths higher than for nonwhites. Setting aside the nonwhites brings the mental illness frequency among the indicated subsample of 371 white persons, by our calculation, to about the 16% point.

Attention is next drawn to the Baltimore classification process. For one thing, the complete examination in clinic was made by internists (rather than psychiatrists), who had many somatic conditions to check systematically and apparently were short both in clinic time for focused psychiatric inquiry and in prior training for secure psychiatric observation, reporting, and evaluation. Explicit at least is that the Baltimore mental disorder rate is beset with potentially serious problems of underreporting, as the monograph authors are at some pains to indicate in the following passages:

1. It was recognized that the number of cases of a particular disease uncovered is closely related to the thoroughness of the examination.[9]

2. With a large number of physicians participating . . . it was not feasible to develop rules governing the recording of diagnoses. . . . The physicians were therefore asked to record all conditions, acute or chronic. . . . Under this general directive, there was, as anticipated, a very wide variation in the kinds of conditions which physicians recorded (and presumably did not record) as diagnoses.[10]

3. The method of arriving at diagnoses probably is a more significant factor (affecting) the prevalence (rate) of mental disorders . . . than most other diseases discussed in this report. The examining internists diagnosed a mental disorder as they chose, with or without a psychiatric consultation or psychometric testing.[11] It was recognized that there would be differences in physicians' *interest in and*

---

[8] *Chronic Illness in a Large City: The Baltimore Study* (1957), p. 97.

[9] *Ibid.*, p. 384.

[10] *Ibid.*, p. 391.

[11] The authors report that only psychiatric consultations were sought, and for only 14 (1.7%) of the 809 examined sample subjects (*ibid.*, p. 390). Given that the examiners were internists in the main, this is not exactly a reassuring index of psychiatric interest.

willingness to diagnose mental disorders. The records, therefore, were subsequently reviewed by a psychiatrist and classified by diagnosis and severity of impairment. . . . In this review, there became apparent substantial differences among examining physicians in the *completeness of recording of information* bearing on mental disorders. The review resulted in the deletion of about one-third of the cases which had been diagnosed (as mental disorders) by examining physicians, on the basis that the information *recorded* did not adequately support the diagnosis. To the extent that the deletion of cases by the reviewing psychiatrist was due to *incomplete recording of evidence* by the examining physician, the data presented here *understate the prevalence.* [All italics added.][12]

Thus, in the Baltimore clinical study, the recording of psychiatric diagnoses and supporting evidence depended entirely upon the motivations of the examining internists to venture a diagnosis beyond their professional competence and, if they so ventured, to inscribe the evidence in sufficient volume and detail to satisfy the specialized and exacting, but previously undefined, criteria of the reviewing psychiatrist.

Under these circumstances, it appears likely, first, that cases of mental pathology in the Baltimore sample examined went unrecognized by the physician, or, if recognized, were unrecorded. Their number is of course unknown. Second, among the many cases of recorded pathology that were subsequently rejected by the reviewing psychiatrist, it is likely that a number reflected inadequate probing for or recording of supporting details, rather than absence of mental illness. On the basis of a 16% mental morbidity rate above derived for the subsample of Baltimore age 15 to 64 whites, we can estimate that prior to such review and rejection this morbidity rate stood at about 24%.[13] Represented in the latter rate would be the "false positives" correctly rejected by the reviewing psychiatrist, but *not* the "false negatives" that were overlooked or maldiagnosed or left unrecorded by the examining internists (and unreviewed by the reviewing psychiatrist). If these two different kinds of errors should happen more or less to cancel each other out, a matter on which evidence is lacking, the estimated 24% morbidity rate would seem to stand as approximately accurate.

The original mental disorder rate of 10.9% reported for the Baltimore sample examined in clinic appears to be distant indeed from the Midtown sample finding of mental impairment in a frequency of 23.9%. We have now demonstrated that the apparent discrepancy between the two studies is not real. When the Baltimore sample is demographically matched to the Midtown sample, the illness rate, on evidence reported, must be adjusted from 10.9% to 16%. And if identifiable errors of underreporting and overreporting of mental pathology should balance out, it appears possible that the true frequency might approach 24%, or near identity with the Midtown rate.

However, any Baltimore frequency would suffer from the further damag-

---

[12] *Ibid.*, p. 96. Throughout the volume, the authors are critically aware of methodological problems in, and lessons to be learned from, the Baltimore investigation.

[13] This estimate assumes that the one-in-three rejection of diagnoses cases by the reviewing psychiatrist, reported for the examined sample as a whole, more or less applies to the subsample of interest here.

ing fact that 44% of the Baltimore sample whites originally selected for clinical examination did *not* participate in the study.[14] With so large a defection, the bias potential in the studied sample itself is serious indeed. The Baltimore investigators' method of applying "weights" in an effort to compensate for observed biases in age, sex, and racial composition[15] altogether fails to correct for the possibility that participants in the underrepresented groups may be unrepresentative of the many non-participants on the crucial index of mental pathology rate. Specifically, if the mentally ill predominantly chose not to submit to the requested medical examination in clinic, then the 24% morbidity frequency estimated above as possible—for the Baltimore age 15 to 64 white subsample actually studied—may be an understatement by a considerable margin. All in all, in the face of this haunting unknown, it must be submitted that the Baltimore mental disorder rate is altogether too inconclusive to be used in judging the tenability of the mental morbidity finding of the Midtown Study.

A more promising benchmark may be elicited from America's World War II experience with military-age men. In the most comprehensive review of that experience made available to the date of this writing, Brill and Beebe[16] focus on "the manpower pool of about 26 million men who were in the ages of 18-37 in 1941, plus those reaching their 18th birthday in the succeeding four years." The quoted authors divide this pool of men into three segments: (1) served in Armed Forces, (2) medically disqualified for such service, and (3) granted occupational or other deferment from such service. For each segment they estimate the prevalence of "psychoneurosis, pathological personality, and other psychiatric disorders" and "psychiatric defects, mental or educational deficiency." In the three indicated segments, these total 4.7 million men (excluding the category "neurological defects") or 18.1% of the entire pool.

This datum, of course, refers to the entire national population of military-age men. A closer match to the Midtown male population can be drawn from wartime Selective Service rejections on psychiatric grounds at the well-documented Boston Regional Induction Station.[17] Relative to all examinees, we know that the station's psychiatric rejection rate was 10.6% during the early months of the war[18] and 21.3% in August, 1945.[19]

---

[14] *Chronic Illness in a Large City: The Baltimore Study* (1957), p. 209.

[15] That is, these varyingly underrepresented groups in the studied sample were arithmetically reconstituted to accord with their representation in the population universe. In this process it was apparently assumed that the unknown mental disorder rate of *nonparticipants* from a given demographic segment would approximate the rate known for *participants* from the same segment.

[16] N. Q. Brill and G. W. Beebe, *A Follow-up Study of War Neuroses* (1955), pp. 322–33.

[17] The region covered was eastern Massachusetts.

[18] R. W. Hyde, and L. V. Kingsley, "Studies in Medical Sociology: The Relations of Mental Disorders to Population Density," *New Eng. J. Med.*, vol. 23, no. 17 (Oct. 26, 1944), pp. 571–577.

[19] S. A. Stouffer, *et al.*, *Measurement and Prediction*, Studies in Social Psychology in World War II, vol. iv (1950), p. 551.

We also know that the national psychiatric rejection rate fluctuated appreciably through the war years with shifts in standards and military demands for manpower. We can assume that the Boston station's rate fluctuated similarly, probably around 16%—the middle point in the above range. On the basis of a 1942 study of the station's examinees we can adjust this median rate to about 17.5% for white men from the high-density areas of metropolitan Boston. If we could also take into account the unrecorded psychiatric cases screened out *before* reaching the station's examiners, and also the subsequent recorded and unrecorded psychiatric discharges from the armed services, the over-all rate would almost certainly turn out to be not less than 20%.

To achieve a better-fitting match to this military-age, white Boston population, we might look at the age 20 to 39 males in our Midtown sample. And there we find an over-all prevalence of impairment in a frequency of 19.5%. The chances are 95 in 100 that this rate stands somewhere between 15.1 and 23.9% in the corresponding segment of the Midtown population universe.

We would not be understood to attach any large significance to the seeming concordance between the Boston frequency of mental morbidity, as just worked out, and Midtown's. It is universal knowledge that initial Selective Service psychiatric examinations were usually brief and superficial, and evaluation was hardly geared to a realistic formulation of psychological balances required to cope with the military environment. From the viewpoint of military manpower needs, therefore, such screening may have discarded too many men who could have been fitted to a limited service function of some kind. However, its very superficiality and an accompanying set of intense social pressures for acceptance in the armed forces, together argue that few of these men could have been rejected except on psychiatric grounds that were sufficiently telling by the criteria of civilian experience.[20]

From this comparison of the Baltimore, Boston, and Midtown data we do *not* draw the inference that *over-all* mental morbidity rates in the three populations were demonstrably alike. Although we made several adjustments in the data to enlarge comparability, remaining uncontrolled are several large intercommunity variations: (1) known differences in such elements of demographic composition as socioeconomic standing and ethnic origin—which could not be analytically controlled because of lack of necessary information; (2) known gross differences in the operating circumstances of the psychiatric examination and evaluation process; and (3) probable differences in professional criteria for differentiating the mentally ill from others. On all these counts, it remains impossible to make any generalizations about relative magnitudes of *over-all* mental pathology in the three analyzed populations.

Nonetheless, we have introduced the two comparison populations to sug-

---

[20] This probability finds particular reinforcement in the case of the Boston induction station from the fact that it was served by a corps of psychiatrists out of the area's distinguished medical schools.

gest, despite appearances to the contrary, that they offer no evidence to support a view of Midtown mental morbidity rate as out of line with previous relevant research experience.

On Interpreting the Incidence of Mental Illness

BERNARD ROSENBERG

A short time ago there appeared a 126-page monograph modestly entitled "Psychosis and Civilization" and written by Herbert Goldhamer and Andrew Marshall. This rather specialized statistical study, which would ordinarily be discussed only in the technical journals, was reviewed, somewhat surprisingly, in *Commentary* (December, 1953) by Nathan Glazer, who voiced an unqualified admiration for the work. I say, somewhat surprisingly, because *Commentary* in its "Study of Man" department often criticizes social science research and seldom applauds it. That Glazer should have felt so enthusiastic about this little book is cause for a certain curiosity.

"Psychosis and Civilization" is, within limits, an admirable job. It happens, however, that the hypothesis of its authors—that the rate of insanity is now no greater than it was a century ago—remains unproved. It remains unproved, not because they have failed to explore all the *available* data, but because it is an unprovable hypothesis. One cannot determine with any degree of accuracy the actual incidence of psychosis, and to be guided solely by the rate of first admissions to mental hospitals, as Goldhamer and Marshall have been, is nearly as misleading as to judge our crime rate by the prison population.

But putting such objections to one side for a moment, and assuming that Goldhamer and Marshall do show that the frequency of psychosis is constant, it is worth our while to see how variously such a dubious conclusion can be interpreted. For example the authors say, "Our findings give us warrant for emphasizing not that mental health is just as good today as it was in the past, but rather that mental health was just as bad in the past as it is now." However, when these findings are popularized and politicized the emphasis, especially in *Commentary,* is reversed. Then it appears that since we will always have the mad with us, there is nothing so particularly stressful about our society as to derange a large percentage of Americans. The appeal that a highly vulnerable piece of social research has for the politically complacent is not hard to understand.

SOURCE: Bernard Rosenberg, "Mental Hospitals and Social Theorists" *Dissent,* 1:3 (Summer, 1954), pp. 62–66. Reprinted by permission.

Glazer paraphrases the authors—up to a point; and thereby does them an injustice. He writes:

All we can conclude, they say, is that there has been no great change in the conditions causing psychosis in this country in the past hundred years. . . . Another conclusion, they point out, is compatible with these results: that is, that in psychosis we deal with a condition which is independent of environmental circumstances, a condition dependent on heredity or physiological aberration, which, like some physical diseases, strikes a certain proportion of the population.

Goldhamer and Marshall do say something like this, but they add something else which Glazer fails to mention:

Theories that view the functional psychoses as resulting from repressions of basic human drives and as the consequence of trauma developing in early intimate personal and familial relationships, may possibly be thought of as being more especially consistent with our findings.

This is acadamese, of course. Yet it points clearly enough to environmental factors and away from hereditarianism.

To misappropriate the Goldhamer-Marshall book in support of a genetic theory of psychosis, even one that reinforces our self-satisfaction, is to make an unwarranted deduction based on fragmentary evidence. The authors speak of a tendency, sometimes referred to as a law, according to which the probability that disturbed persons will be hospitalized is inverse to their distance from a mental hospital. Those farthest removed from psychiatric centers are not necessarily the most immune to breakdown, but they are least likely to be institutionalized. In Arkansas there are only two mental hospitals and in that state the official rate of psychosis is low. In Massachusetts there are excellent facilities for mental patients and the records indicate a correspondingly high rate of psychosis. Does anyone care to argue that there is something about Arkansans—their physique, their hormonal balance, the amount of oxygen in their brains—which decisively differentiates them from residents of Massachusetts? Governor Dewey has asked the New York State Legislature for an appropriation of $350,000,000 to be used for mental health. Suppose all of it were spent on new institutions: there would be a sudden leap in the reported number of psychotics. But this would tell us very little about the actual distribution of mental disease, except that many—an indeterminable percentage—of its victims go without professional care.

Goldhamer and Marshall assert that, "The various conditions inhibiting admissions to mental hospitals were at least no less in Massachusetts of 1855–59 than they are currently in the United States as a whole." It follows that any estimate of psychosis in the population at large is guesswork. Practically all mental hospitals are crowded, many have long waiting lists. In short a certain proportion of people are known to be psychotic and yet go uncommitted. Full records of how many individuals apply for admission to mental hospitals are lacking, but if we could add those who do apply and are turned down for reasons of space to those who are accepted, the statistical picture would look quite different. Nor would we have exhausted the possibilities. For there are certainly psychotics who never apply or are never committed to mental hospitals.

It is relevant to consider the rural-urban differential. S. Kirson Wineberg indicates that, "The standardized rates for schizophrenia during 1933, based upon the 1930 population, show 1.92 times more schizophrenics committed from urban than from rural areas." How does one interpret such facts? Either the statistics are faulty and farmers are just as susceptible to schizophrenia as urban dwellers, or social conditions *do* affect sanity. If the former, then Goldhamer and Marshall must be taken with a grain of salt; if the latter then no genetic theory of psychosis can be seriously entertained. Landis and Page report that for the years 1915–20 rates of schizophrenia in New York State increased steadily with size of city. The rates varied from 11.7 per 100,000 inhabitants in cities between 20,000 and 50,000 to 21 in New York City. With manic-depression the differences are less marked, but still plainly discernible.

All that Goldhamer and Marshall have really shown is that public and private expenditure for mental disorder is proportionately the same at present as it was a hundred years ago—at least in Massachusetts. (They have already been chided for confusing that New England state with all of civilization.) If this is so, I find it appalling that we should not have invested more heavily in research and treatment programs. Leopold Bellak, in his comprehensive survey of schizophrenia, points out that it is a scourge more serious than cancer since it usually strikes in early adult life whereas the degenerative diseases commonly occur at an advanced age. About fifty per cent of the total resident population of mental hospitals are schizophrenic. Since approximately one-half of all hospital beds in the nation are occupied by mental patients, and schizophrenics constitute one-half of these, Dr. Bellak suggests that every fourth or fifth bed available is occupied by a patient suffering from dementia praecox.

Is all this irremediable? Short of Nazi-style eugenics, there are three possible answers: (1) Yes, because some people are just born that way; (2) No, because the whole phenomenon is biological and can be dealt with mechanically, through such means as shock treatment; (3) No, because the problem is biosocial and where machines have failed other methods are beginning to work. That the last answer should still be an unpopular one puzzles me a great deal.

Ours is a middling age. We have a middle class society, a middle-brow culture, and a middle-of-the-road government. A false aura of Aristotelian wisdom has been cast over the whole civilization. With all that, when a centrist position is really indicated those who embrace moderation in the abstract, choose this occasion to throw it overboard. Our constitutions differ drastically, but any of us may become psychotic. No one who takes lysergic acid diethylanide at Boston Psychopathic Hospital fails to experience insanity. Nevertheless, we are differentially endowed, perhaps from birth, surely thereafter; one man's predispositions are not the same as another's. If X is unhinged he may become a paranoid while Y exhibits symptoms of cyclothymia. None of this takes places *in vacua*. Something precipitates the disorder: war, bereavement, guilt, conflict—something. If precipitating factors can be minimized by a reconstitution of the society that breeds them, it is safe to say that personality disorganization will decline. If, however, you believe there is no essential difference between American society and, let us say Congolese Bantu society where Ellsworth Faris reports "the relative absence of insanity," then nothing needs to be reconstituted unless it be the body chemistry and the brain tissue of disturbed individuals.

The insane used to be doomed; nothing could be done for them aside from the provision of more or less brutal custodial care. By now we are supposed to have progressed far beyond any theory of diabolic possession. Nevertheless, it often seems as if nothing except terminology has actually changed. About twenty years ago shock treatment was discovered and quickly swept the psychiatric field where, more often than not it continues to be used promiscuously. A good many practitioners have finally felt some revulsion against this so-called therapy whose use causes quick remissions and quick readmissions. It is no longer widely regarded as a panacea. One uses shock to establish rapport, to pierce the patient's gibberish, to bring him within reach. And when he relapses, one shocks him again. What harm this may do no one knows, but therapists who have had success in the direct analysis of psychotics contend that those who have been subjected to excessive shock are by far the hardest to cure.

Despite this chastening experience, the psychiatric Old Guard are undismayed. Their presuppositions are perhaps more popular than ever. I recently took a guided tour through one of Massachusetts' more "progressive" mental hospitals and was struck with the fact that nearly every other patient had a bandaged head. Lobotomy, lobectomy, lately topectomy, and other forms of emotional decapitation which do not diminish intelligence (they merely take the spark out of life) have become increasingly common. Psychiatrists are reported in the press to be working on a magic pill that, when consumed in the proper quantity, will restore the demented to health and happiness. It is still the devil, which smells as medieval by any other name, that needs to be exorcised.

Laurence K. Frank has suggested, however, that society is the patient. So long as we persist in denying this, it will be impossible to adopt a curative *or* a therapeutic program of any fundamental value. Clearly, we need not tamper with our sick society if psychosis—and who knows how many other forms of pathology?—are, as Glazer so happily puts it, "independent of environmental circumstances." What may not be so obvious is that, within such a narrow framework, even intelligent therapy for individual patients, limited as its possibilities may be, is also very nearly blocked.

If severe mental disorder is nothing but a biological phenomenon, machines, pills, and surgical instruments are the appropriate means for dealing with it. On the other hand, if psychosis is a personality problem ordinarily triggered by a crisis embedded in our tension-ridden society, then psychotherapy is surely indicated. Furthermore, practitioners like John Nathaniel Rosen, Frieda Fromm-Reichmann, and Harry Stack Sullivan have had success in treating schizophrenics without benefit of shock or tips from the pharmacopeia. Rosen goes to the heart of the matter in "Direct Analysis" when he observes:

Early years of training in pathology prompted me to describe the deteriorated schizophrenic in . . . organic terms, although at no point along the line have I ever been persuaded that there exists in these patients an organic or even a constitutional factor that could begin to fulfill the criteria of Koch's postulates. In each case, in accordance with well-known authors, I also found environmental factors of such distressing intensity that, if they could be duplicated, I believe they would produce the same type of psychosis in many other individuals as that which was produced in the unfortunate victims.

The above would seem to be a firm link in the chain of progressive approximations of the truth; and if writers in liberal journals such as *Commentary* prefer to suppose that psychosis is "independent of environmental circumstances" that may well be because they are committed to the view that American society—call it capitalism, socialism, what have you—is nearly the best of possible worlds. But social currents have a way of changing, and scientific evidence has a way of accumulating. Given another twist of the *Zeitgeist*, the views I have quoted from Rosen may even gain general acceptance.

Crime as an American Way of Life

DANIEL BELL

I

In the 1890's, the Reverend Dr. Charles Parkhurst, shocked at the open police protection afforded New York's bordellos, demanded a state inquiry. In the Lexow investigation that followed, the young and dashing William Travers Jerome staged a set of public hearings that created sensation after sensation. He badgered "Clubber" Williams, First Inspector of the Police Department, to account for wealth and property far greater than could have been saved on his salary; it was earned, the Clubber explained laconically,

SOURCE: "Crime as an American Way of Life," *Antioch Review*, 13:2 (Summer, 1953), pp. 131–154. Copyright by Antioch Press. Reprinted by permission.

through land speculation "in Japan." Heavy-set Captain Schmittberger, the "collector" for the "Tenderloin precincts"—Broadway's fabulous concentration of hotels, theaters, restaurants, gaming houses, and saloons—related in detail how protection money was distributed among the police force. Crooks, policemen, public officials, businessmen, all paraded across the stage, each adding his chapter to a sordid story of corruption and crime. The upshot of these revelations was reform—the election of William L. Strong, a stalwart businessman, as mayor, and the naming of Theodore Roosevelt as police commissioner.

It did not last, of course, just as previous reform victories had not lasted. Yet the ritual drama was re-enacted. Twenty years ago the Seabury investigation in New York uncovered the tin-box brigade and the thirty-three little MacQuades. Jimmy Walker was ousted as Mayor and in came Fiorello La Guardia. Tom Dewey became district attorney, broke the industrial rackets, sent Lucky Luciano to jail and went to the Governor's chair in Albany. Then reform was again swallowed up in the insatiable maw of corruption until Kefauver and the young and dashing Rudolph Halley threw a new beam of light into the seemingly bottomless pit.

How explain this repetitious cycle? Obviously the simple moralistic distinction between "good guys" and "bad guys," so deep at the root of the reform impulse, bears little relation to the role of organized crime in American society. What, then, does?

I I

Americans have had an extraordinary talent for compromise in politics and extremism in morality. The most shameless political deals (and "steals") have been rationalized as expedient and realistically necessary. Yet in no other country have there been such spectacular attempts to curb human appetites and brand them as illicit, and nowhere else such glaring failures. From the start America was at one and the same time a frontier community where "everything goes," and the fair country of the Blue Laws. At the turn of the century the cleavage developed between the Big City and the small-town conscience. Crime as a growing business was fed by the revenues from prostitution, liquor and gambling that a wide-open urban society encouraged and which a middle-class Protestant ethos tried to suppress with a ferocity unmatched in any other civilized country. Catholic cultures rarely have imposed such restrictions, and have rarely suffered such excesses. Even in prim and proper Anglican England, prostitution is a commonplace of Piccadilly night life, and gambling one of the largest and most popular industries. In America the enforcement of public morals has been a continuing feature of our history.

Some truth may lie in Svend Ranulf's generalization that moral indignation is a peculiar fact of middle-class psychology and represents a disguised form of repressed envy. The larger truth lies perhaps in the brawling nature of American development and the social character of crime. Crime, in many ways, is a Coney Island mirror, caricaturing the morals and manners of a society. The jungle quality of the American business community, particularly at the turn of the century, was reflected in the mode of "business" practiced by the coarse gangster elements, most of them from new immigrant families, who were "getting ahead," just as Horatio Alger had urged. In the older, Protestant tradition the intense acquisitiveness, such as that of Daniel Drew, was rationalized by a compulsive moral fervor. But the formal obeisance of the ruthless businessman in the workaday world to the church-going pieties of the Sabbath was one that the gangster could not make. Moreover, for the young criminal, hunting in the asphalt jungle of the crowded city, it was not the businessman with his wily manipulation of numbers but the "man with the gun" who was the American hero. "No amount of commercial prosperity," once wrote Teddy Roosevelt, "can supply the lack of the heroic virtues." The American was "the hunter, cowboy, frontiersman, the soldier, the naval hero." And in the crowded slums, the gangster. He was a man with a gun, acquiring by personal merit what was denied to him by complex orderings of a stratified society. And the duel with the law was the morality play *par excellence*: the gangster, with whom rides our own illicit desires, and the prosecutor, representing final judgment and the force of the law.

Yet all this was acted out in a wider context. The desires satisfied in extra-legal fashion were more than a hunger for the "forbidden fruits" of conventional morality. They also involved, in the complex and ever shifting structure of group, class and ethnic stratification, which is the warp and woof of America's "open" society, such "normal" goals as independence through a business of one's own, and such "moral" aspirations as the desire for social advancement and social prestige. For crime, in the language of the sociologists, has a "functional" role in the society, and the urban rackets—the illicit activity organized for continuing profit rather than individual illegal acts—is one of the queer ladders of social mobility in American life. Indeed, it is not too much to say that the whole question of organized crime in America cannot be understood unless one appreciates (1) the distinctive role of organized gambling as a function of a mass consumption economy; (2) the specific role of various immigrant groups as they one after another became involved in marginal business and crime; and (3) the relation of crime to the changing character of the urban political machines.

III

As a society changes, so does, in lagging fashion, its type of crime. As American society became more "organized," as the American businessman became more "civilized" and less "buccaneering," so did the American racketeer. And just as there were important changes in the structure of business enterprise, so the "institutionalized" criminal enterprise was transformed too.

In the America of the last fifty years the main drift of society has been toward the rationalization of industry, the domestication of the crude self-made captain of industry into the respectable man of manners, and the emergence of a mass-consumption economy. The most significant transformation in the field of "institutionalized" crime was the increasing relative importance of gambling as against other kinds of illegal activity. And, as a multi-billion-dollar business, gambling underwent a transition parallel to the changes in American enterprise as a whole. This parallel was exemplified in many ways: in gambling's industrial organization (e.g., the growth of a complex technology such as the national racing wire service and the minimization of risks by such techniques as lay-off betting); in its respectability, as was evidenced in the opening of smart and popular gambling casinos in resort towns and in "satellite" adjuncts to metropolitan areas; in its functional role in a mass-consumption economy (for sheer volume of money changing hands, nothing has ever surpassed this feverish activity of fifty million American adults); in the social acceptance of the gamblers in the important status world of sport and entertainment, i.e., "café society."

In seeking to "legitimize" itself, gambling had quite often actually become a force against older and more vicious forms of illegal activity. In 1946, for example, when a Chicago mobster, Pat Manno, went down to Dallas, Texas, to take over gambling in the area for the Accardo-Guzik combine, he reassured the sheriff as to his intent as follows: "Something I'm against, that's dope peddlers, pickpockets, hired killers. That's one thing I can't stomach, and that's one thing the fellows up there—the group won't stand for, things like that. They discourage it, they even go to headquarters and ask them why they don't do something about it."

Jimmy Cannon once reported that when the gambling raids started in Chicago, the "combine" protested that, in upsetting existing stable relations, the police were only opening the way for ambitious young punks and hoodlums to start trouble. Nor is there today, as there was twenty or even forty years ago, prostitution of major organized scope in the United States. Aside from the fact that manners and morals have changed, prostitution *as an industry* doesn't pay as well as gambling. Besides, its existence threatened the tacit moral acceptance and quasi-respectability that gamblers and gambling have secured in the American way of life. It was, as any operator in the field might tell you, "bad for business."

The criminal world of the last decade, its tone set by the captains of the gambling industry, is in startling contrast to the state of affairs in the two decades before. If a Kefauver report had been written then, the main "names" would have been Lepke and Gurrah, Dutch Schultz, Jack "Legs" Diamond, Lucky Luciano, and, reaching back a little further, Arnold Rothstein, the czar of the underworld. These men (with the exception of Luciano, who was involved in narcotics and prostitution) were in the main industrial racketeers. Rothstein, it is true, had a larger function: he was, as Frank Costello became later, the financier of the underworld—the pioneer big businessman of crime, who, understanding the logic of co-ordination, sought to *organize* crime as a source of regular income. His main interest in this direction was in industrial racketeering, and his entry was through labor disputes. At one time, employers in the garment trades hired Legs Diamond and his sluggers to break strikes, and the Communists, then in control of the cloakmakers union, hired one Little Orgie to protect the pickets and beat up the scabs; only later did both sides learn that Legs Diamond and Little Orgie were working for the same man, Rothstein.

Rothstein's chief successors, Lepke Buchalter and Gurrah Shapiro, were able, in the early '30's, to dominate sections of the men's and women's clothing industries, of painting, fur dressing, flour trucking, and other fields. In a highly chaotic and cut-throat industry such as clothing, the racketeer, paradoxically, played a stabilizing role by regulating competition and fixing prices. When the NRA came in and assumed this function, the businessman found that what had once been a quasi-economic service was now pure extortion, and he began to demand police action. In other types of racketeering, such as the trucking of perishable foods and water-front loading, where the racketeers entrenched themselves as middlemen—taking up, by default, a service that neither shippers nor truckers wanted to assume—a pattern of accommodation was roughly worked out and the rackets assumed a quasi-legal veneer. On the water-front, old-time racketeers perform the necessary function of loading—but at an exorbitant price, and this monopoly was recognized by both the union and the shippers, and tacitly by government. (See my case study "The Last of the Business Rackets," in the June, 1951 issue of *Fortune*.)

But in the last decade and a half, industrial racketeering has not offered much in the way of opportunity. *Like American capitalism itself, crime shifted its emphasis from production to consumption.* The focus of crime became the direct exploitation of the citizen as consumer, largely through gambling. And while the protection of these huge revenues was inextricably linked to politics, the relation between gambling and "the mobs" became more complicated.

IV

Although it never showed up in the gross national product, gambling in the last decade was one of the largest industries in the United States. The Kefauver Committee estimated it as a twenty-billion-dollar business. This figure has been picked up and widely quoted, but in truth no one knows what the gambling "turnover" and "take" actually is, nor how much is bet legally (pari-mutuel, etc.) and how much illegally. In fact, the figure cited by the committee was arbitrary and arrived at quite sloppily. As one staff member said: "We had no real idea of the money spent. . . . The California crime commission said twelve billion. Virgil Peterson of Chicago estimated thirty billion. We picked twenty billion as a balance between the two."

If comprehensive data are not available, we do know, from specific instances, the magnitude of many of the operations. Some indications can be seen from these items culled at random:

—James Carroll and the M & G syndicate did a 20-million-dollar annual business in St. Louis. This was one of the two large books in the city.

—The S & G syndicate in Miami did a 26-million-dollar volume yearly; the total for all books in the Florida resort reached 40 millions.

—Slot machines were present in 69,786 establishments in 1951 (each paid $100 for a license to the Bureau of Internal Revenue); the usual average is three machines to a license, which would add up to 210,000 slot machines in operation in the United States. In legalized areas, where the betting is higher and more regular, the average gross "take" per machine is $50 a week.

—The largest policy wheel (i.e. "numbers") in Chicago's "Black Belt" reported taxable net profits for the four-year period from 1946 through 1949, after sizable deduction for "overhead," of $3,656,968. One of the large "white" wheels reported in 1947 a gross income of $2,317,000 and a net profit of $205,000. One CIO official estimated that perhaps 15 per cent of his union's lower echelon officials are involved in the numbers racket (a steward, free to roam a plant, is in a perfect situation for organizing bets).

If one considers the amount of betting on sports alone—an estimated six billion on baseball, a billion on football pools, another billion on basketball, six billion on horse racing—then Elmo Roper's judgment that "only the food, steel, auto, chemical, and machine-tool industries have a greater volume of business" does not seem too far-fetched.

While gambling has long flourished in the United States, the influx of the big mobsters into the industry—and its expansion—started in the '30's when repeal of Prohibition forced them to look about for new avenues of enterprise. Gambling, which had begun to flower under the nourishment of rising incomes, was the most lucrative field in sight. To a large extent the shift from bootlegging to gambling was a mere transfer of business operations. In the East, Frank Costello went into slot machines and the operation of a number of ritzy gambling casinos. He also became the "banker" for the Erickson "book," which "laid off" bets for other bookies. Joe Adonis, similarly, opened up a number of casinos, principally in New Jersey. Across the country, many other mobsters went into bookmaking. As other rackets diminished, and gambling, particularly horse-race betting, flourished in the '40's, a struggle erupted over control of racing information.

Horse-race betting requires a peculiar industrial organization. The essential component is time. A bookie can operate only if he can get information on odds up to the very last minute before the race, so that he can "hedge" or "lay off" bets. With racing going on simultaneously on many tracks throughout the country, this information has to be obtained speedily and accurately. Thus, the racing wire is the nerve ganglion of race betting.

The racing-wire news service got started in the '20's through the genius of the late Moe Annenberg, who had made a fearful reputation for himself as Hearst's circulation manager in the rough-and-tumble Chicago newspaper wars. Annenberg conceived the idea of a telegraphic news service which would gather information from tracks and shoot it immediately to scratch sheets, horse parlors, and bookie joints. In some instances, track owners gave Annenberg the rights to send news from tracks; more often, the news was simply "stolen" by crews operating inside or near the tracks. So efficient did this news distribution system become, that in 1942, when a plane knocked out a vital telegraph circuit which served an Air Force field as well as the gamblers, the Continental Press managed to get its racing wire service for gamblers resumed in fifteen minutes, while it took the Fourth Army, which was responsible for the defense of the entire West Coast, something like three hours.

Annenberg built up a nationwide racing information chain that not only distributed wire news but controlled sub-outlets as well. In 1939, harassed by the Internal Revenue Bureau on income tax, and chivvied by the Justice Department for "monopolistic" control of the wire service, the tired and aging Annenberg simply walked out of the business. He did not sell his interest, or even seek to salvage some profit; he simply gave up. Yet, like any established and thriving institution, the enterprise continued, though on a decentralized basis. James Ragen, Annenberg's operations manager, and likewise a veteran of the old Chicago circulation wars, took over the national wire service through a dummy friend and renamed it the Continental Press Service.

The salient fact is that in the operation of the Annenberg and Ragen wire service, formally illegal as many of its subsidiary operations may have been (i.e. in "stealing" news, supplying information to bookies, etc.) gangsters played no part. It was a business, illicit, true, but primarily a business. The distinction between gamblers and gangsters, as we shall see, is a relevant one.

In 1946, the Chicago mob, whose main interest was in bookmaking rather than gambling casinos, began to move in on the wire monopoly. Following repeal, the Capone lieutenants had turned, like Lepke, to labor racketeering. Murray ("The Camel") Humphries muscled in on the teamsters, the operating engineers, and the cleaning-and-dyeing, laundry, and linen-supply industries. Through a small-time punk, Willie Bioff, and union official George Browne, Capone's chief successors, Frank ("The Enforcer") Nitti and Paul Ricca, came into control of the motion-picture union and proceeded to shake down the movie industry for fabulous sums in order to "avert strikes." In 1943, when the government moved in and smashed the industrial rackets, the remaining big shots, Charley Fischetti, Jake Guzik, and Tony Accardo decided to concentrate on gambling, and in particular began a drive to take over the racing wire.

In Chicago, the Guzik-Accardo gang, controlling a sub-distributor of the racing news service, began tapping Continental's wires. In Los Angeles, the head of the local distribution agency for Continental was beaten up by hoodlums working for Mickey Cohen and Joe Sica. Out of the blue appeared a new and competitive nationwide racing information and distribution service, known as Trans-American Publishing, the money for which was advanced by the Chicago mobs and Bugsy Siegel, who, at the time, held a monopoly of the bookmaking and wire-news service in Las Vegas. Many books pulled out of Continental and bought information from the new outfit, many hedged by buying from both. At the end of a year, however, the Capone mob's wire had lost about $200,000. Ragen felt that violence would erupt and went to the Cook County district attorney and told him that his life had been threatened by his rivals. Ragen knew his competitors. In June 1946 he was killed by a blast from a shotgun.

Thereafter, the Capone mob abandoned Trans-American and got a "piece" of Continental. Through their new control of the national racing-wire monopoly, the Capone mob began to muscle in on the lucrative Miami gambling business run by the so-called S & G syndicate. For a long time S & G's monopoly over bookmaking had been so complete that when New York gambler Frank Erickson bought a three months' bookmaking concession at the expensive Roney Plaza Hotel, for $45,000, the local police, in a highly publicized raid, swooped down on the hotel; the next year the Roney Plaza was again using local talent. The Capone group, however, was tougher. They demanded an interest in Miami bookmaking, and, when refused, began organizing a syndicate of their own, persuading some bookies at the big hotels to join them. Florida Governor Warren's crime investigator appeared—a friend, it seemed, of old Chicago dog-track operator William Johnston, who had contributed $100,000 to the Governor's campaign fund—and began raiding bookie joints, but only those that were affiliated with S & G. Then S & G, which had been buying its racing news from the local distributor of Continental Press, found its service abruptly shut off. For a few days the syndicate sought to bootleg information from New Orleans, but found itself limping along. After ten days' war of attrition, the five S & G partners found themselves with a sixth partner, who, for a token "investment" of $20,000 entered a Miami business that grossed $26,000,000 in one year.

V

While Americans made gambling illegal, they did not in their hearts think of it as wicked—even the churches benefited from the bingo and lottery crazes. So they gambled—and gamblers flourished. Against this open canvas, the indignant tones of Senator Wiley and the shocked righteousness of Senator Tobey during the Kefauver investigation rang oddly. Yet it was probably this very tone of surprise that gave the activity of the Kefauver Committee its piquant quality. Here were some Senators who seemingly did not know the facts of life, as most Americans did. Here, in the person of Senator Tobey, was the old New England Puritan conscience poking around in industrial America, in a world it had made but never seen. Here was old-fashioned moral indignation, at a time when cynicism was rampant in public life.

Commendable as such moralistic fervor was, it did not make for intelligent discrimination of fact. Throughout the Kefauver hearings, for example, there ran the presumption that all gamblers were invariably gangsters. This was true of Chicago's Accardo-Guzik combine, which in the past had its fingers in many kinds of rackets. It was not nearly so true of many of the large gamblers in America, most of whom had the feeling that they were satisfying a basic American urge for sport and looked upon their calling with no greater sense of guilt than did many bootleggers. After all, Sherman Billingsley did start out as a speakeasy proprietor, as did the Kreindlers of the "21" Club; and today the Stork Club and the former Jack and Charlie's are the most fashionable night and dining sports in America (one prominent patron of the Stork Club: J. Edgar Hoover).

The S & G syndicate in Miami, for example (led by Harold Salvey, Jules Levitt, Charles Friedman, Sam Cohen, and Edward (Eddie Luckey) Rosenbaum was simply a master pool of some two hundred bookies that arranged for telephone service, handled "protection," acted as bankers for those who needed ready cash on hard-hit books, and, in short, functioned somewhat analogously to the large factoring corporations in the textile field or the credit companies in the auto industry. Yet to Kefauver, these S & G men were "slippery and arrogant characters. . . . Salvey, for instance, was an old-time bookie who told us he had done nothing except engage in bookmaking or finance other bookmakers for twenty years." When, as a result of committee publicity and the newly found purity of the Miami police, the S & G syndicate went out of business, it was, as the combine's lawyer told Kefauver, because the "boys" were weary of being painted "the worst monsters in the world." "It is true," Cohen acknowledged, "that they had been law violators." But they had never done anything worse than gambling, and "to fight the world isn't worth it."

Most intriguing of all were the opinions of James J. Carroll, the St. Louis "betting commissioner," who for years had been widely quoted on the sports pages of the country as setting odds on the Kentucky Derby winter book and the baseball pennant races. Senator Wiley, speaking like the prosecutor in Camus's novel, *The Stranger,* became the voice of official morality:

Senator Wiley: Have you any children?
Mr. Carroll: Yes, I have a boy.
Senator Wiley: How old is he?
Mr. Carroll: Thirty-three.
Senator Wiley: Does he gamble?
Mr. Carroll: No.
Senator Wiley: Would you like to see him grow up and become a gambler, either professional or amateur?
Mr. Carroll: No . . .
Senator Wiley: All right. Is your son interested in your business?
Mr. Carroll: No, he is a manufacturer.
Senator Wiley: Why do you not get him into the business?
Mr. Carroll: Well, psychologically a great many people are unsuited for gambling.

Retreating from this gambit, the Senator sought to pin Carroll down on his contributions to political campaigns:

SENATOR WILEY: Now this morning I asked you whether you contributed any money for political candidates or parties, and you said not more than $200 at any one time. I presume that does not indicate the total of your contributions in any one campaign, does it?

MR. CARROLL: Well, it might, not, Senator. I have been an "againster" in many instances. I am a reader of *The Nation* for fifty years and they have advertisements calling for contributions for different candidates, different causes. . . . They carried an advertisement for George Norris; I contributed, I think, to that, and to the elder La Follette.

Carroll, who admitted to having been in the betting business since 1899, was the sophisticated—but not immoral!—counterpoint to moralist Wiley. Here was a man without the stigmata of the underworld or underground; he was worldly, cynical of official rhetoric, jaundiced about people's motives, he was—an "againster" who believed that "all gambling legislation originates or stems from some group or some individual seeking special interests for himself or his cause."

Asked why people gamble, Carroll distilled his experiences of fifty years with a remark that deserves a place in American social history: "I really don't know how to answer the question," he said. "I think gambling is a biological necessity for certain types. I think it is the quality that gives substance to their daydreams."

In a sense, the entire Kefauver materials, unintentionally, seem to document that remark. For what the Committee revealed time and time again was a picture of gambling as a basic institution in American life, flourishing openly and accepted widely. In many of the small towns, the gambling joint is as open as a liquor establishment. The town of Havana, in Mason County, Illinois, felt miffed when Governor Adlai Stevenson intervened against local gambling. In 1950, the town had raised $15,000 of its $50,000 budget by making friendly raids on the gambling houses every month and having the owners pay fines. "With the gambling fines cut off," grumbled Mayor Clarence Chester, "the next year is going to be tough."

Apart from the gamblers, there were the mobsters. But what Senator Kefauver and company failed to understand was that the mobsters, like the gamblers, and like the entire gangdom generally, were seeking to become quasi-respectable and establish a place for themselves in American life. For the mobsters, by and large, had immigrant roots, and crime, as the pattern showed, was a route of social ascent and place in American life.

VI

The mobsters were able, where they wished, to "muscle in" on the gambling business because the established gamblers were wholly vulnerable, not being able to call on the law for protection. The Senators, however, refusing to make any distinction between a gambler and a gangster, found it convenient to talk loosely of a nationwide conspiracy of "illegal" elements. Senator Kefauver asserted that a "nationwide crime syndicate does exist in the United States, despite the protestations of a strangely assorted company of criminals, self-serving politicians, plain blind fools, and others who may be honestly misguided, that there is no such combine." The Senate Committee report states the matter more dogmatically: "There is a nationwide crime syndicate known as the Mafia. . . . Its leaders are usually found in control of the most lucrative rackets in their cities. There are indications of a centralized direction and control of these rackets. . . . The Mafia is the cement that helps to bind the Costello-Adonis-Lansky syndicate of New York and the Accardo-Guzik-Fischetti syndicate of Chicago. . . . These groups have kept in touch with Luciano since his deportation from the country."

Unfortunately for a good story—and the existence of the Mafia would be a whale of a story—neither the Senate Crime Committee in its testimony, nor Kefauver in his book, presented any real evidence that the Mafia exists as a functioning organization. One finds police officials asserting before the Kefauver committee their *belief* in the Mafia; the Narcotics Bureau *thinks* that a worldwide dope ring allegedly run by Luciano is part of the Mafia; but the only other "evidence" presented—aside from the incredulous responses both of Senator Kefauver and Rudolph Halley when nearly all the Italian gangsters asserted that they didn't know about the Mafia—is that certain crimes bear "the earmarks of the Mafia."

The legend of the Mafia has been fostered in recent years largely by the peephole writing team of Jack Lait and Lee Mortimer. In their *Chicago Confidential*, they rattled off a series of names and titles that made the organization sound like a rival to an Amos and Andy Kingfish society. Few serious reporters, however, give it much credence. Burton Turkus, the Brooklyn prosecutor who broke up the "Murder, Inc." ring, denies the existence of the Mafia. Nor could Senator Kefauver even make out much of a case for his picture of a national crime syndicate. He is forced to admit that "as it exists today [it] is an elusive and furtive but nonetheless tangible thing," and that "its organization and machinations are not always easy to pinpoint." His "evidence" that many gangsters congregate at certain times of the year in such places as Hot Springs, Arkansas, in itself does not prove much; people "in the trade" usually do, and as the loquacious late Willie Moretti of New Jersey said, in explaining how he had met the late Al Capone at a race track, "Listen, well-charactered people you don't need introductions to; you just meet automatically."

Why did the Senate Crime Committee plump so hard for its theory of the Mafia and a national crime syndicate? In part, they may have been misled by their own hearsay. The Senate Committee was not in the position to do original research, and its staff, both legal and investigative, was incredibly small. Senator Kefauver had begun the investigation with the attitude that with so much smoke there must be a raging fire. But smoke can also mean a smoke screen. Mob activities is a field in which busy gossip and exaggeration flourish even more readily than in a radical political sect.

There is, as well, in the American temper, a feeling that "somewhere," "somebody" is pulling all the complicated strings to which this jumbled world dances. In politics the labor image is "Wall Street," or "Big Business"; while the business stereotype was the "New Dealers." In the field of crime, the side-of-the-mouth low-down was "Costello."

The salient reason, perhaps, why the Kefauver Committee was taken in by its own myth of an omnipotent Mafia and a despotic Costello was its failure to assimilate and understand three of the more relevant sociological facts about institutionalized crime in its relation to the political life of large urban communities in America, namely: (1) the rise of the American Italian community, as part of the inevitable process of ethnic succession, to positions of importance in politics, a process that has been occurring independently but almost simultaneously in most cities with large Italian constituencies— New York, Chicago, Kansas City, Los Angeles; (2) the fact that there are individual Italians who play prominent, often leading roles today in gambling and in the mobs; and (3) the fact that Italian gamblers and mobsters often possessed "status" within the Italian community itself and a "pull" in city politics.[1] These three items are indeed related—but not so as to form a "plot."

VII

The Italian community has achieved wealth and political influence much later and in a harder way than previous immigrant groups. Early Jewish wealth, that of the German Jews of the late nineteenth century, was made largely in banking and merchandising. To that extent, the dominant group in the Jewish community was outside of, and independent of, the urban political machines. Later Jewish wealth, among the East European immigrants, was built in the garment trades, though with some involvement with the Jewish gangster, who was typically an industrial racketeer (Arnold Rothstein, Lepke and Gurrah, etc.) Among Jewish lawyers, a small minority, such as the "Tammany lawyer" (like the protagonist of Sam Ornitz's *Haunch, Paunch and Jowl*) rose through politics and occasionally touched the fringes of crime. Most of the Jewish lawyers, by and large the communal leaders,

---

[1] Toward the end of his hearings, Senator Kefauver read a telegram from an indignant citizen of Italian descent, protesting against the impression the committee had created that organized crime in America was a distinctly Italian enterprise. The Senator took the occasion to state the obvious: that there are racketeers who are Italian does not mean that Italians are racketeers. However, it may be argued that to the extent the Kefauver Committee fell for the line about crime in America being organized and controlled by the Mafia, it did foster such a misunderstanding. Perhaps this is also the place to point out that insofar as the relation of ethnic groups and ethnic problems to illicit and quasi-legal activities is piously ignored, the field is left open to the kind of vicious sensationalism practiced by Mortimer and Lait.

climbed rapidly, however, in the opportunities that established and legitimate Jewish wealth provided. Irish immigrant wealth in the northern urban centers, concentrated largely in construction, trucking and the waterfront, has, to a substantial extent, been wealth accumulated in and through political alliance, e.g. favoritism in city contracts.[2] Control of the politics of the city thus has been crucial for the continuance of Irish political wealth. This alliance of Irish immigrant wealth and politics has been reciprocal; many noted Irish political figures lent their names as important window-dressing for business corporations (Al Smith, for example, who helped form the U.S. Trucking Corporation, whose executive head for many years was William J. McCormack, the alleged "Mr. Big" of the New York waterfront) while Irish businessmen have lent their wealth to further the careers of Irish politicians. Irish mobsters have rarely achieved status in the Irish community, but have served as integral arms of the politicians, as strong-arm men on election day.

The Italians found the more obvious big city paths from rags to riches preempted. In part this was due to the character of the early Italian immigration. Most of them were unskilled and from rural stock. Jacob Riis could remark in the '90's, "the Italian comes in at the bottom and stays there." These dispossessed agricultural laborers found jobs as ditch-diggers, on the railroads as section hands, along the docks, in the service occupations, as shoemakers, barbers, garment workers, and stayed there. Many were fleeced by the "padrone" system, a few achieved wealth from truck farming, wine growing, and marketing produce; but this "marginal wealth" was not the source of coherent and stable political power.

Significantly, although the number of Italians in the U.S. is about a third as high as the number of Irish, and of the 30,000,000 Catholic communicants in the United States, about half are of Irish descent and a sixth of Italian, there is not one Italian bishop among the hundred Catholic bishops in this country, or one Italian archbishop among the 21 archbishops. The Irish have a virtual monopoly. This is a factor related to the politics of the American church; but the condition also is possible because there is not significant or sufficient wealth among Italian Americans to force some parity.

The children of the immigrants, the second and third generation, became wise in the ways of the urban slums. Excluded from the political ladder—in the early '30's there were almost no Italians on the city payroll in top jobs, nor in books of the period can one find discussion of Italian political leaders—finding few open routes to wealth, some turned to illicit ways. In the children's court statistics of the 1930's, the largest group of delinquents were the Italian; nor were there any Italian communal or social agencies to

---

[2] A fact which should occasion little shock if one recalls that in the nineteenth century American railroads virtually stole 190,000,000 acres of land by bribing Congressmen, and that more recently such scandals as the Teapot Dome oil grabs during the Harding administration, consummated, as the Supreme Court said, "by means of conspiracy, fraud and bribery," reached to the very doors of the White House.

cope with these problems. Yet it was, oddly enough, the quondam racketeer, seeking to become respectable, who provided one of the major supports for the drive to win a political voice for Italians in the power structure of the urban political machines.

This rise of the Italian political bloc was connected, at least in the major northern urban centers, to another important development which tended to make the traditional relation between the politician and the protected or tolerated illicit operator more close than it had been in the past. This is the fact that the urban political machines had to evolve new forms of fund-raising since the big business contributions, which once went heavily into municipal politics, now—with the shift in the locus of power—go largely into national affairs. (The ensuing corruption in national politics, as recent Congressional investigations show, is no petty matter; the scruples of businessmen do not seem much superior to those of the gamblers.) One way urban political machines raised their money resembled that of the large corporations which are no longer dependent on Wall Street: by self-financing —that is, by "taxing" the large number of municipal employees who bargain collectively with City Hall for their wage increases. So the firemen's union contributed money to O'Dwyer's campaign.

A second method was taxing the gamblers. The classic example, as *Life* reported, was Jersey City, where a top lieutenant of the Hague machine spent his full time screening applicants for unofficial bookmaking licenses. If found acceptable, the applicant was given a "location," usually the house or store of a loyal precinct worker, who kicked into the machine treasury a high proportion of the large rent exacted. The one thousand bookies and their one thousand landlords in Jersey City formed the hard core of the political machine that sweated and bled to get out the votes for Hague.

A third source for the financing of these machines was the new, and often illegally earned, Italian wealth. This is well illustrated by the career of Costello and his emergence as a political power in New York. Here the ruling motive has been the search for an entrée—for oneself and one's ethnic group —into the ruling circles of the big city.

Frank Costello made his money originally in bootlegging. After repeal, his big break came when Huey Long, desperate for ready cash to fight the old-line political machines, invited Costello to install slot machines in Louisiana. Costello did, and he flourished. Together with Dandy Phil Kastel, he also opened the Beverly Club, an elegant gambling establishment just outside New Orleans, at which have appeared some of the top entertainers in America. Subsequently, Costello invested his money in New York real estate (including 79 Wall Street, which he later sold), the Copacabana night club, and a leading brand of Scotch whiskey.

Costello's political opportunity came when a money-hungry Tammany, starved by lack of patronage from Roosevelt and La Guardia, turned to him for financial support. The Italian community in New York has for years nursed a grievance against the Irish and, to a lesser extent, the Jewish political groups for monopolizing political power. They complained about the lack of judicial jobs, the small number—usually one—of Italian Congressmen, the lack of representation on the state tickets. But the Italians lacked the means to make their ambitions a reality. Although they formed a large voting bloc, there was rarely sufficient wealth to finance political clubs. Italian immigrants, largely poor peasants from Southern Italy and Sicily, lacked the mercantile experience of the Jews, and the political experience gained in the seventy-five-year history of Irish immigration.

During the Prohibition years, the Italian racketeers had made certain political contacts in order to gain protection. Costello, always the compromiser and fixer rather than the muscle-man, was the first to establish relations with Jimmy Hines, the powerful leader of the West Side in Tammany Hall. But his rival, Lucky Luciano, suspicious of the Irish, and seeking more direct power, backed and elected Al Marinelli for district leader on the Lower West Side. Marinelli in 1932 was the only Italian leader inside Tammany Hall. Later, he was joined by Dr. Paul Sarubbi, a partner of Johnny Torrio in a large, legitimate liquor concern. Certainly, Costello and Luciano represented no "unified" move by the Italians as a whole for power; within the Italian community there are as many divisions as in any other group. What is significant is that different Italians, for different reasons, and in various fashions, were achieving influence for the first time. Marinelli became county clerk of New York and a leading power in Tammany. In 1937, after being blasted by Tom Dewey, then running for district attorney, as a "political ally of thieves . . . and big-shot racketeers," Marinelli was removed from office by Governor Lehman. The subsequent conviction by Dewey of Luciano and Hines, and the election of La Guardia, left most of the Tammany clubs financially weak and foundering. This was the moment Costello made his move. In a few years, by judicious financing, he controlled a bloc of "Italian" leaders in the Hall—as well as some Irish on the upper West Side, and some Jewish leaders on the East Side—and was able to influence the selection of a number of Italian judges. The most notable incident, revealed by a wire tap on Costello's phone, was the "Thank you, Francisco" call in 1943 by Supreme Court nominee Thomas Aurelio, who gave Costello full credit for his nomination.

It was not only Tammany that was eager to accept campaign contributions from newly rich Italians, even though some of these *nouveaux riches* had "arrived" through bootlegging and gambling. Fiorello La Guardia, the wiliest mind that Melting Pot politics has ever produced, understood in the early '30's where much of his covert support came from. (So, too, did Vito Marcantonio, an apt pupil of the master: Marcantonio has consistently made deals with the Italian leaders of Tammany Hall—in 1943 he supported Aurelio, and refused to repudiate him even when the Democratic Party formally did.) Joe Adonis, who had built a political following during the late '20's, when he ran a popular speakeasy, aided La Guardia financially to a considerable extent in 1933. "The Democrats haven't recognized the Italians," Adonis told a friend. "There is no reason for the Italians to support anybody but La Guardia; the Jews have played ball with the Democrats and haven't gotten much out of it. They know it now. They will vote for La Guardia. So will the Italians."

Adonis played his cards shrewdly. He supported La Guardia, but also a number of Democrats for local and judicial posts, and became a power in the Brooklyn area. His restaurant was frequented by Kenny Sutherland, the Coney Island Democratic leader; Irwin Steingut, the Democratic minority leader in Albany; Anthony DiGiovanni, later a Councilman; William O'Dwyer, and Jim Moran. But, in 1937, Adonis made the mistake of supporting Royal Copeland against La Guardia, and the irate Fiorello finally drove Adonis out of New York.[3]

La Guardia later turned his ire against Costello, too. Yet Costello survived and reached the peak of his influence in 1942, when he was instrumental in electing Michael Kennedy leader of Tammany Hall. Despite the Aurelio fiasco, which first brought Costello into notoriety, he still had sufficient power in the Hall to swing votes for Hugo Rogers as Tammany leader in 1945, and had a tight grip on some districts as late as 1948. In those years many a Tammany leader came hat in hand to Costello's apartment, or sought him out on the golf links, to obtain the nomination for a judicial post.

During this period, other Italian political leaders were also coming to the fore. Generoso Pope, whose Colonial Sand and Stone Company began to prosper through political contacts, became an important political figure, especially when his purchase of the two largest Italian-language dailies (later merged into one), and of a radio station, gave him almost a monopoly of channels to Italian-speaking opinion of the city. Through Generoso Pope, and through Costello, the Italians became a major political force in New York.

That the urban machines, largely Democratic, have financed their heavy campaign costs in this fashion rather than having to turn to the "moneyed interests," explains in some part why these machines were able, in part, to support the New and Fair Deals without suffering the pressures they might have been subjected to had their source of money supply been the business groups. Although he has never publicly revealed his political convictions, it is likely that Frank Costello was a fervent admirer of Franklin D. Roosevelt and his efforts to aid the common man. The basic measures of the New Deal, which most Americans today agree were necessary for the public good, would not have been possible without the support of the "corrupt" big-city machines.

---

[3] Adonis, and associate Willie Moretti, moved across the river to Bergen County, New Jersey, where, together with the quondam racketeer Abner, "Longie" Zwillman, he became one of the political powers in the state. Gambling flourished in Bergen County for almost a decade but after the Kefauver investigation the state was forced to act. A special inquiry in 1953 headed by Nelson Stamler, revealed that Moretti had paid $286,000 to an aide of Governor Driscoll for "protection" and that the Republican state committee had accepted a $25,000 "loan" from gambler Joseph Bozzo, an associate of Zwillman.

VIII

There is little question that men of Italian origin appeared in most of the leading roles in the high drama of gambling and mobs, just as twenty years ago the children of East European Jews were the most prominent figures in organized crime, and before that individuals of Irish descent were similarly prominent. To some extent statistical accident and the tendency of newspapers to emphasize the few sensational figures gives a greater illusion about the domination of illicit activities by a single ethnic group than all the facts warrant. In many cities, particularly in the South and on the West Coast, the mob and gambling fraternity consisted of many other groups, and often, predominantly, native white Protestants. Yet it is clear that in the major northern urban centers there was a distinct ethnic sequence in the modes of obtaining illicit wealth, and that uniquely in the case of the recent Italian elements, the former bootleggers and gamblers provided considerable leverage for the growth of political influence as well. A substantial number of Italian judges sitting on the bench in New York today are indebted in one fashion or another to Costello; so too are many Italian district leaders—as well as some Jewish and Irish politicians. And the motive in establishing Italian political prestige in New York was generous rather than scheming for personal advantage. For Costello it was largely a case of ethnic pride. As in earlier American eras, organized illegality became a stepladder of social ascent.

To the world at large, the news and pictures of Frank Sinatra, for example, mingling with former Italian mobsters could come somewhat as a shock. Yet to Sinatra, and to many Italians, these were men who had grown up in their neighborhoods, and who were, in some instances, bywords in the community for their helpfulness and their charities. The early Italian gangsters were hoodlums—rough, unlettered, and young (Al Capone was only twenty-nine at the height of his power). Those who survived learned to adapt. By now they are men of middle age or older. They learned to dress conservatively. Their homes are in respectable suburbs. They sent their children to good schools and had sought to avoid publicity.[4] Costello even went to a psychiatrist in his efforts to overcome a painful feeling of inferiority in the world of manners.

As happens with all "new" money in American society, the rough and ready contractors, the construction people, trucking entrepreneurs, as well as racketeers, polished up their manners and sought recognition and respectability in their own ethnic as well as in the general community. The

---

[4] Except at times by being overly neighborly, like Tony Accardo, who, at Yuletide 1949, in his elegant River Forest home, decorated a 40-foot tree on his lawn and beneath it set a wooden Santa and reindeer, while around the yard, on tracks, electrically operated skating figures zipped merrily around while a loud speaker poured out Christmas carols. The next Christmas, the Accardo lawn was darkened; Tony was on the lam from Kefauver.

"shanty" Irish became the "lace curtain" Irish, and then moved out for wider recognition.[5] Sometimes acceptance came first in established "American" society, and this was a certificate for later recognition by the ethnic community, a process well illustrated by the belated acceptance in established Negro society of such figures as Sugar Ray Robinson and Joe Louis, as well as leading popular entertainers.

Yet, after all, the foundation of many a distinguished older American fortune was laid by sharp practices and morally reprehensible methods. The pioneers of American capitalism were not graduated from Harvard's School of Business Administration. The early settlers and founding fathers, as well as those who "won the west" and built up cattle, mining and other fortunes, often did so by shady speculations and a not inconsiderable amount of violence. They ignored, circumvented or stretched the law when it stood in the way of America's destiny, and their own—or, were themselves the law when it served their purposes. This has not prevented them and their descendants from feeling proper moral outrage when under the changed circumstances of the crowded urban environments later comers pursued equally ruthless tactics.

I X

Ironically, the social development which made possible the rise to political influence sounds, too, the knell of the Italian gangster. For it is the growing number of Italians with professional training and legitimate business success that both prompts and permits the Italian group to wield increasing political influence; and increasingly it is the professionals and businessmen who provide models for Italian youth today, models that hardly existed twenty years ago. Ironically, the headlines and exposés of "crime" of the Italian "gangsters" came years after the fact. Many of the top "crime" figures long ago had forsworn violence, and even their income, in large part, was derived from legitimate investments (real estate in the case of Costello, motor haulage and auto dealer franchises in the case of Adonis) or from such quasi-legitimate but socially respectable sources as gambling casinos. Hence society's "retribution" in the jail sentences for Costello and Adonis was little more than a trumped-up morality that disguised a social hypocrisy.

Apart from these considerations, what of the larger context of crime and the American way of life? The passing of the Fair Deal signalizes, oddly, the

---

[5] The role of ethnic pride in corralling minority group votes is one of the oldest pieces of wisdom in American politics; but what is more remarkable is the persistence of this identification through second and third generation descendants, a fact which, as Samuel Lubell noted in his *Future of American Politics*, was one of the explanatory keys to political behavior in recent elections. Although the Irish bloc as a solid Democratic bloc is beginning to crack, particularly as middle-class status impels individuals to identify more strongly with the G.O.P., the nomination in Massachusetts of Jack Kennedy for the United States Senate created a tremendous solidarity among Irish voters and Kennedy was elected over Lodge although Eisenhower swept the state.

passing of an older pattern of illicit activities. The gambling fever of the past decade and a half was part of the flush and exuberance of rising incomes, and was characteristic largely of new upper-middle class rich having a first fling at conspicuous consumption. This upper-middle class rich, a significant new stratum in American life (not rich in the nineteenth century sense of enormous wealth, but largely middle-sized businessmen and entrepreneurs of the service and luxury trades—the "tertiary economy" in Colin Clark's phrase—who by the tax laws have achieved sizable incomes often much higher than the managers of the super-giant corporations) were the chief patrons of the munificent gambling casinos. During the war decade when travel was difficult, gambling and the lush resorts provided important outlets for this social class. Now they are settling down, learning about Europe and culture. The petty gambling, the betting and bingo which relieve the tedium of small town life, or the expectation among the urban slum dwellers of winning a sizable sum by a "lucky number" or a "lucky horse" goes on. To quote Bernard Baruch: "You can't stop people from gambling on horses. And why should you prohibit a man from backing his own judgment? It's another form of personal initiative." But the lush profits are passing from gambling, as the costs of coordination rise. And in the future it is likely that gambling, like prostitution, winning tacit acceptance as a necessary fact, will continue on a decentralized, small entrepreneur basis.

But passing, too, is a political pattern, the system of political "bosses" which in its reciprocal relation provided "protection" for and was fed revenue from crime. The collapse of the "boss" system was a product of the Roosevelt era. Twenty years ago Jim Farley's task was simple; he had to work only on some key state bosses. Now there is no longer such an animal. New Jersey Democracy was once ruled by Frank Hague; now there are five or six men each top dog, for the moment, in his part of the state or faction of the party. Within the urban centers, the old Irish-dominated political machines in New York, Boston, Newark, and Chicago have fallen apart. The decentralization of the metropolitan centers, the growth of suburbs and satellite towns, the break-up of the old ecological patterns of slum and transient belts, the rise of functional groups, the increasing middle-class character of American life, all contribute to this decline.

With the rationalization and absorption of some illicit activities into the structure of the economy, the passing of an older generation that had established a hegemony over crime, the general rise of minority groups to social position, and the break-up of the urban boss system, the pattern of crime we have discussed is passing as well. Crime, of course, remains as long as passion and the desire for gain remain. But big, organized city crime, as we have known it for the past seventy-five years, was based on more than these universal motives. It was based on certain characteristics of the American economy, American ethnic groups, and American politics. The changes in all these areas means that it too, in the form we have known it, is at an end.

Changing Criminals: The Application
of the Theory of Differential Association

DONALD R. CRESSEY

Sociological theories and hypotheses have had great influence on development of general correctional policies, such as probation and parole, but they have been used only intermittently and haphazardly in reforming individual criminals. Since sociology is essentially a research discipline, sociologist-criminologists have devoted most of their time and energy to understanding and explaining crime, leaving to psychiatrists and others the problem of reforming criminals. Even the sociologists employed in correctional work have ordinarily committed themselves to nonsociological theories and techniques of reformation, leading the authors of one popular criminology textbook to ask just what correctional sociologists can accomplish which cannot be accomplished by other professional workers.[1]

Perhaps the major impediment to the application of sociological theories lies not in the nature of the theories themselves but, instead, in the futile attempt to adapt them to clinical use. Strictly speaking, the now popular policy of "individualized treatment" for delinquents and criminals does not commit one to any specific theory of criminality or any specific theory of reformation, but, rather, to the proposition that the conditions considered as causing an individual to behave criminally will be taken into account in the effort to change him. An attempt is made to diagnose the cause of the criminality and to base the techniques of reform upon the diagnosis. Analogy with the *method* of criminal medicine (diagnosis, prescription, and therapy) is obvious. However, by far the most popular interpretation of the policy of individualization is that the *theories*, as well as the methods, of clinical medicine must be used in diagnosing and changing criminals. The emphasis on this clinical principle has impeded the application of sociological theories and, it may be conjectured, success in correctional work.

The adherents of the clinical principle consider criminality to be an individual defect or disorder or a symptom of either, and the criminal as one unable to canalize or sublimate his "primitive," antisocial impulses or

SOURCE: Reprinted from "Changing Criminals: The Application of the Theory of Differential Association," in *American Journal of Sociology*, vol. LXI (September, 1955), by Donald R. Cressey by permission of The University of Chicago Press. Copyright, 1955, by The University of Chicago Press. Pp. 116–120.

[1] Harry Elmer Barnes and Negley K. Teeters, *New Horizons in Criminology* (New York: Prentice-Hall, Inc., 1951), p. 644.

tendencies,[2] who may be expressing symbolically in criminal behavior some unconscious urge or wish arising from an early traumatic emotional experience,[3] or as a person suffering from some other kind of defective trait or condition.

In all cases the implication is that the individual disorder, like a biological disorder, should be treated on a clinical basis. An extreme position is that criminality actually is a biological disorder, to be treated by modification of the physiology or anatomy of the individual. However, the more popular notion is that criminality is analogous to an infectious disease like syphilis—while group contacts of various kinds are necessary to the disorder, the disorder can be treated in a clinic, without reference to the persons from whom it was acquired.

Sociologists and social psychologists have provided an alternative principle on which to base the diagnosis and treatment of criminals, namely, that the behavior, attitudes, beliefs, and values which a person exhibits are not only the *products* of group contacts but also the *properties* of groups. If the behavior of an individual is an intrinsic part of groups to which he belongs, attempts to change the behavior must be directed at groups.[4] While this principle is generally accepted by sociologists, there has been no consistent or organized effort by sociologist-criminologists to base techniques or principles of treatment on it. Traditionally, we have emphasized that sociologists can make unique contributions to *clinical* diagnoses, and we have advocated the development of a "clinical sociology" which would enable us to improve these diagnoses.[5] But here we reach an impasse: if a case of criminality is attributed to the individual's group relations, there is little that can be done *in the clinic* to modify the diagnosed cause of the criminality. Moreover, extra-clinical work with criminals and delinquents ordinarily has merely extended the clinical principle to the offender's community and has largely ignored the group-relations principle. For example, in the "group work" of correctional agencies the emphasis usually is upon the role of the group merely in satisfying the needs of an individual. Thus the criminal is induced to join an "interest-activity" group, such as a hiking club, on the assumption that membership in the group somehow will enable him to overcome the defects or tendencies considered conducive to his

---

[2] Sheldon and Eleanor T. Glueck, *Delinquents in the Making* (New York: Harper & Bros., 1952), pp. 162–63; see also Ruth Jacobs Levy, *Reductions in Recidivism through Therapy* (New York: Seltzer, 1941), pp. 16, 28.

[3] Edwin J. Lukas, "Crime Prevention: A Confusion in Goal," in Paul W. Tappan (ed.), *Contemporary Correction* (New York: McGraw-Hill Book Co., 1951), pp. 397–409.

[4] Cf. Dorwin Cartwright, "Achieving Change in People: Some Applications of Group Dynamics Theory," *Human Relations*, IV (1951), 381–92.

[5] See Louis Wirth, "Clinical Sociology," *American Journal of Sociology*, XXVII (July, 1931), 49–66; and Saul D. Alinsky, "A Sociological Technique in Clinical Criminology," *Proceedings of the American Prison Association*, LXIV (1934), 167–78.

delinquency.[6] Similarly, in correctional group therapy the emphasis is almost always on the use of a group to enable the individual to rid himself of undesirable psychological disorders, not criminality.[7] Even in group-work programs directed at entire groups, such as delinquent gangs, emphasis usually is on new and different formal group activities rather than on new group attitudes and values.

The differential association theory of criminal behavior presents implications for diagnosis and treatment consistent with the group-relations principle for changing behavior and could be advantageously utilized in correctional work. According to it, persons become criminals principally because they have been relatively isolated from groups whose behavior patterns (including attitudes, motives, and rationalizations) are anticriminal, or because their residence, employment, social position, native capacities, or something else has brought them into relatively frequent association with the behavior patterns of criminal groups.[8] A diagnosis of criminality based on this theory would be directed at analysis of the criminal's attitudes, motives, and rationalizations regarding criminality and would recognize that those characteristics depend upon the groups to which the criminal belongs. Then, if criminals are to be changed, either they must become members of anticriminal groups, or their present pro-criminal group relations must be changed.[9]

The following set of interrelated principles, adapted in part from a more general statement by Dorwin Cartwright,[10] is intended as a guide to specific application of the differential association theory to correctional work. It is tentative and directs attention to areas where research and experimentation should prove fruitful. Two underlying assumptions are that small groups existing for the specific purpose of reforming criminals can be set up by correctional workers and that criminals can be induced to join them. The first five principles deal with the use of anticriminal groups as *media* of change, and the last principle emphasizes, further, the possibility of a criminal group's becoming the *target* of change.

1. If criminals are to be changed, they must be assimilated into groups which emphasize values conducive to law-abiding behavior and, concurrently, alienated from groups emphasizing values conducive to criminality. Since our experience has been that the majority of criminals experience

---

[6] See the discussion by Robert G. Hinckley and Lydia Hermann, *Group Treatment in Psychotherapy* (Minneapolis: University of Minnesota Press, 1951), pp. 8–11.

[7] See Donald R. Cressey, "Contradictory Theories in Correctional Group Therapy Programs," *Federal Probation*, XVIII (June, 1954), 20–26.

[8] Edwin H. Sutherland, *Principles of Criminology* (New York: J. B. Lippincott Co., 1947), pp. 6–9, 595, 616–17.

[9] Cf. Donald R. Taft, "The Group and Community Organization Approach to Prison Administration," *Proceedings of the American Prison Association*, LXXII (1942), 275–84; and George B. Vold, "Discussion of *Guided Group Interaction in Correctional Work* by F. Lovell Bixby and Lloyd W. McCorkle," *American Sociological Review*, XVI (August, 1951), 460–61.

[10] *Op. cit.*

great difficulty in securing intimate contacts in ordinary groups, special groups whose major common goal is the reformation of criminals must be created. This general principle, emphasized by Sutherland, has been recognized and used by Gersten, apparently with some success, in connection with a group therapy program in the New York Training School for Boys.[11]

2. The more relevant the common purpose of the group to the reformation of criminals, the greater will be its influence on the criminal members' attitudes and values. Just as a labor union exerts strong influence over its members' attitudes toward management but less influence on their attitudes toward say, Negroes, so a group organized for recreational or welfare purposes will have less success in influencing criminalistic attitudes and values than will one whose explicit purpose is to change criminals. Interesting recreational activities, employment possibilities, and material assistance may serve effectively to attract criminals away from pro-criminal groups temporarily and may give the group some control over the criminals. But merely inducing a criminal to join a group to satisfy his personal needs is not enough. Probably the failure to recognize this, more than anything else, was responsible for the failure of the efforts at rehabilitation of the Cambridge-Somerville Youth Study workers.[12]

3. The more cohesive the group, the greater the members' readiness to influence others and the more relevant the problem of conformity to group norms. The criminals who are to be reformed and the persons expected to effect the change must, then, have a strong sense of belonging to one group; between them there must be a genuine "we" feeling. The reformers, consequently, should not be identifiable as correctional workers, probation or parole officers, or social workers. This principle has been extensively documented by Festinger and his co-workers.[13]

4. Both reformers and those to be reformed must achieve status within the group by exhibition of "pro-reform" or anticriminal values and behavior patterns. As a novitiate, the one to be reformed is likely to assign status according to social position outside the group, and part of the reformation process consists of influencing him both to assign and to achieve status on the basis of behavior patterns relevant to reformation. If he should assign status solely on the basis of social position in the community, he is likely to be influenced only slightly by the group. Even if he becomes better

---

[11] Sutherland, *op. cit.*, p. 451; Charles Gersten, "An Experimental Evaluation of Group Therapy with Juvenile Delinquents," *International Journal of Group Psychotherapy*, I (November, 1951), 311–18.

[12] See Margaret G. Reilly and Robert A. Young, "Agency-initiated Treatment of a Potentially Delinquent Boy," *American Journal of Orthopsychiatry*, XVI (October, 1946), 697–706; Edwin Powers, "An Experiment in Prevention of Delinquency," *Annals of the American Academy of Political and Social Science*, CCLXI (January, 1949), 77–88; Edwin Powers and Helen L. Witmer, *An Experiment in Prevention of Delinquency—the Cambridge-Somerville Youth Study* (New York: Columbia University Press, 1951).

[13] L. Festinger *et al.*, *Theory and Experiment in Social Communication: Collected Papers* (Ann Arbor: Institute for Social Research, 1951).

adjusted, socially and psychologically, by association with members having high status in the community, he is a therapeutic parasite and not actually a member until he accepts the group's own system for assigning status.

5. The most effective mechanism for exerting group pressure on members will be found in groups so organized that criminals are induced to join with noncriminals for the purpose of changing other criminals. A group in which criminal A joins with some noncriminals to change criminal B is probably most effective in changing criminal A, not B; in order to change criminal B, criminal A must necessarily share the values of the anticriminal members.

This process may be called "retroflexive reformation"; in attempting to reform others, the criminal almost automatically accepts the relevant common purpose of the group, identifies himself closely with other persons engaging in reformation, and assigns status on the basis of anticriminal behavior. He becomes a genuine member of this group, and at the same time he is alienated from his previous pro-criminal groups. This principle is used successfully by Alcoholics Anonymous to "cure" alcoholism; it has been applied to the treatment of psychotics by McCann and Almada; and its usefulness in criminology has been demonstrated by Knopka.[14] Exconvicts have been used in the Chicago Area Projects, which, generally, are organized in accordance with this principle, but its effect on the ex-convicts, either in their roles as reformers or as objects of reform, appears not to have been evaluated.

6. When an entire group is the target of change, as in a prison or among delinquent gangs, strong pressure for change can be achieved by convincing the members of the need for a change, thus making the group itself the source of pressure for change. Rather than inducing criminals to become members of pre-established anticriminal groups, the problem here is to change anti-reform and pro-criminal subcultures, so that group leaders evolve from among those who show the most marked hospitality to anti-criminal values, attitudes, and behavior. Neither mere lectures, sermons, or exhortations by correctional workers nor mere redirection of the activities of a group nor individual psychotherapy, academic education, vocational training, or counseling will necessarily change a group's culture. If the subculture is not changed, the person to be reformed is likely to exhibit two sets of attitudes and behaviors, one characteristic of the agency or person trying to change him, the other of the subculture.[15] Changes in

---

[14] Freed Bales, "Types of Social Structure as Factors in 'Cures' for Alcohol Addiction," *Applied Anthropology*, I (April–June, 1942), 1–13; Willis H. McCann and Albert A. Almada, "Round-Table Psychotherapy: A Technique in Group Psychotherapy," *Journal of Consulting Psychology*, XIV (December, 1950), 421–35; Gisela Knopka, "The Group Worker's Role in an Institution for Juvenile Delinquents," *Federal Probation*, XV (June, 1951), 15–23.

[15] See Edwin A. Fleishman, "A Study in the Leadership Role of the Foreman in an Industrial Situation" (Columbus: Personnel Research Board, Ohio State University, 1951) (mimeographed).

the subculture probably can best be instigated by eliciting the co-operation of the type of criminal who, in prisons, is considered a "right guy."[16] This principle has been demonstrated in a recent experiment with hospitalized drug addicts, whose essentially antireform culture was changed, under the guise of group therapy, to a proreform culture.[17] To some extent, the principle was used in the experimental system of prison administration developed by Gill in the Massachusetts State Prison Colony.[18]

Drug Addiction: Enforcement and/or Treatment

CHARLES WINICK

The last few years have seen narcotics programs which are both more punitive and less punitive than has been customary, and both extremes have reported considerable success. A number of vocal exponents of permitting physicians to supply drugs to addicts at low cost have aroused considerable sentiment for their point of view (Lindesmith, 1957). It has been repeatedly urged by various legislative committees that this approach be tried on a limited basis, but to date it has not. The employment of such a procedure involves some ambiguous questions of medical ethics. Physicians have generally believed, along with the late distinguished narcotics authority, Dr. Kenneth W. Chapman, that "drugs are not good for anyone . . . giving drugs to all addicts is a last resort. . . ." Physicians would have the responsibility of deciding which addicts were incurable and what their dosage should be, and whether such a dosage should be increased if the user wanted more than the amount prescribed for him.

Another procedure for liberalizing treatment procedures, and one which has been tried experimentally with limited success, has been the psychotherapy of addicts on an ambulatory basis, while they are still on drugs. Such procedures leave the question of cessation of drug use up to the patient,

---

[16] See Hans Riemer, "Socialization in the Prison Community," *Proceedings of the American Prison Association,* LXVII (1937), 151–55.

[17] James J. Thorpe and Bernard Smith, "Phases in Group Development in Treatment of Drug Addicts," *International Journal of Group Psychotherapy,* III (January, 1953), 66–78.

[18] Howard B. Gill, "The Norfolk Prison Colony of Massachusetts," *Journal of Criminal Law and Criminology,* XXII (September, 1937), 389–95; see also Eric K. Clarke, "Group Therapy in Rehabilitation," *Federal Probation,* XVI (December, 1952), 28–32.

SOURCE: Charles Winick, "The Drug Addict and His Treatment," in Hans Toch (ed.), *Legal and Criminal Psychology* (New York: Holt, 1961), pp. 376–379. Reprinted by permission.

with no coercion from the psychotherapist. Using such procedures, the Musicians' Clinic in New York reported that all its jazz musician-addict patients were off drugs for an average of thirty months, three years after the commencement of voluntary out-patient therapy. These patients were given treatment on an ambulatory basis, while still on drugs, and it was up to them to handle the problem of their addiction. The clinic grew out of the experience of another experiment in voluntary treatment, the Narcotic Addiction Research Project, which resulted in a working classification of addicts into two categories: those who function effectively on drugs, and those who do not function well and want to get off drugs but are "hooked" (Nyswander, Winick, *et al.*, 1958).

At the other extreme, there have been a number of proposals for making more stringent the current practices for coping with drug addicts. One direction, followed by some states, including New Jersey, has been to make it a misdemeanor to be a drug addict. New Jersey requires a convicted narcotics offender to register with the police and to keep the police posted on changes of address. This procedure seems to have resulted in an increase in the number of narcotics arrests, with some addicts going to states with less stringent penalties. The District of Columbia has made hospitalization for addicts compulsory and has established a high-security ward for addict patients.

The city of Oakland in California has experimented with the Nalline test for determining whether a person has taken drugs prior to the administration of the test. In a person who has taken an opiate in the day or so previous to administration of the synthetic drug Nalline, there will be a measurable dilation of the pupils as well as a miniature withdrawal reaction after taking a small dosage of Nalline. In Oakland the test is used to establish whether a convicted former drug user is or is not using drugs. Some physicians have objected to its use on the ground that it is a kind of chemical conscience, and that this kind of external threat is likely to interfere with any ongoing therapeutic relationship which a former drug user may be attempting to establish. Oakland authorities, however, report not only a decline in addicts but also a sharp decline in crimes usually associated with addiction, which they feel is related to their use of the Nalline test. In the three-year period (1955–58) since they began using Nalline, for example, they report a 21 percent decline in robberies, a 13 percent drop in burglaries, a 47 percent falling off in stealing from automobiles, and 25 percent fewer prostitution offenses.

The experience of Oakland has renewed interest in a suggestion made by a number of law-enforcement officials, and especially by Commissioner Harry J. Anslinger of the Federal Bureau of Narcotics. He has suggested that there be compulsory commitment of the drug addict (Anslinger, 1957). Such a law, Commissioner Anslinger notes, "would have to be enacted by state legislatures; it could not be federal because of the Constitution. . . ." The commissioner has documented the extent to which very severe sentences on peddlers have led to a substantial decline in the number of addicts arrested in such states as Ohio. He has consistently opposed providing drugs to addicts on any clinic basis, pointing to his estimate of one addict in 400 in America before the passage of the Harrison Act, whereas there is now one in 3,000. This decline in the proportion of addicts, the commissioner feels, is a reflection of the efficacy of the Harrison Act and is the best retort to the critics of his bureau's procedures.

The argument for compulsory treatment has received some support from the experience of the New York State Department of Parole's experimental project for providing close supervision to a limited number of parolees who had been in prison for narcotic violations. After three years, 42 percent of this group which received the supervision had remained off drugs, suggesting that this kind of intensive case work in an authoritarian setting may be effective with some former drug users.

Another development in the enforcement of drug-addiction laws has been the introduction, in a number of jurisdictions, of legislation which removes the judge's discretion in issuing sentences to drug users by providing for mandatory minimum sentences with no probation. This has raised the question of how police can reward the informers on whom they must depend for the bulk of arrests of other narcotics violators, if they cannot promise them a suspended sentence for cooperating and identifying their source of supply. Most arrested narcotics users will not cooperate by naming other users or sellers, but there are some who will. In some cases they may be encouraged to buy narcotics for their own use, so that police can watch them making the purchase and so arrest the seller. There have been cases in which drug-using informers were paid by the police in drugs, and thus maintained in their addiction.

Although many officials believe that it is unethical for police to promise anything to an informer, a substantial proportion of narcotics violators are arrested through such procedures. The growing inability of the police to promise informers a light sentence, because of the growing tendency toward mandatory minimum sentences, will surely focus new attention on the ethical and civil liberties aspects of arrests for drug violations as the question of how informers are to be paid becomes increasingly urgent. Recent court decisions have questioned the propriety of evidence obtained through wiretapping and have also raised important questions related to narcotics enforcement, since many narcotics arrests are based on wiretaps.

It is a sign of healthy differences in a controversial field that so many differences of opinion exist on the subject of dealing with addiction. Available facilities have, however, not kept up with the interest in discussing the addiction problem. The extent to which the problem is ignored in practice can be seen in the almost total lack of beds for adult addicts in the large cities which have the major problems of addiction. In the municipal hospitals of all three of these cities (New York, Chicago and Detroit) combined, there are not even one hundred beds for many thousands of addicts. The poor results so far obtained with treatment of addicts should not be discouraging, any more than poor results in schizophrenia or cancer research are keeping us from an extensive program of research and treatment in these fields. Unless we can mount the kind of concerted research and treatment program which ultimately led to the Sabin and Salk polio vaccines, our treatment of narcotics addiction will continue to be a rebuke to twentieth-century America. . . .

12. SEGREGATION AND SOCIAL RELATIONS

A Case of Interracial Marriage

ST. CLAIR DRAKE AND HORACE R. CAYTON

Mr. and Mrs. Brown live in a new two-story brick building in one of the better Negro residential districts. Their house is very attractively furnished, and the whole atmosphere is one of middle-class respectability. Mrs. Brown works in a downtown office in a supervisory position. Her husband is a railroad waiter. Their combined income makes it possible for them to maintain a standard of living comparable to that of most middle-class white couples. They are about forty years of age, and have been married for about twenty years.

Mr. Brown was born in Kentucky, the son of one of the wealthiest farmers in that section of the state. Both of his parents had been slaves. He has Negroid hair and light brown skin. Probably he has as much white as colored blood. He went through prep school, and then attended a small Negro college for a time. Later he came to Chicago, and there met his future wife. They became acquainted through a Negro girl who was passing for white in the office in which Mrs. Brown worked. After the two young women had been intimate friends for some time, the Negro girl told Mrs. Brown her secret, and invited her to her home. At that time, Mrs. Brown was engaged to a white man who lived on the North Side in Chicago. Mrs. Brown said: "When I went to this girl's home, Mr. Brown was often there. I don't know what attracted us to each other, but music was one common bond. After I had seen Mr. Brown for some time at this girl's house, we became very fond of each other. We decided not to see each other any more, and didn't for four months. But after my brother left town, we did see each other again and finally married."

One of the first problems that faced Mrs. Brown was informing her relatives of her marriage. "I was married three months before I decided to tell my sister," she recalled. "On that day we saw a hard-looking blonde woman

with a dark Negro. My sister remarked, 'Isn't that terrible?' I didn't tell her
of my marriage then, as I had planned, but I told her a week later. She said,
'Sis, are you happy with him?' I told her that we were very happy together,
and she said, 'That's all that matters.' "

Mrs. Brown did not, however, tell her other relatives of her marriage for
a long time—not until it became necessary for her to support them:

"I rented an apartment for them on University Avenue [in a white neigh-
borhood]. That's when I told my mother about my marriage. But I didn't tell
my brother, even then. For a while I was the only one that was working in
the family, and it became necessary for my mother, sister, and her three
children to live with us. My sister didn't like it because the baby used to
climb all over Mr. Brown, but she got over it after she had gotten to know
him. My brother, who was in the Army, disapproved strongly of my marriage
when he found out about it. He was in the Philippines and I know that
while he was there he lived with a Filipino woman. Yet he thought it was
terrible that I married a Negro. He said it was terrible, but he sent my husband and me cards on Christmas and on our birthdays. I told my sister that
if she saw him, she should tell him I thought it was terrible that he lived
with a native woman without marrying her, and then left her heartbroken
when he returned to America. He said later that he would like to see me
six feet underground. I wrote him a letter and told him that I still loved
him, no matter what he thought. Then I told Mother never to mention me
to him, as if I were dead.

"About two years later my brother 'phoned. I asked him to come over and
he came. I put him and Mr. Brown together in the parlor. They talked and
became acquainted. Mr. Brown told him that I was not supporting him,
that he had always worked, and that I was working because I wanted to.
My brother saw that my husband was not a bad fellow. For a year and a
half after that, until he left town, he didn't miss a Sunday with us."

A major problem which Mrs. Brown faced from the first was the problem
of keeping her job. She did not tell any of the office people about her marriage, and was constantly in fear of being discovered. A number of embarrassing incidents occurred, and she tells how she handled them:

"One day my husband called to drive me home from work. Just as he was
about to start the car, I saw my boss. I told my husband to stop and asked
my boss if he was going to the station I was going to. I was in the back seat
and Mr. Brown was in the front. I introduced Mr. Brown to my boss, but
didn't say who he was.

"Another time my husband was teaching me how to drive the car. I must
have been talking about something intimate because we were both laughing.
We were both sitting in the front seat. One of our salesmen drove right up
next to our car and saw me. I told Mr. Brown to stop. I talked with the
salesman and told him I was trying to learn to drive, but wasn't having much
success. I always make it a point to stop and talk whenever I am with my
husband and someone I know from the office sees us, else they might wonder
what we are doing together and tell others what they have seen."

The Browns assert that this subterfuge is carried on only for economic reasons, for both feel that they would lose their positions if it were known that they were married. "We have to be very careful in going out," they said. "We have a car and go together often. The only thing that bothers us is that we can't introduce each other as husband and wife." Outside of Chicago, where there is no fear of detection, they have made many trips, including several cross-country expeditions, and while on these, they ate in white restaurants and stayed in white hotels. "If Mr. Brown's skin were a little lighter," remarked his wife, "we could go anywhere together."

In summarizing her attitude toward interracial marriage Mrs. Brown said:

"I think that anyone is foolish to plunge headlong into an interracial marriage without careful consideration. My sister married a Negro she had met in our home. We were all opposed to it for it was a foolish marriage. I wouldn't have wanted my sister to marry that man if he had been white, because he wasn't at all worth while, but it makes it even worse to marry a man like that who is colored. If I weren't married to a Negro and had a daughter, I wouldn't like her to make a point of intermarriage. I wouldn't want her to marry just *any* colored man."

Although the Browns have no children, they have these observations to offer about the offspring of intermarriage:

"Don't you think the children of interracial marriages are finer people than most people? I think they are generally more intelligent than either white or colored. I think the white race needs a little mixture of the Negro. The Negro is more carefree and easy going than the white person, and the white can use some of this characteristic."

Mrs. Brown continued:

"Don't you think that, if a good friend of a white person married a Negro, that person would think more of colored people? They would think that some colored people would be worth while or their friend would not have married one. I know one girl at the office whom I finally told of my marriage. She didn't like colored people and thought interracial marriage was terrible. Since then she has come to my house and met Mr. Brown, and she thinks he is a fine man."

Mrs. Brown does not, however, minimize the difficulties involved in interracial marriage:

"If you do make an interracial marriage, you have to think a lot of each other. We like each other enough to forget the world. The high-class colored person doesn't care to mix with white. Many people have the idea that any colored man would like to marry a white woman. That isn't true."

The majority of the Browns' friends are white and are connected with the Bahai group. It is with these people that they spend most of their leisure time:

"We go to the Bahai meeting as often as we can. I'd say we go three or four times a month. We drive to the temple in Winnetka every Sunday in the summer and go to the downtown meeting twice a month. We go to their homes and they come to ours. We have white and colored friends here together."

Their membership in the Bahai church seems to be the great stabilizing force in the lives of the Browns. It gives them a circle of associates which allows them to defy the mores of the general society and helps them to circumvent some of the difficulties of their marriage. In talking about her religion, Mrs. Brown contrasts the attitude of the Episcopal Church, to which she formerly belonged, with that of Bahai:

"I used to belong to the Episcopal Church. One day I met a bishop whom I used to know well. He asked me why he didn't see me at church any more. I told him that I went to the Bahai Temple on Sundays. He said that I was getting away from the Christian church. I said that it is simply the Christian religion brought up to date. Then the bishop said, 'There is something in your life that you are not telling me.' I said, 'Yes, there is. I'm married.' 'There is nothing unusual about that,' the bishop said. I said, 'No, but my husband is colored.' I asked him what he thought about it, and he said, 'I'm shocked.' Then he asked me if I was happy, and I said that I was. Then I asked the Bishop if I could go to his church with my husband. He said that as an individual he would have no objections, but that the congregation would object. I told him that was the difference between his church and the Bahai."

Mrs. Brown's religion has not only acted as a means of justifying her behavior, but has fired her with a sort of crusading zeal to think of intermarriage as the solution to the problem of color. "I think interracial marriage will do a lot to break down prejudice," she said. "I can truthfully say we've been very happy. Other interracial couples that I know have also."

Like most of the wives of interracial marriages interviewed in this study, Mrs. Brown was sensitive about her respectability:

"I think that the truth is what will help us interracial people. Of course there are some we can't speak highly of. They are the ones that get in the news. Everyone knows about Jack Johnson's wives. But if you see an interracial woman like Mrs. Sampson, who has raised a family and has always led a quiet, decent life, it never gets in the newspaper."

The Problem: The Social Meaning of Discrimination

AARON ANTONOVSKY

This chapter is an attempt to develop a sociological theory of discrimination. Much work has been directed toward the study of prejudice; many

SOURCE: Prepared especially for this volume.

AUTHOR'S NOTE: Appreciation is expressed to Dr. Don J. Hager for his careful critical reading of this paper and his many helpful suggestions.

studies describe the extent and costs of discrimination. But no systematic theoretical framework has been developed which can be applied to the way in which discrimination is initiated, perpetuated, and expressed in the United States.[1]

In this paper we will, first, analyze the nature of discrimination; second, consider its impact on the life chances of its victims; and third, discuss the problems involved in breaking down discriminatory practices.

I. THE NATURE OF DISCRIMINATION

DISCRIMINATION AS A SOCIAL RELATIONSHIP. Discrimination may be defined as the effective injurious[2] treatment of persons on grounds rationally irrelevant to the situation. Individuals are denied *desired* and *expected* rewards or opportunities for reasons that have no relation to their capacities, merits, or behavior, but solely because of membership in an identifiable outgroup. Although a discriminatory relationship bears similarity to a caste system, it is fundamentally different: in both, the victims are barred, in some degree, from access to such values as housing, jobs, educational facilities, full participation in culture, and voting. In a caste system, however, those excluded accept the barriers as legitimate; whereas in discrimination, there is a conflict because the outsiders desire and feel they have a right to the rewards and opportunities which the insiders tend to monopolize. The former find it necessary to challenge this monopoly. This conflict is not primarily the result of a failure in communication; on the contrary, the two contending groups are well informed about their differences in status and power. They share the same goals—even though they do not achieve them equally.[3] Thus, whenever discrimination prevails, it is always accompanied by tension, challenge, aggression and defense, and flux.

Certain conditions are necessary before discrimination will emerge and persist: (1) There must be scarcity of rewards and opportunities, both material and psychic. The greater the scarcity, the greater the pressure for

---

[1] The memorandum prepared by the United Nations Commission on Human Rights, *The Main Types and Causes of Discrimination* (New York, 1949); the writings of Gunnar Myrdal and Robert M. MacIver; Robin M. Williams, Jr., *The Reduction of Intergroup Tensions* (New York, 1947); and Chapter V of Morroe Berger's *Equality By Statute* (New York, 1952) are among the works which have had an important impact on the thinking in this field.

[2] Legally, discrimination may refer to preferential, rewarding treatment. Such treatment always implies its converse. Most discussions of discrimination have been limited to its negative aspects, for it is these which constitute the core of the social problem of discrimination.

[3] St. Clair Drake and Horace Cayton, *Black Metropolis* (New York, 1945), on pp. 120–127, implicitly adopt this position in discussing Negro-white relations in Chicago. Tension, they point out, arises when both desire the same goals but there is disagreement on whether Negroes should have access to these goals. Where the two agree—*either* in not having the same goals, for example, purely private social relations or, on the other hand, in providing equality of access, for example, to theatres—there is no tension.

recourse to discrimination. (2) But scarcity is—beyond the sheer subsistence level—a culturally defined concept. There would be no such pressure unless both insiders and outsiders agreed upon the desirability of the scarce values. (3) In order for discrimination to operate, there must be an unequal distribution of power, which enables the insiders to impose their monopoly and perpetuate it. *Thus scarcity, shared goals, and unequal power are the necessary conditions for discrimination.* Under such conditions, discrimination will become a reality given sufficient motive.

DISCRIMINATION AND THE SOCIAL STRUCTURE. We have distinguished between discriminatory relations and a caste system by pointing to the shared values in the former. At the same time, we must distinguish between a discriminatory pattern and sporadic, peripheral incidents of discrimination. For example, one may question whether Jew-Gentile or Catholic-Protestant relations in the United States are any longer predominantly discriminatory in character. Despite medical school quotas, country club exclusion, certain housing patterns, job barriers, and so forth, access to opportunities and rewards is generally open to Jews and Catholics; moreover, most of them have learned how to circumvent what restrictions exist by finding substitute gratifications and exploiting interstitial opportunities. (The question of latent prejudice, that is, what may happen in a crisis, is another problem.) On the other hand, America does assign a *subordinate status* (in fact, if not in principle) to Negroes, Puerto Ricans, Mexican-Americans, Indians, and Oriental-Americans. These groups are regarded as inferior and, by virtue of prejudice and discrimination, remain relatively deprived and in isolation.

There is an important distinction, too, to be made concerning the centrality of discrimination in the social and psychic structure of a society. The economic, political, and psychic life of the white South has, in large measure, been predicated upon anti-Negro prejudice and discrimination. In the North, on the other hand, while anti-Negro discrimination is intense and pervasive, its elimination would not require a radical change in the structure of society. This is no reason for being sanguine. While it is true that the nature of our economic and political life is not built upon the subordinate status of minority groups, patterns of housing occupancy and of voluntary associations are. Perhaps the greatest distinction between North and South is to be found in the centrality of psychic dependence on discrimination by the majority group in the South.

In any case, an examination of the *pervasiveness, intensity,* and *centrality* of discrimination in a social system contributes to an understanding of its consequences.

DISCRIMINATION AS AN INSTITUTION. The failure to perceive that discrimination is a system of social relations underlies the over-emphasis of research on the psychological factor of prejudice. Whatever its psychological origins, discrimination takes place largely outside the realm of the conscious decisions and the freedom of choice of individual persons. It is more than the sum and the individuals who discriminate; it is an institution with a life of its own. While we lack sufficient evidence for a full understanding of the social arrangements that create and perpetuate the institution of discrimination, we have theoretical notions to guide us in the search.

There is, first of all, the *weight of the past.* Traditional patterns—so long as they appear to serve a function—are not easily upset. Thus, the fact that one has never hired Negroes, never lived in a mixed neighborhood, or never admitted Jews to a fraternity continues to carry weight. Habits of the past are not easily extinguished.

Second, social behavior is predominantly *role-playing.* Acceptable behavior is based upon the expectations attached by society to the roles people occupy. Thus, be the individual a personnel director, guidance counselor, politician, or real estate broker, whatever his personal inclinations he tends to act as he is expected to act in his position. Only when he receives an indication that the expectations are changed, can he be expected to behave differently. (Simply put, the individual who tries to behave differently, that is, in a nondiscriminatory manner, without group sanction, is likely to meet with opposition and hostility.)

Third, there are *isolating mechanisms,* that is, patterns which operate to prevent the victims of discrimination from access to the necessary tools to break down the barriers. Obstacles to voting, inadequate educational facilities, apathy-producing poverty, "legal" harassments, exclusion from unions, and other manifestations of discrimination are ways of keeping minority group members from acquiring effective means to challenge the system. The Negro who does not live in an area where neighbors might inform him of a good job opportunity, or who is excluded from an informal plant clique, is isolated from possible rewards.

Fourth, law and other *social sanctions* often serve to maintain and perpetuate discrimination. The direction in which this operates depends on the climate of opinion and the dominant values of a community. Men are bound, voluntarily or involuntarily, by restrictive covenants, pressure of alumni, associations of business, and other groups.

A fifth factor, often ignored, is the *institutionalized evasion* of antidiscriminatory policies. There is often a gap between policy formulation and administrative execution. Intentional evasion, lackadaisical enforcement, and ineffective communication may often subvert the intent of law and policy.

Sixth, *anticipatory fears*—held by neighbors, colleagues, work group, the public—often operate to prevent modification of discrimination. These fears may, of course, be real or rationalizations.

Uniting and reinforcing the mechanisms of discrimination is an *ideology,* which is invoked to justify the inferior status of the excluded group. It expresses beliefs about the inferiority of the minority and deals in stereotypes. Given some easily visible characteristic, such as color, language, or dress, the barriers tend to become more rigid and the ideology more intense. All perceptions tend to become distorted in the direction of justifying discriminatory behavior. Social patterns of discrimination do not invariably precede the formulation of such an ideology. Rather, the two reinforce one another. The stereotypes are incorporated into everyday life: in literature (*Uncle Tom's Cabin*), in children's games and songs ("catch a nigger by the toe"), in the mass media (Amos and Andy, Aunt Jemima), in the Negro domestic, and in the prejudicial discourse of parents. The social result is to prepare the child for discrimination in his adult roles. Where prejudice is not intense or immediate, where other reasons are compelling, we make individual exceptions—"you're a white nigger"—exceptions that actually do not upset systemic discrimination, but reinforce it. For by noting the exception, we affirm the rule.

Perhaps the most insidious aspect of discrimination as an institution is its feedback character: what has been called the self-fulfilling prophecy, or the principle of cumulation.[4] Discrimination vitiates the power and knowledge of its victims, so that they may often be unable to take advantage of the facilities and opportunities which do exist to combat it. It may lower their levels of aspiration, and it produces a degree of objective support for the original rationalizations. It would be an oversimplification to assume that this vicious circle encompasses all factors; for then, we would expect discrimination to spread and harden into a caste system. Other factors modify these tendencies, but they negate neither the significance of the feedback nor its consequences.

THE FUNCTIONS OF DISCRIMINATION. The word "function" may be used in various ways: on the one hand, it may refer to the motives of behavior; on the other, it refers to its consequences.[5] A complete analysis of discrimination can only be achieved if both its impelling reasons and its consequences are examined. Let us first consider the former.

Discrimination rests upon several motives, personal and social. First, there is the possibility of *direct economic social or political benefit* through exploitation. The Southern landowner who, as a member of the Board of Elections, prevents Negroes from voting and thus from exercising political power, may thereby increase his profit margin through rigged laws and judicial practices. Second, there is the gain that derives from *monopolistic control over desired values;* for example, the union that restricts membership and thus gains economic advantage for its members.

Third, there is discrimination that is motivated by fear of loss, or *negative profit*. This rests upon the discriminator's presumption that he will be punished by failing to discriminate. The employer, the union official, the real estate broker, the admissions committee of a club or medical school, the

[4] Gunnar Myrdal, *An American Dilemma* (New York, 1944), pp. 75–78; Robert K. Merton, "A Social Psychological Factor (The Self-Fulfilling Prophecy)," in Arnold Rose (ed.), *Race Prejudice and Discrimination* (New York: Knopf, 1951), ch. 50.

[5] Robert K. Merton, *Social Theory and Social Structure* (Glencoe, Ill.: Free Press, 1949). Chap. 2, discusses the distinction between manifest and latent functions—intended and unanticipated consequences—at great length.

emloyment agency, may or may not be prejudiced, but they discriminate because they assume that their economic or status interests will suffer if they do otherwise, since they believe themselves to be dependent upon a prejudiced work force, membership, body of alumni, clientele, or colleagues.

"... A STRANGE CASE OF JUBILATION"

Late in 1960 the Department of Labor issued a study, "The Economic Situation of Negroes in the United States." It noted that in 1939, non-white workers earned, on the average, 41 per cent as much as whites. Not a little elation greeted this announcement. Some of the editorialists cited these statistics as indicating that slow and steady progress was being made. (At this rate, the Negro would reach parity with the white some time well after the year 2000.)

To begin with, the figures were somewhat more optimistic than the reality. Part of the Negro gain reflected the shift of rural Negroes to cities and Southern Negroes to the North. In both cases, the people involved increased their incomes by going into a more prosperous section of the country. But within each area their relative position remained the same at the bottom. Then, the statistics take a depression year (1939) as a base for comparison, and contrast it to a year of recession (1958). This tended to exaggerate the advance because Negroes in 1939 were particularly victimized.

Another important aspect of the problem was obscured by the sweeping comparisons most editorialists made between the 1939 and 1958 figures. Even the Department of Labor statistics themselves indicate that the major gain was made during World War II (the increase from 1939 to 1947 was from 41.4 per cent to 54.3 of the white wage). In the postwar period the rate of advance slowed to a walk. Moreover, most of the optimism was based on figures for Negro men. When the women are included, and when one takes a median family income from the Current Population Reports, Negroes rose from 51 per cent of white family income in 1947 to 57 per cent in 1952—and then declined back to the 1947 level by 1959.

But even without these qualifications, the fact is stark enough: the United States found cause for celebration in the announcement that Negro workers had reached 58 per cent of the wage level of their white co-workers. This situation is deeply imbedded in the very structure of American society. ...

SOURCE: Reprinted with permission of the Macmillan Company from *The Other America: Poverty in the United States* by Michael Harrington. Copyright 1962 by Michael Harrington. Pp. 72–73.

A fourth type of gain is that which, by pandering to prejudice, *diverts hostility* which might otherwise be directed against the discriminator. The employer who establishes himself as a "right guy" by discriminating in hiring or upgrading, by exploiting the prejudices of the labor force, may thereby divert attention from other grievances.

In all these cases, the discriminator benefits from the persistence of discriminatory policies. It should be noted, however, that once discrimination becomes institutionalized, it may be perpetuated even though its agent no longer receives any significant gain.

To these types of discrimination should be added the *prejudice-motivated* type. Here there is psychic gain for the discriminator rather than or in addition to financial profit or avoidance of loss. The employer who doesn't hire a Negro, even though he may be the most competent candidate for the job, simply because he hates Negroes, may take a material loss, but his action provides him with psychic income.

For discrimination to exist, one or another of these motives (which are not mutually exclusive) must be present under the conditions of scarcity, shared goals, and unequal power discussed earlier. Motivation without power is insufficient to effect discrimination. To understand the perpetuation of discrimination, however, it is useful to examine its "functions" in the sense of its consequences. There are those who are in no position to exercise, apply, or extend discriminatory practices, for example, the workers in a factory whose union does not have control of hiring and upgrading; poor whites in the South; landlords who own only dwellings in Negro sections; Protestant and non-Italian Catholic applicants to medical school. Yet because discrimination benefits them, materially and psychically, they lend tacit support to discriminatory patterns. This is significant because, if sufficiently numerous, such beneficiaries promote a climate of opinion that strengthens the hold of discrimination and makes it all the more difficult to eradicate. One of the major questions for research lies precisely in determining who benefits from discrimination, and in what ways, among those who hold power and those who do not.

What is often overlooked is that discrimination may also be functional for the victim. The Negro in America may in large measure be freed of one source of guilt; powerless, he need not share in the guilt of the powerful; a second-class citizen, he is relieved of full responsibility. With the road to advancement blocked or partially blocked, the victim of discrimination may not suffer the anxieties and frustrations, particularly for the many who fail, of being involved in the struggle to get ahead.[6] The Negro entrepreneur or professional may also benefit from discrimination, which gives him a captive market.[7]

Were discrimination unequivocally rewarding—materially and psychically —it would indeed be a Herculean task to eradicate it. Discriminatory social patterns, however, invariably have negative consequences not only for the victim, but for the community, and even for the discriminators.

---

[6] As the Elmira study demonstrates, however, Negroes, subjected to the impact of mass media, as well as for other reasons, are hardly immune to mobility drives.

[7] See E. Franklin Frazier, *Black Bourgeoisie* (New York, 1957), for a discussion of the vested interest of the Negro middle class in segregation.

Obviously, discrimination has destructive consequences for its victims, though far more is known about its effects on the Negroes in the South than about its impact upon Negroes and other minority groups in the North. The cost of discrimination to the national community has, fortunately, received thorough analysis in the symposium edited by Professor MacIver[8] (though further documentation, particularly covering the eight years since the appearance of MacIver's volume, is needed). The tension it creates in the community is demonstrably destructive and wasteful, but we know little, even today, about its costs in terms of social disorganization, mental and physical illness, absenteeism, noncooperation with authority, and the like. Informed commentators have discussed the disastrous international implications of discrimination in the United States; others have called attention to the costs of discrimination to poor Southern whites and to unorganized workers, two segments of the population often in ardent support of discrimination. Most recently, the tight labor market has made segments of management sensitive to the waste of manpower in which discrimination results.[9] Discrimination as an institution is clearly less than successful, even judged by its own ends.

II. EQUALITY OF LIFE CHANGES

A problem of status

The central consequence of discrimination to its victims is a systematic, pervasive inequality of life chances. The term "life chances" refers to the typical chance of the members of a social group for acquiring goods, external living conditions, and personal life experiences.[10] The rules of the game—whatever the rules are in a given society—do not apply to the member of an excluded group. He always bears the burden of being in this group, even if an occasional exception is made for the individual. This is what makes discrimination a problem of *status* rather than of welfare alone. For even were our society wealthy enough to assure a good living to all Negroes, provide them with adequate houses, and so forth, their life chances would still be unequal. It is only when the individual is treated as an individual, with freedom of choice and equality of opportunity, that the consequences of a subordinate status are resolved.

Discrimination and cultural equipment

Discrimination (or its absence) is not the only factor involved in the distribution of life chances. The life chances of the members of a minority group are affected by their cultural equipment and environment. This in-

---

[8] Robert M. MacIver (ed.), *Discrimination and National Welfare* (New York, 1949).

[9] This is a central thesis of Eli Ginzberg, *The Negro Potential* (New York, 1956).

[10] The concept of "life chances" is, of course, that of Max Weber. See Hans H. Gerth and C. Wright Mills, eds., *From Max Weber: Essays in Sociology* (New York, 1945), pp. 180–81.

cludes such things as the opportunity to learn the language of their host culture; the capacity, in the light of their cultural background, to take advantage of existing opportunities; conceptions of time, "success," mobility, work, morality; their possession of appropriate skills, associations, and educational attainments. There is no doubt that cultural equipment plays a major role, over and above discrimination, in determining the life chances of Negro migrants from the South or of Puerto Rican in-migrants.

Cultural equipment played a similar role in the life of earlier immigrants to the United States. However, in due course of time, through the process of acculturation, the weight of the cultural baggage brought by immigrants and the cohesive pressure of the immigrants community dissolved, and the immigrants—or, more likely, their children and grandchildren—became integrated into the American social structure. Class position replaced ethnic origin in determining life chances. The discrimination which every immigrant group encountered as "strangers" tended to disintegrate in time, in the absence of physical characteristics that set them apart.

The relation of discrimination to cultural equipment has a variety of effects on life chances. On the one hand, language differences, different value orientations, lack of contacts, and the like, may hamper the minority group in the effective confrontation of discrimination. On the other hand, the opportunity to modify cultural equipment is limited by past experience with discrimination.

Thus discrimination sometimes produces a "reaction formation": its victims retreat to the safety of the old culture and ghettoes, abandoning efforts at overcoming the barriers to integration. This retreat becomes a "return," a value in itself, and continues even after the barriers are removed. Since full participation in the larger society offers greater rewards, however, the breakdown of discrimination is ultimately decisive for most members of a minority group in the determination of their life chances.

Discrimination in the past may also have had more permanent consequences. To take advantage of existing opportunities, children and youth must grow up in an environment which allows them to develop their individual potentialities, which provides them with models of success that they can emulate, which equips them with tools and skills, and which enables them to develop the aspirations and self-confidence that lead to maximum growth. Thus, for example, the lack of self-esteem among Negroes that derives from long experience of cultural and economic deprivation makes it difficult for many Negroes today to perform effectively tasks requiring self-confidence. The discrimination which has in the past militated against the existence of a stable Negro family environment makes it difficult for Negro children to acquire the benefits of family stability or parental encouragement.

The responsibility of a society committed to the values embodied in the American Creed—particularly to the equality of life chances—as well as the pragmatic desire to eliminate the undesirable social problems which arise from the existence of minority status dictate the need for efforts to overcome the social and psychological effects of a long history of discrimination.

Discrimination and low incomes

The most direct expressions—though not necessarily the most painful, particularly in times of prosperity—of the inequality of life chances imposed upon the victims of discrimination are seen in economic indices and in housing and health standards. In a society which has not succeeded in eradicating poverty, minority groups are likely to be disproportionately concentrated in the low-income brackets. This disproportion is not greatly reduced by private and public welfare activities. Only the end of discriminatory barriers promises to resolve this inequality.

There is no necessary hard-and-fast relationship between discrimination and low incomes. In the first place, a group may be disproportionately poor because it occupies an immigrant status. The crucial questions are: how rapidly does it overcome poverty? To what extent is its disadvantage maintained because of discrimination?

Second, discrimination may be largely limited to certain areas of life, for example, social and public accommodations, which may have only a minimal effect on the persistence of poverty, undesirable as such discrimination may be on other grounds. While there is an indubitable connection between discrimination in resort areas and segregated schools, the latter are of far greater gravity and significance in perpetuating low-income status.

Third, an outcast group may come to fulfill a central function in the economy so that, though it is disliked, feared, and avoided, its income level is high. This can result from two factors: the performance by the rejected group of important functions which are closed, on religious-cultural or status grounds, to the majority; and the exploitation by the group of hitherto undeveloped opportunities in the economy. The latter factor, of great importance in a dynamic and secular society, requires that such groups develop inclinations and abilities which equip them to seek out and develop new avenues of employment in the economy.

In actual practice, however, discrimination in most cases tends to keep most of its victims at low income levels. It does so directly, in preventing adults from obtaining decent jobs and homes or chances for improving their skills and competence. It does so indirectly, as suggested above, in preventing the establishment of an environment for youth which equips them with the skills and courage necessary for exploiting educational and social opportunities. Moreover, the dead weight of history, of the attitude that "things have always been this way," tends to vitiate the desire and the attempts to ameliorate the situation.

Heretofore we have used "poverty" or "low incomes" in objective terms, referring to insufficient purchasing power to maintain a socially acceptable minimum standard of living. In America today, a family is considered poor when it cannot purchase the food required for a healthy diet as defined by nutrition experts; cannot afford housing which has separate rooms for parents and adolescents of different sexes, and indoor toilet and plumbing facilities; and has inadequate access to proper medical care, and so on. The Sub-Committee on Low Income Families of Congressional Joint Committee has accepted the figure of $2,000 annual family income (or $3,000 for urban families) as a mark below which a family is considered poor.

This figure is subject to refinement. It can only be valid on the assumption that all people pay the same price for similar commodities, a manifestly untenable assumption where discrimination in housing, resorts, and so forth, exists. It implies a relatively rational pattern of expenditures. Obviously, the poverty-line figure must be adjusted to the number of people to be supported by a given income and to the number of people in a family who have to work to attain a given income.

There is also, however, the subjective aspect of poverty. We have in mind the image of the average American family presented by mass media. The impact of these media, projecting cultural, social, and material goals which many families, in good measure because of discrimination, cannot reach, is to make these families feel poor. With this approach, one's conception of who is to be included in the low-income bracket would expand considerably.

One cannot, in other words, inculcate in a population the desire to have certain things, a given level of aspiration, and deny their poverty when their desires are not satisfied, simply because they surpass a relatively arbitrary income level. Inequality of life chances not only results in low levels of living; it also creates intense frustration and tension when—assuming the minority group has come to share the aspirations of the majority for a given standard of living—this standard cannot be realized.

Mobility, "success," class, and discrimination

In our vertically stratified democratic society, achieving what we have come to call the "American Dream" rests upon a particular concept of mobility and success. There are a few places available at the top of the economic, power, and prestige hierarchies. It is morally incumbent upon all of us to strive for the top positions in these hierarchies. Ideally, perfect competition would allow those in each generation who possessed the best combination of drive, talent, training, and luck to reach the top. (There are, of course, relative degrees of "moral perfection" or "success.") The educational system is geared to this system of values, and youngsters are urged and prepared to participate in the race for mobility.

If we accept this view of success uncritically, then we might also accept the view that discrimination is simply an irrelevant element in the competition to get to the top. Those who see the problem in this light urge minority members to adopt middle-class goals, patterns, and values and urge society at large to give them an equal chance at success.[11] Thus, emphasis is directed

---

[11] There is no doubt that this conception of success presents a problem relevant to *all* youth in our society, and not only to minority youth.

toward securing admission to country clubs, high-priced housing areas, and executive and professional positions for the most "capable" (that is, the most middle-class) minority group members.

This concept of success, though not wholly irrelevant to the central problem of discrimination and low incomes, in essence obscures its major dimensions. Success can have a completely different connotation, emphasizing the achievement of satisfying levels of living by everyone, rather than the high ascent of the few. The central problem for minorities would then be that of full participation in the life and problems of *whatever social class they are in*. Concretely, this means acquisition of industrial skills, full rights of union membership, the procurement of education and training commensurate with ability, and access to moderate housing areas and white-collar and lower managerial positions. Abstractly, it means a sense of their own dignity and worth at whatever social level they find themselves. In other words, the orientation becomes one of decency, comfort, security, stability, and dignity for the many. Once this is achieved, the few who are so motivated will—as will some majority group members in their position—seek to attain middle- and upper-class status.

The function of symbols and role models must also be considered. It is often contended that the apathy and lack of self-confidence characteristic of many minority group youngsters stems in part from a lack of adequate models as well as from an all-too-realistic appraisal of their life chances. These characteristics, in turn, tend to vitiate antidiscrimination efforts. Traditionally, the Jackie Robinsons, Ralph Bunches, and George Washington Carvers have been extolled as providing models whom Negro youngsters can emulate. Such men doubtless are—and justly—an important source of group pride. Moreover, they are unquestioned successes. But they are highly gifted men functioning in fields (athletics, science, and so forth) that are hospitable to talent—but a kind of talent that is not possessed in quantity by either the majority or the minority. One might well question the relevance of such symbols to the overwhelming number of minority group youngsters. For all but a minute handful, aspirations based on such models are self-defeating. If, on the other hand, one's own father or other relatives have achieved security, respect, and satisfaction, or one can point to the teacher, union official, successful artisan, or laboratory technician of one's own group, emulation becomes more meaningful, realistic, and feasible.

Moreover, there are further grounds for skepticism regarding the use of highly successful individuals as symbols in antidiscrimination efforts. All too often the exception is hailed as evidence of liberalism and promotes an unrealistic view of the status of the minority group as a whole. One must also inquire into the characteristics of certain types of minority group "success" models. Can we speak of discrimination having been overcome when a Negro engineer or sales supervisor or foreman occupies his position not simply because he is competent, but because he is outstanding, is ingratiating, has no "chip on his shoulder," is extraordinarily polite, or is willing to accept responsible but nonsupervisory positions? In other words, one who is not treated as any other individual, but who is rewarded not only because he has the requisite characteristics for the job or house, but because, "knowing his place," he becomes accepted? Such success is often achieved at the cost of self-respect and dignity, extraordinary hard work, and the repression of characteristics which would be perfectly acceptable in majority group members. One may doubt the desirability and efficacy of this kind of success model.

III. THE BREAKDOWN OF DISCRIMINATION

Accommodation

Theoretically, one way to bring about the end of discriminatory relations would be for the minority group to relinquish their claims and aspirations to equal opportunities in the struggle for life chances, that is, to accommodate to a caste status. This is, in essence, what happened in part at the end of the nineteenth century in the North as well as in the South. A second alternative would be the establishment of a quota system: such and such a percentage of a minority group may be admitted to the universities, managerial positions, and so forth. But the American culture continues to promote and reinforce the idea that access to material and psychic satisfactions are to be possessed and enjoyed by *all* the people. Moreover, the last decade and a half of nearly full employment and the possibility of geographic mobility have strengthened the demand for equality of opportunity. There is no longer any serious possibility that any minority will reject this expectation. (It seems equally obvious that a third alternative—a biracial state or minority nationalism—is no longer a remote possibility.)

When minority groups in a society reject caste or quasi-caste status, what are the factors that will advance or impede the breakdown of discrimination?

Minority discontent

Minority discontent with discrimination is essential to this breakdown. Its effectiveness, however, requires a strength which, in turn, demands organization and leadership. The minority which transforms its aggression into self-hatred, which spends its energies in intraminority strife and status-seeking, which fails to develop a competent leadership, and which neglects to involve the majority of its members in opposing discrimination thereby diminishes its potential power and resources. But even the most efficient mobilization of minority power is not sufficient to affect sweeping changes in social relations. Economic boycotts and political pressures by a minority act as gadflies and irritants, but not as decisive levers of social change. (This does not deny the importance of such action in enhancing the pride, solidarity, and self-esteem of the minority.)

General environmental factors

Social action directed against discrimination does not take place in a vacuum. Its success or failure is related to prevailing conditions and social developments. It would require extensive analysis to determine the conditions that would facilitate the breakdown of discrimination, but certain of these conditions are already evident.

We have noted the relationship between discrimination and the conflict over scarce values and goods. It is obvious that an economy of full employment and an expanding productive capacity lessens the pressure to discriminate. It does not, however, resolve discrimination in job upgrading, nor is it necessarily accompanied by an adequate housing supply. As we approach abundance, however, discrimination that results from conflict over the attainment of scarce values subsides.

Industrialization (of agriculture as well) likewise aids in the reduction of discrimination. This is true not only because greater abundance is achieved through industrialization, but because it depends upon the rational and universal distribution of skills, resources, and purchasing power. Where there are formalized rules and regulations, where impersonal profit-making or efficiency guides conduct and decisions, then prejudice-motivated, irrational discrimination can more easily be attacked. Thus, where upgrading is based on average competence and seniority, rather than on personal factors, the minority group member experiences improved job and upgrading opportunities.

External threats to national security tend to modify internal conflict and increase solidarity, particularly with respect to full utilization of manpower. This factor may, however, be a double-edged sword: does the hostility directed toward an external target necessarily diminish the amount of internal hostility? On the contrary, may not hostility once aroused be pervasive and nonselective, aiming at "enemies" inside as well as outside the state?

Somewhat more clear-cut in its effects is the degree of existing tension in a society. The greater the general tension and frustration, the higher the anxiety level, the greater is the temptation to resort to discrimination.

Thus, it would seem that antidiscrimination efforts must necessarily be allied with efforts to achieve an abundant, secure, and relaxed society.

The value context

We know that the most effective way of achieving any social behavior pattern, at least in a free society, is for consensus to underlie both the goals of the behavior and the means for its attainment. In other words, a successful antidiscrimination effort depends, in part, upon the existence of a unified climate of opinion. Fortunately, in our case, we possess an official, public commitment to democratic values. Every American school child is taught the precepts of democracy. Two gaps exist, however: that between goals and means; and that between belief and action. The current state of affairs points up the need to sharpen the awareness of this conflict of norms in the hearts of our citizens: to stress that in order to have full democracy, concrete equality of opportunity must be granted. This would, of course, intensify the guilt feelings of those who violate, even passively, democratic values. Some would react with greater bigotry, rejecting democratic goals. There are those, however, who would find it possible to relinquish discriminatory behavior, bringing means into accord with goals.

The first step is getting larger segments of the population to accept and commit themselves, formally and explicitly, to democratic goals and to the means by which they are attained. State law and statements of voluntary and corporate bodies are steps in this direction. The discriminator or supporter of discrimination must be made to feel increasingly isolated and antisocial. This is one important way of getting him to conform.

A law that is in conformity with accepted values has a good chance of being obeyed. Widespread publication of the existence of the law is a second step toward achieving a democratic climate of opinion.

Not all segments of the population, though, are equally important, since power is distributed unequally. Thus it is most essential that power groups in industry, labor, and public bodies accept and affirm their adherence to democratic tenets. As authorities, they can convince others; as power-wielders, they can help translate belief into action. For example, union leadership, imbued with a democratic-humanitarian ideology, can go far to eradicate discrimination from its area of influence.

Guilt and the acceptance of a democratic ideology are not the only bases for adherence to equalitarian values. Moral suasion can be supplemented by pragmatic considerations. The taxpayer, the union organizer, the profit-seeking executive, the welfare worker, and others may be converted by reference to the high cost of discrimination.

Translating values into action

Conversion is not enough, however. Unless antidiscriminatory policies are made part and parcel of the ways of doing things, and not dependent upon the good will and caprice of individuals, they are often bound to be ineffective. Values must be embodied in policy and procedures, and policies supported by enforcement mechanisms and adequate personnel. Constant evaluation must be made of the effectiveness of antidiscrimination policies.

Making discrimination "uneconomic"

The notion that "crime does not pay" has yet to eradicate crime, no matter how harsh the punishment and how effective the policing powers, for the

"GEORGIA HAS THE NEGRO AND HARLEM HAS THE JEW"

. . . When the Negro hates the Jew *as a Jew* he does so partly because the nation does and in much the same painful fashion that he hates himself. It is an aspect of his humiliation whittled down to a manageable size and then transferred; it is the best form the Negro has for tabulating vocally his long record of grievances against his native land.

At the same time, there is a subterranean assumption that the Jew should "know better," that he has suffered enough himself to know what suffering means. An understanding is expected of the Jew such as none but the most naïve and visionary Negro has ever expected of the American Gentile. The Jew, by the nature of his own precarious position, has failed to vindicate this faith. Jews, like Negroes, must use every possible weapon in order to be accepted, and must try to cover their vulnerability by a frenzied adoption of the customs of the country; and the nation's treatment of Negroes is unquestionably a custom. The Jew has been taught—and, too often, accepts —the legend of Negro inferiority; and the Negro, on the other hand, has found nothing in his experience with Jews to counteract the legend of Semitic greed. Here the American white Gentile has two legends serving him at once: he has divided these minorities and he rules. . . .

Both the Negro and the Jew are helpless; the pressure of living is too immediate and incessant to allow time for understanding. I can conceive of no Negro native to this country who has not, by the age of puberty, been irreparably scarred by the conditions of his life. All over Harlem, Negro boys and girls are growing into stunted maturity, trying desperately to find a place to stand; and the wonder is not that so many are ruined but that so many survive. The Negro's outlets are desperately constricted. In his dilemma he turns first upon himself and then upon whatever most represents to him his own emasculation. Here the Jew is caught in the American crossfire. The Negro, facing a Jew, hates, at bottom, not his Jewishness but the color of his skin. It is not the Jewish tradition by which he has been betrayed but the tradition of his native land. But just as a society must have a scapegoat, so hatred must have a symbol. Georgia has the Negro and Harlem has the Jew.

SOURCE: James Baldwin, "The Harlem Ghetto," in *Notes of a Native Son* (New York, Beacon, 1955), pp. 69, 71–72. Reprinted by permission of the Beacon Press, copyright © 1955 by James Baldwin.

simple reason that crime is not always engaged in because one thinks it will pay. But discrimination often is. By making it uneconomic—where union recognition is denied, where government contracts are not consummated, where no alternative housing exists, where fines and publicity are concentrated—discrimination can be effectively combatted even prior to conversion to democratic values.

Other possibilities for action

Three other areas would seem to be relevant to the breakdown of discrimination. The first is related to the effects of past discrimination. We have noted that one of the consequences of discrimination lies in the measure of truth it gives to prejudice. An employer, ready to hire a member of a minority group, may not find one with adequate skills, for appropriate training has been denied in the past. Special efforts, then, must be devoted to such areas. This suggests that guidance, special help, and training of minority youth may pay off far more in terms of equality of life chances than a similar investment in a program focused on discrimination against adults. (The two are, of course, not mutually exclusive.) Central to this problem is the absence of success models for minority youth. If they cannot identify with their parents and relatives, who have been unsuccessful because of discrimination, society must make provision for identification with others of their own group.

The second area is related to the first. The breakdown of stereotypes is involved in the breakdown of discrimination, though one need not necessarily precede the other. Whatever truth past discrimination has given to the stereotype must be eradicated. Stereotypes—irrational beliefs though they are—can also be dealt with *under certain conditions* by the rational presentation of evidence to the contrary. Where no great stake in holding to the stereotype exists, where it is contradicted in interaction with minority group members under conditions of equality, where reason can operate— stereotypes can be either eradicated or repressed. We should not belittle the latter possibility; most liberals, brought up in a discriminating society but brought to liberalism for various reasons, still retain their stereotypes and prejudices, but they *do not act on them.* This is a major gain in antidiscriminatory efforts. Perhaps the most effective way stereotypes can be overcome is the development by minority group members of new identifications. When a Negro comes to be seen as a union member, an actor, a member of a PTA, a Methodist, or a neighbor, the stereotypic set of the observer is weakened for all Negroes. Nonetheless, stereotypes are basically irrational; they remain even when exceptions are made and cannot be expected to disappear prior to the disappearance of discrimination. This suggests the wastefulness of overinvestment in antistereotypic education, particularly since discrimination is not primarily a psychological phenomenon.

Finally, we must see the struggle against discrimination as a long-term affair. Concomitant with it—and relevant to the problem of life chances— are efforts to by-pass discrimination. There are gaps waiting to be filled in our economy, as well as new areas of activity where discrimination has not yet set in. Taking advantage of these is the primary responsibility of minority group leadership. But the majority of the society which fostered discrimination has a responsibility to do its share in guiding its minorities to such potential areas of success.

Intellectual Perspective and Adjustment
to Minority Status

MELVIN SEEMAN

In the study of the consequences of social marginality, two opposed, though not mutually exclusive, viewpoints find clear expression: on the one hand, that marginal status is a misfortune involving inescapable psychological penalty; and, on the other hand, that substantial good may flow from the fact of marginality. This paper adopts the latter view, and presents empirical evidence bearing on the possibility of such positive consequences.

The significance of this evidence lies partially in the fact that the negative view is now so dominant in the literature. One could document at length Riesman's contention that "we tend all too often in social science to look at the punishing aspects of such phenomena as alienation, marginality and social mobility."[1] The theme which emerges from this negative view is nicely put by Jessie Bernard at the outset of her paper on "biculturality":

There is no happier fate for any man than to live his life in a culture never challenged, a culture he is never called upon to justify; to eat and speak and dress and pray without ever realizing that there are other ways of doing these simple things.[2]

Though the negative stance toward marginality is more abundant and powerful in impact, the alternative view has, nevertheless, a respectable history: Park, Simmel, and Veblen are among those who have stressed the potential good that may issue from the fact of marginality. Simmel, for example, treats the "stranger" as a marginal person, and one consequence of this marginality is the "objectivity of the stranger":

He is not radically committed to the unique ingredients and peculiar tendencies of the group and therefore approaches them with the specific attitude of "objectivity." But objectivity does not simply involve passivity and detachment; it is a particular structure composed of distance and nearness, indifference and involvement. . . . Objectivity may also be defined as freedom: the objective individual is bound by no commitments which could prejudice his perception, understanding, and evaluation of the given.[3]

SOURCE: Melvin Seeman, "Intellectual Perspective and Adjustment to Minority Status," *Social Problems*, 3:3 (January, 1956), pp. 142–153. Reprinted by permission.

[1] D. Riesman, *Individualism Reconsidered*, Glencoe, Ill.: Free Press, 1954, p. 159.

[2] J. Bernard, "Biculturality: A Study in Social Schizophrenia," in *Jews in a Gentile World*, I. Graeber and S. H. Britt, eds., New York: Macmillan Co., 1942, p. 264.

[3] Georg Simmel, *The Sociology of Georg Simmel*, K. H. Wolff, ed., Glencoe, Ill.: Free Press, 1950, pp. 404, 405.

In a sense, Simmel and Veblen are the points of origin for the thesis advanced here. Our thesis is that marginal status (in the present case, the position as Jew in a Gentile world) provides the opportunity for the development of perspective and creativity in the realm of ideas, and that the realization of this opportunity depends upon the individual's adjustment to marginality.[4] We incorporate, in what follows, both Simmel's view of the marginal person as one who is uniquely equipped to challenge the "givens" in society; and Veblen's view that the marginality of the Jew, in particular, has been an important factor in his emergence "as a creative leader in the world's intellectual enterprise":

It is by loss of allegiance, or at the best by force of a divided allegiance to the people of his origin, that he finds himself in the vanguard of modern inquiry. [Such intellectual enterprise] presupposes a degree of exemption from hard-and-fast preconceptions, a skeptical animus, *Unbefangenheit,* release from the dead hand of conventional finality. The intellectually gifted Jew is in a peculiarly fortunate position in respect of this requisite immunity from the inhibition of intellectual quietism. But he can come in for immunity only at the cost of losing his secure place in the scheme of conventions into which he has been born, and at the cost, also, of finding no similarly secure place in that scheme of Gentile conventions into which he is thrown.[5]

We are not here interested in the question of whether the Jew has, as Veblen argues, contributed "more than an even share to the intellectual life of modern Europe"; but in the question of whether marginality of any kind (using the Jews as a clear case in point) can be one of the conditions for the development of intellectual perspective. Our guess was that a successful experience with marginality increases the likelihood of high perspective. The guess is one which can be rationalized as a simple learning phenomenon: the individual whose attempt to accommodate to the conflict in values which marginality imposes is reinforced by success will, by the same token, learn the value of (and technique for) questioning "givens" and seeking new solutions.

INSTRUMENTS, SCORING PROCEDURE, AND SAMPLE

To test such a notion, we developed two major instruments for use with a Jewish sample. One of these was an Incomplete Sentences Blank (ISB) composed of 28 stems to be made into sentences by the respondent. Four-

---

[4] This same view has been nicely put by Riesman: ". . . our problem becomes one of seeing what positions in society are conducive, more or less, to insight and choice. Whether marginality fosters insight and choice depends, of course, on the given case. Marginality can freeze people with anxiety or nostalgia, while the absence of marginality can give people so much power that they need not choose, but can make all the other people choose." (*Op. cit.,* p. 163.)

[5] T. Veblen, *Essays in Our Changing Order,* New York: Viking Press, 1934, pp. 225–227.

teen of the stems were Jewish-relevant in content (e.g., "Jewish radicals . . ."; "Passover . . ."); and fourteen were neutral stems ("I regret . . ."; "I secretly . . ."). The neutral and Jewish stems were alternated, with the neutral stems providing an index of general personality adjustment as distinct from adjustment to minority status.[6]

The second instrument consisted of six brief descriptions of problem situations. The subjects were asked to "state and discuss your reaction to such a situation in *twenty-five or more words.*" Each situation dealt with a controversial issue involving multiple value viewpoints from which the social conflict might be approached. The first of these six items is reproduced here in full:

Legislators, parents and professional educators have been concerned about the menace of comic books to children. Many communities are searching for a way of handling this problem, with censorship being a key issue. What stand would you take in this issue? Why?

The remaining five situations dealt with enforcement of the Supreme Court's desegregation ruling, inter-religious dating, homosexuality in athletics, a legitimate but unwanted child being put up for adoption, and Communist authorship of a physics text used in the high schools.

The responses to these six situations were scored on a five-point "Scale for the Measurement of Intellectual Perspective." The scale is intended as an index of creativity in intellectual approach, where "creativity" is defined essentially as "the capacity to make the given problematic." Thus, scale point 1 is used for responses which treat "values as standardized givens"; and scale point 5 for responses which treat "values as experimental emergents." But since these two rather cryptic definitions of the end points of the scale were hardly enough for scorers to use in judging responses to the situational items, a set of descriptions of each of the five positions on the scale was worked out. Those descriptions are presented as Figure 1.[7] The three descriptions were intended for clarification only: each situational item received one score—a score which, as we proceed from 1 through 5, represents an increasing degree of readiness to entertain an uncategorical, multi-

[6] The original form of the ISB, with 38 stems, was developed by Milton Feiner and used by him in a master's thesis. (M. Feiner, *Adjustment to Minority Group Status and Perspectival Freedom,* unpublished master's thesis, on file in the library at The Ohio State University, 1953.) The neutral stems were modelled after the items in the Rotter Incomplete Sentences Blank, a test designed to measure personality conflict. (J. B. Rotter and J. Rafferty, *Manual for the Rotter Incomplete Sentences Blank,* New York: Psychological Corporation, 1950.)

I wish to express my special thanks to Mr. Feiner, who served as one of the judges for the Jewish-relevant responses—a laborious and difficult task, indeed, since it involved over 1000 individual judgments on 72 protocols. I am indebted also to Mr. Walter Mischel for the judgments on the "neutral" stems, and to Mrs. Frances Mischel for the major share of scoring and computation on this project.

[7] The situational items and the perspective scale were worked out in collaboration with Mary L. Bach, who used this scale in a master's thesis. (M. Bach, *The Relationship between Measurements of Self-Insight and Value Perspective,* unpublished master's thesis, on file in the library at The Ohio State University, 1955.)

ple-value perspective toward situations which are inherently complex. The respondent's total score on intellectual perspective was simply the sum of his six item scores. To minimize contamination, each of the six items was scored independently.

"Minority maladjustment" and "conflict" scores were derived from the responses to the ISB. The 14 neutral items of this test were scored for "conflict" on a seven-point continuum, according to the method described in the Rotter manual.[8] Scoring was performed by an advanced graduate student in clinical psychology.

The individual's maladjustment to minority status was obtained by scoring the 14 Jewish-relevant stems of the ISB on a five-point scale.[9] Here, only the end-points of the scale were defined; the scale as used by the judges appears in Figure 2. The total score on minority maladjustment is an index of the extent to which the individual responds to his minority position with efforts at escape and denial (assimilationist responses) or at defense (chauvinist responses), as against a positive acceptance of the fact of marginality without over-reaction to stereotyes. The view of adjustment embodied in this scoring borrows heavily from Lewin's analysis of self-hatred among Jews[10] and from Clement Greenberg's essay on Jewish chauvinism.[11] Lewin was concerned almost exclusively with the individual who manifests escape tendencies, but Greenberg argues that this overtly anti-Jewish adjustment may be matched on the other side by the so-called "positive Jew" who "asserts, seeks out, and revels in his Jewishness." About this type, Greenberg says:

> But what do I see when I take a longer look? That the Jewishness of so many of these "positive" Jews is truculent and very sensitive to criticism; and that it is also aggressive and uncharitable; that it points to itself too challengingly and has too little patience with conceptions of Jewishness other than its own . . . It is this absence of ease that makes me suspect that a certain familiar psychological mechanism is at work here. By projecting it upon others and attacking it violently in others, these "positive" Jews may be exorcising from their own consciousness an image of the Jew that is no less "negative" than that in the mind of the most cringing "assimilationist."[12]

The description of minority adjustment given in Figure 2 attempts to put these conceptions to work in empirical fashion. The view of adjustment which the scale represents clearly involves certain value premises—as, for that

---

[8] *Op. cit.*

[9] In this case, and in the scoring of conflict, responses were scored over the entire protocol, on the theory that the meaning of the relatively short item responses could be better assessed with the total group of responses in view. This procedure represents, in a sense, a calculated risk of contamination in the interests of surer meaning for brief responses.

[10] C. Greenberg, "Self-Hatred and Jewish Chauvinism," *Commentary*, 10 (November, 1950), 426–433.

[11] K. Lewin, *Resolving Social Conflicts*, New York: Harper and Bros., 1948, pp. 186–200.

[12] *Op. cit.*, p. 427.

FIGURE I.   *A Scale for the Measurement of Intellectual Perspective*

SCALE POINT 1	2	3	4	SCALE POINT 5
1. Scorer Judgment A given value, alternative, or position taken as obviously right, unconditional, categorical. Shows no awareness of the relevance of multiple values to the situation. *Treats values as standardized givens.*	Shows awareness of other positions and values; but clear commitment to one.	Recognizes the legitimacy of other positions, in spite of own commitment; the "un-decideds" also go here.	Shows clear evidence that alternatives are possible for him; that under different conditions, different choices may be made; that multiple values are involved in decision.	Seeks a creative alternative which synthesizes the viewpoints possible. *Treats values as experimental emergents.*
2. Inferred Thought Process "X is the only possible right way."	"I think X is right; but I know some people think Y is right."	"I think X is right; but after all you have to take into account that some people hold to Y and they may have some justification for their view."	"I think you have to weigh the values that may be involved from a number of points of view, and realize that your decision is not an absolute choice but relative to the situation; under the circumstances I choose X; but I can conceive of myself choosing Y, and my choice is a choice of relative goods."	"I think there are a number of right ways of dealing with this, and a number of important values involved—the job is to find a solution that may go off the beaten path and may in the process set a new standard without sacrificing any one good for another."
3. Presumed Behavior Tendencies *Behavior is a function of standardized right answers.*	*Behavior is a function of choice between tenable and untenable alternatives (the latter being considered in some degree but rejected).*	*Behavior is a compromise between a "right" position and a legitimate minority view not personally subscribed to.*	*Behavior is a function of seen multiple ends which may be served in complex social situations.*	*Behavior is a function of the search for new solutions where multiple tenable values are involved.*

FIGURE 2.   *A Rating Scale for Minority Maladjustment*

	SCALE POINT 1	2	3	4	SCALE POINT 5
1. *Identification with Jewishness*	Jewishness not categorically rejected; but accepted with neither belligerence nor defensiveness				Categorical identification, or categorical rejection (by way of idealizing of Jewish membership and associations; or rejection of "bad" Jews)
2. *Treatment of stereotypic qualities*	Stereotypes of either own group or outgroup are not accepted as adequate basis for response: there is qualification; causal review; speculation; search for the meaning of differences, rather than outright acceptance or rejection of stereotypes				Stereotypes are accepted with no qualification as the basis for response, either by way of approval or disapproval of the quality seen
3. *Conflict over Jewishness*	Openly discussed; or takes the form of admitted difficulties to be positively and rationally assessed				Denial of conflict; or exaggeration of personal doubt or persecution

matter, does the "conflict" scale and, indeed, any measure of maladjustment. So long, however, as these premises are clear, and the scoring derived from them reliable, the reader may judge for himself how far he wishes to go in accepting the implications of the data presented in the following section.

A total of 70 usable protocols was obtained from a fairly diversified sample of respondents. The original plan was to distribute the questionnaires to a random list of persons contributing to the United Jewish Appeal in the city of Columbus, Ohio. It quickly became clear, however, that an adequate return could not be achieved in this way, partly because of the length and difficulty of the instruments. Out of a total of 100 questionnaires distributed to the random list, only 20 complete forms were returned. The following groups were then personally contacted and their aid enlisted: two groups of members of Jewish women's organizations; a social club and an evening class at the local Jewish Center; and a student group meeting at the university center for Jewish students. The returns from these groups averaged 64%, a total of 87 questionnaires having been distributed among them.[13]

TABLE I. *Inter-Scorer Agreement and Split-Half Reliabilities of the Minority Maladjustment, Intellectual Perspective, and Conflict Scales*

	INTER-SCORER CORRELATIONS		CORRECTED SPLIT HALF RELIABILITY**	
	N	r	N	r
Minority Maladjustment	72	.73	72	.79
Intellectual Perspective	18	.68	75	.86
Conflict	*	*	53	.73

* Since considerable material is already available on the reliability of "conflict" scoring, and since the judge in this case was thoroughly familiar with the use of the Rotter manual, no multiple judging for "conflict" was attempted.
** The correlation between odd and even halves of each test was corrected by the Spearman-Brown prophecy formula.

The reliability of judgments, as well as total score reliabilities in the conventional sense, are always a primary question in work of this kind, where

---

[13] We have, obviously, no measure of marginality, but we assume that by the very nature of the sample, we are dealing with individuals who have had to come to terms in some fashion with their marginal status as minority members. There are a number of problems which cannot be adequately discussed in this limited space, and one of these is the unclarity of the concept of marginality itself. We use it here as essentially synonymous with minority position, where minority is defined as a group against which categorical discrimination is practiced, and where, by implication, the minority individual is oriented toward the differing norms of both the minority and the majority group, while the full rewards of both are not accessible.

A second problem which cannot be explicated lies in the perspective scale. This scale, being oriented toward the individual's treatment of values, concerns only one kind of intellectual perspective. Further, we do not mean to imply that the behavior which we have labelled as scale point 5 is always the most desirable. This is a situationally relative matter; there are presumably times and circumstances in which "creativity" is not a functional response.

open-ended material is scored. The agreement among independent judges and the corrected split-half reliabilities for the three major scores are presented in Table 1. All of the available evidence indicates that the judgments and the scores used here have a satisfactory reliability.

RESULTS

The correlations of primary interest—those among the three main variables of minority maladjustment, intellectual perspective, and conflict—are presented in Table 2. They show, first, a significant inverse association, as we

TABLE 2.   *Correlations among Minority Maladjustment, Intellectual Perspective, and Conflict Scores* (N = 70)

	MINORITY MALADJUSTMENT	INTELLECTUAL PERSPECTIVE
Intellectual Perspective	—.44*	—
Conflict	.03	.03

* Significant at the 1% level of confidence.

anticipated, between minority maladjustment and intellectual perspective. The "highs" in minority maladjustment, who have not solved the problems which their marginality imposes, are low in intellectual perspective; while the "lows," who have experienced marginality and resolved it, are high in intellectual perspective. Second, they show no association between conflict and minority maladjustment, indicating that the minority score is a fairly specific index of the individual's reaction to marginality rather than a measure of general personality adjustment.

Since our thesis is that successful experience with marginality, not personality conflict in general, is a crucial factor in the development of perspective, the independence here established between the two measures is important. It is an independence, too, which makes considerable sense on logical grounds, since the sources of personality conflict are so varied, and so often unconnected with marginality (as in the case of many intra-family difficulties, for example). At any rate, we discover here that conflict and minority maladjustment are independent, and that the latter, not the former, is significantly tied to intellectual perspective.[14]

---

[14] Feiner's results (*op. cit.*), based on a sample of 66 Jewish respondents, are rather consistent with the data given in Table 2, but there are some important differences. He used the well-known "F" scale as his measure of intellectual perspective. Feiner reports an *r* of .72 between "F" and minority adjustment. This correlation is considerably higher than the r given here, though consistent in direction. Between conflict and minority maladjustment his correlation was .37 (significant at the 1% level), while the obtained r between conflict and "F" was .27 (significant at the 5% level). It was largely because of our dissatisfaction with the use of the "F" scale to measure intellectual perspective that the scale described above was developed.

Beyond this bald statement of relationships, however, several important considerations remain. It might be asked, for example, whether the correlation of —.44 between minority maladjustment and perspective is consistent from item to item in the perspective scale. The correlations of minority maladjustment with responses to each item of the perspective scale are given in Table 3, where considerable consistency in association with all items is indicated. This consistency is all the more notable when we recall that the six items of the scale were scored "blind"—i.e., the consistency is presumably not a function of scorer "halo."

T A B L E   3.   *Correlations between Minority Maladjustment Scores and Item Responses on Intellectual Perspective (N = 70)*

ITEM NUMBER	ITEM CONTENT	r
1.	Comics and the problem of censorship	—.49*
2.	Enforcement of desegregation	—.27**
3.	Adoption of unwanted children	—.32*
4.	Inter-religion dating and marriage	—.32*
5.	Homosexuality in athletics	—.36*
6.	Communist authorship of physics text	—.25**

* Significant at the 1% level of confidence.
** Significant at the 5% level of confidence.

A more crucial question, however, is whether the relationship between minority maladjustment and intellectual perspective holds regardless of the schooling, occupational level, or age of the respondent. The relevant r's needed for partial correlation are given in Table 4, and the partial correlations themselves in Table 5. The relationship between minority maladjustment and intellectual perspective remains quite stable when the influence of these three possible "hidden factors" is eliminated. In all three instances, the key correlation retains its statistically significant character. This does not

T A B L E   4.   *Years of Schooling, Occupational Prestige, and Age of Respondents Correlated with Minority Maladjustment and Intellectual Perspective (N = 70)*

	MINORITY MALADJUSTMENT	INTELLECTUAL PERSPECTIVE
Years of Schooling	—.35*	.43*
Occupational Prestige**	—.22	.35*
Age	.14	—.21

* Significant at the 1% level of confidence.
** Prestige scores were obtained by rating the respondent's occupation (or husband's occupation) by reference to an extended North-Hatt scale. (National Opinion Research Center, "Jobs and Occupations," in *Class, Status, and Power*, R. Bendix and S. M. Lipset, *eds.*, Glencoe, Ill.: Free Press, 1953, pp. 411–426.)

TABLE 5. *Partial Correlations between Minority Maladjustment and*
Intellectual Perspective with Schooling, Occupational
Prestige, and Age Held Constant (N = 70)

VARIABLE HELD CONSTANT	PARTIAL CORRELATION	"t" VALUE
Years of Schooling	−.34	2.983*
Prestige	−.40	3.545*
Age of Respondent	−.43	3.877*

* Significant at or beyond the 1% level of confidence. The significance of partial r was computed according to the procedure described in McNemar. (Q. McNemar, *Psychological Statistics*, New York: John Wiley & Sons, 1949, p. 227.)

demonstrate, of course, that minority adjustment *causes* high perspective, but it seems clear that there is *some reliable relationship* between the two.

In order to explore more fully the nature of that relationship, the total sample was divided into four adjustment types: assimilationists, chauvinists, ambivalents, and adjustors. In scoring the Jewish-relevant items, all responses which deviated from the adjustment end of the scale, and which could be clearly typed as assimilationist or chauvinist in tendency, were so designated. Responses were scored "assimilationist" when they reflected the premise that Jewish differences are the root of the minority's troubles and these differences should, therefore, be done away with. For example, in completing the stem "Jewish doctors . . . ," one respondent wrote: "seem to judge each other by the amount of money they make." Chauvinist responses, by contrast, reflect the premise that Jewish differences are either inherently superior or require extravagant defense. In response to the same stem, "Jewish doctors . . . ," a characteristic chauvinist response was: "are very brilliant." Thus, a given response might be scored "3—chauvinist," while another, equally indicative of maladjustment, might be scored "3—assimilationist."

The "chauvinist" type category was made up of the 17 respondents scoring highest on minority maladjustment in the chauvinist direction; similarly, the 17 highest scorers in the assimilationist direction constituted the "assimilationist" category. Two of the more ambiguous cases were omitted to provide equal n's in an analysis of variance design. Then the 17 lowest scorers on minority maladjustment were labelled "adjustors," and the remaining 17 cases, neither low in maladjustment nor conspicuously high in either a chauvinist or an assimilationist direction, were termed "ambivalents."

The mean scores and standard deviations for each of these types on the three major variables of perspective, conflict, and minority maladjustment are presented in Table 6. The data on minority maladjustment are given for purposes of inspection only (the breakdown into types being itself dependent upon this score), and these data may be dismissed with one comment. The mean scores on minority maladjustment vary as the selection procedure dictates—i.e., the adjustors are low, while the chauvinists and assimilationists are high—but it is notable that the chauvinists and assimilationists are equally high in maladjustment.

TABLE 6. *Means and Standard Deviations of Scores on Intellectual Perspective, Conflict, and Minority Maladjustment, by Adjustment Types*

ADJUSTMENT TYPE	N	INTELLECTUAL PERSPECTIVE		CONFLICT		MINORITY MALADJUSTMENT	
		MEAN	S.D.	MEAN	S.D.	MEAN	S.D.
Adjustors	17	4.76	1.80	4.35	1.97	1.24	1.00
Chauvinists	17	2.71	1.32	4.76	2.01	6.18	3.88
Assimilationists	17	4.23	2.65	5.76	2.01	5.82	2.09
Ambivalents	17	3.76	2.42	4.24	1.99	4.35	1.28

It is, however, the perspective and conflict scores in Table 6 which are of greatest interest. Both the means and the standard deviations for "intellectual perspective" vary widely among adjustment types. The standard deviations, in fact, turned out to be significantly different at the 5% level of confidence, and it was necessary to apply a square root transformation to the original perspective scores to meet the conditions for an analysis of variance among adjustment types. With the data thus transformed, an analysis of variance was conducted to determine whether the adjustment types differ significantly in intellectual perspective. The resulting "F" ratio of 1.935 does not reach a statistically significant level.

As far as perspective is concerned, therefore, there are two outcomes of this analysis by type. Although, apparently, the four types do not differ significantly in their average level of intellectual perspective, there are differences among types in the amount of variation in perspective (i.e., in the clustering or spread of scores). In this light, the data of Table 6 are suggestive. The assimilationists score substantially the same as the adjustors in intellectual perspective, but their scores are the most variable of the four types. The chauvinists, on the other hand, do have the lowest score on intellectual perspective,[15] and, at the same time, their scores vary the least. Our sample here is quite small, given the four-way typology; but there is a sense, it seems, in which Greenberg may be perfectly correct in his doubts about the "positive" Jewish adjustment. Judged, at least, in terms of consequences (and here intellectual perspective is viewed as one such consequence), the chauvinists are not only the poorest in perspective, but they are homogeneously so.[16]

If we look, now, at the data on "conflict" in Table 6, the pattern found in

---

[15] Bernard, *op. cit.*, p. 271.
[16] The leads provided by this analysis are not dissipated when the three relevant control variables of age, occupational prestige, and education are brought into the picture. A comparison of the four adjustment types on these variables indicates the following: (a) for all three variables the standard deviations among types are homogeneous; (b) for age and occupational prestige, there are no significant differences of means among types; and (c) for education, the mean differences among types are significant at the 5% level (F = 3.918), but the comparison of greatest interest here, that between assimilationists and chauvinists, yields a critical ratio which is not significant (t = 1.854).

the over-all correlations is repeated in the analysis by types—i.e., the pattern of no association. The standard deviations do not differ significantly, nor are there significant differences of means among the four adjustment types. Apparently, general personality conflict is consistently unrelated to the main issues in our analysis.

THE PROBLEM OF "INAUTHENTICITY"

One further type of scoring was attempted. For each respondent, a "conversion" score was computed, indicating the number of times a neutral stem on the ISB was completed with Jewish-relevant material. With 14 neutral items, the theoretical range of this conversion score was from zero to 14; the obtained range was from zero to 12. The engaging aspect of this score, as with all indirect measures, is that the respondent has little opportunity to "manipulate" his replies, since the very existence and meaning of the score is relatively hidden.

It is difficult to give a definitive label to the conversion score, but one way to describe it is through the concept of "inauthenticity," a notion first introduced by Sartre. For Sartre, "what characterizes the inauthentic Jews is that they deal with their situation by running away from it; they have chosen to deny it . . ."[17] This is only one form of "inauthenticity," however. The more general referent of the term is *over-reaction to the occupancy of a given status.*

An adequate general definition of "over-reaction" is, of course, difficult to provide, but instances of it point fairly clearly to the phenomena which "inauthenticity" is intended to cover: the female scientist who guides her behavior as scientist (e.g., in a discussion of physical principles) by letting her position as a woman intrude into the decision as to what she should or should not say; or, more pertinently, the Jew who guides his behavior by the stereotype of the "bad Jew," and reveals extreme sensitivity to the behavior of other Jews.[18]

The conversion score represents an effort to explore empirically this idea of inauthenticity conceived as over-reaction to status position. Viewed in this way, the extremes in conversion are of major interest, since it is possible to "over-react" in two ways: to evade the issue of one's Jewish status by permitting no overlap between the neutral stems and the relevant stems; or to over-assert, by allowing the fact of Jewishness to determine response to all of the items regardless of their neutrality.

---

[17] J. P. Sartre, *Anti-Semite and Jew*, New York: Schocken Books, 1948, p. 93.

[18] Rinder and Campbell have analyzed some of the very real difficulties, both moral and conceptual, which the term "inauthenticity" presents. Their view is closely allied to the one presented here. At one point, for example, commenting on the Greenberg paper (*op. cit.*), they say: "In this insightful and perceptive essay, Greenberg has tried to show how both the Jewish chauvinist and the Jew manifesting self-hatred share the same motivational anomaly; namely, the behavior of both suffers from over-reference to the fact of their Jewishness." I. D. Rinder and D. T. Campbell, "Varieties of Inauthenticity," *Phylon*, 13 (December, 1952), 271.

The question, then, is whether the conversion score—taken as a measure of inauthenticity—is significantly associated with degree or type of minority maladjustment. We would not anticipate, however, simple straightline relationships, since the extreme cases of conversion (whether low or high) are seen as being more alike, insofar as inauthenticity is concerned, than the middle group who convert to some extent. As one would guess, following this logic, the linear *r*'s between conversion and the three major variables in this study are quite low and statistically insignificant: the correlation of conversion with intellectual perspective is .09; with minority maladjustment, .03; and with conflict, .21. Nor, on the other hand, was there a significant departure from linearity of relationship, a departure which the logic of the argument *would* lead us to anticipate in the case of minority maladjustment and intellectual perspective. The correlation ratio between conversion and intellectual perspective was .33; between conversion and minority maladjustment, .36. Neither of these ratios reaches the .05 level of significance, though the trend of the relationship in both cases is in the expected direction (high and low conversion associated with high maladjustment and low perspective).

The analysis of conversion scores by adjustment types was based upon the information given in Table 7. As with the perspective scores, the conversion

T A B L E 7.   *Means and Standard Deviations for Conversion Scores by Adjustment Types*

ADJUSTMENT TYPE	N	MEAN	S.D.
Adjustors	17	1.59	1.75
Chauvinists	17	2.29	2.98
Assimilationists	17	1.88	2.08
Ambivalents	17	1.06	1.35

data show no difference in mean scores for the several types (again, using transformed data), but the standard deviations are significantly different at the 5% level of confidence (chi square = 8.895). These results conform to expectation, in that there is no sure ground (where conversion extremes are equally inauthentic) to anticipate *mean* differences, but there is ground for expecting the spread of scores on conversion to vary. It is notable that the two groups which show the widest spread are the chauvinists and the assimilationists, the two groups which, on *a priori* grounds, are most likely to be "inauthentics."

These results on "conversion" tell us very little of a substantial nature about the relation of inauthenticity to minority maladjustment or intellectual perspective. As exploratory results they may nevertheless be important, for two reasons. First, they do suggest that the concept of inauthenticity can be usefully explored as an aspect of minority life. With a larger sample (where the correlation ratios, for example, would be less suspect due to a small number of cases in some of the arrays) and with supplementary information by way of interviews, there is ground for hope that this concept, heretofore exclusively a vehicle for the essayist, may be made empirically productive. Second, the consistency of some of the findings on conversion (where the respondent was totally unaware of the meaning or existence of the measure) with the results given earlier in this paper suggests that we are not dealing here with a fictitious association between minority maladjustment and perspective produced by the simple fact that some of our respondents are "sharper" than others in guessing what a "good" response is on the two instruments developed in this study.

CONCLUSION

No one would assert that this work has verified the assertions by Park, Simmel, Veblen, and others about the positive consequences of marginality. We have, at best, made these assertions more plausible. At the same time, we have laid out some tools and directions for further inquiry.

Such inquiry is surely one of the crucial tasks in the sociology of knowledge, since it bears directly on the relationship of social position to creativity in intellectual work. There are many kinds of marginality—including national, sexual, religious, economic, and a host of other brands. We need, especially in these days when conformity rather than creativity is the rule, to examine with care, as well as with hope, any doctrine which directs our attention to such marginalities as potential sources of insight and perspective.

The Slum—"Internal Colonialism"

BERNARD ROSENBERG

Some years have passed since a humorist named Henry Morgan first remarked that: "The housing shortage is an ugly rumor—circulated by people who have no place to live." There are few observers who understand better than Charles Abrams how valid that sad quip still is. The New York State Rent Administrator, a long time student of housing, has presented us with a massive documentation of the problem in his recent book, *Forbidden Neighbors*.[1] Formal social science, with its penchant for the trivial, has a

SOURCE: Bernard Rosenberg, "The Slum—'Internal Colonialism,'" *Jewish Frontier*, 23:4 (April, 1956), pp. 16–19. Reprinted by permission.

[1] *Forbidden Neighbors: A Study of Prejudice in Housing* by Charles Abrams. Harper and Brothers, New York, 1955, 404 pp., $5.

good deal less to say about contemporary American culture than can be found between the covers of this book. One needs passion as well as detachment, a sense of irony and some subtlety to survey the scene before us. Abrams has them all in good measure.

At the moment, residential patterns reveal a new trend, which has not yet been widely recorded, toward exclusiveness in previously mixed areas. Under the circumstances, it is well to be reminded of a *presegregation* past, when not so long ago, in the American metropolis:

It was fashionable for the mansion folk to have their Negro housekeepers live in the house across the alley, if not within the houses themselves. The type of structure was more reliable than the type of neighbors in gauging wealth and status. In smaller cities, too, old and young, Catholic and Protestant, Negro and white, well-born and humble, all lived in the same general area without loss of face or position.

All this has changed for the worse in every section of the United States. After a brief period of fluidity, the post-Civil-War South gradually imposed nearly every stigma of caste upon its Negro population. The classic tabus, *connubium* and *commensality*, prohibiting intermarriage and informal association, were firmly established by law and by custom. The Negro's subordinate status was symbolized in his forced obedience to an elaborate protocol governing all forms of intercourse with the upper caste. However, white Southerners never mistook physical propinquity for ritual contamination. They accepted Negro neighbors as much as the black Mammies who raised their children. Discriminatory in every other way, whites did not feel the need for residential segregation which, like other manufactured goods, had to be imported from the North.

The American ghetto, as a semi-voluntary institution, originated in the big city. There the foreign-born huddled together in ethnic islands that were also patches of the Old Country, and there they tarried for awhile. Those who had arrived earlier moved up to "areas of second settlement," to Suburbia, and respectability. Then, to replace them, came minorities with a higher visibility, some from abroad, but most from other parts of the country. Soon, Negroes, Puerto Ricans, and other dark-skinned settlers found themselves stuck fast in decrepit tenements from which there seemed, and seems, to be no escape.

Real *apartheid* came only in a state like Florida, the swamp that grew into a playland, where phenomenal growth occurred in a forty year span largely as the result of Northern migration. By 1950 Miami had risen from a town of 5000 to a city of 250,000. A trickle of whites from Alabama and Georgia brought segregation in schools, churches and transportation. Whites from north of the Mason-Dixon line contributed their own brand of neighborhood segregation, and a fine rapport was achieved—after the manner of South Africa. It is a nice question whether we are resegregating in fact faster than we are desegregating on paper. In Miami there are only about 40,000 Negroes left. The rest have been pushed out of town (which is unusual; elsewhere they are being pushed into town; whether the pressure is centripetal or centrifugal would appear to be a side issue.) When you try to pull down barriers you have just erected, this is what happens:

. . . Two Miami builders named Wiseheart and Bouvier decided to build a 400-unit FHA private project for whites on the white side of the wall, and a Negro project on the black side to be called Carver Village. Since the Negro project was inside the wall no one objected. But the white dwellings remained half empty, so the owners, sensing the larger profit in Negro rentals, decided to rent some of these units to the home-hungry Negroes.

The intolerable invasion by Wiseheart and Bouvier, misidentified as Jews, could be met in only one way: by dynamite. That instrument of terror was used indifferently in Florida throughout most of 1951 to blow up homes, whether occupied or not, to blast synagogues and to attack churches.

Florida is but one of several case studies Abrams reports; Cook County, Illinois, Detroit and Dearborn, Mexican communities in the Southwest, and Puerto Rican anthills in New York City are a few others. Each one is a valuable summary of the trend from bad to worse. In Washington, D. C., Negroes at the time of their emancipation operated many businesses, paid $650,000 in taxes, and lived decently. Certain occupations, like those in the tobacco industry, were open to Negro freedmen while slavery existed, and barred to them thereafter. In the Midwest, it was only from about 1915 that "privileges" in theaters, hotels, cafes and other public places were denied. Restoring such rights has been an uphill battle. While engaged in winning it, we have been distracted from another front where few victories can be claimed.

One-third of the housing in America is sub-standard, just as it was more than twenty years ago when FDR first came to power. But the poor quality of dwellings is less serious than the overcrowded conditions they conceal. Abrams quotes an American missionary who, probably without exaggeration, describes Harlem housing conditions as worse than anything he had seen in China. Nor could Moscow, where cramped quarters are the norm, surpass New York's Puerto Rican sections for the degree to which they approximate pig pens, fleabags and rabbit hutches. These are the same slums built sixty years ago to accommodate the nineteenth century immigrant who never had to suffer quite so acutely in tenements that were built to provide shelter at rents he could afford. Now they are in the possession of landlords whose annual yield is as high as 100% on investment, and the tenant must pay up to $60 a month per room in an incredibly dilapidated environment. Nor can the Puerto Rican in this prosperous era when he is able to earn a living, buy his way into a better environment. 20,000 Puerto Ricans have been absorbed into the garment industry; 16,000 into hotel and restaurant employment. If their position is difficult now, with practically full employment, what will it be if the color-line persists when they are more fully Americanized?

Besides the stationary ghetto, there is what Abrams refers to as the mobile ghetto, a novel American phenomenon. In it can be found the two-way immigrant who comes to do stoop labor and leaves. The hobo and Hobohemia are gone. Instead, we have the migratory worker and his portable slum. Membership is restricted to certain citizens and aliens, Mexicans, Negroes, Puerto Ricans, Bahamians and a scattering of other minorities willing to accept two or three dollars for a day's hard labor. They constitute a major segment of the vast rural proletariat that has only recently come into being. Hundreds of thousands of Mexicans cross the border into California and Texas, without benefit of social security, minimum wages, or any other official protection for themselves or social services such as schooling for their children. They pick the crops, get arrested, and are sent back home. Here we have unbridled exploitation: no job standards, no housing, no sanitation, no medical facilities.

These are the wetbacks. The drybacks, Mexican-Americans legally admitted to the U.S., sometimes urgently solicited to come, are not much better off. "In San Antonio, the west-side Mexican slum of 60,000 is called 'the largest solid bloc of underpossessed in the United States.' Slum life, exploitation, segregation, and social subordination are virtually complete." But the migratory worker, white and dark, citizen or alien, is even less privileged. While everything booms but the guns, "He sleeps on the ground, in a cave, under a tree, or in a chicken house." In Los Angeles County, Abrams found a Mexican community composed of homemade huts put together from such homely materials as burlap, cardboard, and corrugated scrap. Of course, there was "no plumbing, drainage or screening and no running water." In Imperial County, where Mexican children represent the highest proportion of victims, the infant death-rate from diarrhea, enteritis, and dysentery is seven times higher than the statewide average. While our surplus food rotted in surplus warships and warehouses, "A physician told the President's Commission of the frequent cases of pellagra and 'ordinary starvation' due to the diet of cornmeal and rice and 'very little else.' In one Texas camp, 96 per cent of the children had not consumed any milk whatsoever in the last six months while eight out of every ten adults had not eaten any meat in six months."

The Mexican sites are deliberately placed outside city limits in inconspicuous places, on unbeaten paths where they are not likely to be seen. This practice does not materially differ from that of the Nazis who threw a sop to the public conscience by hiding concentration camps. People are encouraged to wear blinders and thus to develop a kind of tunnel vision. Whether one chooses to see it or not, this nasty business is what Abrams calls it, namely, *internal colonialism.* Part of the configuration is familiar enough: a socially debased native laborer working hard for pitiful wages under subhuman conditions. But, "the difference between the traditional and the new colonialism is that our colonial natives are kept with us within distance when we want them—and then driven out of the community when no longer needed. They go back to the 'colony' at the season's end, often under armed guard."

When an alliance is formed between federal agencies, homebuilding and improvement associations, banks, insurance companies, neighborhood clubs and weekly papers—that burgeon as fast as dailies disappear—when city planning and slum clearance are used as devices to evict minorities and make their lot still more insufferable, and when it can be said that since 1935 "less than 1 per cent of new dwelling construction was for the nonwhite families who comprise 10 per cent of the population," then truly, a situation with dangerous potentialities exists.

13. WORK AND EMPLOYMENT: AUTOMATION

The Closing of Maryland #1

HARVEY SWADOS

It was only a couple of years ago that the coal dust problem was so bad in St. Michael that a civic committee was formed to cope with it. "I was used to not recognizing my husband, to say nothing of the other men who'd come out of the mine and wave to me," says one miner's wife. "But the coal dust got so bad that it lay over the town like a pall. Everything was covered with it, and we got worried, not just about silicosis down in the mines, but about what it was going to do to all of us right out on the streets."

The dust too was a by-product of mechanization, a result of the automatic miners chewing away furiously hundreds of feet under the earth, and the company informed the committee that there was no point in investing the large sum that would be necessary to abate the nuisance, since it was already losing money on every carload of coal being taken from Maryland #1. All too soon thereafter the mine closed down, and the dust stopped sifting through the streets. The committee·was disbanded. . . .

Most of the miners have been used to seasonal operations, working winters and taking off summers, and for quite a long time they assumed that this was to be just another layoff. But then the summer was over, fill-in jobs elsewhere in the area did not seem to be available, and the company took out its expensive automatic equipment and moved some of it down to Maryland Shaft #2, half a dozen miles away at Wilmore. At that point the miners and their families began to face up to the reality of their prospects, and habits began to change. The first item to stop moving at the general store was dog food. After the dog food gathered dust, it was the bottled baby food in the

SOURCE: From "The Miners: Men Without Work," in *A Radical's America*, by Harvey Swados, by permission of Little, Brown and Co.—Atlantic Monthly Press. Copyright © 1959 by Harvey Swados.

little glass jars that stayed on the shelves. A while after that, the shopkeeper himself gave up and locked his doors forever.

The saloons are still going in St. Michael's Hotel, the Workers' Educational & Social Club, the American Legion Hall, and the old boathouse, but many of the whisky drinkers have switched to beer, many of the beer drinkers have switched to Squirt, and even more do not show up at all nowadays in the saloons.

"I used to spend between forty and fifty dollars every two weeks in the saloons," says one miner. "Now I never go any more. It's one thing to be a good fellow when you have it—it's a little different when you have no job."

The town barber, a horn-rimmed young man in a starched white shirt who is on the school board and looks startlingly middle-class in a community that is overwhelmingly working class, stares at his cigar and muses over his beer at the Legion Hall. "I bear no resentment to the miners who don't come in any more to have me cut their hair. I guess if I'd been out of work as long as they have, I'd ask my wife to cut my hair too."

Some of the miners have managed to get jobs elsewhere. Hampered by the fact that their skills—and even more than their easily-acquired skills, such intangible assets as courage, fortitude, esprit de corps and insouciance in the face of continuous danger—are not readily transferable to other trades, they have been absorbed only in lower-paying jobs. Those who came from other communities and only boarded in St. Michael have gone home. A few have gotten into the steel mills, but not many. A few more have gotten construction work and jobs with the State Highway Department, but again not many; the men point to the million-dollar addition to the high school plant now going up with only seven miners among the construction crew, and they claim that it is impossible to get such a job without "politics." A number of the miners are now working, often for a third or less than what they used to earn, as orderlies in hospitals and institutions, and as janitors and stockmen in big stores. Some have tried to relocate—at least one man has been back and forth to California twice tracking down rumors of steady employment there—only to return to home grounds when jobs haven't materialized. Practically everyone, they say, would come rushing back to St. Michael if Maryland #1 were to reopen, even those few who have gotten good-paying jobs elsewhere (a man with seniority is allowed up to three weeks to re-apply for his job). Mining is something that gets in a man's blood, and a coal mine is a man's world in a way that a department store or a mental hospital can never be.

It is truly ironic that a substantial proportion of these men, who pride themselves on their ability to live with danger, to work hard, fight hard, drink hard, love hard, are now learning housework and taking over the woman's role in the family.

What happened was terribly simple. When it became apparent that the mine was not going to reopen, the men signed up for unemployment insurance and their wives began to look for work. Committees were set up—as they have been, hopefully, sometimes pathetically, in similarly depressed areas in Kentucky, West Virginia, Illinois and Michigan—to see what could be done about bringing in new businesses that could provide employment. The ones that did come to the Western Pennsylvania area were those that could benefit not only from tax rebates, low rents, cheap utilities, and other enticements, but also from a substantial pool of people hungry for work—almost any kind of work at almost any kind of wage. Now there are in the area a scattering of small garment factories, brassieres, shirts, shirtwaists, children's wear, all employing not men but women to bend over their sewing machines.

So the women go out to work in the new factories at minimum wages and the men stay home, running the washing machines and the vacuum cleaners, doing the shopping and the dusting, often baby-sitting, occasionally cooking and scrubbing. There are variations. Some wives hire themselves out as cleaning women to middle-class homes in other towns while their husbands serve as cleaning women at home. There are rebellions too. One husband sits in the saloon waiting for his wife to finish her shift and come after him at midnight, which she does, standing in the doorway in her pedal-pushers, her arms folded, smiling tiredly but firmly until he shoves back his chair, finishes his beer, and walks her home. He insists on playing his role as a man even if he cannot do his work as a man, and one can only guess as to whether his wife loves him any less than do those women whose husbands have taken to drowsing in front of the TV after they have finished the dishes and await their wives' return from the factory. But these are for the most part younger women; it is hard for a woman in her fifties to keep up with the production pace in a factory, and a number of them have had to give it up and reluctantly rejoin their husbands on the rockers or the porch steps.

What else does a man do besides keep house and rock, and hang around the saloon, after he has been out of work for fourteen months? One miner says, "I've been going from town to town, city to city, every place within a hundred miles of here, looking for work. I know it's a wild goose chase. I'm too old. My own boy is thirty-two, or maybe thirty-three, with three kids of his own, and *he* can't find work. One or two places where he could have had work as a carpenter, he couldn't get a journeyman's card in the union. So what chance do I stand? Just the same, I keep trying—it keeps me occupied."

One would think, as one gets closer to the workers themselves than Washington, D. C., that there would be a greater awareness of their problems and a deeper searching for possible answers. The office of District 2 of the UMW, which includes the miners of St. Michael, is located in the county seat of Ebensburg, Pa. about seventeen winding miles from St. Michael. It has taken over an old mansion in the better part of town and it is staffed by Lewis appointees.

A visitor walks in and asks why so many men are being laid off in the district. Because they were unfortunate enough to be stuck in uneconomic low-seam mines which do not adapt to mechanization as well as the mines of District 5 or West Virginia. But even with a six per cent increase in tonnage nationally, men are being laid off everywhere. Then what is the answer?

"I don't really know."

Once again, there is the story of efforts to attract new industry, with its usually turning out to be light industry, employing women. As for the men in District 2 who are still working, with the exception of the captive mines, working hard to stockpile metallurgical coal in expectation of a steel strike, they are averaging three days a week, and glad to have jobs, with the prospect of occasionally picking up a fourth or fifth day of work. The fact is simply that with three days of work the operators take out all the coal they can sell: which is one more reason for the cutbacks.

What about the men who aren't working?

"They don't come in here, so we don't get any complaints at the office. We're not in touch with them."

And what will happen when the unemployment insurance runs out?

"I don't know how they'll get along."

The truth is that no one really does know. The barber of St. Michael may be as close to the truth as anyone when he observes that the men were so stunned by the closing of the mine that they are still in a state of shock, and unable to face the reality that they may never again be able to work at their chosen trade.

Automation and the Automobile Worker

WILLIAM A. FAUNCE

Few developments in American industry have ever attracted as much attention as has automation. There have been congressional hearings, hundreds of conferences, and thousands of newspaper and magazine articles dealing with the possible consequences of automation for American society. This concern has not yet, however, manifested itself in a comprehensive program of research designed to discover what the effects of automation may actually be. To the extent that social scientists have become concerned with the problem at all, their attention has been focused primarily upon the possibility of technological displacement of workers and its attendant problems. The question of individual and organizational adjustments to the changes in

SOURCE: William A. Faunce, "Automation and the Automobile Worker," *Social Problems*, 6:1 (Summer, 1958). Reprinted by permission.

production techniques has received much less attention. This paper is not concerned with the problems of workers who have lost their jobs as a result of automation but with the adjustment problems of what is currently a much larger group of workers: those who are still working but who have recently experienced the changes in their jobs resulting from the introduction of automated machinery. We will consider, first, the nature of the changes in the job of the individual worker in the automated plant and then the effect of these changes upon work satisfaction and attitudes toward industrial work.

The research upon which this paper is based was conducted in 1956 and 1957 in one of the most highly automated automobile engine plants in Detroit. It involved interviews with a random sample, stratified by department size and job classification, of 125 workers from the four most highly automated departments of this plant. All of the workers interviewed had had experience with non-automated machining operations in the older plants of the company and had been working on automated jobs in the new plant for approximately two years at the time of the interviews. These workers were asked to compare their last previous non-automated job with their present job in terms of job content, working conditions, patterns of social interaction, and work satisfaction.

Perhaps the most important change which has occurred in the job of the machine operator on automated production lines is the reduction in the amount of materials handling required. In the old, non-automated plants of the company, over 80 per cent of machine operator jobs involved some handling of materials. In the new plant only 44 per cent of the workers reported that their job involved materials handling. A majority of this 44 per cent were workers in departments where smaller parts were machined and, in many instances, automatic loaders were added to the transfer machinery so that the materials handling involved only the feeding of small parts into a loader. Even for those workers whose jobs still involved some materials handling, automation has considerably changed job content. For those workers in departments where no materials handling was involved, this aspect of the change represented an even more substantial difference from the old jobs where, in many instances, it was necessary to handle crankshafts, cylinder blocks or other heavy engine parts.

A second important change reported in jobs on automated lines was that workers no longer actually operated the machines and therefore no longer had any control over the work pace. Most of the workers in the old plants using conventional machining techniques operated the machines in the sense that they pulled down a lever or in some other way actuated the machining process. Because they controlled the machine, they were able to regulate the pace of the work within the limits prescribed by the established production quotas. As long as production quotas were met, workers were able to vary work pace in such a way as to be able to work ahead and take a break.

With the advent of automation, the long trend toward decreasing control of work pace by the industrial worker has almost run full course. Only two workers in the sample of workers interviewed reported that they actually operated a machine in the sense described above. Significantly fewer workers reported that they were able to work at their own speed on their automated job and significantly fewer indicated they were able to work ahead and take a break on these jobs.

A third change reported in job content on automated lines was in the amount of attention required by the job. Many jobs in the old, non-automated plant could be reduced to a series of repetitive manual operations requiring only surface mental attention. In addition, since the work pace was controlled by the machine operator, there were periods between machining operations when no attention was required by the job. In contrast, in the new, automated plant, many jobs required more or less constant attention to gauges or panels of lights throughout the day or as long as the transfer machines were in operation. The consequences of not attending closely to the job were more serious in automated production departments because more things could go wrong with automated machinery and this machinery was much more costly than conventional machines. Also, a breakdown of a transfer machine was often the signal for a confluence around the machine of the superintendent, general foreman, engineers, repairmen, and other white collar or "blue collar with tie" workers from all parts of the plant. This is a consequence to be assiduously avoided from the viewpoint of most of the workers interviewed.

A fourth type of change in the job of the machine operator on automated jobs, which deserves mention particularly because of the amount of attention it has been given in discussions of the consequences of automation, is the amount and type of skill required on the job. The opinion of management in the automated plant was that no new or greater skill was required of machine operators. Accordingly, there was no special training programs set up for these workers. The responses of the workers were generally consistent with this view. A comparison of the amount of training time reported on the old jobs and the automated jobs revealed no significant differences. Likewise, there was little difference between the two jobs in the amount of time estimated by workers that it would "take a new man to learn their job." In response to the question, "Would you say your job gives you a chance to use your abilities, or is the job too simple to let you use your abilities?," little difference was found between the old jobs and on the new jobs in the number reporting that the work required ability.

There would seem to be little reason to suppose on a basis of the differences in job content that greater skill would be required with the automated machinery. It would seem in fact, because many of the manual skills required with conventional machining techniques are no longer needed, that the converse may well be true. In response to the direct question, "Which job, your old job or your present job, requires more skill?," however, a larger proportion of workers indicated that their present jobs in the automated plant required more skill. In view of the evidence to the contrary, this response would seem to be an unrealistic appraisal of the skill requirements of the job.

Some workers may have felt that their automated jobs required more skill because of the change in the type of skills involved. Fifty-three per cent of the responses of workers who felt that their present job in the automated plant allowed them to use their abilities identified ability on the job with alertness or attention. Most of the remaining responses were general responses suggesting that there was a lot to know about automated machinery. Fifty-one per cent of the responses of workers who felt their old jobs required ability dealt with the fact that in the non-automated plant it was necessary to inspect the parts as they were machined. Thirty-one per cent of the responses dealt with the skills required in setting, loading, or operation of the old machines.

A general assessment of the data suggests that somewhat different but probably no greater skills are required of *machine operators* in the automated plant. It should be emphasized, however, that we are comparing similar or identical job classifications here on automated and non-automated operations. There was actually a higher proportion of skilled to semi- or unskilled workers in the automated plant because of the larger number of skilled maintenance workers and "trouble shooters." The data reported here do not suggest that the automation of conventional machining techniques does not require new and greater skills or that the work force is not up-graded in the sense that the proportion of skilled to less skilled workers increases, but rather that the whole work force is not necessarily up-graded and that some jobs in automated plants may actually call for less skill than before.

A number of other ways in which the job of the machine operator has or has not changed merit some mention. It has been frequently suggested that automation increases the amount of responsibility of the industrial worker. His responsibility is increased in many instances because his work accounts for a larger share of the total production process and in most instances because machinery investment per worker and the cost of mistakes has increased. Our data suggest that the workers also *feel* that their new jobs involve more responsibility. Over twice as many workers indicated that their jobs in the automated plant involved more responsibility than their previous, non-automated jobs and over three times as many workers indicated that their present, automated jobs were more important.

The question of the amount of fatigue resulting from the two types of jobs should be further clarified. It was obvious from the responses to other questions that many workers felt fatigued at the end of a day working in the automated plant. This fatigue, however, was described as the result of the constant attention required by the job and not as a result of physical effort expended. It is possible that in responding to the question, "Which job is more physically tiring?," some workers did not distinguish between fatigue resulting from the amount of attention required and fatigue from physical effort. If this distinction had been more clearly made, an even greater proportion would probably have reported the non-automated job to be more physically tiring.

It has been frequently suggested that automation will result in a considerable improvement of working conditions. The automated plant has been described as a cleaner, safer, quieter, and generally more pleasant place in which to work. The data suggest that this is not the case in the automated plant in which this study was conducted. Working conditions apparently varied considerably from department to department in the automated plant and, while they were improved on some jobs by the introduction of automated machinery, they appear to have actually become worse on others.

In addition to the changes in job content in the automated plant, there has been a considerable change in the social milieu of the worker on the automated line. The effects of automation upon in-plant social structure in the plant studied will be dealt with in detail in another paper. It is sufficient for our purpose here to note that there was a decrease in opportunity for social interaction, that the interaction which occurred took place within smaller groups of workers, and that there was less apt to be identification with a particular work group in the automated plant. Relations between workers and supervision were also affected by the introduction of automated machinery. The workers reported closer and more frequent supervision and a change in established informal patterns of worker-foreman relationships in the direction of increased formality with increased use by the foreman of the authority vested in the role.

We shall now consider how these changes in the job of the automobile worker have affected his attitude toward work in the automated plant. The effects of the changes in patterns of social interaction upon work satisfaction will be discussed first and then the reactions of the workers to the changes in job content will be considered.

On a basis of previous research, it might be hypothesized that a decrease in opportunity for social interaction and an increase in amount of supervision would be sources of dissatisfaction with automated jobs. The data collected in this study support these hypotheses.

A difference significant at the .01 level was found in the amount of social interaction reported by workers who were satisfied and by those who were not satisfied with their jobs in the new plant. This difference is accounted for by the large proportion of workers not satisfied with their automated job who reported frequent social interaction on their previous job and infrequent social interaction on their present job. Of those who were satisfied with their present job over half reported frequent social interaction on both jobs. That frequency of opportunity for social interaction was a factor in the worker's general evaluation of the total job is suggested by the fact that significantly more of the workers who indicated a preference for automated as opposed to non-automated jobs had some opportunity for social interaction on their present automated jobs. Also, significantly more of the respondents who preferred non-automated jobs indicated that they used to get together socially off the job more often with friends from that job, while almost 60 per cent of the workers who preferred their automated job reported no difference between the jobs in this respect. An example of the type of response showing dissatisfaction with this aspect of automated jobs is the attitude expressed by one worker who responded to the question, "Is there anything else about your present job which is different from your old job?," by stating, "There are not so many workers around . . . that's why it (the automated job) is more boring and lonesome."

The relationship between type of leadership and group productivity and morale has been demonstrated by research in a variety of situations from the early experiments of Kurt Lewin with children to more recent studies in the industrial setting. The data from this study also suggest that type of supervision is a factor in work satisfaction on the automated line. A significant difference was found between the number of workers who preferred their old, non-automated job and those who preferred their present job in terms of the amount of supervision desired with a larger proportion of those who preferred non-automated jobs reporting that they would rather have less supervision than they were getting on their automated job.

A significantly larger proportion of the workers who preferred their old, non-automated job also reported that it was easier to get along with the foreman on that job. In addition to the effect of type of supervision on worker preference for one type of job or the other, the responses to questions dealing with level of work satisfaction on each job suggest that differences in type of supervision affect worker attitudes toward the job. A significantly larger proportion of the workers who were not satisfied with their present, automated job but satisfied with their previous non-automated job indicated that it was easier to get along with the foreman on their previous job.

In general, the data suggest that the social structural changes which can be attributed to the change in production technology were sources of dissatisfaction with jobs in the automated plant. Two other aspects of jobs in the automated plant with which workers were dissatisfied will be considered now, and then those changes in job content which the workers regarded as improvements over jobs in plants using conventional machining techniques will be discussed.

One apparent source of *dissatisfaction* with job content in the automated plant may be labeled feelings of *alienation* (if it is possible to borrow this Marxian term without its overtones of Hegelian mysticism). The worker on the automated line is alienated in the sense that he no longer has control over the machine and the work pace, machining skills previously acquired are no longer of use, and it becomes increasingly difficult to identify what the transfer machines does as *his* work. The following quotations from interviews may illustrate this feeling:

(I don't like) the lack of feeling responsible for your work. The feeling that you're turning out more work but knowing it's *not yours really* and not as good as you could make it if you had control of the machine like before.

It's a completely different feel of work. On my old job, I controlled the machine. On my present job, the *machine controls me*.

It is reasonable to expect that workers who have had long experiences with conventional machining operations will feel alienated from their work when placed on a job where they need only push a button or watch a panel of lights and where they may not even see the operation being performed in an enclosed transfer machine. The most frequent response given as a reason for feeling satisfied with non-automated jobs was that on these jobs the operator controlled the work pace and that it was possible to vary work pace and take a break. The third most frequent response dealt with the fact that the old, non-automated job required machining skills. When workers who indicated a preference for non-automated over automated jobs were asked the reasons for their preference, 31 per cent of the responses referred to control of work pace and the feeling of responsibility for one's own work. All of these responses may be interpreted as reflecting the general feeling of alienation from one's work expressed in the quotations cited above, and this feeling appears to be one of the important sources of dissatisfaction with automated jobs.

Another source of job dissatisfaction on the automated line was the feeling of tension or anxiety reported by some workers. These increased tensions were apparently attributable to a combination of factors involving the increased speed of production, the constant attention required, and the cost of mistakes and frequency of breakdowns of automated machinery. The following comments from interviews may be cited as illustrations of this feeling:

> You are very rushed on automation. You are under *pressure all the time*. That's why it's so hard to learn and some can't do it—can't stand the pressure.
> (Automation is) just different all the way through. You've *got to be aware all the time* and push the right button. If you push the wrong one it could cost around $13,000 and is very dangerous. I pushed a wrong button and stuff flew all over. I was lucky but it cost the company $13,000 to fix the machine.

Thirty-three per cent of the responses expressing dissatisfaction with automated jobs dealt with either the amount of attention required by the job or the fast pace of production. Twenty-five per cent of the responses of workers who indicated a preference for non-automated jobs dealt with the feeling that too much attention was required by the automated job or that too much tension was involved. Responses expressing concern for the cost of mistakes and the frequency of breakdown of automated machinery were frequent and occurred as parts of responses to many different questions in the interviews. The feelings of anxiety resulting from these characteristics of automated jobs appear to be a common source of dissatisfaction with these jobs.

Only one factor stood out as a reason given for satisfaction with automated jobs or for a preference for these jobs. That factor was the decrease in amount of materials handling involved in the work in the new plant. Over 68 per cent of the reasons given for a preference for automated jobs dealt with the fact that there was less materials handling and less physical work involved on these jobs. Approximately 45 per cent of the responses indicating satisfaction with automated jobs involved mention of the fact that no materials handling was required. Responses suggesting dissatisfaction with jobs involving materials handling accounted for 29 per cent of the reasons given for dissatisfaction with non-automated jobs. These responses were by far the most frequent response categories for each of the above questions.

Some of the reasons for the significance attached to this aspect of the change in job content by workers on automated lines should be mentioned. Significantly more of the workers who preferred automated jobs reported that the non-automated jobs were more physically tiring (P is less than .001). Apart from the differences in the amount of physical effort and fatigue involved on the two jobs, however, work involving hard physical labor is generally regarded as low status work in our culture. The data from this study suggest that the traditionally high status jobs in industry, i.e., non-production jobs like repairman which involve more skill and less physical effort, are also high status jobs in the automated plant. The only new high status job which appeared in the new plant was the job of "console operator" which involved no more physical effort than is required to stand and watch a panel of lights for eight hours. While the traditional pattern of status relationships was not appreciably altered, there is some evidence of an "upgrading" of the whole system with most jobs in the automated plant being regarded as more prestigeful than jobs in the older plants using conventional machining techniques.

Some further evidence of this change is suggested by the fact that irrespective of place of origin (North–South or urban–rural), Negroes in the sample were significantly more satisfied with automated jobs than were white workers and a significantly higher proportion of reasons given by this group for this preference involved mention of decreased need for materials handling. Since Negroes are more often assigned low status jobs involving heavy manual labor, the change to jobs perceived as being more important and which involve less physical effort might represent a more important status change for this group than for white workers in the new plant. For whatever reasons, it is clear that for almost all workers the most important source of satisfaction with the change to automated jobs was the reduction in the amount of materials handling required.

Workers on some jobs in the automated plant, particularly those most highly automated, reported some other ways in which the change to automation represented an improvement. Some types of automated jobs were reported as more interesting primarily because of the greater complexity of the transfer machinery. Because of this complexity, some workers also reported that the new jobs were more challenging and commented that there was a lot to know and learn about the operation of the machines. The challenge of understanding the operation of the automated equipment was apparently a source of satisfaction with the job regardless of whether such knowledge was necessary for the performance of the job. In most instances it was not required. A majority of workers and especially those workers on the most highly automatic machines felt that their jobs involved more responsibility, and most of these workers listed increased responsibility as a source of work satisfaction and as a reason for a preference for automated jobs. A majority of workers also felt that their automated jobs were more important and, of these workers, a majority indicated a preference for jobs in the automated plant.

Data were collected in this study in three other areas generally considered in analyses of work satisfaction, i.e., amount of skill involved, pay and working conditions, and job security and promotional opportunities. No clear pattern of differences between automated and non-automated jobs appeared in the data in the extent to which any of these factors served as sources of work satisfaction or dissatisfaction. Skill requirements and working conditions apparently varied from job to job sufficiently in both the old and the new plants that automation did not produce a clear pattern of change in attitudes toward these aspects of the job. The same system of job classification and the same pay scale were in use in both the automated and non-automated plants so that satisfaction with this aspect of the job was also not affected by the change. Neither was there any great difference perceived in opportunity for promotion in the two kinds of plants.

The data regarding job security were of particular interest because of the widespread conviction that automation will result in displacement of workers. The workers interviewed in this study apparently share this conviction. Almost 90 per cent of the sample were of the opinion that automation would result in increased unemployment. There was little evidence, however, that these workers felt that their jobs were less secure because of the change. It is probable that, in industries like the automobile industry where there are both automated and non-automated plants in operation, it is in the non-automated plants that workers may feel that their jobs are less secure as a result of the change.[1]

Thus far in the analysis of work satisfaction on automated lines we have compared the reasons given for satisfaction or dissatisfaction with automated and non-automated jobs and the reasons given for a preference for one job or the other. Another way of approaching the problem is to compare the most highly automated jobs in the new plant with the least automated jobs. Perhaps the most appropriate way of dividing jobs in the automated plant on this basis is to compare jobs involving materials handling with jobs which do not. When a comparison of this kind is made, the findings are generally consistent with those previously discussed. For example, workers whose jobs involved no materials handling reported less frequent opportunity for social interaction within smaller work groups. Workers on these jobs also said their jobs were more important, less monotonous, and less physically tiring. Finally, as previously noted, significantly more workers whose automated jobs involved materials handling preferred non-automated jobs.

---

[1] Mann and Hoffman have reported that this was the case in the industry in which their studies of automation have been conducted. (F. C. Mann, and L. R. Hoffman, "Individual and Organizational Correlates of Automation," *Journal of Social Issues*, 12 [1956], pp. 7–17.)

Because the work force in the automated plant was relatively homogeneous with respect to the kinds of information gathered about the personal characteristics of the respondents, very few differences were found in the types of workers who were satisfied or dissatisfied with automated jobs. Specifically, the sample of workers interviewed was relatively homogeneous with regard to age, marital status, family size, income, and length of residence in Detroit, and no differences in amount of work satisfaction were found when the data were broken down in terms of these variables. The finding that Negro workers were more satisfied with automated jobs than were white workers was discussed previously. Irrespective of race, workers with more education tended to be less satisfied with automated jobs. While the range in number of school years completed was not large, it may be that more highly educated workers were more perceptive of the discrepancy between the complexity of the automated machinery and the simplicity of the operations performed by the machine operator and felt more acutely the alienation from their work previously discussed.

The only other difference found was between workers with rural or urban backgrounds. Significantly more workers with rural backgrounds were dissatisfied with automated jobs and preferred non-automated jobs. The number of workers with rural backgrounds was only a small proportion of the total sample, however, and this group did not differ significantly from urban workers in terms of any of the reasons given for satisfaction or dissatisfaction with automated jobs identified in this study. The adjustment of industrial workers of rural backgrounds in the urban labor market is an area which merits further research.

The extent to which the sources of work satisfaction on automated jobs compensated for the dissatisfactions previously identified is difficult to assess. Sixty-six per cent of the respondents reported that they were either completely or well satisfied with their old, non-automated jobs with the remainder indicating dissatisfaction to some degree. A slightly smaller proportion, 59 per cent, reported being completely or well satisfied with automated jobs. On the other hand, in response to the question, "Would you rather work on automatic transfer machines as you do now, or on a non-automated job?," approximately 72 per cent of the respondents indicated that they preferred their present jobs. This finding should, however, be interpreted with caution. Since all of the respondents were working in the automated plant at the time of the interviews, it is possible that those workers most dissatisfied with automated jobs would have quit or been transferred from this plant before the sample was drawn. It should also be noted that the transfer of workers to the automated plant was on a basis of seniority from a list of workers who indicated a preference for the transfer. On the other hand, turnover rate was not high in the automated plant and the initial statement of preference of workers for transfer to the automated plant was not based upon any previous experience with jobs on automated machinery. If the attitudes of these workers may be regarded as representative of the attitudes of automobile workers in automated plants, it would appear, since the proportion of workers who preferred automated jobs was so high and because those workers whose jobs were most highly automated were most satisfied with these jobs, that the general preference of automobile workers may well be for automated jobs.

This preference does not mean, however, that the reduction in amount of materials handling or the increased feelings of responsibility and importance on the automated job make the tension on the job less acute, eliminate the feelings of alienation from work, or cause the social isolation of the worker to be any more pleasant. The question of whether there are problems of human adjustment to changing production technology and the question of how these adjustments may be facilitated are not less important because workers may be generally favorably disposed toward the change.

Generally a change which is perceived as increasing the importance and amount of responsibility of a job could be expected to affect the relative importance of work in the life of the worker, the effect of work upon self-image, or the worker's perception of the general status of industrial work. The extent to which this is true of the change to automated machining processes is open to question. Generally accepted and clearly defined norms with which industrial machine operators might evaluate their jobs have not developed as a part of the value framework of industrial social systems. The absence of such norms is due in part to the absence of a clearly defined status hierarchy of "blue collar" jobs. The characteristics of a good job may be much more clearly perceived by a file clerk as he looks up the promotional "ladder" in the management bureaucratic hierarchy than by a sweeper as he looks around him at other jobs in the plant to which he may aspire. In the automated plant, where changes in the job of the industrial worker have so recently occurred, norms for evaluating work experience may be expected to be even less a part of the general value system. There is also some evidence from this study that the range of the status hierarchy is even more compressed in automated than in non-automated plants so that such norms may be even less likely to emerge.

A more important way in which automation may affect the worker's general attitude toward his work, however, is the change in the relation of the worker to the machine. In the older, non-automated plants, where the worker controlled the machine and the work pace, there was still some feeling apparent that it was the worker who was producing the automobile engine parts being machined in these plants. This feeling was no longer apparent in the automated plant. While workers felt that jobs in the automated plant were more important, it should be noted that these responses were primarily concerned with the importance of the part produced and of the automated machine process. The increased feelings of responsibility were related for the most part to the complexity and cost of the machine tended by the worker. Those workers who reported that their automated jobs involved more skill were reacting primarily to the increased complexity of the automatic transfer machinery and not the increased complexity of the operations performed by the worker on the job. To the extent that the worker perceives that it is the machine and not the worker which produces the engine parts, it is the machinery and not the worker which has achieved added importance as a result of automation. It must not have escaped the attention of many workers that the numerous visitors to this automated plant were escorted through the plant in order to see machines at work and not men at work.

It is possible that the social isolation, alienation from work, and increased work tensions resulting from automation may be characteristic only of a phase in the development of the automatic factory. The kinds of operations performed by the machine operators in this study may no longer be necessary with further refinement of automatic machine processes and reactions to automation might be different for workers having no previous experience with non-automated machinery. While the automobile engine plant in which this study was conducted was among the most highly automated heavy manufacturing plants in operation at the time, it is generally agreed that we stand only at the threshold of the age of automation. It is precisely because this millennium has not yet arrived, however, that there is need for study of the effects of automated equipment upon workers in the offices and plants in which it is being introduced. It is only through knowledge acquired through such research that the necessary individual and organizational adjustments to technological change can be facilitated.

Automation and the White-Collar Worker

JACK STIEBER

The Bureau of Labor Statistics has studied the effects of the introduction of an electronic computer in a large life insurance company.[1] This was a company which had been experiencing considerable growth in business volume and shortages and high turnover of clerical personnel, most of them women. The company had an announced policy of not laying off or downgrading workers when mechanical changes were introduced. Of the 800 employees in the divisions using the new computer, 198 were directly affected by the change. Employment of clerical and statistical workers was scheduled to be decreased from 198 to 85 over a period of two years—a reduction of 57 per cent. Of the 106 employees released by the time the study was made, 87 had been transferred to other jobs, eighteen resigned (most of them to get

SOURCE: Jack Stieber, "Automation and the White-Collar Worker," *Personnel* (November–December, 1957). Used by permission of the American Management Association.

[1] *Studies of Automatic Technology; No. 2—The Introduction of an Electronic Computer in a Large Insurance Company* (October, 1955), U. S. Department of Labor.

married) and one retired. None were laid off. Twenty persons were required to operate the computer—nine were employees in the original division using the computer, ten came from other divisions, and one man was hired from the outside. Of the 85 employees working directly with the computer or in related jobs, only five had been upgraded to skilled work from lower level positions; 71 were performing the same work as before or were on work of comparable skill; and nine men were employed as programmers and had been brought into the division from the computer planning group established earlier by the company. An indirect effect of the company's advent into the use of electronic data processing equipment was the establishment of a new division to plan for the installation of computers in other operations of the company. This division employed about 60 people with skills and aptitudes in the fields of programming, project analysis, and logical processes. None of the people in this new division came out of the department directly affected by the computer installation studied by the BLS. Except for a few persons trained by the computer manufacturer, all personnel in the electronic installation division were given on-the-job training.

In a second study, also conducted in a life insurance company, the installation of an electronic computer resulted in decreasing the work force affected from 539 to 406—about 25 per cent.[2] There were no layoffs in accordance with company policy. In contrast to the BLS study findings, this researcher reported considerable upgrading in terms of job content and skills. Average weekly salaries in the affected department were increased, reflecting a redistribution of employment in favor of the higher labor grades. The conversion to the new equipment was handled almost entirely by company people, with only four hires from outside—three technicians and one IBM computer expert.

The third study was made in the accounting department of a public utility which had installed an IBM 650 computer and was planning to follow it with a higher level computer—the IBM 705. The report from which this summary was taken was an interim one, and it stressed the effects of the new equipment on management.[3] The author, Floyd Mann, suggests that consideration of an electronic computer installation calls for a rethinking of the entire operation on the part of management. A change of this kind opens up a re-evaluation of long-standing routines which had not previously been questioned. It presents an opportunity to think through again the fundamental purposes of the organization's functions and the means of accomplishing them. Greatest over-all economies from electronic equipment will be realized if as many operations as possible are adapted to the computer, instead of someone using the equipment to do present operations somewhat

---

[2] *Proceedings of Seventh Annual Meeting of IRRA*, "Administering Technological Change in a Large Insurance Office—A Case Study" by Harold F. Craig, pp. 129–139.

[3] *Man and Automation*, The Technology Project, Yale University, New Haven, Conn. (1956), "Impact of Electronic Accounting Equipment on the White-Collar Worker in a Public Utility Company" by Floyd C. Mann, pp. 32–39.

more rapidly and efficiently. Actually, many economies achieved in this company when the electronic equipment was introduced were not directly related to the equipment and could have been accomplished without it. However, such changes do not often occur until there is a "psychological unfreezing of the situation" through the injection of a new element into the existing situation—in this case, the installation of an electronic data processing machine.

Mann suggests that one of the reasons why automation in insurance and public utility companies has had little or no serious repercussions is that there is more time available to cushion the effects of the change. There is less urgency in the day-to-day competitive economic position of such companies than is faced in many manufacturing industries. Also, a factor is the large proportion of women employed in these concerns, to whom work has a different and—the author implies—a less important meaning than to male workers who are generally the sole or major wage-earner in their families.

Experience in other companies and in the government has borne out the above findings with respect to (1) substantial displacement of clerical employees in departments in which computers are installed, (2) absorption of displaced employees in other operations without layoffs, (3) preference for using existing personnel rather than hiring outside experts to plan for and operate the computer, (4) expectations of continued growth in total employment but at somewhat slower rate than in past, and (5) necessity of management's taking a fresh approach to its purpose and functions in order to make optimal use of an electronic computer. Most companies believe that office automation will result in an upgrading of jobs and employees, but quantitative information is rarely supplied on this point.[4]

At Michigan State University, a group which includes an economist, a psychologist, and two graduate research assistants has been working in the Labor and Industrial Relations Center on a project to determine the effects of automation on jobs and people.[5] The first studies are being conducted in one medium-sized and one large automobile insurance company. Both have recently installed IBM 650 computers. Only very tentative findings are available at this time. I shall emphasize findings which differ from or add to those outlined above with respect to other research and experience.

On an over-all company basis, there has probably been some rise in the level of skill required to perform jobs in the departments affected by the computer. But this is reflected in only a few jobs. Underwriters now spend less time on routine tasks involved in processing new applications in one company and policy renewals in the other. Much of this work is performed by the computer, which leaves underwriters more time to work on more difficult

---

[4] *Automation for Industry*, University of Alabama, (1956), "Automation in Prudential" by Harry Schnobel, pp. 35–43.

[5] In addition to the author, Einar Hardin of the Economics Department; Eugene Jacobson, Psychology Department; Gloria Cheek and Don Trumbo, research assistants, are involved in the project.

applications and renewals requiring the use of judgment in making a final determination. Field agents should also benefit from the new equipment because of a reduction in paper work formerly required of them and now done at the regional office or home office. This should allow them more time for customer contacts and servicing which, it is hoped, will be reflected in an increase in business volume.

On the other hand, the introduction of the IBM 650 computer in the insurance companies under study has been accompanied by a multiplication of IBM cards (which function as permanent records) and an increase in the work of file clerks.[6] Other routine jobs, such as keypunch operator and card-sorter, have seen little or no reduction in work load. This effect of office automation has not been noted in other studies but is likely to be found in most concerns using smaller-scale electronic computers. While higher-level machines almost invariably use magnetic tape for recording and feeding data into the machine, thus cutting down substantially on the use of punch cards and related tasks, small- and even medium-sized computers depend much more on cards.[7] Since the use of lower-level computers is expected to grow rapidly in businesses which cannot economically utilize high-speed machines, this distinction is an important one. While this finding is favorable for the employment of clerical workers, it will counteract, to a degree, the desirable trend towards job enlargement and upgrading.

How has the computer been received by employees, and what are their attitudes towards technological change in general? Answers to these questions may have a bearing on the potential for unionization of white-collar workers, in addition to their being of assistance to managements in planning for computer installations.[8] In order to obtain this information, we recently administered a comprehensive questionnaire to the entire work force of one of the companies under study. Some observations based on this questionnaire may be of interest.

Technological change in general was viewed as desirable by an overwhelming proportion of workers; changes in job processes and content were also regarded favorably. A substantial proportion believed that machines have replaced workers in insurance companies generally during the last two years, but very few thought that this would happen to them. In fact, almost 80 per cent expected that the total number of people doing their "kind of job" would increase during the next five years. These replies are not too surprising, in view of the expressed policy of this company that no employees would be laid off because of the introduction of new machinery.

With respect to the impact of the computer itself, 15 per cent felt that their

---

[6] Such cards are to be distinguished from other punch cards which are used in preparation of summary reports and statistical data. These cards may be discarded after use and do not have to be filed.

[7] Howard S. Levin, *Office Work and Automation*, New York: Wiley, p. 75.

[8] None of the insurance companies reported on in this paper was organized by labor unions.

work had been "greatly changed," and only 6 per cent reported being promoted or transferred as a result of the new equipment. Most changes were of such a nature as to require less than one month to get "used to the change." Of considerable interest to me was the feeling of a substantial number of employees (about 40 per cent in most cases) that during the past year their jobs had become more secure, more interesting and more responsible, required greater skill and accuracy, and contained more variety. But, except for its impact on variety of job content, less than half of these employees ascribed these changes to the electronic computer. This suggests that change may be a "normal" characteristic of office jobs and that the computer was only another element in a total situation undergoing more or less constant change instead of being the radical innovation that many have taken it to be.

In the management area, there was complete willingness to exchange information on the computer and its use among insurance companies which operate in some of the same geographic areas and compete directly with one another for customers. At first blush, one might say this is not very surprising, since the computer manufacturer could supply any information requested by a potential user. In actual practice, however, computer-users almost invariably state that they have "discovered" uses for their machines which were never suggested by the manufacturer. Since this equipment is rented or purchased in order to cut costs, increase efficiency, and contribute towards business growth, normal entrepreneurial behavior might lead to a closer guarding of unique uses of the machine, even if the advantage might be short-lived. The fact that there is a free exchange of computer information among competing firms indicates a form of competitive behavior (or lack thereof) which is worthy of further study.

Despite this open-door policy on computer information, it is interesting to note that the two companies studied use their IBM 650's for different purposes. One utilizes its machine primarily for policy renewals, while the other processes new applications, but not renewals, on the machine. In time, both companies will probably extend their machines to other uses, but their initial needs seem to be different.

Work tends to gravitate toward the computer wherever it may be located. In the medium-sized insurance company, the computer is located in the home office, which has resulted in a flow of paper work from the field offices to headquarters. In the large company, each regional office has an IBM 650, which has caused a transfer of work toward the regional offices both from below (state and district offices) and above (the home office).

This indicates that one cannot generalize regarding the effects of office automation on centralization or decentralization of business operations. It is to be expected that as computers of varying capabilities and costs become available, companies will be able to exercise considerable freedom of choice in deciding which type of equipment will best serve their needs and be in harmony with management philosophies with respect to centralization or decentralization of operations.

Conclusions

Office automation will affect primarily white-collar workers engaged in clerical occupations. These tentative conclusions apply principally to this group of some 8.5 million workers.

E M P L O Y M E N T : Because of high turnover, labor shortages, a large proportion of women, and a prevalent management policy of no layoffs, the effects of automation in the office promise to raise fewer immediate problems than in industry generally. The long-run employment outlook for white-collar office workers is more doubtful. The ability of white-collar occupations to continue to absorb an increasing proportion of the total labor force, as they have in the past, cannot be taken for granted. The increased productivity which will result from office automation will not necessarily be accompanied by greater employment opportunities for white-collar workers. An analysis of experience in manufacturing for the period 1952–1955 indicates that there is no automatic relationship between increases in employment and increases in productivity. Stephen Raushenbush found that of twenty manufacturing industries, only five increased employment requirements at approximately the same rate as their increases in output per man-hour; seven industries actually decreased employment, despite increased productivity and increased volume of output; and eight industries increased employment much less rapidly than productivity.[9] If office automation helps to close the productivity gap between service industries and manufacturing, it is questionable whether these industries, which employ the bulk of white-collar workers, will be able to absorb as many newcomers into the labor force as they have in the past.

O C C U P A T I O N A L D I S T R I B U T I O N : The effects of office automation on skill requirements and upgrading of jobs and workers have probably been exaggerated. There should be some rise in the occupational level of office work generally, but most workers will continue to do much the same work as before or work requiring about the same skills as their previous jobs.

N E W J O B O P P O R T U N I T I E S : With few exceptions, such new jobs as will be created in offices by automation can be filled by upgrading or transferring existing personnel. However, workers whose jobs will be eliminated will not necessarily, or even generally, be qualified to fill the new jobs. People responsible for operating and programming for computers must understand both the machine and the business in which it is to be used. Most companies seem to prefer training employees who are acquainted with their operations in the use of the computer, rather than the other way around. There will be pressures for higher educational institutions to train programmers and other skilled personnel on a large scale, which, in my opinion, should be resisted.[10] There is no evidence that, except for some high-level

---

[9] Stephen Raushenbush, *Productivity and Employment 1955–1965*, Washington, D.C.: Public Affairs Institute, 1956, pp. 35–37.

[10] The Technology Project, *op. cit.* "Installation of Automatic Office Equipment and the Manufacturer," pp. 17–22.

computers, skill requirements for these jobs are beyond the capabilities of a high school graduate with a logical mind who understands the operations of tabulating machines and is intimately acquainted with the operations of the firm using the equipment. Such people are generally available in offices of a size large enough to consider the installation of an electronic computer.

E M P L O Y E E   A T T I T U D E S : As long as companies follow the practices of those studied of not laying off personnel displaced by new office equipment and promoting from within wherever possible, the employee response to office automation is likely to be favorable. This suggests that unions should not count on automation to ease their task of organizing white-collar workers. It may even make organizing more difficult, since the workers to be persuaded are those who continue to be employed (some at better paying jobs) and not those who have difficulty finding jobs due to office automation. In this connection, it is curious that, despite the current emphasis in the labor movement on understanding the problems of white-collar workers,[11] unions have not made more use of social psychologists or sociologists who might be of assistance in this area. Unions have employed full-time lawyers, publicists, and economists to good advantage for many years; why should they not use others trained in fields which are not within the special competence of labor leaders or organizers?

M A N A G E M E N T : The way in which managements use electronic data processing equipment may affect not only the operations of their business organizations but may also influence employment. If these machines are used primarily to do existing work more rapidly with fewer people, the consequences for employment of white-collar workers are obvious. If, on the other hand, the approach is one of taking a fresh look at all operations, functions, and purposes of the business in order to see how automation can be used to further business objectives without regard to existing practices, the results are likely to be more favorable both for business and for employment. The fact that the latter approach is becoming more prevalent is a hopeful sign for the future.

Man, Work, and the Automated Feast

B E N   B .   S E L I G M A N

Automation is said to have ancient beginnings. To be sure, the technology from which it stems goes back several centuries, at least. Automatic devices

---

[11] Address by John Livingston before the Conference on Problems of the White-Collar Worker, AFL–CIO, December 13, 1956.

SOURCE: *Commentary*, 1:34 (July, 1962). Copyright by the American Jewish Committee. Reprinted by permission.

in the middle 18th century included a mechanical loom for the manufacture of figured silks; James Watt's steam engine utilized a fly-ball governor which controlled the speed at which his contrivance operated; and it has been suggested that automation's basic concept—the linkage of machines—is evident in the detachable harpoon head of the Eskimo. Yet to assert that automation is simply the latest link in a great chain of industrial history obscures what is patently a new phenomenon. In the old days, industrial change developed through fission: division of labor was the key to progress and work was made available to a huge pool of unskilled persons who in the main had been forced to migrate from farm to city. Today, it is precisely these unskilled, together with semi-skilled and even some of management's people, who are displaced and poured back into the pool. Furthermore, automation represents a marked acceleration of change with so cumulative a force that this alone spells a profound difference from what went on before.

Automation is already moving with a rapidity that threatens to tear apart existing social and organizational structures; according to some observers, it will even alter the habits of thought that men have up to now prided themselves on. Such a prospect is perhaps not surprising when we consider the cataclysmic results of the 18th century's Industrial Revolution: the changes then were so swift as to constitute a whole new phenomenon. And Marx and Weber and Sombart had shown convincingly how human and social transformation accompanied technological transformation.

Now, new industrial functions, new economic forms, new work habits, and new social headaches are being created in ways that signify a kind of dialectic leap. Even John Diebold, who claims to have invented the word "automation" and whose ebullient advocacy of computer technology has done much to spread the gospel, confesses: "I believe that [automation] marks a break with past trends, a qualitative departure from the more conventional advance of technology that began with jagged pieces of flint and progressed up to the steam engine."

Why is this so? Up to recent times, technology simply sought to substitute natural force for animal or human force. In the early days, primacy of place was given to windmills and waterfalls. Then came metallurgical discoveries; and the screw and the lathe made possible the machine, essentially a contrivance which man could watch in action. But man remained at the center of the whole business, essential to both operation and control, still more or less the maker and master of materials. With automation, man not only loses irrevocably his function as *homo faber*; he no longer even possesses the character of *animal laborans*. At best, he is a sometime supervisor of a flow process. Actual control is removed from him and given to an electronic contraption whose feedbacks and servomechanisms make it possible to produce goods and manipulate information in a continuous system, without human participation.

To realize what automation implies, we must examine the kinds of machines employed and see what they do to people and organizations. Essentially, today's scientific upheaval comprises four aspects: the conversion of industrial materials into a flow; the setting of uniform standards so that output can be treated as a flow; the utilization of electronic computers with built-in feedbacks to enable the exercise of automatic control; and the application of new energy sources to the whole process. Thus, raw materials, which represent the "input" of an industry, must be handled without human hands, as in a modern meat-packing plant. Production, at one time a series of discrete steps, is completely integrated by means of transfer machines. In some cases, computers tied to cams or templates can make the producing machine follow a predetermined pattern with greater accuracy and sharper tolerances than were dreamed possible in the heyday of the skilled machinist. Computers, into which all sorts of complex information can be fed by "programmers," automatically correct errors. A wide range of goods is now produced in this startling manner—chemicals, automobiles, steel, glassware, electric bulbs, television sets, beverages, and drugs, to name a few. Factories are able to function 24 hours a day, 365 days a year, while manpower needs are reduced dramatically. And with the development of nuclear energy for industrial power, manufacturers no longer need to be near their source of raw materials; they can set up their plants closer to markets, or—if they are seeking to escape the union organizer—in the most isolated of places. Yet one industry necessarily must relate itself more intimately with the next; a seamless web envelops all the entrepreneurs and their works.

There is no lack of Panglossian attempt to assuage our concern. In the long run, we are told (who lives that long?), natural economic forces will work out the necessary adjustments. A shorter work week might stem from automation, suggest some experts; but at the thought that men might work less than the ordained forty hours a week, all kinds of people, from Secretary of Labor Arthur Goldberg down, immediately explode with great cries of anguish. Or we are told that human desires are insatiable: demand will grow, enough to reabsorb men displaced by machines—which calls to mind an apocryphal conversation between Henry Ford II and Walter Reuther. "How," said Ford, as he revealed his automatic factory, "are these machines going to pay you dues, Walter?" "How," replied Reuther, "will they buy your autos?"

We are assured that more jobs will be created by new industry, that higher skills will be required, that economic stability will be guaranteed by automation. There are pitifully few facts available to support these euphoric hopes. More likely a vast trauma awaits us all, to use Irving Howe's phrase. Then why automate? The underlying motives were exposed with unaccustomed bluntness in one of the trade journals recently when an automation advocate wrote: "[Machines] don't call in sick; they don't talk back; they work early and late and without overtime; they don't get tired; and last, but far from least, they don't line up at the cashier's window every week for a slice of the operating funds."

The automobile industry illustrates how an integrated set of machines can function. There the engine production line, for example, consists of a series of drilling, boring, and milling operations connected by transfer machines which move the engine blocks from one point to the next. Tolerances are checked automatically; if something is awry, the whole line is stopped by an electronic device. Or one can see an automatic assembly machine put the components of a television set on a printed board and then solder them into place. These are repetitive operations and their economic justification stems from the replacement market. There is not much of a style factor here and such model changes as do occur can be handled with relative ease. Yet even where variation in the product is essential, as in machine tools, the operation still can be made automatic.

The machine tool industry, mainly a congeries of small shops employing highly skilled labor, has notoriously resisted innovation. But since it is now so closely allied to Air Force and Space technology, it has been impelled willy-nilly by the needs of the armed forces to the adoption of newer techniques. Formerly, a human operator worked from blueprints, controlling his equipment with a variety of jigs and templates. To avoid waste, and perhaps because he was concerned with craftsmanship, he worked slowly. But now, all the variables can be "programmed" into computers, and with the technique known as "numerical control" these electronic brains direct the same cutting tools, handle the same jigs and templates once operated by the machinist. Most important of all, this sort of automation is economically feasible for small lots in which there are changes in product design.

The key here is feedback, the simplest case of which is the home thermostat turning a furnace on and off in order to maintain a constant room temperature. In essence, signals are sent from one part of the automated line to another, correcting errors, shifting power loads, or modifying the speed of the line. No human need adjust gauges or read thermometers or press buttons. Feedback or servomechanisms do a better control job then humans, especially when many elements are involved. Whereas the human eye can follow the motion of a gauge at about two cycles a second, a servomechanism does about 100 a second. Now, marry feedback to a computer and automation is complete. The computers, really giant adding machines and calculators, receive information from the gauges and thermometers, analyze the data, and then transmit new instructions to other gauges and instruments.

Computers, whose basic concept goes back to Blaise Pascal, were developed in their electronic form during World War II to help guns hit their targets more efficiently. There are two basic types—the analog and digital computer. The former is a kind of electronic slide rule able to apply higher mathematics to problems of rates of change in various flows. However fast it might have been, for the engineer, mathematician, and operations researcher it was not fast enough. So the digital computer was devised, a machine that employs the binary number system and consequently can only add and subtract. This is no impediment, for like an electronic abacus, the digital computer sends its impulses forward at an unbelievable speed, giving it a marked advantage over the analog machine. Moreover, digital computers have "memory" drums in which data can be stored for future use. The electrical pulses in a digital computer last less than one-millionth of a second. Information can be extracted from the memory drum in about ten-millionths of a second.

Of course, a considerable amount of human brain power is expended before the computer can be put to work. This is the science of programming. Instructions are written on a process sheet, then coded and entered on tape. That is, English is translated into machine language. The control unit of the system then "reads" the tape, gives forth with the appropriate electrical impulses, and sets the servomechanisms to work. One writer compared the operation to an old-fashioned player piano in which the punched holes in the roller actuate the hammers to bang out either the "Basin Street Blues" or a Beethoven sonata.

Lending a nightmarish quality to these developments is the current scientific talk about artificial intelligence. Machines, it is said, can be built to recognize certain patterns and can learn to plan simple tasks. While the computer may be something of a moron, awaiting instructions from a human Ph.D., the fact that an electrical contrivance can be made to learn anything is astonishing enough. If a heuristic or generalized solution is sufficient, then a thinking computer is no longer science fiction. Chess-playing machines are at least feasible: the only problem seems to be that they would have to review the outcomes of all possible plays and that might take centuries. Perhaps that is what makes them morons.

The names one often sees bandied about—PERT, ALGOL, COBOL, GECOM, SURE—are merely abbreviations for specific programming methods, each utilizing one or more computer installations constructed by Burroughs, Bendix, Rand, or IBM. PERT, for example—Program Evaluation and Review Technique—is based on the concept of a tree network with alternatives to be considered at each node of the tree. Since the computer works so much faster than the human mind and also uses stored information, it can review the accumulating cost of a flow process at each step and then direct the sequence of decisions along the critical or least-cost pathway. PERT originated in the Polaris Missile Project when it became essential to keep track of some 11,000 contractors and subcontractors. Again, military need provided the research motive. So complex can these matters become that the Defense Department had to work out a standardized pidgin English to coordinate programming.

It is sometimes said that the considerable investment in these systems precludes all but the largest firms from employing them. This is not so. Any number of consulting services are available for smaller concerns to meet data-processing needs, and some firms have set up cooperative research centers. Span, Inc. is one such co-op doing the bookkeeping for a number of insurance companies in Hartford; Tamcor maintains brokerage records in New York, and IBM, the biggest of them all, makes its equipment available to all comers through 70 locations around the country. In fact, the latter is now compiling tape libraries, dubbed by one journal "computer laundromats." Thus, the new technology is available to anyone who wants to make use of it.

All this must be worthwhile, for rental costs run from $12,000 a year up and outright purchase of computer equipment can cost millions. Some $2 billion has been invested in computers by private companies since 1950, and this does not include what the government has spent. It is estimated that by 1970 computer sales will hit $500 million a year or about 2½ times present outlays. When the Pennsylvania Railroad automated its Conway, Pa. yards, it expected to recoup its $34 million cost within three years. At Ford, 9 workers at 3 machines putting holes into crankshafts replaced 39 workers at 39 machines. A Philco plant reduced its work force by 25 per cent by using printed circuitry. A computer engineer once remarked that he could cut one man off the payroll for every $5,000 spent on automated equipment. And finally, the initial cost of installing a computer system, according to Wassily Leontief, comes to no more than 6 per cent of total plant investment. The value of the new technology seems undeniable.

By now "Detroit" automation is quite well known. Automatic machines, linked by transfer equipment, move engine blocks through a complete manufacturing process, performing 530 precision cutting and drilling operations in 14½ minutes as compared to 9 hours in a conventional plant. The Chrysler Corporation's recent breakthrough on computer "balancing" of assembly lines, essentially a "combinatorial" problem, now defines each job so rigidly that little liberties like a worker's taking a few minutes out for a smoke become serious impediments to the smooth flow of cars. An automated power plant in Louisiana saved $175,000 in fuel, $100,000 in maintenance, $1.5 million in eliminating delays and mishaps, and $500,000 in labor. A Jones & Laughlin sheet-plate mill turns out strip at the speed of 70 miles an hour with no labor other than the supervision of engineers. Punch-card systems in a reversing roughing mill modify ingot shapes, and the computer even "remembers" what to do when the forms have to be changed. Foundry work, traditionally a hand operation, is now being tied to the computer. In petroleum and chemicals, the story is almost ancient: as far back as 1949 catalytic cracking plants were turning out 41,000 barrels a day with instruments and only a few workers to watch gauges. In a Texaco refinery the computer controls 26 flow rates, 72 temperatures, 3 pressure levels, and 3 gas combinations. General Electric uses segmented "automation," that is, batch production, for motors of varying models up to 30 horsepower. Ribbon machines make 800 electric bulb blanks a minute, running without end, and requiring only one worker who stands by to make an occasional adjustment.

Even in the office and retail store, one finds evidence of the new technology. Although office work has expanded tremendously since 1910 (today 17 per cent of the labor force is found in the office as compared to 5 per cent fifty years ago), it is precisely the enormous quantity of paper work and routine operation that makes automation feasible here. Banks, utilities, insurance companies, and government bureaus have eagerly made room for yards of the new equipment—so much faster is the computer than the old-fashioned bookkeeper and clerk. As a result, office work no longer is the growth industry it was—at least in terms of jobs. One California firm, studied by Mrs. Ida R. Hoos, put only two accounting operations on a computer and promptly eliminated 300 out of 3,200 office jobs and drastically altered the functions of some 980 others.

In retailing, automation starts with inventory and accounting records. Sales data are transmitted to control centers where billing, inventory, and credit information is stored. Bad credit risks are automatically checked and information returned to the sales clerk before the package can be wrapped. Sylvania and IBM have been working on automatic check-out counters for supermarkets—the number of cash registers would be reduced, as well as the number of workers. Ferris wheels, conveyor belts, chutes, and slides, all controlled by electronic computers, deliver garments from receiving platforms to stockrooms and even return the merchandise to the ground floor if necessary. Eventually we will pay our traffic penalties to a computer: in Illinois, records of driver violations are stored in a computer and the fines calculated by machine.

This, then, is the automated feast. Tasks are accomplished with unimaginable speed. Decisions are made by coded instructions and errors quickly detected. Facts are stored and extracted from memory drums. The machines learn and "perceive": they analyze stock market conditions; establish rocket flight patterns before the shot is fired into space; write television scripts that compare favorably with what is now available; compose music; translate; and play games. They combine high technical competence with just enough of an I.Q. to keep them tractable. They do precisely the kind of work to which junior executives and semi-skilled employees are usually assigned.

No slur is intended here, for in addition to the ordinary worker it is the middle manager, the backbone of the average corporation, who will be most affected by automation. He has a bleak future indeed, when computers relay information to each other, do all the scheduling, and control manufacturing from inception to the point at which the product is packaged and rolled onto a box car. It is rather the archon of industry—as Edward Ziegler has dubbed him—who ultimately wins out, for with the elimination of both plant and office staff, this man at the very top gains even tighter control over the decision-making process. The sort of organizational looseness that prevailed prior to the advent of the computer is eliminated, and corporate structure becomes more formal, more "integrated," since with the computer there must be greater "cooperation." The number of links in the chain of command is reduced drastically; vice-presidents are soon out of a job. No less an authority than Herbert A. Simon of Carnegie Tech has said that by 1985 machines can dispense with all middle echelons in business. Production planning is handed over to the digital demon, while both the middle manager and the displaced worker drive taxicabs. The sociologist may very well ask, whither the American dream of status and success?

Quite often, the computer engineer tries to build his own empire within the corporation. Fresh to the ways of business life, he has unabashedly played havoc with established relations. He and his programmer cohorts, cutting across all divisions, have often ignored and undermined the authority of department heads and vice-presidents. Many middle management people in automated companies now report that they are awaiting the ax, or if more fortunate, retirement. Bright young men leave for non-automated firms, hoping to reach the top elsewhere before the computer catches up with them. Sometimes the new elite does lose out: it has not been unknown for a computer installation to be yanked as a result of corporate internecine warfare.

Usually though, archon and engineers are in complete accord. With the computer creating certain expectations, the firm must operate through a series of highly rigid sequences. Flexibility has been dispensed with, for the whole plant is now a single technical structure in which total performance must be "optimized." The engineer examines each step in the process solely in terms of efficiency—industrial logic of the most unremitting kind takes primacy of place. Under automation, the engineer or mathematician is *the* skilled man in the plant, while workers, those who remain and those who do not, are expected to adjust with equanimity to a situation for which they have had no responsibility. In fact, the engineer's attitude quite often is tough and hard, too much so for ordinary men: what the worker doesn't know, says he, won't hurt him. The scientists appreciate only "facts": the human problems of an industrial system frequently have little meaning for them. Unlike the organization men of the 50's, they are usually "inner directed," disturbers of the corporate peace, free-booters in pursuit of the idols of efficiency. Since the latter is measured by high profit and low cost, such scientific ruthlessness meets the approval of the archon. The latter really doesn't know what the scientist is doing: top management merely voices a faith based on payoff. Thus the programmer, who often assumes the aspect of a medieval alchemist, runs his own show, designing projects, cutting corporate red tape with abandon, and advising the industrial relations department that labor displacement is "none of your business." At best, the engineer can parrot some devotee of the conventional economic wisdom by repeating that automation creates new demand and new jobs, upgrades the worker and inspires everyone with its challenge. There must be a certain glory in the marvels of automation: but the men who once worked in the chemical plants, oil refineries, and steel mills are now out of sight and out of mind.

Between 1953 and 1960, a million and a half jobs disappeared. In one plant, studied by Floyd Mann of Michigan State University, automation reduced the work force by half. In the electrical industry, output increased 21 per cent between 1953 and 1961, while employment declined 10 per cent. There was a loss of 80,000 production jobs in steel during the decade of the 50's. In the shift from aircraft to missiles, 200,000 jobs went down the technological drain. For the 5-year period 1955–1960, production workers in automobile factories were down 21 per cent. All this displacement occurred in an affluent society that itself went through four postwar recessions each of which left behind an increasingly hard-core residue of unemployment—3 per cent in 1951–53; 4 per cent in 1955–57; and 5 per cent in 1959–60.

Full employment for the next 10 years means creating 12 million new jobs—25,000 a week, or almost double the number of new openings in the 1947–57 decade. Extending the period to 1961, we find that output rose 65 per cent while the number of production and maintenance jobs declined. True, white collar workers increased 7 per cent, but now automation is making them just as insecure. If we assume that demand in the 60's will expand at the same rate as it did in 1947–57, then output by 1970 may very well be 50 per cent greater. However, if the present rate of productivity is maintained, then the number of required man-hours will have increased by 12 per cent, providing only 75 million jobs at the end of the decade. Thus, about 8 million persons, 10 per cent of the labor force, will have no work. And this is a moderate forecast, for should the secular growth rate fall below 3 per cent per annum, as is conceivable, output will have gone up about 40 per cent. Add to this the effects of automation, and the job increase by 1970 may be only 2 million, leaving a residue of perhaps 10 million persons without jobs.

Is this so weird a tale? The ever optimistic Bureau of Labor Statistics' chief, Ewan Clague, recently admitted to an Arden House conclave that 200,000 jobs a year would be lost through "disemployment by automation." He found that in 70 per cent of manufacturing industries such "disemployment" comprised four-fifths of the jobs lost. And his estimate did not include computer displacement among white collar workers.

The unions now know what automation can do to them. No matter how strong the security clause in a collective bargaining agreement, the serious drop in membership for most internationals is a harbinger of approaching catastrophe. Further, it is so much easier now for plants to escape to communities where unionism seems to represent little threat. And in such towns, management does not worry about a labor supply, for under automation what need is there for workers? There are also related problems for the unions: What happens to seniority? How about pension rights? Can traditional unionism with its roots in craft concepts cope with an industry whose shape has assumed the form of a process? Is the programmer a part of the bargaining unit? Or does his role in decision-making place him in management's ranks? And how effective is the strike when a handful of engineers can operate the whole works? This last question was answered in Port Arthur, Texas, where about 3,700 production workers walked off the job at an oil refinery, leaving 600 white collar employees and supervisors behind to run the plant at 65 per cent of capacity. One labor relations man was reported to have said: "Maybe they ought to have removed a couple of transistors."

Some have argued that the displaced can be directed to jobs in the service and white collar fields. What jobs? Automation, as we have already noted, has been moving into these fields in the last three years just as rapidly as elsewhere. In 1960, at the Census Bureau, 50 technicians plus a battery of com-

puters did the work that it had taken over 4,000 statisticians to do in 1950.
The little black code numbers now appearing on bank checks inform us that
our accounts are debited, credited, and cleared by a scanning device hooked
into a computer. It is poor consolation, moreover, to be told that employment
adjustments will be made via the A & P route—attrition and pregnancy—for
this is an admission that there really are no jobs for those who want to work.

The notion that all who have been displaced by machines will quickly find
new employment is a cheerful thought, something like whistling while walking through a cemetery. Some years ago, such cheerfulness was quite common, even among labor leaders. Walter Reuther's early speeches all but
embraced the computer, so high was the regard for technology, so powerful
the belief in growth and progress. The Joint Economic Committee's 1955
report on automation urged laissez-faire, for no serious problems were en-
visioned. In the short space of seven years, hesitation and doubts have cropped
up. There is no longer the ancient and well-regarded optimism that more
machines mean expanded employment elsewhere or that automation will up-
grade workers. It is evident, rather, that the new technology enforces a
deterioration of skills for the great mass of workers and offers only the social
junk pile for the unskilled and untutored.

What is the solution? Frankly, there is none, at least none of a definitive
character. The numerous suggestions for dealing with the pressing problems
that stem from automation are all piecemeal, pecking at a spot here and a
point there. No amount of federal fiscal tinkering will meet the immediate
needs of those who are attached to a dying industry. Economic growth, while
essential, will not of itself put to work again the idle coal miner, ex-machinist,
and troubled bookkeeper whose jobs have vanished like the first atom bomb
tower. Administration economists believe that automated unemployment can
be solved by turning on ordinary Keynesian tap valves: it's all a matter of
failing effective demand, they assert. There seems little awareness in important circles that the American economy is undergoing deep-rooted and subtle
structural changes and that it will take massive economic and social therapy
to assuage the hurt.

The AFL-CIO has been advocating a series of measures, including meaningful retraining programs, especially for workers over forty, area redevelopment, better unemployment insurance, an improved national placement
service, special help to relocate the "disemployed," higher pensions, and even
shorter hours. But will we—American Management, American unions, Congress, the administration—really expend the necessary hard thought? Don
Michael doubts it, for it is unlikely, says he, that ". . . our style of pragmatic
making-do and frantic crash programs can radically change in the next few
years. . . ." It is hard to disagree.

Consider the retraining effort. A case of too little, if not too late, it is hardly
a roaring success. In West Virginia, the federal pilot scheme plus the state's
own 22-month-old program have been able to uncover new jobs for only half
the 3,000 "graduates." Most of the others simply returned to the ranks of the

unemployed. In Pennsylvania, 1,760 persons enrolled in retraining courses in 1957. Of these, 884 completed their re-education, 741 obtained new jobs. The state had a half million unemployed at the time.

Where private enterprise undertakes some corrective steps, it is usually found that a labor union had been doing the prodding, as in the meat-packing industry. Yet when 433 workers were laid off in Armour's Oklahoma City plant, only 60 could qualify for retraining and those who did secure new employment had to accept a lower rate of pay. Some firms are genuinely disturbed about the effects of automation. For example, U. S. Industries, a manufacturer of electronic equipment, and the machinists union have agreed upon a jointly managed fund to study the entire question. The company's president, John Snyder, at least acknowledges that each one of his machines sends 60 workers scurrying to the unemployment insurance offices. Incidentally, one of U. S. Industries' contributions is the invention of automatic equipment to train displaced workers for typing and similar tasks.

There have been other experiments in adjustment. Some take the form of liberal severance-pay allowances. One of the earliest such schemes, though not related to automation per se, was the famous 1936 Washington Agreement between the railroad companies and the unions. Displaced workers receive 60 per cent of their average pay as severance compensation for periods as long as five years whenever mergers occur. In cases of relocation, moving expenses are paid and losses resulting from forced sale of homes reimbursed. More recently, another generous plan was agreed upon by TWA and its navigators, who if replaced by automatic instruments will receive $25,000 plus $400 a month for three years as severance. In addition, the now footloose navigators will be given free lifetime travel passes on the airline. Thus they will have at least acquired mobility and will be able to search for jobs in all corners of the globe. Yet such measures offer no genuine solution: they are mere palliatives, for they fail to confront the fundamental question—what does a man do with his time, either during the temporary period of affluence, or when the windfall resources will have given out, or for that matter, even when he has not been detached from industry?

Not every arrangement exhibits a handsome concern for the displaced. In the coal fields a contemptible alliance between John L. Lewis and the operators has cast adrift almost 300,000 miners. The coal industry, caught between the grinders of competitive fuels and high operating costs, was thoroughly run-down by the mid-40's. Deciding not to worry any more about the unemployed at the pits, Lewis acquiesced in rapid technological change. Output per day rose from 6.4 tons in 1949 to 14.4 tons in 1961; one ton of coal now requires less than half the labor it did a decade ago. At the Paradise, Kentucky coal field an automatic shovel larger than the Statue of Liberty strips 200 tons of material in one scoop. In Harvey Swados's words, Lewis decided to trust to time and mortality to resolve the problem of the unemployed. And so the coal industry no longer suffers from economic decay. With a return on investment of 7.5 per cent, it compares favorably with steel and oil. To hasten the day when his union can depend upon a healthy industry for its 40-cent per ton royalty, Lewis directed the mine workers to invest in sundry mine operations and even lent $35 million to Cyrus Eaton, whose interests include peace movements as well as coal. Of course, it would have been troublesome to apprise the membership of these transactions, so all the deals were carried through with great secrecy, only to be smoked out last year in a Tennessee lawsuit. At a recent convention of the union, an innocent delegate who suggested that perhaps something might be done for the un-employed was ". . . verbally torn to pieces by a buckshot charge of oratory from John L. Lewis himself." Declining dues are amply compensated for by investment returns in banks, mines, railroads, and power plants. Meanwhile, 300,000 miners continue to rot in the idle towns of Pennsylvania and West Virginia.

This sort of cooperation could set a strange trend if other unions were to adopt the Lewis formula. One that did is Harry Bridges's West Coast Long-shoremen's International. Several years ago, the ILWU signed an agreement with the Shipping Association that was hailed as a reply to automation. Indeed, the retirement benefits are quite munificent and the pay scale was increased somewhat, but at the same time the employers were given the go-ahead signal to install a whole range of technological improvements which will virtually exclude entire blocs of workers not yet ready to retire. More-over, the new work rules, extracted by the employers as a price for the higher pay and liberalized pensions, have intensified work loads on the docks virtually to the human breaking point.

Thus, one comes back to an immediate step, which though not by any means a "solution," nevertheless offers a practicable way for mitigating some of the effects of automation—the shorter work week. Mere mention of this is apt to send a shudder down the backs of administration economists and devotees of the conventional wisdom. Expressing their horror at the thought that man should have even more leisure than he now enjoys, the latter urge that a shorter work week means less production and higher costs. And in the present context of growthmanship, this is unthinkable. Arthur Goldberg, whose grasp of legal subtleties contrasts sharply with his simplistic formula-tions of economic issues, warned the International Ladies' Garment Workers' Union recently that fewer hours per week would ". . . impair adversely our present stable price structure [and] make our goods less competitive both at home and abroad. . . ." The enormous productive capacity of America's industry was conveniently forgotten, a capacity so enhanced by automation that it can more than compensate for the alleged loss of output. And this is to say nothing about the quality and content of contemporary "production"— that would require another essay. The point to observe now is the curious inner tension of an industrial system whose fundamental Puritan outlook demands an incessant, unremitting outpouring of goods (for what?) while at the same time it imposes dreary idleness and dismal futures on those to whom the cornucopia is directed. We may well ask, what is the feedback in this insane circle?

But to return to the shorter work week—a cursory review of its history would demonstrate how completely reasonable it is. Prior to 1860, the rule was dawn to dusk with as much as 72 hours as the weekly standard. Demands for a shorter span were met with the contention that 12 hours a day, 6 days a week had been divinely ordained in order to strengthen worker morality. Three decades later the work week had been shortened by 12 hours. In 1910, the average ranged from 51 to 55 hours, and at that time a work force of 34 million produced a Gross National Product of about $37 billion. The work week continued to shrink: in 1920, it was 48 hours; in 1929, 44 hours; and since 1946, 40 hours. By 1955, the labor force had almost doubled while GNP increased 10-fold as compared to 1910. And all the time the work week kept declining, about 13 hours in a 45-year span, or roughly 15 minutes a year.

Was anyone hurt? Did productivity lag? Has technology been impeded? The depression years aside, whatever unemployment did occur would have been unquestionably greater without the steady drop in hours. A continuation of this secular decline would cut back the normal work week by one hour every four years. According to one estimate, this might create about a million jobs a year which, together with the normal increase in job openings, could really begin to cut into the displacement caused by automation. When Harry van Arsdale of the New York electricians' union obtained a 5-hour day, he was savagely flayed for selfishness and lack of patriotism. Even the labor movement felt embarrassed. Arsdale insisted that he was only seeking to "spread the work." Now it seems, according to Theodore Kheel, the industry's arbitrator, that well over 1,000 new jobs will be made available as a result of the union's action.

What has happened in agriculture presents, in a sense, an object lesson we ought to heed. As W. H. Ferry remarked in a perceptive paper on affluence and plenty, the farm is technology's most notorious victory. Here abundance has become an economic catastrophe. So advanced is our agricultural establishment that even the 10 per cent of the labor force it now employs is too much. Farm output increased 77 per cent between 1910 and 1954, while land used for crops went up only 15 per cent. During the same period, labor on farms as measured by man-hours dropped over 30 per cent. This suggests an almost threefold rise in productivity. According to the late John D. Black, a leading farm expert, the major element in this change unquestionably was the substitution of machine power for muscle power. Yet the economic and political thrust of our system is such that 70 to 80 per cent of the federal government's spending on agriculture goes to counteract the price impact of an ever accumulating surplus.

The parallel between farm and industry is startling. There is enough grain in storage to feed everyone from Maine to Hawaii, but some 50 million Americans barely manage to subsist, even today. The steel industry functions at 65 per cent of capacity, or thereabouts, while thousands of able-bodied men are shoved aside by automation. Strategic curtailment of production is employed, like the farm parity program, to distort the genuine capacities of our economy. Technology, rather than man, becomes the central focus of existence, and at the same time that it destroys, for example, the belief in the family farm, it seemingly ought to compel a desiccated concept of resource allocation and optimum production to retire in favor of a philosophy of distribution. But we really have no adequate social theory to deal with the latter. The ideas of a Galbraith, a C. Wright Mills, a Paul Goodman, or a Harvey Swados deal only with aspects of the problem. We await to be told what is happening to us, what we need to do. And even then we shall not listen.

It is of course a common cliché that scientific advances have outrun our capacity to deal with them. Technology, the practical and material basis of life, has acquired a tidal force of its own which threatens to inundate human thought. Moreover, modern technology, as evidenced by automation, manifests no orderly growth. Its leads and lags, its uneven development, create new power centers that result in unaccustomed strains. To be sure, this has happened before, but always at immense human cost. It is this that the high priests of automation fail to grasp, while those of us who are merely bystanders can only hope that society will eventually catch up with the engineers and scientists and archons of industry who see only a handsome profit in what the machine can do. . . .

The correspondents[1] fall into three distinct classes: (1) engineers for whom the·shock of recognition induces a state of grandiloquent nitpicking and a continuing refusal to face up to automation's social consequences; (2) young professors of business administration whose training in conventional wisdom has launched them into perpetual maunderings through the bogs of post-classical economics; and (3) serious persons who while disagreeing with some of my observations have indeed sought to grapple with the core of the problem.

Let me dispose first of the engineers: (One wrote to me privately, saying: "The social problems of automation *must* be solved! They *will* be solved!" Nice sloganeering, but how?). . . . While the engineers are arguing about when is a computer not a computer, they forget all about the ultimate consequences of the new technology—the creation of a vast economic and social underworld, a subculture of poverty enclosing a fourth of the population to which automation *per se* now contributes to the tune of 200,000 idle souls a year. Perhaps they feel about this as did a visiting English economist who told a group of West Coast academicians: "They're only Negroes, Puerto Ricans, and itinerant farmers."

Now, according to the professor of business administration, there is no such thing as Detroit automation, computers and feedback are mere science fiction, the Cleveland auto plant is a Potemkin village built by Henry Ford II, the unemployed in Detroit and Omaha and Pittsburgh displaced by machines are out of work because they're just plain lazy or uneducated, and the initials IBM stand for something like "intercontinental ballistic missile." Seriously,

---

[1] Reply by Mr. Seligman to discussion of his article appearing in the Letters from Readers Department of *Commentary* (December, 1962), pp. 533–34.

where has he been, lo these last ten years? Hasn't he seen any of the new installations in industry, let alone all the data-processing equipment in offices, banks, and retail stores? Has he ever talked with a worker displaced by a machine? Is he so unaware of the research efforts of the computer manufacturers that he believes bookkeepers to be a surviving breed? Ah yes, the professor teaches middle managers. The poor professor soon won't have anyone to teach.

. . . I consider the Lewis-Bridges response despicable because of its undercurrent of desperate cynicism. [The] understandable defense of the ILWU contract does not tell us what happened to the "B" men and the casuals on the docks. These workers—several thousand of them—are not "fully registered" and therefore unable to enjoy the handsome benefits won by Bridges for his "regular" longshoremen. This may seem a great victory for the ILWU, but it sounds somewhat hollow. I should think that the sort of approach employed by the Machinists' and Packinghouse Workers' Unions in bargaining on technological change makes more sense: at least the latter were concerned with *all* their members, not solely the elite. And they are exploring such avenues as retraining and relocation. As to the evidence on work loads, I choose to take the word of Harvey Swados, who was there.

. . . Does [this correspondent] suggest that displaced workers can be upgraded to become teachers and technicians? Obviously, this is silly: the prospect rather is for massive unemployment in the lower depths and shortages elsewhere. The latter may very well continue to afflict us simply because our society does not know how to secure what it needs.

An important lesson may be drawn from a debate such as this: the willingness to drift is as patent in technology as in politics and the cold war. Such is the nature of our time and such is its tragedy.

POSTSCRIPT: The above article evidently fluttered the dovecotes of a baker's dozen of *Commentary* readers who wrote angry letters to the editor. By far the greater number of correspondents appeared to be engineers of one sort or another who, ignoring the central discussion of automation's social and economic impact, seized upon what I now realize was an ambiguous description of the analog computer. Instead of saying that the analog "operates much as a desk calculator," I should have written that it does the job of that useful office machine, but in a kind of slide rule fashion. Whereas the latter uses distances and markings to represent numbers, the analog employs voltage variations. This technical imprecision on my part was the signal for an interesting attack—interesting in its utter disregard of the main points of the discussion. Not one of the engineers addressed himself to automation and unemployment, the impact on middle management, alterations in organizational structure or the role performed by the new breed of computer scientists in the corporation. Perhaps it was the latter description that irked them. If this is indeed the case, as I suspect it is, then what a commentary on the engineer mentality today!

PRE-AUTOMATED WORK—PASTURES OF PLENTY

The migrants

These people who travel the fields come from the classically dispossessed groups. They are Texas Mexicans, Southrn Negroes, Puerto Ricans, winos from skid row, Oakies from the thirties who stayed on in the culture of poverty. On the East Coast some 50,000 move from Florida to the North, most of them Negroes. From Texas come 75,000 who travel to the Mountain States and the Northwest. These are primarily of Mexican extraction. In the rich wheat fields from Texas to Canada, 50,000 work. On the Pacific Coast another 100,000 are on the move. The Braceros number some 40,000 a year.

Taken all in all, men, women, children, and counting the Braceros there are around 2,000,000 human beings who live and work under inhuman conditions. In 1959 the Secretary of Labor computed the average Bracero wage, which is a fair index of what all of these people are paid: it came to $.50 an hour. In the same period a congressional study estimated that a family of Texas migrants, with five workers in the field, would make just over $3,000 a year. That means $600 to each worker for a full year's work. . . . (p. 55)

Life in California

California agriculture is the richest in the nation, and its agricultural sufferings is perhaps the most spectacular. People work ten-, eleven-, and twelve-hour days in temperatures over one hundred degrees. Sometimes there is no drinking water; sometimes big common barrels of it are used. Women and children work on ladders and with hazardous machinery. (The Industrial Welfare Commission was told in 1961 that 500 children are maimed each year.) Babies are brought to the fields and placed in "cradles" of wood boxes. . . . (pp. 49-50)

Far to the South, in the Imperial Valley of California, the living is, if anything, more terrible than in Stockton. A friend of mine wrote me of some of the people there. One family he described lives in a shack and sleeps on flattened pasteboard boxes on the floor. There is no heat, and since the man of the house has been driven out of the fields by Braceros there is often no food. The mother is breastfeeding her infant—and her four-year-old as well—since that is the only way he will eat. (In this detail there is an eerie echo of the occasion in *The Grapes of Wrath* when the young girl breastfeeds a starving Oakie man. That scene was set almost thirty years ago.) . . . p. 51)

Americans and Braceros

I drove past the fields with an organizer from the Agricultural Workers Organizing Committee of the AFL-CIO. He had grown up in this area and

---

PRE-AUTOMATED WORK—PASTURES OF PLENTY (*cont.*)

had known the field as a child. As we passed each farm, he told me who was working there. Whenever he saw a group of Braceros, his voice became sharp.

"They are poor people," he said. "That is why they come here, and work for so little. The growers get them cheap, and they know that the union can't organize them. So that keeps the rates down for the American workers. We don't want to hurt these poor people; they are like us. But it is no way to help them to hurt us. Let the government work out some kind of a deal with Mexico for aid, or something like that. But let the American farm workers have a decent living without having to hate other poor people." . . . (p. 50)

SOURCE: Reprinted with permission of the Macmillan Company from *The Other America: Poverty in the United States* by Michael Harrington. Copyright 1962 by Michael Harrington.

14. KNOWLEDGE: LIMITATION ON ITS PRODUCTION AND USE

Science as a Vocation

MAX WEBER

. . . In our time, the internal situation, in contrast to the organization of science as a vocation, is first of all conditioned by the facts that science has entered a phase of specialization previously unknown and that this will forever remain the case. Not only externally, but inwardly, matters stand at a point where the individual can acquire the sure consciousness of achieving something truly perfect in the field of science only in case he is a strict specialist.

All work that overlaps neighboring fields, such as we occasionally undertake and which the sociologists must necessarily undertake again and again, is burdened with the resigned realization that at best one provides the specialist with useful questions upon which he would not so easily hit from his own specialized point of view. One's own work must inevitably remain highly imperfect. Only by strict specialization can the scientific worker become fully conscious, for once and perhaps never again in his lifetime, that he has achieved something that will endure. A really definitive and good accomplishment is today always a specialized accomplishment. And whoever lacks the capacity to put on blinders, so to speak, and to come up to the idea that the fate of his soul depends upon whether or not he makes the correct conjecture at this passage of this manuscript may as well stay away from science. He will never have what one may call the "personal experience" of science. Without this strange intoxication, ridiculed by every outsider; without this passion, this "thousands of years must pass before you enter into life and thousands more wait in silence"—according to whether or not you succeed in making this conjecture; without this, you have *no* calling for science and

SOURCE: *From Max Weber: Essays in Sociology*, ed. and trans. by Hans H. Gerth and C. Wright Mills (New York: Oxford U. P., 1946), pp. 134-156 (excerpted). Copyright 1946 by Oxford University Press, Inc., Reprinted by permission.

you should do something else. For nothing is worthy of man as man unless he can pursue it with passionate devotion.

Yet it is a fact that no amount of such enthusiasm, however sincere and profound it may be, can compel a problem to yield scientific results. Certainly enthusiasm is a prerequisite of the "inspiration" which is decisive. Nowadays in circles of youth there is a widespread notion that science has become a problem in calculation, fabricated in laboratories or statistical filing systems just as "in a factory," a calculation involving only the cool intellect and not one's "heart and soul." First of all one must say that such comments lack all clarity about what goes on in a factory or in a laboratory. In both some idea has to occur to someone's mind, and it has to be a correct idea, if one is to accomplish anything worthwhile. And such intuition cannot be forced. It has nothing to do with any cold calculation. Certainly calculation is also an indispensable prerequisite. No sociologist, for instance, should think himself too good, even in his old age, to make tens of thousands of quite trivial computations in his head and perhaps for months at a time. One cannot with impunity try to transfer this task entirely to mechanical assistants if one wishes to figure something, even though the final result is often small indeed. But if no "idea" occurs to his mind about the direction of his computations and, during his computations, about the bearing of the emergent single results, then even this small result will not be yielded.

Normally such an "idea" is prepared only on the soil of very hard work, but certainly this is not always the case. Scientifically, a dilettante's idea may have the very same or even a greater bearing for science than that of a specialist. Many of our very best hypotheses and insights are due precisely to dilettantes. The dilettante differs from the expert, as Helmholtz has said of Robert Mayer, only in that he lacks a firm and reliable work procedure. Consequently he is usually not in the position to control, to estimate, or to exploit the idea in its bearings. The idea is not a substitute for work; and work, in turn, cannot substitute for or compel an idea, just as little as enthusiasm can. Both, enthusiasm and work, and above all both of them *jointly*, can entice the idea.

Ideas occur to use when they please, not when it pleases us. The best ideas do indeed occur to one's mind in the way in which Ihering describes it: when smoking a cigar on the sofa; or as Helmholtz states of himself with scientific exactitude: when taking a walk on a slowly ascending street; or in a similar way. In any case, ideas come when we do not expect them, and not when we are brooding and searching at our desks. Yet ideas would certainly not come to mind had we not brooded at our desks and searched for answers with passionate devotion.

However this may be, the scientific worker has to take into his bargain the risk that enters into all scientific work: Does an "idea" occur or does it not? He may be an excellent worker and yet never have had any valuable idea of his own. It is a grave error to believe that this is so only in science, and that things for instance in a business office are different from a laboratory. A merchant or a big industrialist without "business imagination," that is, without ideas or ideal intuitions, will for all his life remain a man who would better have remained a clerk or a technical official. He will never be truly creative in organization. Inspiration in the field of science by no means plays any greater role, as academic conceit fancies, than it does in the field of mastering problems of practical life by a modern entrepreneur. On the other hand, and this also is often misconstrued, inspiration plays no less a role in science than it does in the realm of art. It is a childish notion to think that a mathematician attains any scientifically valuable results by sitting at his desk with a ruler, calculating machines or other mechanical means. The mathematical imagination of a Weierstrass is naturally quite differently oriented in meaning and result than is the imagination of an artist, and differs basically in quality. But the psychological processes do not differ. Both are frenzy (in the sense of Plato's "mania") and "inspiration." . . .

In contrast with these preconditions which scientific work shares with art, science has a fate that profoundly distinguishes it from artistic work. Scientific work is chained to the course of progress; whereas in the realm of art there is no progress in the same sense. It is not true that the work of art of a period that has worked out new technical means, or, for instance, the laws of perspective, stands therefore artistically higher than a work of art devoid of all knowledge of those means and laws—if its form does justice to the material, that is, if its object has been chosen and formed so that it could be artistically mastered without applying those conditions and means. A work of art which is genuine "fulfilment," is never surpassed; it will never be antiquated. Individuals may differ in appreciating the personal significance of works of art, but no one will ever be able to say of such a work that it is "outstripped" by another work which is also "fulfilment."

In science, each of us knows that what he has accomplished will be antiquated in ten, twenty, fifty years. That is the fate to which science is subjected; it is the very *meaning* of scientific work, to which it is devoted in a quite specific sense, as compared with other spheres of culture for which in general the same holds. Every scientific "fulfilment" raises new "questions"; it *asks* to be "surpassed" and outdated. Whoever wishes to serve science has to resign himself to this fact. Scientific works certainly can last as "gratifications" because of their artistic quality, or they may remain important as a means of training. Yet they will be surpassed scientifically—let that be repeated— for it is our common fate and, more, our common goal. We cannot work without hoping that others will advance further than we have. In principle, this progress goes on *ad infinitum*. And with this we come to inquire into the *meaning* of science. For, after all, it is not self-evident that something subordinate to such a law is sensible and meaningful in itself. Why does one engage in doing something that in reality never comes, and never can come, to an end?

One does it, first, for purely practical, in the broader sense of the word, for technical, purposes: in order to be able to orient our practical activities to the expectations that scientific experience places at our disposal. Good. Yet this has meaning only to practitioners. What is the attitude of the academic man towards his vocation—that is, if he is at all in quest of such a personal attitude? He maintains that he engages in "science for science's sake" and not merely because others, by exploiting science, bring about commercial or technical success and can better feed, dress, illuminate, and govern. But what does he who allows himself to be integrated into this specialized organization, running on *ad infinitum,* hope to accomplish that is significant in these productions that are always destined to be outdated? This question requires a few general considerations.

Scientific progress is a fraction, the most important fraction, of the process of intellectualization which we have been undergoing for thousands of years and which nowadays is usually judged in such an extremely negative way. Let us first clarify what this intellectualist rationalization, created by science and by scientifically oriented technology, means practically.

Does it mean that we, today, for instance, everyone sitting in this hall, have a greater knowledge of the conditions of life under which we exist than has an American Indian or a Hottentot? Hardly. Unless he is a physicist, one who rides on the streetcar has no idea how the car happened to get into motion. And he does not need to know. He is satisfied that he may "count" on the behavior of the streetcar, and he orients his conduct according to this expectation; but he knows nothing about what it takes to produce such a car so that it can move. The savage knows incomparably more about his tools. When we spend money today I bet that even if there are colleagues of political economy here in the hall, almost every one of them will hold a different answer in readiness to the question: How does it happen that one can buy something for money—sometimes more and sometimes less? The savage knows what he does in order to get his daily food and which institutions serve him in this pursuit. The increasing intellectualization and rationalization do *not,* therefore, indicate an increased and general knowledge of the conditions under which one lives.

It means something else, namely, the knowledge or belief that if one but wished one *could* learn it at any time. Hence, it means that principally there are no mysterious incalculable forces that come into play, but rather that one can, in principle, master all things by calculation. This means that the world is disenchanted. One need no longer have recourse to magical means in order to master or implore the spirits, as did the savage, for whom such mysterious powers existed. Technical means and calculations perform the service. This above all is what intellectualization means. . . .

What stand should one take? Has "progress" as such a recognizable meaning that goes beyond the technical, so that to serve it is a meaningful vocation? The question must be raised. But this is no longer merely the question of man's calling *for* science, hence, the problem of what science as a vocation means to its devoted disciples. To raise this question is to ask for the vocation of science within the total life of humanity. What is the value of science?

Here the contrast between the past and the present is tremendous. You will recall the wonderful image at the beginning of the seventh book of Plato's *Republic:* those enchained cavemen whose faces are turned toward the stone wall before them. Behind them lies the source of the light which they cannot see. They are concerned only with the shadowy images that this light throws upon the wall, and they seek to fathom their interrelations. Finally one of them succeeds in shattering his fetters, turns around, and sees the sun. Blinded, he gropes about and stammers of what he saw. The others say he is raving. But gradually he learns to behold the light, and then his task is to descend to the cavemen and to lead them to the light. He is the philosopher; the sun, however, is the truth of science, which alone seizes not upon illusions and shadows but upon the true being.

Well, who today views science in such a manner? Today youth feels rather the reverse: the intellectual constructions of science constitute an unreal realm of artificial abstractions, which with their bony hands seek to grasp the blood-and-the-sap of true life without ever catching up with it. But here in life, in what for Plato was the play of shadows on the walls of the cave, genuine reality is pulsating; and the rest are derivatives of life, lifeless ghosts, and nothing else. How did this change come about?

Plato's passionate enthusiasm in *The Republic* must, in the last analysis, be explained by the fact that for the first time the *concept,* one of the great tools of all scientific knowledge, had been consciously discovered. Socrates had discovered it in its bearing. He was not the only man in the world to discover it. In India one finds the beginnings of a logic that is quite similar to that of Aristotle's. But nowhere else do we find this realization of the significance of the concept. In Greece, for the first time, appeared a handy means by which one could put the logical screws upon somebody so that he could not come out without admitting either that he knew nothing or that this and nothing else was truth, the *eternal* truth that never would vanish as the doings of the blind men vanish. That was the tremendous experience which dawned upon the disciples of Socrates. And from this it seemed to follow that if one only found the right concept of the beautiful, the good, or, for instance of bravery, of the soul—or whatever—that then one could also grasp its true being. And this, in turn, seemed to open the way for knowing and for teaching how to act rightly in life and, above all, how to act as a citizen of the state; for this question was everything to the Hellenic man, whose thinking was political throughout. And for these reasons one engaged in science.

The second great tool of scientific work, the rational experiment, made its appearance at the side of this discovery of the Hellenic spirit during the Renaissance period. The experiment is a means of reliably controlling experience. Without it, present-day empirical science would be impossible. There were experiments earlier; for instance, in India, physiological experiments were made in the service of ascetic yoga technique; in Hellenic antiquity, mathematical experiments were made for purposes of war technology; and in the Middle Ages, for purposes of mining. But to raise the experiment to a principle of research was the achievement of the Renaissance. They were the great innovators in *art,* who were the pioneers of experiment. Leonardo and his like and, above all, the sixteenth-century experimenters in music with their experimental pianos were characteristic. From these circles the experiment entered science, especially through Galileo, and it entered theory through Bacon; and then it was taken over by the various exact disciplines of the continental universities, first of all those of Italy and then those of the Netherlands.

What did science mean to these men who stood at the threshold of modern times? To artistic experimenters of the type of Leonardo and the musical innovators, science meant the path to *true* art, and that meant for them the path to true *nature*. Art was to be raised to the rank of a science, and this meant at the same time and above all to raise the artist to the rank of the doctor, socially and with reference to the meaning of his life. This is the ambition on which, for instance, Leonardo's sketch book was based. And today? "Science as the way to nature" would sound like blasphemy to youth. Today, youth proclaims the opposite: redemption from the intellectualism of science in order to return to one's own nature and therewith to nature in general. Science as a way to art? Here no criticism is even needed. . . .

Under these internal presuppositions, what is the meaning of science as a vocation, now after all these former illusions the "way to true being," the "way to true art," and "way to true nature," the "way to true God," the "way to true happiness," have been dispelled? Tolstoi has given the simplest answer, with the words: "Science is meaningless because it gives no answer to our question, the only question important for us: 'What shall we do and how shall we live?'" That science does not give an answer to this is indisputable. The only question that remains is the sense in which science gives "no" answer, and whether or not science might yet be of some use to the one who puts the question correctly.

Today one usually speaks of science as "free from presuppositions." Is there such a thing? It depends upon what one understands thereby. All scientific work presupposes that the rules of logic and method are valid; these are the general foundations of our orientation in the world; and, at least for our special question, these presuppositions are the least problematic aspect of science. Science further presupposes that what is yielded by scientific work is important in the sense that it is "worth being known." In this, obviously, are contained all our problems. For this presupposition cannot be proved by scientific means. It can only be *interpreted* with reference to its ultimate meaning, which we must reject or accept according to our ultimate position towards life.

Furthermore, the nature of the relationship of scientific work and its presupposition varies widely according to their structure. The natural sciences, for instance, physics, chemistry, and astronomy, presuppose as self-evident that it is worth while to know the ultimate laws of cosmic events as far as science can construe them. This is the case not only because with such knowledge one can attain technical results but for its own sake, if the quest for such knowledge is to be a "vocation." Yet this presupposition can by no means be proved. And still less can it be proved that the existence of the world which these sciences describe is worth while, that it has any "meaning," or that it makes sense to live in such a world. Science does not ask for the answers to such questions.

Consider modern medicine, a practical technology which is highly developed scientifically. The general "presupposition" of the medical enterprise is stated trivially in the assertion that medical science has the task of maintaining life as such and of diminishing suffering as such to the greatest possible degree. Yet this is problematical. By his means the medical man preserves the life of the mortally ill man, even if the patient implores us to relieve him of life, even if his relatives, to whom his life is worthless and to whom the costs of maintaining his worthless life grow unbearable, grant his redemption from suffering. Perhaps a poor lunatic is involved, whose relatives, whether they admit it or not, wish and must wish for his death. Yet the presuppositions of medicine, and the penal code, prevent the physician from relinquishing his therapeutic efforts. Whether life is worth while living and when—this question is not asked by medicine. Natural science gives us an answer to the question of what we must do if we wish to master life technically. It leaves quite aside, or assumes for its purposes, whether we should and do wish to master life technically and whether it ultimately makes sense to do so.

Consider a discipline such as aesthetics. The fact that there are works of art is given for aesthetics. It seeks to find out under what conditions this fact exists, but it does not raise the question whether or not the realm of art is perhaps a realm of diabolical grandeur, a realm of this world, and therefore, in its core, hostile to God and, in its innermost and aristocratic spirit, hostile to the brotherhood of man. Hence, aesthetics does not ask whether there *should* be works of art.

THE INTELLECTUAL AS ACADEMIC MAN

Most social scientists are of necessity academic men, and working within the academic institutions of the twentieth century often poses formidable obstacles to the pursuit of science as a vocation as Weber conceived it. This is particularly true in the United States, where the governing boards of these institutions are made up of businessmen and similar lay groups. Thorstein Veblen was only one of many social scientists who have found it difficult, at times, to carry on their proper business of posing embarrassing questions about the social order, but he was the first to thoroughly scrutinize the American university as itself a source of bias in scientific research.

THE INTELLECTUAL AS ACADEMIC MAN (*cont.*)

Something of the flavor of his classic study, *The Higher Learning in America,* will be evident in this brief excerpt:

With the exception of archaeological inquiries and the study of law, as commonly pursued, these moral or social sciences are occupied with inquiry into the nature of the conventions under which men live, the institutions of society,—customs, usages, traditions, conventions, canons of conduct, standards of life, of taste, of morality and religion, law and order. No faithful inquiry into these matters can avoid an air of scepticism as to the stability or finality of some one or other among the received articles of institutional furniture. An inquiry into the nature and causes, the working and the outcome, of this institutional apparatus, will disturb the habitual convictions and preconceptions on which they rest, even if the outcome of the inquiry should bear no colour of iconoclasm; unless, indeed, the inquirer were so fortunate as to start with an inalienable presumption that the received convictions on these matters need no inquiry and are eternally right and good; in which case he does best to rest content at his point of departure. Scepticism is the beginning of science. Herein lies the difference between homiletical exposition and scientific inquiry.

Now, on these matters of habit and convention, morality and religion, law and order—matters which intimately touch the community's accepted scheme of life—all men have convictions; sentimental convictions to which they adhere with an instinctive tenacity, and any disturbance of which they resent as a violation of fundamental truth. These institutions of society are made up of the habits of thought of the people who live under them. The consensus of the unlearned, or unscientific, as regards the scientific validity of inquiries which touch these matters means little else than the collective expressions of a jealous orthodoxy with respect to the articles of the current social creed. One who purports to be a scientist in this field can gain popular approval of his scientific capacity, particularly the businessmen's approval, only by accepting and confirming current convictions regarding these elements of the accepted scheme of life with which his science is occupied. Any inquiry which does not lead to corroboration of the opinions in vogue among the unlearned is condemned as being spurious and dangerously wrong-headed; whereas an unbiased inquiry into these things, of course, neither confirms nor disputes the scheme of things into which it inquires. And so, at the best, it falls into the same class with the fabled Alexandrine books that either agreed with the Koran or disagreed with it, and were therefore either idle or sacrilegious.

SOURCE: Thorstein Veblen, *The Higher Learning in America* (New York: Sagamore Press, 1957), pp. 131–132. (First published in 1918.)

Consider jurisprudence. It establishes what is valid according to the rules of juristic thought, which is partly bound by logically compelling and partly conventionally given schemata. Juridical thought holds when certain legal rules and certain methods of interpretations are recognized as binding. Whether there should be law and whether one should establish just these rules—such questions jurisprudence does not answer. It can only state: If one wishes this result, according to the norms of our legal thought, this legal rule is the appropriate means of attaining it.

Consider the historical and cultural sciences. They teach us how to understand and interpret political, artistic, literary, and social phenomena in terms of their origins. But they give us no answer to the question, whether the existence of these cultural phenomena have been and are *worth while*. And they do not answer the further question, whether it is worth the effort required to know them. They presuppose that there is an interest in partaking, through this procedure, of the community of "civilized men." But they cannot prove "scientifically" that this is the case; and that they presuppose this interest by no means proves that it goes without saying. In fact it is not at all self-evident.

Finally, let us consider the disciplines close to me: sociology, history, economics, political science, and those types of cultural philosophy that make it their task to interpret these sciences. It is said, and I agree, that politics is out of place in the lecture-room. It does not belong there on the part of the students. If, for instance, in the lecture-room of my former colleague Dietrich Schäfer in Berlin, pacifist students were to surround his desk and make an uproar, I should deplore it just as much as I should deplore the uproar which anti-pacifist students are said to have made against Professor Förster, whose views in many ways are as remote as could be from mine. Neither does politics, however, belong in the lecture-room on the part of the docents, and when the docent is scientifically concerned with politics, it belongs there least of all.

To take a practical political stand is one thing, and to analyze political structures and party positions is another. When speaking in a political meeting about democracy, one does not hide one's personal standpoint; indeed, to come out clearly and take a stand is one's damned duty. The words one uses in such a meeting are not means of scientific analysis but means of canvassing votes and winning over others. They are not plow-shares to loosen the soil of contemplative thought; they are swords against the enemies: such words are weapons. It would be an outrage, however, to use words in this fashion in a lecture or in the lecture-room. If, for instance, "democracy" is under discussion, one considers its various forms, analyzes them in the way they function, determines what results for the conditions of life the one form has as compared with the other. Then one confronts the forms of democracy with nondemocratic forms of political order and endeavors to come to a position where the student may find the point from which, in terms of his ultimate ideals, he can take a stand. But the true teacher will beware of imposing from the platform any political position upon the student, whether it is expressed or suggested. "To let the facts speak for themselves" is the most unfair way of putting over a political position to the student.

Why should we abstain from doing this? I state in advance that some highly esteemed colleagues are of the opinion that it is not possible to carry through this self-restraint and that, even if it were possible, it would be a whim to avoid declaring oneself. Now one cannot demonstrate scientifically what the duty of an academic teacher is. One can only demand of the teacher that he have the intellectual integrity to see that it is one thing to state facts, to determine mathematical or logical relations or the internal structure of cultural values, while it is another thing to answer questions of the *value* of culture and its individual contents and the question of how one should act in the cultural community and in political associations. These are quite heterogeneous problems. If he asks further why he should not deal with both types of problems in the lecture-room, the answer is: because the prophet and the demagogue do not belong on the academic platform.

To the prophet and the demagogue, it is said: "Go your ways out into the streets and speak openly to the world," that is, speak where criticism is possible. In the lecture-room we stand opposite our audience, and it has to remain silent. I deem it irresponsible to exploit the circumstance that for the sake of their career the students have to attend a teacher's course while there is nobody present to oppose him with criticism. The task of the teacher is to serve the students with his knowledge and scientific experience and not to imprint upon them his personal political views. It is certainly possible that the individual teacher will not entirely succeed in eliminating his personal sympathies. He is then exposed to the sharpest criticism in the forum of his own conscience. And this deficiency does not prove anything; other errors are also possible, for instance, erroneous statements of fact, and yet they prove nothing against the duty of searching for the truth. I also reject this in the very interest of science. I am ready to prove from the works of our historians that whenever the man of science introduces his personal value judgment, a full understanding of the facts *ceases*. But this goes beyond tonight's topic and would require lengthy elucidation.

I ask only: How should a devout Catholic, on the one hand, and a Freemason, on the other, in a course of the forms of church and state or on religious history ever be brought to evaluate these subjects alike? This is out of the question. And yet the academic teacher must desire and must demand of himself to serve the one as well as the other by his knowledge and methods. Now you will rightly say that the devout Catholic will never accept the view of the factors operative in bringing about Christianity which a teacher who is free of his dogmatic presuppositions presents to him. Certainly! The difference, however, lies in the following: Science "free from presuppositions," in the sense of a rejection of religious bonds, does not know of the "miracle" and the "revelation." If it did, science would be unfaithful to its own "presuppositions." The believer knows both, miracle and revelation. And science "free from presuppositions" expects from him no less—and no more— than acknowledgment that *if* the process can be explained without those supernatural interventions, which an empirical explanation has to eliminate as causal factors, the process has to be explained the way science attempts to do. And the believer can do this without being disloyal to his faith.

But has the contribution of science no meaning at all for a man who does not care to know facts as such and to whom only the practical standpoint matters? Perhaps science nevertheless contributes something.

The primary task of a useful teacher is to teach his students to recognize "inconvenient" facts—I mean facts that are inconvenient for their party opinions. And for every party opinion there are facts that are extremely inconvenient, for my own opinion no less than for others. I believe the teacher accomplishes more than a mere intellectual task if he compels his audience to accustom itself to the existence of such facts. I would be so immodest as even to apply the expression "moral achievement," though perhaps this may sound too grandiose for something that should go without saying.

Thus far I have spoken only of practical reasons for avoiding the imposition of a personal point of view. But these are not the only reasons. The impossibility of "scientifically" pleading for practical and interested stands—except in discussing the means for a firmly given and presupposed end—rests upon reasons that lie far deeper.

"Scientific" pleading is meaningless in principle because the various value spheres of the world stand in irreconcilable conflict with each other. The elder Mill, whose philosophy I will not praise otherwise, was on this point right when he said: If one proceeds from pure experience, one arrives at polytheism. This is shallow in formulation and sounds paradoxical, and yet there is truth in it. If anything, we realize again today that something can be sacred not only in spite of its not being beautiful, but rather because and in so far as it is not beautiful. You will find this documented in the fifty-third chapter of the book of Isaiah and in the twenty-first Psalm. And, since Nietzsche, we realize that something can be beautiful, not only in spite of the aspect in which it is not good, but rather in that very aspect. You will find this expressed earlier in the *Fleurs du mal,* as Baudelaire named his volume of poems. It is commonplace to observe that something may be true although it is not beautiful and not holy and not good. Indeed it may be true in precisely those aspects. But all these are only the most elementary cases of the struggle that the gods of the various orders and values are engaged in. I do not know how one might wish to decide "scientifically" the value of French and German culture; for here, too, different gods struggle with one another, now and for all times to come. . . .

But enough of these questions which lead far away. Those of our youth are in error who react to all this by saying, "Yes, but we happen to come to lectures in order to experience something more than were analyses and statements of fact." The error is that they seek in the professor something different from what stands before them. They crave a leader and not a teacher. But we are placed upon the platform solely as teachers. And these are two different things, as one can readily see. . . .

Finally, you will put the question: "If this is so, what then does science actually and positively contribute to practical and personal 'life'?" Therewith we are back again at the problem of science as a "vocation."

First, of course, science contributes to the technology of controlling life by calculating external objects as well as man's activities. Well, you will say, that, after all, amounts to no more than the greengrocer of the American boy. I fully agree.

Second, science can contribute something that the greengrocer cannot: methods of thinking, the tools and the training for thought. Perhaps you will say: well, that is no vegetable, but it amounts to no more than the means for procuring vegetables. Well and good, let us leave it at that for today.

Fortunately, however, the contribution of science does not reach its limit with this. We are in a position to help you to a third objective; to gain *clarity*. Of course, it is presupposed that we ourselves possess clarity. As far as this is the case, we can make clear to you the following:

In practice, you can take this or that position when concerned with a problem of value—for simplicity's sake, please think of social phenomena as examples. *If* you take such and such a stand, then, according to scientific experience, you have to use such and such a *means* in order to carry out your conviction practically. Now, these means are perhaps such that you believe you must reject them. Then you simply must choose between the end and the inevitable means. Does the end "justify" the means? Or does it not? The teacher can confront you with the necessity of his choice. He cannot do more, so long as he wishes to remain a teacher and not to become a demagogue. He can, of course, also tell you that if you want such and such an end, then you must take into the bargain the subsidiary consequences which according to all experience will occur. Again we find ourselves in the same situation as before. These are still problems that can also emerge for the technician, who in numerous instances has to make decisions according to the principle of the lesser evil or of the relatively best. Only to him one thing, the main thing, is usually given, namely, the end. But as soon as truly "ultimate" problems are at stake for us this is not the case. With this, at long last, we come to the final service that science as such can render to the aim of clarity, and at the same time we come to the limits of science.

Besides we can and we should state: In terms of its meaning, such and such a practical stand can be derived with inner consistency, and hence integrity, from this or that ultimate *weltanschauliche* position. Perhaps it can only be derived from one such fundamental position, or maybe from several, but it cannot be derived from these or those other positions. Figuratively speaking, you serve this god and you offend the other god when you decide to adhere to this position. And if you remain faithful to yourself, you will necessarily come to certain final conclusions that subjectively make sense. This much, in principle at least, can be accomplished. Philosophy, as a special discipline, and the essentially philosophical discussions of principles in the other sciences attempt to achieve this. Thus, if we are competent in our pursuit (which must be presupposed here) we can force the individual, or at least we can help him, to give himself an *account of the ultimate meaning of his own conduct.* This appears to me as not so trifling a thing to do, even for one's own personal life. Again, I am tempted to say of a teacher who succeeds in this: he stands in the service of "moral" forces; he fulfils the duty of bringing about self-clarification and a sense of responsibility. And I believe he will be the more able to accomplish this, the more conscientiously he avoids the desire personally to impose upon or suggest to his audience his own stand.

This proposition, which I present here, always takes its point of departure from the one fundamental fact, that so long as life remains immanent and is interpreted in its own terms, it knows only of an unceasing struggle of these gods with one another. Or speaking directly, the ultimately possible attitudes toward life are irreconcilable, and hence their struggle can never be brought to a final conclusion. Thus it is necessary to make a decisive choice. Whether, under such conditions, science is a worthwhile "vocation" for somebody, and whether science itself has an objectively valuable "vocation" are again value judgments about which nothing can be said in the lecture-room. To affirm the value of science is a presupposition for teaching there. I personally by my very work answer in the affirmative, and I also do so from precisely the standpoint that hates intellectualism as the worst devil, as youth does today, or usually only fancies it does. In that case the word holds for these youths: "Mind you, the devil is old; grow old to understand him." This does not mean age in the sense of the birth certificate. It means that if one wishes to settle with this devil, one must not take to flight before him as so many like to do nowadays. First of all, one has to see the devil's ways to the end in order to realize his power and his limitations.

Science today is a "vocation" organized in special disciplines in the service of self-clarification and knowledge of interrelated facts. It is not the gift of grace of seers and prophets dispensing sacred values and revelations, nor does it partake of the contemplation of sages and philosophers about the meaning of the universe. This, to be sure, is the inescapable condition of our historical situation. We cannot evade it so long as we remain true to ourselves. And if Tolstoi's question recurs to you: as science does not, who is to answer the question: "What shall we do, and, how shall we arrange our lives?" or, in the words used here tonight: "Which of the warring gods should we serve? Or should we serve perhaps an entirely different god, and who is he?" then one can say that only a prophet or a savior can give the answers. If there is no such man, or if his message is no longer believed in, then you will certainly not compel him to appear on this earth by having thousands of professors, as privileged hirelings of the state, attempt as petty prophets in their lecture-rooms to take over his role. All they will accomplish is to show that they are unaware of the decisive state of affairs: the prophet for whom so many of our younger generation yearn simply does not exist. But this knowledge in its forceful significance has never become vital for them. The inward interest of a truly religiously "musical" man can never be served by veiling to him and to others the fundamental fact that he is destined to live in a godless and prophetless time by giving him the *ersatz* of armchair prophecy. The integrity of his religious organ, it seems to me, must rebel against this. . . .

The fate of our times is characterized by rationalization and intellectualization and, above all, by the "disenchantment of the world." Precisely the ultimate and most sublime values have retreated from public life either into the transcendental realm of mystic life or into the brotherliness of direct and personal human relations. It is not accidental that our greatest art is intimate and not monumental, nor is it accidental that today only within the smallest and intimate circles, in personal human situations, in *pianissimo,* that something is pulsating that corresponds to the prophetic *pneuma,* which in former times swept through the great communities like a firebrand, welding them together. If we attempt to force and to "invent" a monumental style in art, such miserable monstrosities are produced as the many monuments of the last twenty years. If one tries intellectually to construe new religions without a new and genuine prophecy, then, in an inner sense, something similar will result, but with still worse effects. And academic prophecy, finally, will create only fanatical sects but never a genuine community.

To the person who cannot bear the fate of the times like a man, one must say: may he rather return silently, without the usual publicity build-up of renegades, but simply and plainly. The arms of the old churches are opened widely and compassionately for him. After all, they do not make it hard for him. One way or another he has to bring his "intellectual sacrifice" that is inevitable. If he can really do it, we shall not rebuke him. For such an intellectual sacrifice in favor of an unconditional religious devotion is ethically quite a different matter than the evasion of the plain duty of intellectual integrity, which sets in if one lacks the courage to clarify one's own ultimate standpoint and rather facilitates this duty by feeble relative judgments. In my eyes, such religious return stands higher than the academic prophecy, which does not clearly realize that in the lecture-rooms of the university no other virtue holds but plain intellectual integrity. Integrity, however, compels us to state that for the many who today tarry for new prophets and saviors, the situation is the same as resounds in the beautiful Edomite watchman's song of the period of exile that has been included among Isaiah's oracles: "He calleth to me out of Seir, Watchman, what of the night? The watchman said, The morning cometh, and also the night: if ye will enquire, enquire ye: return, come."

The people to whom this was said has enquired and tarried for more than two millennia, and we are shaken when we realize its fate. From this we want to draw the lesson that nothing is gained by yearning and tarrying alone, and we shall act differently. We shall set to work and meet the "demands of the day," in human relations as well as in our vocation. This, however, is plain and simple, if each finds and obeys the demon who holds the fibers of his very life.

The Intellectual and the Language of Minorities

MELVIN SEEMAN

I

The signs of deep concern about the contemporary position of the intellectual in America are not hard to find. To be sure, as Merle Curti has stressed in his presidential address to the American Historical Society, anti-intellectualism—in one form or another—has a long history in American life.[1] But in recent years the situation of the intellectual has not resembled the mere continuation of a somewhat consistent and historically routine negativism. The current sense of urgency regarding the definition of the intellectual's role has found expression in a wide variety of places: from *Time* magazine's alarm about the "wide and unhealthy gap" between the American intellectuals and the people to a series of symposiums which have appeared in the *Journal of Social Issues,* in the book edited by Daniel Bell entitled *The New American Right,* and in the thoughtful British Journal, *Encounter.*[2]

Yet, in spite of this volume of words, and the talent of those involved, it is still possible to agree with Milton Gordon's remark that "the man of ideas and the arts has rarely been studied seriously as a social type by professional students of society."[3] Whether, as some have argued, this retreat from self-analysis reflects a basic disorder in the scientific study of man is debatable enough; but the fact is clear that the research techniques which have been applied to nearly everybody else—from the hobo to the business elite—have rarely been applied to ourselves.[4]

SOURCE: Reprinted from "The Intellectual and the Language of Minorities," in *American Journal of Sociology,* vol. LXIV (July, 1958), by Melvin Seeman by permission of The University of Chicago Press. Copyright, 1958, by The University of Chicago Press, Pp. 25–35.

[1] "Intellectuals and Other People," *American Historical Review,* LX (1955), 259–82.

[2] Cf. S. S. Sargent and T. Brameld (eds.), "Anti-intellectualism in the United States," *Journal of Social Issues,* Vol. II, No. 3 (1955); D. Bell (ed.), *The New American Right* (New York: Criterion Books, 1955); and *Encounter,* Vols. IV and V (1955).

[3] "Social Class and American Intellectuals," *A.A.U.P. Bulletin,* XL (1955), 517.

[4] The roster of those who have recently written, more or less directly, on the problem of the intellectual would comprise a list of the contemporary great and near-great in a variety of humanistic and social science fields (not to mention the physical sciences): e.g., Schlesinger and Hofstadter in history; Parsons and Riesman in sociology; Tolman and Fromm in psychology. Two well-known older works that embody the spirit of self-study are those by Znaniecki (*The Social Role of the Man of Knowledge*) and Logan Wilson (*The Academic Man*). There have, of course, been many commentaries on the intellectual, especially in the more or less Marxist journals; but I am referring here to the more formally analytic mode of investigation.

This paper is a report on one such study of ourselves, its aim being to determine how intellectuals in the current social climate deal with their identity as intellectuals and, beyond that, to suggest what difference it may make if this identity is handled in different ways.

The empirical base for this report was obtained through relatively unstructured interviews (on the average about one hour in length) with all the assistant professors teaching in the humanities and social science departments of a midwestern university.[5] These interviews were not content-analyzed in any statistical sense but were simply examined (as the illustrations in the next section will show) for patterns of response.

The total number of persons interviewed was forty. They came, in the number indicated, from the following departments: Economics (7), English (6), German (2), History (4), Law (1), Mathematics (3), Philosophy (4), Political Science (2), Psychology (4), Romance Languages (3), and Sociology-Anthropology (4). The sample included no one from the physical or biological sciences, from the engineering and applied fields, or from the creative arts; and, when an appropriate level in the staff hierarchy had been selected, there was no further sampling problem. Co-operation was good: of a total of forty-five persons listed in the university directory at the assistant-professor level, only one refused to be interviewed (and four were unavailable because of assignments out of the city).

The procedure in the interviews was consistent though not standardized. There was no attempt to get answers to preformed questions. We engaged, rather, in a conversation regarding a letter which outlined a plan for exploring the situation of the intellectual today. The letter was not mailed; it was read by the respondent at the start of the interview and served in this way as a common stimulus object. The body of the letter, which carried my signature, follows:

There is considerable evidence (though debatable evidence, to be sure) that the role of the intellectual has become increasingly problematic in American life. Such evidence includes: (1) the widespread expression of anti-intellectual attitudes; (2) the increasing pressure for conformity in intellectual work; and (3) the typical isolation of the intellectual in community life. These current trends are presumably matters of considerable moment to university people who are uniquely concerned with the social conditions under which intellectual activity is carried forward.

It seems to me that some effort to assess the problem among ourselves is in order; and that such an effort might proceed initially by calling together small, informal groups of faculty members to clarify issues and get an exchange of view-

---

[5] It seemed wiser, with a limited sample, to hold staff level constant rather than sample all levels of permanent staff. The assistant-professor group was chosen for two reasons: (1) it was large enough to provide suitable frequencies, yet small enough to be manageable without taxing time and finances, and (2) it is, in the institution studied, basically a tenure group like the higher ranks but presumably less involved in official committee work and graduate work and therefore more likely to give the time required for interviewing.

points. This letter comes as an invitation to you to participate in one of these discussions on the current situation of the intellectual. The discussion would include four or five other persons from the humanities and social sciences, and would take roughly one hour of your time. Since several discussions are planned, I would consider it part of my responsibility to provide you with some type of analytical summary of the sessions held—in effect, a research report.

Let me emphasize that the purpose of these discussions is not to canvass possible lines of action, but to achieve a clarification of issues on matters which are clearly controversial.

Would you indicate whether you wish to be included in the list of discussants by returning this letter to me with the appropriate notation?[6]

After the respondent had read the letter, he was encouraged to comment freely on any aspect of it; then each of the three points listed in the first paragraph of the letter was discussed; and, finally, I raised the question, "Do you classify yourself as an intellectual?"

The latter question raises for us, no less than for the respondents, the matter of definition. As a first approximation, I defined the intellectuals as a group for whom the analysis of ideas in their own right (i.e., for no pragmatic end) is a central occupation. The group I chose to interview was taken as a sample of intellectuals, in spite of the fact that some would surely not qualify on more stringent criteria (e.g., their degree of dedication to the life of the mind or the quality of their intellectual work). The sample is defensible, however, on the ground that by social definition—whether he or his colleagues prefer it or not—the university professor teaching in the humanities or social sciences is probably the prime case of intellectual endeavor (i.e., of non-pragmatic and ideological pursuits). Thus, we are concerned with the self-portrait of those who, by social definition at least, are intellectuals.[7]

---

[6] The italicized portion of this letter was underlined in the original; but in one-half of the cases a more action-oriented statement was substituted for the underlined portion given here. The two types of letters were randomly alternated in the interviewing program. In the second version, the underlined sentence read: *"Let me emphasize that the purpose of these discussions is not only to achieve a clarification of issues on matters which are clearly controversial; but also to canvass suitable lines of action."* In all cases, at the end of the interview, the respondent was asked to comment on what his reaction to the letter would have been if the alternative not presented to him had been used. The variation in letter style is mentioned here for the sake of completeness; it is not directly relevant to the treatment of the interviews reported here. The proposed discussions never took place, owing to both the press of time and a certain lack of enthusiasm—a lack which the remainder of this paper may make more understandable.

[7] This assertion, obviously, is an assumption, since the public definition of an intellectual is not a matter of empirical record, so far as I know. One could hold, further, that, if they are not so designated, they should be—that, in the ideal university, the group I have described would be identifiable as intellectuals in the sense of my stated definition. That definition has its difficulties, to be sure. For example, one might ask why an intellectual cannot believe that (or behave as if) ideas are of more than simply aesthetic interest, that ideas have consequences, and that the analysis of them serves a "pragmatic" end. A host of names come to mind of persons who would appear to have indorsed this view and whom we would presumably not wish to dismiss as intellec-

II

In a certain sense the chief finding of this study consisted of a "surprise": the unanticipated discovery of the extent to which these intellectuals use the language and mechanisms of minority status to describe themselves and their situation. It may be suggested that this should have been no surprise—that arguments quite consistent with this have been advanced in many places. And to some degree that is true.

In a recent well-publicized paper in *Harper's*, for example, a French writer had this to say:

It seems to me that the attitude of the American intellectual in comparison with his European counterpart is based on frustration and an inferiority complex. I am continually meeting people who tell me that the intellectual in Europe enjoys a position which, if not happier, is at least more dignified than that of the intellectual in America. . . . Whose fault is this? They go on to tell me that the fault rests with the American people, who have no appreciation for things of the intellect. I wonder whether it is not also in great measure the fault of the American intellectuals themselves.[8] .

In a similar vein Riesman and Glazer have commented that "the opinion leaders among the educated classes—the intellectuals and those who take their cues from them—have been silenced more by their own feelings of inadequacy and failure than by direct intimidation."[9] And Marcus Cunliffe, describing the United States intellectual for *Encounter* magazine, concludes: "Altogether, there has been an unfortunate loss of self-respect. Some intellectuals have felt that, wrong about communism, they must be occupationally prone to be wrong about everything."[10]

But the point is that comments of this kind do not constitute evidence; and, indeed, it is possible, if one questions the evidence, to treat such comments

tuals—e.g., Marx, Lenin, Jefferson, among others. The best provisional answer to this, I should think, would be that being an intellectual is not the designation for a person but for a role and that many who play the intellectual role, and play it well, are also deeply involved with the course of societal and individual development. One does not need to say, therefore, that Marx was not an intellectual because he was also a revolutionary.

In any event, though this definition does not thoroughly solve matters, it does suggest a line of approach and clarifies, perhaps, the senses in which our sample may or may not be considered as members of the class. To my mind it is much less important to determine whether they are, so to speak, "in" or "out" of the category than it is to recognize that they are candidates in several senses: (1) in public definitions of them; (2) in their personal self-definitions; and (3) in the definition of a university ideal. The issue is nicely captured in Randall Jarrell's fictional *Pictures from an Institution*, where he says of an academic man: "He had never been what intellectuals consider an intellectual, but other people had thought him one, and he had had to suffer the consequences of their mistake" (p. 110).

[8] R. L. Bruckberger, "An Assignment for Intellectuals," *Harper's*, CCXII (1956), 69.
[9] D. Riesman and N. Glazer, "Intellectuals and the Discontented Classes," *Partisan Review*, XXII (1955), 50.
[10] "The Intellectuals: II. The United States," *Encounter*, XX (1955), 31.

themselves as reflections of a kind of minority-style indictment of one's own group (like the Jew who agrees that "we" are too clannish, the intellectual says that "we" are too weak in will). Furthermore, the comments we have cited do not provide a systematic view of the specific forms of minority language which intellectuals employ in discussing themselves. Our empirical task here is to indicate that such minority references are surprising, indeed, in their frequency and to make a start toward a categorization of the forms these references take.[11]

The clearest of these forms may be labeled *the direct acceptance of majority stereotypes*. Like the Negroes who have accepted the whites' definition of color and who choose "light" among themselves, our respondents appear eager to validate the outsider's negative view of them. One need only read these forty protocols to emerge with a collective self-portrait of the soft, snobbish, radical, and eccentric intellectual who is asocial, unreliable, hopelessly academic, and a bit stupid to boot. It is impossible to cite here the evidence for all this; but each of the stereotypes in the previous sentence has a parallel affirmation in the interview material. These affirmations are, to be sure, frequently hedged with restrictions and limitations—we are dealing, after all, with a group of highly trained qualifiers. But the significant thing is that the respondents take this opportunity to affirm the stereotype; and this affirmation is typically set in a context which makes it clear that the stereotype, rather than the qualification, has a competing chance to govern behavior. Let me give some examples:

If there is anti-intellectualism in our community, I feel frankly we are to blame. If we can't throw off our infernal need for preaching and dictating, they have a right to damn us, and we have no answer but our human fallibility [C-1].[12]

---

[11] A word is in order about the meaning of "minority" and the occasion for "surprise." On the latter I am aware of the fact that many occupational groups (and certainly "notorious" ones—e.g., policemen, farmers, or traveling salesmen) develop somewhat negative images of themselves. But two special conditions make this case, it seems to me, somewhat different. First, we are dealing with a high status group (note, for example, their generally high placement in the North-Hatt prestige scale); and, second, we are dealing with a group whose very function, in good part, is the objective analysis of society and its products. On these grounds, I would argue that it is not enough to dismiss the problem by saying that all occupations reflect negative self-images or that the problem approach in the stimulus letter occasioned the results obtained. The question is: What occupations have stereotypes about them, in what degree, and how are these stereotypes handled by the incumbents, with what consequences? This is the broader problem to which this paper is addressed.

With regard to "minority": I use it here to designate a group against which categorical discrimination is practiced. A minority, in this view, is determined not by size but by the behavior of being subjected to categorical discrimination. It should be clear, however, that I am not attempting to prove that intellectuals *are* a minority in this sense but that they use the typical language and forms of the classical minority groups in their self-descriptions.

[12] The source of each quotation from the interviews is identified by an assigned case number so that the reader may note the spread of the illustrations. Departmental identi-

It's pretty difficult for the intellectual to mix with people. They feel ill at ease. Many intellectuals are not very approachable; perhaps his training is not complete enough. The intellectual may be more to blame for that than anyone else [C-2].

My general attitude is that some of the intellectuals are so concerned with academic freedom that it kind of tires me. And, I think, this sometimes adds up to wanting more freedom than anybody else—the kind of freedom to be irresponsible. [And later, when asked whether the letter should include the action alternative, this subject said:] It shouldn't be in there, because basically I think that except in the most long-run sense there is not a thing you can do. Maybe we can breed a new line of professors [C-3].

We could go on here, if space permitted, about "the snobbishness we are all guilty of" and about the "queer birds" who "make a profession of being different" and "don't have sense enough to pour sand out of a boot" (these quotations coming from four different protocols). This direct acceptance by intellectuals of the negative stereotype regarding intellectuals follows the pattern of the minority "self-hate" which Lewin has described in the case of the anti-Semitic Jew[13] and which has been clearly expressed in Negro color attitudes.[14]

A second, and somewhat less extreme, variety of minority attitude may be labeled *the concern with in-group purification*. This label points to language and behavior which are guided by the idea that the minority's troubles are rooted in the misguided ways of a small fraction among them. The parallel with traditional minorities reads: for the Jews, it is the "bad" Jew—the one who is, indeed, aggressive and loud—who breeds anti-Semitism; and, for the intellectuals, it is the radical, asocial types who are responsible for the group's difficulty. Thus, on the radical issue, one respondent, speaking of his effort to establish a research contact downtown, said:

I realized we had one or two strikes against us because we were from the university. We had to have people vouch for us. We don't enjoy the best reputation down there; we're blamed for the actions of a few who make radical speeches and seem to overgeneralize [C-4].

Another respondent, speaking of an "extreme liberal" in his college, remarked:

I've got nothing against it, but the average man might translate this [liberalism] over to our college. In this sense, he does a slight disservice to the college [C-5].

---

fications are avoided, though these would be of some interest, to preserve anonymity. There is, I presume, every reason to believe that the frequency and subtlety of minority responses will vary among universities and departments—by region, eminence, and the like. But it also seems reasonable to believe that the bulk of American universities are not substantially different from the one involved here.

[13] K. Lewin, *Resolving Social Conflicts* (New York: Harper & Bros., 1948), pp. 186–200.

[14] M. Seeman, "Skin Color Values in Three All-Negro School Classes," *American Sociological Review*, XI (1946), 315–21.

Similarly, on scores other than radicalism there are expressions of the view that the position of the intellectuals turns on the "impure" behavior of the intellectual himself. One respondent, discussing anti-intellectualism in general, remarked that we could lick the problem:

If we had people getting out and who really did mix, as speakers and members. . . . I've worried about this: would I be willing to be in an organization if I were only a member? We get to be president and vice-president all the time. It doesn't do any good to be in and be officers; in order to get over the thought of us as intellectual snobs, we have to be satisfied to be just members [C-6].

This quotation highlights one interesting result of this concern with the "impure"—and a result which, again, has a clear minority flavor. The intellectual becomes involved in the need to prove that the impurity really is not there (or, at the very least, that the intellectual in question is not one of the "impure" few). We are familiar with the Jewish person who is inordinately careful to demonstrate in his own behavior that Jews as a group are not what the stereotype says; and Anatole Broyard has nicely described the various forms that Negro "inauthenticity" of the same type may take (e.g., what he calls "role inversion" is a careful and extreme negation of precisely those qualities embodied in the Negro stereotype—"cool" music and passive behavior, for example, being a negation of the primitive, hot, carefree quality in the Negro stereotype).[15]

The interviews reveal a similar concern with disproving the stereotype. Thus, one respondent, discussing possible action alternatives, commented:

We could, of course, go out and make talks to various groups—show them that intellectuals really aren't bad guys [C-7].

Another, speaking about the isolation of the intellectual, said:

Well, in neighborhood isolation, there's a lot of it due to their initial reaction —when they find out you're a professor they slightly withdraw, but, if you continue to make connections, then they find out you're a human being [C-5].

Still another person commented:

If we mixed more, and became known as people as well as college teachers, maybe it would be better. Frequently, the antipathy to college teachers melts when they meet you personally; though we do have a tendency to carry our classroom personality into other areas [C-8].

A third major category of minority-like response may be titled *the approval of conformity*. In a certain sense, of course, the pattern just described is a specialized form of conformity; for its main aim is to emphasize the conventional as against the divergent aspects of the intellectual's behavior. But the pressure for conformity goes beyond this. It involves the same kind of passive, conservative, and attention-avoiding behavior that Lewin has described as

---

[15] "Portrait of the Inauthentic Negro," *Commentary*, X (1950), 56–64.

prototypical for minority leaders, his "leaders from the periphery."[16] And, in the long run, this pressure for conformity leads to assimilationism—to the very denial of any significant observable differences on which minority status may rest. As far as the more traditional minorities are concerned, the classic Adorno volume on prejudice and personality has put one part of the conformist case as follows:

Since acceptance of what is like onself and rejection of what is different is one feature of the prejudiced outlook [i.e., of the authoritarian personality], it may be that members of minority groups can in limited situations and for some period of time protect themselves and gain certain advantages by conforming in outward appearance as best they can with the prevailing ways of the dominant group.[17]

As with these minorities, we find that there is considerable commitment to conformity among intellectuals and that this is expressed variously as a need to adjust, to avoid controversy, or to assimilate and deny differences entirely. Thus, one respondent, discussing the conformity question raised in the letter said:

On that, I can't say I've experier.ced it. I'm in a pretty safe field. . . . [He then described a book of readings he had collected and said that there was a short passage from a well-known writer which had been taken out before publication.] There's no use stirring up trouble. I don't think it was a lack of courage on my part. We thought—that is, the editor and I—that it was too touchy. It's a very beautiful thing, but we took it out [C-9].

Another individual, discussing the community life of the intellectual, noted that they often do not take an active part and added:

Part of that is good, in that they are lending the prestige of the university when they do take part, and shouldn't be doing that. I don't want to be written up in the paper as Professor X of university holding a certain opinion. I've deliberately refrained from expressing political opinion [C-5].

Still others appear to argue for conformity by denying that there is a difference to which the notion of "intellectual" points:

I don't feel any different from my electrician-neighbor [C-10].

I get a kind of inferiority complex if they call me "professor"; I know that my work with the intellect is on the same level in the eyes of the man in the street as, say, a chain-store manager [C-11].

Or else there is insistence that it is important for the intellectual to assimilate or disguise himself more successfully. Thus, one respondent, speaking of occasions when he makes public addresses, said:

When I go out and meet these people, I try to fit myself into their realm, into the climate of the various groups [C-12].

---

[16] *Op. cit.*, p. 196.
[17] T. W. Adorno *et al.*, *The Authoritarian Personality* (New York: Harper & Bros., 1950), p. 974.

Another gave, as part of his recipe for the intellectual's behavior, the directive:

He should adjust his personality so he can mix in better with the person who isn't an intellectual [C-2].

And one I have quoted before, speaking of the intellectual's isolation in community life said:

You must make concessions. I would find it pretty hard to have contacts, for example, in places like Wilder's *Our Town* or Anderson's small Ohio town, but I couldn't accuse the people in the town of being anti-intellectual; it's probably my fault. If you make ,a certain amount of concession, you will find a way [C-11].

There are other comments which are less clear in their conformist implica-tions—for example, more than faintly guilty remarks to the effect that "my neighbors see me home in the early afternoon and wonder just what it is I do in my job" (C-13). On the whole, there is considerable evidence in these protocols that the typical minority response of conformity is found in a variety of forms among intellectuals.[18]

The fourth category of response represents the extreme of minority assimi-lation from the standpoint of the individual, namely, *the denial of group membership*. Like the name-changing Jew and the Negro who "passes," many intellectuals find means to hide or escape their unwelcome identity. An inter-viewee nicely described this pattern as follows:

One consequence of anti-intellectualism is for some intellectuals to deny that they are intellectuals. This is a behavioral denial; it's part of the psychological revolution, the adjustment trend. . . . The pressure to be well-adjusted is high, and so he becomes non-intellectual and begins to deny in some respects that he is an intellectual [C-15].

The evidence in the interviews indicates that the retreat from membership is a substantial one and takes many forms. Indeed, one of the real surprises, during the course of these interviews, was the rarity of real acceptance of intellectual status. This non-acceptance is revealed in several ways. First, there is the frequency with which this freely offered remark appears: "Intel-lectuals, I hate the word!" Second, there are the direct denials to the ques-tion, "Do you consider yourself an intellectual?" A complete listing of the protocol responses on this point would reveal a quite consistent, though subtly

---

[18] Two of the respondents themselves commented on this "trimming of sails" in the university setting. One, for example, after noting an increase in anti-intellectual pres-sures, said:

"If you work at the university, you want the outside to be as non-controversial as possible; to say, 'Look at me, I'm just like anybody else.' This is part of the general line of not hurting the university by getting in the news in negative ways" (C-14). Another person, in similar vein, remarked:

"The intellectual is assuming more of the role of the non-intellectual and seeks to be a part of the gang—denies that he's different" (C-15).

varied, attern of maneuvering, all aimed at being counted out—the kind of "Who, me?" response one gets from the obviously guilty.[19]

Thus, one respondent said:

That's a word that always does bother me. I don't think of myself so. It's a self-conscious word that sets us apart from the rest of the population. The only thing that sets us apart, in fact, is that we have gone to school longer than some, and there are doctors who have gone longer and we don't consider them intellectuals [C-10].

Another said:

I don't apply it to myself. I never use it myself. It's sort of snobbish [C-17].

And still another:

I would [use the designation "intellectual"] in the professional sense only. . . . Professionally, I suppose we can't avoid it. Only in the very narrow professional sense, in the sense that we are trying to improve the intellect of students, I suppose it applies. I don't see how a university professor can escape the narrow meaning of the term [C-1].

And, finally, one respondent clearly recognized the social definition of himself yet reflected no eagerness in his personal definition:

I suppose I would [consider my self an intellectual]. . . . I don't know if I am twenty-four hours a day, but still I suppose my work would be classified or considered an intellectual. . . . I teach the best I can, and certainly I'm classified as an intellectual by the community, my neighbors, and my colleagues [C-9].

A third kind of denial of membership is shown in the efforts that are made to avoid having one's affiliation publicly known. Thus, one respondent said:

When I'm away from the university, I usually have plenty of dirt under my nails, or I'm getting a harvest. Some of us fool ourselves into believing that the stain of our profession doesn't follow us. I can work with a carpenter for several weeks, and he has no notion I'm a university professor. I take a foolish pride, I suppose, in this [C-1].

Another remarked:

By training we get so we show contempt for those who overgeneralize, as in the Rotary, and we don't want to be in arguments all the time so we stay away. And how often do we go out of the way to announce that we're college professors. I don't conceal it; but I don't volunteer it. It would change your relation to the group [C-4].

---

[19] Even where there is acceptance of the "intellectual" label, there is sometimes a suspicious belligerence about it. One respondent, who vigorously denied the validity of the view embodied in the stimulus letter and felt that anti-intellectualism was a fictitious problem, said: "You need to live your life as if you were proud of it—talk it up" (C-16).

Thus, in one way or another, many of our respondents indicate that they do not cherish either their name or their identity as intellectuals; and they adopt a language of evasion and anonymity which is minority-like, indeed. Though one may argue that this rejection of the name is not, after all, so terribly important, it seems to me more reasonable, in this case, to see the "naming trouble" as an essential part of the status involved.[20]

The fifth, and last, category of minority-like response can be designated *the fear of group solidarity*. This label indicates behavior whose essential function is similar to the conformist response; namely, behavior calculated to keep the majority's attention off the minority as such. In our intellectuals this typically takes the form of strong resistance to any clearly identifiable group action on the group's problems; the answer lies, rather, in individual goodness. One respondent, in fact, while stating the case against group action, made the minority tie himself:

The notion of action involves the whole place of the intellectual in society. In addition, direct action puts us in the position of special pleading. It's like a Jew going out and talking about anti-Semitism [C-7].

Another said:

Individual action seems more feasible. One has to measure one's forces and deploy them properly. . . . If you try to organize a society for X, Y, or Z, and you have the right people on the letterhead, maybe you're O.K.; but otherwise you're considered radical. Many things can be carried out without anybody knowing there is an organization [C-18].

Still another remarked:

I'm frankly very much afraid of any action that has the label of the organized action of the intellectuals—not afraid of what they might do, but of public reaction. It ought to be unorganized [C-19].

Many of those interviewed seem committed to "having an effect the individual way" and are against "forming an organization that's militant." They wish, in a certain sense, to be (as one respondent [C-20] described himself) "the kind of social actionist who never appears to be one." I am interested here not in asserting that the strategy of organizational effort is a sounder strategy but in noting that the arguments against it frequently reflect a desire —common in other minorities—not to become too visible or too aggressive in one's own interest.

---

[20] On a similar point Everett Hughes has written in an essay titled "What's in a Name": "Words are weapons. As used by some people the word 'Hebrew,' for example, is a poisoned dart. When a word is so expressively used, we are face to face with no simple matter of social politics, but with part of the social process itself. This is, in part, what Durkheim had in mind in his long discussion of collective symbols and concepts. Words, he pointed out, are not merely something that happens along with the social process, but are its very essence. Naming is certainly part of the social process in inter-ethnic and racial relations" (*Where Peoples Meet* [Glencoe, Ill.: Free Press, 1952], p. 139).

III

Neither the quotations nor the theories given above exhaust the minority language in these protocols. Moreover I have intentionally failed to analyze or report in any fulness the more "positive" remarks on the intellectual's role in society or on the anti-intellectualism within university life itself (as one person put it [C-21]: "the destruction of the intellectual community within the university"). It was, in fact, only after the interviews were almost completed, and the variability in self-definition became ever more striking, that it was clear we might treat intellectual status directly, as one which presents a standard problem in minority adjustment.

I have argued elsewhere that marginalities of this kind provide the opportunity for the development of perspective and creativity—an opportunity whose realization depends upon the adjustment which is made to marginal status.[21] In this earlier study, using the Jews as a case in point, I found that favorable adjustment to marginality was, indeed, associated with what was called "intellectual perspective"; and it now seemed possible to apply the same general logic to this sample of intellectuals.

Certainly many have asserted that there is an inherent alienative potential —an inescapable degree of marginality—in the intellectual role; and the assertion usually follows that the individual's style of adjustment to this marginality affects his performance as an intellectual. The usual view, of course, is that those who are "frozen" by this marginality and who retreat into conformity are less creative as intellectuals. Cunliffe, almost incidentally, makes this tie between mode of adjustment and creativity in advancing his distinction between two types of American intellectuals, whom he calls the *"avant-garde"* and the *"clerisy"*:

So, if there have been many alienated Western intellectuals since 1800, whom I will label the *avant-garde*, there have also been others, [the "clerisy"] of similar intellectual weight, though as a rule of less creative brilliance, who have remained more or less attached to their society.[22]

The discovery, in the interviews, of so many and so varied responses to this marginal aspect of the intellectual's position suggested the possibility of testing, in a small-scale empirical way, such common assertions about the consequences (or correlates) of the intellectual's adjustment to marginality. The hypothesis to be tested parallels that given in the earlier paper on the Jews as a minority; namely, that those intellectuals who have successfully adjusted to the marginal character of their role—those who, let us say, reveal a minimum of our five minority-style attitudes toward themselves as intellectuals—will be, in turn, the more creative workers in their respective crafts.

For a provisional glimpse of such a test, and to illustrate at the same time

---

[21] M. Seeman, "Intellectual Perspective and Adjustment to Minority Status," *Social Problems*, III (1956), 142–53.
[22] *Op. cit.*, p. 25

one possible utility of the descriptive categories developed in the previous section, I attempted to score the forty protocols for evidence of commitment to, or rejection of, each of the five categories. At the same time, I asked a group of persons in the various departments (in all cases, men of higher academic rank than the individual in question) to judge the professional creativity of those interviewed. Creativity here refers to the ability to make the "given" problematic: the ability to challenge the routines and to provide alternatives to the standardized "right answers" in the respective fields.

Unfortunately, though expectedly, the free-response character of the interviews led to some serious limitations as far as the present more quantitative interest is concerned. For example, on two of the five minority categories (No. 2, "concern with in-group purification," and No. 5, "fear of in-group solidarity") more than one-third of the protocols received a score of 3, which indicated a lack of substantial evidence in the interview; and, in addition, among the remaining two-thirds of the cases, there was a very poor numerical split between "high" versus "low" adjustors on these two categories.

In view of these limitations, I shall not attempt to present what would amount to a complete, but premature, account of the adjustment ratings and creativity judgments.[23] But it is of illustrative interest to note what happened on the three remaining "minority response" categories where a more reasonable split between high versus low adjustment was obtained. "High" adjustment refers to a tendency to reject the use of the indicated minority-like modes of response in self-description; "low" adjustment refers to a tendency to embody the indicated minority-type response. Table 1 reveals what was obtained when individuals who scored 3 (no evidence) on each category were eliminated and when the high and low adjustors were compared on their average creativity. The data in Table 1 are read as follows: For the twelve persons who scored either 4 or 5 on category 1 (i.e., whose responses were antithetical to the acceptance of majority stereotypes about the intellectual), the mean creativity score was 3.27, with a standard deviation of 0.65. For the

---

[23] I am indebted to Mrs. Frances Mischel, a graduate student in sociology and anthropology, for the two hundred "minority" ratings (five ratings on each of forty protocols). These ratings were "blind" as far as identification of individuals or specialty fields was concerned. They were done as independently as possible, as far as the five categories are concerned, to minimize "halo." A total of 120 creativity judgments by colleagues were secured; and the evidence suggests that there is substantial agreement among them. Both the adjustment and the creativity ratings were made on five-point scales. For minority adjustment, the scale read as follows: 1—very much evidence of this; 2—some evidence of this; 3—no evidence one way or the other; 4—some evidence of rejection of this mode of response; 5—clear evidence of rejection of this mode. The creativity scale ran simply from 1 ("low in creativity") to 5 ("high in creativity") and was accompanied by a full-page explanation of both the meaning of creativity in this context and the method to be used in making the ratings. It should be clear that the term "adjustment" does not refer to the standard psychological meaning of the term; it designates only whether the respondent reflects or does not reflect the five categories of response described here. Thus, "high adjustment" refers to those who scored either 4 or 5 on the given category; "low" refers to a score of 1 or 2 on the category.

TABLE I. *Mean Creativity Scores and Standard Deviations for Individuals Scored High versus Low on Three Categories of Minority Response to Intellectual Status*

ADJUST-MENT GROUP	CATEGORY 1—ACCEPT-ANCE OF STEREOTYPES			CATEGORY 3—APPROVAL OF CONFORMITY			CATEGORY 4—DENIAL OF MEMBERSHIP		
	N	MEAN	S.D.	N	MEAN	S.D.	N	MEAN	S.D.
High ..	12	3.27	0.65	16	2.74	0.84	13	2.48	1.02
Low...	13	2.54	1.19	15	2.53	1.35	15	2.34	1.06

thirteen persons who scored low in adjustment on this same category (i.e., who revealed a clear tendency to accept negative stereotypes), the mean creativity score was 2.54, with a standard deviation of 1.19.

The differences in creativity between adjustment groups are consistently in the direction of higher ratings for those who do not use the minority-style response to intellectual status. Though the N's are small, and the differences are not uniformly great, the trend is clear, and the difference between adjustment groups for Category 1 is statistically significant.[24]

I do not take this as an unequivocal demonstration of the hypothesis in question. For one thing, there are other variables of considerable relevance (e.g., the age of the respondent) that cannot be controlled adequately in a sample of this size; and, in addition, questions remain open about the reliability of the adjustment ratings.[25] But for purposes of illustration the trend revealed in Table 1 is of considerable interest, for it suggests that the minority orientations I have attempted to specify here may be treated (provisionally, at least) not simply as categories of description but as relevant factors in the performance of the intellectual role as such.

It is customary, of course, to conclude by noting the need for further research—in this case, research on the forms and consequences of anti-intellectualism. But there is one crucial thing.—To find, as we have, that many intellectuals adopt, without serious efforts to build a reasoned self-

---

[24] A test of the homogeneity of the two variances for the adjustment groups yielded an F ratio which approximated the 0.05 level of significance and raised doubt about the wisdom of pooling the variances for the two groups in computing the t test between the creativity means. The obtained t ratio for the test of Category 1 was 1.841, a figure which is significant at the 0.05 level using a one-tailed test. Neither of the two remaining categories yielded a significant t. The method used to test for homogeneity of variance and for the significance of the difference between means is given in A. Edwards, *Statistical Methods for the Behavioral Sciences* (New York: Rinehart & Co., 1954), pp. 271–74.

[25] The question of reliability of rating may not be a serious problem. The same judge who did the ratings in this case was also used in the previously mentioned study of Jewish adjustment; and in that case the ratings of two independent judges, completing a task quite similar to the rating task involved here, were quite reliable (see the paper cited in n. 21 above). I have not deemed it essential for purposes of this illustration to compute another reliability figure for the judge in question.

portrait, an essentially negative, minority view of themselves and to find, in addition, some plausible ground for believing that this failure in self-conception is not independent of role performance—gives a special cast to the usual call for research. Thus it would seem essential to recognize that this research must include, if we may call it that, an "inward" as well as an "outward" orientation—that is, we must presumably conduct two related research operations: a study of the attitudes that others take toward intellectuals as well as a more intensive study of the intellectuals' attitudes toward themselves. A serious effort along those lines might yield considerably more than the usual research project; it can become an opportunity for self-discovery.

The Effect on Academic Goods of Their Market

WARREN G. BENNIS

Research in the physical sciences is perhaps more certain to be directed toward useful ends than research in humanistic fields, because the former is most commonly carried on in organized laboratories, where consultation is almost inevitable and a consensus of opinion as to what is worthwhile is easily formed, and has its effect on the investigator, whereas in most humanistic and social subjects the researcher can work in comparative isolation.—J. FRANKLIN JAMESON[1] (1927).

As the design engineers in an industry feel harried by the demands and expectations of product engineers who want to produce, and the sales engineers who want to sell, so the design engineers of social science are under the pressures just indicated from the production and sales staff who insist on putting on the social science assembly line what is still necessarily in the handicraft and mock-up stage. In many quarters, the promoters of social science have aroused such unfillable expectations as to risk a disillusioning bust of the whole enterprise.—DAVID RIESMAN.[2]

In less than two decades we have seen the emergence in the United States of a new industry: the organized production of new social knowledge. While Slichter and other economists cite the rise of industrial, mostly physical,

SOURCE: Reprinted from "The Effect on Academic Goods of Their Market," in *American Journal of Sociology*, vol. LXII (July, 1956), by Warren G. Bennis by permission of the University of Chicago Press. Copyright, 1956, by the University of Chicago Press. Pp. 28–33.

[1] Cited in F. A. Ogg, *Research in the Humanistic and Social Sciences* (New York and London: Century Co., 1928), p. 17.

[2] "Observations on Social Science Research," from *Individualism Reconsidered* (Glencoe, Ill.: Free Press, 1954), p. 475.

research as one of the main developments in the national economy, the use of teams of social scientists working on practical problems has turned social research into a million-dollar business.[3] Although comprehensive and comparable statistical data on the growth of social science research are nonexistent, certain clues indicate the magnitude of this development: (1) The combined expenditures for social research of the twenty largest universities in 1928 would probably support only one present-day university research organization.[4] (2) While the government disbursed practically no funds for social research twenty-five years ago, in 1952 eleven million dollars was spent on psychological research alone. (3) The National Science Foundation estimates that a hundred million dollars was spent on research in the social sciences in 1953.

Perhaps the most important circumstances in stimulating large-scale programs of research are the increased specialization of the social disciplines which has created a need for interdisciplinary and team research,[5] the magnitude of world problems, the proved usefulness of social science findings for policy-makers, the availability of large sums of money from foundations and the United States government, and the quantifiability of social data. These developments have created sweeping changes in the structure of social research. A new type of intellectual organization is emerging, replete with big budgets and the growing pains of managerial responsibility. The purpose of this paper is to examine an organization which has been under study by the author for over fifteen months and describe its chief organizational syndrome: exposure to market forces.

The organization, the "Hub," is located in a large university, is under the

---

[3] Sumner Slichter, address at the Business Executive Conference at the University of Omaha, Omaha, Nebraska, May 15, 1953.

[4] Ogg, *op. cit.*, reported that the following universities spent under $350,000 on social research in 1926–27: California, Chicago, Illinois, Indiana, Kansas, Michigan, Minnesota, Missouri, Nebraska, Harvard, Yale, Columbia, Johns Hopkins, and Cornell. The total budget of the research organization which will be described here is larger; indeed, it maintains the largest budget in the College of Social Studies.

For accounts of the growth of expenditures in social science, see H. Alpert, "National Science Foundation," *American Sociological Review*, XIX, No. 2 (1954), 208; R. G. Axt, *Federal Government and Financing Higher Education* (New York: Columbia University Press, 1952); B. Barber, *Science and the Social Order* (Glencoe, Ill.: Free Press, 1952), p. 132; W. G. Bennis, "The Structure of Social Science: An Organizational Study" (paper read at the American Sociological Society Annual Meetings, Urbana, Ill., September 9, 1954), pp. 2–3; L. P. Lessing, "National Science Foundation Takes Stock," *Scientific American*, March, 1954; *Federal Funds for Science: National Science Foundation, 1950–52* (Washington: U.S. Government Printing Office).

[5] The Russell Sage Foundation, Brookings Institution, and the Social Science Research Council stress this development as one of the most significant in the social sciences in the last two decades. See M. Graham, *Federal Utilization of Social Science* (Washington, D.C.: Brookings Institute, 1954), pp. 18–21; *Effective Use of Social Science Research in the Federal Services* (New York: Russell Sage Foundation, 1950), p. 21; *The Social Sciences in Historical Study* (Social Science Research Council Bulletin 64 [1954], pp. 31–33).

jurisdiction of its College of Social Studies, and is equivalent to an academic department. Its growth was spurred both to strengthen the social sciences at the university and to offer social scientists the opportunity to influence the nature of American foreign policy by tackling problems of major interest to the government. Hence its main activity centers around international affairs and economic development.

The total personnel numbers about eighty-five: twelve equivalent to full or associate professors, twenty-six research associates, twenty research assistants (chiefly graduate students), twenty-two secretaries, and four administrative assistants. These persons are connected with one or the other of two main research projects: a Development program to examine three countries with contrasting geographical and economic environments and a Communications program to study the interaction of words, impressions, and ideas which affect the attitudes and behavior of different peoples toward one another. Each program has its own director who attempts to co-ordinate the activities of the staff prescribed by the research goals.

The Hub is almost completely dependent upon outside financing by a large private foundation.[6] An indication of the anxiety concerning the granting of funds was shown in the Hub's 1953–54 Annual Report, the first sentence of which reads: "The most important event in the life of the Hub last year was the receipt at the year-end of a substantial grant from the foundation for the conduct of research. This grant removed a major uncertainty which had hovered over a major portion of the Hub's forward planning. . . ."

The program on Communications has been established with a four-year grant, while that on Development has been awarded a grant on a year-to-year basis. While even four years is short, considering the gestation period of research, the Development project was threatened by the yearly scrutiny of the foundation and by its annual uncertainties. For the preceding two years the foundation had not announced the grant until the end of May.

MARKET VERSUS TASK ORIENTATION

One chief conception of work in a research organization varies with the degree of control the organization maintains over exogenous forces—in this particular case, market forces. Where financial security provides protection from the market, the organization and the scientists within it are safe from the vagaries of the market. This situation we call "task-orientation." Where there is little protection from the market place, the organization becomes intimately concerned with financial matters. Attention, for sheer sake of

---

[6] Since the field work for this paper was completed, i.e., during the very early days of the organization's life, important changes have been made toward a more permanent footing of research projects. The Hub director and other officers, fully aware of the problems of tenuous short-term financing, submitted a proposal urging a long-term commitment, and a five-year grant was issued by the foundation just as this study was closing.

survival, is diverted from the task to the sponsors of research. This we call "market-orientation."

Unless there is some degree of insulation from competitive and market pressures on the science organization, professional standards are likely to be lowered, if not entirely rejected. In industrial laboratories, firms with large research budgets and some modicum of protection from the market have an opportunity to offer their scientists more freedom and hence more opportunities for "pure" research.[7] If the market structure of a particular project is insecure and tenuous, the individual researcher faces a peculiar type of role conflict: duty as a scientist qua scientist and the demands of the market. Putting it differently, he is torn between organizational demands and his own professional demands. Hans Zinnser once described how the competitive milieu affects scientific performance in medical work:

It puts a premium upon quantitative productiveness, spectacular achievement and practical success, which will bring administartive applause, often because of its advertising value in institutional competition. These tendencies, to be fair, are in every university known to be resisted by the men who have the determining influence; but the psychology of the situation is too logical to be offset by individual idealism, the natural pressure too strong.[8]

The thesis presented here is that the Development program, because of its tenuous financing, is market-oriented while the Communications program is task-oriented. How was this difference in forces (market structure) reflected in the data?

THE PROBLEMS

One of the questions asked of all Hub researchers in the course of an interview was "What do you consider the three main problems of research at the Hub?" The 186 responses were then categorized in five classes: organizational, external, substantive, bureaucratic, and interpersonal. We are concerned here with the "external problems" category, which deals specifically with those issues concerned exclusively with "instability and uncertainty due to precarious relations with the sponsor of research." Almost 30 per cent of the total responses fell into this category. The Communications staff made the fewest responses in this category (four times) and when they did, barely mentioned the foundation. The following representative responses were made by the Development staff:

"I would take a job at X college in preference to the Hub based not on criteria of teaching over research but just that the Hub's future is not as certain as X college."

---

[7] W. Bennis, "Role Conflict and Market Structure" (Massachusetts Institute of Technology, 1953) (mimeographed).

[8] Cited in L. Wilson, *Academic Man* (Oxford University Press, 1942), pp. 206–7.

"One of the major problems here has been and continues to be the uncertainty of the budget. You have to know the scale of funds before you can plan. We got only a fraction of what we had planned for. Now we're looking for other funds, etc. We cannot recruit too well because we cannot make a firm offer. If we had a budget—a firm budget—we would have no personnel problems."

"The main problem here is doing research and justifying ourself to the foundation. The thing that's annoyed me the most is that we spend so much time looking at our navel without doing anything—except justifying our existence."

"The main problem is the uncertain environment. This is an uneasy life . . . tougher than a real university life . . . this time-uncertainty and shoestring operation. If I were given dough when I first came here—say so many thousand per annum, I may have hired not *better* people but people more akin to project needs."

"I have to spend up to 25 per cent of my time working on the foundation submission."

"The tightest pressure I've felt is the annual soul-searching with the foundation. I've been through it two years now and it wears me out."

"Ever since January, tension has been awful. Everyone has been watching, waiting, and, in general, usurping valuable time because of the terrible fear of not getting the contract renewed because of budget cuts. This takes a large part of group conversation."

"I'VE JUST RECEIVED WORD FROM THE FOUNDATION THAT . . ."

Few members of the Hub, according to responses to a cartoon,[9] were free of anxiety concerning relations with the foundation. In point of fact, of the eighteen cartoons used, the one dealing with foundation relations attracted the second highest responses, twenty-five completions. This particular cartoon depicted five men seated around a table, one of whom is shown saying, "I've just received word from the foundation that. . . ." Those interviewed were asked to complete the statement of the speaker by filling in the space above the speaker's head. In addition to the straight-line box extending over the speaker, there was a cloudlike "bubble" over another member's head. Subjects were also asked to supply a response in this space to the speaker's statement but to consider it an unspoken, private thought. Thus, with a device borrowed from the cartoonist, it was possible to derive public or "overt" responses as well as private or "covert" reactions. Of nineteen overt statements, seventeen dealt specifically with the question of grants. Moreover, Table 1

---

[9] These cartoons evolved out of the problem areas mentioned by Hub members in the initial interviews. The most prominent problems were reduced to simple sketches which allowed for "projections" by the subjects. The original impetus for the use of cartoons was made by H. A. Shepard, and June Moyer is responsible for the drawing.

TABLE I.   *Attitudes toward Foundation (N = 25)*

OVERT RESPONSE		COVERT RESPONSE	
Grant was awarded	8	Insecurity from uncertainty	13
Grant was cut	9	Hostile to foundation	3
Other	2	Personal insecurity stemming from	
	––	fragile situation	7
Total	19		––
		Total	23

shows that in their covert remarks thirteen subjects revealed anxiety about financing.

Again there was a clear distinction between responses from the Communications project and those from Development. Of the seven responses showing "severe" insecurity in the covert box, six were made by Development personnel. By "severe" we mean that the individual voiced serious personal problems as a result of foundation vagaries, such as: "My job will be lost" or "Whew! Another year accounted for. . . . At last." This is not to say that the Communications staff was unconcerned about the foundation. But, judging from their responses, they tended to react more *aggressively* to the foundation. At the same time they were less worried about *personal* insecurities and more concerned with having "to revise my work" or deleting research problems of great interest. In short, while the Development staff was anxious about the possible loss of a job, the Communications group was concerned with the research goals. Examples of cartoon responses are shown in Table 2.

In addition to the data presented here the effects of the situation upon project functioning were reflected in the Communications program in the following ways: (1) more perceived freedom and scope for the staff member; (2) less time spent in writing up research proposals and progress reports; (3) greater satisfaction with the work in progress.[10] Perhaps equally important was the impression gained that more frequent offhand, somewhat parenthetical allusions to the foundation were made by the Development program. Many of these remarks were humorous. It can be argued that they were a mechanism for dealing with tension. This argument is strengthened by the fact that there seemed to be an increase in these remarks as the time drew near for the foundation decision. The following are examples:

STAFF MEMBER (*pointing to foundation proposal which is nearing completion*): "There it is—about seven thousand dollars a page. . . . We have talked of matters serious—but of that—it is a matter of life and death."

(*Backing up intellectual point*): "All I'm saying is what our submission to the foundation says."

CHAIRMAN OF SEMINAR: "Well, that settles it!"

[10] These data were taken from the author's unpublished doctoral dissertation, "The Social Science Research Organization: A Study of the Institutional Practices and Values in Interdisciplinary Research" (Massachusetts Institute of Technology, Department of Economics and Social Science, 1955).

TABLE 2.　　*Overt and Covert Responses to Cartoon*

OVERT　　　　　　　　　　　　　　　　COVERT

Communications Program Responses

". . . they'll give us half the money we asked for."

"Oh God! Some jerks have no sense of the realities of life. We'll either have to get more money or revise our objectives completely."

". . . have cut our grant in half."

"There goes our non-economic research!"
"Here we go! Another 'revision.' "

Development Program Responses

"The Development grant will probably come up for action at the May meeting of the Board of Directors."

"How can you run a research outfit with all this uncertainty and delay? That foundation is all 'snafu'd' and unless they get straightened out they're not going to measure up to X or Y foundations—no matter how much money they have."

"We will not be given a final answer to our submission until mid-summer. By that it seems as if our request will be cut in part even if finally accepted."

"Planning research under foundation sponsorship is uncertain!"

"They are greatly pleased with our plans and will cut our request only ·by 75%."

"We still got away with murder! (Will I keep *my* job?)"

"They will continue the present subsidies through the coming year."

"I'm delighted. That means my own subsidization will continue unimpaired."

"We sent off the submission to the foundation and, after we totaled up what all the problems of development would cost, found that it would break the foundation, so we cut it down a little."

"Why are we studying X country? Well, the last time this came up we had to hunt around for a slip of paper. Unfortunately today I couldn't find that, so I have to give you my own ideas for it. Where is the submission?"

Usually one does not think of knowledge and research findings in terms of the pricing mechanism, but it does offer insight in understanding the difficulties of organized research. Because of methods of financing, the Development group was in a more "competitive" position than was the Communications group, which was protected from the market forces for at least four years. While the latter was aware of the foundation's importance, the Development personnel saw the foundation as a towering, overshadowing Jehovah. (One of the Development directors once substituted the name of the foundation in the phrase, "God willing!") Each year during the last two years, with growing intensity from January to May, the question asked by the Development personnel has been, "Will the funds come through?" More indirectly, "What does the foundation want from us?" Or "How can we make our research proposals so attractive that we can get funds other institutions won't get?"

Without stretching the analogy, there was a good deal of concern with a form of market activity, "product differentiation." This was evidenced when a project group from the Hub visited a neighboring research group financed by the same foundation and working on the same country. The latent function of this trip, it can be argued, was to look over the "competitor," to insure the marketing of a unique and more appealing product. The effects of the anxiety over uncertain economic returns were reflected in various ways. At times it took the form of advanced gamesmanship, that is, how to impress the foundation and still keep the research plans fluid. As one member put it: "They [the foundation] want a research proposal now, but, after all, our hypotheses will come only after six months or so." Indeed, one of the most important functions of the Hub director was to keep a balance between the pressures of exogenous influences (demands of the country under study, foundation, users of research) and the pressures made upon him by individual researchers to keep insulated from market demands.

Another effect of the uncertain environment was the attitude toward the foundation. In reality the foundation exerted no pressure on the substantive efforts of the Hub. However, social and objective realities in this case were not consonant. Thus various individuals felt that the foundation placed unbearable constraints on research proposals; that the main problem at the Hub, as one member quoted before said, "was doing research and having to justify ourself to the foundation."

We see here a tendency, not uncommon in an organized milieu, to project blame upward and away.[11] This tendency may be exacerbated in social research, where uncertainty and the unknown are daily companions, where physical and social comparisons are ambiguous, and where authority is not definite. Hence the foundation, much as in the other cases, the civil service or "bureaucracy," may be made the scapegoat.

---

[11] Paula Brown's study of a government laboratory indicates that people tend to attack and blame the far-off civil service and that there is a "reluctance to accept responsibility for making decisions easily rationalized." Thus the projection of blame upward ("Bureaucracy in a Government Laboratory," *Social Forces*, XXXII, No. 3 [March, 1954], 266). For a laboratory experiment showing somewhat similar social processes see L. Festinger, "A Theory of Social Comparison Processes," *Human Relations*, VII, No. 2 (May, 1954), 119.

Some Social Functions of Ignorance

WILBERT E. MOORE AND MELVIN M. TUMIN

Ignorance is commonly viewed today as the natural enemy of stability and orderly progress in social life. It is equally commonly believed, as a corollary, that any increase in knowledge automatically brings with it an increase in benefits to mankind. As a result education, as the formal technique of imparting this knowledge to the uninformed, has become elevated in many lay and professional circles to the status of a panacea for all of man's ills.

This enthusiasm for education, and for the "rational" approach which is considered its handmaiden, is found throughout the social sciences. That sociologists share this enthusiasm is indicated by the readiness with which, as applied scientists, they advocate such things as enhanced knowledge on the part of prospective marriage partners; improved lines of communication in industry; increased awareness of community and national affairs; greater knowledge about the "real" meaning of such terms as race and nationality; increased sensitivity to personal differences and the nuances of interpersonal relations; and therapeutic treatment of neuroses through giving the patient a knowledge of the sources of his anxieties.[1]

The rationalistic bias, which finds its way into many sociological writings of the last half century, may, however, be contrasted with several developments in social science that have served to diminish the importance ascribed to rational, scientific knowledge. Two of these may be singled out for special mention. The first has been the careful study and analysis of the functions of magic, ritual, and superstition in social organization. This culminates, perhaps, in the findings of Malinowski concerning the role of magic as a means for providing a subjective and socially sanctioned security with regard to anxiety-producing features of the physical and social environment.[2]

SOURCE: Wilbert E. Moore and Melvin M. Tumin, "Some Social Functions of Ignorance," *American Sociological Review*, vol. 14 (December, 1949), pp. 787-95. Reprinted by permission.

AUTHORS' NOTE: The authors wish to express their thanks to Harry C. Bredemeier, Don J. Hager, Paul K. Hatt, and Marion J. Levy, Jr., and to students in a graduate theory seminar, who have aided by criticism of preliminary drafts of this paper.

[1] It should not be overlooked here that there is an essential ambivalence concerning the role of knowledge. For, despite the institutionally sanctioned emphasis on education and on "facing the facts," there is considerable "folk" acceptance of the contrary idea that "where ignorance is bliss, it is folly to be wise," or, in a more popular formulation, "what I don't know can't hurt me."

[2] See especially Bronislaw Malinowski, "Culture," in *Encyclopaedia of the Social Sciences*, 4:621–645; Malinowski, "Magic, Science and Religion," in Joseph Needham, ed., *Science, Religion and Reality*, New York: The Macmillan Co., 1925, pp. 19–84. The latter paper has been reprinted in the volume of Malinowski's essays, *Magic Science, and Religion* (Boston: Beacon Press; Glencoe, Ill.: Free Press, 1948).

The second development has been the distinction between irrational and nonrational orientations, and the recognition of the high importance in society of ultimate values and attitudes toward them. This development is exemplified especially in the works of Pareto and Parsons.[3]

The first of these developments calls attention to a widespread type of social action that functions as a "satisfactory" alternative to complete knowledge and perfect control. And, since resort to magic is so generally distributed throughout human society, there is at least some doubt that it is likely to be eliminated by any predictable expansion of knowledge and technique.

The second development emphasizes the fact that empirical knowledge and ignorance do not in combination exhaust the socially significant orientations of the individual to his environment. It thus helps to distinguish clearly between ignorance, on the one hand, and ultimate, including superempirical, values, on the other.

Neither of these developments, however, has included an explicit examination of the role of ignorance as such. Both have served to narrow and redefine its relation to other types of orientations. But in both there is some implication that genuine ignorance, as distinct from knowledge on the one hand and nonrational beliefs and values on the other, is only a disturbing element in social action and relations, and is accordingly subject to successive constrictions in importance.

It is the central purpose of this paper to examine explicitly some of the contexts in which ignorance, rather than complete knowledge,[4] performs specifiable functions in social structure and action. Some of the observations that will be made have already been recognized in the literature. It is suggested, however, that their significance has ordinarily been missed, since they provide uncomfortable exceptions to the prevailing rationalistic emphasis in sociological writing.

The central theorem of this paper holds that, quite apart from the role of ultimate values and the attitudes relative to them, perfect knowledge is itself impossible, and an inherently impossible basis of social action and social relations. Put conversely, ignorance is both inescapable and an intrinsic element in social organization generally, although there are marked differences in the specific forms, degrees, and functions of ignorance in known social organizations.

The following attempt to classify the sociological functions of ignorance is necessarily rudimentary and primitive. There is unquestionably some, and

---

[3] See Vilfredo Pareto, *The Mind and Society* (New York: Harcourt, Brace and Co., 1935, 4 vols.); Talcott Parsons, *The Structure of Social Action* (New York: McGraw-Hill Book Co., 1937).

[4] Ignorance is to be taken here as simply referring to "not knowing," that is, the absence of empirically valid knowledge. "Perfect knowledge" is considered as the totality of all knowledge ideally available to man in general, and not simply that which is believed available within any context of social action. Ignorance may refer to past, present, or future conditions or events, as long as valid knowledge is conceivably available. For the purposes of this paper, ignorance is to be kept distinct from "error," whether of fact or of logic, and from the act of *ignoring* what is known.

perhaps considerable, overlapping among the various categories. It is to be hoped that the greatest portion of this overlapping is due to the fact that attention will be focussed on primary functions in specific action contexts, ignoring, for purposes of classification, the secondary and derivative functions. It is also possible that further investigation and analysis would reduce the variety of specific functions to more general principles.

THE STRUCTURAL FUNCTIONS OF IGNORANCE

1. *As Preservative of Privileged Position*

The function of ignorance that is most obvious, particularly to the cynical, is its role in preserving social differentials. However, a purely cynical view is likely to overlook the extent to which the continuity of any social structure depends upon differential access to knowledge in general, and, *a fortiori,* to specialized knowledge of various kinds. In many instances, of course, the counterpart of ignorance on the part of the outsider is *secrecy* on the part of the possessor of knowledge. Some of the outstanding examples of this general function of ignorance are summarized in the following paragraphs.

a. THE SPECIALIST AND THE CONSUMER. Ignorance on the part of a consumer of specialized services (for example, medical or legal advice) helps to preserve the privileged position of a specialized dispenser of these services. This is in some measure a byproduct of the division of labor, and theoretically the same persons may occupy super-ordinate or subordinate positions as one or another service or skill is demanded. However, there are both theoretical and empirical bases for concluding that some persons whose skills are both scarce and functionally important will occupy a generalized superior status.[5] Although that status is not solely the product of the ignorance of others, in concrete instances it is partially maintained by such ignorance.

One evidence of the function of ignorance as a preservative of privileged position lies in the situation where the consumer acquires, through continuous exposure to the services of the specialist, a sense of his own ability to deal with his problems, and thus to dispense with the services of the specialist (e.g., where we learn how to treat common colds, simple fevers, and bruises, and where we learn how to send stern notes concerning contractual obligations). Thus the range of situations in which the special services are believed to be required is altered from the original position.

On the other hand, the specialist commonly develops devices to protect himself against this sort of attrition. A common device is that of specialized and possibly esoteric vocabulary, or the use of instruments and techniques not intrinsically required for the solution but seemingly so.[6] However, the

---

[5] Kingsley Davis and Wilbert E. Moore, "Some Principles of Stratification," *American Sociological Review*, 10: 242–249, April, 1945.

[6] Indeed, in the field of medicine and psychiatry it is not necessary that the alleged technique or treatment be the empirically valid means; health may be restored as a

central point remains that real or presumed differential knowledge and skills are inherently necessary to maintain mutually satisfactory relationships between specialist and consumer.

b. THE SPECIALIST AND THE POTENTIAL COMPETI- TOR . Another facet to the preservation of the privileged position of the specialist is perhaps worthy of special mention. It was noted in the preceding paragraphs that the specialist's position may be endangered by "the patient becoming his own physician." A related danger is that the privileged position of the specialist will be so attractive that too many competitors will appear in the market. This is simply another, and more common, way of saying that ignorance operates to protect the specialist from potential competitors. Per- haps the commonest devices for guarding against this danger are "trade secrets" and their protection through the control by the specialists themselves of training and thus of access to the privileged positions. Examples in con- temporary society are to be found in the limited access to certain professions and in the restriction of apprenticeship on the part of various craft unions. Although often justified as a means for protecting technical standards, these restrictions appear also to preserve a sharp distinction between the knowl- edge of specialists and the ignorance of aspirants. For the society as a whole the result may be a restriction in essential services, either directly through limitation of the number of specialists or indirectly through increasing costs so that other goods or services must be sacrificed by the consumer.

c. ROLE DIFFERENTIATION AND THE MAINTENANCE OF POWER . In any society internal social order is in part maintained by allocating statuses and differentiating roles along lines of age, sex, and gen- eration. These differentials serve as hooks on which differences in life- chances are hung, and the result is that differentials in knowledge also fall along these lines. In non-literate societies, this tends to result in a monopoly of skills on the part of the elders and the consequent monopoly of power in their hands. It also results in sexual division of special skills, providing females with sources of power that their physique would not otherwise give them, and providing males with a source of power that acts as a balance to the power inherent in the female's control of sexual access.

The universal diffusion of age-respect as an organizing principle of social relations in primitive societies is functionally dependent upon and com- patible with differential distribution of skills and knowledge along age lines. Since most primitive societies surround these differentials with traditional

---

result of the fact of treatment rather than of the specific content. It is not even neces- sary for the specialist to know the source of his success. The important point is that the consumer must rely upon the superior knowledge of the specialist, whether or not that knowledge is genuine or even understood. For example, it is common among psychoanalysts to operate on the assumption that neuroses may be treated by digging out the sublimated facts, and facing up to them squarely. It seems quite probable that therapeutic success, in at least some cases, may depend upon the ritual efficacy of treatment and not upon complete knowledge; indeed there are factually and rationally impossible situations to which this is the only effective solution.

sanctions, and since knowledge of alternatives is highly limited, the situation is essentially stable.

The contrasting case in Western civilization serves further to document these contentions. In Western society there is an observable attrition in parental control over children and an equalization of power as between the sexes, in part because of the accessibility of extra-familial sources of knowledge and skill. Where the young can learn skills independently of the instruction of their parents, and where females have an increasing access to economic independence, there tends to be a marked attenuation of the power based on the former parental and male monopolies of knowledge and skills. It should be noted, however, that the extra-familial access to knowledge and skills (and the power derived therefrom) is by no means unlimited. Censorship, whether by State or Church, is one obvious form of limiting access to knowledge as a means of preserving power structures.

d. AVOIDANCE OF JEALOUSY OVER UNEQUAL RE-WARDS. Ignorance operates to maintain smooth social relations by preventing jealousy and internal dissension where differential rewards to approximate status equals are not based on uniformly known and accepted criteria. It is a common administrative rule of formal organizations that salaries are confidential. The efficacy of this rule may rest upon the existence of special treatment and individual agreements, which, if known, would give rise to intramural bickering. It may also rest upon the lack of absolutely objective criteria of performance, so that the person not equally rewarded may claim as bias what is in fact a difference of judgment. Whether the confidential differentials are based on favoritism, meeting outside offers, or some commonly acceptable criteria that are debatable in their application, ignorance of the differentials serves a positive function where either the public statement of the criteria or their open application to particular cases would create difficulties.

This principle also applies outside of formal organizations. Even invitations to dinner or other "social" events are commonly confidential if the criteria of inclusion and exclusion are not both self-evident and defensible. Within the family, younger children, who are likely to regard themselves as the equals of their older brothers and sisters, may be kept in ignorance of the privileges of the latter as a device less fraught with potential conflict than the principle of age differentials.

e. SECRECY AND SECURITY. As a general principle, ignorance serves to maintain the security of the individual or of the social system as a whole wherever knowledge would aid an actual or potential enemy. This principle is commonly understood, although in somewhat different terms, with reference to national security. However, the principle operates in other contexts also. The success of a military or law-enforcement undertaking, and the security of its participants, may depend upon the element of *surprise*. Indeed, any power structure may depend in part upon ignorance not only of its specific activities, but also of its basic intentions. Even the security of the individual may depend upon ignorance by others of personal attributes or past experiences that have no intrinsic bearing on his present status but which would be regarded unfavorably if known: for example, the technical Negro who is passing for white, the reformed exconvict, the person below or above the required age for his position, the illegitimate child subsequently adopted.

2. As Reinforcement of Traditional Values

a. ISOLATION AND TRADITIONALISM. Traditional behavior depends in part upon ignorance of alternatives. The classical case of ignorance reinforcing traditional behavior is the significance of isolation from new stimuli in the maintenance of the round of customary practices in primitive and peasant societies. It is likely, however, that isolation alone does not account for the failure to explore alternatives; having achieved some kind of working equilibrium, such a system is not likely to foster inquiry. There is no "good" reason why it should do so, and ample reason, in terms of continued stability, why it should not. However, no social system is without internal strains and dissident elements; it is here especially that ignorance of alternatives helps preserve the existing order of things. It is also possible that knowledge and acceptance of alternatives would result in a more stable set of relations.

The same generic phenomenon is found in any society in the isolation of the individual from new ideas. Where the individual's notions of right and wrong are rigidified, susceptibility to new knowledge and influences is minimized. The "conservative" is a short-hand term for this phenomenon. As this equilibrium may also have its weak points, ignorance may be necessary to preserve whatever balance has been achieved.

b. IGNORANCE OF NORMATIVE VIOLATIONS. Another way in which ignorance serves to protect the traditional normative structure is through reinforcing the assumption that deviation from the rules is statistically insignificant. This is especially crucial in those situations where there is a strong tendency to deviate which is repressed but which would be expressed if it were known that deviation was statistically popular rather than limited. This is perhaps particularly true of sexual conduct,[7] but may occur with respect to any system of norms that is subject to considerable pressure or internal strain. In a sense, therefore, the normative system as such may suffer more from knowledge of violations than from the violations themselves.[8]

---

[7] It is not unlikely that one by-product of the public reaction to the Kinsey report may be that the knowledge of the widespread practice of some hitherto tabooed sexual acts will materially stimulate further participation with less guilt in these acts. This in turn raises questions as to the implications of such knowledge of the divergence of ideal and actual behavior for the socialization of future generations.

[8] On the other hand, knowledge of violations of strongly-supported norms may lead precisely to a reassertion of convictions that might otherwise suffer the attritional effect

A similar conclusion may derive from a somewhat different functional context. There is the possibility that various activities are contrary to particular normative prescriptions, yet perform a function in the maintenance of the approved structure as a whole. Ignorance of violations would thus serve to prevent outraged suppression of these functionally significant practices, of which perhaps the most common examples are prostitution and gambling.[9]

C. REINFORCEMENT OF GROUP MANDATES. Ignorance also serves to reinforce ultimate values and heighten the sense of community through induction of subservience of individual to group interests. This is made possible in part by active or passive barriers to knowledge of the consequences of following individual as against group mandates. All socialization processes in all human societies operate to reduce curiosity and knowledge about the presumed socially dysfunctional alternative of pursuing individual tendencies. These processes act so effectively in most cases that the matter rarely appears as a matter of choice, much less as a conflict. All social groups thus require some quotient of ignorance to preserve "esprit de corps."

3. *As Preservative of Fair Competition*

Most competitive systems, whether in economic production and exchange or in games of chance and skill, assume not only a uniform range of knowledge and rational skill but also an explicit or implicit ignorance. Thus the idea of the "free competitive market" assumes equal initial access on the part of all concerned, and an impersonal limitation on advantage of all participants. In such a situation, differential access to knowledge gives inequitable advantages and destroys the freedom and fairness of competition. Similarly, the rationale of an open-class system of stratification assumes equality of opportunity, which includes as a major element equal access to knowledge and technical training requisite for class mobility. The normative justification of the system is thus endangered by notable inequalities of access to knowledge, *unless there is an effective range of ignorance about this also.*

There is, however, in the impersonal market system a more fundamental role of ignorance, rather than of equally limited knowledge that might in principle be extended to equally perfect knowledge. To keep the system genuinely and impersonally competitive, each competitor must *not* know all the policies and decisions of his competitors. Such knowledge would unavoidably destroy the bases of competition either through the creation of

---

of indifference. This is the famous principle elaborated by Emile Durkheim. See his *On the Division of Labor in Society*, trans. by George Simpson (New York: The Macmillan Co., 1933), pp. 80–105. This possibility does not remove the significance of ignorance as a component of various situations, but does emphasize the importance of other conditions.

[9] See Kingsley Davis, "The Sociology of Prostitution," *American Sociological Review*, 2: 744–755, October, 1937. The functional role of gambling is well analyzed in a forthcoming study by Edward C. Devereux, Jr.

overwhelming power combinations or, in other circumstances, making the outcome so certain that no further action would be required.[10] Indeed, the inability to predict results, whether from simply inadequate or from structurally barred knowledge, is a prerequisite to many situations of competition and conflict. Illustrations of this principle range all the way from poker games and athletic events to armed warfare.

4. As Preservative of Stereotypes

Viewed from the standpoint of the individual actor, all social behavior is directed toward stereotypes of other social units, representing greater or lesser degrees of abstraction or misconception of the precise and complete characteristics of the other units. So-called primary and informal groups tend to reduce the role of stereotypes to a minimum by great emphasis on wide ranges of personal knowledge and involvement, whereas formally structured relations in their nature emphasize the stringently limited role of the actor. Even in the former case, however, ignorance of the *full* range of individual characteristics and motivations is not only factually present, but also intrinsically necessary. The most intimate of friends are happily ignorant of some of each other's habits and thoughts. In fact, an important element of socialization involves acquisition of the habit of appearing to conform to the expected stereotypes demanded in standard situations.

a. BUREAUCRATIC ORGANIZATION. The general principles discussed in the preceding paragraph have a special relevance in formal bureaucratic structures, which by their nature depend narrowly and precisely defined roles and, therefore, personalities. The nature of the established relations among individuals in such organizations is such as to foster ignorance of "irrelevant" personal characteristics, and indeed to require such ignorance whenever knowledge would impair impersonal fulfillment of duties. The rules that define authority and function are such as to make possible the cooperative interdependence of actual or potential personal enemies, just as in the military services the subordinate is required to "salute the uniform and not the man." Similarly, in state-entertaining a strict protocol makes it unnecessary and probably inadvisable to inquire into the personal merits of attending officials.

It is also well known, of course, that in strictly bureaucratic organizations, where membership constitutes an occupation and frequent face-to-face con-

---

[10] Although not formulated exactly in this way, this point emerges from the application of the theory of games to economic behavior in John von Neumann and Oskar Morgenstern, *Theory of Games and Economic Behavior*, 2nd ed. (Princeton: Princeton University Press, 1947). See also Morgenstern, "The Theory of Games," *Scientific American*, 180 (5): 22–25, May 1949. The function of ignorance in the market is explicitly treated in Morgenstern, "Perfect Foresight and Economic Equilibrium," a mimeographed translation of "Vollkommene Voraussicht und wirtschaftliches Gleichgewicht," *Zeitschrift für Nationalökonomie*, 6: 337–357, August, 1935.

tact is the rule, the expected ignorance is subject to attrition by greater familiarity and the establishment of "informal" procedures and relations. These are likely to be based upon characteristics and attitudes irrelevant and possibly inimical to the formal expectations, although they may be more effective components of the operating organization than are the official and limited expectations. The continuity of the organization thus depends upon an effective balance between the ignorance required for orderly procedure and the knowledge acquired by participants.

b. ETHNIC AND CLASS STEREOTYPES. Among the more commonly recognized stereotypes that at least partially thrive on ignorance, are those relating to ethnic groups and other minorities that may be the object of scapegoat reactions. It is true that "education in the facts" often does little to remove the prejudice that supports, and the discrimination that expresses, the stereotype. It may nevertheless be asserted that knowledge that the facts do not support one's stereotype may significantly affect the quantity and quality of intensity with which these stereotypes are held and acted upon. Maintenance of the stereotype in the face of superior knowledge then at least involves the cost and strain of additional rationalization.[11]

The element of ignorance in stereotypical behavior is also illustrated in reference to class. It appears that the notion of "typical class behavior" is a most significant basis of social action precisely at those points where there is least knowledge of the actual heterogeneity internal to "classes." This may be stated in a more general way. The idea that there are characteristics and attributes common to a social class is likely to be most firmly believed precisely by those farthest removed, in the class structure, from the class in question. In a highly complex open-class system, most relationships between status unequals take place not in the general context of inter-class relations, but in specific contexts of bureaucratic superior and inferior, landlord and tenant, professional and client. Many of these relationships may specifically rule out questions of general inequality (as in market relations), and in others the ranks of the actors may vary with the context of the action. It is only where the specific attributes of individuals and the specific contexts of action are unknown, ignored, or irrelevant that the more general category of class is likely to have any significance. Yet for certain limited purposes social action may be structured along class lines as long as the stereotype with its component of ignorance is maintained.

5. *As Incentive Appropriate to the System*

a. ANXIETY AND WORK. There are a variety of situations in which ignorance of present rating or future chances is used as a device to create

---

[11] Where the affective component of the stereotype is weaker, knowledge may serve to reduce the effectiveness of the stereotype or actually remove it as one of the action premises of the individual. In this connection, see the interesting study by Gordon Allport and Bernard M. Kramer, "Some Roots of Prejudice," *Journal of Psychology*, 22: 9–39, July, 1946.

anxieties and spur activity in a competitive system. Thus, in a bureaucratic organization rules are ordinarily thought of as giving predictability. However, they may be so constructed and applied as they relate to persons in the lower strata that prediction is difficult and the worker is expected to be motivated by his insecurity.[12] With slight modification, the principle would appear to fit the situation of students, but more especially of their teachers. Indeed, to the extent that risk, uncertainty, and insecurity have ignorance as a common component and anxiety as a common incentive, the principle is a general feature of the rationale of competition.

It is easy to see that the principle, so generalized, has a point of diminishing or negative returns, varying with the circumstances. There is unquestionably an attrition of motive when anxiety is prolonged, owing to the way anxiety typically produces personal disorganization and is thus disruptive of the organization required for efficient performance.[13]

b. THE ALEATORY PRINCIPLE. Ignorance also operates as an incentive in a quite different context from that just discussed. Here attention is directed to the role of "new experience" in human life, where the attractiveness of the new experience depends in part upon the uncertainty of the outcome. Certainly the attractiveness of many games of chance, as well as of those games and sports where chance may equalize or offset known differences in skill and performance, rests in large measure on their unpredictable outcome. In fact, there is some rough evidence that ignorance of the future in recreational activities assumes an especially significant role where routine (read: perfect predictability) and boredom are characteristic of work assignments and where there is a sharp break between working time and leisure time.

THE INTERPLAY OF IGNORANCE AND KNOWLEDGE

Knowledge and ignorance may for some purposes be viewed as polar antipodes on a continuum. Seen this way, there is an objective relationship between them that is at least analytically independent of any actor's definition of the situation.[14] That relationship may be described in the following terms: For every increase in what is known about a given phenomenon there is a corresponding decrease in what is unknown. In any actual situation of social action, however, this analytical relationship between the known and

---

[12] See Alvin W. Gouldner, "Discussion" of Wilbert E. Moore, "Industrial Sociology: Status and Prospects," *American Sociological Review*, 13: 382–400, August, 1948, at p. 398.

[13] See Allison Davis, "The Motivation of the Underprivileged Worker," in Willian F. Whyte, ed., *Industry and Society* (New York: McGraw-Hill Book Co., 1946), pp. 84–106.

[14] This continuous distribution of knowledge and ignorance makes many of the observations in this paper reversibly viewable as functions of limited knowledge rather than of ignorance.

the unknown is conditioned by the fact that social actors always know at least somewhat less than the totality of what is theoretically knowable. At least in some contexts, therefore, recognition of ignorance by the actor is prerequisite to the acquisition of knowledge, and may itself be regarded as a gain in knowledge.

Where there is a felt need, by an individual or group, for a solution to a problem, ignorance can operate as a factor dynamic to social change. There is, of course, no intrinsic directionality in ignorance or its recognition which determines that empirically valid rather than invalid solutions will result. But each of these alternative possibilities has differential consequences for the later interplay of ignorance and knowledge. For, by and large, those "solutions" which are psychologically reassuring but empirically invalid or superempirical may simply postpone the crisis or problem situation. And since in doing so they may distract attention from and possibly hide the source of the problem, it can also be said that they tend tacitly to institutionalize those crises or problems where psychological reassurance is not by itself sufficient.

On the other hand, it may also be said that while empirically valid solutions do eliminate the specific problems to which they are relevant, they by no means reduce the inherently problematic character of social life and are not therefore more *generally* final in the reassurance they provide. For, there is *no* exception to the rule that every time a culture works out an empirically valid answer to a problem, it thereby generates a host of derivative problems, if only in terms of the social reorganization required to incorporate the new solution.[15] In one sense, then, the difference reduces to one where the maintenance of ignorance institutionalizes old problems and the acquisition of knowledge makes continuous the introduction of new problems. The dynamic role of ignorance in social change is thus played in the recognition of its existence and the subsequent formulation of answers, whether empirically valid or not.

SUMMARY NOTE

Ignorance is not a simple analytical element, but rather a more or less hidden component of situations usually discussed in other terms. It follows that the categories of function treated here are not entirely homogeneous. Thus, in some instances such as market competition ignorance may be viewed as an element or condition within a circumscribed system. In other instances such as the maintenance of national security, ignorance may be a necessary

---

[15] See Robert K. Merton, "The Unanticipated Consequences of Purposive Social Action," *American Sociological Review*, 1: 894–904, December, 1936. This holds as well in the structure of scientific theory as it does in the structure of social relations. For an expansion of this notion see Merton, "The Bearing of Empirical Research upon the Development of Social Theory," *American Sociological Review*, 13: 505–515, October, 1948.

condition for outsiders. In all these instances, however, the problem is one of shifting perspective, since maintenance of position or the existing relationships may be viewed within a narrower or broader frame of reference.

Functional analysis must distinguish elements necessary for *any* social structure and those necessary within particular, given configurations. If a single society is taken as the unit of reference, then it may be necessary to distinguish the whole and the part. Known societies are not so neatly intermeshed as to assure that a particular function of ignorance within a segment of society (for example, the privileged position of the specialist with regard to potential competitors) is favorable to other segments, or to the society as a whole.

If the foregoing observations are sound, it follows that ignorance must be viewed not simply as a passive or dysfunctional condition, but as an active and often positive element in operating structures and relations.

What Do Americans Think?

BERNARD ROSENBERG

Samuel Stouffer's *Communism, Conformity and Civil Liberties* is an extraordinarily revealing book.[1] It tells us a great deal, perhaps more than was intended, about plain and fancy Americans at midcentury. Stouffer has crammed his report with data scrupulously gathered and cross-checked by the trained personnel of two large polling organizations. The methodology is impressive and so are the findings which have been presented in clear tabular form. That these findings might distress some of his readers occurred to the author; it would depend, he said, on the color of their spectacles. Since his own are of a rosy hue, what we frequently get is a grim fact followed by a chirpy interpretation. This can be rather trying, and in the end, exasperating.

The most provocative question asked in this survey is: What kinds of things do you worry about most? It was addressed to a national cross-section of Americans in 1954 just when the Army-McCarthy imbroglio seemed to monopolize their attention (although a significant number of them, nearly one third, were unable to *name* Senator McCarthy.) These are tense times. This is the Age of Anxiety. The alphabetical bombs may be dropped. Even a people who scorn the worrier have a right to wrinkle their brows. And

---

SOURCE: Bernard Rosenberg, "What Do Americans Think?" *Jewish Frontier*, 22:7 (July, 1955), pp. 6–10. Reprinted by permission.

[1] Samuel A. Stouffer, *Communism, Conformity and Civil Liberties* (New York: Doubleday, 1955).

they are worried, but "even by the most generous interpretation of occasionally ambiguous responses," less than 1% are worried about civil liberties. World problems, including the danger of war, did not evoke a spontaneous answer from more than 8% of them. In *Look Magazine,* where Stouffer gave the public a foretaste of these facts, he suggested that they were not signs of indifference. The American can be very concerned about baseball, but he does not lie awake nights worrying about it. The same goes for peace and freedom. Stouffer wishes us to understand that we are not jittery. A great calm lies upon the land.

The American people are not unduly perturbed about domestic communism; they merely want to suppress it. The idea of freedom for Communists, atheists, or Socialists is obnoxious to most of those whose desire for civil liberty is no greater than their interest in it. 13% say they personally feel less free to speak their minds than in the past, but of these only five percent are much put out about that loss. In this materialist-secular society, 60% of the public favor removal from their libraries of books against religion, and 84% would not allow the nonreligious to teach in a college or university. As of 1953, 45% would deny Socialists the right to publish, and those who would forbid newspapers to criticize our form of government stood at 42%. Moreover, there has been a steady upward curve of political intolerance in the past ten years. *Nothing* bothers us, least of all the loss of our freedom.

Says one respondent, "I don't worry about world problems. When trouble gets here I can take it. I'm paying taxes for someone to do my worrying for me." Another, "I don't worry about things like politics, because we have people who are paid to do that kind of worrying." Still another, "I worry about my health. Other worries I leave to Papa. He's got the brains in the house." Which should comfort Papa who probably leaves it to his Papa in the White House, especially if the subject is how to handle Communists. This procedure can be undertaken with confidence since of those who said they looked for counsel to the President, only 19% claimed to know well what Eisenhower's viewpoint is.

Not everyone is entirely carefree. In the land of plenty one finds a disturbing preoccupation with money matters. Many Americans find that they have health problems. (Only 10% assert that they have absolutely no problems.) Whatever their general optimism, Stouffer finds that oldsters take a dimmer view of the future than youngsters. High medical bills have apparently soured the aged and brought them to ruminate now and then on the mortality of man. Stouffer correlates the relative gloom of old people with their indisposition to tolerate political dissent. They also have less education than the young whose threshold of tolerance is somewhat higher.

A percentage distribution favorable to those with most schooling e.g., college graduates, as less anti-libertarian than high school graduates, makes Stouffer exceedingly hopeful. After all, the United States, with its birthrate going up, has a great many young people, and more of them will be going to school than ever before. Formal schooling has been on the increase for some time, surely to an unparalleled degree in the past ten years, and our civil liberties have undergone concomitant shrinkage over that period. In the thirties, there were far fewer "educated" people, but many more who would abide nonconformist neighbors. If education were the decisive variable, we should have had very little tolerance in the past and a great deal now. Also, it ought to be noted that, although more babies are being born in the fifties than in the thirties, life expectancy keeps going up at the same time. This means we have an aging population whose pressure has been great enough to wring at least one small Social Security concession from a President not yet inclined to meet the needs of children. And persons in their sixties, seventies, and eighties, who do not look to the future as cheerfully as they should, are more intolerant than their offspring. One factor would seem to balance the other. Stouffer points out that there is no way of telling whether the present generation will turn out differently in its old age. Still, the kids *are* better educated. They have been coerced first by the state and then by the drive for success into attending more classes for a longer time than their parents. This might make them better democrats. Stouffer believes that it will. He would be entitled to his opinion except for collateral evidence cited in his own study.

Polling data show that while the better educated are more tolerant than the less educated, *both* classes of the population have tended to become less tolerant in recent years. For example, the proportion of college-educated people who would deny freedom of speech to a Communist increased from 31% to 71% between 1945 and 1953, while the corresponding proportions among less educated people increased from 42% to 78% (*which is pretty close to equivalence. B. R.*)

Can it really be said that ". . . higher education makes for greater tolerance of human differences, whether ideological, racial or cultural," as Stouffer supposes? Does higher education inevitably produce optimists? If so, what kind of higher education can it be? One's guess is that if the intellectuals were polled separately, they would turn out to be the most saturnine group in America, and the one most devoted to freedom. Stouffer points out that lack of optimism is related to prejudice. The proof supporting this proposition is very weak indeed. He admits it is now considered too simple to postulate fear of the future, frustration and personal anxiety as the cause of hostility toward out-groups, but lends some credence to the theory as a partial explanation. Since J. M. Gillespie and Gordon Allport have found that American youth express a more optimistic outlook on the future than do the youth of other nations, they should be a bit less prejudiced than their opposite numbers abroad. Neither in ethnic nor in political relations does this seem to be so. However, if optimism led to tolerance, it would certainly be fortunate that so few citizens are exercised about the threat of war, for if they were, the people might become anxious, frustrated, pessimistic, Un-American, and possibly conscious as well.

There is a basic fallacy that may have skewed the analysis of these results in a peculiar direction, namely, that political intolerance is comparable to or identical with ethnic intolerance. Stouffer frequently speculates about the connection, and occasionally takes it for granted. Nevertheless, "On specific questions relating to free speech for Socialists and Communists, (according to a National Opinion Research Center study, 1953) the South was not consistently different from the North." Certainly the South is more racist than the North, but it is not more politically restrictive. On Stouffer's scale, the Far West is more tolerant than any other region. Still, in states like California, Arizona, and New Mexico ethnic discrimination directed at Orientals, Indians, Spanish-Americans, Mexicans, Filipino-Americans, Okies, Arkies, and Negroes has flourished much more than in other parts of the United States.

In a massive study of ethnic prejudice, Adorno and his co-workers contended that intolerant people have a common or similar "authoritarian" character structure which predisposes them to hate minority groups. Whatever limited validity this thesis may have with reference to one phenomenon, it obviously does not apply to all others. Earlier inquiries have indicated that women are slightly more tolerant of Jews and Negroes than men. This study shows conclusively that at all educational levels and in every region women are less tolerant of political deviation than men. It should follow, if the psychic factor is relevant, that females are more authoritarian than males. The interviewers tested for this possibility by asking such questions as, "If a child is unusual in any way, his parents should get him to be more like other children. Do you agree or disagree?" Women *agree* less often than men. They evidently want to be permissive with their children and repressive with the rest of us. A shock-proof consciousness is necessary not to be appalled by this situation. Women as mothers, public-school teachers, and Sunday school teachers, do enormously more than their spouses to shape and disfigure American society. The instruments of socialization have long been feminized. It would require a maximum of adolescent rebellion—which, when there is any nowadays more often takes criminal than political form—to shake off these anti-democratic values.

America is in the midst of a church-going, if not a religious, revival. Here as elsewhere, women are in the vanguard. They not only attend services more regularly than men, but are gradually taking over sacerdotal functions. Feminism is beginning to triumph in the pulpit. Several leaders of Reform Judaism have suggested that their movement emulate the liberal Protestant sects which have granted ladies of the cloth a position equal to that of clergymen. It is therefore not too surprising that church-goers should be less tolerant than non-church-goers.

"Dangerous" ideas, which can be much more freely aired in the metropolis, are least tolerable to the residents of small towns. Fine. The rural exodus has been going on for a century and continues unabated. When Stouffer looks at a narrow sector like this, he forgets the total picture, and allows himself to cheer too soon. Americans have been getting more citified, but less tolerant for some time. Similarly, Stouffer finds that one reason for the educated person's greater hospitality to strange notions is that "Schooling puts a person in touch with people whose ideas and values are different from one's own. And this tends to carry on, after formal schooling is finished, through reading and personal contacts." Dr. Gallup will soon publish his material on the reading habits of college graduates. Unhappily, they do not confirm Stouffer's vision of the "educated" man as reader. Contacts he has. So do most city dwellers who rub shoulders with a variety of people. Does the mixture make for greater tolerance at the market place of ideas, as Stouffer believes? Is the destruction of community life by a migratory people what it takes to maintain civil liberties? Then no one qualifies as superlatively as the American who moves about so much that, to outsiders, he seems like a victim of the St. Vitus dance. Tocqueville a hundred years ago in his treatise on this civilization, entitled a classic chapter, "Why Americans are So Restless in the Midst of Their Prosperity." They don't stand still for very long. Whether it gets them anywhere is debatable. Max Lerner has this to say about internal mobility in his forthcoming book:

A government study of migrant families in 1937 showed that in a great industrial center like Detroit, which draws constantly on new sources of labor, four out of five people had not lived in the same dwelling for five years. (*By 1943, the people of Detroit had rubbed shoulders long enough to precipitate a race riot as an expression of their new-found tolerance. B.R.*) While this is extreme, it was true before the housing shortage tightened changes of residence, between a fourth and a half of Americans in the big cities used to change their quarters from year to year. Inside the same state there had been a constant movement from farm to town, especially of the women; and from town to the big city, of the men as well. The crucial mobility however is out of state, and the census figures use residence in some state other than that of birth as the index of migration. In these terms there has been a rapid increase since 1890 of the proportion of native Americans living outside the state of their birth, with the current percentage somewhere around twenty-five percent.

It is not his rootedness that makes a political bigot of the average American nor *wanderlust* that renders the average "community leader" more flexible than his followers. Stouffer has ingeniously separated leaders from the led, and pins much of his abundant hope on the former. The following example is characteristic of a consistent pattern. Question: If some people in your community suggested that a book he (a Socialist) wrote favoring government ownership should be taken out of your public library, would you favor removing the book or not? Response:

	Favor	*No Opinion*	*Not Favor*
Leaders	18%	3%	79%
Cross-Section	35	13	52

Although other polls do not divide the population as Stouffer has, it is pertinent to cite certain trends they trace. In 1943 when leaders and opinion-makers like Luce, Hearst, Zanuck, and Willkie were praising Soviet Russia, two Americans out of five would have prohibited any Communist Party member from speaking on the radio. By 1948, Stouffer remarks, the proportion was up to 57%; by 1952 it had risen to 77%; and in a survey conducted by NORC in January, 1954, the figure was 81%. It is to be doubted that the public at large was very far removed from its leaders on an issue like this one.

As for politicians, two quotations in the sample itself should suffice. One is from the chairman of a Republican County Central Committee in New Jersey, "Well, I have to be careful because of my position. I have to be careful not to express liberal views which run counter to ideas which have been built up for the public." A New York State mayor says, "I'm in politics, and there's no point in saying something that can be attacked unless you must." Such statements have the ring of truth about them. There are two conceptions of democratic leadership, one more ideal than real, the other operative in most areas of American political and cultural life. According to the first, a leader formulates an opinion, presents it to his constituents, tries to persuade them that he is right, and failing that, suffers defeat at the polls or the box-office. What actually happens in most cases is quite different: the leader, candidate for office, movie producer, etc., does everything in his power to ascertain what people want, and then works furiously to supply it. His own personal proclivities, if he has any—and the nation does not abhor a vacuum in the White House or on Capitol Hill or in Radio City—are immaterial. All this is inherent in mass culture which has never before been so thoroughly exploited as by "Ike" Eisenhower, Dickie Nixon, Robert Montgomery, Charlie Wilson and all the other stars in our national galaxy. Indeed, the major impetus behind poll-taking, attitude and opinion testing is to serve just this purpose. *Vox populi vox dei.* Foster Furcolo and a score of Democratic office-seekers like him who probably detest McCarthyism could not afford to say so in 1954 when they were running for the Senate. If by now they are a trifle bolder, it is because McCarthy's fortunes have sunk, thanks very little to them.

In short, Stouffer's belief that community leaders will change a deplorable condition on their own initiative seems to be without warrant. One can only hope that they do not read this study which makes the inarticulate prejudice of Americans all too explicit. An able demagogue might find out how far behind *the peepul* he really is. Some years ago a writer on the trade magazine *Tide* reported his experience with the question, "Are you in favor of or opposed to incest?" As Robert Cobb Myers reports it, forty percent of the people had no opinion and 33.5% were in favor. Would it be madness to follow such "opinion"? It rests on a misunderstanding of the word, incest? Hardly more so than the comments recorded by Stouffer rest on a misunderstanding of the word, Communist. Eighty-one percent of the national cross-section said that American Communists constituted a danger at the present time. Of these approximately 8% defined the danger as sabotage, 8% as espionage, and 28% as subversion (conversion of other people and spreading ideas). The community leaders are even more apprehensive about ideas, 36% of them listing subversion as the primary danger. An Indiana housewife says, "They're creeping in in places and poisoning the minds of young people in education with things that are contrary to the Bible." A government official, District of Columbia, "I think some elements of Communist ideology have been sold to people in the newspaper field and they peddle it daily in their columns. So people in influential places have adopted some of those ideas, especially the idea the state should control the instruments of production." A lady from Massachusetts, "Communists get children into cellars, educating them in warfare, and training them to go into secret places." The professional insight of a physician from California, "They are poisoning the minds of our kids in school." A Texas clergyman, "They teach people against Christianity, ungodly things, and this is against our country. We believe in Christianity." A woman in Pennsylvania, "In different communities I've heard there are Communist school teachers and ministers. Young minds catch onto these things through their influence. Hitlerism proved that it's the youth of the country who can be instilled with these ideas." Finally we might mention this *bon mot* of a Michigan lawyer, "Communism and Socialism are the same thing and are being taught in this country."

Stouffer says that the idea of converting Americans to Communism, which recurs so often in these comments, may come as a surprise to those "who believe that the era of making any appreciable number of Communist converts in this country has long since passed." There never was such an era, and the unrealistic estimate of danger should surprise nobody familiar with public opinion in America. "In so far as the ideas so widely prevalent about *current* subversion of thought, especially of our youth, are exaggerated or untrue, a tremendous challenge is presented to leaders of American public opinion to correct the misapprehension." But Stouffer has already shown that the leaders suffer more from this misapprehension than the general public. Wherewith shall they correct?

Three percent of the cross-section said they knew a person who admitted he was a Communist, but another 10% said they knew somebody who acted suspiciously enough to make them think he was a Communist. What were some of the grounds for suspicion? "He was always talking about world peace . . . I saw a map of Russia on a wall in his home . . . I suspect it from his conversation and manner. He was well educated and had a high disregard for the mentality of others . . . Her activities in distributing literature about the United Nations . . . He wrote his thesis in college about Communism . . . He brought a lot of foreign-looking people into his house . . . A distant relative of mine. Is a scientist, an atheist, and down on everything." These are typical of only 10%, but their babblings are not pleasant even to Stouffer who, nevertheless, manages to exclaim, "Nobody could sit down and read through the filled out questionnaire in this study without coming to the conclusion that most of the seemingly intolerant people are good, wholesome Americans."

What we have here on the one hand, is a ringing vote of no-confidence in the American system by a cross-section of Americans, and on the other, a vote of total confidence, by Stouffer, in the American people. Many of them are drawing logical inferences from false premises because the information they get is false. Tell them the truth, give them the facts, and they will know. This Platonic doctrine of evil as illusory since there is only ignorance to be dispelled by knowledge, sits strangely on the modern empirical sociologist. It may have come, not from Greek philosophy, but from discredited, if well intentioned, efforts to educate people out of racial prejudice. Again, education as a panacea second to none, remains the cornerstone of good wholesome Americanism.

Marie Jahoda and Eunice Cooper, among others, have shown that attempts to banish racial intolerance by propaganda and education may boomerang so as to intensify the original feeling. Confront the anti-Semite with pro-tolerance literature, and he will often hate Jews more than ever. At the very least, prospects for enlightenment are slim indeed. One psychologist has put the matter succinctly by saying that facts don't change attitudes, but contrariwise, attitudes change facts. When Otto Klineberg wrote *Race Differences* twenty years ago, he set forth a systematic refutation of all racist absurdities, and recommended education to give them the permanent lie. Latterly, like most of his colleagues, he has given up this simple solution. These days, Klineberg likes to tell the following story as an illustrative anecdote: A psychotic is convinced that he is dead. The psychiatrist tries every device he can think of to dissuade his patient. Nothing works. At last the doctor asks, "Dead men don't bleed do they?" Patient says, "No." Thereupon the doctor pulls out a hypodermic needle, plunges it into the patient's arm, and blood begins to spurt. Says the patient, "I guess they do." The psychologist, Irene Pierce, who used to teach in a large Eastern university, tells of the bright Southern graduate student she used to have there. He had a blind-spot, his anti-Negro bias. So Professor Pierce gave him *Race Differences* to read. He took the book home and carefully absorbed its contents, afterwards remarking, "Well, what can you expect of a Jew?"

Besides formal education, Stouffer sees another pedagogical force operating on the side of greater tolerance. He gets rhapsodic about the phenomenal growth of mass communications. "In a single evening television carries the viewer on a magic carpet to all parts of the world." The magic carpet to oblivion where we are turned into a pulpy manipulable mass, is to be the vehicle of our political salvation! "Even if confidence in the FBI is quite high, we have evidence that there is room for improvement in that confidence." Let Walter Winchell have every TV channel, and the job will be done. But first, let us buy Samuel Stouffer a new pair of spectacles with which to view television and the American scene.

15. POLITICS:
PARTICIPATION AND
DEMOCRATIC
INSTITUTIONS

Political Apathy: Its Social Sources
and Subjective Meaning

DAVID RIESMAN AND NATHAN GLAZER

Among thoughtful people today there is increasing discussion of political apathy. The discussion of apathy—and its converse, the "responsibility of the citizen"—has overflowed the boundaries of traditional political science and become the concern of the sociologist, the psychiatrist, the social psychologist, and, recently, the atomic scientists. From Gosnell's studies of nonvoting to the recent interest in the "no-opinion vote" in public opinion polls, from *Middletown* to recent studies of participation in voluntary associations, we have become increasingly aware that many millions of Americans remain aggressively unattached to the political events and discourse of their locality, their nation, and the world; that millions of others pay only casual attention; and that millions more only observe the game of politics as they would a horse race. Yet during recent decades politics has become increasingly impor-

SOURCE: "Criteria for Political Apathy" by David Riesman and Nathan Glazer from *Studies in Leadership*, edited by Alvin W. Gouldner. Copyright 1950 by Harper & Row, Publishers, Incorporated. Reprinted by permission of the publishers.

AUTHORS' NOTE: The research project on character and political apathy in America of which this previously unpublished article is one outcome has been conducted by the senior author under the auspices of the Yale University Committee on National Policy. We are very much indebted to the Committee, and to the Carnegie Corporation which financed the work, for the opportunity to pursue these inquiries. This article has been read in an earlier version by a number of friends who made many helpful suggestions. We would like to express our appreciation particularly to Professors Reuel Denny and Herman Finer of the University of Chicago, and Dr. Henry M. Pachter of New York City, for their very careful and critical readings.

tant as a mode of conscious manipulation of the social environment; and complaints arise that people begin to flee from politics just when politics matters most for them.

It is not easy to separate from current complaints about political apathy those themes which represent old problems—for instance, traditional middle-class concern with lower-class indifference to politics—and those which may represent perceptions of new types or meanings of apathy. The division between an active leadership and a passive multitude, in almost all spheres of life, has been almost universally observed; many social theories assume it is inevitable, and some that it is desirable. *Yet such a generalization may obscure differences in the relative size of the passive multitude at different times; in the reasons for its passivity; in the intensity of its indifference; and in the subjective feelings which accompany the apathy.* It is our thesis that, while the proportion of the passive may not have increased in recent decades, and even declined (Bryce commented on the passivity of the American multitude, and there is some evidence that participation, as contrasted with spectator-ship, was low in the alleged heyday of the town meeting)—while, we say, the numbers of the apparently passive may not have increased, *we do believe that there have been far-reaching changes in the reasons for passivity and in the types of apathy that have resulted.* . . .

WHAT IS POLITICAL APATHY?

THE DEVELOPMENT OF INDICES FOR APATHY. While the preceding discussion is largely based on historical-philosophcial reflections, we turn now to an account of our search for the proper criteria or indices for apathy and involvement to be used in analyzing our own interview material—some 150 long interviews—as well as data gathered by public opinion researchers largely for purposes other than the study of character and apathy. We can ask people today, as we cannot ask the dead, what politics means to them—though we do not have to take what they say at face value—and we can try to see, by careful analysis of their fully recorded responses, what role politics plays in their psychic economy, at present, what role it plays in their group adjustment, and, within limits, what role it might play under changed social-psychological conditions.

Our investigation is only in its initial stage. We still do not fully grasp what apathy and involvement mean to people, let alone know how to detect these attitudes "operationally" in our interview material. Nevertheless, we feel that discussion of possible criteria may be advanced even by the report of inconclusive efforts.

Apathy in our usage refers to a fairly complex psychological orientation, closely related to historical developments both directly, through the impact of the changes we have touched on in the preceding section, and indirectly (by means of the character structures "created" or favored by a given historical setting). Faced with such complexity, the tendency in social science is to seek for a simple index or criterion which will stand for, or register, the complex phenomenon. Thus, industrial morale may be measured by absentee-ism, anomie by suicide rates, the success of propaganda by bond purchases. The most apparent index for apathy is also some simple behavioral one such as voting, participation in certain political activities, attention to media trans-mitting political information, and so on. These behavioral indices are the first type of criterion for political apathy we will consider. As we shall see, the use of this type of index raises very sharply the danger of losing sight of the complexities of the problem to which the index points.

POLITICAL ACTIVITY AS AN INDEX OF APATHY. Four difficulties arise in equating apathy with inactivity, and in equating involve-ment with activity. The first is that an index based on activity does not help us to distinguish cases in which that activity is carried on for apolitical pur-poses. The second is the possible class bias of observation: stamping certain things the middle class does, or does more easily, as "activity." The third is the possible bias in favor of the more temperamentally energetic: the index will be an inadequate measure of varying social-psychological meanings if it is affected by physiologically-grounded factors. The fourth difficulty in using some form of activity as an index lies in the human meaninglessness of activity as such, apart from purpose: we could not infer purpose, which gives changing meaning to the activity, from the index alone.

1. *Activity and apolitical uses.* While an apathy characterized by listless-ness and lethargy may have its roots in neurosis, as in the case of a person whose energies are occupied with internal conflicts, individual and social neurosis might also lead to frantic political activity, as an escape from the self—an activity which we would also tend to label as "apathetic" in view of its quality and its origins, its use of politics as a "phobic screen" for the play of irrational affects. If one of the hypotheses one wishes to consider is that such "apolitical" political activity is on the increase, or widespread, an em-phasis on formal political activities as the index to apathy will be of little use.

2. *Activity and social class.* We sought for an index which would not be simply representative of middle-class judgments as to the political style of the lower class; and while we thought it altogether likely that, in any scale, the middle class would on the whole rank as less apathetic than the lower class, we wished to reduce class-relative factors to a minimum.[1]

---

[1] While Gallup and other pollers occasionally ask questions such as "do you have a cold?" or "are you happy?" that are not class-typed, little has been done in public opinion research to develop and ask questions concerning politics in the widest sense that are not class-typed. To do this would require some knowledge of all political domains and interests in all social groups. How large this order is we can estimate from Kinsey's work. Sex is something we can be pretty sure exists in every human being, and its forms and meanings on the physical level to which Kinsey confined himself are not limitless. Yet the Indiana group found they had to learn the sex-lingo and sex-style of an enormous variety of people before they could ask questions which got home to their interviewees. Beyond that, they had to convince respondents that the interview was meaningful and that Kinsey and his coworkers understood what the respondents had to say. Kinsey, moreover, did not go beyond overt sex activity, whereas a question-naire on politics would have to encompass all the intangibles which even quite limited definitions of politics imply.

We did not need evidence from our interviews to establish the obvious fact that political activity today is a matter very largely of clique affiliation and class position. At an urban progressive school where we had a group of interviews made, virtually everybody sent telegrams to congressmen, circulated petitions, and campaigned both in the presidential election and in the off-years. But our interviews seemed to us to show that most of these young people were nonetheless apathetic, in that their relationship to politics was apolitical—a matter of desperate need for group conformity and prestige and in some instances a phobic sphere as well. In many of these cases, we think that the individual, his adolescent fling in politics behind him, will settle into his business or professional life with a decreasing political interest unless there, too, it happens to be stimulated by group pressures. On the other hand, we had a group of interviews done among seniors in an urban trade school, where virtually no one had engaged in the slightest political activity, and where the level of political information was so abysmally low that one boy did not know to what party Truman belonged. Yet in a few of these cases the respondent indicated some awareness of those political developments which mattered for him personally: the draft, the chances for war, the outlook for labor unions. For these people, their adolescence is not, as so often with the middle class, a peak of political interest; when they enter the working force, they may be brought by their unions and their life-situations into some concern with politics.

Even then, however, the lower-class adult will find himself limited in his political activity by his class position, in subtle as well as obvious ways: he is apt to be more tired in the evening, and cannot take time off for meetings in the afternoon (unless he is a shop steward); he does not have a secretary, even if he is a leader in a local union, to type memoranda and make appointments; indeed, he is often ill at ease in handling such middle-class routines as telephone calls and memoranda; lower-class women with children find it of course still more difficult to be active politically. To be sure, the spread of education, the rise of unions and of other more or less formal associations, the increase in experience with government and corporate forms and routines—these developments are increasing the ability of the lower-class person to "act middle class," and to handle himself in the formalized aspects of political activity.

Studies of participation and nonparticipation in voluntary associations provide evidence that lower-class groups are in general more "privatized" than upper-class groups, no matter what forms of interest and participation are included in measuring lower-class participation. (So far as we know, however, no one has tried to see if lower-class men participate less in clique activity centering around sports, drink, and gambling; compare William F. Whyte's *Street Corner Society* and James West's *Plainville*, U.S.A.) Low-income people have very low participation in nonpolitical groups of any formal sort, and frequently have very little interest in matters that might be said to affect them directly. The experience of the Neighborhood Center for

Block Organization in East Harlem is instructive in these matters: despite two years of active effort on the part of trained psychiatrists and social workers, it proved impossible to stimulate neighborhood groups in a slum area to deal even with the most pressing problems of daily life, such as housing-law violations, lack of playground space, and police protection. Although even slight coöperative efforts were impressively successful in improving neighborhood conditions, only about 2 percent of the residents—and these often the most psychologically disturbed—could be induced to participate in any group activity. Why this was the case is obscure—at the cordial invitation of the Center, we along with other social scientists have been trying to find out—but there would seem to be evidence that the conditions of lower-class life do not train people in the motivations and techniques, taken for granted in some sections of the middle class, which underlie coöperative activity. This is a point which converges with Ullmer and Mills' analysis of "Class Structure and Civic Leadership." Put another way, this brings us back to our earlier point, that activity, including political activity, in the lower class requires much more effort, and seems therefore much more fruitless, than in the middle class. With an index which simply measures gross activity, the lower class will simply disappear from consideration and the index will not do much to cast light on class differences in political apathy. Of course, it still remains desirable to explore further the relationships between class and clique position, on the one hand, and various types of political activity, on the other. (On class and clique determination of voting behavior, see Lazarsfeld, Berelson, and Gaudet, *The People's Choice*, excellent for its techniques and stimulating for its suggestiveness.)

3. *Activity and temperament.* Activity is relative not only to class and clique situations but also to temperament differences between individuals; we use "temperament" here to mean such things as native energy-level (apart from its directly psychic components), sanguinity, gregariousness, good health. The problem is that our focus of interest is not on apathy as a universal human phenomenon but on apathy as a social, a historical product. While the distribution of different kinds of temperament in different populations may well be connected with social and historical changes—see, for instance, the brilliant paper by Margaret Mead, "The Concept of Culture and the Psychosomatic Approach" (*Psychiatry*, 10, 1947, 57-76)—in the present state of psychosomatic knowledge, we prefer to get involved as little as possible in questions of temperament, limiting ourselves to those parts of personality and its expressions that are generally considered social in their determination. To isolate apathy as a product of social factors and history rather than of individual temperament is difficult in any case, but it would be even harder if we limited ourselves to the study of activity alone.

4. *Activity and purpose.* There is, finally, the consideration that political activity may be relative not only to a person's temperament and clique situation, but also to the context of his available political world of the moment. We can hardly call apathetic the behavior of someone who, fully aware of

and completely involved emotionally in politics, yet decides not to be active, for want of meaningful activity at the time. Inevitably, we cannot survey political activity over a lifetime, much of it not yet lived, but must ask questions about the moment, the contiguous past, and the immediate future. Dipping in with an interview, our record of activity—as any behavioral index—must be incomplete and may be misleading. Since we view apathy as, among other things, a disproportionate relationship between means and ends—too much activity as well as too little—we cannot assume, because activity goes on, that it makes any human sense. For great numbers of people today, political activity is little more than an inherited ritual or routine, varying according to class demands and psychological needs.

5. *Activity as related to affect and competence.* We can sum up the foregoing paragraphs by saying that activity may conceal as much as it reveals about political apathy. Yet it would go much too far to say that activity is irrelevant to an estimate of the political involvement of an individual. We cannot use it as an independent criterion without a great deal of further clarification. But we have found that we could use the record of activity, as it was revealed in an interview, as evidence in evaluating the individual's position on two other indices, those of affect and competence. It was these more "psychological" measures of apathy, rather than the "behavioral" one of activity, that seemed to give us a closer approximation to the quality of apathy itself, as our interviews revealed it. Certainly it is harder to work with such intangibles as (in our terminology) affect and competence, than with the (apparently) hard reality of activity. Yet the fact is that apathy itself is intangible: we cannot reduce it to an operational factor which we know does not include a good part of the meaning of our original object of study. We felt we must strive for criteria commensurate with our problem rather than shape our problem to the most readily available criteria.

If we are to understand apathy as "passionless existence"—one of the definitions given in the Oxford Dictionary—we need not explain why affectlessness (in the way the term is used by psychoanalysts) can be used as a criterion of political apathy. One might ask whether affectlessness is not a synonym for apathy. However, if we look at the pole opposite to political apathy, and consider the meaning and implications of political "concern" or "involvement," we will see immediately that affect or passionate existence is not a sufficient criterion to measure what we find. Concern and involvement imply awareness, appropriateness; yet passion may be blind, disproportionate. These considerations lead us to add to affect as an index of apathy another term: competence; and, as we shall see, to classify as "apathetic" according to our criteria those who, while ranking high in affect, are low in competence. Conversely, those who possess both affect and competence we term "involved," that is, nonapathetic.

We turn in the following two sections to a discussion of these criteria of affect and competence. Thereafter, we develop an additional set of criteria which, especially for the more politicized respondents, may be helpful in differentiating among affects, and hence among apathies.

POLITICAL AFFECT AS AN INDEX OF APATHY. These
two dimensions, affect and competence, are obviously closely related. Just as
the affect of the competent differs from the affect of the incompetent, so the
competence of those of genuine affect differs from the competence of those
who lack affect; the effort at distinction here faces problems similar to those
of distinguishing between "cognitive" and "emotive" elements in intelligence.

At any rate, the use of these two indices simultaneously could give us four
polar relationships: (1) those high in both dimensions; (2) those low in
both; (3) and (4) those high in one and low in the other. Accordingly, we
defined as (1) "involved" the person who combined high and genuine affect
with competence; all others we classified as "apathetic." Thus we grouped in
the apathetic category those (2) whose high affect and low competence indicated an "indignant" relationship to politics (it might also be an "enthusiastic" one); those (3) who were high in competence and affectless, and
whom we termed "inside-dopesters"; and those low in both affect and competence, whom we called (4) the "indifferent."

These four types were, we suspected, related both to class position and to
character structure; we expected, for instance, to find "inside-dopesters" in
upper middle-class urban circles, "indignants" in rural and small-town Protestant areas. We do not yet have the sample that would permit us to test these
hypotheses, though we have found interviews which illustrate them.

Affect is, of course, an intangible. It can be probed by projective tests such
as the Rorschach, but these will not tell us very much about *political* affect,
as distinguished from affect in other spheres of life. Specific answers to direct
questions concerning political affect are, however, of more help than one
might suppose. Thus, when we ask people what in politics gets them indignant
or excited and how long they stay that way; what in politics makes them feel
good or bad; whether they can get as worked up about politics as about other
things in life; and so on—when we ask these direct questions, even rather
non-commital answers, followed up by exploratory probes, are often quite
revealing. A direct positive or negative answer to the first question bearing
on affect, or to the whole series, may be belied by later answers in the series,
or other parts of the interview.

For example, all the students in the progressive high school already referred
to claim that politics makes a difference in the way they live, and that they
get indignant about political happenings. However, the content of the answer
gives us clues about the real nature of their alleged affect. We quote several
responses to the question whether politics makes a difference:

> Not directly, but in a way I think it does; but in discussion with friends or
> parents I can usually take ideas or get facts from the discussion. In this way,
> these discussions make a difference.

> It makes no difference physically but it changes my mind—if I met someone
> who violently disagreed with me on an important issue it is bothersome for
> friendship. It affects me in this way.

Here politics is among other things a function of social intercourse in a
group which makes "politics" obligatory. The first one quoted can "take ideas

or get facts from the discussion"—for him politics is perhaps a means for self-improvement. The respondent who tells us that disagreement in political matters might be "bothersome for friendship" also volunteers that "if just two people were left in the world, they would still fight."

Working, then, both with what the interviewee tells us directly about his political affects and with what he "gives" of them without meaning to, we try to reconstruct the history of the individual's political affect, much as the archaeologist, working with fragments, tries to reconstruct a culture.

An individual may rate himself high, or low, in affect in contrast to his milieu. Hence, to understand what he tells us, we have to understand something of the milieu, if we are to make comparisons which transcend a limited group. Moreover, individuals differ very much in the style by which they express affect, or repress it. Possibly, we cannot avoid here the interjection of temperament factors, such as the distinction between choleric and sanguinic types—compare Jan Stapel, "The Convivial Respondent" (*Public Opinion Quarterly*, 11, 1947, p. 524). The popular folklore has it that "still waters run deep": people may feel deeply and yet not express this feeling by accepted patterns of gesture or speech. Contrariwise, the folklore would have it that easily surfaced affects are not genuine, but this, too, will vary, not only with individuals, but also according to the conventionalized mode of expression of affect in the particular group. So we must know something of what may be expected in the milieu to interpret the individual's idiosyncratic modification of group styles in vaunting affect or concealing it. It follows that we need a group portrait of political affect before we can draw the lineaments of the individual.

But, of course, we learn of the group in part through the individuals who compose it, just as we learn of the individual in part from single answers to questions which then become interwoven with other answers. Thus, the method weaves back and forth, from the single answer to the whole interview, and from the single individual to the whole group of which he is a part. This is far from simple. Yet it is the kind of judgment which we constantly make in life—indeed, on which our lives and fortunes often depend—and which novelists and biographers must make when they tackle political subjects.

In this way, we try to arrive at a qualitative description of political affect, in all its subtleties and variations, as well as to judge whether it is, on the whole, high or low. The gamut of affects is wide: there is the affect of aggressive or sadistic types, who look for opportunities of releasing indignation onto politics; the affect of people who live in a slightly paranoid and autistic world; the affect of people with little staying power and the affect of those with great explosive power; the high affect of those whose roles as political leaders of certain groups require them to maintain a chronic political stance (which may feel "sincere" to them); the high, though repressed, affect of disillusioned folk who fear political affect and therefore deny it.

One crucial issue in all this is the source of the affect displayed in politics.

Harold Lasswell, in *Psychopathology and Politics,* asserted that political behavior, if it is to be understood psychologically, must be understood in terms of affects arising in the personal ("primary") sphere and becoming displaced onto available ("secondary") political symbols. In a crude form, the notion that personal frustrations and tensions are displaced onto politics has become increasingly a part of our popular folklore and science; the personal experience of everyone offers examples. Professor Lasswell's more provocative question is rather whether *all* affect expressed in a political sphere must be considered as deriving from a personal tension or frustration. Perhaps in some ultimate or definitional sense there can be no other source for affect; and yet there is no question that we can distinguish between those in whom a clear link shows between the personal tension and its political expression, and those who seem to respond with emotion to the event itself. We may, that is, distinguish between an "idling" affect which seeks for justification or rationalization in politics, and an affect which is a reaction to specific political developments; the distinction here is analogous to the one Erich Fromm draws between idling and reactive hatred in *Man For Himself.* While such a phenomenological distinction does not answer the question as to the ultimate source of affect, it does indicate that there are different kinds of political affect, and we know from our experience of life that these different kinds may have different consequences.

This was, then, the first refinement we introduced in the use of affect as an index to apathy: where the affect expressed in politics is closely and directly linked to a personal tension—where the affect is "blind," so to speak, expressed on an available political object rather than directly aroused by the object—we did not consider that subject as showing affect in the political realm. Or, more precisely, we did not consider him politically "involved" if his affect was of this sort even if he might be considered politically competent —but, obviously, this very decision leads us away from any quantitative or quasi-quantitative use of either affect or competence as isolable criteria.

Finally, we found ourselves compelled to deal with still other elusive problems of the quality of affect. Our tendency had been to call those who show a great deal of affect without corresponding competence "indignant" types, but in some cases we felt that they were more properly called "enthusiasts." Moreover, "indignation" itself can be of different sorts: it can have the quality of an outlet for idling hatred and malaise which Svend Ranulf describes in his essay *Moral Indignation and Middle Class Psychology;* or it can represent a deeply human reaction to threat or atrocity. Often the presence or absence of competence would permit us to distinguish between these two types of indignation, but this is not always so.

POLITICAL COMPETENCE AS AN INDEX OF APATHY. In dealing with affect as an index we did not raise the question of how one defines politics, though obviously the problem of displacing affects which arise elsewhere onto politics implies a distinction of spheres between what is "politics" and what is "elsewhere." However, in establishing standards for political competence, it is even more necessary to define what we mean by politics.

1. *What is "politics"?* There is a great deal to be said for a "meteorological" definition—the term is that used by Kris and Leites in the paper previously cited—perhaps an "entertainment" or "consumer's" definition: "interest in the world around one." In this sense, in terms of one's ability to react to events that do not affect one directly, but which are "interesting," one would be justified in testing for competence on the "politics" of the numbers game for the lower-class men, on tenement-house intrigues for lower-class women, and so on. In another sense, however, these things often do affect people in the lower class, at least immediately, more than a presidential election—in fact, we cannot speak of apathy, in its conventional use, in referring to someone who cannot affect the outcome of a political event, and who cannot be affected by its outcome.

An interest or consumer definition of politics would permit us to set up indices for political competence that would be relative to the interests of each social group; that is, each class or group would have a different index. As a practical matter, this would be exceedingly difficult—it would require determining what is important and interesting to a particular class, relative to that class, rather than in terms of what is important and interesting to another class. But apart from such considerations, such a definition of politics and hence of political competence would ignore our view that politics *does* determine the condition of people's lives today—including lower-class lives. And, as already stated, we believe that an awareness of those power-forces in the world which do matter for people, an awareness of the human potentialities for changing the social environment in the general interest—an awareness, that is, which transcends mere consumer's "interest," mere meteorology—is a human need whose satisfaction is important for individual psychic health. Of course there may be other, still more imperative needs.

One could also consider another type of judgment of competence which would be no less relativistic than a judgment in terms of local patterns of interest or consumption. By this test, one would be judged "competent" if one were able to perform the political tasks dictated by one's group milieu and party affiliation. Thus, the government official would be "competent" if he could handle the political news in the way demanded of him by his job, no matter how fragmentary his awareness of the long-run political forces in which his department, his class, and his country were caught. And the young Stalinist, knowledgeable on how to get Marcantonio reëlected, would be "competent" by the standards of his outfit—and even "incompetent" if he possessed the grasp of Marxist fundamentals demanded of an earlier generation of Communists and feared by the present generation. But, obviously, such complete relativism as this, which would equate the "functionally rationalized" with the rational (in Karl Mannheim's terms), would again be to deny our value premise: namely, that politics matters for people, irrespective of the ideology in which it is clothed in a particular culture and time

THE VOTER AND LOCAL GOVERNMENT IN
TWO STABLE DEMOCRACIES

Although there have always been among us believers in strong central government, our governmental system, as compared to the British, has been extraordinarily weak and decentralized. This has been particularly true of state and local government. The general idea seems to have been that no one should govern, or failing that, that everyone should govern together. The principle of checks and balances and the division of power, mitigated in the Federal government by the great powers of the presidency, were carried to extreme lengths in the cities and states. As little as fifty years ago, most cities were governed by large councils, some of them bicameral, and by mayors who could do little but preside over the councils. There was no such thing as a state administration. Governors were ceremonial figures only, and state governments were mere congeries of independent boards and commissions. Before anything could be done, there had to occur a most elaborate process of give and take (often, alas, in the most literal sense) by which bits and pieces of power were gathered up temporarily, almost momentarily.

It was taken for granted that the ordinary citizen had a right—indeed, a sacred duty—to interfere in the day-to-day conduct of public affairs. Whereas in Britain the press and public have been excluded from the deliberations of official bodies, in the United States it has been common practice to require by law that all deliberations take place in meetings open to the public. Whereas in Britain the electorate is never given an opportunity to pass upon particular projects by vote, in the United States it usually is. In Los Angeles, according to James Q. Wilson, "The strategy of political conflict is more often than not based upon the assumption that the crucial decision will be made not by the City Council of Los Angeles, the Board of Supervisors of the county, or the legislature of the state, but by the voters in a referendum election."

Los Angeles is an extreme case, but the general practice of American cities, a practice required by law in many of them, is to get the voters' approval of major expenditures. The New York City government, one of the strongest, is now having to choose between building schools and making other necessary capital expenditures; it cannot do both because the voters of the state have refused to lift the constitutional limit on debt. Such a thing could not happen in London; there all such decisions are made by the authorities, *none of whom is elected at large.*

SOURCE: Edward C. Banfield, "The Political Implications of Metropolitan Growth," *Daedalus*, 1:90 (Winter, 1960), pp. 69–70. By permission of the American Academy of Arts and Sciences.

and of the tasks or busywork demanded by that ideology. Our judgments of what is apathy, and of its subcomponents, must be based upon a standard which, while relative to long-term historical developments, does not fluctuate with party politics and anti-rationalist slogans; to that extent, our definitions of politics, hence of political competence, aim at a degree of universal validity, independent of culture and class.

Thus we are led to define politics, not in terms of mere passive interest nor in terms of roles demanded by one's station in life, but in terms of the human need for understanding the social environment and even of improving it. We define it, that is, in terms of our two levels of political awareness and action: the reflective and utopian and curious one, and the day-to-day struggle for the lesser as against the greater evil; to be judged competent one must have some grasp of both these levels.

2. *Distinguishing real from spurious competence.* Even when, for practical purposes, we limited our inquiries as to competence to the more traditional fields of politics, we still found it difficult to distinguish between an individual's awareness of real forces and superficial, atomistic consumption of political data. We had to distinguish between political reality and political illusion, even if that illusion was couched in conventionally "realistic" terms; inevitably, it is we who had to decide which is which, on the basis of our own political values and comprehension.

But in important respects we felt it necessary that our judgment of competence be relative. We could not judge everyone by the standard of a professor of political science; conversely, and perhaps unfairly, we expected more of the professor than of someone with (theoretically) less opportunity to acquire competence. We asked in each individual case: what could we expect, in terms of political awareness, in view of this individual's ability to deal with rather abstract matters, an ability partly native and partly learned? We also asked: what sort of awareness would this individual *need* in order to function in a satisfying way in "his" world? We asked a small-town person about rather more localized political matters than an urban person; we tried to discount, as far as possible, local and regional differences in distribution of the mass media. In every case, we tried to reduce, except for comparative purposes, questions of specific fact or opinion, such as are usually asked on polls, and to find questions which brought out the individual's ability to evaluate political forces. Since to some degree all of us live in the same world, these questions were identical for all people we interviewed, except insofar as we modified them to give the less articulate or intelligent a chance to respond.

This effort to allow for differences between rural and urban, and between articulate and inarticulate, raises many of the same complications as the effort to allow for class differences—ethnic differences also are important— and, of course, these various sets of differences overlap. In small-town and rural Vermont, where we had a group of interviews made, people are in easy contact with local and even state officials. Social distance between the politically influential and the noninfluential is small; indeed, many of the patterns of political meaning persist which we described above as typical for the nineteenth century. As against this, urban lower-class people, in our small number of interviews, seemed ordinarily to have no face-to-face contacts with officials; some of them, however, had a kind of taxi-driver wisdom and were more "knowing" than the Vermonters—less likely, for instance, to think that the interviewer must be a Communist because he asked questions about politics. Here, too, we do not have an adequate sample to permit comparisons; and in any case, we repeat, we have not solved the technical difficulties of developing a questionnaire to tap differential meanings of politics in the barely explored variety of American subcultures—what a political cosmology, for example, is wrapped up in the phrase: "Go fight city hall!"

In an effort to do this, however, we have asked people, for instance, what image they had of a political person, and of a nonpolitical person; whether they changed their minds about politics and when and why; whether they thought war or depression easier to avoid; whether they thought experts or the man in the street had better judgment; whether they trusted people, and whom they trusted on political questions. We asked whether they thought their country, their school (for people in school), and their family was democratic, and how they could tell; what groups they felt had interests in common with themselves, and what groups antagonistic interests; and who they thought ran the country. Finally, we presented people with a series of political "dilemmas" and asked them what they would do if, for example, they came into possession of information which showed that "their" candidate in an election was corrupt, and if disclosure of such information would enable the other side to win; we said nothing about what their candidate stood for.

We did find, with our small haul of 150, that people in various social strata, urban and rural, young and old, felt they could take a crack at our questions and dilemmas. We did not have, as in the usual political questionnaire, a cluster of "don't knows" at the bottom of the socio-economic scale. Middle-class people, to be sure, had greater facility on some of the questions, but they were not likely to have thought in terms of all of them; for instance, they were usually challenged by the question as to their image or picture of a person very much interested in politics. This type of challenge is important, for it enabled us to use the interview as a sort of projective test, by seeing the kind of verbal and nonverbal (e.g., gestural) performance it elicited in sequence. It helped us, on the one hand, to get through the veneer of opinionatedness in the middle class and, on the other hand, to evoke what political competence there was in our lower-class respondents.

COMPETENCE   AND   AFFECT   AS   CRITERIA.   We have worked intensively with some twenty interview protocols, and in each case made as complete a record as we could of all the grounds of our judgments, as we sought to determine apathy or involvement by the application of our criteria of competence and affect. (At the same time we made a judgment of character structure, on the basis of a typology which we do not touch on here, and compared character structure and political orientation.) We found in our use of these criteria that often we could not make separate judgments of each as easily as we could make a judgment of apathy or involvement directly. We found ourselves, moreover, moving away from primary attention to the specific questions which had been designed to reveal competence and affect respectively, and making instead judgments which treated the whole interview as a *Gestalt*; that is, all parts of our comprehensive questionnaire—covering popular culture, attitudes toward family and friends, philosophical values and many other things as well as politics—entered into and enriched our judgments.[2] Moreover, when we worked with the interviews, we discovered that in addition to employing our concepts of affect and competence, we were also tempted to smuggle in other criteria that were not explicit in our initial theoretical scheme. We were in the position, so frequent in social science, where our indices, despite our care to make them adequate to the complexities we were seeking to measure, turned out in many cases to be too mechanical to cover the whole range, the nuances and subtleties, of apathy and involvement. These difficulties arose, and our scheme of affect-competence seemed least illuminating, in the case of those who had fairly elaborate political ideologies, and who lived in politically saturated milieus. There ideology itself demanded that one be concerned with political events (just as in certain other environments ideology demanded the opposite), and a certain kind of competence could be avoided only by a remarkably high impermeability to the group.[3] Because general attitudes and orientations could be assumed, the range within a given orientation became exceedingly important.

In this situation, our recourse was to develop an additional set of criteria which, taken together with affect and competence rather than replacing them, would embrace more of the interview material and of our theoretical framework. This set of criteria was based on interview data we had originally planned virtually to disregard, namely, the detailed political ideology of the respondent. We had believed that in America—whatever might be found elsewhere—ideology is almost entirely a function of milieu, bearing little if any relation to individual character or to the psychological roots of apathy and involvement. Our view was, in other words, that party and ideological positions in America do not bespeak a psychological choice: ordinarily the individual has no choice but to take the ideology offered him in his family, class, clique, and region.

Yet our interviews showed us that while this was on the whole true, there were crucial differences in the nuance and emphasis with which the ideology was expressed by each subject in our more highly political groups of respondents. We believed these differences to be significant both for revealing character structure and revealing apathy or involvement. We therefore developed, on the basis of our study of a variegated group of interviews, some general

---

[2] Cf., e.g., Werner Wolff, *The Expression of Personality* (1943), p. 9: ". . . specific statements about personality items are often less accurate than free descriptions."

[3] Rose Laub Coser has been engaged in analyzing for varieties of affect and competence a group of twenty-three interviews with the entire second-year class of students in a coeducational, progressive urban private school. Her preliminary analysis reveals that those who, on a series of questions, show competence and alertness vis-à-vis politics are those who also exhibit the least interpersonal tensions with their classmates.

concepts of the way in which the coloring of one's ideology—more or less irrespective of its nominal content—may be related to an underlying apathy.

A set of criteria based on nuances of political statement inevitably will not be applicable to large numbers of people: first of all, to those who present virtually no political statements or opinions—and there are many of these— and then to those in whom these statements are very simple or primitive. However, our criteria, as will be seen in a moment, refer to such general categories that they might also be applied to views on family relations, education, and similar topics which have political bearing or implications, and we have often done this, though here, too, we run into some difficulty where views are not elaborated. Nevertheless, the main use of this set of categories was to serve as a refinement on the affect-competence scheme: for most people, the affect-competence scheme described the degree of political involvement or apathy sufficiently; but for those for whom politics is a focus of interest, the affect and competence categories were too gross, and a direct analysis of ideology permitted somewhat closer approximation. Moreover, these additional criteria directly introduced into our analysis of the interviews our judgments, set forth in the preceding section, on the need for a political orientation which combined elements of detachment and of attachment to one's time-bound and culture-bound milieu.

In what we have said, the reader may feel that our use of the term "apathy" is too idiosyncratic and complex, even in the light of scientific awareness that definition is an essentially arbitrary device. And, indeed, our choice of the term "apathy" rather than a word of less common use or of our own coinage is frankly polemical. It is a way of stating our conviction that current conceptions about apathy—seen in terms of failure to vote, to send telegrams, to inform oneself about politics, etc.—greatly oversimplify the problem of finding adequate ways for relating people to politics on its various levels. To seek an increase in formal political activity and information as such, without too much concern for the meaning of that activity or information, is self-deceiving. For it may blind one to the historical changes in the significance of politics for the individual which, in our opinion, have led to an increase in unconscious apathy, an apathy arising as a result of congruent changes in social structure and character structure, as well as in the political sphere alone. These changes are reflected in slight changes of ideology and of modes of expression of affect; these are possible clues to long-term developments whose consequences in political behavior have not yet become fully manifest —clues to the latent dynamics of politics.

To be sure, not all apathies are alike, and the "apathy" of the active is obviously different from the "apathy" of the quiescent. Nevertheless, in using the same term for both, we are seeking to emphasize functional similarities—primarily the inappropriateness of the political outlook or behavior of all the apathetic ones.

It is, moreover, not only apathy which is misconceived, but its opposite which we call "involvement." Here, too, we think that changes may be under way in those individuals and groups who are seeking for possible new modes of relatedness to politics. Our effort is to formulate criteria which will permit us to distinguish inappropriate and apolitical orientations, no matter how well rationalized and disguised, from orientations which might satisfy the need of modern men to meet their altered political situation with competence and fitting affect.

FURTHER CRITERIA FOR APATHY AND INVOLVEMENT

The criteria set forth below are meant to supplement, primarily for the more politicized respondents, the criteria of affect and competence. They are not yet exhaustive. Taken together, however, they help to differentiate apathetic, apolitical approaches to politics from involved and appropriate responses. They do *not* determine the correctness or misguidedness of an individual's political position: people can be mistaken without being judged apathetic, and conversely, they can be "right" despite a basic apathy. For any political position, then: (1) concern with human ends is less apathetic than concern with institutional means; (2) concern with what has been or potentially can be personally experienced is less apathetic than concern with remote items, access to which is gained through impersonal agencies of information diffusion; likewise, the ability to personalize and concretize distant events is less apathetic than the ability to report them; (3) concern with the welfare of self-and-others is less apathetic than concern exclusively with the self or exclusively with others; (4) concern with trends and elements that are not in the focus of attention of the mass media is less apathetic than exclusive concern with what is in their momentary focus; (5) ability to take a critical or independent view of authority[4]—its assertions of fact, and claims to special treatment or consideration—is less apathetic than unquestioning acceptance or rejection of these assertions and claims because of their authoritative source.

Obviously, these criteria overlap at a number of points. We have made no attempt to use them as a scale; to say, for instance, that we judge a person nonapathetic if he ranks high on three out of five. Rather, they constitute a check list of things to be looked for in characterizing the political style of a person. We say a few words in illustration and explanation of each.

HUMAN ENDS V. INSTITUTIONAL MEANS. When we ask people what could be done to make war less likely, some answer in terms of changing people, and some in terms of changing institutions; still others, of course, say that war is inevitable. But we cannot interpret such answers directly in terms of our criterion: it is the personal variant of a given ideological frame that tells us something about individual political orientation. Thus,

---

4 "Authority" here must be taken in terms of the individual's group and not in any general sense; obviously, the authorities to which an obedient Stalinist, Zionist, Catholic, or Democrat submits are not the same.

if a politically sophisticated respondent emphasizes nationalization of industry, centralization of planning, control over industry, breakup of cartels, etc., with what seems to us a disproportionate emphasis on the specific institutional instrument rather than the human end, we become suspicious and wonder whether his interest in the human end may not be an excuse for his desire to institute a particular set of more or less belligerent means. We cannot tell this, we repeat, from the position itself. To be sure, some ideologies are so constricted that acceptance of them amounts to a virtual choice of totalitarian means; yet we can imagine a racist who puts more emphasis on freedom for the allegedly subject race than on means for destroying or controlling an oppressor race, and we can conceive of a Nazi who, before 1939, emphasized the strength-through-joy program, the end of unemployment, new motor roads and the *Volkswagen*, and who through all-too-human error, failed to see the necessary implications of other Nazi goals.

Conversely, acceptance of an ideology that exalts ends without reference to conceivable human means may tend toward apathy, as we think is the case with some current versions of pietism and quietism. For ends cannot be too serious when the problem of implementation is lightly regarded. We do not mean, of course, that one must always have means available before one can justify speculation about ends; it is again a question of the "two levels" of political relatedness we discussed above.

Though such questions seem highly theoretical,[5] the issue boils down to a fairly simple one: does the person possess, in the realm of politics, the "normal" human ability to differentiate ends from means? To take a common instance in everyday life, we are critical of the person who makes a compulsive ritual out of behavior that should serve convenience—keeping a house neat, for example. So, too, in political life, we find people whose aim of getting rid of "dirt"— municipal corruption, excess profits, un-American activities, etc.—has become a dangerous and compulsive ritual, blind to human priorities and consequences. Flight into politics typically uses political means without appropriate relationship to human ends.

THE PERSONALIZED AND CONCRETIZED V. THE IM-PERSONAL AND REMOTE. The very nature of modern politics is such that we cannot form our political judgments on the basis of personal experience alone. If we try to do this, we will simply be applying "parataxic" frames of reference to the world. This misapplication is typical of the philistine, of the ethnocentric person who, in art, "knows what he likes," and in politics insists on judging everything that happens by the norms of his own morality, his own family, his own unquestioned way of life. Such a person is also one who makes the semantic error, discussed by S. I. Hayakawa,[6] of asserting firmly that "pigs is pigs" and can never be anything else: *he* knows

---

[5] For fuller discussions, see "Some Observations on Community Plans and Utopia" in *Yale Law Journal*, 57 (1947), 173.

[6] "The Revision of Vision," *ETC.: A Review of General Semantics*, IV (1947), 258.

a pig when he sees one. Probably the lower-class person, less sophisticated, is more likely than the upper-class person to fall prey to these fallacies.

Increasingly, however, people tend to make the opposite error, and it is with this that our second criterion deals. While the world that influences us is enormous, and while we must depend almost entirely on reports that we read or hear in order to evaluate it, we are inclined to apathy if we fail to measure these reports, wherever we can, by our personal identification with the described situation. When, for instance, we read that the Russian people have greeted with joy a decree lengthening hours of labor, because this permits them to do more for the beloved Stalin, we can use our own experience to discount the report as at least in part exaggerated. Of course, this personal reference may lead us into error: people are different; nevertheless, by means of this natural and widely used control, a large part of the political can be assimilated to personal experience.

We found in our interviews, however, a number of people—largely in the urban upper-middle class, young, and much concerned with politics—who did precisely the opposite: they were attracted by what was most abstract and remote; they parroted events and attitudes in the same forms and terms in which the mass media (for their class) present them; it never occurred to them to use their own experience, their own likes and dislikes, as a norm. We might suggest that this strand of apathy is a trained incapacity of the educated. These same people knew all about the disasters of the last years; they claimed great concern, great affect. Yet in many instances we found that the events which made an impression were those which the respondent could not possibly have assimilated in terms of personal experience. In such cases we were sometimes able to see that the reason for the apparent political concern lay in anxieties about group conformity patterns or in the use of politics as an escape from exigent and unconscious problems of the self.

It is in judging such cases that the problem of differential exposure to the mass media becomes important. The ability to react to the remote may have been stimulated by, say, a vivid "March of Time" or CBS broadcast. Similarly, other sources, at school or elsewhere, might sensitize an individual to connections which will seem remote only to the less sensitive observer.

More typically, however, the mass media operate on a level of spurious personalization of events, which are made concrete and chummy by playing up personalities and local color. Thus it is apparent that this criterion is closely linked with the fourth one (see p. 553, below): concern with what is not in focus as against concern only with what is in the focus—and the conventional style of perception—of the relevant clique or media.

To avoid misunderstanding, we should emphasize that we are not equating political involvement with immediacy in time and space, and political apathy with physical or temporal remoteness. It is not apathy but its opposite to react strongly to Plato's *Apology*, for example, or to an account of misery on Okinawa. Rather, our point is simply that one's own experience, enriched by sensibility and imagination, is with all its weaknesses the only safe yardstick for judgment—paradoxically, it furnishes the only escape from solipsism. Indeed, we believe that many political disasters of our own time and of earlier times have resulted because of people's acceptance of political ideologies which their own experience might have disproved, had they trusted it or resorted to it. Programs of sacrifice and war can be put over just because people, failing to do this, act like "statesmen," applying *raison d'état*, and never, like kings, saying "*l'état: c'est moi.*"

CONCERN WITH SELF-AND-OTHERS V. CONCERN WITH SELF-OR-OTHERS. This criterion is closely linked to the one we have just discussed; it too demands that the individual see himself in the context of others and others in the context of himself. But by the use of this criterion we wish to make explicit our judgment, set forth above, that both selfishness and selflessness are obstacles to political involvement. As to the former, if we find an interview record which formulates the view that the respondent can achieve happiness for himself at whatever cost to others—or for his group or nation, at whatever cost to other groups or nations—we suspect first of all his political competence, since all experience suggests the interdependence of human beings and nations, and second, his humanity: otherwise, how could he be happy at the direct expense of others? In fact, these two judgments interlock: the respondent's lack of humanity will lead him to misjudge politics in long-run terms, no matter how effective he may be as an operator; he is apathetic because he does not penetrate to the real forces at work— certain forces, for example, which may tend after a time to reduce the power of the powerful and increase the power of the powerless but sees politics only as the manipulable extension of his own ego and its group or territorial representatives.

If, on the other hand, we find an interview record of a person who thinks only of others, and never of himself or his group, we suspect a fear of facing or knowing the self (and the group), often coupled with a more or less unconscious desire to suffer.

One of our respondents, for instance, asked what he would do if he had six months to live and could do as he pleased, said he would use the "aura of reverence attached to one who has six months to live . . . to improve conditions." His whole interview is filled with references to the suffering of others, but he is oblivious to his own suffering, which leads to his inhuman willingness to make himself an instrument, even in his hypothetical last six months, for meeting unlimited obligations to a rather shadowy "humanity."

The case is extreme; while others among our group of interviews exhibit similar tendencies, selflessness is rationalized more typically in some hard-boiled vein. In all such instances, however, we feel there is something apathetic in a view of politics which fails to connect it with the speaker's own place in the world, and his own claims for happiness. As we all know, modern political leaders have become adept at exploiting the willingness of people to submit to intolerable conditions for some cause; the cause gives meaning to the followers' lives because these are completely lived in the "second sphere" of culturally-given tasks and motivations: there is insufficient attachment to life in the "first sphere" of day-to-day living, let alone sufficient detachment in the "third sphere" of transcending imagination. In much the same way, many leaders who make their careers on the basis of others' sacrifice are themselves "selfless," that is, ascetic; they, too, find meaning only in submission to a cause, though they may appear as highly egocentric.

If one thinks of earlier military heroes and their devoted followings, of earlier fanaticisms and crusades, it is not easy to see what is new in all this. Erich Fromm, in *Escape From Freedom,* pointed to resemblances between the social-psychological conditions which gave rise to the more virulent aspects of the Reformation and those which gave rise to modern fascism. If there are differences, they might be sought in the more limitless nature of modern totalitarian demands, and more effective techniques for their enforcement. Beyond that, we think there may be changes in individual psychology which have removed certain defenses people once had against the internalized voices of the peer-group; moreover, older barriers of property, theology, and class have been largely smashed. Whatever the degree of change, we can at least be sure that there is plenty of political dynamite available to those who can combine the apathy of the selfless and the apathy of the egocentric, sopping up into a political movement the affect of the incompetent and finding places for the technical but often cruel competence of the affectless.

CONCERN WITH WHAT IS NOT IN FOCUS V. CONCERN ONLY WITH WHAT IS IN FOCUS OF CLIQUE OR MEDIA. As throughout this discussion, here, too, our criteria shade into one another. Individuality of the focus of attention is related, on the one hand, to ability to put oneself (but not only oneself) into the figure-ground pattern of politics—our third criterion—and on the other hand, it is related to a critical attitude toward the (generally anonymous) authorities who tell people what their focus of attention should be, which is our fifth criterion. If we define politics in terms, *inter alia*, of efforts to change the social environment, we see that the ability to envisage such change involves originality. This can flow from the actual experiences people have, if they do experience them directly— that is, if they are able to look clear-sightedly at their own conditions and their own way of life. However, <u>most people do not interpret their experience directly, but through the conventional, ideologized accounts of their life that are proffered them by the mass media and by other authorities</u>. This passivity of perception, this permeability, is apathetic, no matter how frantic the concern with the flow of political news. Passivity suffocates the development of alternative and unexpected ways of handling political developments. In our culture, preoccupation with the stream of events as they are culturally perceived is praised as practical. Yet without utopian thought—thought which makes it worth while to apply human effort to the social environment rather than being overwhelmed by it—man's political inventiveness is stunted.

To be sure, not everyone can be a builder of utopias, nor do we expect originality in the sense in which the term is used in scholarship before we judge a person nonapathetic. Rather, our criterion is an effort to evaluate the mode of perception of the person—his ability, as a matter of degree, to criticize and judge pleasant and unpleasant, just and unjust, ways of social living. (Here, and generally, we have profited very much from the discussion in Erich Fromm's *Man For Himself.*) Where this ability is absent, people tend to become increasingly invaded in their individuality of judgment by what they, are told, and by the stream of reportage furnished them through the mass media of communication. Increasingly, the mass media peddle the "inside dope," much like the Fascist agitator portrayed by Leo Lowenthal and Norbert Guterman in *Prophets of Deceit.* Like other opiates, it may make some people jumpy and other people quiescent, but both groups are functionally apathetic in the light of our criteria.

CRITICALNESS OF AUTHORITY V. SUBMISSIVENESS. We have already indicated, in preceding criteria, the sort of nonapathetic orientation a person may have who is able to criticize assertions and demands for attention from authoritative sources: such a person can concern himself with human ends, and can relate events to his own human experience and human desires; he can transcend, if only in slight degree, the way the mass media present political occurrences. And, on the contrary, we have spoken of the apathy indicated by an orientation to politics which is basically submissive, being concerned only with means, messages, and missions. Our fifth criterion deals explicitly with the relationship to authority. Of all our criteria, this one is probably most palpably linked to character structure; though conceivably submissiveness toward authorities of state, school, or religion may be the outcome of a rational, though mistaken, judgment, we usually expect to trace a basis in personality for the attitude.

Even so, it is necessary to distinguish various kinds of submissiveness. In one of our interviews, we came across a second-generation Italian youth, a trade school senior, who exhibited great docility to the middle-class interviewer, to the school officials, and to constituted authority generally. Yet there was nothing intense about this submission; it had the archaic quality of a fatalistic but upstanding and secure peasant, who had no characterological *need* to submit because he genuinely respected authority and took his humble place in the world for granted. Today, this attitude is rare in America, and when we find submissiveness it is usually rooted, not in respect for unquestioned authority, but in a sado-masochistic syndrome of incomplete rebellion and incomplete—and therefore all the more intense—submission. Through the examination of attitudes toward authority, we hope to be able to differentiate between rebelliousness as simply a highly critical attitude toward authority and rebelliousness as an irrational character orientation.

Intense cravings for submission, and irrational rebelliousness—these again are psychological constellations which invite the coming into power of people with destructive and harmful personalities, people who are themselves apathetic in their lack of concern for human ends and their ruthless egocentricity for self or group.

APPLICATIONS OF THE CRITERIA. Out of our 150 interviews, we have taken about 20 for intensive study in the light of our criteria of affect and competence, as well as the further criteria we have just now set forth. We have sought not only to classify the respondent as politically involved or apathetic as the case may be, but also to portray in detail his political orientation as it now appears and as we envisage its possible future courses—to give, so to speak, the political potential of the person. As is evident from the qualitative nature of the criteria, such work involves ransacking the entire interview for clues to the interpretation of the specifically political responses. Moreover, the responses are themselves qualified in meaning by our knowledge of the ideology of the group, perhaps a numerically very small group, to which the interviewee belongs; it would be absurd, for instance, to take at face value the remarks of a small child about killing people, but we would have to see where the child went beyond or gave an idiosyncratic twist to his current peer-group's lingo.[7] We must also, of course, take account of the respondent's age; where, for instance, we have worked with high school students, we must allow for the fact that the political style of adolescence is often not fully formed.

We have found for ourselves that the criteria, in all their elaboration, do permit us to encompass many of the nuances and subtleties of the interview material. To be sure, there are many cases where the interview leaves us in doubt either because our questions and probes did not get beneath the surface or because politics for the individual *is* only surface—he cannot be said to have a political orientation, except embryonically, which is *his*. And of course we expect that people can fool us. We have found people who go through all the motions of affect so convincingly that, on first analysis, we have judged them nonapathetic, only to see on fuller scrutiny that this was a very smooth act. And conversely, we recall one instance of a returned veteran so cynical, so anxious to deny affect, that his interview was filled with brutal remarks; fuller examination revealed the very genuine affect which he was trying desperately, but quite unsuccessfully, to crush: it was apparent, for instance, that he was not submissive, not mass-media oriented, not as selfish as he claimed.

We wish it were possible to set forth here some of our material from our interviews and to show in detail how the protocol may reveal a syndrome of apathy—"indignant," "enthusiastic," "indifferent," etc., as the case may be—in terms of the criteria. However, even one of these discussions is apt to run the length of this article and space forbids including such an illustration. This is unsatisfactory because only through the details can the reader judge the validity of the research procedure. To be sure, this is not "validity" in the technical sense of proof of our results. In a few cases we have sought such proof—never fully adequate of course—by following a respondent up to see whether he fulfills predictions we have made on the basis of the interview.

---

[7] For a fuller account of the method and its difficulties, see our discussion in "Social Structure, Character Structure, and Opinion," in *International Journal of Opinion and Attitude Research*, Vol. 2, Winter, 1948–1949, p. 512.

In other cases, we have tried to check out interpretation against the judgments of others who have had dealings with the subject: this may help test our methods but is hardly probative as to the individual, since all concerned may be deceived.

At the present stage of our work, however, we do not see the interview material as "proving" our criteria, let alone as proving something about the apathy of the Americans. For one thing, we have worked experimentally with some more or less homogeneous groups who were not meant to be representative. For another thing, we are still far from having a satisfactory instrument, in our interviews and methods of analyzing them, for the measurement of potentials for apathy and involvement in individuals; and then, as social scientists do not need to be told, it is a long step from what we call "handicraft" work with individuals to "assembly line" work with groups and social classes. A great deal of investigation by many social scientists will be necessary before we have such tools, and before the problem of using historical categories in social-psychological studies is pushed nearer to solution.

In the meantime, however, interview material can be fruitfully used, we think, to stimulate the development of hypotheses as to historical changes of the sort we have here proposed. We were struck, for instance, to find in a small community in southern Vermont a shading of difference between the way the young people and their elders expressed themselves about national and international political developments. The elders were many of them of the type we call "indignant"— high in affect, low in competence—and their indignation had a curdled quality, not an amiable one, which reminded us of similar folk as described in Granville Hicks' *Small Town*. Despite their actual lack of participation, these elders still felt some sense of relatedness to government, though this showed often only in grievance. Thus, they would tell the interviewer that they felt they ought to take part in politics, and felt guilt for not doing so. And in referring to events, they used the pronoun "I"—"I" think, "I" want, "I" hate, etc. The young people, the teen-agers, on the other hand, had less grievance and less sense of relatedness. They took whatever government gave them, including the draft, with an almost total passivity; it never occurred to them that they *ought* to do anything about it, except obey: they would certainly pass the current loyalty tests! Moreover, their interviews on politics are almost devoid of the pronoun "I"; sometimes the reference is to a group "we," and mostly to a group "they." Perhaps more "socialized," more coöperative than their parents, they do not even make use of the privilege of the underprivileged to gripe, to react—to feel strongly—about what happens to them. They have passed from "indignation" to "indifference," with low affect to match their low competence.

Our sample is much too small to be sure of this divergence. Nor are we sure whether we deal here with changed underlying attitudes, or with age-graded conventions for expressing or repressing affect, or with self-selection of the old who choose to live in small-town Vermont. Beyond that, we cannot be sure that any contemporary matching of old versus young can be taken as establishing historical changes, though it was just for the purpose of studying "older" political styles that we decided on a survey in Vermont. But we are trying to pin down and narrow possible sources of error of this sort as we work with the Vermont material.[8] And each such investigation may be viewed as a step toward the clarification and simplification of our criteria for apathy and involvement, with the hope of settling on some which are more "diagnostic" than others of the social and psychological complex which interests us. As ever, work on the problem weaves back and forth between the field and the study with, occasionally, mutual stimulation and, equally often, mutual discouragement.

One such discouragement lies in the fact, evident from the above discussion, that it is easier to define apathy than to define its opposite, easier to spot and describe negative political orientations and the reasons for them in individual psychology and social situation, than to describe what we feel to be *appropriate* political styles and to see where, if at all, these may be developed and encouraged. Even our few interviews make plain what many know: that there is no want of people to do the dirty work of totalitarian political movements in America; this is a potential in many who are now "indifferent" apathetic types. At the same time, we have come across, out of 150 interviewees, perhaps four or five who could be classified as actually or potentially nonapathetic, and we doubt if a more favorable picture would emerge from a more complete sampling job.

This is not surprising. Character and culture combine to generate apathy. At best, involvement becomes deviant behavior, rational and adaptive though it is in historical perspective. It is rational and adaptive for the individual because, as we have said, it helps to orient him in his world and to satisfy the human need to be political. It is rational and adaptive for the society because, ever since the disillusionments of the last decades, and ever since the discovery, made by many, that America under full employment is not a particularly happy or humanly lively land, we have needed to fire people's imaginations with the possibilities of a major leap to security and freedom. It is to the nonapathetic that we look for such utopian political inventions, and to the recognition and support of those inventions when made by others. To be sure, inventions may be suppressed or ignored; all by themselves, they will not overcome apathy. But in the fate of an invention, as in the fate of a battle, there is often an element of chance. If we take the long historical view, we know that immense consequences have occasionally followed the inventiveness of a seemingly insignificant few. And if, on our other level of awareness, we take only the view of here-and-now, we can defend political involvement because, in our handful of instances, it seems to make the individual better able to face and enjoy life.

---

[8] The survey was made under the direction of Professor Martin Meyerson of the University of Chicago, and his wife, Marge Meyerson. The point about divergences between the young and the old was developed in discussions with them and with Rosalie Hankey, of the University of Chicago, who collaborated on the Vermont interviewing and analysis.

Democracy and Political Participation
in the Emerging Nations

SEYMOUR MARTIN LIPSET

The characteristic pattern of the stable western democracies in the mid-20th century is that of a "post-politics" phase—there is relatively little difference between the democratic left and right, the socialists are moderates, and the conservatives accept the welfare state. In large measure this reflects the fact that in these countries the workers have won their fight for citizenship and for political access, *i.e.*, the right to take part in all decisions of the body politic on an equal level with others.[1]

The struggle for citizenship had two aspects, political (access to power through the suffrage) and economic (institutionalization of trade union rights to share in the decisions affecting work rewards and conditions). The representatives of the lower strata are now part of the governing classes, members of the club. Political controversy has declined in the wealthier stable democracies because the basic political issue of the industrial revolution, the incorporation of the workers into the legitimate body politic, has been settled. The only key domestic issue today is collective bargaining over differences in the division of the total product within the framework of a Keynesian welfare state; and such issues do not require or precipitate extremism on either side.

In most of Latin and Eastern Europe, the struggle for working-class integration into the body politic was not settled before the Communists appeared on the scene to take over leadership of the workers. This fact drastically changed the political game, since inherently the Communists could not be absorbed within the system in the way that the Socialists have been. Communist workers, their parties and trade unions, cannot possibly be accorded the right of access by a democratic society. The Communists' self-

---

SOURCE: Seymour Martin Lipset, "Some Social Requisites of Democracy: Economic Development and Political Legitimacy," *American Political Science Review*, 53:1 (March, 1959), pp. 100–3. Reprinted by permission.

[1] T. H. Marshall has analyzed the gradual process of incorporation of the working class into the body politic in the 19th century, and has seen that process as the achievement of a "basic human equality, associated with full community membership, which is not inconsistent with a superstructure of economic inequality." See his brief but brilliant book, *Citizenship and Social Class* (Cambridge University Press, 1950), pp. 77. Even though universal citizenship opens the way for the challenging of remaining social inequalities, it also provides a basis for believing that the process of social change toward equality will remain within the boundaries of allowable conflict in a democratic system.

image and more particularly their ties to the Soviet Union lead them to accept a self-confirming hypothesis. Their self-definition prevents them from being allowed access and this in turn reinforces the sense of alienation from the system (of not being accepted by the other strata) which workers in nations with large Communist parties have. And the more conservative strata are reinforced in their belief that giving increased rights to the workers or their representatives threatens all that is good in life. Thus, the presence of Communists precludes an easy prediction that economic development will stabilize democracy in these European countries.

In the newly independent nations of Asia, the situation is somewhat different. In Europe at the beginning of modern politics, the workers were faced with the problem of winning citizenship, the right to take part in the political game, from the dominant aristocratic and business strata who controlled politics. In Asia the long-term presence of colonial rulers has identified conservatism as an ideology and the more well-to-do classes with subservience to colonialism; while leftist ideologies, usually of a Marxist variety, have been dominant, being identified with nationalism. The trade unions and the workers' parties of Asia have been part of the political process from the beginning of the democratic system. Conceivably such a situation could mean a stable democracy, except for the fact that these lower-strata rights pre-date the development of a stable economy with a large middle class and an industrial society.

The whole system stands on its head. The left in the European stable democracies grew gradually in a fight for more democracy, and gave expression to the discontents involved in early industrialization, while the right retained the support of traditionalist elements in the society, until eventually the system came into an easy balance between a modified left and right. In Asia, the left is in power during the period of population explosion and early industrialization, and must accept responsibility for all the consequent miseries. As in the poorer areas of Europe, the Communists exist to capitalize on all these discontents in completely irresponsible fashion, and currently are a major party, usually the second largest in most Asian states.

Given the existence of poverty-stricken masses, low levels of education, an elongated pyramid class structure, and the "premature" triumph of the democratic left, the prognosis for the perpetuation of political democracy in Asia and Africa is bleak. The nations which have the best prospects, Israel, Japan, Lebanon, the Philippines and Turkey, tend to resemble Europe in one or more major factors, high educational level (all except Turkey), substantial and growing middle class, and the retention of political legitimacy by non-leftist groups. The other emerging national states in Asia and Africa are committed more deeply to a certain tempo and pattern of economic development and to national independence, under whatever political form, than they are to the pattern of party politics and free elections which exemplify our model of democracy. It seems likely that in countries which avoid Communist or military dictatorship political developments will follow the pattern developing in countries such as Ghana, Tunisia or Mexico, where an educated minority uses a mass movement expressing leftist slogans to exercise effective control, and holds elections as a gesture toward ultimate, democratic objectives, and as a means of estimating public opinion, not as effective instruments for legitimate turnover in office of governing parties.[2] Given the pressure for rapid industrialization and for the immediate solution of chronic problems of poverty and famine through political agencies, it is unlikely that many of the new governments of Asia and Africa will be characterized by an open party system representing basically different class positions and values.[3]

Latin America, underdeveloped economically like Asia, is, however, politically more like Europe in the early 19th century than like Asia today. Most Latin American countries became independent states before the rise of industrialism and Marxist ideologies, and contain strongholds of traditional conservatism. The countryside is often apolitical or traditional, and the leftist movements secure support primarily from the industrial proletariat. Latin American communists, for example, have chosen the European Marxist path of organizing urban workers, rather than the "Yenan way" of Mao, seeking a peasant base.[4] If Latin America is allowed to develop on its own, and is able to increase its productivity and middle classes, there is a good chance that many Latin American countries will follow in the European direction. Recent developments, including the overthrowal of a number of dictatorships, in large measure reflect the effects of an increased middle class, growing wealth, and increased education. There is, however, also the possibility that these countries may yet follow in the French and Italian direction rather than that of northern Europe, that the communists will seize the leadership of the workers,

---

[2] See David Apter, *op. cit.*, for a discussion of the evolving political patterns of Ghana. For an interesting brief analysis of the Mexican "one-party" system see L. V. Padgett, "Mexico's One-Party System, a Re-evaluation," this REVIEW, Vol. 51 (1957), pp. 995–1008.

[3] As this paper was being edited for publication, political crises in several poor and illiterate countries occurred, which underline again the instability of democratic government in underdeveloped areas. The government of Pakistan was overthrown peacefully on October 7, 1958, and the new self-appointed president announced that "Western-type democracy cannot function here under present conditions. We have only 16 per cent literacy. In America you have 98 per cent." (*Associated Press* release, October 9, 1958). The new government proceeded to abolish parliament and all political parties. Similar crises have occurred, almost simultaneously, in Tunisia, Ghana, and even in Burma, which since World War II has been considered one of the more stable governments in Southeast Asia, under Premier U Nu. Guinea has begun life as an independent state with a one-party system.

It is possible that the open emergence of semi-dictatorships without much democratic "front" may reflect the weakening of democratic symbols in these areas under the impact of Soviet ideology, which equates "democracy" with rapid, efficient accomplishment of the "will of the people" by an educated elite, not with particular political forms and methods.

[4] Robert J. Alexander, *Communism in Latin America* (New Brunswick: Rutgers University Press, 1957).

and that the middle class will be alienated from democracy. . . . Considerably more research must be done specifying the boundaries of various societies along many dimensions before reliable comparative analysis of the sort attempted here can be carried out. Although the task obviously presents tremendous difficulties, it is only through such methods that we can move beyond the conventional semi-literary methods of giving illustrative examples to support plausible interpretations.

The data available are, however, of a sufficiently consistent character to support strongly the conclusion that a more systematic and up-to-date version of Aristotle's hypothesis concerning the relationship of political forms to social structure is valid. Unfortunately, as has been indicated above, this conclusion does not justify the optimistic liberal's hope that an increase in wealth, in the size of the middle class, in education, and other related factors will necessarily mean the spread of democracy or the stabilizing of democracy. As Max Weber, in discussing the chances for democracy in Russia in the early 20th century pointed out: "The spread of Western cultural and capitalist economy did not, *ipso facto,* guarantee that Russia would also acquire the liberties which had accompanied their emergence in European history. . . . European liberty had been born in unique, perhaps unrepeatable, circumstances at a time when the intellectual and material conditions for it were exceptionally propitious."[5]

These suggestions that the peculiar concatenation of factors which gave rise to western democracy in the nineteenth century may be unique are not meant to be unduly pessimistic. Political democracy exists and has existed in a variety of circumstances, even if it is most commonly sustained by a limited cluster of conditions. To understand more fully the various conditions under which it has existed may make possible the development of democracy elsewhere. Democracy is not achieved by acts of will alone; but men's wills, through action, can shape institutions and events in directions that reduce or increase the chance for the development and survival of democracy. To aid men's actions in furthering democracy was in some measure Tocqueville's purpose in studying the operation of American democracy, and it remains perhaps the most important substantive intellectual task which students of politics can still set before themselves.

---

[5] Richard Pipes, "Max Weber and Russia," *World Politics,* 7 (1955), p. 383.

Part Four. SOLUTIONS

"What should we do?" is the question put more and more clamorously to sociologists—who, for the most part and in good conscience, find it unanswerable. Still, the question, rising in volume and frequency on every hand, can scarcely be avoided.

Earlier in this book we have suggested that some of our most serious problems stem from a basic pathological condition, that they may be embedded in the very structure of our society, that disease which is exemplified by genocide, mass terror and thermonuclear war goes far toward obliterating all signs of health. If our social situation is nearly as grave as we suspect, then in order to change it, desperate action would seem to be necessary. Indeed, it is perhaps already too late for any action; all "remedies" initiated now or in the near future, could fall far short of meeting our urgent need.

It is not for us as sociologists, with our limited knowledge, to say whether man will survive his "problems" or be overwhelmed by them. We can say, that although the Apocalypse may soon be upon our species, and while there is yet time, a systematic sociological appraisal of methods currently used to "solve" social problems is certainly in order. If nothing more it should help to clarify the nature of those problems and how they might better be conceptualized—while incidentally exposing the inadequate or inept means we too often adopt in our haste to resolve them.

There are many modes of remedial action which are doomed to failure from the outset, no matter how brilliantly conceived they may be. The best remedy cannot work if it is designed to cope with an inaccurately identified problem. When misidentified, the "problem" leads necessarily to inappropriate proposals for action. If taken, the action sometimes produces genuine problems which are also misperceived and misidentified. The original error feeds on itself; trouble waxes; insight wanes.

Thus we commonly concern ourselves with the divorce rate, and fixated upon it, lose sight of the underlying reality, that of family stability and instability in a mercurial world. What is usually called "the crime problem" blinds us to something else, of which it is merely a symptom, namely a chronic disparity between social control and the traditional definition of unlawful acts. Our disinclination (or our inability) to pay for effective social control of criminal behavior begets one of two parallel illusions: either that what we take for granted as criminal is "natural," and that therefore nothing can be done about it, or the converse, that crime is simply evil and must be stamped out no matter what the consequences.

Mass terror and population decimations are not necessarily isolable problems; they might better be defined anew as events integral to certain institutional arrangements in "post-modern" society. These institutional features range from familial socialization to social competition; they enforce a marked tendency toward impersonal, objectified mistreatment of human beings in the interests of a given political policy.

The foregoing examples show the discrepancy between the popular definition of a social problem (by the electorate, the administrative bureaucrats, elected politicians, businessmen in vested interest associations) and the reformulation of a problem by sociological analysis. We wish to suggest a sociological scheme for delineating solutions in relation to the causal explanation, or etiology, of a problem. The schema, "Panaceas and Nostrums," is one which suggests several possible points of departure.

Given a definition of a problem at one etiological level, what are the consequences for its solution if we attack it at another level? As Thomas Gladwin reports, in the first selection reprinted below, Miller's study of psychological intervention seeking to change juvenile attitudes toward authority, adults, school, and middle-class values in a "desirable" direction, showed no significant reduction of the delinquency rate. In terms of our schema, delinquency so conceived is a problem of level 4 but Miller's attempts to deal with it were at levels 2 and 3.

Panaceas and Nostrums

SOURCES POSITED	PANACEAS PRESCRIBED
Etiological Levels	*Social Action Examples*
1. BIOLOGICAL (Genetic, physiological, constitutional)	MEDICAL (Eugenics, plastic surgery, vitamins, tranquilizers)
2. PSYCHOLOGICAL (Personality, regression, aggressivity, frustration, etc.)	ADJUSTMENT (Change of persons by means of therapy, psychiatry, counseling, etc.)
3. SOCIAL PSYCHOLOGICAL (Learning, reference group, interactions)	EXPERIENCE BY (a) contact with others (b) indoctrination through mass media (c) education
4. SOCIAL STATUS (Group attributes or strata attributes)	LEVELING (Expand opportunities for disadvantaged strata, e.g., group work, birth control, etc.)
5. SOCIAL INSTITUTIONS (Neighborhood, community, area aggregates)	SOCIAL REORGANIZATION (Urban renewal, political action, public health, bureaucratic reorganization, legislation, warfare)
6. SOCIAL VALUES (Norms, traditional attitudes)	INDOCTRINATION (Adult education, public relations, propaganda)

Gladwin's article demonstrates that there has to be a logical relationship between the etiological conception of a problem and intelligent attempts to do something about it.

I

The discrepancy already noted between a popular definition and the sociologically analyzed redefinition of social problems can be applied to a number of seemingly insoluble and generally recognized problems so serious that they might extinguish or, at least, cripple our society.

The problem of establishing and maintaining the peace of the world has been obscured in its common definition by sloganeering ("Better Dead than Red," "Peace with Honor"), and by assigning scapegoats ("It's the fault of Germans, Russians, Chinese"—when not Japanese, or all foreigners). The "solutions" which follow seem simple, and they are simple-minded. For example, "If we abolish the munition makers, we could then disarm." (George Bernard Shaw, in the guise of Andrew Undershaft in *Major Barbara,* disposed of that notion some years ago.) The problem of the peace is one which has to be solved in a hard way, as Amitai Etzioni has stated in his book's sloganized title, *The Hard Way to Peace.*[1] This way involves a basic reorganization of our values and institutions. The Great Powers have to find acceptable techniques of shifting from an escalation of the arms race into a world devoted to Professor Seymour Melman's peace race.[2] This requires answering such questions as how do we allocate the resources and energies now expended on arms to peaceful uses? Do we concentrate on underdeveloped areas, or do we focus upon raising living standards at home? Can we do both in a radioactive world where the safety levels of Strontium 90 and other poisonous products are constantly being revised upwards? Indeed, the schema on p. ooo suggests that we may well be on our way to a biological solution (through genetic destruction of chromosomes and bone marrow) of a problem heretofore defined by the question, can we survive a nuclear war?

The literature on this subject is enormous and ranges from sober evaluation of limited nuclear conflict and what our side can get out of it (for example, Herman Kahn, Edward Teller, and, we suppose, their Russian counterparts) to voices of doom warning us that we must not permit this situation to go on much longer.

In the next article, Richard Korn indicates some of the dilemmas that we face when we try to thrash out problems and suggest solutions. Note, however, that he views solutions through the treatment situation of therapist and clients, whereas Herbert Gans, in his discussion of social planning, suggests a different model. This tendency to go beyond the social worker-

---

[1] Amitai Etzioni, *The Hard Way to Peace: A New Strategy* (New York: Collier Books, 1962).

[2] Seymour Melman, *The Peace Race* (New York: Ballantine Books, 1962).

client model of social action is explored still further by David R. Hunter in his discussion of slums and social work.

The roles of leaders in making decisions which are supported by their followers and actions which arise from these decisions are the topic of Seymour Leventman's selection. Here we see the successes noted by Alvin W. Gouldner in his *Studies in Leadership* and by C. Wright Mills in *The New Men of Power*. They deal with sincerely dedicated leaders committed to a mobility ethos in which personal ascent up the status ladder transcends the original aims of their action. In some such manner, all social movements, ethnic integration, universal education, trade unionism, and political action are made rigid, get organized, and become hierarchically structured. Their leaders use the efficient bureaucratic structure to further their power goals, as well as to meet the aims of their organization. While this process is taken for granted in business, its presence in other areas of organized social action seems to have gone largely unnoticed.

Lest we allow ourselves to be carried away with the grandeur of doing something positive about our serious social problems, Harold Orlans's article, "The Asylum as an American Death Camp" (which appeared originally over fifteen years ago), is a grim reminder of how slowly social change does occur, even when it has been widely endorsed. Erving Goffman's more recent discussion of asylums and total institutions is wholly consistent with the earlier observations of Orlans.

Herbert Gans' article is constructive, but it can hardly be called optimistic. Social planning is possible, but the technical complexities and political obstacles it encounters are more likely to give pause than to fire enthusiasm. In sociological perspective, a program to be rational and effective should seek to foster what Gans names "guided mobility." Urban poverty is not going to be eliminated by physical "renewal" or psychiatrically oriented programs of social meliorism. But if guided mobility offers the best hope, ultimately, it is far harder to implement than the piecemeal programs now in vogue with city planners and social workers. This is a case in which what seems to be the least "practical" procedure may provide some kind of "solution." To know even this much about a social problem is to have departed drastically from the conventional outlook and the conventional wisdom.

Once a social problem has been adequately defined, and seen to be amenable to solution, a policy decision must be made. We choose above all between doing something and doing nothing. A decision to act entails the further choice of the *target* of action, whether to aim at the individual or at the social and institutional organization involved in the problem. Schematically one might view it as follows:

Action	*Target*	
	INDIVIDUAL	SOCIAL STRUCTURE
+	therapeutic intervention	meliorism
−	positive neglect	laissez-faire

If the solutions proposed to real problems are not panaceas for illusory problems, all sensible action requires an estimate of the consequences of a decision to take action. If we are going to do something in order to ameliorate, abolish, allay or aid, we must ask the following:

1. Is the action related in a specific way to the phenomenon we are trying to correct or change?
2. If it is related, how is it related?
3. What will happen if we act?
4. What will happen if we do not act?
5. If we accept a statistically "normal" amount of crime, divorce, mental illness, disease, disaster, political unrest, and economic dislocation, what are its limits?
6. How much pathology should we regard as normal in a given social system?
7. If we act to solve a problem as defined popularly, how much does it cost in social consequences and in money?
8. If we redefine the problem sociologically and act to solve it, how much will it cost?
9. If we do not act, what are the costs?

All ameliorative action requires decisions, and these always entail subsequent decisions based on assumptions about costs, degrees of efficiency in reaching goals, and suitability of goals. Logically and ideally, one should always—though it rarely happens—examine all proposed actions and compare them to the alternative of not acting at all. When we compare action and nonaction we can see that a considered decision to do nothing involves systematic weighing of most of the same questions associated with deciding to act.

WAYS OF ACTING
Doing Nothing and Doing Something

Doing something involves:
1. Definition of a problem and its boundaries.
2. Specification of objectives.
3. Selection of appropriate means of attaining objectives.
4. Evaluation of effectiveness of action.

Doing nothing involves:
1. Definition of a problem and its boundaries.
2. Specification of objectives.
3. Selecting, or opting for lack of action, doing nothing as the appropriate means of attaining objectives.
4. Evaluation of the effectiveness of nonaction.

One can frequently make a rather attractive case for doing nothing, on three grounds: (1) Spontaneous recovery rates in many social problems involving behavior seem to give better results than recovery rates linked with specific actions. (2) Actions on a problem may result in undesired consequences and other problems that would not arise if we did not act. (3) Many actions based on inadequate understanding are irrelevant to the real problems.

But, in the contemporary world there are strong, although not necessarily scientific, reasons for preferring action to inaction. Political considerations, ego-satisfactions, cross-pressures of interest groups—all enter into decisions to act rather than stand pat. Utopian visions may sometimes becloud harsh realities and impel actions not consonant with careful or logical analysis of the facts. On the other hand, inaction does brake action solely for the sake of action.

An abundance of information available limits action. Given a general state of ignorance, one can act in any manner whatsoever—without fear of exposure.[3] Much information will generally slow down decisions to act, especially so with respect to such social problems as we have considered in this volume. When our information is contradictory, inconsistent, and incomplete, and it usually is, thoughtless action may be impeded for that reason.

In part, this accounts for our capacity to make it appear that social actions are occurring when in reality they are being delayed or diverted. Studying a problem at length is a favorite method of handling pressures to act. Often the problem will change; contemplated and pressured action can then be safely forgotten; it no longer applies; the problem is redefined.

Another popular mode of avoiding action while apparently engaging in it is to remove everyone from the situation. A revolt breaks out in Hungary or Poland. Crush it and the problems that give rise to revolution, while still there, are no longer defined as such. The affected population has been destroyed. In more democratic societies, as a rule, such extreme measures are avoided. In dealing with the problem of slums, poverty, and their attendant phenomena of crime, disease, illiteracy, and disorganization, we have used urban renewal. By razing the area and thereby effectively removing the population, we solve the problem of slums by destroying them (although we send their former occupants to create a slum elsewhere).

By far, the most popular way of doing nothing by acting is to individualize problems and treat them as matters which only pertain to individuals. Thus, we tend to define problems as medical and psychiatric or as matters of individual morality. Since this means, in effect, that we are asking persons ·to adjust to their lot while we counsel, cajole, and persuade them, the problems remain but perception of the problems is translated from the social sphere of action to the domain of individual initiative.

This seems to be the critical area of dispute in solving social problems. It pervades all matters of public concern and finds its expression in the preachments of organized religion, medicine, and law, as well as in the basic patterns of socialization at home and in school.

Adjustment is the goal, and if individuals can achieve it, then our actions

---

[3] See Moore and Tumin, p. 516.

or inactions are justified. There are real costs in this position since adjustment may also mean apathy, gloom, and loss of interest even in matters of social survival. Adjustment does not mean satisfaction and since satisfactions in living are what count to most of us, it may be that we prefer to die rather than adjust to lives of dissatisfaction and frustration. So far, actions initiated by men of good and ill will have not solved our most elemental problems—those of human survival, famine, disease, senseless premature death, and widespread dissatisfaction—in an equitable manner throughout the social structure.

A case in point is the very much greater incidence of drug addiction in this country, where legislation has intensified the problem, by contrast with England and Wales, where the problem is negligible. Why should the Briton be thirty-four times less likely to use narcotics than the American? Wilkins ingeniously interprets the disparity as due (in part) to differences in social definition of narcotics addiction. It is a criminal vice, in the official American view, while the British have always perceived it as a sickness. Is it possible that our appraisal of need—it *must* be suppressed—has produced both the motive and the structure of opportunities (lacking in Great Britain, since drugs may be prescribed by physicians) that make for a large-scale social problem? If so, it is clear that a policy of responsible nonaction should always be held open as possibly the better alternative. The more dramatic forms of coping with deviant behavior judged by some to be intolerable may actually encourage it, and thus create a "social problem" where none of such magnitude existed before.

16. CAUSE AND CURE: MATCHING LEVELS

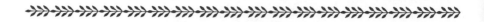

Strategies in Delinquency Prevention

THOMAS GLADWIN

Alarm over increases in juvenile delinquency is reaching acute proportions, and has created inescapable pressure on schools, police, social agencies, and governments to do something about delinquency. In particular, the alarm, and therefore the pressure, focuses on delinquency in lower-class urban populations. Presumably this is because delinquency is more prevalent in these populations, and also because lower-class delinquents display more of the physical violence which so distresses middle-class people. The question, then, is posed with increasing insistence: What can or should be done about delinquency in big city slums?

Current theoretical formulations on juvenile delinquency in the United States are phrased in largely sociological terms, emphasizing the interplay between personality structure and social institutions. Action programs based on these formulations select one or more strategic points around the circle of causality at which to intervene, and thereby hopefully to break the circle. Most commonly, manipulation is attempted with respect to the psychological links in the chain. Programs of this sort have largely been directed by social workers, with the assistance of psychiatrists and psychologists. The aim is to alter self-defeating attitudes and perceptions, and to redirect social energy toward more constructive goals which will hopefully prove more satisfying and less frustrating. However, in actual practice the relationship of a worker with lower-class clients is usually structured in terms of the psychoanalytically-oriented clinical training of the worker, and the goal of the relationship becomes one of draining off or deflecting acute psychological and social tensions. In essence, the worker tries to make conformity tolerable.

This strategy of psychological manipulation of individuals or groups has come under increasing criticism, especially with respect to lower-class delinquency. It has been pointed out that professional intervention based on a

SOURCE: Leonard J. Duhl (ed.), *The Urban Condition* (New York: Basic Books, Inc., 1963), pp. 267–275. Reprinted with permission.

psychotherapeutic model has little impact on the basic social and cultural conditions which channel psychological needs in troublesome directions. This criticism states in effect that lower-class people develop self-defeating attitudes because they are in fact defeated by their society.

An additional argument against this kind of psychological intervention is provided by Walter B. Miller's findings in working with lower-class gangs, that while it was possible to change many psychological attributes—attitudes toward authority, adults, education, and to some extent general middle-class values—in a desirable direction, no significant reduction was achieved in the rate of delinquent acts.[1]

However, the dilemma of the social agencies has recently led to experiments with massive assaults on the social environment. These generally propose saturation of a lower-class neighborhood with multiple and varied services intended to alleviate simultaneously all of the various social limitations which the proponent of the plan views as serious. There are numerous obvious criticisms which can be leveled at the strategies of this sort thus far proposed. Most are so expensive in both money and professional requirements that they offer little hope of providing in themselves a strategic model of subsequent usefulness elsewhere.

The answer to this objection is that new insights and ideas will be found and proven effective, and that these can then be applied selectively and less expensively in other areas. However, the proposed programs are so global that their evaluation also tends to be global, and it becomes very unlikely that the specific impact of any single program component can be isolated and measured. Therefore even if these programs are demonstrably successful, their benefits will be largely limited to the affected area or community.

Perhaps we must recognize that juvenile delinquency *as such* is not directly amenable to programs of prevention or amelioration. If we accept this, we can contemplate programs which will achieve a more critical and economical focus upon selected components of the problem of the lower-class adolescent, with the expectation that in the long run delinquency rates will drop proportionately as one after another of the forces pressuring these adolescents is relieved. Juvenile delinquency is not a distinct social disease or syndrome. It encompasses a number of different kinds of behaviors. Furthermore, the behaviors defined as delinquent are by no means the only ways in which adolescents can or do respond to their many-faceted dilemmas. Juvenile delinquents are simply those individuals or groups who happen to react to a situation in ways which the larger society views as threatening. In contrast, the youth who enters military service, for example, may thereby achieve temporary relief from his difficulties, but his behavior is not considered delinquent.

Equally we must recognize that the pressures and blockages are by no

---

[1] Miller, W. B., "The Impact of a 'Total Community' Delinquency Control Project," *Soc. Prob.*, 10:168–191, 1962.

means perceived and experienced in the same way by everyone. One adolescent may feel frustrated and discriminated against because he cannot go to college or because he is unable to get a white-collar job, and therefore feel he must somehow vent his frustration, or at least escape from his dilemma. But another may have set his heart on being a long-haul truck driver and feel no frustration whatever.

The challenge, then, is to identify those attributes of the social environment which are perceived by the largest number of lower-class adolescents as unfair limitations upon them. If we can find realistic ways to relieve these limitations (which are usually very real) we may hope to reduce progressively a succession of those social pressures which cause some youths to react with behaviors we call delinquent.

However, any strategic alternative to a direct attack on delinquency must meet at least two conditions. One is that the alternatives be realistically feasible and within reach of available financial and professional resources. The second is that the goal of any new program must be high enough in the hierarchy of middle-class values so that the self-evident worth of the new program will justify its substitution for the original aim of simply preventing delinquency as such.

One goal meeting these requirements would be a substantial increase in the number of lower-class adolescents who complete high school and attain a regular and educationally respectable diploma. A diploma is not the cure for all the problems of any lower-class youth, and at best would be unattainable for many, but a substantial proportion of the population of our concern have the ability and would unquestionably be much better off if they could complete high school satisfactorily. It is therefore worth examining with some care the potential value and feasibility of starting the attack on the lower-class dilemma with a focus on the academic achievement of lower-class youths in high school.

Middle-class values link education not only to occupational opportunity but also to the formation of good character. High school dropouts are related in the popular view directly with delinquency—even though many adolescents leave school for the respectable purpose of entering productive employment. Similarly, the first question likely to be asked by enforcement officers or judges if a boy gets in trouble is, "How is he doing in school?" Clearly, a program goal of improving school performance and participation meets the criterion of self-evident worth as a substitute for, or an indirect approach to, delinquency prevention as such.

From what we as social scientists know of the lower-class dilemma, a valid high school diploma is clearly of ever increasing importance to an adolescent for at least two closely related reasons. It is in the first place a testimonial to "good character," and in fact during its acquisition many middle-class behaviors and attitudes are necessarily acquired. It reflects a willingness to conform.

It is also an essential, even though not in itself sufficient, key to the middle-class opportunity structure. This results from the continued dwindling of the skilled labor market and the increasing requirement of a high school diploma for consideration for even a semi-skilled job. And of course without a diploma from high school, college is also out of the question.

The difficulty is that lower-class children are lacking not so much in educational opportunities as in the capability or readiness to utilize these opportunities. Schools are available. In lower-class areas the teachers may not be quite as good but they at least meet minimum requirements. To some degree, the inability to capitalize on opportunities is recognized in planning for lower-class students. However, the response is usually an attempt to adapt the school to the child, rather than the reverse.

Thus it is frequently stated that schools demand middle-class behaviors, and that this handicaps the lower-class child. This is undoubtedly true, but the answer is not necessarily to relax the demands. If we recognize that a high school diploma acts as a badge of middle-class respectability, the schools must continue to demand middle-class behaviors. At the risk of appearing cynical, when I see a negligible relationship between the content of the average high school curriculum on the one hand, and the abilities required in the jobs for which a high school diploma is demanded on the other, I believe we are forced to conclude that the *primary* value of the diploma is as a certificate of socialization. It certifies that the holder of a diploma will respond in predictable ways to the expectations of middle-class employers.

There is real danger in pressuring schools to meet the lower-class child at his own level. Successful school participation requires above all working fairly hard and steadily at tasks which at best are often dull, in order to achieve a very distant reward, the diploma. In other words, in order that academic learning itself be achieved, the student must accept the necessity of hard work and delay in reward and gratification—behaviors which lie at the heart of middle-class values. Equipped to work within these values, lower-class youths can and do move upward. Without them they are more than likely to fail in school and to spend their lives in underprivileged poverty.

The problem therefore is not primarily one of making the schools more accepting of lower-class adolescents and their behaviors (although certain unnecessary rigidities could be relieved), but rather of preparing lower-class children to accept and fit into middle-class society. Part of this, of course, consists in effecting changes in elementary school curricula which will develop thinking styles better adapted to the requirements of curriculum in the higher grades, but this is a separate and complex problem. Even more important, for many lower-class children, is the development of more positive values and attitudes toward schooling and teachers such that they will be willing to modify their behaviors to conform to teachers' expectations, and yet will not in the process suffer a disastrous loss of status in the eyes of their peers.

It is hard to believe that the massive reality of the meaning of a high school diploma is unknown to lower-class youth. They must all know slightly older boys, in particular, who have found the doors to good jobs permanently closed to them for lack of a diploma. The reality is constantly restated in the mass media, in recruiting and employment offices, and in a thousand other ways. Yet equally constant is the expression of negative attitudes toward schools among lower-class adolescents.

The contrast between the perceived value, even necessity, of schooling, set against consistent attitudinal devaluation of the school, almost certainly reflects a thinly veiled rationalization. The need for rationalization emerges from a belief, based on long experience and shared by many lower-class adolescents, that sooner or later their academic careers will inevitably end in failure. Their school performance has been unsatisfactory and subject to criticism. As a social experience, school has been so humiliating that there is no realistic basis for expecting personal acceptance by teachers. In other words, the lower-class student sees the cards stacked against him.

Here it is useful also to bear in mind that an increasing number of studies have pointed out the quite limited future-time orientation which obtains in much of the lower class. The inability to implement plans or hopes discourages realistic thinking about one's status in the years to come. It is more comfortable, and often psychologically essential, to live from day to day. Only by stripping the future of reality can life appear tolerable. Yet I am convinced that any program which offered some measure of meaningful help and encouragement in school, and which could demonstrate some achievement or reward in return for the expenditure of energy or the demonstration of willingness, would find acceptance among large numbers of lower-class children from junior high school onward. I also believe—despite the hostility and rejection of school by these adolescents, which we see every day—that the relief from a perhaps unconscious sense of defeat would improve their outlook and behavior in school and out. They would, in effect, become less likely to undertake the acts we call delinquent. A few examples can be cited which point tentatively in this direction.

In a primarily lower-class Negro enclave known as Ken-Gar in a middle-class white area of Montgomery County, Maryland, school achievement was revealed as conspicuously poor when the schools were integrated, and delinquency was fairly high. A group of white adults from the surrounding area organized a program on a voluntary basis to tutor and encourage the Ken-Gar children in all grades. School achievement rose rapidly, high school drop-outs decreased, adults developed more interest in the schooling of their children, and there appears to have been some decrease in juvenile delinquency. Recently the success of this venture led to the county board of education hiring a full-time program director for Ken-Gar, and another person who is developing similar programs among other underprivileged groups in the county.

Neighborhood House, in a very depressed and apathetic Negro slum area of Richmond, California, instituted a Study Hall Project. They set up a center for evening study, organized as a social center but with supervision and some tutorial help with homework. Although it is not yet clear what effect this has had on academic achievement, it has resulted in a striking change among neighborhood youths with respect to homework. Whereas in the past anyone who brought books home from school was obviously a square, now one has to account for oneself if books are not brought home. It is fashionable to study, or to seem to study, and with this half the battle is won. At the same time school personnel are aware of this project and are pleased by it. This undoubtedly affects favorably the response of teachers toward these students and increases the possibility of their social acceptance by the teachers, quite aside from objective academic achievement.

Another example is provided by the Work-Study Program of the University of Southern California Youth Studies Center, conducted in the Santa Monica schools. This is a program which combines a half day of study with a half day of (often subsidized) employment and vocational counseling. This program has apparently had some success in keeping students, who were selected as imminent drop-outs, in school. But the really interesting development is that in its second year the students began complaining that the academic part of the program was not sufficiently rich.

The most ambitious undertaking of this sort to date is the Higher Horizons program in New York City schools in underprivileged neighborhoods. With its exploratory predecessor, "Project 43," this has been evolving and expanding since 1956. It has included help with school work, counseling with parents and with teachers, class trips and cultural activities, and a variety of other approaches to helping students do better in school and feel better about schooling. There has been an explicit attempt to develop in the students the idea of planning for their futures, and the recognition that education is not only a necessary but also a possible part of such planning. Starting with two high schools it has expanded into elementary schools and into additional junior high and high schools. Careful evaluation demonstrates striking gains in almost all areas of school achievement and a reduction in school misbehavior, truancy, and drop-outs. Although out-of-school behavior, including delinquency, has not been evaluated, it is hard to believe that this has not been improved also.

These examples are only straws in the wind. They certainly do not exhaust the possibilities for ingenious programs. They encourage the belief, however, that very rewarding possibilities exist for programs which will actively focus on the negative attitudes toward education which pervade and infect the lower-class adolescent subculture in most cities. Opening up the possibilities for academic success at least to the point of getting through high school, with the change in values and behavior which this implies, will certainly not solve all the problems of lower-class youth, nor even touch some of the causes of juvenile delinquency. But it does offer a real hope for increasing access to the opportunity structure of our society for substantial numbers of lower-class persons, with a very modest social agency investment. As such, it is a strategy which should receive serious attention.

17.   EXPERT AND POLITY: RECONCILING WISH AND PRESCRIPTION

The Private Citizen, the Social Expert, and the Social Problem:
An Excursion Through an Unacknowledged Utopia

RICHARD KORN

Though the state of Israel has been in existence since 1948 we met on every hand large numbers of the Orthodox who still pray for the deliverance of the Promised Land. When we suggested that the two-thousand year promise had already been fulfilled they rejected our interpretation with scorn. Perhaps they were wiser than we knew. In their preference of eternal hope they may have grasped the wisdom of the savant who said that achievement is the death of endeavor and the birth of disgust. The dream they dreamed could not be destroyed by 2000 years of frustration. They were not prepared to risk it now with the one thing that is more fatal to hope than disappointment: success.

—Excerpt from an unpublished travel journal

1. The Unnoticed Arrival of a Millenium

Those of us who have hoped for the millenial day when an applied science of human behavior would be granted authority to cope with most social problems may be unprepared to recognize that the Millenium has in many places already arrived, silently and almost unnoticed. The evidence is all around us.

Consider, for example, the quiet revolution which has taken place in the handling of certain types of criminals. Psychiatrists have for many years protested the traditional legal treatment of offenders, particularly of the criminally insane and the sexually deviated. Among the many faults they

---

SOURCE: Prepared especially for this volume.

found with conventional procedures was the requirement that the legal apparatus could be set in motion only after an actual crime had been committed. Would not the citizens be better protected if those with the skill to detect antisocial tendencies were granted the authority to identify the potentially dangerous before they transgressed—instead of standing helplessly by until the criminals actually carried out their crimes against unsuspecting, undefended victims?

Thanks in part to the unremitting urging of many psychiatrists, the citizenry of several states need no longer stand helplessly by. By 1949 a number of states had adopted "sex psychopath" laws enabling the authorities to incarcerate suspected potential offenders without the requirement that they prove or even charge the defendant with commiting a criminal act. Once adjudicated a sex-psychopath, the suspect is confined in a mental hospital or correctional institution and required to remain until he is pronounced "cured" or safe enough to release. In this connection Drs. Gutmacher and Weihofen have written:

> If analysis of the convict's personality indicates that he cannot safely be released, he may have to spend the rest of his life under legal supervision of some kind, even though the only crime he has actually committed was a minor one.[1]

By 1950 at least thirteen states had adopted laws which embodied some or all of the provisions described above—a conservative index of the extent to which psychiatry had established its position in the innermost fortress of the law itself.[2] Four years later one of the more influential architects of the victory was still invoking a millenium which had, in large part, already arrived:

> Criminals should be classified on the basis of their psychological propensities and the inner structure of their personalities. Neither the law nor the warden is fit to pass on the corrigibility or incorrigibility of a given criminal. Those who mete out the revenge of society on the transgressor are by their nature and training unfit to develop a deep psychological insight into the psychological dynamics of a given criminal's behavior. Only specially trained clinical workers who understand the psychopathology of the nonpsychotic offender can be entrusted with the evaluation of the criminal.[3]

---

[1] M. S. Guttmacher, and H. Weihofen, *Psychiatry and the Law* (New York: Norton, 1952), p. 445.

[2] These innovations have not been established without serious and determined resistance on the part of defenders of the traditional legal order. One unremitting legal critic, an attorney, writes about the application of the statute in Washington, D.C.: "Recently it was reported that 'of the sex psychopaths now at the St. Elizabeth Hospital, five or six are exhibitionists whose offense was exposing themselves to men. From present prospects (it was noted by hospital officials) they probably won't respond to treatment, which means that under the act they will be kept there for the rest of their lives'." (Edward De Grazia, "The Distinction of Being Mad," University of Chicago Law Review, 22 (1955), p. 352).

[3] G. Zilboorg, *The Psychology of the Criminal Act and Punishment* (New York: Harcourt, 1954), p. 129.

The foregoing citation may serve as an introduction to the broader dimensions of our subject: the social expert at large. In the few sentences with which he suggests the appropriate role of the clinician in crime, Dr. Zilboorg has offered a prescription applicable to a far wider universe of discourse. He has actually described not one role but three and in doing so he has provided an implicit working model for the analysis of the relations between the social expert, the private citizen and social problems of many kinds. The working assumptions implicit in this model may be spelled out in detail:

1. The model sets up a trichotomy consisting of a small, relatively organized confraternity of experts with special and exclusive skills, a large body of private citizens lacking these skills and an indeterminate number of persons or problems requiring the services of these skills.

2. With this trichotomy established, it is suggested that certain relationships between these groups are appropriate. These relationships are posited on the acknowledgement that the expert group alone possesses the skill or will to ameliorate the difficulties of the citizens in need of help. Corollary to this acknowledgement is the implication that persons with certain categories of problems cannot help themselves and cannot be helped by means of direct interaction with other private citizens.

3. In the definitions of the roles governed by these assumptions, the expert is given the status of operator and prescriber, the person in need the status of patient or client and the private citizen is given the task of supporting the expert in his work and referring the person in need of help to his care.

2. The Medical Model of the Social Expert

Recognizably, this definition of roles derives its model and inspiration from a profession in which a similar structuring of roles has achieved high social prestige, presumably because it has brought society great benefits. This profession is, of course, *medicine*—and its institutional roles of doctor and patient. Generalizing this relationship to problem areas other than physical health, one derives the conception of "society-as-patient" and the ancillary conception of the social practitioner as the physician of society.

Within this context, the particular content of the problems and remedies may vary widely without any significant change in the formal structure of the relationships. The problems may be "political," "economic," or "social"— and the practitioner, accordingly, may function as a professional politician, economist or social engineer. In each situation, however, the model of society —as patient and expert—as physician has similar implications. One of these derives by analogy from the medical injunctions against self-prescription by the patient and unauthorized treatment by the unqualified. Since the expert alone has the skills to prescribe for society, it follows that the citizens at large should confine their task to that of providing that number of experts which is adequate for treating these numbers of their fellow citizens in need of help. To the extent that a sufficient number of experts are made available for the skilled, professional treatment of social problems, the direct obligation of citizen-to-citizen in these matters may be reduced. Ideally, a stage may be reached when the sole obligation of the private citizenry is to support by their taxes and contributions a sufficient number of experts, agencies, and institutions to treat all categories of social problems.

3. *The Argument in Support of the Medical Model of the Social Expert as an Operator upon Society*

a. THE ARGUMENT OF A SOCIALLY NECESSARY DI-VISION OF·LABOR. Perhaps the most basic argument derives from the observation that the human problems of a complex civilization are as much beyond the grasp of the individual citizen as are its technical and material problems. The increasing power of man-in-general over his environment and the decreasing control by men-in-particular of their personal destinies is a universal paradox of the modern age. Despite the obvious price paid for specialization in the decline of individual self-sufficiency, the complexities of modern life will probably continue to require an even greater division of labor; short of catastrophe, the paradoxical trend seems irreversible.

Nevertheless, while the division of labor has placed men in an unprecedented state of dependency on one another, it has simultaneously liberated them from many of the old necessities and limitations imposed by physical nature. Is it not equally possible that a similar specialization in the field of social relations holds the promise of the same kind of liberation from the primordial limitations of human nature? If the citizen can now rely with confidence on the electrician, the plumber and the engineer to keep his material house in order, if he can rely on the doctor and public health specialist to keep his body in repair, may he not with equal confidence anticipate the day when the social sciences will provide equally competent practitioners to deal with his personal and social problems?

Such, at any rate, is the alternative offered by those who believe that an applied social science can solve the problems and salvage the casualties created by unbridled human initiative and ingenuity. Before examining this alternative we might recall that neither the problem, as posed, nor the solution, as offered, is in any fundamental way novel to human thought. The dream of imposing order upon the chaos of uncontrolled human initiative has been advanced by thinkers as separated in time as Plato, Thomas More and Thorsten Veblen—and by theorists as remote in political ideology as Karl Marx and Elton Mayo, founder of the "human relations" school of industrial psychology centered at the Harvard School of Business. Consider the solution proposed by Mayo in his influential book, *The Human Problems of an Industrial Civilization*:

> The world over we are greatly in need of an administrative elite who can assess and handle the concrete difficulties of human collaboration . . . If at all the

critical posts in communal activity we had intelligent persons . . . very many of our difficulties would dwindle to the vanishing point.[4]

In advancing his proposal of all power to the administrative elite, Mayo did not hesitate to discover both a community of problems and a community of solutions with the methods of the Soviet state. Refusing to be misled by ideological superstructures, he asserted the essential similarity of the managerial techniques of American capitalists and the Soviet management of a whole society. In each country the managers were faced with the same problems:

The rapid pace of industrial development, uninformed by human research or knowledge, dispersed the last possibilities of collaborate and social effort and imposed upon the workers a low level of human organization from which social participation and social effort were excluded. This low-level organization, like trade unionism, also represents a conservative and reactionary attempt to conserve human values; its chief symptom is "stalling," a procedure apparently resented as much by the workers themselves as by management. Since this seems to be as characteristic of Russia as of the United States, it is probable that the human problems involved are fundamental and contain no "political" element. Again it may be said that the question is not who is to control, but, rather, what researches are essential to the development of intelligence in control.[5]

The problems, then, are not political at all: it is a question of control or perish. And the processes which the Soviets have accelerated as a matter of principle may be identical to those in which we are caught, despite our contrasting principles and opposed ideology. Moreover, just as the problems are similar, so will the solutions converge: we should not be confused by slogans:

Socialism, Communism, Marxism would seem to be irrelevant to the industrial events of the twentieth century. These doctrines probably express the workers' desire to recapture something of the lost human solidarity. But Russian communism, however, although it claims this purpose, seems to be expressive of twentieth century methods rather than of an ideal of human solidarity.[6]

In his appraisal of the Soviet experiment—the most thoroughgoing subordination of human relations to the ideals and techniques of social engineering—the American founder of the human relations approach does not conceal his respect for the engineering efficiency of Stalin's program of the enforced collectivization of Soviet agriculture. In what may yet become appreciated as the most revealing acknowledgment ever made by an oracle of modern American industry, Mayo, writing in 1933, speaks admiringly as one human engineer of another:

The violent uprooting of peasants and workers to take them to a distant scene, the quick and final determination of disputes, are in part perhaps Slavonic and

---

[4] E. Mayo, *The Human Problems of an Industrial Civilization* (New York: Viking, 1960) (1st ed., 1933), p. 177.

[5] *Ibid.*, p. 174.

[6] *Ibid.*

in part due to the critical nature of the present developmental stage. But the conceptions of work and industrial organization which such methods express are more nearly related to the engineering logic of the twentieth century than to Marx's dictatorship of the proletariat.[7]

Mayo's salute to the engineering logic of Soviet communism was warmly returned 30 years later by Chairman Khrushchev on the occasion of his address to the National Association of Manufacturers in 1960. In the course of his speech, which featured a mutually favorable comparison of Soviet and American industrial methods, Chairman Khrushchev extended to the industrialists an invitation to live and work in the Soviet Union, promising them not only higher pay but a higher status than they now held in a country which inadequately employed their talents. During the same period in which Khrushchev was expressing his approval of American industrial methods the amicable spirit of his tour was marred by one jarring note: a bitter clash with Walter Reuther of the United Auto Workers.

Mayo's call for an administrative elite has been endorsed by a number of later social thinkers, among whom may be counted the recent president of the American Sociological Society, Professor Talcott Parsons. Writing in 1950, Parsons asserts:

> Under American conditions, a politically leading stratum must be made up of a combination of business and non-business elements. The role of the economy in American society and of the business element in it is such that political leadership without prominent business participation is doomed to ineffectiveness and to the perpetuation of dangerous internal conflict. It is not possible to lead the American people against the leaders of the business world. But at the same time, so varied now are the national elements which make a legitimate claim to be represented, the business element cannot monopolize or dominate political leadership and responsibility. Broadly, I think, a political elite in the two main aspects of "politicians" whose specialties consist in the management of public opinion, and of "administrators" in both civil and military services, must be greatly strengthened.[8]

b.   THE SCIENTIFIC FOUNDATIONS FOR THE ROLE OF THE EXPERT AS THE OPERATOR ON SOCIETY. Those favoring the installation of a specialized elite of experts with authority to restore order, rationality and health to the social organism cite, as their inspiration and example, the achievements of the physical sciences. In these sciences the rigorous exploitation of a small number of basic ideas enabled their discoverers to think their way through the apparent diversity of things and to grasp an underlying unity. In the course of their explorations they uncovered many of the hitherto hidden levers of the physical world and placed them in the hands of men to manipulate as they willed. These achieve-

---

[7] *Ibid.*, p. 175.
[8] T. Parsons, "Social Strains in America," in D. Bell (ed.), *The New American Right* (New York: Criterion, 1955), pp. 139–140.

ments also inspired another aspiration: a faith that the mainsprings of human thought and action were equally reducible, equally simple, equally graspable —and might be manipulated for human purposes.

Researches guided by this aspiration occupy increasing numbers of behavioral scientists. We are indebted to William F. Whyte for the following composite of views expressed at several scientific conferences held under the auspices of a number of large corporations:

> If we draw into our group increasing numbers of hard-headed students, some of whom are not afraid of mathematics, and if we have faith and daring, we can build a science of man. . . . The conditions which determine human happiness are discoverable to scientific methods and are to a major extent capable of realization. . . . More than ever, the world's greatest need is a science of human relationships and an art of human engineering based upon the laws of such science. We should, to put it brutally, pay more attention, first to the scientific aspects of our problems rather than to the philosophical ones. . . . Although human relationship problems are extremely complicated, *science is gradually reducing them to simple fundamentals through which these complexities are reduced to factors that respond to direct and simple treatment* [italics supplied].[9]

The scientific validity of the program projected by these conferees rests on the demonstrability of two assumptions, namely (1) that the apparent complexities of human thought and action can be reduced to a limited number of simple fundamentals and (2) that human behavior can be controlled by means of "direct and simple treatment."

The first requirement of this program—the discovery of the simple "mainsprings" of human behavior—has not been fulfilled. Curiously enough, the second requirement—the control of men by other men—has *frequently* been fulfilled, and its fulfillment has never been hampered by the lack of scientific knowledge. Before turning to this discrepancy between theory and practice— a subject we must discuss at some length—we might first consider the evidence on which the first and more basic assumption relies.

This first assumption—the simplicity of the fundamentals of human action —rests, entirely by analogy, on faith that the physical universe may still be explained and described in terms equally fundamental and "simple." Unfortunately, when one turns from the writings of social scientists to the writings of contemporary physical scientists for evidence of this claim, one meets with a startling and embarrassing disappointment. The physical scientists themselves no longer share an unbroken faith in the "simplicity" of the material world. With reference to this issue, the renowned physicist Bridgman has written:

> The immediate question for us here is one of fact: does nature seem to be getting intrinsically simpler as we get toward small scale phenomena? There is much room for difference of opinion here; personally I feel that this expected simplicity is not in evidence, at least to the extent that we could desire. . . .
> It must be remembered that a certain *simulation of simplicity* is inevitable as

---

[9] W. H. Whyte, *The Organization Man* (New York: Doubleday, 1957), p. 27.

we approach the limits of experimental knowledge, whatever the actual structure of nature, *for the mere reason that near the limit our possible experimental operations become fewer in number, and our concepts fewer also.* The question which we are trying to answer has, therefore, its real meaning only in terms of the possible future. Do we believe that if we drive in our stakes at a certain point on our present frontiers, this point will gradually, as physics advances, become possessed of a continually richer experience, so that nature at this point will appear increasingly complicated? Or do we expect a termination of this process of expansion fairly soon? *It seems to me that as a matter of experimental fact there is no doubt that the universe at any definite level is on the average becoming increasingly complicated, and that the region of apparent simplicity continually recedes.* (italics supplied)[10]

Nevertheless, in the face of the fact that the drafts they have drawn on the treasury of the physical sciences can no longer be endorsed by the bank itself, many social scientists continue to transact their theoretical business without regard to the bankruptcy of their credit.

Consider the following description by a sociologist of the "subject matter" of his field:

Sociology is concerned with "the behaviors of those electron-proton configurations called societal groups, principally human groups." These operate on the basis of the conversion of energy into human behavior—a conversion which "takes place through the well-known metabolic process on the combustion of fuel, in this case called food."[11]

On a rather more lofty level of analysis, Professors Parsons and Bales announce their discovery that certain of the properties of human action may be derived, theoretically, from the classical laws of motion. As usual, the evidence for this contemporary astrological notion that human behavior is "fundamentally" determined by the same laws that govern the fall of apples and the flight of the stars, is based entirely on analogy:

The reason this seems probable is that classical mechanics had three fundamental laws of motion and operated in terms of a three-dimensional space. Moreover, the first three of our generalizations are clearly analogous to the three Newtonian laws. . . . If all this, which frankly involves a speculative element, is correct, then it would seem likely that there is a very important analogy between the scheme we have developed . . . and the classical mechanics. [They then go on to describe the "laws" of social phenomena in terms of a virtually literal transcription of the Newtonian principles of inertia, action and reaction, etc.][12]

It seems ironic that the student seeking a coherent account of social phenomena must turn from the writings of sociologists-who-write-like-physicists to the writings of a physicist who insists that sociology must be written in

---

[10] P. W. Bridgman, *The Logic of Modern Physics* (New York: Macmillan, 1948), pp. 204–205.

[11] G. Lundberg, as paraphrased in D. Martindale, *The Nature and Types of Sociological Theory* (Boston: Houghton, 1960), p. 120.

[12] T. Parsons, R. Bales, and E. Shils, *Working Papers in the Theory of Action* (Glencoe, Ill.: Free Press, 1953), p. 102.

the language of sociology. Gently rebuking the naive scientism of the mechanistic sociologist, Bridgman reminds us that the behavioral sciences will never grow up by holding on, like frightened children, to the apron-strings of Mother Physics.

Here more than ever do we have to abandon the impersonal objective approach which we have found increasingly inapplicable in the progression from logic through mathematics and physics to psychology. Even more than in psychology is it difficult to make situations repeat or to execute controlled experiments. Here is a field where truly "emergent" properties occur, in the sense that when an individual becomes a member of a group he will act in ways which could not have been anticipated from an exhaustive knowledge of his behavior in an environment containing not more than one other individual.[13]

Nevertheless, the increasing complexity of the physical foundations of material nature does not trouble those whose models of human nature and behavior are based on the analogy of a clock-like machine obeying the consistent laws of classical mechanics in a clock-like social universe. Events described in mechanical terms have a number of properties which make the analogy particularly attractive. In the first place, mechanical processes are reversible. One can arrest their action at any time and in any state, and turn it back to an earlier state as one turns back the movement of a clock by reversing the mainspring. Similar parts moreover, are *interchangeable* from the largest to the smallest components, so that one can construct identical wholes from similar pieces. Finally, and perhaps most gratifying of all, neither the parts nor the wholes change their essential character in different combinations because their basic constituents are discrete and impermeable. Even when they merge to form novel combinations with novel properties, they can always be reduced to their original elements, just as a chemical compound is reduced by the appropriate processes of chemical analysis.

A number of these advantages would be lost if the models were patterned on other than mechanical systems—thermodynamics, for example. "We note," writes the physicist Henry Margenau, "that all strictly mechanical laws imply reversibility, whereas the laws of thermodynamics do not."[14] Mechanical models cannot be applied to electrodynamics. Strikingly, they do not apply to biological systems.

But it is not necessary that a model reproduce the substantial characteristics of its subject as long as it can duplicate its functional characteristics. One may appropriately conceive of human behavior in mechanical terms so long as one's operations, concepts and observations are consistent with each other and the predictions made from them confirm expectations. As an operational model, the mechanistic conception of the organism and its behavior may,

---

[13] P. W. Bridgman, *The Way Things Are* (Cambridge, Mass.: Harvard U. P., 1959), pp. 249–250.
[14] H. Margenau, *The Nature of Physical Reality* (New York: McGraw, 1950), p. 161.

under certain circumstances, be useful. The experimental psychologist speaks of establishing a conditioned response in the organism and then extinguishing it. The imagery here suggests the mechanical operations of insertion and removal, that is, *reversibility*. Though these terms cannot presume to describe what is actually happening within the organism, they can be used to describe what happens to the conditioned and deconditioned animal after the experimenter has performed certain operations.

Evaluation at this point encounters a dilemma. We confront a model which is obviously inappropriate to the substantial reality of any organism that we know. But the theory drawn from that model is quite adequate for describing and predicting how the experimental animal will behave in response to certain operations by the experimenter. How is this possible?

On analysis the dilemma resolves itself. The theory does not describe the organism at all. What it describes is the experimenter's dealings with the organism, his operations upon it and their consequences. Irrelevant to the nature of the organism, it is quite relevant to the behavior of the scientist. And it is quite useful, since it enables him to view the organism and to deal with it strictly on his, the scientist's own terms.

c. APPROPRIATENESS OF THE MECHANICAL MODEL AS A RATIONALE FOR CONTROL. We suggested earlier that the first requirement of the program—the understanding of the "mainsprings of human action"—is, in the last analysis, irrelevant to the realization of the second part—the control of human behavior "by direct and simple treatment." This control has frequently been achieved in times past, by means of measures which were not less effective because they lacked a scientific rationale. The failure to develop a *theory* capable of reducing the complexity of human behavior to scientific comprehensibility by no means precludes the development of a program which limits human variability on the level of action. This "other way" of reducing the complexity of human behavior is to simplify the alternatives in which human variability can express itself in the first place.

A similarly rigorous procedure provided experimental psychologists with what they considered to be a highly satisfying account of the motivational life of the rat. The wished to discover which of the "basic drives" of the rat had primacy: thirst, hunger, or the "maternal drive." In order to find answers to these questions—and to these questions only—they induced hunger in the rat by starving it, thirst by denying it water and, another kind of stress in it by denying it access to its recently born young. They then placed the variously deprived experimental animals in a situation in which the only way they could reach the goal objects—water, food, and their young—was by traversing an electrically charged grid. The degree of shock the rat would endure before refusing to cross the grid in order to reach the goal and satiate the three different drives defined their relative strengths.

The elegance of this procedure lay in the effectiveness with which it limited the alternatives open to the experimental subjects. Starving the animal prior to the test of the hunger drive insured that hunger would be dominant in its motivation during that experiment; denying it water insured that thirst would be dominant during the experiment measuring the thirst drive. Denying access to the goal except by crossing the charged grid effectively limited its repertoire of responses. In these ways the "complexity" of the rat was reduced by reducing the rat, the variability of its responses was reduced by simplying its environment—*and the problem of knowledge was simplified by simplifying the object of knowledge.*

The hospitality of the mechanical model to an ideology and program of total social control becomes more and more apparent. In a clock-like social mechanism the whole cannot function except by a perfect coordination of the parts. But perfect coordination requires that the parts surrender their autonomy and subordinate their activity to the functioning of the whole. Growth, innovation, individuation, the overcoming of limits—the supreme values of a biological system—become inappropriate. But these are precisely the values which typically distinguish the human personality in its free state, and it is for this reason that a thoroughgoing ideology of social control must recognize them as principal targets and adversaries. As Elton Mayo correctly saw, operations restricted to political and economic objectives merely manipulate the symptoms. The only effective way to control the disruptive forces of human creativity is to control and simplify the source: the human personality itself.

Guided by this insight, Mayo refers nostalgically to the nearly perfect collaboration found in primitive collectivities. Citing the anthropological works of Malinowski, A. R. Brown, and Lloyd Warner he writes:

> Amongst the Australian aborigines their method of living involves an almost perfect collaboration drilled into the members of the tribe in such a fashion that a kinship relation, a social ceremony, an economic duty become signals or commands to act or respond in a certain manner. I say "drilled into" members of a tribe, because although individual actions, as with a regiment of soldiers, are intelligently related to the actions of others and to the situation, yet no member of the tribe can expound the system and its grounds as a logic. The tribe responds to situations as a unit; each member knows his place and part although he cannot explain it.
>
> . . . A century of scientific development, the emergence of a considerable degree of social disorganization—these and certain effects of education have led us to forget how necessary this type of nonlogical social action is to achievement and satisfaction in living.[15]

The hospitality of these views to a totalitarian political ideology seems obvious, and the logic of Mayo's respect for the engineering efficiency of Stalin and his rejection of trade-unionism appropriately foreshadow Khrushchev's tribute to the members of the National Association of Manufacturers and his clash with Walter Reuther. The human engineers understand each other and recognize the common enemy.

---

[15] E. Mayo, *op. cit.*, p. 172.

The social psychologist Gordon Allport has summarized the issues:

Up to now the "behavioral sciences," including psychology, have not provided us with a picture of man capable of creating or living in a democracy. These sciences in large part have imitated the billiard ball model of physics, now of course outmoded. They have delivered into our hands a psychology of an "empty organism," pushed by drives and molded by environmental circumstance. . . . But the theory of democracy requires also that man possesses a measure of rationality, a portion of freedom, a generic conscience, propriate ideals, and unique value. We cannot defend the ballot box or liberal education, nor advocate free discussion and democratic institutions, unless man has the potential capacity to profit therefrom. In *The Measure of Man,* Joseph Wood Krutch points out how logically the ideas of the totalitarian dictatorships follow from the premises of "today's thinking" in mental and social science. He fears that democracy is being silently sabotaged by the very scientists who have benefited most from its faith in freedom of inquiry.[16]

Allport's words point to a profound disjuncture of ends and means. Few scientists would dispute that the ultimate goal of science is to increase the understanding, enrich the creativity and promote the self-determination of the individual. Increasing the power of human agency requires that men liberate themselves from all forces which tend to compel them, to limit them, to simplify them. These forces include the designs, the purposes, the powers of other men. A social science whose major goal is to engineer adjustment and conformity, whose major experimental interest is to explicate the determinate, one-way domination of the social environment over the generalized human organism, is little concerned with experiments which seek to explore how individuality can be developed and how creativity can be matured. The interest is largely the other way. Instead of inspiriting the individual to change the conditions which seek to subordinate and limit him, he is called on to participate in a program which seeks to adjust him to it: in a word, he is called on to merely limit himself.[17]

The reactionary character of this program is self-evident, and its proponents have, with some appropriateness, been described as the "servants of power."[18] One might question whether the social structure is so perfect, the distribution of life-chances so equitable and the rewards of the system so fulfilling that men should resign themselves to their indefinite subordination to it.

4. *Alternative Models of the Social Expert*

If, on the contrary, the ultimate objective is the enlargement of men's powers of self-realization—of which the achievements of science are among

---

[16] G. Allport, *Becoming* (New Haven, Conn.: Yale U. P., 1955), p. 100.

[17] The nonreciprocal character of this call to conformity is striking. It brings to mind Lincoln's acid comment to the effect that he never met a slave-owner who was so enthusiastic about slavery that he would himself wish to become a slave.

[18] C. Loren Baritz, *The Servants of Power* (Middletown, Conn.: Wesleyan U. P., 1960).

the supreme examples—it becomes appropriate to ask how social science can further the realization of this objective.

The evidence of the relationship between learning and performance suggests that the development of self-determination *in* individuals depends on the exercise and experience of self-determination *by* individuals. It cannot be conferred or fabricated because it is, in itself, not an end-state but a process. As Simmel suggests:

> To a great extent, freedom consists in a process of liberation; it rises above a bond, contrasts with a bond; it finds its meaning, consciousness, and value . . . as a reaction to it.[19]

Like insight, like thought itself, it requires a problem to confront, a difficulty to overcome and the freedom to explore and develop the alternatives through which the obstacles may be overcome. Hence, it is utterly paradoxical to believe that it can be facilitated by procedures which, at one extreme, make the obstacles insuperable and render effort futile or, at the other extreme, destroy the problems by enforcing the solutions, rendering the effort unnecessary.

We are dealing at bottom with the fateful consequences of three different attitudes toward the Other. We can do things *to* him, in which case he becomes an object. We can do things *for* him, in which case he becomes a de-

Alternative Models of the Social Expert

	EXPERT AS OPERATOR	EXPERT AS PRESCRIBER	EXPERT AS CO-LEARNER
Action of expert	Does *to* client what client cannot do	Does *for* client what client cannot do for himself	Transactional sharing of learning Does *with* the client what client can ultimately do for himself
Role of client	Total passivity Client as object	Dependency Client as dependent	Active Participation Reciprocity, client as colleague
Relational aspects	Superiority-inferiority; dominance-submission—nonreciprocity	Superordination-subordination Nonreciprocity	Equality Exchangeability of roles Mutuality
Typical statuses	Surgeon-body of patient	Ruler-subject Parent-child	Brothers Friends
Expert's skills are	Arcane, uncommunicable, forbidden to client	Translated only into commands	Fully shared

[19] G. Simmel, in K. Wolff, *The Sociology of George Simmel* (Glencoe, Ill.: Free Press, 1950), p. 122.

pendent. Or we can do things *with* him, in which case he has the opportunity to become self-sufficient, and to enter a plane of equality with us. Whatever the content or intent of the action, it is the relationship between the actors that is crucial—and their consequences define the differences between domination, dependency and self-realization in the political, economic, and social realms as well as in the interpersonal.

Long ago Aristotle justified kingship on the basis of the necessary dependency of the child on the father. Humanity is indebted to Rousseau for his exposure of the incompleteness of the analogy:

Children are bound to their father for only just so long as they feel the need of him for their self-preservation. Once that need ceases the natural bond is dissolved. From then on, the children, freed from the obedience which they formerly owed, and the father, cleared of his debt of responsibility to them, return to a condition of equal independence. If the bond remains operative, it is no longer something imposed by nature, but has become a matter of deliberate choice. The family is a family still, but by reason of convention [i.e., agreement] only.[20]

The goal of the father, then, is that his children grow up and become equal with him; the goal of the teacher is that the pupil learn how to instruct himself, so that the relation of tutelage shall end. To permit or create a social order in which a minority of expert human beings limit the knowledge and the alternatives of the rest on the grounds that they are incapable of determining their own salvation is to create a self-fulfilling prophecy of interminable tutelage, and to return mankind to another dark age in the name of a new fanaticism miscalled science.

We may now return to that model of the social expert which defines him as the physician of society and society as his patient. As we have seen, this model accepts as its working premise the assumption that the individual citizens cannot be equipped with sufficient knowledge and skill to solve their major interpersonal problems on a person-to-person basis. An unequal trichotomy is thus perpetuated, placing the expert in the position of authority and responsibility, the private citizen in a situation of relative irresponsibility, and the person in need in a position of dependency. A universal application of this model would shift the locus and responsibility for the solution of problems of human relations from the Dyad to the Triad: I—Thou would be replaced by I—He and They, and in most situations of stress the obligations of direct interhuman accommodation would be resolved into a universal *privatism* on the one hand, and a universal *professionalism* on the other, with authoritative intervention compelling the resolution. In the course of this trend the social distance of each from the others would immeasurably widen and the relations of dependency, irresponsibility and authority would become irrevocably institutionalized.

It is at least an arguable proposition that many of our social problems are exacerbated by social distance and by the decrease of situations enabling

---

[20] Jean-Jacques Rousseau, *The Social Contract*, trans. by H. J. Tozer (1924), Book I, Section II.

contact and reciprocity on an equal give-and-take basis with our fellow citizens. It is also arguable that the roles of patient and client, in their passivity, their dependency and lack of mutuality contribute to the perpetuation of the illness. Studies of institutional adjustment, whether in prisons, hospitals and other settings suggest that situations which limit the alternatives and forestall the possibilities of reciprocity between the *cared-for* and the *caring* contribute powerfully to the continuance of the need for care.[21] It may well be that the status of patient is half the disease.

The trend toward the increasing segregation of the social conscience within the responsibilities of a more and more exclusive minority of professional experts, the increasing isolation of those being served from the contact, the notice and, hence, the concern of the rest of the citizens, have already moved us far in these directions. The delegation of the obligations of mutual aid to impersonal, nonmutual social agencies has effectively removed the problems of the poverty-stricken from the consciousness of many. The poor are still with us—but they are less and less of us: they are welfare clients. They are, we can now assume, being adequately taken care of. The reformatories and prisons have relieved us of the responsibility of personally coping with the angrier victims of social neglect and abuse. They too are still with us, and their number is increasing. Over a hundred years ago a Boston shoemaker, John Augustus—a private citizen, not an expert—revolutionized correctional treatment by taking beggars, prostitutes, and petty thieves into his home, procuring jobs for them and creating a situation from which they could move toward self-sufficiency. His revolution has since been institutionalized in the form of *probation*—and half destroyed in the process. In any event, his record has never been equalled. We no longer take offenders into our homes: they too are being cared for by experts. But from time to time they are released and repay our kindness with base ingratitude. As for the confused, the depressed, those of us who have lost their direction in the race we are all running—and who litter the race track, cluttering our steps—they too are still with us but no longer of us: they are mental patients and the experts are taking care of them too.

Having closed our doors to the poor, the bad, and the mad, we may now withdraw even further into the privacy of our individual lives and wait, next to our family bomb shelters, for the political experts to solve the rest of our problems. And what of those experts themselves? How broad is their compassion for the weight of conscience we have consigned to them: how immune are they to the indifference around them?

5. *The Human Service Bureaucracies*

These questions lead inevitably to the most sensitive and hence most neglected phase of this cycle of public irresponsibility, individual privatism

---

[21] Cf., Erving Goffman, *Asylums*, (New York: Anchor Books, 1961).

and professional expertism: the consequences for the specialist himself. As the universal consultant, executive, practitioner, and administrator, the successor of the omnipresent functionaries of kings, he presides over a larger secular realm than was ever ruled by Caesar and Charlemagne. When to these secular powers he lends the force of his influence as the arbiter, executor, and heir of the collective conscience, he rules simultaneously over a moral realm vaster than the Churches of Peter and Justinian. Combining in his professional person the roles of doctor, priest, and magician, he performs for an audience whose faith in their new religion of science invests him with an awe and a license rarely granted to prophets and sages in the most credulous ages of human history.

How has he fared under the burden of these responsibilities? How has he used the freedom granted him by the fact that his lore, being incomprehensible or forbidden to the public, is also immune from their specific evaluation? Has he a weightier sense of obligation—is he equally immune from considerations of self-interest and personal expediency? In a word, has he succeeded in solving the moral dilemma unsolved by the kings and priests who preceded him: the absolute corruption of absolute power?[22]

a. THE MORAL CAREER OF THE HUMAN SERVICE FUNCTIONARY. In a stably organized mass society, the human service functionary typically performs his secular and sacred roles as a member of one of a vast, interlocking complex of organizations which, collectively, might be titled the Human Service Bureaucracies. The candidate is selected, trained, and ultimately placed within this complex and functions thereafter under its discipline and with its sufferance.

As a novice, the candidate typically brings little more than his qualifications, his enthusiasm, and a faith, reflected to him by the rest of the citizens, that his chosen profession can redeem the lost, sick, or needy committed to its care. His passage from the stage of novice to the status of mature professional is marked, like any rite of passage, by a series of shocks, incommunicable illuminations, and disillusionments. It is, in fact, his stoic and unprotesting acceptance of these disillusionments as "facts of life" rather than as moral crises which marks him in his colleagues' eyes as fully "matured."[23]

---

[22] The combined roles of doctor and priest make the human-service functionary a beneficiary of two powerful traditions. As a dedicated, unselfish servant of mankind— a priest—his motives are above suspicion. As a scientist, he is granted complete control over his laboratory and his materials. Statuses in this combined category are routinely granted a degree of authority unique in a democracy and found nowhere else in it. Dean Roscoe Pound has written, "The powers of the Star Chamber were a trifle in comparison with those of our juvenile courts and courts of domestic relations." Similarly, a welfare worker, with his unquestioned authority to grant or withhold aid, has the power of life and death over a hungry relief applicant.

[23] In one of his cartoons, Peter Arno portrays the dean of a theological seminary imparting a final word of wisdom to an eager graduate. The text, as I recall it, reads something to this effect: "My son, if you want to get ahead in this business, there are two subjects you'll have to steer clear of: Politics and Religion."

One of the earliest and more bitter of these disillusionments is the realization that his profession cannot fulfill the mission assigned to it by the larger society. Should he become unduly disturbed by this insight, he is likely to be told by his older colleagues or mentors that the larger society is itself to blame for this. This explanation is, of course, not without a convincing degree of validity. A community which has dismembered itself in the course of surrendering many of its vital person-to-person responsibilities to the ministry of a self-governing elite is not easily to be recalled from its indifference by the ministers themselves. It is therefore quite acceptable and "safe" to tell the community that crime, mental disease and poverty are community problems requiring community solutions.

When and if the young professional persists in questioning why his colleagues do not more vehemently and urgently communicate their problems to the public, he very quickly is confronted with his second major disillusionment. He learns that his colleagues, though quite aware of their own ineffectuality, are quite opposed to sharing this awareness with the public. Public support and confidence require that the myth of effectuality and competence be maintained at all costs. If public confidence is undermined, the security and prestige of the profession will be endangered.

It is then that the novice learns of the great unwritten law of bureaucracy: *Do Nothing to Embarrass the Organization*. He becomes aware that his organization, like all bureaucracies, lives in a perpetual state of crisis created by the knowledge that its inadequacies or derelictions may become known and result in its disenfranchisement. This crisis of self-knowledge keeps a vicious cycle in perpetual motion. The defensive efforts required to conceal inadequacies and put off the day of reckoning render the organization more and more inefficient. As inequities and injustices multiply, the knowledge of them spreads, and an inordinate amount of time and energy must be expended to extenuate or explain them away. Clients must be silenced or placated; failing that, the organization must vitiate the effect of their complaints by maintaining a good public image.[24]

Staff members who become aware of organizational felonies must be silenced. The most effective technique is to involve them in complicity; the potential accuser must be transformed into a compliant and rewarded accomplice: the knowledge of crimes must become a guilty knowledge. In this manner, complicity in the bureaucracy's injustices becomes a precondition to personal advancement: one is promoted if he proves he is "reliable." In this process, "trustworthiness" becomes redefined as a demonstrated readiness

---

[24] Gerver and Bensman describe the importance of bureaucratic experts whose main function is public reassurance: "[As] the public becomes increasingly distant from the administrative and substantive aspects of [the organization's] work . . . (it is) presented with symbols of organization especially manufactured by interpretive and symbolic experts. Thus a halo of science, efficiency, service, and results is associated with bureaucratic organization for the purposes of those who control it. In common parlance this is known as 'public relations' both in its broadest and narrowest sense." (I. Gerver and J. Bensman, "Towards a Sociology of Expertness," *Social Forces*, 32:233 [1954]).

to betray the public trust on behalf of the organization, while defense of the public and client is defined as organizational treason.

It is in the course of grasping these relationships that the human service functionary must cope with the severest disillusionment of all: the knowledge that the organization can survive only at the expense of systematically betraying the responsibilities it was designed to fulfill. If he is a policeman, the functionary must live with the knowledge that the largest single category of persons systematically and daily violating the law are his fellow policemen. If he is a mental-health worker, he must accept the fact that the largest single aggregate of persons engaged in the daily mistreatment of the mentally ill are his fellow employees at the mental hospital. If he is a correctional specialist, he must work with the awareness that prisons, reformatories, and training schools constitute society's most comprehensively organized and effective means for preventing rehabilitation. If he is a welfare worker, he must work with the realization that neither the landlord nor the loan-shark can compete with the relief agency in its readiness to crush the souls of the poor.

b. THE MORAL ALTERNATIVES. The human service functionary who refuses to define these conditions as "facts of professional life" will find his alternatives clearly delimited both in terms of available acts and foreseeable consequences.

If he is willing to sacrifice his personal and professional scruples for the purposes of the organization, he will be well rewarded. If he serves these purposes with unusual distinction, he may even be presented to society as a public benefactor—an honor reserved only for the most deserving.

If he chooses to serve the community to the neglect or disregard of the organization's purposes, he will be defined as a traitor and may be expelled not only from the organization but from the profession as well. His obituary has already been written; he can read it, if he wishes, in Ibsen's *Enemy of the People.*

If he elects to remain in the organization, avoiding what complicity he can in its misdemeanors, and doing what quiet good he can in spite of them, he may be tolerated—but only if his good works are relatively ineffectual and do not obstruct the organization's more pressing business: its self-aggrandizement. But he must then content himself with the prospect of permanent low status on the brink of expulsion.

He has one further alternative: to fight the system and denounce it. Though the rewards of this choice are largely philosophical, he can enjoy them in good company. He can, if he wishes, follow the example of the philosopher Alexander Herzen, who refused to go to his grave without proclaiming the guilty secret. In a spirit of unbearable revulsion, he pronounced the diagnosis of his intellectual generation: "We are not the doctors. We are the disease."

Slums and Social Work

or

Wishes and the Double Negative

DAVID R. HUNTER

"I don't want no Jaguar."

"I ain't got no use for them ivy league clothes."

"Hell, man, who wants to be leanin' on the rail of that boat goin' on some faggy cruise."

"Yeah, man, those things are for them cats who got it made. They ain't for the likes of us. We better adjust our aspirations to our reality expectations so them ads don't bug us so."

Anyone overhearing that dialogue between two Negro boys, idly leafing through the *Saturday Evening Post* while waiting in the dimly lit corridor of the juvenile court for their hearing on the theft of a car, would know he'd better make an early appointment with the head shrinker because he was out of touch with reality. Such a dialogue might take place on some earth, but not this one.

This earth, and more particularly our own part of it, has the following characteristics (partial list):

. . . a social class structure (or continuum if you will).

. . . some people having made it, some feeling that they are going to make it, and some knowing they are not.

. . . some of our population (more than most people think) having limited access to the success goals established by the dominant value system, while at the same time receiving messages from all sides that failure to achieve these goals is bad. This is where the wishes and the double negative come in. The "limited access" part of our population is the lower class, one of the identification tags of which is the common use of the double negative. The wishes are the aspirations of the outs to be in and the down to be up, aspirations the frustration of which lead to trouble.

. . . recent movements of people which have exacerbated social problems and cast them in high relief. Movement of poor, ill-educated people from rural areas to the city where the first stop is the inner city, replacing the suburban-bound upwardly mobile. Thus a piling up of expensive "problems" in the inner city plus relatively fewer human and financial resources with which to cope.

SOURCE: Prepared especially for this volume.

. . . strong subcultures which have arisen out of conditions of exclusion and alienation and which function both as defense for the occupants and as their prison.

Those two boys epitomize all these things. They are lower class, they use double negatives; their opportunities are blocked because they are Negro, because they are ill-educated, unskilled, poorly motivated; they live and move in a subculture that makes them think and act in ways that make it ever more difficult to break out; their subculture helps to teach them self-defeating adaptations to the world around them. Their parents came to the big city from Alabama ten years ago equipped with third-grade education to cope with urban life. Their great grandfathers were torn from their families by the slave market, thus establishing the matriarchal family and the weak male figure. They are quite aware of the fact that the chances of their ever "making it" are slim indeed.

These boys, their sisters, and their white, Puerto Rican, or Mexican counterparts set the agenda of social problems in the American city for 1964.

The question is: what does social work have to do with all this?

There is unease abroad about this question. Unease as much within the trade as outside.

All of us find ourselves in frequent conversations where we wonder: where are the Jane Addamses, where are the Julia Lathrops? Where is Jacob Riis? Where are the old war horses who had profound concern and understanding for their fellow man in his individuality and uniqueness, but who also saw him in his social, political, and economic context. They saw him in his place in the social hierarchy, pushed ahead or held back by his circumstances, shaped by the powerful forces of his milieu. They saw injustice, inequality, and deprivation writ big and tackled them big.

Somehow today it is hard for us to escape a feeling of powerlessness and ineffectuality. The big things are getting away from us. We seem to be occupying ourselves in the recesses and eddies of the main stream. But we can't push out of our consciousness the awareness that the main stream is racing on out there and threatens to suck in the flotsam.

Our society is different now from Jane Addams' time. Perhaps its complexity is such that there is no possibility of the individual hero and prophet, the fighting reformer. We know more now than Jane Addams knew about human behavior; we are able to be much more scientific about the things we do.

Is it possible that we have been, to a degree, seduced by that knowledge? Is it possible that scientism and professionalism have subtly pushed social work into another ball game in another park?

Is it possible that, in Roy Sorensón's words, social work has become "too much of a technical service, focusing too much on deep-dish therapy, based on borrowed concepts, divorced from the culture in which we live which is doing more to people than are their psychic maladjustments?"

I think it is.

This attitude is not so heretical. It is shared by many of our colleagues.

It isn't altogether a matter of preoccupation with little goals as against big goals, or with more malleable lumps of clay instead of rocks. It is perhaps fairer to say that what is involved here is the ascription of too great a degree of universality to certain fields of theory, out of which logically has come the attribution of inflated powers to certain methods, and their application in situations or to problems to which they are in fact irrelevant.

It would be fun here today to scold and view with alarm, but I doubt that that would accomplish much beyond unloading some of my own hostilities. Anyway, that's been done before and it really is past that time. Social workers don't need to be scolded on this score. They are the ones asking the questions. It needs no one of any great perception or courage to get on the band wagon and waggle an admonitory finger.

The hard job to be done is the identification of some of the points at which social work seems to be disconnected from the critical forces of our society followed by suggestions of ways in which the connection might be re-established. I will not be so immodest as to claim that my list of suggestions will be exhaustive. Far from it. Illustrative at most.

I suppose at this point I should stress explicitly what has been implicit up to now. That is my own view of what the basic mission of social work is. There may not be universal agreement on this, and it is only fair to make my own frame of reference quite clear.

I believe the mission of social work is twofold: first, to identify, with the help of other disciplines, the faults in our social organization and machinery which cause some people to be out of kilter and unfulfilled; to mobilize other intellectual disciplines and social institutions to correct these faults; to be interpreter, organizer, promoter, gadfly, facilitator, and leader in this endeavor. Second, it is to provide specialized skills for direct intervention in the lives of some of the victims of the faults.

Against this definition I would like now to look at some of the areas in which it seems to me social work has some problems.

The Problem of the Illusion of Services

This is a term I learned from Richard Cloward and it says a lot about the lack of connection between many agencies and reality. Some agencies suffer from an illusion of service, others create it to attract support.

One well-known example of this is the claim of many youth-serving agencies to be preventing delinquency without the slightest evidence that this is so. On the contrary a little digging beneath the glossy pages of the fund-raising leaflets usually shows either that the most delinquency-exposed youth are not touched by the agency, or that, if they are touched, the touch has little effect on their delinquency. They may use the gym with gusto and then step outside to violate the societal norms.

Another embarrassing example is the family case-work agencies which raise money with at least the implication, if not the outright claim, that they are helping the poor. As a generalization this is not so either. The clientele of the better family case work agencies has gotten less and less poor over the years and more and more middle class. We have paid a lot of verbal attention to the multi-problem families recently, but there has not been a commensurate increase in service to such families by the agencies which are the bearers of the highest professional competence in social work. Far from it.

But now, what to do about it?

At the minimum, every agency has an obligation to examine itself and its clientele to see clearly just what it is doing to whom. This is important from a practical as well as an ethical point of view. There is plenty of evidence around the country of restiveness on the part of givers to voluntary agencies. Might some of this be due to this very problem of illusory claims? This certainly is not the only contributor to the restive condition, but it may well be an important one. Following such an examination, care should be taken to fit the public image to the reality of agency function. This isn't going to be easy to do because some fund raisers will fear that if you do that too honestly you'll lose some contributions.

If, after such examination, the agency sees that it has been victimized by an illusion of service which is not a reflection of reality, and if the agency wishes to change the reality rather than its label and public image, a different kind of exercise is then called for.

In the instance of a case work agency, it will need to work through such questions as: How can we better go to where our untouched, but desired client group is: in the housing project; in the indigenous organization; in the public school; in the places where young and old spend their nonworking time; on the street? How must we modify what we do under the label of "case work": what balance is best between providing concrete services and counseling or relationship treatment; how much time is spent with one individual or family; to what degree can the professional case worker work *through* other less highly trained people; can there be a better discrimination among the elements making up the case work functions so that some of the elements can be identified and performed by less highly trained or even nonprofessional people; can the client group be more involved in decision making even within the agency and its function?

In the case of a group work agency, it will have to face up to the problem of the "baddies" and the "goodies." Are troublesome youngsters going to be excluded so as not to disrupt the program? Or will the agency which claims to prevent delinquency either stop putting forth the claim or adjust itself drastically to fit into the complex of institutions and systems which must mesh to equip the youngster and provide him with the essential opportunities he needs to become integrated with the larger society?

If such an agency decides to fit itself to its label rather than take the easier course of just changing the label, it will in all likelihood have to undertake a searching analysis of the field within which it is working in order to recast its function. The first step of course is to decide whether or not it should exist. By the very fact of its existence, is it preventing the assumption of what may be essentially a public responsibility by the community? There aren't very many examples of decisions not to exist. One dramatic one occurred in Oakland, California, where the settlement houses were deeded to the City Department of Recreation. If the agency decides to exist, but with a different character, it must decide if it's in the right part of town. Demography and urban renewal have left a lot of agency buildings out in left field. Hull House in Chicago has to decide right now what it is and where it's going to go, since everything around it is being wiped out and a university installed.

In city after city, institutions and agencies, including churches, have awakened to the fact that they are abandoning the inner city. There are increasing service needs on the periphery and in the suburbs, but does this call for abandonment of the core?

The Problem of Limited Theoretical Horizons

Although essentially eclectic in its construction of the theoretical foundation for function, social work has been too limited in its field of choice. It has shopped too exclusively at the stores of the psychic sciences and too rarely dropped in at the supermarket to select from the sociology, political science, anthropology, social psychology, and economics shelves. This is changing, but hasn't gone so far that it's not worth saying a little something about it.

This is saying in another way what has been alluded to earlier. Too often the response of social work to symptomatic behavior has been ineffective for two reasons: first, a tendency to focus unduly on the symptom; and, second, a tendency to misinterpret what the symptom is a symptom of.

Take unmarried motherhood. This could be regarded, for example, as a means of establishing her womanhood by a girl whose parents have always implicitly denied it. On the other hand, it could be viewed as a reflection of a culture pattern which has been shaped by social and economic forces of the past which shattered stable family structure and weakened the role of the father. The pattern continues since conditions persist in which Negro men have difficulty in achieving a status which will permit them to be a proper head of a family. But sex goes on.

The point here is that unmarried motherhood represents many different things and doesn't always happen for the same reasons. But it happens more often for certain reasons than for others. It should be the responsibility of any group which concerns itself with unmarried motherhood, and this is certainly one of social work's main dishes, to look beyond individual service to the big picture. Who are most of the unmarried mothers? Taking into account the contributions of all the relevant disciplines, what are the best ideas about what gives rise to unmarried motherhood as a problem for the individual and for society? Conclusions about this being arrived at, what are the strategies for intervening in these processes in ways most likely to pay off in reduction of the problem? What are the best kinds of services which need to be rendered to the immediate victims—yes, but far beyond this, what must be done to prevent the problem, *as a problem* (if everybody had babies out of wedlock and the state automatically provided for their upkeep, this particular problem wouldn't exist)? This is the point at which the creative role of social workers can come in. A number of intellectual disciplines have something to contribute to the analysis of this problem, and can provide hints about strategies of intervention. Social work, on the firing line of direct contact with the problem and responsibility for doing something about it, can do more than it has to exploit these interdisciplinary insights and draft a battle plan which calls for more relevant kinds of action, not only by social welfare agencies, but also by the schools, by public housing authorities, by employment offices, and many other institutions.

Delinquency is another area in which social work has tended to emasculate its own efforts by taking too narrow a theoretical base for its actions. This, too, is changing, but has far to go. Stated simply, and one is always susceptible to the charge of oversimplification in a paper of this kind, troublesome behavior by youth has been linked too predominantly to individual psychological disturbance presumed to arise from intrafamilial tension. Remedial action then has been planned on the basis of that diagnosis. What is missing in the diagnosis, of course, are the influences of peer group, social class values, minority group alienation, concepts of anomie, relative deprivation, availability of legitimate channels to success, and a few other ideas which will certainly turn your therapeutic stew sour if not taken into account.

The Problem of Social Class and Social Work

Social work has not done very well about the problem of social class. I don't think it has understood concepts of social class too well in the first place. At least, it has not emphasized them very much in its charter and training. This has been a blind spot which has frustrated much sincere effort. The primary victims of this have been case workers who have labored to establish communication, to nurture insight, and to stimulate movement in a lower class family with little success. Casework simply hasn't been very successful with lower-class families. The technique apparently requires in the client a readiness to look to intrapersonal and intrafamilial conditions as sources of difficulty, when lower-class culture, or the culture of poverty, says the real devils are fate and luck. In other words, "That's the way the cookie crumbles."

For our purposes, it is not necessary to be very precise about how many classes there are, or whether it is really a continuum. It is sufficient for us here to recognize class differences and the fact that membership in society at one level or another substantially affects your life chances; that there are indicators, such as speech patterns, of what class you belong in; that different classes have different ways of looking at things, and that it is very difficult really to communicate across class lines.

This being so, what can social work, manned by middle-class people, do about it in terms of its own mission?

For one thing, social work training and agency practice must pay more attention to class and culture: what they are; what they mean in terms of values; how people in different class and culture spheres look at things differently; what this means in terms of differential response to social work techniques which have been developed perhaps too "culture free." We wish IQ tests could be more culture free; not so social work techniques.

Another thing that social work can do is consciously recruit its army from more than just the "middle class." Recruit some soldiers from the classes which produce most of the social problems. This will mean some redefinition of social work functions, some adjustment of job descriptions, and the invention of some new functions. I will have more to say on this further on. Suffice it to emphasize here the importance of the social work mission being carried out by a multiclass army.

The Problem of Professionalism and Training

This is a very touchy subject. Anyone who ventures to say anything other than "we need more professionally trained social workers" is inviting excommunication. But we'll never get near the issues unless we raise the questions, so here goes.

I believe that we have gone too far in insisting that the social work mission can properly be performed only by people with graduate professional education. This is deliberately overstated to highlight the issue, but it does not exaggerate the tone and tenor of the main push within the profession.

I believe that in manning the brigades to perform its mission, social work is challenged to move beyond its single-minded concentration on graduate professional training. This obviously is needed, and much more of it than there now is. But more attention needs to be given to two other training targets, perhaps equally as important. One is the infusion of social work insights and methods in the training of other disciplines and professions. School teachers, police, medical personnel, city planners, public housing personnel could all use some of this. The other is training for sub- or nonprofessional personnel. This is where one's fancy can really take flight. The first necessary step is some fresh and uncluttered thinking about who the other people in the environment are who might help the social worker in influencing that environment and the client group.

First comes to mind the client group itself. There is little question that clients are people. However, there seems to have been some question in the past that they are multidimensional: that they are more than objectives of service. Now we are beginning to see that they are people of influence, that they have potential skills which if cultivated and mobilized can considerably lengthen the reach of the professional. This can mean "delinquent" boys, it can mean mothers of dependent children, it can mean "newcomers" to the city, it can mean the aged. It can mean the tired and discouraged, who, if called upon to perform meaningful roles in the social work mission may become less tired and discouraged themselves.

There are the "indigenous." Many of the "indigenous" are "significant others" with considerable power and influence among client groups. With a little bit of the right kind of training, who is to say they cannot measurably help social workers change the problem-producing environment? It is perhaps nearer the truth to say that it can't be done unless they are on board.

There are others who have a lot to do with what happens in a particular setting whose roles need to be realistically assessed and training created for them where possible so that those roles can be as productive as possible. Turnkeys in prison, candy store operators in the slums, inspectors from city departments, filling station operators and mechanics, and high status kids in school are a few examples. Social work can help to identify these people, creatively plan for their cooperative action, train them.

Aside from the hard and creative thinking that must underlie any attempt to mobilize the cooperative action of nonprofessional people for the social work task, standing in the way of this will be the fear that such people will almost surely botch the job, if not do actual harm, if they haven't had professional training. This is a risk, but in the light of the potential values to be gained from such an exercise, it is a risk worth taking and trying to cope with.

The Problem of Exclusivism and Limited Use of the Power Base

Social workers have tended to figure out the solutions to individual and social problems too exclusively in social work terms. This results in ineffectiveness and social workers talking to social workers. The problems with which social work is supposed to cope are made in many arenas. Enhanced effectiveness requires social work to operate in as many of these arenas as possible as close to decision making as possible.

Urban renewal is one of these arenas. Social workers need to be very aggressive about getting in on this act to insure that decisions are not made on the basis of real estate and fiscal considerations alone. Mortgage banking is another arena where basic decisions are made concerning what color people shall live where which very directly affect social work. Welfare agencies have a lot of powerful people on their boards, but too often the influence these people can wield in the community is mobilized only in support of the narrowly defined agency function. The basic value system professed by social work needs to permeate considerably more than the agencies defined as devoted to welfare. If social work doesn't push for this, it allows itself to be devalued and ultimately vitiated.

The school is another arena. The function of the school is to educate. Fair enough. But anyone who is not trying to duck a responsibility knows full well that that means more than teaching the three R's in the classroom. Social work can well work much more closely with teachers, school administrators, and school boards toward making schooling more meaningful, particularly for slum children. The educational process is a full-time, day and night affair, which goes on in the school building, on the street, in the home. This idea is dramatically highlighted by Bruno Bettelheim when he says: "No child ever learned to read in school! He learned to read at home, or in the street reading signs and listening and asking questions."

Social workers can help vastly to knit school and community together, and school and family. Anything done under this heading has high value, since education is of such crucial importance in our society. The channels to upward mobility will be progressively harder to find for those with little or inadequate education. Many of the problems handed to social work can be traced to blocked opportunities for upward reach.

There is more and more readiness among forward-looking school people to look beyond the child to the parent and to the community. In many cities this is more than a readiness. It is a practice. But it is still rough around the edges and everywhere needs development. Social work must play a vigorous role in this development, performing roles suitable to its capacities, planning for services and facilities with the school, sharing insights with school personnel, and learning in turn from them.

The school with its wide dispersion, its universality, its access to the young and changeable is certainly one of the key institutions for the better integration of all people in society. This is another way of saying the school is a potentially potent factor in the prevention of social problems. Only the blind in the social work profession will fail to work with it, help it, learn from it, and be helped by it.

The Problem of Social Work and Social Planning

The place of social workers in social planning is one which demands some soul-searching and head-knocking.

I believe it is possible to discern something disquieting for social work across the country. It is that in those communities where the most dynamic social planning is going on the play is being taken away from Health and Welfare Councils. This, it seems to me, can be traced to the fact that despite the changes of name that have been made in most places, these councils in the main are still limited by three things: they still tend to be representative of agencies rather than the community; they tend to be dominated by private, voluntary health, and welfare interests; they tend to be concerned with coordination of social services rather than with social problems. Obviously, this varies from place to place, but more often than not the initiative and leadership seems to come from somewhere else when a community begins to wake up to the need for more comprehensive planning and action if any impact is to be made on the massive problems which now reside in the slums and gray areas of the inner city. Somehow, too many councils seem to have become so conventionalized that they have been unable to broaden their scope effectively to encompass the system within the city that must be meshed: public services, economic opportunity, education, physical redevelopment, racial and social class residential patterns, as well as services for the socially disabled.

There are some new organizational patterns emerging in response to the need for broad planning and action. It is to be hoped that alert social work leadership will be in the front ranks in these developments.

The Problem of Accountability

The last item on my list is as difficult and as challenging as the rest. Social agencies have a real problem of holding themselves accountable before the public for what they claim to do. No one will deny for a moment the great difficulty of measurement in human behavior and social relations, but social agencies are at a point in history when they must make a serious effort to do better at this than they now do. In reality very few make any such effort. To be sure there are statistics galore about how many cases were handled, how many interviews held and recorded, how many in attendance at the center during a given period, how many foster home placements, and so on. These are the things that are easy to measure, but they are not the objectives of the agencies. What needs to be done better is to define agency purposes in as objective terms as possible and measure performance against these purposes. A foster home placement means nothing if it doesn't last very long, or if the foster family turns out to be inadequate and unable to contribute to the rearing of a truly independent person. The recorded attendance at a golden age center doesn't mean very much if the people who go there are the ones who have a good deal of initiative anyway and would be out being useful or hobnobbing somewhere, center or no center, while the real isolates and lonesome ones wither away in their rooms.

By setting up clear standards of accomplishment, agencies will be serving a better purpose in the long run anyway than by obfuscation. It is a great temptation to make reports as glowing as possible when you have to justify your existence. But if these reports keep on being glowing and yet the problems generally persist and are visible all around, the public is entitled at least to bewilderment. The public is entitled to know what can't be accomplished by present methods and institutions as well as what can.

These seem to me to be some of the reasons why we can't confidently feel that social work is engaged effectively enough with the most pressing social problems of the day.

Minority Group Leadership:
The Advantages of the Disadvantages

SEYMOUR LEVENTMAN

THE PROBLEM

In *The Study of Sociology*, Herbert Spencer observed that social institutions tend to become self-propagating, independent of their original causes. Institutions may be maintained when they "perform some other function than that intended or no function at all."[1] Applied to the alleviation of human misery, these notions allowed Spencer to note that programs designed to solve social problems may themselves become obstacles to the problems' eventual resolution. The tendency for ameliorative movements to become problems in themselves is the general concern of this paper. We concentrate especially on minority group leadership in American society.

Minority group leadership presumably represents a force working for the good of society, especially minority group members. Frequently, however, these leaders display a propensity to perpetuate the social inferiority of their own people. We are interested in the nature of such leadership as it affects and is a product of relations between particular minority and majority groups. The major contention is that minority leaders tend to become alienated from the groups and ideals they allegedly represent. They work instead to protect their exclusive enjoyment of certain privileges and advantages resulting from the continued inferiority of their own people. Minority leaders continually must seek new *raisons d'etre* as they act to eliminate the initial conditions that brought about their existence. We emphasize that these patterns are not necessarily the result of insidious plots by evil-minded leaders to undermine their peoples' highest aspirations. Rather, the tendency to protect their "vested interests"[2] in the "advantages of the disadvantages"[3] is a function of the strains and tensions built into the role of minority leader itself.

These strains are produced by the conflicting principles on which the role is based. The minority leader must be acceptable to his own people, but his position depends ultimately on his acceptance by the majority. He "leads"

SOURCE: Prepared especially for this volume.

[1] Herbert Spencer, *The Study of Sociology* (New York, 1896), pp. 17–18.

[2] To the author's knowledge, E. Franklin Frazier was the first to call attention to the "vested interests" of minority leaders in his article, "Human All Too Human," *Survey Graphic*, 36 (1947), pp. 74–75, 99–100.

[3] A phrase originated by H. B. Frissell, second principal of Hampton Institute. Quoted in Gunnar Myrdal, *An American Dilemma* (New York, 1944), p. 794.

but is the most led of persons. In his tenuous position he must pacify both groups. He must integrate their conflicting demands, those of the minority group requiring commitment to its most cherished values, including claims for social equality, and those of the majority group requiring acceptance of its values, including maintenance of its dominant position. The minority leader must negotiate between "selling out" his own people by overcompromising their demands and threatening the power of the majority by overdemanding social equality. Although his position rests on "two centers of gravity," it is the majority group whose judgment of his acceptability ultimately matters. In making the demands of both groups palatable to each other, the minority leader therefore must pay more homage to the majority since it is the group that "runs things" in society.

TYPES OF MINORITY GROUP LEADERSHIP

We will examine three types of minority group leaders: the *charismatic*,[4] the *functional*,[5] and the *professional*. The charismatic minority leader is endowed with special personal characteristics that set him apart from his people and qualify him to lead them out of bondage or to adjust to it satisfactorily. The performance of this self-styled role to which the leader was "called" requires considerable virtuosity, especially in handling the more mundane affairs of politics and economics. He has a vision of social equality, a mission to lead his people toward that nirvanic state, and the ability to successfully transmit his zeal for his goals to a following of minority group aspirants as well as majority group members who want to be assured of the temperate nature of the leader's claims to social ascendancy. Leadership here depends upon a mergence of highly personal qualities and appropriate social conditions that reinforce and legitimize the leader's right to his position. Booker T. Washington is an interesting example since, though he was initially charismatic, he eventually developed features of the other two types.

The role of the functional leader depends on his position in an association or activity devoted to such neutral or nonracial causes as education, religion, or the protection of economic interests of particular group or classes. Because of the prestige, power, and contacts with the wider society gained from such a position, he is drawn into the fray and becomes a race leader. A. Philip Randolph, head of the Brotherhood of Sleeping Car Porters, is an example of this type. When personal qualities become even less important and leadership becomes a career based on specialized training and skill, the professional emerges. This type of leader is likely to be a human relations expert adept

---

[4] See Max Weber, *The Theory of Social and Economic Organization*, trans. by A. M. Henderson and T. Parsons (New York, 1947), pp. 358–363, for a discussion of charismatic leadership. See also pp. 353–363 for a discussion of the routinization of charisma, which is especially pertinent to the present treatment.

[5] For a discussion of this type, see E. Franklin Frazier, *The Negro in America* (New York, 1959), pp. 547–548.

at a rational application of general principles to a variety of minority situations. This individual, with a college degree in minority leadership, is apt to be an anonymous employee or director of a social agency rather than an eminent public figure. Such a leader is to be found in any number of Jewish defense agencies, particularly the Anti-Defamation League.

Several general features of this typology may be noted. All types share the same alleged goal—the social advancement of the groups they represent. But the types vary in tactics, from the personal exhortations of the charismatic leader serving as the moral conscience of society to the rational methods of the career-oriented expert. Furthermore, these types are by-products of particular minority groups and their characteristic statuses in society. We might hypothesize that the lower the status of the minority group, the greater the likelihood of its leadership being the charismatic type. The higher the status, the greater the probability for its leadership to be professional. The American Negro has gone through the charismatic stage, is now largely in the functional stage, and is approaching the professional. The American Jew is now in the professional stage and has already experienced an even more advanced development—the bureaucratization of leadership.

Early in the history of a minority group, when its structure is not fully crystallized, there is a leadership vacuum. This was the case of the post-Emancipation Negro who was free but had no awareness of the course of action to take to implement his freedom and relieve his plight as a second-class citizen. It remained for a leader to emerge who promised advancement to the Negro while making "safe" demands that did not threaten the racial *status quo* favoring the whites. This set the stage for the ascendancy of Booker T. Washington. It is significant that his name is known and revered by all school children, few of whom are familiar with such names as W.E.B. DuBois. In fact, the *only* Negro leaders who are generally recognized as such are those acceptable to the whites. The "real leaders"[6] are to be found at the grass roots level and include countless numbers of anonymous individuals whose demands for direct action to bring about full equality render them "unsafe" to carry on the work of the racial *status quo*. As Frazier puts it, "Only those Negroes who fit into the white man's conception of the Negro will be built into giants."[7]

THE CHARISMATIC LEADER

Booker T. Washington was one of these "giants." Born into slavery, Washington taught himself to read and write before entering Hampton Institute at the age of sixteen. At this institution, a Negro college founded by the American Missionary Society, he acquired a unique combination of pietistic practicality and mistrust of scholarly learning that became the guiding prin-

---

[6] James Baldwin, "The Dangerous Road Before Martin Luther King," *Harper's* (February, 1961), p. 40.

[7] E. F. Frazier, *The Negro in America*, p. 569.

ciples in his life's work of teaching Negroes to be "good people." Hard work, frugality, and Christian character were the cornerstones of his personal philosophy, while he tempered the Negro protest by emphasizing duty over right and pragmatic power bargains over demands for full-scale equality. Believing that the Negro's heart and hand should receive priority over his mind, Washington founded Tuskegee Institute in 1891 to provide vocational and moral training for Negroes.[8] Minimizing the potentiality of the intellect in education, Washington claimed that Negroes profit most by conforming to white preconceptions as much as possible. The major result of his approach was to educate Negroes to contentment as second-class citizens.

An adept fund-raiser, Washington befriended many of the leading public figures of his day, such as Presidents Roosevelt and Cleveland and philanthropists Carnegie, Eastman, and Rosenwald. To obtain and maintain their support, he argued for Negro equality in particularly appeasing tones. Characteristically, his speeches portrayed not the "sins" of the white man but the faults of his own race. His tactical philosophy was especially well expressed in the Atlanta speech of 1895. Addressing himself to Negroes, Washington exhorted them to "cast down your bucket where you are. . . . It is at the bottom of life that we must begin not at the top. No race can prosper till it learns there is as much dignity in tilling a field as writing a poem."[9]

Addressing whites, Washington assured them, "In all the things that are purely social we can be separate as the fingers, yet, one as the hand in all things essential to mutual progress."[10] He added, "The wisest in my race understand that agitation of questions of social equality is the extremist folly in that progress in the enjoyment of all the privileges that will come to us must be the result of severe and constant struggle rather than of artificial forcing."[11]

Washington's remarkable ability to please all sides made him a "natural" leader. To whites, his position represented acceptance of Negro subordination, while to Negroes his skill as racial arbitrator resulted in obtaining favors and concessions from whites. Small but significant opposition came from a group of Negro intellectuals led by W.E.B. DuBois, who admonished Washington for "selling out" and advised Negroes to stay out of his "dangerous net" which stood for "submission and slavery."[12] Rejecting Washington's conciliatory attitude, DuBois and his followers formed the Niagara Movement in 1905, which demanded full social and political equality for Negroes as well as complete cultural assimilation. Foreshadowing a strategy that was to develop a half century later, the movement was short-lived and eventually led to the formation of the National Association for the Advancement of

[8] Oliver C. Cox, "Negro Leadership in the United States," in Alvin Gouldner (ed.), *Studies in Leadership* (New York, 1950), pp. 235–239. G. Myrdal, *op. cit.*, pp. 726–727, 739–742.

[9] Booker T. Washington, *Up from Slavery* (New York, 1956), p. 155.

[10] *Ibid.*, p. 157.

[11] *Ibid.*, p. 158.

[12] O. C. Cox, *op. cit.*, p. 260.

Colored People in 1910. As Myrdal says, "Its main importance was that it brought into open conflict and wide public debate two types of Negro strategy, one stressing accommodation and the other raising the Negro protest."[13]

Realistic as Washington's tactics may have been for his day, he influenced two important areas of Negro life, education and leadership, in ways that did not entirely improve the condition of the Negro in American society. His educational philosophy led to a Negro school system which, as Lomax puts it, ". . . produced a flood of miseducated Negroes who, almost by second instinct, acquiesced in segregation and all the indignities that went with it."[14] Washington also established precedents at the racial bargaining table for generations of Negro leaders. Whatever concessions the leaders carried away was done with the understanding that they in turn would influence the Negro masses in the direction desired by the dominant white group. Cox and Myrdal both indicate that Washington's control of the choice of Negro leaders was so great he literally monopolized national Negro leadership for several decades.[15]

Washington's influence waned as the Negro population became more differentiated, making it less possible for a single individual to represent the entire group. The period between the two World Wars saw great changes in the situation of the American Negro, due especially to urban migration and industrial employment. These critical forces created economic and social cleavages among Negroes to an extent never before known. Negro classes emerged whose members' concern with economic and power interests often exceeded their concern for racial matters from which they had become estranged. One such individual is A. Philip Randolph, head of the Brotherhood of Sleeping Car Porters.

THE FUNCTIONAL LEADER

In January, 1941, Randolph proposed that 10,000 Negroes march on Washington to demand an end to discrimination in defense employment and in the military services. July 1 was set as the date, but after months of announcements, promises, and threats, Randolph called off the march as President Roosevelt established a Fair Employment Practices Commission. Herbert Garfinkle notes, "A. Philip Randolph had a large stake in the success of the FEPC. As head of the Brotherhood of Sleeping Car Porters, the FEPC provided a governmental weapon in his effort to expand the union's jurisdiction over new categories of railroad workers."[16] Randolph threatened a mass protest movement in the hope of pressuring the President into helping him achieve his goal. After prolonged negotiation, the President apparently con-

---

[13] G. Myrdal, *op. cit.*, pp. 742–743. See also Elliott Rudwick, *W. E. B. DuBois: A Study in Minority Group Leadership* (Philadelphia, 1961).

[14] Louis Lomax, *The Negro Revolt* (New York, 1962), p. 36.

[15] O. C. Cox, *op. cit.*, p. 259; G. Myrdal, *op. cit.*, p. 741.

[16] Herbert Garfinkle, *When Negroes March* (Glencoe, Ill., 1959), p. 148.

ceded, but, in so doing, crushed the movement by establishing a toothless FEPC with no enforcement powers.

Randolph voiced his protests through channels which brought him back "into formal alliance with the established organizational leadership, Negro and white."[17] His role shifted from mass action leader to member of the National Council for a Permanent FEPC. The movement eventually lost its mass character and became "one more organization competing for public attention in an increasingly apathetic market."[18] In effect, Randolph participated with the majority group in a carefully regulated, yet game-like, test of its power. The result was a reaffirmation of the power of the majority. An important result of minority group leadership, therefore, is the reinforcement of the dominant power structure which has so weakened as to permit an organized protest of the subordinate group. Protest leadership is possible and effective mainly under conditions of flux in the power structure regulating minority-majority relations.

Recently, we have witnessed precisely this development. The traditional Negro leadership, as represented by the NAACP for example, was more oriented toward the dominant white group than toward its own people. The leader paid lip service to the plight of the "masses," but his actions indicated a greater interest in preserving his own status and that of the "talented tenth" or "exceptional" Negro. But, especially since the end of World War II, a complex of social, political, and economic changes have created a crisis for this kind of leader. As Lomax describes it, ". . . the Negro masses are demanding action, immediately, and leadership organizations are being circumvented when they hesitate or stand in the way."[19] The leadership of Martin Luther King is one response to the crisis.

King is no exception to our typology but overlaps several categories. He is charismatic, but this quality stems largely from his position as religious functionary. His occupation and self-controlled benignity give special force and dignity to his actions, so that, for the first time in Negro history, open protest has become respectable. In accounting for King's effectiveness, we should not overlook the traditional power of the Negro Church and the climate of opinion in contemporary American society that favors religion and religious motivations for social actions. King leads a protest movement with ideological trapping of a spiritual mission.

King achieved prominence as a guiding force behind the Montgomery bus boycott[20] of 1955–1956. For the first time, a grass-roots movement of Negroes succeeded in altering certain aspects of the racial balance of power. Yet these changes were more apparent than real since the basic power structure remained unaltered. Though threatening white dominance, the incident may

---

[17] *Ibid.*, p. 149.

[18] *Ibid.*, p. 117.

[19] L. Lomax, *op. cit.*, p. 157.

[20] N. W. Walton, "Walking City—A History of the Montgomery Boycott," *Negro Historical Bulletin*, 20:16–20, 27–33, 102–110, 147–52; 21:75–76.

have strengthened this power by publicly suggesting that the dominant group is sufficiently secure to permit the subordinate group's gaining an occasional advantage. Negroes now sit next to whites on buses but travel to their usual low paying, low status "Negro" jobs. Neither schools, parks, playgrounds, nor other public facilities in Montgomery are integrated. Despite a temporary lapse, the dominant group did not relinquish its power but continues to control the most critical life chances of the Negro minority. Such a deep-seated movement as the Montgomery boycott apparently resulted in nothing more than the integration of buses.

King's effectiveness in this and other movements may lead to eventual estrangement from his followers rather than to identification with them. As he becomes a force to reckon with, King is drawn into a complex network of intergroup relations in which he is likely to be co-opted by the "brotherly love" and status offerings of the dominant group. Simmel observes that social mobility results in the draining off of the minority group's reservoir of talent and leadership. He describes a situation in Spanish-Colonial America in which the Spanish offered gifted and troublesome native rebel leaders legal patents to join white society. Once assimilated into the ruling class, the native leader's superiority over his fellows is replaced by apparent equality with the dominant group.[21] King may confront a similar situation, though his ties to the Negro community remain strong as interaction and apparent acceptance by whites reinforces his status among Negroes.

Nevertheless, success brings him closer to the periphery of the Negro community where, subject to increasing majority controls, he becomes a "nominal" leader with reduced efficiency at improving the lot of his people.[22] Meanwhile, pressures emanating from his own community are already beginning to modify his effectiveness. After Montgomery, King returned to his home community of Atlanta under an apparent agreement which calls for him to concentrate largely on national matters and leave local affairs to the entrenched Negro power structure.[23] Furthermore, his connection with the Southern Christian Leadership Conference, an organization of Southern (Negro) clergymen dedicated to instigating nonviolent protest in Southern cities, has created new conflicts for him. In reality, there are two Kings, the "symbolic leader" and the "organization man." As symbolic leader, he inspired one of the most important revolts in Negro history. As organization man, he acceded to pressures exerted by Adam Clayton Powell in a personnel disagreement forcing the resignation from the Southern Christian Leadership Conference of one of King's most able associates.[24] He inspired the Albany, Georgia, desegregation movement in 1962, but after being jailed and promising to remain there till changes occurred, the came out on bond. This action

---

[21] Kurt Wolff (trans.), *The Sociology of Georg Simmel* (Glencoe, Ill., 1950), p. 281.
[22] See Kurt Lewin for a discussion of the "leader from the periphery," *Resolving Social Conflicts* (New York: Harper, 1948), p. 193.
[23] L. Lomax, *op. cit.*, p. 84.
[24] J. Baldwin, *op. cit.*, p. 42.

dealt a severe blow to the spirit of revolt in Albany.[25] However, the most important consideration of all may be King's role in narrowing the gap between "official" leadership, such as that of the NAACP and grass-roots movements of young Negroes.

THE PROFESSIONAL LEADER

Negro leadership tends to be a nonprofessional activity of persons recruited from the upper strata of Negroes. King and others are "amateurs" compared to the professional leaders of Jewish defense agencies that protect the social reputation of Jews in the general community. In the ghettos of Eastern Europe, leadership depended upon sacred learning and scholarship. In the acculturated American Jewish community, leadership depends upon wealth and prestige derived from such secularized activities as fund-raising.[26] But there is a new leader, a special type of organization man. He is particularly skilled at converting complex race issues into neat, marketable commodities to be packaged, publicized, and sold under the label "Brotherhood." Rarely is he a native of the community in which he works which represents only a temporary stop in a career pattern of occupational mobility. As "strangers," professional leaders act as detached observers protected against community pressures by their expertise and the national organizations they represent. But high status Jews influence the strategies of professional leaders by controlling the latter's access to the power and pursestrings of the local community. This results in an alliance between lay and professional leaders whereby the professionals serve as spokesmen for their high status brothers in various affairs of status. Generally, the concerns of professional leaders are those of high status Jews, for example, social discrimination in clubs, organizations, and exclusive resorts. Problems of low status Jews, such as discrimination in jobs and schools, are neglected as "passé," no longer critical in a successful middle-class community.

The decline of anti-Semitism and the improved status of Jews threaten the persistence of professional Jewish leaders unless they discover new *raisons d'etre* in the plight of other minorities. In so doing, they are not likely to forget that "The best way of retaining the masses' attention and making them proud of their leaders is the provocation of persecution incidents rather than far flung issues."[27] Synagogue bombings or other displays of anti-Semitism may be "bad" for the Jews but "good" for defense agencies which thrive in hostile situations. The strategy these agencies sometimes utilize is illustrated in a recent school crisis in Virginia. The Richmond Anti-Defamation League disseminated pro-integration literature, thus involving Richmond Jews in the desegregation issue. An editorial in the *Richmond News* charged the ADL

---

[25] L. Lomax, *op. cit.*, p. 99.
[26] See Judith R. Kramer and Seymour Leventman, *Children of the Gilded Ghetto* (New Haven, Conn., 1961), pp. 99–101.
[27] Robert Michels, *Political Parties* (Glencoe, Ill., 1949), p. 166.

with deliberately associating all Jewry with compulsory integration. The editorial claimed the ADL would (as it did) take subsequent criticism of its position as evidence of anti-Semitism. And having thus "stirred up defamation of the Jews, it could then combat it with gusto, uncovering anti-Semitism under every segregated school."[28]

The instructions of the national ADL opposed the wishes of local Jews who desired to remain silent on the question of desegregation. Though sympathetic to Negroes, Southern Jews are unwilling to set themselves off from the dominant white society to which they aspire. The desegregation issue is secondary to that of community status. Jews have spent years working in Community Chest and other civic activities in an "effort to show their Christian neighbors that they too belong. If Jews now stand apart from the dominant group, they fear they may jeopardize the prestige and position they have worked so long to secure."[29]

The professional leader uses the community to enhance the prestige he derives from his occupation. He is adept at clarifying issues and guaranteeing that his services will be required to solve minority problems. However, he cannot solve these problems so efficiently as to threaten the persistence of this community which he needs to test and display his human relations skills. The leader thus may perpetuate his role by engaging in activities independent of (though not necessarily opposed to) his original functions.

SUMMARY AND CONCLUSIONS

Minority group leadership can be a social problem in its own right. The leader's role is such that often he perpetuates rather than resolves the problem that brought about his existence. The most serious problem he faces is the successful achievement of his avowed goal of social equality for his people. Indeed, he may lose sight of this goal because of intervening and conflicting interests. Due to its dependent power position, any rights the minority group attains are "favors" granted by the majority. Attempting to gain these favors, minority leaders must use tactics and ideologies acceptable to the majority. The distinction between favors granted to the minority and those to the leader himself are often blurred. In time, minority leaders form a separate stratum that bridge the minority and the majority communities and claim for themselves exclusive rights to the critical values of both communities.

While solidifying their personal gains, minority leaders thus become increasingly alienated from their own groups, often representing class interests having little relation to their original purpose. This is especially the case as minority leadership becomes increasingly professionalized, subsequently, distinctions between "radical" and "conservative" leaders are no longer relevant; "trained" and "nontrained" are more accurate designations.

[28] Murray Freedman, "Virginia Jewry in the School Crisis," *Commentary*, 47:20–21.
[29] *Ibid.*, pp. 18–19.

The consequences but not necessarily the intentions of minority leadership are often detrimental to the minority group. Intergroup relations are too complex for any person or stratum to plan and control the outcome of a particular tactic, even a manipulatory one. Just as many advantages accruing to minority groups are fortuitous and unplanned, so are the negative effects of their leadership. Structural factors, such as changing economic and political institutions, often are more crucial than the subjective intentions of particular individuals.

18. ENDS AND MEANS: OUTMANEUVERING THE APPARATUS

An American Death Camp

HAROLD ORLANS

The Nazi death camps apparently shocked some people to whom such sights were new—people with jobs, orderly (if crowded) transportation to and from the jobs, and polite pleasures evenings and sabbath. People who believe that silk and concrete define civilization and that death is an accident, were disturbed by the human incinerators, the methodical piles of corpses, salvaged underwear, human hair (for mattresses) and human fat (for soap). There followed readily the rationalization that Germans are specially perverse.

Now, I do not pretend to offer a sufficient explanation of the German death camps. Nothing, however, is clearer than that Germans are ordinary human beings, that regimentation is a normal aspect of industrial society, and that the carnage of Auschwitz was as consistent and logical an outgrowth of such a society as are subways, burlesque, and packaged meat.

At any rate, that is the contention of this article. To support it, two courses are open: either one can prove that the Germans are normal human beings and that their death camps operated as do other social institutions; or one can show that other people, generally accepted as normal—e.g., ourselves—have institutions which, in their own way, can be regarded as incipient death camps. I have adopted the latter course, and the institution I am going to describe is an American state insane asylum.

Clearly, the asylum, at worst, is a faint copy of Auschwitz. Indeed, it bears a more striking resemblance to a concentration than to a death camp; and there are those who will insist that I am distorting the entire picture, and that the asylum contains notable humanitarian elements. But I am not concerned with drawing a complete picture of asylum life; nor do I assert

SOURCE: Harold Orlans, "An American Death Camp," *Politics* (Summer, 1948), pp. 162–167, 205. Reprinted by permission.

that there is an *identity* between the American asylum and the German death camp. I am, instead, interested in certain similarities of social process in both institutions, and my thesis is that the American asylum manifests, in embryo, some of the same social mechanisms which in Germany matured into death camps (and that, by inference, a similar chain of historical circumstances could lead to the development of death camps here). I will not argue the thesis at this point. First I would like to present a description of some aspects of life in an American asylum, so the reader can evaluate the evidence for himself, and then I will return to a discussion of the subject.

One final introductory statement should be added. I worked fourteen months in this insane asylum (as well as five months in another), and everything I say is based upon personal observation and recorded notes. The consolation that this particular asylum is atypical or representative of a backward section of the country is unavailable since, on the contrary, the asylum is distinctly superior to the average state institution and is located in a pleasant town near a great Northern metropolis. Some of the conditions which will be described may have been temporarily aggravated by a shortage of help arising from the war. But, in any case, these conditions *existed*, these events *have happened*, and readers are welcome to whatever consolation the facts afford.

The Insane Asylum

"Insane asylum" is not the popular designation; legal and medical authorities and the initiated public prefer "state hospital." A hospital, however, is a place where people go of their own volition to be treated for a while and then leave; but there are few transients here, and forceful commitment is common. Aside from the steady crop of alcoholics with delirium tremens who either die shortly after admission or respond to paraldehyde dosage and enforced continence and are discharged in a few weeks (to repeat the cycle interminably) most patients remain for a long time. Many remain for life. It is with these long-term inmates who constitute the major population of the asylum that we are principally concerned.

Bewildered, violent, apathetic, or plaintively cooperative, each patient enters the admission ward as an individual, wearing his own clothes, and possessing his own type of insanity. He may rebel at the asylum order, complain about the rising time and the food, the restrictions on smoking and shaving; he may try hard to learn the routine, or he may be utterly oblivious of it; he may ask questions or energetically propound his delusions; but he remains an individual, angular and alive, striving to live his disordered life as best he can purpose.

A year later, he wears strange, old, wrong-size clothes, he has lost his pride and sense of shame, he is thoroughly obedient and observes the routine listlessly, and even his eccentricities are somehow dulled and passionless. He has no privacy, no freedom, no friends, no occupation, no pastime; and he has no hope. In short, he has been institutionalized.

He has been stripped of all belongings, and even his asylum clothes must be returned each night. (They are rolled into a ball and placed on the floor of the roach-infested washroom until morning. Going to the toilet at night, he walks barefoot and naked, or in his underwear.) He has no place to store the smallest article except, perhaps, a small cupboard which serves the entire ward, and which only the attendant can open.

His world is bounded by barred windows, locked doors, and bare walls standing along long wooden corridors which creak underfoot. Small rooms and a larger dormitory open off these corridors, holding rows of narrow cots often wedged so close together they must be entered by climbing over the footboards. This is where he lies at prescribed hours—he is not allowed in the room before a set evening hour, and he is ousted from it early each morning.

During the day, he eats three meals of watery and often poisonous slop (hardly a week passes without an outbreak of diarrhea; the average cost of these meals is 8¢ a piece), he plods down the corridor and back, kneading into its pine ruts a thin compost of wax, spittle, dust, urine, and excrement; he stands against the bare plaster wall; he stares through the grates of the window; seats himself on a hard chair; walks, pisses; returns slowly to his chair where he sits, contemplating his shoe; asks the attendant for a cigarette; mutters or shouts at himself or the ceiling; walks the long corridor, returns and sits again; and sits, and sits and does absolutely nothing, waiting out motionless hours. A hundred other ward inmates live the same climaxless life, each in the solitude of his insanity, day after interminable day unto death.

To fashion this life, to guard 3,000 inmates and perpetuate the policies of the institution, a social system has evolved whose crude, medieval quality is rivalled by that of few others in the land. Let us examine the various hierarchies of this system.

Inmates

At the base are the ordinary inmates. This base is unique among social systems in that there is no cohesion, no organization among its human particles. Rarely, a tie may form between two more rational inmates, or between two with complementary delusions. But there is no interlinkage of such ties, and the inmate mass remains fragmented and leaderless, unable to engage in any type of cooperative activity without the direction of others. It is for this reason that two attendants are able to dominate any number of inmates, because they are never challenged by more than one at a time. Upon one occasion, another attendant and myself were struggling to put a violent paretic into a strait-jacket, when he burst forth with a most logical and impassioned plea to the silent crowd of inmates which surrounded us: "Come on, fellows, don't let them do this to me! What do you stand around for?

There are so many of us and only the two of them. If you don't help me now, they'll get you next." I was new on the job then, and watched the circle of inmates with anticipation. Not one person moved a limb, or altered a gesture, or spoke a word in response; nor did anyone offer to assist us; each simply stood and watched as he might watch a passerby through a window—something was happening, and it was so seldom that anything happened to watch, but each man remained bound by his insanity.

In a sense, the inmates are not really part of the asylum social plant. They are more the raw material which it processes.

Worker Patients

The proletariat of the asylum is the worker-patient class whose labors exceed those of all other personnel combined. Members of this class are generally more rational than their fellow inmates, and have more hope of leaving the asylum alive. For many, work constitutes a way of gaining favor with the authorities and eventually winning a coveted parole home. For others, without this hope, there is only the consolation that the work itself affords, and a few privileges with which they may be rewarded—some extra tobacco or food, or the right to shine the attendant's shoes.

The worker-patients work 10-12-14 hours a day, 6-7 days a week, some without pay, some for about $12 a month. They furnish the heavy manual labor to operate the inefficient asylum laundry (to estimate how delectable this job is, think of continually sorting mountains of sheets soiled with urine and feces), the vast eating hall (dispensing food and washing dishes), the farm, the coal furnaces in the power and heating plant; and they do most of the work required to keep the place neat and orderly: making the beds, washing and waxing the floors and furniture, sorting the "linen," raking leaves from the grounds in the fall and shovelling snow from the paths in winter. The worker-patient is proud of the work he does and grows furious if an attendant mistakes him for an ordinary inmate. Should an inmate get in his way or refuse to obey his order, he will cuff him about and curse disdainfully until the nuisance is removed.

Attendants

Above the worker-patient, at the lowest level of the free-labor hierarchy and the most numerous class of asylum personnel, is the attendant, also known by the elevating title of "psychiatric aide." A century ago he was called a *keeper,* and this term still conveys his essential function. He is the man with the keys, the man who keeps the inmates locked up. There are a dozen doors on every ward at which worker-patients bang to be admitted or let out, or through which inmates must be conveyed at meal time, and to receive visitors; the medication room, the supply room, the closets and wash rooms must be locked or unlocked as the occasion may demand. The keys are the symbol of his status in the asylum, and many attendants devise an elaborate chain to sport them with proper dignity, and spend a great deal of time idly twirling the keys on this chain.

During the time I was at the asylum, attendants were working 54 hours a week for a salary which varied from $720 to $944 plus maintenance (the fare was little better than that given inmates), which may indicate their status in society at large. Within the asylum, they must sign an agreement which states that "the superintendent . . . has the right to inspect my rooms, trunks, bags, packages, or other receptacles at any time," and instant dismissal may follow the violation of petty regulations. Attendants wear a distinctive uniform and eat in a room separate from nurses or doctors (who, in turn, eat separately from each other). They must rise and remain standing when a nurse or doctor is present, and their official instructions read: "Never discuss your physician or any superior officers, nor criticize any orders they may have given."

It is not surprising, therefore, that, placed in immediate authority over a hundred inmates, each in the image of a man, the attendant takes a certain relish in this authority. There is one thing he exacts from all inmates, and that is obedience. (And subservience. "Make them call you 'Mister,'" one attendant—a C.O., incidentally—early advised me. "Although they're crazy, it gives you a pyschological edge.") When he tells them to get up in the morning, they are to get up; when he tells them to line up for dinner, to dress or undress, to produce a sample of urine, or to stop drumming on the window sill, they had better oblige, or else—. Unfortunately, the inmate is demented and does not understand what is expected of him. Searching for a familiar house or engaging an old enemy, he may resent this interruption and revile or (God help him) even raise his hand against the intruder. Seldom does an inmate have sufficient contact with reality deliberately to disobey a command. The conflict which ensues would be comical if the results were not so serious to the offender.

For there is only one result, invariably. To preserve the attendant's tender self-esteem, and because it is genuinely difficult *not* to treat an insane person as one would a normal man, and because, at the same time, the attendant half-recognizes the inmate to be insane and fears the consequences of irresponsible behavior, the inmate must either be compelled to obey the command or he must be humbled. If a shove or a blow will suffice, the inmate gets off easy. If not, he may be thrown upon the floor, beaten, choked to unconsciousness (a choice grip, passed on from attendant to attendant and used daily with abandon, is the necklock-from-the-rear which, applied forcefully, constricts the lateral blood vessels of the neck, stopping the flow of blood to the brain and rendering the victim insensible in a matter of seconds), tied in a strait jacket, or given a hyoscine-morphine-cactus injection that puts him out for several hours. Or he may be killed.

One small group of asylum murders occurs this way by the natural extension of disciplinary measures. I would not carry discipline so far myself, and generally worked with a friend who felt the same way, so I was present at no such murder and will not describe one here, though I have heard them described by co-workers. A typical account of such a murder is given by Frank L. Wright, Jr., in his authoritative *Out of Sight Out of Mind* (p. 100), which has recently been published by the National Mental Health Foundation (1520 Race St., Philadelphia, 2, Pa.) and which is earnestly recommended to all readers of this article. Also related in this book (p. 107) is the murder by sedation of 36 patients at one asylum.

The attendant spends only a fraction of his time beating inmates. Much, often most of his day is spent in idleness and his usual goal is to so regulate ward affairs as to insure himself the greatest possible amount of leisure; his ideal is a quiet ward with old-time inmates, accustomed to the discipline. And, then, from time to time, the attendant works. But the subject of his work *is* the inmate, and this is how another death-camp mechanism has arisen in the asylum. For there are many inmates, and few attendants, and in the press of numbers inmates are stamped as so much tin. No cruelty is intended thereby but it is, nevertheless, effectively administered; the inmate is in the position of the cow in an immaculate slaughter house—any visitor can see for himself that the place is clean.

Incidents selected to illustrate these conditions may appear trivial. But incidents in asylum life are generally trivial. There is no one event which, by itself, changes the conditions of an inmate from that of a man to that of an object. Dehumanization is a slow, cumulative process. Nor is there always one event which can be called "murder"; killing by attrition is more common: the asylum attacks periodically, the victim weakens and revives, and no one can say when it was that death first gained its hold.

The weekly shower is such a "trivial" instance. Once a week, two or three attendants strip, shower, and dress all the inmates on their ward in the space of an hour or so. This means that 100 men in various stages of mental and physical decay, averaging 55-60 years old and uniformly feeble, are lined up, undressed, pushed under a spray of water (and a good deal of pushing is usually required to speed the process and to keep inmates from wandering off), and treated quickly, roughly, and casually. The attendants have a job to do, a standardized procedure facilitates the job, and their behavior is almost exactly the same as it is when they wash a row of chairs.

The twice-weekly shave is another instance. Regulations forbid inmates to shave themselves. (One of the more ludicrous aspects of asylum morality is the pains which are taken by the administration to prevent suicide while doing everything possible to discourage life). But there was only one barber. He operated with a straight razor—because of professional pride—and never took more than one minute per shave. Since the inmate often offered resistance, three or four attendants would be on hand to restrain him; a first class battle might be fought, the inmate might lose half his skin and bleed profusely from razor cuts, but he was always shaved.

Then there are cases involving individuals. One old man, whose belly was deeply furrowed with wrinkles, tried constantly to crawl into bed. But no inmate was allowed to remain in bed without the nurse's approval—it disarrayed the sheets—and we were always pushing him out. One day he finally lay down long enough to bring up a great round half-congealed blob of dark-red blood about the diameter of your head, and then to go unconscious and to die. I believe the doctor then decided that he had had a stomach cancer. One young Jewish inmate was half-starving because bread was the only kosher food he could get. Many many incontinent, bed-ridden old men were hurried to death by the indifference of nurses and attendants to their care. Lying for long hours on urine-soaked sheets, they would develop bed sores that ate deep into the tissues of buttocks and back. I remember one man who must have been 80; he had been a farmer and still had great reserves of strength; all day and night he would call out, "Here, here. Here kitty paper, kitty. Hoo-hoo. Ho-ho. Come kitty, come my cat. . . . The cat is sitting there on the chair. Take the cat off and give me the chair so I can milk." This man rotted away, the flesh of his back turning into a pulpy mass of pus and blood whose stench drove visitors from the ward. It is only just to acknowledge that I was one of the attendants who helped to kill him, and there were many others we wished dead so that we would be spared the trouble of waiting on them. Fluids are important in preserving the resistance of bed-patients, and few received the necessary quantities of water or nourishment—we gave them little by mouth, and the doctors gave them none intravenously. It was quite a game, though, to try and keep inmates from dying during the second half of each shift, in order to avoid having to prepare the corpse for the undertaker; and then we forced fluids upon them and, if successful, gloated to the attendants who relieved us when we went off duty.

The attendants had closer contact with the inmates than did any other class of asylum personnel. They were a motley, frustrated lot—middle-aged bachelors, or childless, if married; often alcoholics or homosexuals. They did not have their own respect.

Nurses

Above the attendant is the nurse. It is difficult to generalize about nurses solely on the basis of my experience, because in the entire asylum wing where I worked, which contained over 500 inmates and included the male infirmary and admission ward, there was only a single nurse, on the day shift. But from contact with nurses at other institutions, as well as from certain published reports, the following remarks appear justified.

During their initial period of contact with inmates, when they are still students or fresh out of school, nurses generally display a positive interest in their patients' welfare. Even trifling cuts and ailments receive their prompt attention and, within the restrictions imposed by the conditions of their work in the asylum's ponderous social machine, they attempt to treat inmates as human beings. This is more possible for the nurse than it is for the attendant, because she sees the inmate only intermittently; in effect, she may occupy a sheltered pocket in the asylum wherein she can preserve for a time the ethics of her profession and the shape of her own personality. In one veterans' mental *hospital* with which I am acquainted, where nurses are not over-worked and where their social and physical surroundings are comparatively pleasant, even older nurses of long experience often did not develop the callousness and brusk manner so common in their profession.

But the asylum machine grinds constantly against all rough edges, and ultimately the average nurse comes, after a series of abrasions, to fit the role apportioned to her. It is not the story-book role of a white-clad woman of mercy; it is more the role of a hired mechanic in a municipal junk-yard, who does not care if the abandoned wrecks rust away. She tries to give as few medications as possible, and she has no interest in her patients as individuals. As the functionary in charge of ward arrangements, her major concern is to see that beds have been made in accordance with precise regulations, that floors have been swept, and that inmates are in their proper places. Three trifling episodes may convey the nature of her role:

Once, together with a nurse, I was changing the sheets of a bed occupied by a feeble old man. The top of the sheet fell over his upturned face. I moved to uncover it, whereupon the nurse, who was busy making a square corner at the foot of the bed, said: "Don't worry about him. Just get the sheet right."

At another asylum, one nurse pushed a female inmate to the washbowl. The inmate said, "Don't you dare push me!" "Why," replied the nurse, "You're just a *patient*; but *I'm* a *nurse!*"

And at another, the nurse told a new attendant, "In the back ward you will find a man lying in a cot. Be sure to watch him and let me know if and when he dies. I hope he goes by tonight. We want to use his bed."

Doctors

The doctor heads the asylum hierarchy that has direct contact with inmates. During the period under review, the active staff consisted of some ten doctors (neglecting the superintendent and assistant superintendent, who devoted all their time to administration). Since the starting salary was $2520, it is perhaps understandable that the asylum did not attract the highest calibre physician, and that only one of the ten was a psychiatrist. Nevertheless, these doctors are responsible for all measures designed to alleviate the mental and physical ailments of 3,000 inmates.

The measures are minimal or nil.

Most inmates receive no mental treatment whatsoever; for them, the asylum is only a prison and a death house.

Some inmates do improve sufficiently to be discharged, but there can be little doubt that the bulk of these effect recovery in response to natural inner forces rather than to asylum "therapy." Virtually no psychotherapy is prac-tised; such therapy as is administered is almost exclusively of a physical nature, because of the belief of the medical staff that insanity is largely caused by organic, constitutional factors, and because physical measures can most readily and economically be imposed upon a mass of patients without the necessity for over-fine discrimination between one patient and another.

Electric shock treatments meet these specifications well, and a dozen or more inmates were usually being subjected to this benevolent torture. To say the least, the atmosphere in which convulsions were induced was any-thing but friendly, however much it might satisfy those psychoanalysts who regard the expiator or punishing aspects of shock therapy as the basis of its efficacy. The doctor was in a rush, the nurse was in a rush, the large room was strewn with recumbent, heavy-breathing, semi-conscious men in various stages of recovery from their comas, while four or more attendants were on hand to insure that inmate resistance did not throw this assembly-line-for-the-manufacture-of-unconsciousness off schedule.

The malarial fever treatment of general paresis was given in a number of cases, but I have no information on how adequately it was administered.

This brings us to mechanical and chemical restraint or "sedation," the only measures we have not yet mentioned that might conceivably be interpreted as "mental treatment." The most common form of restraint at this asylum is the camisole or strait-jacket. State law, printed on the back of each restraint order, reads: "Mechanical restraint is to be employed only for satisfactory surgical or medical reasons, or to prevent a patient from injuring himself or others. Mechanical restraint shall be employed only on the signed order of a physician . . . and a physician shall always be present at the first application of restraint. . . . No patient in restraint shall be left unattended, and the restraining apparatus shall be removed each 3 hours, so as to permit change of position, exercise of the limbs, and attention to cleanliness and the ex-cretions."

All of these provisions are constantly violated: inmates are placed in strait-jackets as punishment for offending their superiors; attendants regularly strap inmates into a jacket and then apply for the physician's order, which is invariably granted; not once in fourteen months did I see a doctor present at the first application of restraint; and the strait jacket is often not removed for days at a time.

Since seclusion rooms are unavailable, chemical "sedation" is freely used as a disciplinary agent to keep inmates from disturbing the quiet of the ward, especially at night. Violent inmates are doped up for days on end with HMC and morphine injections or oral ministrations of sodium amytal or nembutal; convulsions occasionally result from overdosage.

This completes our summary of the asylum provisions for "treatment" of mental illness, though I have heard that a program of lobotomy operations has recently been inaugurated with some fanfare. (Amputation of the head will, doubtless, come next.)

A similar situation exists in regard to the treatment of physical ailments. The health of inmates deteriorates rapidly after entry (seclusion and poor diet alone would ensure this, not to mention disease contagion and the general decline in spirit), and no concerted effort is made to maintain it. Fortunate inmates enjoy an occasional mass walk on the grounds in good weather; many, however, get their only taste of fresh air on narrow porches through screens dark with dust and dried spittle. Even a program of periodic weighing or other health inspection is lacking, and persons infected with TB may circulate on the wards for a year before being detected and isolated.

Usually an ailment goes unnoticed until it develops to such a point that the attendant or nurse becomes aware of it and notifies the doctor. What is done thereafter depends to some extent upon the personality of the doctor involved. One doctor, thorough and conscientious in administering medication, was disliked by his colleagues for setting them such a standard of performance. Most doctors, like most attendants, tried to get by with as little work as possible, and the longer they remained at the asylum the more adept they became at avoiding work. Two doctors with whom I had close contact afford excellent examples.

One inmate with bladder distension went uncatheterized for over 30 hours at a stretch, because they were too lazy to take care of him sooner. Another inmate suffered for two weeks while gangrene spread up his foot and penis and the ward was kept awake nightly by his groaning, before they paid any attention to repeated reports of his condition (immediate amputation was then decided upon, and the man died twelve hours after the operation). Inmates with pneumonia died simply because of lack of medication.

The doctors especially resented being called (rather awakened) during the night, although one or the other was theoretically always on duty. When temperatures running from 100-104° were reported to them by phone, the invariable reply was a standard order of sulfa pills and soda bicarb; on these occasions, the doctor never made a personal visit to the ward. Their general attitude to patients may be indicated by an episode:

One summer night, a newly admitted alcoholic went into convulsions some time after having been put into a strait jacket; I took his temperature: it was up to the top of the thermometer, at 110°. I phoned the doctor, who ordered a shot of coramine. I ran to the surgery room, hunted up a vial of coramine, found a hypodermic and a needle, ran back to the man, now obviously on the way out, and gave him the injection in the arm. Three minutes later he was dead. Twenty or thirty minutes later the doctor showed up.

His exceptional zeal was due to the fact that any inmate who dies within twenty-four hours of admittance is automatically classified as a coroner's case, and the present inmate had been young and strong and very much alive upon entry. The supervisor primed me to say that everyone had done everything that could possibly have been done for the deceased. But the coroner's investigation was so perfunctory he did not ask me a single question. Some matters he neglected to investigate were the connection between strapping a strait jacket on a sweating alcoholic on a warm night and his subsequent heat stroke, the whereabouts of the doctor during and subsequent to the application of the strait jacket, and the absence, on the infirmary ward of this "hospital," of anyone who was qualified to administer emergency medical treatment.

Discussion

We are now better able to discuss the similarity of some social mechanisms in the Nazi death camps and the American insane asylum.

First, there is the matter of public indifference to atrocities despite a general knowledge of them. The American public is as guilty here as was the German people. Exposes of insane asylums have been published with monotonous regularity for years (see, for instance, the novels of Jane Hillyer, William Seabrook, Margaret Wilson, Mary Jane Ward, etc.), numberless investigating committees have conducted investigations, but the callous inhumanity of these institutions persists unaltered. Indeed, the asylum I have described is one in which Clifford Beers was an inmate over forty years ago and where he experienced cruelties that, in part, later led him to found the Mental Hygiene movement. And although psychiatric science has made considerable advances since that day, the social structure of the insane asylum and the ill-treatment and murder of its inmates by attendants and doctors remains substantially the same today that it was then.

How has it been possible for the asylum to persist unchanged, how was it possible for the death camps to exist? How was it possible to get men to work in death camps? One answer which has been advanced is that it was not ordinary Germans, but specially sadistic SS men who ran the camps. Undoubtedly there was selection of personnel at Auschwitz, just as there is an automatic selection of the kind of men who work in insane asylums in this country. But this answer is not satisfactory: SS members were human beings; the attendants, nurses, and doctors at the asylum are ordinary human beings; as is the writer (who also was involved in these atrocities); and every one of the thousand and more conscientious objectors who worked in American asylums during the war was personally involved in similar atrocities.

The simple factor that seems to explain the phenomenon might be called "getting used to things." The longer an attendant works at the asylum, the longer a man works in the death camp, the more indifferent does he become to the business at hand, the more mechanical and unemotional become his murderous operations. "It was bad at first, *but we got used to it*," said the paymaster at the Nazi death camp. That death is the product of these operations makes not the least bit of difference psychologically. Men who handle the dead daily—morticians, doctors, hangmen, gravediggers, butchers, soldiers —are traditionally unconcerned with their merchandise, while the uninitiated citizen or child is shocked by sight of the corpse. The period of first introduction to the scene of slaughter would, then, usually be crucial in determining whether or not a man will continue to endure it; selection of personnel can serve to increase the likelihood that this test of transition is successfully met. (This is not to deny that psychological tensions will, in some circumstances, build up gradually so that, e.g., a soldier may crack under the strain of successive battles after facing death bravely in his first encounter.)

In the asylum, it is a common experience that the incoming attendant is more humane in his dealings with inmates than are older attendants, and the longer he remains the more callous he becomes. Clifford Beers made a similar observation:

"I recall the advent of a new attendant—a young man studying to become a physician. At first he seemed inclined to treat patients kindly, but he soon fell into brutal ways. . . . That the environment in some institutions is brutalizing, was strikingly shown in the testimony of an attendant at a public investigation in Kentucky, who said, 'When I came here, if anyone had told me I would be guilty of striking patients I would have called him crazy himself, but now I take delight in punching hell out of them.'" (*A Mind That Found Itself*, pp. 165-6)

Conscientious objectors who worked in asylums during the recent war gradually took over a large part of the code and conduct of regular asylum employees, including cruel and vulgar behavior which did not fit happily with their pacifist ideology.[1] The instance parallels the unconscious assumption by anti-fascist inmates in German concentration camps of the character and ideology of their Nazi keepers. (See Bruno Bettelheim, "Individual and Mass Behavior in Extreme Situations," *Journal of Abnormal and Social Psychology*, Oct. 1943.) The moral I would draw is that the social mechanism is stronger than any individual's will, and there are situations from which only physical escape can ensure the maintenance of the individual's integrity. When an individual remains in a situation such as that of an asylum, the army, prison, a concentration or death camp, it is inevitable that, to a greater or lesser extent, he sacrifices those values acquired by earlier experience which do not accord with the role he must play in the new situation. Similar, but milder, sacrifices would seem to be inevitable in less extreme situations.

Allowing the parallelism between the psychology of the working staff of the asylum and the death camp, a difference in their type of work still remains. The work of a death camp is to kill men and to dispose of their

---

[1] That CO's exerted a humanizing influence upon asylums and have become a force for reform through the publicity they have given to existent conditions is, of course, true; but the other half of the equation, the brutalization of CO's by their experience, has been insufficiently stressed. Some CO's who volunteered for asylum work found themselves unable to stomach the violence that went with it, and requested transfer to other units. Those who remained were soon absorbed into the system, learning to hate and punish, to loaf, to enjoy their authority over those beneath them and to resent the authority of superiors. One of the most rational inmates with whom I became friendly, a weaver who had murdered his daughter, once made this very observation: "You boys all come here with ideals, but you change after awhile and become like everyone else."

corpses methodically and efficiently. <u>The work of an asylum is to imprison men methodically, and only occasionally to kill them.</u> The ultimate test of similarity between the death camp and the asylum lies in the nature of the murder that is committed in the latter institution.

Murder by the attendants' beating of inmates is reprehensible both to the society outside the asylum and even, to some degree, to the society within it. The action of attendants involved in this type of murder seems more comparable to the disciplinary action of a police force than to the systematic operations of death camp guards.

It is in the murder by neglect of decrepit old men that, I believe, the closest analogy is to be found with death camp murders. The asylum murders are passive; the Auschwitz murders active (although once the factory was set going, largely passive too); but otherwise their logic is the same. The aged, insane paupers of the American asylum are surely the most pitiful members of American society; but no one will give them more than pity, and they also evoke feelings of abhorrence and fear. Asylums are institutions which have been created to remove this sight from our eyes. If the death rate at asylums were to be reduced, the yearly dollar and cents cost of their upkeep would be very much higher than we have thus far been willing to pay. In effect, the judgment of American society has been to murder its elderly insane. This was the same judgment that German society rendered against its Jews.

On the Pacific islands of Tonga, where a class society prevailed, it was believed that only the souls of noblemen are immortal. The debasement of the life of lower classes in industrial society was described by Engels and Dickens in England a century ago. Cannibalism was practised by *Sinanthropus pekinensis;* slavery, sacrifice, exploitation and murder of designated social classes are popular human practices during both war and peace, and the victims often cooperate in achieving their own demise. Jew hatred has been common in the Western world for at least 2,000 years. Did the death camps do more than make various generic theories explicit?

The problem of what to do with its senile population is faced by every human society, and the answer is always given in terms of prevailing cultural forms. The authoritarian structure, impersonalized operation, and standardized products of asylum and death camp appear, in this light, as a macabre caricature of the modern mode of production.

[The following exchange of letters between Orlans and Dwight MacDonald, then editor of *Politics*, appeared as an appendix to the article.—EDS.]

Is there not a greater qualitative difference between the American mental hospital and the Nazi death camps than Orlans recognizes? The latter seem to me irrational for this reason: the Nazis took millions of people who were not dangerous to them and, at a big expenditure of manpower, rolling stock, materials, etc., killed them because of their race alone. A rational course would have been to let the Jews alone unless they threatened the regime enough to justify the effort of killing them; the death camps were not even useful as propaganda—to strike terror in others, like the concentration camps—since their existence was carefully concealed. The authorities who run our asylums, on the other hand, don't go out and pull in victims; they have the insane dumped on them, and must do something about them; as you show, the most convenient thing to do is to first reduce them to subhuman objects, and then help them perish as speedily as possible; this is abhorrent, of course, but rational, since it's the easiest way out for normal, callous, lazy men. The Nazis went to great and needless trouble in creating *their* camps.—D.M.

I cannot agree that the death camps were any less (or more) rational than asylums. Reason may be said to guide human activity when, an end clearly in view and reality correctly appraised, measures are taken to achieve the end most economically. But:

(1) I believe, with Weber, that all human ends (values) are partly irrational for, although (or because) they can be explained historically, their choice is essentially arbitrary so far as the individual is concerned, and hence not dependent solely either upon reason or functional utility. All culture partakes of this nature; not logic but social and personal structure and history determines that our goals shall be to kill Japanese, Germans, Jews, or lunatics; to seek transmigration of souls or a socialist utopia; ascetic or sensual pleasures; and impeachable logic is used to defend all of these goals. Human behavior is more often devious than direct, and visitors to foreign lands always wonder why the natives do things this way instead of that; culture channels the course of human effort like an old river, which now and then wears through an ox-bow or overflows or finds a new bed, but mainly wanders rather pointlessly to the sea.

(2) Having appointed a goal, inadequate knowledge often intervenes to make its efficient realization impossible. Can the politician or citizen be expected to behave more rationally than social scientists or historians, the more honest of whom confess that they know little about society or personality?

Nazi ideology was obviously irrational in asserting as true what science had found false, but since this assertion served a function in Nazi society it can also be considered rational according to the devious logic of history. Given a drive of Jew hatred, it seems to me eminently rational to kill Jews. How would the reader go about killing several million Jews, if he were in Hitler's position, with the ideology, resources and experience that Hitler and his aides had at their disposal? I think his solution would be similar to the one the Nazis adopted. That this solution may have seriously weakened the Nazi war effort is possible (but not certain), and evidence of the fact that human goals frequently conflict in a manner not easily resolved. The roundabout manner in which the asylum kills inmates strikes one at first as irrational (a gas chamber would be more efficient); but knowledge (or hindsight) of American society makes it apparent that no shorter course is, at present, practicable; indeed a longer course may one day be adopted. I know very little about Nazi society; if I knew more, the reasons for the course which it pursued at Auschwitz would be clearer to me—H.O.

This reply misses my point. I did not question the rationality of the Nazis' ends, but of their means. Nor did I deny that anti-semitism was a rational means to the end they had in view. Even killing the Jews *might* have been rational as a means to their end, which was to make the Germans, and themselves as the quintessential leaders of the Germans, the master race of Europe and, ultimately, the world. The Jews, in 1942-44 when the death camps were instituted, *might* have threatened the Nazis by their active sabotage or counter-violence; but they didn't. Or they *might* have been framed up by the Nazis on such charges, as the defendants were in the Moscow Trials, to serve as scapegoats for the shortcomings of the regime; in which case, their mass slaughter would have been widely publicised for propaganda purposes. But this was not done either: the death camps were *concealed* by the Nazis, from the Germans as well as from the rest of the world. Hence one must conclude that killing six million Jews served merely to alleviate the personal neurotic difficulties of the Nazi bigshots; it was, true, rational from this standpoint, just as handwashing every five minutes is rational from the standpoint of certain compulsive neurotics—i.e., it in fact does give a momentary relief from tension.

Nor is the point whether the Nazi death camps were rationally organized for mass killing—for, of course, they were—but rather whether it was rational to institute them at all. This latter point hardly exists so far as the American asylum is concerned: the moneyless insane are dumped on them—where else in this inhuman society we live in?—and they must be disposed of somehow. The methods adopted, as definitively described by Orlans, are as rational as they are ethically horrible. Both the death camps and our own asylums are indices of barbarism; but there *is* a difference—and one that favors American as against Nazi society—between letting sick people die through callous neglect and gathering up and exterminating, at great expenditure of manpower and materiel, millions of people who are healthy (hence no burden on society) and politically passive (hence no threat to society's rulers). To equate the one with the other seems to me stretching things too far.—D.M.

I've little to add to what I said above. I don't think one can fruitfully separate ends and means, or the rationality of the inception and operation of the camps. Macdonald's comparison with the compulsive neurotic seems to me good, although we must allow for the possibility that some preposterously simple and rational reason (like the high cost of plate glass and losses which German insurance companies suffered from anti-Jewish pogroms, as Melvin Lasky suggests in the August *Commentary*) played a part in the business. But how much sense does it make to talk of a neurotic *society,* when there is no broader normative realm (except the rather irrelevant realms of nature and history, whose main norm is survival) with which a society meshes and against which it may be measured? Compulsive neurotics, anal sadists, epileptics (as among certain primitive groups), or homosexuals may ride horse on a culture and swing off in their direction, but only someone who sets up rules for the race can tell which culture has won it.—H.O.

Social and Physical Planning for the Elimination of Urban Poverty

HERBERT J. GANS

City planning has traditionally sought community betterment through so-called *physical* methods, such as the creation of efficient land use and transportation schemes, the sorting out of diverse types of land use, and the renewal of technologically obsolescent areas and buildings to achieve functional, as well as esthetically desirable, arrangements of structures and spaces. This paper deals with a new planning concept which places greater emphasis on economic and social methods of improving community life. In some places it is called human renewal; in others, community development; in yet others, social planning. Although none of the names is quite appropriate, the programs to which they refer are of crucial importance to the future of the city, for they seek to do away with—or at least to decimate—urban poverty and the deprivation that accompanies it. If these programs succeed, they are likely to have a lasting impact on city planning and on the other professions concerned with planning for community welfare.

The fight against poverty is not new, of course, and, in fact, the elimination of urban deprivation was one of the goals of the founders of modern city planning. The planning movement itself developed partly in reaction to the conditions under which the European immigrants who came to American cities in the mid-19th century had to live. The reduction of their squalor was one of Frederick Law Olmstead's goals when he proposed the building of city parks so that the poor—as well as the rich—might have a substitute rural landscape in which to relax from urban life. It motivated the Boston civic leaders who first built playgrounds in the slums of that city, and the founders of the settlement house movement, notably Jane Addams, who argued strongly for city planning. It also sparked the efforts of those who built model tenements to improve the housing conditions of the poor. And Ebenezer Howard had this goal in mind when he proposed to depopulate the London slums through Garden Cities.

Most of these planning efforts were not aimed directly at the reduction of poverty and deprivation, but sought to use land planning, housing codes

SOURCE: Reprinted, with some revisions by its author, from *Washington University Law Quarterly* (symposium issue on land-use planning) vol. 1963, no. 1 (February, 1963), pp. 2–18. An earlier version of this paper was read to the 1962 Conference of the American Institute of Planners, Los Angeles, October 17, 1962, and appears in American Institute of Planners, *Proceedings of the 1962 Conference* (Washington, D.C.: The Institute, 1963), pp. 176–190.

and occasionally zoning to eliminate slums and reduce densities in the tightly
packed tenement neighborhoods. The apotheosis of this approach—slum
clearance—followed upon the arrival of the newest wave of poor immigrants:
the Southern Negroes, Puerto Ricans and Mexicans who came to the city
during World War II and in the post-war era. After a decade of noting the
effects of the federal slum clearance program, however, some observers became concerned because while this method was eliminating slums, it was not
contributing significantly to the improvement of the slum dwellers' living
conditions.

In many cases, the reduction in the already short supply of low cost housing
brought about by slum clearance, together with faulty or nonexistent relocation planning sent slum dwellers into adjacent slums or forced them to
overcrowd declining areas elsewhere. But even where slum clearance was
accompanied by adequate relocation programs, the housing of poor people
in decent low cost dwellings did not solve other—and equally pressing—
problems, such as poverty, unemployment, illiteracy, alcoholism, and mental
illness. Nor could rehousing alone do away with crime, delinquency, prostitution, and other deviant behavior. In short, it became clear that such physical
changes as urban renewal, good housing, and modern project planning were
simply not enough to improve the lives of the poverty-stricken.

As a result, planners and "housers" began to look for non-physical planning
approaches.[1] In this process, they made contact with other professions that
are concerned with the low-income population, for example, social workers.
Working in tandem with them and others, they have developed new programs, bearing the various names indicated above. Most often they have been
referred to as social planning, a term that had been coined by social workers
to describe the coordination of individual social agency programs carried out
by such central planning and budgeting agencies as the United Fund.[2]

Although the term has already received considerable attention in city
planning circles, I prefer to use another term. Insofar as the programs seek
to aid low income people to change their fortunes and their ways of living,
they are attempts to guide them toward the social and economic mobility that
more fortunate people have achieved on their own. For this reason, the programs might best be described as planning for *guided mobility*.

Such programs are now underway in many American cities. Some are
designed as programs in juvenile delinquency prevention, which have come
into being under the aegis of the President's Committee on Juvenile Delinquency and work mainly with young people.[3] Others are oriented toward

---

[1] Another impetus came from the fact that several cities scheduled urban renewal
projects in their skid row areas, and programs to "rehabilitate" its residents were
developed as part of the relocation plan.

[2] The term has also been applied to plans which attempt to outline social—that is,
non-physical—goals for the entire society, a procedure that would be more aptly called
societal planning.

[3] Of these, the leading program is New York's Mobilization for Youth. This is
described in Mobilization for Youth, Inc., "A Proposal for the Prevention and Control
of Delinquency by Expanding Opportunities" (New York, Dec. 1961, mimeographed).

low income people of all ages, and since planners have been most active in these, the rest of the article will deal primarily with such programs.[4] Although most of the programs are just getting started, some over-all similarities between them are apparent. Needless to say, any generalizations about them are preliminary, for the programs are likely to change as they progress from initial formulation to actual implementation.

The guided mobility plans and proposals which I have examined have four major programmatic emphases:

1. to develop new methods of education for children from low income and culturally deprived homes, so as to reduce functional illiteracy, school dropouts and learning disabilities which prevent such children from competing in the modern job market in adulthood;

2. to reduce unemployment by new forms of job training among the young, by the retraining of adults and by the creation of new jobs in the community;

3. to encourage self-help on an individual and group basis through community organization methods that stimulate neighborhood participation; and

4. to extend the amount and quality of social services to the low income population. Among the latter are traditional casework services, new experiments for giving professional help to the hard-to-reach, multi-problem family and the provision of modern facilities and programs of public recreation, public health and community center activities.

The educational phase of guided mobility includes programs such as Higher Horizons, which attempt to draw bright children from the culturally restrictive context of low income environments, and to offer them the academic and cultural opportunities available to bright middle class children. There are also programs to help average and backward youngsters, using remedial reading and other devices to guide them during the early school years, so that they will develop the skills and motivations to stay in school until high school graduation. The occupational phase of the plans includes job programs which will employ young people in useful community projects, and in quasi-apprentice programs in private industry, as well as various voca-

---

[4] Examples of the many such plans are: Action for Boston Community Development, "A Proposal for a Community Development Program in Boston" (Boston, Mass. Dec. 1961, mimeographed); Action Housing, Inc., ". . . Urban Extension in the Pittsburgh Area" (Pittsburgh, Pa. Sept. 1961, mimeographed); City of Oakland, "Proposal for a Program of Community Development" (City of Oakland, Cal. June and Dec. 1961, mimeographed); Community Progress, Inc., "Opening Opportunities: New Haven's Comprehensive Program for Community Progress" (New Haven, Conn. April 1962, mimeographed); and Department of City Planning, "A Plan for the Woodlawn Community: Social Planning Factors" (Chicago, Ill. Jan. 1962, mimeographed). My comments about the plans below are based on a number of published and unpublished documents which I have examined, as well as on discussions about existing and proposed plans in which I have participated in several cities. My description of these plans is, in sociological terminology, an ideal type, and does not fit exactly any one of the plans now in existence.

tional training and retraining programs for young and old alike. Meanwhile, added effort is scheduled to attract new industries, and thus to bring new jobs to the community.

The extension of social services, and the community organization phase of the programs use decentralization as a means of reaching the high proportion of low income people who usually abstain from community contact. The provision of social services to the hard-to-reach will be attempted by bringing programs to the neighborhood level, with neighborhood directors to supervise the process. In addition, the social agencies plan to coordinate their services, so that individual agencies working with the same individual or family know what the other is doing, and duplication and contradictions can be avoided. More neighborhood facilities will also be established, including community schools, public health clinics and recreation centers, sometimes grouped in a "services center," so that people will be encouraged to come there when they need help.

The decentralizing of community organization activities is intended to create a sense of neighborhood and an interest in neighborhood self-help. Community organizers will work in the neighborhood for this purpose, and will try to involve "natural leaders" living in the area, who can act as a bridge between the professionals, the city and the neighborhood population.

This is a very general description of the programs. In actuality, each community has a somewhat distinctive approach, or a different emphasis in the selection of programs, depending partly on the lineup of sponsoring agencies. But some city planners who have become interested in guided mobility programs are still preoccupied—and sometimes too much so—with traditional physical planning approaches, notably two: the realization of a neighborhood scheme—originally devised by Clarence Perry[5] and consisting of a small, clearly bounded residential area, built up at low density, with auto and pedestrian traffic carefully separated, considerable open space, and with a combination elementary school and neighborhood meeting place in its center; and the provision both in such neighborhoods and in the larger community of a standard array of public facilities for recreation, health, education, culture, and other community services.

The concern with neighborhood is of course traditional in city planning, and even the new challenge of finding non-physical ways of helping the low-income group has not diverted the planner from it. In some cities, guided mobility plans are thus almost appendages to physical planning programs, based on the traditional belief that the rebuilding of the city into a series of separate neighborhoods to encourage a small-townish middle class form of family life is a proper solution even for poverty. Elsewhere, the program may be an appendage of urban renewal activities, the main intent still being the upgrading of the physical neighborhoods. Thus, guided mobility is used partly to organize the neighboorhood into undertaking—or helping the city

---

[5] Clarence A. Perry, "The Neighborhood Unit," *Regional Survey of New York and Its Environs*, vol. 7 (New York: Committee on Regional Plan of New York and Its Environs, 1929), Vol. 7, pp. 22–140.

with—this task. But in most cases, the neighborhood emphaiss is based on a genuine concern that one of the causes of urban deprivation is to be found in the poor quality of neighborhood life.

The provision of public facilities is also a traditional planning emphasis, dating back to the days when the planner was an ally of the reformers who were fighting for the establishment of these facilities. Out of this has come the belief that public facilities are crucial agencies in people's lives, that up-to-date facilities and programs will encourage intensive use of them and that this in turn will help significantly in achieving the aims of guided mobility planning.

Despite the intensity of the planner's belief in neighborhood and public facility use, there is no evidence that these two planning concepts are as important to low income people as they are to planners. Consequently, it is fair to ask whether such concepts are as crucial to the elimination of urban poverty and deprivation as is signified by their appearance in some guided mobility plans. The answer to this question requires a brief discussion of the nature of contemporary urban poverty.

I I

The low-income population may be divided into two major segments, which sociologists call the *working class* and the *lower class*.[6] The former consists of semiskilled and skilled blue collar workers, who hold steady jobs, and are thus able to live under stable, if not affluent, conditions. Their way of life differs in many respects from those of the middle class; for example, in the greater role of relatives in sociability and mutual aid, in the lesser concern for self-improvement and education, and in their lack of interest in the good address, cultivation and the kinds of status that are important to middle class people. Although their ways are culturally different from the dominant middle class norms, these are not pathological, for rates of crime, mental illness and other social ills are not significantly higher than in the middle class. This population, therefore, has little need for guided mobility programs.

The lower class, on the other hand, consists of people who perform the unskilled labor and service functions in the society. Many of them lack stable jobs. They are often unemployed, or forced to move from one temporary— and underpaid—job to another. Partly because of occupational instability, their lives are beset with social and emotional instability as well, and it is among them that one finds the majority of the emotional problems and social evils that are associated with the low-income population.[7]

---

[6] Herbert J. Gans, *The Urban Villagers* (Glencoe, Ill.: Free Press, 1962), chap. 11. See also S. M. Miller and Frank Riessman, "The Working Class Subculture: A New View," *Social Problems*, vol. 9, (1961), pp. 86–97. The nature and extent of urban poverty is described in Michael Harrington, *The Other America* (New York: Macmillan, 1962), chaps. 2, 4, 5, 7, 8.

[7] An excellent brief description of lower class culture may be found in Walter B. Miller, "Lower Class Culture as a Generating Milieu of Gang Delinquency," *Journal*

In past generations, the American economy had considerable need for unskilled labor, and the European immigrants who performed it were able to achieve enough occupational stability to raise themselves, or their children, to working class or even middle class ways of living. Today, however, the need for unskilled labor is constantly decreasing, and will soon be minimal. Consequently, the Negro, Puerto Rican and Mexican newcomers who now constitute most of the American lower class find it very difficult to improve their condition.[8]

Guided mobility planning is essentially an attempt to help them solve their problems and to aid them in changing their lives. This makes it necessary to find out what causes their problems, what they themselves are striving for and how they can be helped to achieve their strivings.

The nature of the problem is not difficult to identify. For economic reasons, and for reasons of race as well, the contemporary lower class is frustrated—if not barred—from opportunities to hold well-paid, stable jobs, to receive a decent education, to live in good housing or to get access to a whole series of choices and privileges that the white middle class takes for granted.

In addition, some lower class people lack the motivations and skills needed to participate in contemporary society, and more important, which are necessary to accept the opportunities if and when they become available. Moreover, the apathy, despair and rejection which result from lack of access to crucial opportunities help bring about the aforementioned social and emotional difficulties.

There are a number of reasons for these reactions.[9] When men are long unemployed or underemployed, they feel useless, and eventually become marginal members of their family. This has many consequences. They may desert their families, and turn to self-destructive behavior in despair. If male instability is widespread, the woman becomes the dominant member of the family, and she may live with a number of men in the hope of finding a stable mate. The result is a family type which Walter Miller calls female-based, which is marked by free unions, illegitimate children and what middle class people consider to be broken homes.[10] Boys who grow up in such families may be deprived of needed male models, and are likely to inherit some of the

---

of Social Issues, vol. 14 (1958), pp. 5–19. The everyday life of the lower class is pictured in Oscar Lewis, *Five Families* (New York: Basic Books, 1959), and *The Children of Sanchez* (New York: Random House, 1961). Athough Lewis' books deal with the lower class of Mexico City, his portrait applies, with some exceptions, to American cities as well.

[8] For an analysis of the occupational history of the European immigrants and the more recent immigrants, see Oscar Handlin, *The Newcomers* (New York: Anchor Books, 1962).

[9] For a more detailed analysis, see Gans, *The Urban Villagers*, ch. 12, and Institute for Urban Studies, *Social Planning: A New Role for Sociology* (Philadelphia 1962, mimeographed). See also Mobilization for Youth, Inc., *op. cit.* and Walter B. Miller, *op. cit.*

[10] Walter B. Miller, *op. cit.* This family type is particularly widespread in the Negro lower class, in which it originated during slavery.

feelings of uselessness and despair they see in their fathers. In addition, the children must learn at an early age how to survive in a society in which crisis is an everyday occurrence, and where violence and struggle are ever-present. Thus, they may learn how to defend themselves against enemies, and how to co-exist with an alcoholic parent, but they do not learn how to read, how to concentrate on their studies or how to relate to the teacher.[11] Those that do must defend their deviant behavior—and it is deviant in the lower class—against their peers, who, like peers in all other groups, demand that they conform to the dominant mode of adaptation. Also, many children grow up in households burdened with mental illness, and this scars their own emotional and social growth. Out of such conditions develops a lower class culture with a set of behavior patterns which is useful for the struggle to survive in a lower class milieu, but which makes it almost impossible to participate in the larger society. And since the larger society rejects the lower class individual for such behavior, he can often develop self-respect and dignity only by rejecting the larger society. He blames it for his difficulties—and with much justification—but in this process rejects many of its values as well, becoming apathetic, cynical and hostile even toward those that seek to help him.

This overly brief analysis is at present mostly hypothetical, for we do not yet know exactly what it is that creates the lower class way of life. We know that the nature of family relationships, the influence of peers, the kind of home training, the adaptive characteristics of lower class culture, the high prevalence of mental illness and the need to cope with one crisis after another are all important factors, but we do not yet know exactly which factors are most important, how they operate to create the way of life that they do and how they are related to the lack of opportunities that bring them about.

Similarly, we know that lower class people are striving to change their condition, but we do not know exactly for what they are striving. It is clear that they want stable jobs and higher incomes, and there is considerable evidence of an almost magical belief in education and high occupational aspirations for the children, especially among Negroes.[12] The lack of opportunity and the constant occurrence of crises frustrate most of these aspirations before they can be implemented, but they do exist, especially among the women. On the other hand, the failure of settlement houses, social workers and other helping agencies to reach the majority of the lower class population suggests that these people either cannot or do not want to accept the middle class values which these professionals preach and which are built into the welfare activities they carry out. Such programs attract the small minority desirous of,

---

[11] The educational and other problems of the lower class child are described in more detail in Patricia C. Sexton, *Education and Income* (New York: Viking, 1961); and Frank Riessman, *The Culturally Deprived Child* (New York: Harper, 1962).

[12] For the most recent example of this finding, see R. Kleiner, S. Parker, and H. Taylor, "Social Status and Aspirations in Philadelphia's Negro Population" (Philadelphia: Commission on Human Relations, June 1962, mimeographed).

or ready for middle class life, but they repel the rest. A number of social scientists suggest that what lower class people are striving for is the stable, family-centered life of working class culture, and at least one delinquency prevention program is based on such an assumption.[13]

These observations about the nature of lower class life have many implications for guided mobility planning. As a result of the sparsity of knowledge, much research, experiment and evaluation of experience will be necessary in order to learn what kinds of programs will be successful. It is clear that the most urgent need is to open up presently restricted opportunities, especially in the occupational sphere. The guided mobility programs which stress the creation of new jobs, the attack on racial discrimination, education and occupational training as highest priority items are thus on the right track. Even so, new ways of bringing industry and jobs to the community must be found, for conventional programs have not been sufficiently productive. Then, ways of channelling lower class people into new jobs, and keeping them at work even if their initial performance is not as good as that of other people, or of labor saving machines, must be invented. Racial barriers will also have to come down more quickly, especially in those spheres of life and activity most important to lower class people, so that they can begin to feel that they have some stake in society. This too is easier said than done.

Not only is desegregation difficult to implement, but the most successful programs so far have benefited middle class non-whites more than their less fortunate fellows. For lower class people, access to jobs, unions and decent low cost housing is most important, as is the assurance of fair treatment from the police, the courts, from city hall, storeowners and helping agencies. The integration of high priced suburban housing, expensive restaurants or concert halls is for *them* of much less immediate significance.

Also, methods of encouraging motivations and skills, and of maintaining aspirations in the face of frustration must be found. If the matriarchal lower class family is at fault, ways of providing boys with paternal substitutes must be developed. Where the entire lower class milieu is destructive, children may have to be removed from it, especially in their formative years. Treatments for mental illness, alcoholism and narcotics addiction that will be effective among lower class people have to be discovered, and the causes of these ills isolated so that prevention programs may be set up. Schools must be created which can involve lower class children. This means that they must teach the skills needed in a middle class society yet without the middle class symbols and other trappings that frighten or repel the lower class student.[14] Finally, it is necessary to develop urban renewal or other housing programs that will make livable dwellings available to the low income population, within its price range, and located near enough to its places of employment so as not to require unreasonable amounts of travel time and expenditures.

These program requirements demand some radical changes in our ways

---

[13] Mobilization for Youth, Inc., *op. cit.*
[14] See Sexton, *op. cit.* and Riessman, *op. cit.*

of doing things. For example, if lower class people are to find employment, there will need to be economic enterprises not geared solely to profit and to cost-reduction, but also to the social profits of integrating the unemployed. In short, eventually we shall have to give up the pretense that 19th century free enterprise ideology can cope with 20th century realities, and learn to replan some economic institutions to help the low-income population, just as we are now redesigning public education to teach this population's children. Likewise, if lower class people are to become part of the larger society, there must be changes in the way the police, the courts and political structures treat them. To cite just one instance, lower class people must be represented more adequately in local party politics, and their needs and demands must receive more adequate hearing at city hall than has heretofore been the case. Similarly, the professions that now seek to help lower class people will have to be altered so as to be more responsive to how lower class people define their needs, and this may mean the replacement of some professionals by skilled nonprofessionals who are more capable of achieving rapport with lower class clients. Also, urban renewal policy must concern itself less with "blight" removal, or with the use of new construction to solve the city's tax problems, and more with improvement of the housing conditions of the slum dwellers. Changes, such as these, which require redistribution of power, income, privileges and the alteration of established social roles, are immensely difficult to bring about. Even so, they are necessary if urban poverty and deprivation are to be eliminated.[15]

III

Proper guided mobility planning must be based on methods that will achieve the intended goal. If the hypotheses about the causes of urban deprivation are correct, the basic components of guided mobility planning must be able to affect the economy, the political and social structures that shore up poverty and racial—as well as class—discrimination, the foci of lower class culture that frustrate the response to opportunities, notably the family, the peer group, the milieu in which children grow up and the helping agencies that now have difficulty in reaching lower class people, especially the school. Any programs which lack these components, and cannot bring about changes in the position of the lower class population vis-à-vis the institutions named are unlikely to contribute significantly to the aim of guided mobility.[16]

The list of basic components does not include the two that have been especially emphasized by planners: the belief in neighborhood and the impor-

---

[15] For other programmatic statements, see Peter Marris, "A Report on Urban Renewal in the United States," and Leonard J. Duhl, "Planning and Poverty," in Leonard J. Duhl (ed.), *The Urban Condition* (New York: Basic Books, 1963), pp. 113–134, and 295–304, respectively. See also Harrington, *op. cit.*

[16] For a more detailed critical analysis of current guided mobility plans, see Gans, *Social Planning.*

tance of public facilities. This omission is not accidental, for I do not believe that these two concepts are of high priority. Indeed, it is possible that they may divert guided mobility programs from the direction they ought to take.

By focusing programs on neighborhoods as spatial units, planners are naturally drawn to what is most visible in them, the land uses, buildings and major institutions, and their attention is diverted from what is hardest to see, the people—and social conditions—with problems. It should be clear from the foregoing analysis that the program must concentrate on the people and on the social and economic forces which foster their deprivation, rather than on neighborhood conditions which are themselves consequences of these forces.

Moreover, too much concern with neighborhoods may cause the programs to seek out the wrong people: the working class segment of the low income population rather than the lower class one. This may happen for two reasons. First, the planner often finds it difficult to distinguish between areas occupied by working class people, and those occupied by lower class people, mainly because his concept of standard housing blinds him to differences between low rent areas, usually occupied predominantly by the former, and slums, which house the latter.[17] Also, working and lower class people sometimes live together in the same planning area, especially if they are non-white, and a neighborhood focus makes it difficult to reach one without the other. This is undesirable because—as I noted earlier—the working class population does not need guided mobility, whereas the lower class population needs it so badly that all resources ought to be allocated to it.

Even so, these drawbacks would not be serious if neighborhood planning could achieve the aims of guided mobility. But this is not the case, mainly because people's lives are not significantly influenced by the physical neighborhood. The important aspects of life take place within the family, the peer group and on the job, and the neighborhood does not seem to affect these greatly. Moreover, although middle and working class people do sometimes participate in neighborhood activities, this is not true of lower class people.[18] Not only do they shy away from organizational participation generally, but because of their great transience they do not spend much time in any one area. More important, since life is a constant struggle for survival and an endless series of crises, lower class people are often suspicious of their neighbors, and even more so of the landlord, the storeowner, the police and the

---

[17] Herbert J. Gans, "The Human Implications of Current Redevelopment and Relocation Planning," *Journal of the American Institute of Planners*, vol. 24 (1959), pp. 15–25, or *Urban Villagers*, chap. 14.

[18] Generally speaking, middle class people participate in formal neighborhood organizations to a much greater extent than other classes, although their social life often takes place outside the neighborhood. Working class people are less likely to participate in formal organizations, but most of their social activities take place close to home. For a discussion of working class attitudes toward the neighborhood, see Marc Fried and Peggy Gleicher, "Some Sources of Residential Satisfaction in an Urban 'Slum'," *Journal of the American Institute of Planners*, vol. 27 (1961), pp. 305–315.

local politician. They harbor similar feelings toward most other neighborhood institutions and local public facilities.

Thus, the lower class population's involvement in the neighborhood is at best neutral, and more often, negative. Yet even if it were more positive, the components of neighborhood planning and the provision of the entire range of modern public facilities can contribute relatively little to solving the problems which concern lower class people the most. To a poverty-stricken family, the separation of car and pedestrian traffic, or the availability of park and playground within walking distance are not very crucial; their needs are much more basic.

This is not to reject the desirability of such planning concepts, but only to say that given the present condition of lower class life, they are of fairly low priority. The location and equipment of the school is much less important than the presence of the kinds of teachers who can communicate with lower class children, and a conventional public health facility is much less vital than an agency that can really help a mother deserted by her husband, or a person who must cope with mentally ill family members.

The standard neighborhood-and-facilities planning package cannot even contribute significantly to the improvement of the lower class milieu. The significant components of this milieu are other people, rather than environmental features, and until these other people are socially and economically secure enough to trust each other, the milieu is not likely to improve sufficiently to prevent the perpetuation of past deprivations on the young growing up within it.

In short, it seems clear that the kind of neighborhood scheme sought through traditional planning and zoning methods cannot be implemented among lower class people until the basic components of guided mobility programs have been effectuated. A stable, peaceful neighborhood in which there is positive feeling between neighbors assumes that people have good housing, the kind of job that frees them from worrying about where the next meal or rent money will come from, the solution of basic problems so that the landlord, the policeman or the bill collector are no longer threatening and the relief from recurring crises so that they can begin to pay some attention to the world outside the household. Similarly, only when people feel themselves to be part of the larger society, and when they have learned the skills needed to survive in it, will they be able to take part in school or community center activities, or to develop the ability to communicate with the staff of a health clinic. In short, the programs which the neighborhood planner proposes cannot come about until more basic problems have been solved; they are consequences of the elimination of urban poverty rather than devices for it.

Neighborhood planning is necessary, of course, but what is needed is of a social and political type which supports the community, state, and federal programs for the elimination of poverty. Thus, the methods required to help the low income population develop the skills and attitudes prerequisite to survival in a modern society must reach into the neighborhood and the street in order to recruit people who do not, for one reason or another, come by themselves into public facilities established for such programs. Also, local political activity must be stimulated so that low income people can use the one power they have—that of numbers and votes—to make their wishes heard at city hall and in Washington. This differs considerably from the need for "citizen participation" often called for by planners and community organization experts; that has usually been defined as citizen consideration of—and consent to—professionally developed programs, or civic activity which is decidedly non-political. The kind of local citizen participation that is needed is quite political, however, and since its aim must be to change the political status quo, it is unlikely that community organizers, who are after all employees of the existing political institution or of establishment-dominated welfare agencies, will be able to encourage such activity even if they are personally willing to do so. Hopefully, enlightened civic leaders and politicians will eventually realize that the low income population must be more adequately represented in the political process, but in all likelihood, they will resist any change in the existing political alignments until they have no other choice. Thus, the initiative for local political activity must come from the areas in which low income people live. But whoever the initiating agencies may be, these are the types of neighborhood planning that are required to do something about urban poverty.

I V

The incompatibility of traditional city planning aims and the basic components of guided mobility programming is not to be blamed on one or another set of planners, nor indeed is it a cause for blame at all. Rather, it stems from the history and nature of modern city planning, and from the basic assumptions in its approach. The description of two of these assumptions will also shed some light on the relationship between social and physical planning and their roles in the improvement of cities.

The first of these assumptions is the belief in the ability of change in the physical environment to bring about social change. Planners have traditionally acted on the assumption that the ordering of land uses, and improvements in the setting and design of buildings, highways and other physical features of the community would result in far-reaching improvements in the lives of those affected. The validity of this assumption has been seriously questioned in recent years, and indeed, the rise of what has been called social planning is one expression of this questioning.[19]

But the traditional city planning approach can also be described in another way, as being *method-oriented*. By this I mean that it has developed a repertoire of methods and techniques which have become professionally accepted, and which distinguish planning from other service-giving professions. As a

---

[19] See, for example, Irving Rosow, "The Social Effects of the Physical Environment," *Journal of the American Institute of Planners*, vol. 27 (1961), pp. 127–133.

result, the planner concerns himself largely with improvements in these methods. In this process, however, he loses sight of the goals which his methods are intended to achieve, or the problems they are to solve. Thus, he does not ask whether the methods achieve these goals, or whether they achieve *any* goals.

This concern with method is not limited to the planning profession; it can be found in all professions. The attempt to maintain and improve existing methods is useful if the goals are traditional ones, or if the profession deals only with routine problems. But it does not work as well when new goals are sought, and when new problems arise. As I have already noted, improvements in neighborhood planning cannot contribute significantly to the new problems of the city, or to the new goal of eliminating urban poverty.

What is needed instead is a *goal-oriented* or problem-oriented approach, which begins not with methods, but with the problems to be solved or the goals to be achieved. Once these are defined and agreed upon, the methods needed to achieve them can be determined through the use of professional insight, research and experiment until the right methods, i.e., those which will solve the problem or realize the goal, are found.[20] This approach was used in the foregoing pages, in which I questioned the usefulness of traditional planning methods and proposed instead programs to cope with the problems of the lower class population—and their causes—as well as programs which would lead toward the goals this population was seeking for itself.

This approach is more difficult to implement than a method-oriented one, because it does not respect accepted methods—unless they work—and because it rejects the claims of professional traditions or professional expertise that are not supported by empirical evidence. It may require new methods and new approaches, and thus can wreak havoc with the established way of doing things. However much the goal-oriented approach may upset the profession in the short-run, in the long run it improves its efficiency and thus its expertise and status, because its methods are likely to be much more successful, thus reducing the risk of professional failure. In an effort as pioneering and difficult as guided mobility planning, a problem and goal-oriented approach is therefore absolutely essential.

The conception of method-oriented and goal-oriented planning can also aid our understanding of the relationship between physical and social planning. In the professional discussions of this relationship, the subject has frequently been posed as social planning *versus* physical planning. Although it is not difficult to understand why the subject has been framed in this competitive way, the resulting dichotomy between social and physical planning is neither

---

[20] This approach is currently receiving considerable attention in planning literature. My discussion is based on an initial formulation by Martin Meyerson, and is treated in more detail in studies conducted by him, John Dyckman, and this writer which are now being prepared for publication. For a summary statement of this approach, see Paul Davidoff and Thomas Reiner, "A Choice Theory of Planning," *Journal of the American Institute of Planners*, vol. 28 (1962), pp. 103–115.

meaningful nor desirable. There are several reasons for rejecting this dichotomy.

First, social planning is said to deal with the human elements in the planning process. When planners talk of the human side of renewal, or of the human factors in planning, they are suggesting by implication that physical planning is inhuman, that in its concern with land use, site design, the redevelopment of cleared land and the city tax base, it has no concern for the needs of human beings. I would not blame physical planners for objecting to this implication, and am surprised that they have not done so.

But even if this implication is inaccurate, the dichotomy has led to another, even more unfortunate implication, which has some truth to it. Every planning activity, like any other form of social change, creates net benefits for some people, and net costs for others. These may be non-material as well as material. Whether intentionally or not, physical planning has tended to provide greater benefits to those who already have considerable economic resources or political power, be they redevelopers or tenants who profit from a luxury housing scheme, central business district retailers who gain, or expect to gain, from the ever-increasing number of plans to "revive downtown," or the large taxpayers who are helped most when planning's main aim is to increase municipal revenues. The interest in social planning is a direct result of this distribution of benefits, for it seeks to help the people who are forced to pay net costs in the physical planning process. Too often, these are poor people, for example, residents of a renewal or highway project who suffer when adequate relocation housing is lacking. Needless to say, this political bifurcation, in which physical planning benefits the well-to-do, and social planning the less fortunate ones, is not a desirable state of affairs either for the community or for planning.

Finally, in actual everyday usage, the dichotomy refers to skills possessed by different types of planners. Physical planning is that set of methods which uses the traditional skills of the city planner and zoning official; social planning, that set favored by sociologically trained planners, by social workers and by other professionals concerned with welfare aims. Yet if the planning activities of each are examined more closely, it becomes evident that the terms social and physical are inaccurate labels. Zoning is considered a physical planning method, but an ordinance which determines who is to live with whom, and who is to work next to whom is as much social—as well as economic and political—as it is physical. So is a transportation scheme which decides who will find it easy to get in and out of the city, and who will find it difficult. Conversely, social planners who urge the construction of more low-rent housing, or argue for scattered units rather than projects, are proposing physical schemes even while they are ostensibly doing social planning. Since all planning activities affect people, they are inevitably social, and the dichotomy between physical and social methods turns out to be meaningless. Moreover, in actual planning practice, no problem can be solved by any one method, or any one skill. In most instances a whole variety of techniques are needed to achieve the goal.

The social-physical dichotomy is a logical consequence of viewing planning as method-oriented, because when methods are most important, there is apt to be competition between the people who are skilled in one method rather than another. All successful professions want to apply the methods they know best, for this permits them to maintain their power and social position most easily.

If planning is conceived as goal-oriented, however, goals become most important and methods are subordinated to the goal. In such a planning process, in which a large number of different methods are used in an integrated fashion, any single method loses its magical aura. Moreover, no goal can be defined so narrowly that it is only physical or only social. In a goal-oriented approach, then, there can be no social or physical planning. There is only *planning*, an approach which agrees upon the best goals and then finds the best methods to achieve them.

This way of defining planning has a number of implications for the future of the professions concerned with planning matters, as well as for the improvement of cities. If professionals continue to emphasize traditional method, when and where it is not applicable, they can easily lose their usefulness, and their professional prerogative for participating in programs of community betterment.

But it is not only the methods which must be reconsidered. Even the goals which are built into these methods are turning out to be less important today. The neighborhood concept has received little support from the clients of planning; the same is true of the planner's insistence on a reduction in the journey to work, which has not been accepted by the journeying populace. Also, in an age of automation and increasing unemployment, the need for economic growth, even if it is disorderly, is becoming more vital than the ordering of growth, and the planner's desire for stability. It is, of course, still important to have efficient transportation schemes, and to locate noxious industry away from residences, but there is less noxious industry than ever before, and for those who are affluent, the inefficiency of the automobile seems to matter little, especially if it is politically feasible to subsidize the costs of going to work by car. And even the concern with land use per se is becoming less significant. In a technology of bulldozers and rapid transportation, the qualities of the natural environment and the location of land are less important—or rather, more easily dealt with by human intervention—and increasingly, land can be used for many alternatives. The question of what is the best use, given topography and location, is thus less important than who will benefit from one use as compared to another, and who will have to pay costs, and how is the public interest affected.

In short, so-called physical planning questions are receding in importance, and socio-economic and political ones are becoming more relevant. This is, of course, why the issue of social and physical planning has been discussed as social versus physical. In the long run, however, it seems clear that the future of city planning lies less in the reliance upon land use plans than in the development of a range of methods that will guarantee the improvement of those aspects of community life that are most in need of improvement.

V

One of the most important tasks in the improvement of cities is the elimination of urban poverty, and of the deprivations of lower class life. Poverty is fundamentally responsible for the slums we have been unable to eradicate by attacking the buildings, and for the deprivations which ultimately bring about the familiar list of social evils. Moreover, poverty and deprivation are what make cities so ugly and depressing, and they hasten the flight of more fortunate people into the suburbs. And this in turn contributes to economic decline, the difficulties of financing municipal services, political conflict, corruption and many of the other problems of the contemporary city.

I would not want to argue that all of the city's problems can be laid at the doorstep of poverty. There are technological changes that affect its economic health, and result in the obsolescence of industrial areas and street patterns. There are political rigidities that inhibit its relations with its hinterland. And the desire of most families to raise their children in low-density surroundings suggests that suburbia is not produced solely by the flight from the city, and would exist without urban poverty. Even so, many of the suburbanites have come to hate the city because of the poverty they see there, and this in turn helps to create the hostility between city and suburb and the political conflict that frustrates schemes for metropolitan solutions.

If planners are genuinely concerned with the improvement of cities, the fight against poverty becomes a planning problem, and one that needs to be given higher priority than it has heretofore received. A beginning is being made in the guided mobility programs that are now in operation, but a much greater effort is needed, both on the local and the federal scene, before these programs can achieve their aim. If such efforts are not made, all other schemes for improving the city will surely fail.

19. ACTION AND NONACTION: APPRAISING NEED

Some Sociological Factors in Drug Addiction Control in England and Wales

LESLIE T. WILKINS

The majority of students of the problem of drug addiction in this country have, at different times, expressed interest in the fact that the British claim that they have no real problems in this area. Some have doubted this claim.

Although I have carried out considerable research projects in prisons, borstals,[1] and approved schools—not to mention probation—and have been concerned with Criminal Statistics for ten or more years, I can say that I have never met any person in the British penal system who has been worried about the use of drugs. The number of addicts who find their ways into prison is extremely small, even if one includes those who smoke the occasional reefer. According to Schur,[2] whose work on the problem of drug control in England is well known, there are about 500 addicts registered. I have no reason to doubt this figure, nor do I doubt his statement that a disproportionate number of these addicts are associated with the medical profession. His description of the facts as he found them accords with my own experience.

Disagreement begins when the "systems" or machinery for addiction control are discussed and when the so called "British system" is interpreted. I do not want to add to the controversy, but to try to throw some light on the problems of interpretation which seem to be posed by those who look favorably on the "British system" and those who do not. I do not want to suggest that there is anything that this country [the United States] could learn from

---

SOURCE: Prepared especially for this volume.

[1] British reformatories for delinquents.
[2] E. M. Schur, *Narcotic Addiction in Britain and America* (Bloomington, Ind.: Indiana U. P., 1962).

the British. I do not think we have been particularly clever. It is possible that conditions could change in Britain and that we might be able to learn from the work which is being done in this country. But the fact remains that we in Britain have been extremely fortunate in avoiding the problems of addiction in the last half century or more.

I will assume that the standard publications giving the official details of the British system of control are known. I can honestly say, as a social scientist, that I have no knowledge whatsoever of any factors which might tend to suggest in any way that these official statements are biassed or incorrect in any detail.[3]

Drug addiction in Britain is regarded as a medical matter, and the medical profession has very considerable freedom to prescribe for any ailment (including addiction) any forms of medical attention, drugs, or treatments that are considered to be desirable for the welfare of the patient. Almost all the population is covered and takes advantage of the National Health Insurance Scheme. I have not seen any recent figures, but I know that the proportion of private patients is so small that it is statistically difficult to obtain a reliable estimate. But the National Health Insurance Scheme cannot be credited with the control of drug addiction, because there were very few addicts before the Scheme became operational. It is possible that the future control of addiction might be facilitated by the Scheme, but that would not be the sort of explanation to interest readers of this book. I could mention, however, that the Ministry of Health maintains a check on "excessive prescribing" by medical practitioners, and will send experts to advise any really outstanding cases. This control covers cost as well as other factors of medical significance.

In the arguments between those interested in addiction control in the United States from various angles, I have noted that much is made of the fact that the British register of addicts is not based on a statutory provision requiring registration. I assume that this "voluntary" nature of the register is often thought to imply that it is hopelessly incomplete. This does not follow. There are many voluntary systems in Britain which seem to work better, even in terms of completeness, than compulsory schemes! Even the Central Criminal Record Office cannot claim statutory provisions for the notification of offenders to New Scotland Yard, but many tests of this register reveal that it is as complete as any enforced scheme would be expected to be, and, indeed it contains somewhat more information than that requested in the proposed list of finger-printable offenses which serve as an informal basis for its compilation. The reason for the voluntary nature of the Criminal Records Office is, of course, that the British policy has always been against any national police force, and although Scotland Yard is often thought of as a national center, in actual fact it is part of the Metropolitan Police who cover most of the London area. The Metropolitan Police, unlike other police

---

[3] *Departmental Committee on Morphine and Heroin Addiction* (London: H.M.S.O., 1926); Ministry of Health Report, *Interdepartmental Committee on Drug Addiction* (London: H.M.S.O., 1961).

forces throughout the country, are responsible to the Secretary of State for Home Affairs. Apart from a Conference of Chief Constables, central control of the local police forces is not exercised; although there are Inspectors of Constabulary, the Chief Constables of the local authorities regulate their own behavior through their Conference. If officials can be persuaded that a particular routine is in the national interest, they normally accept this fact as controlling their own behavior, and enforcement by statute is unnecessary.

This acceptance of national interest as a regulator of official and professional behavior is helpful in the administration in many sectors. I suppose it may spring from the fact that although Britain has no Constitution, we behave in a manner which is, if anything, more strictly in accord with the "unwritten constitution" than we might if one were written. I recall finding the "unwritten constitution" philosophy rather difficult to comprehend when I first began my duties in a government department. That was some eighteen years ago, but I am still not quite used to the idea, perhaps because I get a brainwashing over here in this country from time to time! I recall asking my chief at that time for my terms of reference, and to my surprise I was told that there were none. I was to take due note of precedent, but I could always suggest a modification of precedent if I could think of a good enough reason and back it up with considered argument.

To some extent, I think it is fair to summarize what has been called "the British system" as a lack of system, but I realize that as soon as I use those words they will convey a different meaning to those whose background of experience of systems and lack of systems is derived from a different culture. Precedent, when it is supported by written evidence laid before one at the time of making a decision, is a heavy control, especially when the names included in the files are some of the great names of our history. Perhaps even the informality of the notes on the "minute sheets" (a system not in use in administrative departments here) even adds to the power of conviction of the argument. I remember being concerned a year or so ago with a Parliamentary Question in the House regarding attempted suicide which was still on the statute book at that time as an offense. Some research had been carried out, and the facts were to be presented in the course of the Minister's reply. When the file containing the question came to my office, it came tied with the files containing the precedents. It was a large pile, and, somewhere near the center of the pile was a file in which Winston Churchill had written a minute (an informal note) when he was Parliamentary Under-Secretary to the Home Office. That, I may say, was some little time ago! And there were many earlier papers as well as later ones. None of these precedents were compulsory considerations—one just considers them!

So perhaps the "British system," lack of encoded system though it is, provides a powerful control. Whether it will continue to operate in the same way, it is difficult to say. I rather tend to think that it is a good "lack of system" to hold on to so long as it continues to work. It should enable changes to be made without too much difficulty when changes are needed.

THE PUBLIC IMAGE

I do not think that the unofficial official system which is lacking (!) is the explanation of the absence of addicts in Britain. There are other reasons. May I first make one short and inadequate summary of the theory of perceptual processes upon which my later arguments will be based.

All knowledge is obtained indirectly. The signals we receive through our senses are "codes" which we decode into our experience in different ways. Perception is the process of observing, recording, and organizing the experience one has with people and things. People do not behave with respect to things as *they are,* but to things as they perceive them to be. Indeed, it is doubtful that there is any meaning to discussing "things as they are." There may be some measures of consensus between observers which come to be regarded as "truth," but there are degrees of subjectivity rather than a dichotomy between subjectivity and objectivity. If a coffee table is perceived by a visitor to your home to be a chair or a stool (a mistake one can make with modern furnishings), he may well be expected to sit upon it!

Brill[4] records that Dr. G. Larrimore and he on a visit to England were ". . . unable to find any indication that in fact there exists anywhere in that country the practice of medically maintaining indefinitely otherwise healthy persons on continued doses of opiates under medical supervision." It might be that the perception of the "otherwise healthy person" differs between the observers. Each medical practitioner has his own views on medical matters, and these views are respected in both administration and law. Personally, I doubt that the concept of a person being at the same time "healthy" and an "addict" would fit the British perception of health and addiction. Addiction is, by definition, an illness, and tends to be perceived as such by all authorities. This perception may be the most substantial difference between our countries: not even a crook goes out of his way to get *sick,* although the image of being *wicked* may even seem attractive. Brill continues, "It was clear that the British practice with respect to addicts was not fundamentally different from our own, nor did the British medical views on treatment of addicts differ from our own." I assume that this lack of difference relates only to "medical" factors, for certainly the penal treatments differ and so does public opinion. Perhaps the perceptual differences explain rather more than the procedural differences, even if there are procedural differences. Public opinion may be more important than public policy.

It is, of course, more probable that when an individual takes drugs for the first time his behavior is determined by his *perception* of drug-taking rather than the actual results of drug addiction. It seems unlikely that he would perceive himself as taking on a most expensive habit which will have the consequences it in fact does. Most studies of addiction which I have seen

---

[4] H. Brill, *Great Britain's Treatment Approach to Narcotic Addiction,* White House Conference Paper (September 27–28, 1963), Washington, D.C.

discuss the problems of addiction in terms of the actual function of drug-taking, that is, its function as seen by normal people or the medical profession. But does the perception of the addict, when he is acting in a more or less voluntary manner, agree with this opinion? Cloward and Ohlin,[5] for example, suggest that it is the two-time losers—those who have failed to make a success either of criminal activities or of legitimate ones—who turn to drugs as an *escape*. But are drugs actually *perceived* as providing an escape by the would-be users? If not, how *is* their use perceived? Not what function do they fulfill, but what function are they *perceived* as fulfilling, seems to be the better question. It is, of course, difficult or impossible to find out in retrospect by questioning addicts, and perhaps equally difficult to assess who is likely to turn to drug use in the immediate future and to validate the results of predictive research. But I wish to try to stay with the perceptual model.

In a current work, Freeman[6] suggests that the *perception* of the function of alcoholic liquors differs markedly between those who subsequently become alcoholics and those who do not. Commercial advertisers know how to use the concept of the "image" of their products to make sales, and perhaps the "image" of drugs in Britain explains a large part of the difference. The difference in image may be rather unsubstantial, but it is something we are getting to know more and more about. If, for any reason, the image were to change in Britain, we might have a serious problem on our hands in absolutely no time at all, and our procedures might avail nothing. But this might be a circular argument; perhaps the procedures operate through the image, rather than with respect to matters of more substance?

DRUGS AND ALCOHOLISM

Brill suggests that the difference in addiction rates between the two countries "may be part of a broader question in comparative psychiatry which, for example, also indicates that rates for alcoholism and alcoholic psychosis are lower in the United Kingdom than in the United States." It is certain that the rates for alcoholism are very much lower in England, but exactly how much lower it is difficult to say. Different estimates can be derived from different types of comparisons. Mental hospital admissions in New York State for alcoholic psychosis in 1959 are reported to have been 1,929, while Great Britain had only 531 with a population two and one-half times that of New York State. On this basis, this indicator suggests that the rate for alcoholism is about one-tenth of the rate in the United States.

It is interesting also to note that the Jellinek formula, which estimates alcoholism from various other indices, does not provide good estimates for the United Kingdom. Thus it would seem that the usual correlates of alco-

---

[5] R. S. Cloward, and L. E. Ohlin, *Illegitimate Means and Delinquent Sub-cultures: Delinquency and Opportunity* (Glencoe, Ill.: Free Press, 1961).
[6] H. Freeman, Paper in preparation; private communication.

holism do not apply in Great Britain, and it might be assumed that the usual correlates with drug addiction would not apply. If the usual correlates do not apply, it seems highly probable that the concept of image and the basis of perceptual processes may afford some sort of explanation of the phenomenon. There must be an explanation of large differences of this kind.

Does this mean, as Brill suggests, a broad question "in comparative psychiatry" or is it a social phenomenon? Or, like many other problems, is it one which runs across a number of disciplines in behavioral science? I think that the latter may be the case. I want, in the remainder of this paper, to try to make some contribution to scholarly thinking on this problem. I do not suggest that the observations I shall make will afford a complete explanation of the differences between the British and American cultures and the relationship between the cultural differences and drug and alcoholic addiction, but I think there may be something in some of the features of culture and human behavior which I will try to bring together into a general theory of deviance.

There are a number of postulates which, initially, may seem unrelated to each other upon which I have to rely for the general nature of the argument. In the space available, I shall have to seem somewhat dogmatic.

OPPORTUNITY THEORY

Let me begin by making a statement with which, I hope, all observers of the British "system" will agree. The *opportunities* for obtaining by legitimate means certain quantities of drugs are greater in the United Kingdom than in this country. In this country, the illegitimate opportunities for obtaining drugs are greater than in the United Kingdom. It is generally agreed that the pusher is very rare (or, I think, almost unknown) in Britain. He is not unknown here. Hence in this country, whatever may be said about the legitimate opportunities, it seems fair to conclude that the illegitimate opportunities for obtaining drugs are rather greater than in the United Kingdom. I do not wish to consider the legitimate and illegitimate opportunities in any absolute terms, but only the balance between them. I think it may be said with reasonable certainty that the *balance* between legitimate and illegitimate opportunities differs between our two countries. If one could express the illegitimate opportunities as a percentage of all opportunities, this country would show the higher ratio. I wish, therefore, to consider the likely effect of differential balance between legitimate and illegitimate opportunities in a completely general way in the first instance; then I wish to develop a theory of self-regulatory systems which may explain how a *very small* difference in the *balance* between *types of opportunities* may have a *very considerable effect* on the outcome in respect of many forms of human behavior; and, finally, I will try to apply this general theory to deviant behavior and to drug addiction.

My first postulate is that where the *balance* between legitimate and illegitimate opportunities remains constant, the amount of crime will tend to remain proportional to the *opportunities.*

My second postulate is related to the theory of strategy and states that people do not "play expected values," and in particular, the cultures from which drug addicts tend to come, there will be observed other forms of behavior which indicate a poor appreciation of "utilities" due to distortions of the "expected values." I shall illustrate what I mean by these terms by examples.

My third postulate is that definitions are made by cultures and that cultures vary in their perception of forms of behavior, and that some definitions are vestigial traces of different cultures.

Fourth, since perceptions influence behavior, the definitions (perceptions) of the culture have an influence on behavior of the culture and the subcultures as perceived and defined by the culture itself.

Finally, a model is proposed which reveals an unstable relationship of the nature of a positive feed-back loop. A kind of "servo-system" is produced such that a small amount of difference in the balance will build up to create a large difference in the state of the organization. (This is much the same sort of situation as is utilized in the engineering designs for power steering of cars or control surfaces in aircraft and in many other ways; a negative feedback tends towards stability and damping of the distorting effects however generated, whereas a positive feed-back tends towards instability and an increase in the distorting forces.)

Postulate 1

IF THE BALANCE BETWEEN LEGITIMATE AND ILLEGITIMATE OPPORTUNITIES REMAINS CONSTANT, THE AMOUNT OF CRIME WILL TEND TO REMAIN PROPORTIONAL TO THE OPPORTUNITIES. It is often stated that we live in an affluent society. The amount of wealth is continuously increasing, and with it the amount of crime continues to increase. But gross correlations of this kind are not very convincing. It is difficult to find any crime which is defined sufficiently in terms of behavior characteristics that it would provide a good measure for comparison with increases in opportunities. One fairly satisfactory index of the increase in "opportunities" may be provided by the number of private cars on the roads of a country, and a crime which might be examined to see whether the increase in opportunity was accompanied by an increase in illegal activity might be the number of thefts from cars. Table 1 shows the data for England and Wales for the years 1938–1961, and Chart 1 reveals that the trends follow each other almost too closely. It cannot be held that our moral values have deteriorated in a manner strictly proportional to the increase and decreases in the number of cars on the roads! A more reasonable explanation seems to be that if opportunities increase

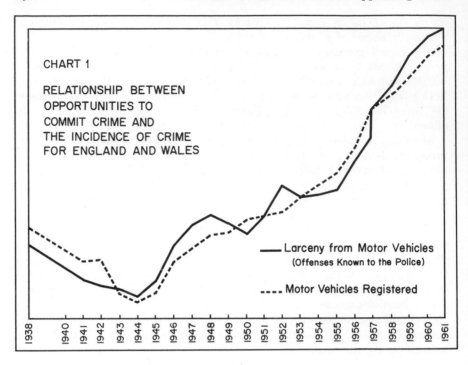

CHART 1

RELATIONSHIP BETWEEN
OPPORTUNITIES TO
COMMIT CRIME AND
THE INCIDENCE OF CRIME
FOR ENGLAND AND WALES

—— Larceny from Motor Vehicles
(Offenses Known to the Police)

···· Motor Vehicles Registered

(that is, the sum of legitimate and illegitimate opportunities) the balance between the taking of illegitimate opportunities and legitimate opportunities will remain constant. The more transfers of money in total, the more legal *and* illegal transfers of money; the more cars, the more thefts from cars, unless the *balance* is changed.

Postulate 2

PEOPLE DO NOT PLAY EXPECTED VALUES. An "expected value" is that derived from the product of the probability and the sum of money or value involved. As Herman Kahn has explained in his exposition of the theory of war in the nuclear age, nations do not play expected values. In a recent broadcast lecture he said:

There is one characteristic many decision-makers have—they do not play expected values. Let me illustrate: Suppose you were Premier of Clotland, and you were told, and believed, that under policy A it was dead certain that you would lose $3,000, but under policy B there was one chance in ten you would lose $300,000, the expected loss is $30,000. Policy C, say, has a one-hundredth chance of losing $300,000,000, expected loss $300,000. If you were a reasonable person you would choose policy A over policy B and policy B over policy C. But if you are a diplomat working on these sorts of diplomatic exchanges where prestige gets

TABLE 1. *Showing the Number of Motor Vehicles Registered and the Number of Thefts from Motor Vehicles Known to the Police between 1938 and 1961. (England and Wales)*

YEAR	MOTOR VEHICLES (IN THOUSANDS)	LARCENY FROM MOTOR VEHICLES
1938	1944	25,281
1939	————	————
1940	1423	11,849
1941	1503	15,672
1942	858	12,180
1943	718	11,084
1944	755	14,509
1945	1487	26,520
1946	1770	32,546
1947	1943	33,984
1948	1961	32,665
1949	2131	30,297
1950	2258	33,156
1951	2380	43,127
1952	2508	41,125
1953	2762	39,739
1954	3100	39,398
1955	3526	43,304
1956	3888	50,782
1957	4187	54,937
1958	4549	68,466
1959	4966	79,899
1960	5526	92,704
1961	5979	112,671

committed, where you have all kinds of public humiliation, you are apt to argue that under policy C there are ninety-nine chances in a hundred that you will get away with it. Therefore, forget about the expected loss! There is a real tendency to underestimate the risk simply because . . . people do not know how to deal with low probability events; they tend to assume they are zero.

In this connection it is interesting also to note the reciprocal of this type of strategy in the attraction of football pools for the majority of the population in Great Britain. Investment (as it is called!) in such pools has only a very small probability of a very large gain, yet the majority of people seem to consider only the size of the prize—the extremely small probability of winning attracts millions of persons and pounds to a most profitable industry to those who run it. No chairman of a board of directors of any company could satisfy his shareholders (or, for that matter, the law) by an explanation of his company's investment policy in the same economic terms as those used by football pool investors. But this does not mean that we must regard the behavior of pools investors as either unpredictable or, given certain modifications in the variables, irrational. A different set of utilities characterizes the different behaviors. It is possible that a similar set of modified utilities characterizes many criminal acts. The remote chance of winning a large prize, the thrill of participation, considerations of prestige, and involvement in the criminal culture doubtless influence criminal strategies in a manner too strikingly similar to the field of politics!

Postulate 3

DEFINITIONS ARE MADE BY CULTURES, AND CULTURES VARY IN THEIR PERCEPTIONS OF FORMS OF BEHAVIOR. THERE ARE VESTIGIAL TRACES OF DIFFERENT CULTURES WITHIN A CURRENT CULTURE. If all persons behaved in exactly the same way within a society, no matter what the form of that behavior, none of the behavior would be defined as criminal, even if by some external standard all the behavior was criminal. A nomadic society has no difficulties within a culture which accepts the nomadic way of life, but this way of life becomes quite unacceptable to a society where land is defined as belonging to people or organizations.

Distinctions between what is perceived as legitimate and illegitimate are made culturally and legally, and the legal definitions tend to follow the cultural definitions. Nonetheless, there are distinctions which are made culturally but not legally, and legal distinctions which are not accepted culturally. This statement excludes those criminal acts which are due to persons whose mental state is such that they would be defined as deviant by *any* form of society and dealt with by some form of exclusion from that society, that is, persons whose acts are defined as not within their control. These persons would be dealt with by medical definitions and not by social definitions, but even in this category social determinants control many definitions and will continue to do so until psychiatric medicine has become more precise.

In general, a religious society will define deviance from the religious norms as heresy, and if perceived as sufficiently deviant, will prescribe some form of punishment; a socialist society will define deviance with respect to its theoretical concepts of collectivism; and an economic society will define certain forms of economic behavior as sufficiently deviant to isolate the offender from the remainder of the society. On a convict island, some of the behavior would still be likely to be defined as deviant and in need of the attention of that society; similarly, in a monastery of saints, some behavior would be defined as deviant. It is clear that all people have some idea of what they regard as deviant or rare events, but no one has any prior knowledge of normality. We have only the sum of our experience against which to measure the unusual or deviant events and to serve as a basis for differential classification. It is as though the human mind had a storage system linked with some classificatory and integrating device which was used for purposes of subjective prediction of behavior and in accordance with levels of expectation.

Any rare event, perceived as either "good" or "bad," say, with a probability of occurrence of less than one in 5,000, is most likely to be perceived as a rare event. Such an event is almost certain to be remarked upon; indeed, it may well be described as "remarkable." Such events will usually call for some action, an action which is also somewhat unusual. Depending upon the way in which the rare event is perceived, and perhaps some personality factors also, the person experiencing the event may write to a newspaper, hold a party, say some special prayers, or demand revenge or punishment. If the event is perceived also by other members of the society as being a rare event, such behavior on the part of the subject will be accepted as "normal," provided that it is perceived as matching the situation. The event was unusual and the response was accepted to be unusual, also. If I am unaccustomed to eating without wearing a jacket and tie, I will perceive a person so acting as acting "abnormally," and, according to my interpretation of the culture patterns and my status within the culture, I will merely take a different seat at the restaurant, go to a different restaurant, or demand that the person be arrested!

It is difficult for a society to retain on its statute books as a law (which is enforced) any concept which is accepted as "normal" behavior by the majority of the population. A society in which 90 per cent of the population are given to gambling will tend to permit gambling, not defining it as deviant but possibly even incorporating gambling (known by a different term!) into its administrative economic system. On the other hand, a society in which a small proportion of the population indulge in behavior which is defined as gambling may well define it as illegal and force those who would participate into illegal opportunity structures. The concept of "local option" whereby laws regarding the sale of alcoholic beverages are determined by local referenda illustrates this point. Here it has been formalized into a system. The divergence between "democratic definitions" and "legal" definitions cannot be maintained at too great a distance for too long.[7] It must be noted, however, that it is not only the actual behavior which conditions the definitions, but also the attitudes of the public toward the definitions. That is to say, laws may remain unamended because they reflect some idealized behavior patterns to which the majority have been persuaded to give lip service. Similarly, although we live today in an economic society, some laws reflect vestigial traces of older religious societies, and indeed older forms of economic society also. Taxi drivers are, within certain cities, still required by law to carry a broom and shovel, and to remain within 15 feet of their "hack"— laws which are still applied to motor vehicles, although remaining from earlier forms of transport. ·

Let us try to construct a suitable mathematical model of this system of "democratic" and "legal" definition concept. Crime is human behavior. Human actions do not divide into bad and good, black and white, crime and

---

[7] The history of prohibition in the United States provides a good example of this fact.

no crime. It is possible to suppose a distribution of human actions as a continuum from very saintly to very sinful. In our society, there are very few acts which are defined as extremely saintly or extremely sinful; the majority of actions are just "normal," and within the limits tolerated by our culture. It is accordingly possible to draw a distribution very similar to that used to describe measurements of general intelligence. In the case of intelligence, very few people are classified as geniuses, and very few as mentally subnormal. (A diagram of the familiar distribution is given as Chart 2.)

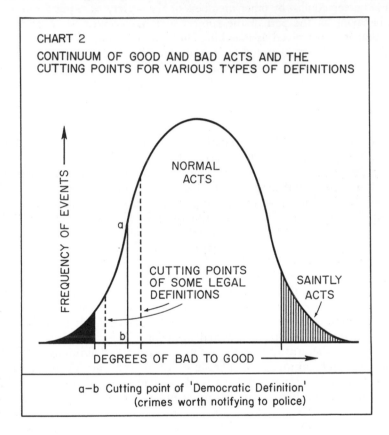

CHART 2

CONTINUUM OF GOOD AND BAD ACTS AND THE
CUTTING POINTS FOR VARIOUS TYPES OF DEFINITIONS

a–b Cutting point of 'Democratic Definition'
(crimes worth notifying to police)

Crimes in the main will be represented by actions at the "bad" end of the scale. It will be obvious that the number of incidents defined as crimes will depend on the point of cutoff. There will be no doubt about the classification of actions which are extremely deviant, but these extremely deviant acts form a rather small proportion of the distribution.

Legal definitions of offenses are quite clear, and there is no intention in this discussion to criticize them when they are used for legal purposes. There is, however, a sense in which all (or nearly all) members of the population could be described as having committed some crime. It is important to note that the cutting point determined by some legal definitions of some crimes will be perceived by some members of the population as being further towards normal than by others, and similarly the majority of the population will perceive some crimes as being nearer to normal than some other crimes. The dotted lines on Chart 2 illustrate the cutting points for certain definitions of crime according to the law, and the line *a-b* represents the cutting point as it might be perceived by the normal middle-class citizen. There are obviously some incidents which are technically described as crimes which the average citizen would not define as anything worth telling the police about.

Postulate 4

SINCE PERCEPTIONS INFLUENCE BEHAVIOR, THE DEFINITIONS MADE BY THE CULTURE HAVE AN INFLUENCE ON THE BEHAVIOR OF MEMBERS OF THE CULTURE AND SUBCULTURES. Perhaps the best way to present some brief support for this postulate is to illustrate the difference between urban and rural cultures, using the model of the normal distribution.

In a village culture, as a community, there is greater tolerance of deviance than in urban cultures, but the deviance permitted to any one individual is greatly restricted. The roles of each member of the village community are specified in considerable detail. A model, somewhat similar to the model provided by the normal distribution, may be used to compare the urban and rural culture. The roles of each member of the village community are specified in considerable detail. There is conduct appropriate to the village blacksmith and the village banker and the village idiot. The blacksmith may not behave like the banker even in his spare time (he may perhaps blow the village church organ on Sunday, but it would be inappropriate for him to play it). If for any reason any member of the village culture deviates from the defined role, his behavior will be interpreted by the village and he will be helped, if help is perceived to be needed, or controlled, if social pressures seem to be required, to re-establish the *status quo*. In the village, each member has information regarding the roles of all other individuals, and the boundary conditions for work and leisure are narrowly defined by the culture. Each narrowly defined role is perceived to have a specific place in the culture; indeed, the tolerance of deviance from the role set for the individual may relate to the tolerance of a wide variety of roles (y) within the culture. Each piece of the mosaic is accepted so long as it stays the same shape. If its shape does not vary greatly, it is easy to see how it fits into the whole, but, if the blacksmith "changes his shape" (that is, fails to stay within the narrow limits of his role), then the structure is seen to be threatened. In the urban culture, far greater variation in role is permitted to each member, but members who are too far out of line are rejected.

Dentler[8] studied deviance and social controls in small work groups in Quaker work camps. These groups were in face-to-face communication. The level of communication was very much greater than that to be expected in the village culture. Dentler's findings confirm the hypotheses suggested in our theory—small groups have specific roles for each member, whereas large groups tend toward anonymity. Dentler suggested that his groups demonstrated that (1) deviant behavior tends to be induced, permitted and sustained, by a given group; (2) deviant behavior functions to help maintain group equilibrium; and (3) groups resist any trend towards alienation of a member whose behavior is deviant.

However, the perception of deviance and the function of deviance differ between large and small groups. The rural culture consists of persons whose roles are known, but the information available to other members of the culture includes more than a knowledge of the role. The individual in the village may be named Smith, and he may be the village blacksmith. In his role he does very useful work for the village community. If Smith died, his son might take over the forge, but if it were sold to a stranger, the stranger ("foreigner") would find it difficult to attract business and the confidence of the villagers. In the urban culture, anybody can be the blacksmith, and anybody may be Smith. In the village culture, the *individual* seems essential to the functioning of the organization in much the same way as Dentler described for his work camps. He notes that the individuals who were perceived as deviant in his groups caused great efforts to be expended on the part of other members of the work group to retain them within the system, although they could leave if they wished. In the urban culture, individuals are expendable if they are replaceable in terms of their *roles*. In the urban culture, it is not Mr. Smith the blacksmith but a "pool of labor" which may or may not include somebody (anybody) possessing the necessary skills.

In the village, "Jack" the village idiot is integrated into the culture, but in the urban culture it is not "Jack" who is dealt with, but the role or stereotype which is perceived. Each member of the village receives some training in the sociology of the village by observation and informal "training on the job." A form of apprenticeship in group management and parish politics is given to all. The training may be in a primitive form of government, but there is a system of passing on of information regarding the role expectations of all within the social system. It is an individualized sociology at the level of anecdote and folk lore, but *information about the system is fed into the system.* And perhaps, even more important, the information covers the whole system, and this information is seen to be relevant. By contrast, the information available to the urban dweller, as part of his experience, is more restricted. The information available to members of the village culture enables them to make predictions of behavior over a wider range of events than the infor-

---

[8] R. A. Dentler, and K. T. Erikson, "The Function of Deviance in Groups," *Social Problems*, 7: 98–107.

mation available to the urban resident. They know that the village idiot drools, but they knew his father, and they know that he has never done anybody any harm, and so on. Transfer the village idiot to an urban setting, and he will have to be removed and cared for professionally. Maybe he is better cared for, but the community has lost *information* which was available to the villagers.

Thus there are systems which can tolerate (deal with) wider ranges of behavior than others. In terms of the probability calculus, the value of x in $x\sigma$ differs with respect to individuals and systems. In the village, x is small for individuals but larger for the system, whereas, within the urban culture, x is larger for individuals and smaller for the system. This model must now be extended from the static to the dynamic frame of reference.

PROGRESSIONS—BAD AND GOOD

It has been noted that definitions of deviance relate to information and cultural experiences of individuals and types of systems. It has also been noted that communities of both saints and sinners would tend to define a certain quantity of behavior as deviant. The degree of deviance $x\sigma$ would, in general, determine the nature of the action taken, and the value of x was likely to vary between individuals and cultures.

It appears, however, that once a subsection of the general distribution has been cut off by definition as not being within the system, the cutoff sector begins to form its own distribution of values, and to define $x\sigma$ values with respect to its own central tendency. The model proposed is illustrated by Chart 3. The cutoff sector of the general distributions seems to develop a centrifugal force which drives the new subset further apart from the parent population.

This is an important feature of the general model, but it is possible to give only one or two illustrations of the working of this principle. Mannheim and Wilkins[9] showed that treatment in "open" borstal institutions appeared to be more successful in reducing recidivism than treatment in closed (secure) institutions, after making full allowance for the fact that the "open" institutions received better risk groups. Croft and Grygier,[10] using sociometric analysis, found that, in most classes in the schools they studied, delinquent boys were rejected by others (had more enemies), that truants were isolated (had few friends), and that the boys rated by the teachers as behaving badly were disliked by other boys. In other words, in most cases they found that the choices on their sociometric scales tended to follow the values of the teachers. But, in the classes reserved for "backward" children, the situation was different. Conforming behavior was unrelated to socio-

---

[9] H. Mannheim, and L. T. Wilkins, *Prediction Methods in Relation to Borstal Training* (London: H.M.S.O., 1955).

[10] I. J. Croft, and T. Grygier, (1956) "Social Relationships of Truants and Juvenile Delinquents," *Human Relations*, 9 (1956), pp. 439–466.

CHART 3
EVOLUTION OF SUB-CULTURAL AND DEVIANT SOCIAL SYSTEMS

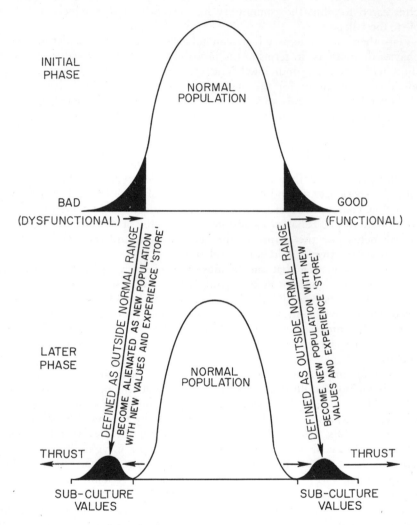

metric status. Both truants and delinquents were more popular in the "backward" classes. Moreno and Jennings had earlier reported that in prisons and reformatories the most popular individuals tended to have had an outstanding record of antisocial activity.

It would appear that a group which has been *defined* to be, or defines itself to be, cut off from the general "norms" develops its own norms which tend to reveal some centrifugal force away from the distribution of values from which they have themselves been rejected. The definitions, as we have noted earlier, relate to both systems and to perceptions of individuals.

THE GENERAL MODEL

Although it is realized that the arguments put forward in presenting the model have been inadequate to support the theory in any detail, the following dynamic system may be proposed:

1. Certain types of information and certain systems lead to more acts being defined as deviant to the extent that the individual is "cut off" from the values of the parent system.
2. The definition leads to more action taken against those perceived as deviant, and the individuals so labelled begin to perceive themselves as deviant.
3. The self-perception and the action taken by the general society lead to isolation and alienation of the groups defined as deviant.
4. The deviant groups develop their own values running counter to the values of the parent system, which has defined them as "outlaws."
5. The centrifugal forces thus developed within the deviant group lead to more deviant behavior by the alienated groups.
6. The increased deviance demonstrated by the deviant groups (resulting from the centrifugal force, results in more forceful action by the conforming groups against the nonconformists.
7. Thus information of this kind received by the conforming groups about the behavior of the nonconformists (as in 6) leads to more acts and back to (1) and round and round again.

This is not too surprising. Indeed it would be surprising if people who are excluded by a system were to continue to regard themselves as part of the system excluding them. But if this is a fair model of the system, some surprising deductions can be made from the theory.

It would, for example, appear that the sanctions applied by a society to its deviants may seem to them to be so extreme that they become alienated from that society. The rejection of an $x\sigma$ deviant, if the value of x is not large, may act as an information set modifying his own tolerance ($x\sigma$) through his "store"—that is, his experience of the culture. If a society truncates its "normal" distribution at low values of x, it seems that it will reduce the cohesiveness of its own social order. Or simply, lack of tolerance by a society for behavior which is not completely intolerable may defeat its own ends, not only through the devaluation of sanctions (although this is important) but by inducing a self-definition of deviance where such a definition is not justified in terms of the social dysfunction of the behavior.

The lower class may find defenses against middle-class value systems which cannot have any meaning for them, by setting up other value systems. They will insulate themselves from those value systems in which they cannot hope to achieve and establish systems which will determine for them some needed hierarchical structure. It may be at this point that the balance between the legitimate and illegitimate opportunities begins to have a second, and perhaps even more powerful, effect than that relating to definitions.

A POSITIVE FEED-BACK SYSTEM

If these forces exist, it is not necessary to show that they are large. The important feature of this type of model is that it represents an *unstable system*. Small, initial differences in the network can build up of their own momentum into quite large forces. Very small forces which tend to regulate towards stability can similarly make very large adjustments in the total situation. The aircraft pilot exerts only a small force on his control column to produce minor changes in the control surfaces which are then fed back to build up much larger forces. Until quite recently, there was often trouble with lateral instability with early marks of designs due to the critical nature of feed-back systems.

How may this theory relate to the difference between the problem of drug addiction in Great Britain and the United States of America? The following are possibilities:

1. The "image" of the use of drugs in Great Britain is different, and the "image" of the addict differs.
2. The "image" of the police is also certainly different.
3. Small differences in the control systems could generate a large difference in "image," which could amplify the effects of the official controls.
4. Less action is defined as "crime" in Great Britain, and fewer people are defined as "criminal," whatever the "objective" differences may be.
5. The *balance* between legitimate and illegitimate means for obtaining drugs differs.
6. The information "set" (or folk lore—it does not have to be true!) modifies behavior. It may be, as Dr. Brill points out, quite untrue that there are differences in the systems of controls between our two countries (I do not wish to debate this point), but the existence of a different set of *beliefs* is quite enough to change behavior.

It is possible, then, that the success of Great Britain in limiting the use of drugs to a very small proportion of the population is built upon some very slender foundations. I am not myself convinced that "perceptual processes" and "images" are slender foundations. Advertising agents know how difficult it is to change the image that the public may have formed of their products and those of their competitors, even though the manufacturing processes and all other details may be exactly similar. The difference between Great Britain and this country may be based on something like the same basis that determines which sort of gas one buys for his car, or the brand of cigarettes one smokes. Looked at one way, these determinants are slender, but they are extremely strong.

CONCLUSIONS

I said I would not presume to offer advice. I will not offer differential advice, but I would suggest that if this theory of deviance is true, or even substantially true, then there are certain factors which might assist any society to control deviance.

The following could be the best strategy:
1. Define as "deviant" the minimum number of actions which are regarded as dysfunctional, and hence reduce the number of people who are defined as "deviants."
2. Consider the "image" presented at different levels of social integration of the control systems which that society employs.
3. Insure that its social controls, and particularly its sanctions, do not become devalued (in the same way as money becomes devalued).
4. Try to insure that all levels of society are able to select legitimate means to obtain legitimate ends.

I would suggest that these points of strategy follow from the theory and are completely general. How right they are depends upon the strength of the theory when subjected to rigorous testing in terms of its practical consequences.

Finally, one light-hearted comment to emphasize the main content of my thinking. I am not (yet!) a member of the Athenaeum[11]; my image of that club is doubtless distorted. Certainly, I do not feel myself bound to follow its rules and regulations unless and until I am elected to membership. If I had been "black-balled" from any club, I should, I am sure, take an even lesser interest in its rules and regulations! Perhaps a society can control effectively only those who perceive themselves to be members of it.

---

[11] The highest status club in the United Kingdom.